Isabel of Spain:
The Catholic Queen

Warren H. Carroll

Christendom Press
Front Royal, VA

All inquiries should be addressed to:
Christendom Press, Front Royal, VA 22630.

Library of Congress Cataloging-in-Publication Data
Carroll, Warren Hasty.
      Isabel of Spain: the Catholic queen / Warren H. Carroll.
            p. cm.
      Includes bibliographical references and index.
      ISBN 0-931888-42-5 (hbk.)
      ISBN 0-931888-43-3 (pbk.)
      1. Isabella I, Queen of Spain, 1451-1504. 2. Spain—History—Ferdinand and Isabella,
1479-1516. 3. Spain—Kings and rulers—Biography. I. Title.
DP163.C3 1991
946'.03'092—dc20
[B]
                                                        91-4903
                                                        CIP

DEDICATED

To my mother

GLADYS HASTY CARROLL

who first taught me the greatness a woman can achieve
and the strength of character and goodness and virtue
which a woman can have, and inspire in a man,
and so prepared me one day,
in the autumn of her life and mine,
to write this biography of Isabel of Spain, the Catholic Queen

Acknowledgments

I would like to express my deepest appreciation to several people without whose help this biography of Queen Isabel would not have been possible, or would have been much more difficult to prepare and less comprehensive and accurate in its coverage:

Regina Graham of Baltimore, Maryland, for her generous financial support of the project for this book which enabled me to travel to Spain in the spring of 1988 to do research for it there, and examine the places important in Isabel's life, and their geographical setting;

Rev. Alphonsus Maria Duran, postulator for the cause of the canonization of Queen Isabel in the United States, and his assistants in the Militant Sons and Daughters of Our Lady of the Epiphany (Miles Jesu), for obtaining several books from Spain containing indispensable source material on Isabel, and for encouraging me to undertake and complete this work;

Dr. Maria Barone, Chairman of the Department of Foreign Languages at Christendom College, for her assistance with difficult translations from fifteenth-century Spanish;

Robert Morey and Thomas Ashcraft, for their good company and penetrating questions and comments as they travelled about Spain with me while I made first-hand examinations of some of the sites of the action described in this book;

my beloved wife Anne, for her unfailing encouragement and critical reading of each chapter as soon as it was completed.

The map of Spain on page viii is from *Spain: A Companion to Spanish Studies* edited by P.E. Russell. It is used by permission from Methuen & Co., London.

The publication of this book is supported by a grant from Daughters of Isabella.

Contents

MAP   viii

1. THE LONGEST CRUSADE (711-1451)   1

2. PRINCESS ALONE (March 1453-September 1468)   17

3. A PRINCE COMES (September 1468-December 1474)   41

4. RALLY TO THE QUEEN (December 1474-February 1477)   73

5. THE QUEEN'S JUSTICE (March 1477-December 1481)   109

6. CRUSADE RESUMED (December 1481-June 1486)   145

7. CRUSADE TRIUMPHANT (July 1486-January 1492)   175

8. COLUMBUS SAILS (January 1492-September 1493)   203

9. ISABEL AT THE SUMMIT (September 1493-October 1497)   241

10. ISABEL ON THE CROSS (October 1497-July 1500)   279

11. DUTY ABIDES (July 1500-November 1504)   307

12. ACHIEVEMENT AND SANCTITY   349

BIBLIOGRAPHY   361

INDEX   369

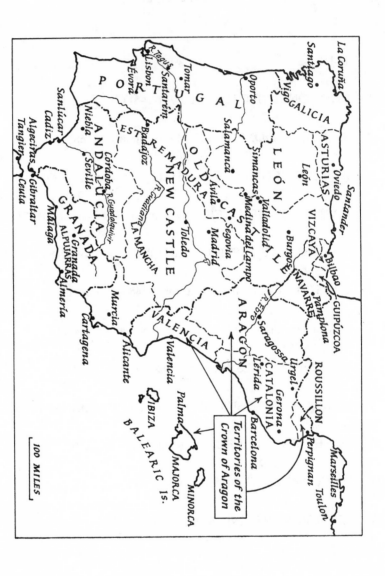

Spain and Portugal in Isabel's Time

100 MILES

to be known in Spain—had seized many lands which had been entirely Christian for centuries: the Holy Land where Christ had walked; Syria where Christians had first been named; Asia Minor which St. Paul had evangelized; Egypt where St. Athanasius, Bishop of Alexandria, had saved the faith from the Arian heresy; North Africa where the peerless genius St. Augustine had been Bishop of Hippo. They had conquered Mesopotamia and Persia; they had marched to the gates of India and China. They had assaulted Constantinople, the greatest city in the world, and almost taken it. Unprepared, shocked, overwhelmed, the Christian kingdom of Spain disintegrated before the invaders. Its King Roderick fought one battle with them. He was totally defeated, and disappeared. His body was never found.

The Moors had no shadow of right to be in Spain at all, to say nothing of mastering and ruling all of it. They meant their conquest to doom the Christian faith there, as it had been doomed for the vast majority of the people in the other countries Muslims had conquered. Why should Spain be different?

But it was—because of one man, and the Lord he trusted. The man's name was Pelayo. He came from the mountains of Asturias to the north. Late in the summer of the year 717 he was one of a party of Christian hostages being taken to the southern city of Córdoba which the Muslim invaders had made their capital for Spain. His sister had been put into the harem of the new Muslim governor of Asturias. On the long southward journey, entirely alone, Pelayo—one man against a world-conquering empire, one man against a tide of history—decided to resist, after all resistance by his people had ceased. He escaped, and called for a rising against the conquerors. At first, almost no one would listen to him. At great peril he made his way back to his mountain homeland in the north. There, during the winter of 718, a few hundred wild skin-clad mountaineers joined him, and an assembly in some forgotten glen elected him king of Spain.

Four years later Pelayo defeated a detachment the Muslim conquerors sent to subdue him, in a last stand at a cave called Covadonga. This guaranteed him possession of his kingdom—a knot of mountain slopes and narrow valleys measuring approximately twenty miles by twenty, which held but a single town, Cangas de Oñis. The Moors scoffed at Pelayo's tiny victory: "What are thirty barbarians perched on a rock? They must inevitably die."[3]

Pelayo's only son Fáfila built a church in Cangas de Oñis, before he was killed by a bear in 739. His daughter Ermesinda married Alfonso I, who had secured another little domain in the Cantabrian Mountains immediately to the east, after Pelayo showed that it could be done. Alfonso I took advantage of civil war among the Moors to enlarge and consolidate the Christian mountain realm, the Kingdom of the Asturias, whose nucleus was Pelayo's domain and

---

[3]Derek W. Lomax, *The Reconquest of Spain* (London, 1978), p. 26.

his, conjoined.   But after Alfonso I's son and successor Fruela I was assassinated, the kingdom of the Asturias became tributary to the Muslim empire, until Fruela's only son, named Alfonso for his grandfather, grew to manhood and claimed his inheritance. He is known to history as Alfonso the Chaste, because he never married, evidently taking a vow of celibacy so as to devote all his life and energy to preserving his Christian remnant kingdom, which the Muslim overlords of the rest of Spain made every effort to destroy. Their armies pierced his last defenses in the mountains of the Asturias, took his capital of Oviedo, reached the northern sea. Fighting on in narrow rocky valleys, year in and year out, he would not yield and he would not despair. He regained Oviedo, restoring with these words a church the Moors had destroyed there: "All is yours, Lord—all we have and all Thou inspirest in us. To thee, Lord—we offer it all to Thee. Your little servant Alfonso presents Thee, as the scanty offering of his poverty, the completed structure of this church."[4] Never yielding, never despairing, Alfonso II the Chaste reigned for fifty years, fixing Christian Spain's destiny and commitment irrevocably upon the reconquest of their homeland from the infidel invaders. When at length he died in 843, he was succeeded by Ramiro I, grandson of the brother of the first Alfonso, who therefore launched a new dynasty.

Ramiro I was the direct ancestor of Isabel the Catholic, across twenty-four generations. Through all those generations the longest crusade went forward. It was in Isabel's body and blood, in her nascent heart and soul, as she lay there in her cradle in the little brick room of the low palace in Song of the High Towers, just as it was in the Spanish air she breathed, the whole culture and environment that would be hers. She would bring that crusade to final victory, and scatter its fruits upon a New World.

Let us review those twenty-four generations through six hundred years of the longest crusade, the generations that shaped Isabel the Catholic and prepared her to serve her people and her God.

The first generation. History tells us little of Ramiro I, who reigned from 843 to 850, except for his lineage, and one extraordinary notice. The year he became king, a party of the marauding Vikings who had terrorized Europe for nearly half a century landed for the first time on the rugged coast of the Asturias near its one port, Gijón. No one, anywhere in Europe, had been able to stand against the Vikings, at least so long as they had access to the sea. Ramiro and his army (whose men had fought all their military lifetimes under Alfonso the Chaste) marched down to the sea to meet the terrible, heretofore invincible invaders. In one smashing blow they drove them back to their dragon ships. The word spread fast; no more Vikings landed on the coast of Asturias.

---

[4]Zacarias García Villada, *Historia eclesiástica de España*, Volume III (Madrid, 1936), pp. 185-186.

The second generation. Ordoño I, son of Ramiro, reigned from 850 to 866. At the eastern edge of his domain, near the present city of Logroño, the Moors had built a great white castle they called Albelda. Ordoño took it in 852. His soldiers swore that the Apostle St. James, patron of Christian Spain, had appeared in person to inspire them as they fought for Albelda the White. Then Ordoño heard that Toledo, the great clifftop fortress city in the center of the country that had been the capital of Christian Spain, was ready to rise against its Moorish rulers. He sent an army to help the rebels—a 200-mile march. They were defeated in 854. Ordoño was not discouraged. The crusade must go on, until all Spain was redeemed. Two years later, in 856, Ordoño reoccupied the old Roman and Christian city of León on the plains below the mountains of the Asturias, and rebuilt its walls.

The third generation. Alfonso III the Great, son of Ordoño, reigned from 866 to 910. The monk-chronicler of Silos wrote of him: "He was famous for his desire to please God."[5] He was a builder who loved peace, the promotion of learning, and especially the propagation of the Faith; frank and outspoken, calm and resolute, with none of the arts of deceit. He was not, at first, known as a warrior. But when in 878 Emir Muhammad of Córdoba rode north with a mighty army to regain the plain of León, Alfonso led a greatly outnumbered body of defenders to the stunted forest around Polvoraría on the Orbigo River. From there he struck from ambush, and won a tremendous victory. After that, for the first time, the Moors asked the Christians of Spain for a truce for several years. The victors placed a stone cross upon the site of the Battle of Polvoraría, and it was said that Our Lady of the Plain, patron of the Catholic people in that region of León, had appeared to her soldiers at the "moment of truth" in the ambuscade. A few years later Alfonso founded the city of Zamora on the reconquered plain of León, holding it against a ferocious Moorish attack in 901. Nine years later, just before Christmas, he died in Zamora after receiving the last sacraments from his confessor, Bishop St. Gennadius of Astorga.

The fourth generation. Alfonso III the Great had five sons. In 909, the next to last year of his life, three of them revolted against him, and he abdicated. Then, in a gesture of humility with few if any parallels in the whole history of monarchy, Alfonso the Great asked his rebel son García—his eldest, the heir to the throne—for troops to make a last campaign against the Moors, as a private warrior. García gave them to him, and did not after all take the royal title for himself until his father died. Four years later García died and was succeeded by his brother Ordoño II, one of the two sons who had remained faithful to their father. Caliph Abdurrahman III (for the Emirs of Córdoba had now taken that title) devastated the eastern part of the Kingdom of the Asturias

---

[5]Ramón Menéndez Pidal, ed., *Historia de España*, Volume VI: "España Cristiana; Comienzo de la Reconquista (711-1038)" (Madrid, 1956), p. 99.

in 920 and won a great battle at Valdejunquera near Pamplona, defeating Ordoño's army there and enabling the Moors to overrun Navarra. The next year Ordoño counterattacked all the way to Madrid.

The fifth generation. Ordoño II died in 924. After a year of turmoil he was succeeded by his son Alfonso IV, a shy and gentle man personally miscast for the iron age in which he had to rule. When his wife, whom he deeply loved, died young and suddenly in 931, Alfonso IV abdicated and became a monk. His brother Ramiro II succeeded him as king. Caliph Abdurrahman III was facing an uprising in the old Christian capital of Toledo, and Ramiro marched to help the rebels. On the way he learned that Alfonso had left his monastery to reclaim his throne—for what reasons, we do not know. Furious, Ramiro had him blinded, sending him sightless to the monastery of Ruiforco, where he lived one last tragic year, directing his soul toward Heaven rather than any longer to the affairs of a bloody and merciless world. Christian Spain mourned the victim monk who had been king and had lost the woman he loved, while speaking as little as they could of their new king. But when Abdurrahman III marched upon them, they rallied to Ramiro's banners and won the mighty victory of Simancas in 939 against odds of three to one. Heavily armored Spanish cavalry struck directly at the person of the Caliph, almost captured him, and drove him in wild flight from the field.

The sixth generation. Ramiro II died in 951 leaving two sons, Ordoño III and Sancho I called the Fat, who reigned in succession. Neither was a competent ruler. During their reigns the upland region around the sources of the Ebro and the Duero Rivers between the plain of León and the mountains of the Basque country became virtually independent and began to be known as Castile.

The seventh generation. Ramiro III, son of Sancho the Fat, was only five years old when his father died—the first minority in the history of the Kingdom of the Asturias. In this turbulent age child-kings were a dangerous liability; while Ramiro did survive until he was old enough to rule in his own right, his kingdom was badly weakened by civil strife, and he proved no match for the military genius who emerged during Ramiro III's minority to lead the Moors in their mightiest effort since the time of Alfonso the Chaste to take over at last the whole of Spain: Almansur, the Victorious. Almansur took Zamora and Simancas; his subjects blamed Ramiro for the losses, deposed him, and began bidding for the conqueror's favor. Ramiro's crippled cousin Vermudo II the Gouty, son of Ordoño III, was proclaimed king, but the real champion of Spanish Christendom in this desperate hour was Count García Fernández of Castile. Fighting relentlessly though losing almost every battle to Almansur, he was finally captured in 995 after receiving a severe wound, and died in captivity in Córdoba. His son, after at first betraying his memory, finally took up his cause and maintained Castilian resistance to Almansur until the Moorish titan died in 1002, after plundering Spain's premier shrine, Santiago de Compostela, and carrying off its bells to Córdoba.

The eighth generation. Vermudo the Gouty died in 999, and once again there was a royal minority; his son Alfonso V was only five. Under the new child-king, Castile and León drew farther apart and were weakened by internal strife; Sancho el mayor of Navarra became the principal ruler of Christian Spain.

The ninth generation. Alfonso V died at 34. He was succeeded as king of León by Vermudo III, another minor, whose sister married Fernando I, son of Sancho el mayor and the king of Castile. Fernando I was a great warrior seeking more unity among the Christian kingdoms of Spain. When Vermudo III, after attaining his majority, would not submit to him, Fernando went to war with Vermudo and killed him. This ugly and destructive internal strife for a time almost completely diverted the attention of the Spanish Christian rulers from the long crusade. But in his later years, beginning in 1055, Fernando turned back to it, calling a great assembly to meet at Coyanza "for the restoration of Christendom"[6] and resuming the war against the Moors, themselves now severely weakened by internal divisions. In 1065, after having reconquered Coimbra in Portugal, Fernando was carried, broken in health, to the cathedral of St. Isidore the Farmer in León for Christmas Mass. The day after Christmas he was brought to the cathedral again, on a litter; he struggled from it to his knees, laid his crown upon the altar, and dropping ashes on his head, declared:

> Thine is the Kingdom and the Power, O Lord! Into Thy hands I render the kingdom I received from Thee and beseech Thee that my soul, which is now being delivered from the turmoil of this world, may find rest in Thy holy peace.[7]

The tenth generation. Fernando I had two able and ambitious sons. The elder, Sancho, inherited a reunited Castile and León; in 1072 he was struck down in the field by a mysterious assassin. The younger brother, Alfonso, then inherited the whole realm; but Spain's most famous knight in all the history of the long crusade, Rodrigo Diaz de Vivar, El Cid, made Alfonso publicly swear his innocence of the assassination before he would take oath to obey and serve him. Alfonso VI hated El Cid for this, but could not do without him; for in 1086, after Alfonso had by trickery taken long-desired Toledo, the ancient Christian capital, from the Moors, a new Muslim army crossed the Straits of Gibraltar from Africa under a commander dedicated once again to completing the conquest of Spain for Islam. Alfonso VI was badly defeated at Sagrajas, but he would not yield; he raised his standard at Astorga at the edge of the

[6]Joseph F. O'Callaghan, *A History of Medieval Spain* (Ithaca NY, 1975), p. 195.
[7]Ramón Menéndez Pidal, *The Cid and His Spain* (London, 1934), pp. 87-88.

mountains where Pelayo and Alfonso the Chaste had made their last stands, called for all to join him, and forgave his enemies who came—even El Cid, who returned to his service and for years held the vital coastal city of Valencia against the African Muslim advance. Alfonso VI, bitter and selfish when his fortunes were in the ascendant, became brave, dedicated, and even generous in defeat; Christian Spain survived. Within weeks of his death in 1109 the Moors assaulted Toledo in force. El Cid was dead, but Spain's second most famous warrior, Alvar Fáñez, held the city while the archbishop led prayers in the cathedral for its salvation, and the new Muslim tide was turned back.

The eleventh generation. Alfonso VI left two daughters, but no son. The elder daughter became the mother of the first King of Portugal; the younger, Urraca, inherited the kingdom of León and Castile. She had one son, another Alfonso, by her first husband, Raymond of Burgundy; then she married Alfonso the Battler, King of Aragon, who reconquered the Ebro River valley from the Muslims after a crusade for this purpose was proclaimed by the Pope. It was intended that their heir would unite León, Castile, and Aragon. But their marriage was disallowed by the Church on grounds of consanguinity and lack of a Papal dispensation, and though they continued to live together for some time despite the annulment, they had no children. Urraca was not loved by her people; during a riot in Santiago de Compostela the townsmen attacked her, ripped off her clothes, and rolled her in the mud. Alfonso the Battler was the hero of the hour; in 1126, the last year of Urraca's reign, he marched all the way across Spain to the mountain-girt Moorish city of Granada in the far south, and though he could not penetrate its walls, he brought back with him more than 10,000 Christians from the area who hailed him as their liberator.

The twelfth generation. Urraca's son Alfonso VII took the title Emperor of Spain when Alfonso the Battler of Aragon died and left his kingdom to three crusading military religious orders of the Church (a bequest ultimately nullified). Though the imperial title did not outlive Alfonso VII, it demonstrated a new sense of the common stake of all Catholic Spain in the long crusade; and throughout his 23-year reign after Alfonso the Battler died, Alfonso the Emperor was the undisputed leader of that crusade. Nearly every year he took the field, marching and countermarching across the dead-flat plains of La Mancha (later famous for the fictional wanderings of Don Quixote), establishing new forts, taking old ones, fighting off Moorish counterattacks, time and again riding with his men through the gateway to the orange-scented lands of Andalusia in the south, the stark rocky defile called Despeñaperros, the Pass of the Overthrow of the Infidel Dogs. Upon its twisting canyon floor, under its looming rocks, Alfonso VII died on the march in 1157, with a new Muslim army and leadership having just arrived from Africa to join in this war that seemed to have no end.

The thirteenth generation. Alfonso the Emperor left two sons. In the most unwise of all his acts, he divided his realm between them, Sancho to have Castile and Fernando, León. Initially there was no conflict; the two brothers solemnly agreed to keep peace with each other, to aid each other against the enemies of either, and above all to maintain the long crusade. They were fortunate in their captains. Sancho III of Castile had Sancho Jiménez, the hunchbacked raider of Avila, who despite his deformity rode hundreds of miles with his men to strike the Moors in Andalusia when and where they least expected it; Fernando II of León had Gerald the Fearless, who would scale the walls of Moor-held towns by a long ladder in the dead of night, accompanied by a mere handful of men, surprise the sentry, and take the town. But after only a single year of rule, Sancho III suddenly died at the age of only 24, leaving a two-year-old child, another Alfonso, to succeed him as King of Castile.

The fourteenth generation. Sancho's son, Alfonso VIII of Castile, was brought up by the Lara family; his uncle Fernando II of León attempted to gain control of him, but was unable to do so. The heroics of Sancho Jiménez and Gerald the Fearless continued; the new Muslim forces thrusting in from Africa were frustrated. Uniquely Spanish military religious orders were founded, with Papal approval, specifically for the long crusade: the Order of Calatrava, named for a key castle guarding the northern approaches to the Pass of the Overthrow of the Infidel Dogs; and the Order of Santiago, named for St. James the Apostle, the special patron of Christian Spain. In 1172 a group of knights from Avila—Sancho Jiménez's home town—joined the Order of Santiago in a body, announcing that their purpose was, first, to complete the Christian reconquest of Spain; then to carry the struggle against the infidel to Morocco; and from there to go on to Jerusalem.[8] By then Alfonso VIII was twenty years old and ruling in his own right. He continued to cooperate well with his uncle Fernando II in León so long as he lived, though Fernando's ambitious son Alfonso IX who succeeded him in 1188 was often hostile. In 1195 another mighty Moorish assault came surging up through the Pass of the Overthrow of the Infidel Dogs and defeated Alfonso VIII in a battle at Alarcos. He escaped with only 20 men, and had to give up Calatrava castle. When Alfonso IX continued to war against his cousin and namesake despite the Moorish threat, Pope Celestine III excommunicated him, and proclaimed a crusade for Spain, urging knights from the rest of Europe to come to help. Alfonso IX finally submitted to the next Pope, Innocent III, who proclaimed the crusade anew. In 1212 Alfonso VIII recovered Calatrava, marched through the Pass of the Overthrow of the Infidel Dogs, and met the Moors at its southern end in what is generally considered the most decisive of all the battles during the long reconquest of Spain, the Battle of Las Navas de Tolosa. A mysterious shepherd (who disappeared afterwards) led the crusading army by night over a secret

---

[8]Lomax, *Reconquest of Spain*, p. 102.

path from the canyon floor up and over a high ridge to take the Moors in the flank. Even so, the battle was fierce and the outcome long in doubt. At one point Alfonso VIII thought all was lost and prepared to die, but the Archbishop of Toledo and primate of Spain, Rodrigo de Rada, told him to be of good hope, that with God's aid the crusaders would triumph that day. And they did.

The fifteenth generation. Alfonso VIII had two children, a boy and a girl. The prince, Henry I, succeeded him, but he was only ten years old and he died three years later, struck in the head by a stone while playing a game. His sister Berenguela married Alfonso IX, so that their children might unite Castile and León; and though this marriage too was annulled for consanguinity and lack of a Papal dispensation, the four children it produced were eventually legitimized. The oldest, Fernando—later canonized, still known throughout all the Spanish-speaking world as San Fernando—succeeded to the throne of Castile when Henry died by the stone, and to the throne of León as well when Alfonso IX died in 1230.

The sixteenth generation. King San Fernando reaped the rewards of the great and (many Spaniards believed) miraculous triumph at Las Navas de Tolosa. He was aided by divisions among the Moors, whose leadership was substantially discredited by their failure in the great battle. Though the southern province of Andalusia had often been raided by the Christians, no part of it had ever been permanently occupied by them since the original Muslim conquest. But in 1233, San Fernando took and held the city of Ubeda south of the Pass of the Overthrow of the Infidel Dogs; and in 1236, called by some of the Christians still living in the Muslim capital of Córdoba to come and rescue them, he rode from city to city in Castile and León rallying his knights for the great enterprise. "Then, 'like an eagle flying on its prey,' he dashed down the Silver Road to Mérida, and across unpacified countryside through muddy roads and flooded rivers to Córdoba."[9] It fell to him within weeks; he entered the city in triumph, to sit on the throne of the emirs and the caliphs, and to send back to the shrine of Santiago de Compostela the bells Almansur the Victorious had taken from it nearly 250 years before. Not content even with this tremendous victory, San Fernando sent his son Alfonso to help King James the Conqueror of Aragon regain Murcia in the southeast from the Moors, and soon pressed on down the valley of the broad, slow-moving Guadalquivir River to the largest city in Spain and one of the largest in Europe: Sevilla, Muslim since the original conquest half a millennium before. In 1247 he created a navy to blockade Sevilla from the sea, brought his army up to besiege it by land, and tightened the noose. By the end of the following year the city capitulated; San Fernando made his triumphal entry three days before Christmas. Fastened to his saddle was an image of the Blessed Virgin Mary he had carried on all his campaigns;

---

[9]*Ibid.*, p. 145.

he left it to the cathedral of Sevilla.

The seventeenth generation. San Fernando died three years after his greatest victory and was succeeded by his son Alfonso X, known as the Wise. He became Spain's lawgiver, a fountainhead of its culture, the first to write and publish extensively in the Spanish language. He put down a Moorish rebellion in the newly reconquered area around Córdoba and Sevilla, and made treaties delineating the borders between Castile (as the kingdom of Castile and León was now generally called) and Portugal on the west, and between Castile and Aragon on the east. The Moors still held Granada, the fertile lowlands to the west of it, the rugged country south from it to the coast, and the lands around the Rock of Gibraltar. The Reconquest was not complete, and Alfonso carried on the long crusade until faced with a rebellion by his second son Sancho, aptly nicknamed the Fierce, who demanded the right of succession when his elder brother Fernando de la Cerda died, instead of letting it go to that brother's boy son. In a tragic ending to a great reign, Alfonso X warred against his son Sancho, even obtaining the help of the Moors in fighting him, until he died in 1284, leaving a will disinheriting Sancho, which was not heeded.

The eighteenth generation. Sancho the Fierce did not betray only his father. The Moors in southern Spain around Gibraltar owed allegiance to the Muslim kingdom of Morocco, while those around Granada formed an independent kingdom. Seeking to reconquer the coastal stronghold of Tarifa near the southern tip of Spain, on Moroccan territory, Sancho IV obtained Granadan help by promising Tarifa to them; but when it was taken, he broke his promise and kept it. The two Muslim nations then united to besiege Tarifa, aided by Sancho's younger brother Juan, who was treating Sancho just as Sancho had treated his father. Renegade Juan called on the commander of Tarifa, Alonso Pérez de Guzmán, to surrender. Sancho IV sent no aid, but Guzmán would not yield. His son had been captured by the Muslims. At Juan's suggestion, the besiegers told Guzmán that his son would be killed if he continued to hold out. Guzmán answered by throwing a sword over the battlements. His son was killed, but Tarifa was held. Ever afterward the dauntless defender was known as Guzmán "el bueno"—Guzmán the Good.

The nineteenth generation. Sancho the Fierce died young, at only 37; his son and heir Fernando IV was nine. The son of Fernando de la Cerda, the eldest son of Alfonso the Wise, still claimed the throne, so there was civil war during Fernando IV's minority. In 1309, at 23 and ruling in his own right, he attacked Algeciras, across the bay from the Rock of Gibraltar, but was repulsed. Three years later he died, leaving a son and heir just two years old: Alfonso XI, later known as the Avenger.

The twentieth generation. During the long minority of Alfonso XI the Moors made some gains; but soon after he began ruling in his own right, at 17 in 1327, he launched a major assault on the kingdom of Granada, capturing several fortresses in its western parts. Thirteen years later a great Muslim army came once again out of Africa, across the Straits of Gibraltar which they still controlled, and laid siege to stoutly held Tarifa. Alfonso the Avenger marched to meet them at the Salado River with an army outnumbered four to one. The day before the battle the Archbishop of Toledo and primate of Spain, Cardinal Gil Albornoz, like his predecessor Rodrigo de Rada before the Battle of Las Navas de Tolosa, preached to the Christian army, inspiring them with the vision and the dream of the longest crusade: the ultimate liberation of their country, which had now been a battleground in the war against the alien conquerors for a full six hundred years. Cardinal Albornoz gave them general absolution and holy communion. They won the battle. Alfonso XI laid siege to Algeciras once more, and this time took it. In 1349 he went on to besiege Gibraltar, the symbol of Moorish dominion in Spain, whose name means "mountain of Tariq," given in commemoration of the leader of the first Moorish invading force in 711. But these were the years of the devastating plague called the Black Death, the worst in history, which killed a third of the population of Europe. The Black Death came to the Spanish camp before Gibraltar, and King Alfonso died of it there, in 1350.

The twenty-first generation. For reasons of state, Alfonso XI had married Princess Maria of Portugal. A son and heir, Pedro, was born of that marriage. But Alfonso disliked his queen, preferring Leonor de Guzmán, a relative of Guzmán "el bueno," the hero of Tarifa. Most of his children were Leonor's. As soon as Alfonso XI died, Queen Maria had her rival executed. Leonor's children hated Pedro, who consented to the execution; and so, increasingly, did the Castilian people, who called him the Cruel, particularly as he proceeded to execute more and more of his relatives by such means as ordering them hammered to death with maces. Married, like his father, to a queen he despised, Pedro the Cruel secretly married his mistress, Maria de Padilla, and lived in bigamy for eight years before ordering the execution of his wife the queen, by whom he had had no children. Maria de Padilla died soon afterward; then Pedro revealed the secret marriage and proclaimed her children legitimate. Now the oldest son of Alfonso XI and Leonor de Gúzman, Henry of Trastámara, stepped forward to claim the throne, on the grounds that he was at least no less legitimate than Pedro's children, and that Pedro by his bloody rule and rejection of the laws of God had forfeited his right to the crown. Each contender called in a potent ally: for Henry, Bertrand du Guesclin, "the Black Eagle," the Constable of France, one of the most famous knights of the late Middle Ages; for Pedro, Edward the Black Prince, heir to the throne of England. Pedro also brought in the Moors to help him. At Nájera on the border of Castile and Navarra the two armies met in battle in 1367, and Pedro prevailed; Henry barely escaped, and du Guesclin was captured. But he was ransomed, the war continued, and two years later at Montiel the verdict was reversed. Henry and du Guesclin won, Pedro was captured, and Henry stabbed him to death with his own dagger. Henry II's reign added little more than footnotes to its bloody beginning. The Moors retook Algeciras and held it for ten years.

The twenty-second generation. Henry II died in 1379 and was succeeded by his son Juan I, aged 21. He married the heiress of Portugal and, when her father died, attempted to take over that country and rule it directly. He was challenged and beaten by John of Aviz and Nun'Alvares Pereira in the Battle of Aljubarrota in 1385, and never really recovered from the blow. He never found time for the long crusade, and in 1390 was killed by a fall from his horse.

The twenty-third generation. Once again there was a royal minority, for Juan I was only 32 when he died, and his son and successor Henry III was eleven. In poor health, he was known as Henry the Ailing. He proclaimed his personal rule at the age of 14, but was unable to do anything about the repeated Moorish raids from Granada; when in 1406 he finally decided to lead a campaign against the Moors, he promptly fell ill and died. However, he did support a unique expedition to the Canary Islands hundreds of miles southwest in the Atlantic, at the edge of the unknown; in 1402 two Norman noblemen in his service sailed to the islands and began their colonization and Christianization.

The twenty-fourth generation. Henry the Ailing was 26 when he died; his son and successor Juan II had been born just the year before. But Henry had a brother, Fernando, known as Fernando of Antequera after he reconquered that Andalusian city from the Moors in 1410, the most important Christian victory in the now very sporadic war of the reconquest since Alfonso XI regained Algeciras in 1344. Fernando of Antequera became the regent for his baby nephew. Fernando's mother, Leonor who had been the wife of Juan I, was the sister of the King of Aragon, Martin the Humane, who died without issue in 1410. Fernando of Antequera was therefore proclaimed King of Aragon, while also having a predominant claim on the throne of Castile if little King Juan should die without issue, or if for any reason he or his issue should be unable to retain the throne. Fernando also held very extensive lands in Castile. In 1416 he died young, like his brother Henry the Ailing; but he left five strong sons. The eldest, succeeding his father as King Alfonso V "the Magnanimous" of Aragon, concentrated on building up Aragon's Italian possessions, extending from the island of Sicily to the southern part of the Italian peninsula, and eventually to the great city of Naples. In 1432 Alfonso V left Spain, never to return; he spent the remaining 26 years of his life and reign as a king in Italy (formally recognized by the Pope as King of Naples in 1443), while his next brother, Juan, ruled for him in Aragon. As for Juan II of Castile, proclaimed of age by the Castilian assembly (*cortes*) in 1419 at the age of fourteen, he was seized by Prince Henry of Aragon (the third son of Fernando of Antequera) the next year, but was soon freed by the shrewd and domineering nobleman Alvaro de Luna, grand-nephew of the indestructibly obstinate antipope of the Great Schism, Pedro de Luna. For no less than 25 years King Juan II of Castile, scion of twenty-three generations of the fighting kings of the longest crusade, was passed back and forth between the princes of Aragon and Alvaro de Luna like a baton or a badminton bird, never in control of his own affairs or those of his kingdom. During one of the periods when the princes of Aragon controlled him, they married him to their sister Maria. She died in childbirth, but the child lived—a son named Henry, who grew into an awkward, uncouth boy who liked animals better than people, and Muslims better than Christians.

At last, in 1445, the contenders for control of the helpless king of Castile met in full-scale battle at Olmedo. Alvaro de Luna, who at this point had the king with him, prevailed over the army of Aragon led by Prince Juan; Prince Henry of Aragon was mortally wounded. De Luna now had a clear field before him, and his domination over the king seemed absolute. He chose a Portuguese princess for Juan II's second marriage, desiring an ally in the west to counter the hostility of Aragon in the east. Juan's new wife was named Isabel. She was young and beautiful, the daughter of Prince John (Joao) of Portugal, a younger brother of Prince Henry the Navigator and first cousin of young King Afonso V of Portugal. Her father had been extraordinarily close to his five brothers and to his sister (for whom she was named), as they had all been to their father, who was that John of Aviz who had won the Battle of Aljubarrota against Juan I of Castile, and to their mother, blonde, lovely, devout Philippa of Lancaster of the royal family of England.

And this Isabel was the 19-year-old girl who lay limp and quiet upon her bed in the little room of the royal residence at Song of the High Towers—this Isabel who inherited through her grandmother the astonishing strength and vigor of the Norman-English Plantagenets, the most prolific and energetic royal house in European history; this Isabel whose uncle Henry the Navigator was a genius and a history-maker, the greatest man of his age as the newborn baby Isabel was to be the greatest woman of hers. But the baby's father was Juan II of Castile, the royal baton passed back and forth between the princes of Aragon and Alvaro de Luna, the feckless king who loved to sing and dance, but, according to the contemporary chronicler Fernán Pérez de Guzmán, "did not wish to involve himself nor to labor one single hour in the governing of his realm."[10]

What of the longest crusade, in the reign of Juan II? He made his obeisance to it in 1431 when he accompanied Alvaro de Luna on a campaign against Granada and watched him defeat the Moorish army at La Higuerela. De Luna was a very competent general; Juan II was not a general at all. But the

---

[10]O'Callaghan, *Medieval Spain*, p. 550.

only consequence of the victory at La Higuerela was the temporary deposition of Muhammad IX "the Left-Handed," king of Granada, by a young rebel of its royal family who had cooperated with the Christians; and within three months of the rebel's coronation he was assassinated, and Muhammad the Left-Handed returned to power. No Christian advance was made. The frontier between Christendom and Islam still stood at Antequera where Juan's uncle Fernando had left it. Not only was the reconquest incomplete; it had made virtually no progress (except for the taking of Antequera) since Alfonso XI the Avenger was struck down by the Black Death at the siege of Gibraltar, 101 years before the birth of the baby Isabel. During those 101 years Castile had had five kings: a monster of cruelty, Pedro; an illegitimate murderer, Henry of Trastámara; a discredited failure, Juan I who was smashed at Aljubarrota; a sickly boy, Henry III the Ailing; and Juan II, the royal baton. So long a period of weakness at the top had spawned a powerful, arrogant, rapacious nobility, and shaken and confused the ordinary people. The longest crusade had not been forgotten, but its torches burned low.

But the heritage was there. Five weak or corrupted generations could not efface the blazing memory and the heaven-storming faith of the crusader kings who had defied the greatest power on earth, fought the longest war in history, and reconquered four-fifths of their country acre by acre from the infidel: Pelayo at Covadonga, crying: "Our hope is in Christ!" Alfonso I, returning in battle array to the great plain of León which had seemed lost forever. Alfonso II the Chaste, making another last stand in the mountains, reigning for half a century of a celibate life consecrated to his people and their God. Alfonso III the Great, defeating the caliph's hosts at Polvoraría with the help of Our Lady and St. James. Ramiro II, hard and cruel, but striking for the person of the Caliph and winning the critical Battle of Simancas. Fernando I, who had called the council for the restoration of Christendom, laying his crown upon the altar to give it back to God. Alfonso VI, planting his standard at Astorga when all seemed lost once again, calling all who would fight on to rally to him, forgiving his enemy El Cid. Alfonso VII, dying on the march through the black ravine on the frontier of Andalusia called the Pass of the Overthrow of the Infidel Dogs. Alfonso VIII, following the shepherd (was he sent by St. James the Apostle himself?) up the secret path which led to victory in the decisive battle of Las Navas de Tolosa. San Fernando, returning the bells of Santiago de Compostela from reconquered Córdoba, riding into great Sevilla at last with the image of Our Lady on his saddle-bow. Alfonso X the Wise, giving laws and learning to his people. Alfonso XI the Avenger winning the Battle of the Salado River against four to one odds, with Cardinal Albornoz's crusading call ringing in his ears, and later stricken by the Black Death while encamped against the infidel foe.

All these were the forebears of the baby who lay in her cradle in the long low palace at Song of the High Towers on that cold April morning of 1451 and heard from afar the joyous peal of the Easter bells, calling the faithful to celebrate the Resurrection of the Lord.

2
Princess Alone
(March 1453-September 1468)

Once again it was Holy Week. Princess Isabel had been born on Holy Thursday two years before; Easter in 1453 came earlier than in 1451, so that her second birthday was more than three weeks away. We know nothing at all of her infancy; the fifteenth century, despite generally excellent recording of public events by chronicles and letter archives, kept no baby books. Only in imagination may we see the tiny figure with red-gold hair and deep blue-green eyes running through the corridors of rusty brick and dark gray stone in the palace at Song of the High Towers—running, because the gravity for which Isabel was later famous would hardly have been hers at two, while the superabundant energy that marked almost all her known life surely already was.

Two is an age before memory. No psychologist even now, half a millennium later, really knows what a child retains from those years beyond the mist. But we know that children of two are vividly conscious of their surroundings and the people in them, and that from time to time they demonstrate a surprising, almost uncanny power of perception.

So we cannot know, any more than Isabel herself later knew, whether she caught any hint, in glance and tone and mien which speak to children of her age far more clearly than words, that her mother had engaged an assassin to kill her father's closest and most trusted friend, who ordered the government of the realm which her father was unwilling or unable to order: Alvaro de Luna, Constable of Castile. Nor do we know how much, if anything, she sensed of the crisis which struck on Good Friday, 1453, when de Luna, goaded past bearing, seized his stalker by the throat atop a tower in Burgos and hurled him over the parapet.[1]

The Queen was in Burgos that day with the King—the flabby, weak-willed, lute-playing King Juan II, who so often did whatever the last person to talk with him asked him to do. In the six years since his marriage, he who was once the plaything of many forces, the badminton bird batted back and forth by many rackets, had become the play of only two: his young wife's, and Alvaro de Luna's. The duel between them had become a duel unto death. Now de Luna

---

[1]Townsend Miller, *Henry IV of Castile* (Philadelphia, 1972), pp. 61-62.

was a murderer, and all Spain knew it; men standing below the tower had seen him fling his victim down. And in the Queen's womb another child was forming; she was six weeks pregnant, and had probably just realized it.[2] This time it might be a son. De Luna was her enemy, and would probably be the enemy of her children. He must go.

Before Good Friday night was done—the dark night of the soul, the night the Lord had been laid in His tomb in Jerusalem—she had persuaded her reluctant, quivering husband to order the Constable's arrest. Three months later, on June 2, he who had been the shield and buckler of a deeply troubled kingdom knelt bound upon a platform in Valladolid. Having refused the traditional blindfold, he gazed with steady eyes—for Alvaro de Luna was a mighty warrior, a protector of his country, a victor over the Moors, a worthy captain in the longest crusade—as the black-clad executioner swung the huge gleaming double-bladed axe that struck off his head.[3]

The King survived his erstwhile friend only just over a year, lamenting him with frequent tears.[4] He felt as though he had cut off his right hand, and sank into a swamp of melancholy from which neither his wife nor even his new son Alfonso, born in November, could rouse him more than briefly. There was no one to take de Luna's place. Designing nobles ringed round the fainting King; whose interests they served he could not tell, but clearly they were not his. His son by his first marriage, strange Henry, had proved impotent; his marriage with Princess Blanca of Navarra had been annulled for non-consummation in May 1453, between de Luna's arrest and his execution. Steadily, hopelessly, King Juan II of Castile—unworthy heir of twenty-three crusading generations—sank. On July 22, 1454, at Valladolid where de Luna had been slain, he died in the night.[5]

Strange Henry was king now, fair game for the noble conspirators—a tragic figure, discredited, a laughingstock, as incapable (though for different reasons) of governing fractious Castile as his father had been. Three-year-old Isabel and baby Alfonso were packed off with their distracted mother to a crumbling old castle at Arévalo in the midst of the Castilian plain not far from Song of the High Towers, on a very limited pension. Isabel of Portugal, ex-queen, was a widow and a dowager at twenty-two; to a large extent she had brought in on herself. Amid the roiling intrigues at Henry's disordered court, no one had time or thought for her. She felt lost, guilty, abandoned. The

---

[2]Prince Alfonso, Isabel's brother, was born on November 14, 1453 (Chronicle of Valladolid, *Colección de documentos inéditos para la historia de España* [hereinafter cited as CODOIN], Volume XIII [Madrid, 1848], p. 21).

[3]Miller, *Henry IV*, p. 62.

[4]Gonzalo Chacón, *Crónica de don Alvaro de Luna*, ed. Juan de Mata Carriazo (Madrid, 1949), p. 434.

[5]Chronicle of Valladolid, CODOIN XIII, 22.

depression that had always haunted her mind, at least since Isabel's birth, gradually gained possession of it. Over the ensuing years, slowly, quietly, the Queen Dowager of Castile went mad—never a raving mania, but sorrow unto despair, and a paralysis of the will.[6]

Her children were, and remained, her only link with reality, even with joy. By their presence, they kept her alive. All through the tumbling rush of events during the years to come, while yet she lived, we shall find them making their way back to Arévalo at every possible opportunity to be with her. From her earliest conscious memories, Princess Isabel knew that this charge was laid above all upon her. She never forgot it, never neglected it, never in all her life spoke ill or condescendingly of the parents who had so spectacularly and completely failed her.

"Honor thy father and thy mother" . . .

For the next eight years after her father's death, Isabel lived (so far as we know, continuously) at Arévalo with her mother and her little brother. Of these vital, formative years we know little more than of her infancy. No one thought she was very important then; no one kept records of her. Teachers came to her from the grand old walled city of Avila, thirty miles away. We know the name of only one of them, Gonzalo Chacón.[7] Significantly, he had been the personal friend and chronicler of Alvaro de Luna, a historian who well knew and understood the longest crusade. To Chacón we may attribute much of the initial awakening in Princess Isabel of awareness and appreciation of that tremendous component of her heritage. Arévalo was a small town; the castle stood on the edge of a countryside only thinly inhabited by farmers barely able to scratch a living from the stony soil. There was not much for a princess to do, as a princess. But Isabel never stood on false dignity, and she was never idle. (We may guess that her mother's long dark silences, the listless torpor of her crippled mind, helped to stimulate this lifelong characteristic of Isabel's.)

She devoured the books her teachers brought to her, but kept her body and her hands busy as well as her mind. She taught herself, or was taught, the technique and art of sewing and embroidery, which she continued to practice all her life. She illuminated her own missal. The broad fields about Arévalo, lush green in spring, golden to brown in the heat of summer, bare and frigid under the lashing winds of winter, might have been made for horses. The princess

---

[6]For the condition of Isabel's mother, the Queen Dowager, see Alonso de Palencia, *Crónica de Enrique IV*, Volume I (Biblioteca de Autores Españoles, Vol. 257, Madrid, 1973), p. 162 (Decada [Dc] I, Libro [Lb] VII, Capitulo [Cp] V), and Galíndez de Carvajal, Crónica de Enrique IV, in Juan Torres Fontes, *Estudio sobre la "Crónica de Enrique IV"* (Murcia, 1946), p. 230. Citations to Palencia are given both in volume and page numbers in the latest edition of his famous Chronicle, published as part of the lengthy series Biblioteca de Autores Españoles, and in the number of the decade, book, and chapter for convenience in consulting earlier editions.

[7]Isabel del Val, *Isabel la Católica, Princesa* (Valladolid, 1974), p. 37.

might be poor, but there would always be a horse for her to ride. Even as a little girl, she became at home in the saddle, learning to keep her back straight and to grip tight with her knees as her steed thundered into a gallop. The tireless young Queen of Castile who could ride two hundred miles through storm and sun and depth of night was shaped on the fields of Arévalo in these hidden years.[8]

Then there was her friend—so far as we know, her only close friend of the Arévalo years: Beatriz de Bobadilla, dark and fiery, daughter of the governor of Arévalo castle, almost exactly her own age. The talks they had, the dreams they shared, lie outside history; but we know that they loved each other all their lives.[9] Isabel was a princess alone; but Beatriz brought her companionship, solace, and in all probability laughter and fun, without which even Isabel's extraordinarily strong personality might have been bent and twisted by isolation and by burdens that childhood should not know.

Above all there was her faith—then, as ever, the center of Isabel's life. Her mother, like all the Portuguese ruling family in these generations of whom we know, was deeply devout. Her malady did not destroy her faith, perhaps even deepened it. (There is no record that she ever sought to take her own life, as depressives often do, but as Catholic doctrine absolutely forbids.) If she could do nothing else for her daughter, she could pass on the Faith to her; and that there is every reason to believe she did.[10] We shall soon see Princess Isabel, in the first shattering crisis of her life at age fourteen, with a faith so strong that she was ready without hesitation, and quite literally, to stake her life upon it. Such a faith is not formed overnight. She must have had it from the beginning, and nurtured it well during those silent years.

Meanwhile the shadows were darkening about King Henry IV of Castile. He was married again in 1455, to Juana of Portugal, but continued to be impotent, the subject of ribald jokes thoroughout the country. His court was a sink of corruption and iniquity, moral and material, which he did nothing to check, and much to favor; the wanton behavior of Queen Juana and her ladies was notorious. He appears to have been a pacifist by principle—a position unknown and almost unimaginable in fifteenth-century Spain. He trusted far too many and gave away far too much. He was essentially incapable of governing, though at times he would turn defiantly on his tormentors: Henry IV was not nearly as weak as his father, but far more neurotic. And at least his father had had Alvaro de Luna to govern for him, until that fatal last year of his reign. Henry had only Juan Pacheco, the Marqués of Villena, the very model of the false friend, the silent traitor, the ruthless schemer who wanted nothing but

---

[8]William Thomas Walsh, *Isabella of Spain, the Last Crusader* (New York, 1930), pp. 7-8.
[9]*Ibid.*, p. 7.
[10]*Ibid.*, p. 6.

wealth and power for himself and would stop at nothing to get them. *"El marqués de Villena,"* ran a satirical couplet of the time, *"nin fabla mala, nin obra buena"*—"The Marqués of Villena, who never speaks ill, nor does well."[11] "History has its fashions," says Townsend Miller crushingly, "but it seems safe to say that no one will ever try to rehabilitate this Marqués of Villena."[12]

For the first nine years of Henry's reign, Villena was fully in control of Castile's public affairs. But Henry, though quite willing then to let Villena govern, was not close to him personally; he gave rich gifts and high offices, which Villena coveted, first to Miguel Lucas, then to Beltrán de la Cueva. Beltrán, a shallow handsome youth of undistinguished lineage who was raised almost overnight to the highest levels of the aristocracy, provoked violent jealousy by his rapid ascent. Restive nobles formed the League of Tudela against Henry. In the fall of 1460 they gained the support of King Juan II of neighboring Aragon, whose family owned vast tracts of land in Castile and had arranged for the marriage of Juan's daughter with Isabel's brother Alfonso, when he should reach marrigeable age. Juan II wanted Alfonso officially declared Henry's heir, on the presumption—apparently sound—that Henry would never be able to have children of his own.[13]

Henry reluctantly agreed. Then in the summer of 1461 came startling, totally unexpected news: Queen Juana was pregnant. Henry insisted that the child was his; Juan of Aragon and his allies spread the report that its father was the hated Beltrán. In fact we do not and cannot know who the father was, though much evidence indicates that he was most unlikely to have been Henry.[14] A legally recognized heir to Henry would destroy all the plans of Juan of Aragon; at 63, he could not wait until the heir grew up to see one of his children married to him or her and thereby to unite Aragon and Castile, which was his great political dream. Therefore it now became very much in the interest of Juan of Aragon to see Henry overthrown—which, in view of Henry's misgovernment and incapacity, did not seem an insuperably difficult task. Any attempt to accomplish it would bring Prince Alfonso, and to some extent Princess Isabel as well, to the center of the action. They were alone, friendless, unprotected. And they were only eight and ten years old, respectively.

So the Marqués of Villena—at this point a firm opponent of Juan II of Aragon and the League of Tudela—called them from Arévalo to court, probably in the winter of 1462.[15] Now that they had become important, he

---

[11]Baltasar Cuartero y Huerta, *El Pacto de los Toros de Guisando y la Venta del Mismo Nombre* (Madrid, 1952), p. 21.

[12]Miller, *Henry IV*, p. 16.

[13]*Ibid.*, pp. 99-116.

[14]*Ibid.*, pp. 64-68, 84-90, 118-121.

[15]Diego Enríquez del Castillo, "Crónica del Rey don Enrique IV," *Crónicas de los Reyes de Castilla*, ed. Cayetano Rosell, Biblioteca de Autores Españoles, Vol. LXX (Madrid, 1878), pp. 119-120 (Cp XXXVII) (hereinafter cited as Enríquez, Crónica,

wanted to keep them closely under his eye.

At the end of February 1462 Queen Juana came to term, and was delivered of a girl who was named for her. (She was to go down in history as Juana "la Beltraneja"—"Beltrán's daughter.") On March 17 she was baptized in Madrid by the primate of Spain, the blustering, belligerent, irresponsible Archbishop Alonso Carrillo of Toledo. Her godfathers were the Marqués of Villena and the French ambassador; her godmothers were Villena's wife—and Princess Isabel.[16]

It was her first public function. The eyes of the kingdom were upon her. She was not quite eleven years old. Could anyone present have imagined that the day would come when this little girl with the pink face and the clear young voice would personally pull down the corrupted power of the gorgeously brocaded Archbishop who presided at the ceremony, and the son and heir of Villena, the mighty grandee who stood beside her?

How much, if anything, she knew or guessed of the dark intrigues which circled round that baptismal font, we have no clue. Probably she felt no more than a vague unease, a sense that all was not as it seemed or should be; for Isabel was all her life extraordinarily frank and direct, despising deviousness. But above all, her attention would have been focussed on the sacrament itself. Whatever fate held in store for this newborn baby—and it was to be tragic indeed—she was a child of God, now joining His family by the waters of salvation. That ten-year-old Isabel most certainly knew, and that she loved to see. We may be sure that she would still have come gladly to that font to stand as godmother, even if some second sight had revealed to her that this baby, in times to come, would be relentlessly used against her by her enemies for ten long and angry years.

The baptism over, Isabel sought and obtained permission to return for a time to Arévalo, to comfort her suffering mother and try to reconcile her to the long periods of separation from her children that must now ensue.[17]

Some of the Castilian nobles flatly refused to swear allegiance to baby Juana as Henry's heir, as law and traditional protocol required; others delayed, or found excuses to avoid doing so. Facing scorn and repudiation, Henry fled to Segovia, the castle-crowned city facing the snow-capped Guadarramas where Isabel's father had been staying when she was born, and from which he did not

---

BAE, LXX). The date is not given, in Enríquez or any other source. It might have been in the fall of 1461, but cannot have been later than the winter of 1462, since Juana's child was baptized March 17 with Isabel present, and Enríquez's account of the baptism follows his mention of Alfonso and Isabel being summoned to court.

[16]Enríquez, *Crónica*, BAE LXX, 120 (Cp XXXVIII); Ramón Menéndez Pidal, director, *Historia de España*, Volume XV: "Los Trastámaras de Castilla y Aragon en el Siglo XV," ed. Luis Suárez Fernández, Angel Canellas López, and Jaime Vicens Vives (Madrid, 1986), p. 240.

[17]Walsh, *Isabella*, p. 23.

come to Song of the High Towers to see his new daughter. Outside Segovia's walls, on the rising mountain slopes, a wall enclosed a thick pine forest known as the glade of Balsaín. Here Henry kept his own private menagerie, a collection of strange and beautiful animals that he loved more than people. Gradually what remained of his court gathered at Segovia, Isabel and Alfonso included.[18]

They soon felt the foul miasma of its moral corruption: the wanton Queen and her shamelesss attendants, the unchecked sodomy among many of the young men. The chronicles imply that Alfonso was drawn into some of this degradation. But, at this point and throughout her life, there is no hint in any record that any of it ever touched Isabel. The Renaissance was a proverbially licentious age, as much in Spain as elsewhere. But Isabel's purity remained untarnished.[19]

Even less than his feckless father did pacifist Henry care for the longest crusade. But there were still men in Castile who had not forgotten it. In the southlands, in this spring and summer of 1462, Rodrigo Ponce de León, the red-haired 19-year-old son of the Count of Arcos, at the head of three hundred lances, fired a hodgepodge of local Andalusian militia with the war-cry of seven and a half centuries of struggle. In April he won a battle against the Moors at Madroño; in May, teamed with the Alcaide of Osuna, he defeated a strong force commanded by Abul-Hassan Ali of Granada; in August, he and the Duke of Medina Sidonia took Gibraltar[20]—one of the symbols of Muslim dominion, named for their first conqueror in Spain, where Alfonso XI the Avenger, the last of Isabel's great warrior ancestors, had died in a besieging camp 112 years before, victim of the Black Death. Mark well this young captain, who bore the name of the supreme hero El Cid: as the Marqués of Cádiz, he will be heard from again. More than any other man except her husband, Rodrigo Ponce de León was to make possible Isabel's victorious completion of the 770-year war of reconquest.

Gibraltar fell to the Christians on August 16. Five days earlier, the rebels of Catalonia—ever-turbulent province of the Kingdom of Aragon—who had been in arms against King Juan for a year and a half, offered their land to Henry. It is hard to imagine why they chose him; they must have seen no farther than that he and King Juan were enemies. Much as he disliked war, Henry snapped at the offer with something close to enthusiasm; at long last,

---

[18]Miller, *Henry IV*, pp. 56-57, 123-124. We do not know when Isabel and Alfonso left Arévalo to rejoin the court, but they were in Segovia by the winter of 1462-63 (Enríquez, Crónica, BAE LXX, 127 [Cp XLVIII]).

[19]Palencia, *Crónica de Enrique IV*, I, 150, 238 (Dc I, Lb VII, Cp I, and Lb X, Cp V).

[20]Historia de los Hechos del Marqués de Cádiz, CODOIN CVI (Madrid, 1893), 162-180; Mosén Diego de Valera, *Memorial de diversas hazañas; crónica de Enrique IV*, ed. Juan de Mata Carriazo (Madrid, 1941), pp. 75-84 (hereinafter cited as Valera, *Hazañas*); Menéndez Pidal, *Historia de España* XV, 243.

somebody actually wanted him. Juan of Aragon, however, was as always far ahead of him. Three months before he had made a treaty with the wily new King of France, Louis XI "the Spider," by which Louis agreed to help Juan subdue the Catalan rebels in return for the province north of the Pyrenees which he coveted though it had historically always been part of Catalonia: Roussillon (in Spanish, Rosellón). Louis sent an army to Barcelona; it was there, besieging the city, when Henry's small force arrived to aid the rebels. Villena urged mediation. Louis, of all people, offered himself as arbitrator. On Villena's recommendation, Henry accepted him. Louis drafted a treaty which awarded Henry a single town in Navarra while requiring him to stay entirely out of Catalonia henceforth. He bought Villena for 12,000 crowns. The perfidious Marqués stamped the treaty with the royal seal. Louis commented that he had not exactly lost his shirt. Then Villena arranged a grandiloquent meeting between the two kings on the frontier, where the wide shallow Bidasoa River flows into the Bay of Biscay, on April 28, 1463. There the treaty was read to Henry for the first time. He was appalled. But his seal was on the document. Villena had put it there, after Henry had trustingly given him the seal. He was betrayed—made to appear to have violated his own promise to the Catalans—in public.[21]

Henry IV of Castile was a psychological cripple, a profoundly disturbed man who often played the fool. But he was not a coward. Through the coiling shadows of his syndromes still shone a gleam of steel from those twenty-four generations of his crusading ancestors. He knew now what Villena had done to him, and set his face against him. Villena was forced out of the court and the government—a fate, to him, worse than death.[22] So he went over to Juan of Aragon and the League of Tudela, to join with them in plotting the overthrow of Henry and his dubious daughter Juana, in the name of Prince Alfonso and Princess Isabel. Of course he did not tell them yet, and would not until his plans matured; the boy was not yet ten, and the girl scarcely twelve.

Though Henry did not yet suspect Villena's new treachery by the end of the year 1463, he knew only too well that Juan of Aragon and his friends among the Castilian nobility wanted him overthrown. Because of Villena, he had lost Catalonia as a counterweight to them; the one remaining possible ally was Portugal. Henry had gone south to Andalusia, probably chiefly to see his old friend Miguel Lucas at Jaén; on the way, in January 1464, he stopped at Gibraltar, which Rodrigo Ponce de León and the Duke of Medina Sidonia had just taken from the Moors, and there he met King Afonso V of Portugal. Henry offered Afonso Isabel's hand in marriage.[23] Afonso was intrigued by the

[21]Menéndez Pidal, *Historia de España*, XV, 242-245; Miller, *Henry IV*, pp. 129-140.
[22]Miller, *Henry IV*, pp. 140-141.
[23]*Ibid.*, p. 145; Menéndez Pidal, *Historia de España*, XV, 255; Enríquez, Crónica, BAE LXX, 131 (Cp LV).

prospect. When, after a long stay at Jaén, Henry returned north, he took Isabel and Prince Alfonso (along with Queen Juana, who was of the Portuguese royal family) to meet the King of Portugal. It was very close to her thirteenth birthday in April 1464 when Isabel met the fat widower of 32, already with two children, at the Bridge of the Archbishop on the main road from Madrid to Portugal.[24]

Isabel, there at the bridge in the wide rolling swale of the Tagus valley in the chill breeze of earliest spring, was utterly alone. Her father was dead. Her mother lay in long-gathering darkness at Arévalo. Her ten-year-old brother depended upon her. Gonzalo Chacón her teacher and Beatriz de Bobadilla her one true friend were far away. To Henry, to Queen Juana, to King Afonso, to Villena, she was a pawn on a chessboard more than she was a human being. In the Lord she loved so much was her only strength.

Afonso at least had the decency to ask her personally to marry him (though contracting a secret marriage treaty with Henry regardless of her answer). Isabel refused. She was not ready for marriage, and was determined—unfashionable though it was in those times—to have a voice in the selection of her own husband. But what she told King Afonso was simply that the great nobles of Castile must first approve her marriage. (These are her first words that history records.)[25] The great nobles of Castile were, by and large, no friends of Henry and Afonso of Portugal. By this answer, in effect, she had summoned their help—and Henry and Afonso were not then strong enough to go against them.

The great nobles of Castile were no more friends of Princess Isabel at that time than the Kings of Castile and Portugal. But, even at thirteen, Isabel's clear steady vision and luminous intellect had already taught her the first hard but supremely important lesson of political survival in the world that is Christ's enemy: divide and conquer. When your enemies are too potent to defeat as a whole, split them apart. When dealing with evil men, that is never very difficult to do.

Yet it is a perilous course, as Isabel soon discovered. For when she called upon the great nobles of the realm, that now meant, above all, Villena. The cold-hearted Marqués was only too willing to respond to her call, confident that he could use and dominate her. He was forty-six years old, in the prime of life and at the peak of his power, a master of intrigue, the Machiavelli of Spain. She was a thirteen-year-old girl who knew nothing—he thought—of the real world. On May 16 he formed an alliance to "protect" her and her brother, to make sure that she did not marry without their consent. The other two founding

---

[24]Enríquez, Crónica, BAE LXX, 132 (Cp LVI); Palencia, *Crónica de Enrique IV*, I, 146 (Dc I, Lb VI, Cp X).
[25]Palencia, *Crónica de Enrique IV*, I, 146 (Dc I, Lb VI, Cp X): Galíndez, "Crónica de Enrique IV," in Torres Fontes, *Estudio*, p. 205.

members of the alliance were Archbishop Carrillo and Villena's own brother, Pedro Girón, Master of the once-crusading Order of Calatrava, by canon law a monk vowed to chastity, whose lust and lechery and multitude of bastards were the talk of Spain, a swaggering bully with a greed matching his brother's and the manners of a swineherd. They were soon joined by Admiral Fadrique; by the Counts of Benavente, Plasencia, and Alba with their vast estates; and by many other grandees—an expanded League of Tudela, henceforth known simply as "the League."[26]

Three times during the next five months Villena and his confederates tried to seize Henry IV and the man on whom he now chiefly depended for protection, Beltrán de la Cueva. (Henry had given Beltrán the most lucrative appointment in Spain, which Villena passionately wanted for himself: the Mastership of Santiago, largest of the Spanish military orders, heir to the wealth given in trust for centuries to maintain the long crusade.)[27] The first time, in May, Villena's men beat down the doors of the palace in Madrid where Henry was then staying (and keeping Alfonso and Isabel in rooms in the tower). But Henry and Beltrán escaped, and Villena pretended he had nothing to do with the attack.[28] The second time, in August, after Henry with Isabel and Alfonso had returned to Segovia, Villena received a royal safe-conduct to come and talk with Isabel. Under that cover he planned to introduce his assassins to the palace, with specific orders to seize the King and slit Beltrán's throat. We would give much to know what Isabel and Villena said to each other during that meeting; but none of our sources gives a hint of it. What we do know is that at the last minute someone revealed the plot to Henry or one of his men. Henry's councillors urged that Villena be killed on the spot (in Isabel's room, perhaps?) but the King rejected that advice; he hated bloodshed. So Villena was able to get away and call off the second attack.[29] Finally, in September, Villena and his henchmen attempted to ambush Henry with 600 horsemen near Villacastín in the Castilian plain, but he was again forewarned and fled back to Segovia, where the local militia rallied to protect him.[30]

So at last Villena and the League had to come out into the open. On September 28, 1464 they issued the "Representation of Burgos," a formal indictment of Henry IV emphasizing his infidelity as a Catholic and toleration of blasphemy and immorality at his court (surely a classic case of the pot calling the kettle black), declaring little Juana "la Beltraneja" illegitimate, and demanding official recognition of Isabel's brother, Prince Alfonso, as heir to the

---

[26]Menéndez Pidal, *Historia de España*, XV, 256; Miller, *Henry IV*, pp. 186-187.
[27]Enríquez, Crónica, BAE LXX, 134-135 (Cp LX-LXI).
[28]*Ibid.*
[29]*Ibid.*, p. 135 (Cp LXII); Miller, *Henry IV*, pp. 152-153.
[30]Enríquez, Crónica, BAE LXX, 136-137 (Cp LXIII); Chronicle of Valladolid, CODOIN XIII, 59-61.

throne of Castile.[31]

It amounted to a declaration of war. Henry called a council of his chief advisors at Valladolid to discuss what to do. The most outspoken councillor was his old teacher, Bishop Lope Barrientos, now an octogenarian; he called, in no uncertain terms, for a fight to the finish. Henry refused, with the most explicitly pacifistic statement of his life: war settled nothing, he said; he would reopen negotiations instead. The surge of strengthened will which had upheld him for the year and a half since the betrayal on the Bidasoa suddenly drained away; Henry's damaged psyche could no longer sustain it. He made an agreement with Villena on October 25 which amounted to surrender: he would recognize Alfonso as his successor, asking in return only that Alfonso promise to marry little Juana (not yet four) when she was old enough; he would deprive Beltrán of the recently granted Mastership of Santiago; he would accept the reordering of the realm by a special commission which Villena would effectively control; finally, he would promise to confess and go to communion once a year. (One is tempted to ask: would Villena so promise?). Prince Alfonso was turned over to Villena; but Isabel remained in Segovia with Henry and Juana.[32] We do not know if this was by her own choice.

When the baronial commission reviewing the government of Castile, meeting at Medina del Campo early in 1465, issued its "Sentence" stripping Henry of most of his royal powers, his courage returned; he denounced the "Sentence" and the agreement, and withdrew recognition of Alfonso as his heir. In March, when Alfonso was in Arévalo visiting his mother, Villena seized the town and proclaimed him king. On April 22, at long last, Henry ordered the confiscation of all Villena's goods, though he lacked the means to see that order carried out. At Villena's suggestion, Archbishop Carrillo and Admiral Fadrique went to Henry to feign repentance and submission. For the next month they confused him, led him astray, and effectively frustrated his efforts to build up the strength of his army.[33] Finally, at the end of May, Carrillo threw off the mask. "Go tell your King," he thundered to the royal courier, "that I am sick of him and everything about him. Now we shall see who is the real sovereign of Castile!"[34]

And so, on June 4, 1465, upon a platform under the walls of Avila, Villena and Carrillo and the leading rebel nobles held a formal ceremony of deposition. A crowned wooden dummy with a sword stood in for Henry. Carrillo took off its crown. The Count of Plasencia took off its sword. The dummy was knocked over and kicked about the platform to shouts of "Down, queer!" Then it was

---

[31]Enríquez, *Crónica*, BAE LXX, 137-138 (Cp LXIV).
[32]*Ibid.*, pp. 139, 141 (Cp LXVI, LXX); Chronicle of Valladolid, CODOIN XIII, 61-65.
[33]Menéndez Pidal, *Historia de España*, XV, 261-267; Miller, *Henry IV*, pp. 164-168.
[34]Enríquez, *Crónica*, BAE LXX, 143-144 (Cp LXXIII).

booted over the edge of the platform into the dust. Prince Alfonso was brought forward. Carrillo placed the crown on his head. The band played. The hirelings cheered. But elsewhere, when they heard what had happened on that platform by the walls of Avila, good men turned away their faces. Henry was a bad king, unfit to govern. But this was worse. What self-respecting country could be ruled under a crown picked off the head of a wooden dummy? What kind of country would treat even a mentally crippled king worse than a whipped dog?[35]

We can imagine how Isabel's heart ached for her little brother when she heard the news. But we cannot imagine her sitting on that platform and receiving that soiled and sullied crown, under any circumstances whatsoever, had the choice been hers.

And the people of Castile—the simple people, whom Isabel had known and loved in her girlhood at Arévalo, who understood and loved her for so many years as few sovereigns have ever been understood and loved—felt exactly as she must have felt. All across the land they rallied to their ugly, groping, failing sovereign, by the thousands and the tens of thousands. Broken reed he might be, but he was King of Castile, heir to twenty-four generations of crusaders. What had been done on that platform at Avila was unforgivable. From knights with armor and lances and pennons to farmers with scythes and clubs, the people of Castile seized their weapons and marched to his aid. Before the summer ended, pacifist Henry commanded an army, sprung as though from the earth itself, of at least 30,000 men. One usually reliable chronicler gives the total as no less than 100,000. When, in July, Archbishop Carrillo brought up a rebel army to take the castle of Simancas (this worldly prelate saw nothing incongruous in a bishop in battle—he fought with gusto, and the accounts of his martial prowess lay special stress on how he emerged from almost every combat covered with blood) its commander, the intrepid Juan Fernández Galindo, defied him with scorn—and held firm. Henry sent his queen and Isabel to Portugal to obtain still more help, and received a promise of it, with the renewed prospect of Isabel's marriage to the Portuguese king.[36]

---

[35]Every chronicler of the age describes the terrible scene at Avila at length: Enríquez, Cp LXXIV (BAE LXX, 144-145); Palencia, Dc I Lb VII Cp VIII (I, 167-168); Galíndez, Chapter 65 (Torres Fontes, *Estudio*, pp. 238-240); Valera, *Hazañas*, pp. 97-99; Chronicle of Valladolid, CODOIN XIII, 67-68; Fernando del Pulgar, *Crónica de los Reyes Católicos*, ed. Juan de Mata Carriazo (Madrid, 1943), I, 4-9. See Townsend Miller's superb description, *Henry IV*, pp. 171-173.

[36]For the reaction in favor of Henry, see Enríquez, Crónica, BAE LXX, 145-148 (Cp LXXV-LXXVIII); Palencia, *Crónica de Enrique IV*, I, 168-182 (Dc I, Lb VII, Cp IX-X and Lb VIII, Cp I-II; Galíndez, "Crónica de Enrique IV," in Torres Fontes, *Estudio*, pp. 240-250; Valera, *Hazañas*, pp. 103-107. The estimate of 30,000 is Valera's; that of 100,000, Enríquez's. For the agreement between Castile and Portugal looking to a future marriage of King Afonso V of Portugal with Isabel, see Antonio de La Torre and Luis Suarez Fernández, eds., *Documentos referentes a las relaciones con*

Yet there can be no substitute for real leadership. Not even the most genuine and justified surge of moral indignation can make up for the lack of it. Henry IV of Castile was constitutionally unwilling or unable to fight. He could not really use an army. The rally in the summer of 1465 saved his throne, but did not end his torment. All it did was to make him strong enough to bring Villena back to negotiate with him again—a willingness Henry was, as always, pathetically eager to reciprocate. Before September ended a truce had been agreed upon, whereupon Henry promptly and totally disbanded his army.[37]

Once again he was in Villena's clutches. And now Castile, with two kings and no order (for, incredibly, the truce had not involved even so fundamental a requirement as the abandonment of Alfonso's claim to immediate possession of the crown), was falling into warlordism and anarchy. The great noblemen, whether for predation or for self-defense, were carving out private fiefdoms and defending them with private armies. Robbers and rapists ravaged the cities; highwaymen and marauding soldiers made most travel impossible; fires raged across abandoned fields; the poor starved to death huddled in their huts.[38] Henry pleaded piteously with Villena to help him do something to halt the devastation and restore order.

But Villena had no pity, only oceanic greed. He and his brother were already the most powerful men in Castile. Now they were aiming even higher, to merge with the royal family itself. In the cold bitter March of 1466 Villena presented new terms to the desperate king. He, of course, was now a loyal subject; but his brother Pedro Girón still held out for Alfonso and the rebels, commanding the biggest army in the southland, in Andalusia. He could persuade his brother to return to obedience to Henry, to enlist his potent army in the King's service, and to supply much money—specifically, 60,000 doubloons—to help restore order in the land. His brother's price was Princess Isabel for his wife. But Henry must decide quickly. Girón was already headed north with three thousand men.[39]

Henry agreed. He seems to have hesitated for no more than a few days at most.

The brothers had obviously planned this coup well in advance; its implementation could not possibly have moved as fast as it did without much prior preparation. There was the requirement for a Papal dispensation; Girón was canonically a celibate monk. The dispensation was obtained, and in a

---

Portugal durante el reinado de los Reyes Católicos (Valladolid, 1958-63), I, 43-57.

[37]Menéndez Pidal, *Historia de España*, XV, 270; Miller, *Henry IV*, pp. 182-183.

[38]Galíndez, "Crónica de Enrique IV," in Torres Fontes, *Estudio*, pp. 261-263; Miller, *Henry IV*, pp. 188-189; Walsh, *Isabella*, p. 43.

[39]Enríquez, Crónica, BAE LXX, 154 (Cp LXXXV); Palencia, *Crónica de Enrique IV*, I, 203 (Dc I, Lb IX, Cp I); Galíndez, "Crónica de Enrique IV," in Torres Fontes, *Estudio*, p. 271; Valera, *Hazañas*, p. 118.

matter of days;[40] it must have been requested before Villena stated his terms to Henry. (And in this act, dispensing a 43-year-old "monk" of the vilest reputation to marry a fourteen-year-old princess, Pope Paul II—often considered one of the better Renaissance Popes[41]—surely made an error very hard to forgive, however little he may have known of the background of the request. What stood on the face of it should have been more than sufficient for refusal. But there is not the slightest indication that Isabel, who believed with all her heart that the Pope is the Vicar of Christ on earth, ever held it against him. It may be one of the clearest proofs of that supernatural charity which is so fundamental a part of sanctity.)

This time there was no way for Isabel to divide her enemies. Even the Pope had decided against her. Girón would arrive in less than a month. He had proclaimed his intention to marry her immediately. She was trapped. Since her father died, before her earliest conscious memories, she had been essentially alone. Now her loneliness was like a vast cavern, engulfing every spark of light. Marriage to Afonso of Portugal, or to a king or prince in some more distant land, little as she desired it, could have been borne. Marriage to Pedro Girón, lecher and despoiler, as totally opposite to Isabel as any human being could be, was beyond bearing.

Many, in such a trap, would have thought of or threatened suicide. But this was Isabel the Catholic. It would never have occurred to her to take her own life. Yet death was the only way out of this crisis. Legend has faithful Beatriz vowing to plunge a dagger into Girón's heart rather than let this obscene union happen. But it is only legend, with no reliable historical evidence to support it; and Isabel would no more have countenanced murder than suicide.[42] Castile had seen more than enough murder since Alvaro de Luna flung her mother's hired assassin over that parapet thirteen years before.

What does a Christian do in a hopeless situation?

He—or she—prays.

And Isabel did pray, as she had never prayed before. A full day and night, on her knees. Over and over, simple, straightforward, direct as Isabel always was. There were just two ways out. She could do nothing about either, except to pray. They could be opened only by the Hand of God.

"Either let him die, or let me die. . . . Either let him die, or let me die. . . . Either let him die, or let me die."[43]

---

[40]Miller, *Henry IV*, pp. 187-188.

[41]Cf. Ludwig von Pastor, *History of the Popes from the Close of the Middle Ages* (St. Louis, 1914), IV, 191-194.

[42]Walsh, *Isabella*, pp. 40-41.

[43]Valera, *Hazañas*, p. 118; Galíndez, "Crónica de Enrique IV," in Torres Fontes, *Estudio*, p. 271; Palencia, *Crónica de Enrique IV*, I, 203-204 (Dc I, Lb IX, Cp I). Third person of indirect quotation changed to direct address in the quotation.

The minutes and the hours passed. Pray without ceasing, Christ had said. Persevere in your prayers, like the woman facing the unjust judge. Pray, and keep on praying.

"Either let him die, or let me die. . . . Either let him die, or let me die. . . . Either let him die, or let me die."

Girón was on the march. By April 13, at the head of his mighty host, he had reached El Berrueco castle, near Jaén. At the hour of vespers a veritable cloud of storks appeared, heading for the castle. Storks do not normally fly in flocks, but these did. They hid the sun, they circled the tower, the flapping of their great wings and their wild weird cries echoed fearsomely in the gloaming. No one had ever seen or heard anything like it. Then they flew on, to the north.[44]

North from El Berrueco rode Girón with his men, into the Sierra Morena, the Dark Mountains. Between the jagged portals framing the most famous defile in Spanish history, gate of reconquerors, home of heroes: Despeñaperros, the Pass of the Overthrow of the Infidel Dogs. (And what else, by his life and goal and fate, was Pedro Girón?) On through the pass, into the dead-flat plain of La Mancha. Across the plain, its grapevines spreading their leaves to the spring sun, until they came to its end at the Sierra de la Virgén, the Mountains of the Blessed Virgin Mary, and stopped for the night at the little town of Villarrubia de los Ojos, Villarrubia of the Eyes. And there they noticed that Pedro Girón, Master of Calatrava, was swaying in his saddle. They helped him down from his horse. Fever was flaring through his body. His throat was burning and filling with alien matter. He called for water, but he could not drink. The next day he grew worse; the next, worse still. Choking, strangling, cursing God with his last breath because He had not let him live to claim his virgin bride, on the third day Pedro Girón died.[45]

For Jesus Christ is King of Kings, and the earth is the Lord's; and prayers to Him are heard.

As Isabel the Catholic had always known, and would never forget.

For five months after this thunderbolt struck, Castile had respite from strife, as Villena, its chief promoter, was totally preoccupied for all that time with the settlement of his brother's vast estates, holdings, debts, and credits. But by the fall of 1466 he was back in action. He proposed to split the kingdom between the two kings, but could not lead even the grasping nobles quite so far as formally to dismember their country. Then, working with Archbishop Fonseca of Sevilla—a prelate, if possible, even less worthy than Archbishop Carrillo of Toledo—he lured Henry into arresting one of his most faithful

---

[44]Valera, *Hazañas*, p. 119.

[45]*Ibid.*; Enríquez, Crónica, BAE LXX, 154 (Cp LXXXV); Palencia, *Crónica de Enrique IV*, I, 204 (Dc I, Lb IX, Cp I); Galíndez, "Crónica de Enrique IV," in Torres Fontes, *Estudio*, p. 272.

supporters, a nobleman named Pedrarias Dávila. In the course of the arrest Dávila received a terrible wound, from which he never entirely recovered. He was an innocent man, as Henry himself soon had to admit. Embittered by pain and betrayal, Dávila changed from one of Henry's most loyal friends to his most relentless enemy. He dogged his footsteps, seeking to kill him or at least to make him suffer.[46]

But Henry had begged his pardon, and thought himself forgiven. When he led a new army into the field which fought the drawn Battle of Olmedo in August 1467 (pacifist Henry had to be lured unsuspecting into the battle by his captains, and fled at the first clash of arms), he left Dávila in his beloved Segovia, where his brother was bishop. Dávila handed the city over to Villena and Carrillo, who brought their army from Olmedo to occupy it.[47]

Alfonso was with them. He and Isabel had not seen each other for three years. Still not fourteen, at a highly impressionable age, Alfonso had been in the company of Villena and Carrillo all that time. With their encouragement of his hostile feelings, Henry had become in his eyes a hated rival. He had heard of the glade of Balsaín. Once in Segovia, he went out to it and personally killed, or ordered killed, every one of Henry's animals except the one he loved the best, a magnificent mountain goat. The mountain goat survived only because Villena told him to spare it.[48] Townsend Miller calls this act of Villena's "his only decent one of which there is record."[49]

The chroniclers tell us that Isabel welcomed the coming of the rebels to Segovia, implying that this was because they were liberating her from captivity by Henry and Juana.[50] But there is no reason whatever to suppose that Isabel thought of Villena, who had done his best to condemn her to a living hell, as a liberator. Surely her joy was not for the treason of Dávila nor for the arrival of the League's army, but because she could at last see her brother again. He needed her desperately. Unfortunately the accounts we have are not chronologically precise enough to tell us whether Alfonso went to Balsaín before or after his reunion with his sister. The slaughter of his animals was psychologically devastating for Henry. It is hard to imagine Isabel approving it; but even if she knew, she might not have been able to keep her brother from it. The effects of three years among robbers and murderers do not wear off in a day.

What Isabel really thought of her "liberators" is revealed with the utmost

---

[46]Menéndez Pidal, *Historia de España*, XV, 274, 277; Miller, *Henry IV*, pp. 190-192.

[47]Menéndez Pidal, *Historia de España*, XV, 279-280; Miller, *Henry IV*, pp. 197-214.

[48]Palencia, *Crónica de Enrique IV*, I, 237 (Dc I, Lb X, Cp IV).

[49]Miller, *Henry IV*, p. 217.

[50]Enríquez, Crónica, BAE LXX, 168 (Cp CI); Palencia, *Crónica de Enrique IV*, I, 232 (Dc I, Lb X, Cp I); Galíndez, "Crónica de Enrique IV," in Torres Fontes, Estudio, p. 308.

clarity by her demand that Villena and Carrillo provide at once a written guarantee of her personal liberty. No doubt rather sheepishly, they did so.[51] Thus protected (by whatever the word of these two scoundrels was worth), she went to work on getting Alfonso out of the bad company he had been keeping. By his birthday in November, if not before, she had brought him away from Segovia to Arévalo, back again with their mother and Beatriz de Bobadilla. In December Isabel and Alfonso went together for about two weeks to Medina del Campo, a rich town which Villena and Carrillo allowed Alfonso to give her. That meant she could choose its administrator. She chose her old teacher, Gonzalo Chacón.[52]

One of the most striking of Isabel's many attributes of greatness as a ruler was her almost unerring judgment of people. She had learned it in a hard school, and learned it well. It was to change the whole history of the world, when applied to a visionary navigator from Genoa named Columbus.

But Isabel was not only a superlative judge of character; she also had the great Christian virtue of forgiveness to a truly heroic degree, along with more than her share of the virtue of prudence. It is not hard to guess what she really thought of Villena and Carrillo. But she could not tell them what she thought, and should do her best not to keep thinking it; otherwise she would be on the road to becoming as devious as they. Christ had said to forgive seventy times seven. She conversed pleasantly with both men. By now they had known her long and well enough to begin to have genuine respect for her intellect, though such men could hardly conceive the full extent of her capacity or of her goodness. In May of 1468, after Isabel had spent five months with her brother in the familiar and healing atmosphere of Arévalo, the two of them went off to the great annual fair at Medina del Campo, her new city—and took Archbishop Carrillo with them.[53]

Imagination staggers before the spectacle of Isabel, grave and quiet and self-possessed beyond her years from her passage through the swarming perils that had so long beset her, growing more lovely every day at seventeen; her still probably rather bewildered and boisterous fourteen-year-old brother; and the towering, caped, loud-mouthed and bloody-minded archbishop, author of so many of their woes, strolling together through the arcades past the gypsies and the jugglers and the fast-talking salesmen at the Medina del Campo fair, the greatest in Spain. What could they possibly have found to say to one another there? But go they did; and it may even have been a memory that Isabel

[51]Menéndez Pidal, *Historia de España*, XV, 280, 286.
[52]Palencia, *Crónica de Enrique IV*, I, 239 (Dc I Lb X Cp V); Juan Torres Fontes, *El príncipe Don Alfonso, 1465-1468* (1973), pp. 128-129; Del Val, *Isabel*, p. 55; Miller, *Henry IV*, p. 219.
[53]Palencia, *Crónica de Enrique IV*, I, 246-247 (Dc I, Lb X, Cp IX); Torres Fontes, *El príncipe Don Alfonso*, p. 133.

cherished—for it was the last time Alfonso could be a boy, and innocently enjoy himself. The end of his young life, so wasted through little or no fault of his own, was at hand.

At the end of June the rebel army was back in action, marching on Toledo which, in the endless seesaw of civil war, had just declared itself for Henry after having previously been controlled by the rebels.[54] Alfonso, their titular commander, had to accompany them. Isabel was there, surely, only because he was. On July 1 the army camped near a tiny village called Cardeñosa. It was Friday. Alfonso was brought a succulent mountain trout for supper. He ate it all. The next morning he could not be roused. Four days later he was dead.[55]

There were rumors of poison; but Henry IV, for all his faults, was no assassin, nor so far as we know were his chief remaining adherents. None of the rebel leaders had the slightest reason for killing Alfonso, whom they all hoped to control and manipulate. The fish may simply have been spoiled; or some medical catastrophe, which that age could not diagnose, may have struck. We shall never know.

And now Isabel was Queen claimant of Castile.

Or was she? Her brother, as King claimant, had never been more than a puppet. But Isabel the Catholic was no man's puppet. In her seventeen years she had seen enough selfish, merciless manipulation of people and of her country to fill a dozen lifetimes. She herself had been saved only by a miracle from the worst of all the instances of this manipulation. Something extraordinary and dramatic had to be done to stop the cycle of destruction, to cut the nets of greed and blind ambition with a sword of fire.

Isabel sent letters and messages to provinces in the kingdom of Castile explaining that she was about to take counsel with the great nobles regarding the succession. These communications made it clear that she would assume her brother's long-standing claim to be Henry's heir, rather than Juana "la Beltraneja." But she did not say whether she intended to be proclaimed as reigning now, thereby accepting the legitimacy of Henry's deposition.[56] She went to the convent of St. Anne at Avila, to pray for guidance and help. She

[54]Menéndez Pidal, *Historia de España*, XV, 282; Miller, *Henry IV*, pp. 222-224.

[55]Enríquez, Crónica, BAE LXX, 178 (Cp CXIV); Palencia, *Crónica de Enrique IV*, I, 250 (Dc X, Lb X, Cp X).

[56]For the general tenor of these letters from Isabel, see Palencia, *Crónica de Enrique IV*, I, 256 (Dc II, Lb I, Cp I). For two specific examples, see her July 4 letter to the Council of Murcia (in which, with Alfonso still living though not expected to recover, she still referred to him as "king") (Torres Fontes, *Estudio*, pp. 505-506); and her July 8 instructions to Lope de Macacho whom she was sending as her emissary to Murcia (Juan Torres Fontes, *Don Pedro Fajardo, adelantado mayor del reino de Murcia* [Madrid, 1953], p. 109). On the careful distinction she made between her claim to the right of succession and a claim to immediate rule, see Luis Suárez Fernández, "En Torno al Pacto de los Toros de Guisando," *Hispania* XXIII (1963), 345-365, and del Val, *Isabel*, pp. 63-65.

surveyed her options and steeled her will.[57] Up to this point in her life, her mission had been to survive, and to help her mother and her brother. Now she had to take her country's destiny in her hands—and the world's. She was still, and more than ever, utterly alone.

Let us look at her, at this hour of decision, as the anonymous chronicler of the next seven years of her life saw her, giving us by far the most vivid description of Isabel we have—obviously drawn from life by one who loved her:

> The Princess had blue-green eyes with long eyelashes, full of sparkle along with great frankness and dignity. High arching eyebrows much enhanced the beauty of her eyes and countenance. Her nose was of a size and shape that made her face more beautiful. Her mouth was small and red, her teeth small and white. Her laughter was quiet and controlled; rarely was she seen to laugh in the customary manner of youth, but with restraint and moderation. In this and in all things the character and honor of womanly virtue shone in her face. She was regarded with such respect that no great prince who dealt with her had the audacity to be in the least discourteous to her. From her childhood she was brought up by her mother in honesty and virginal purity, so that never did her worst enemy find any reason or suggestion to stain her reputation. Her face colored readily under its white skin, and was of royal mien. Her hair was very long and golden-red, and she would often run her hands through it, to arrange it so as better to display the configuration of her face. Her throat was high, full and rounded, as women prefer it to be; her hands were exquisitely graceful; all her body and her person were as lovely as a woman's could be. She was moderately tall. In person and countenance no one in her time touched her perfection, refinement, and purity. Her aspect as she moved, and the beauty of her face, were luminous.[58]

Isabel deliberated no more than a few days at the convent of St. Anne. Her decision was probably already made when on July 20 she appointed her old teacher, Gonzalo Chacón the historian, as head of her household.[59] When Villena and Carrillo appeared before her, urging her to assume the crown as her brother had done, she had her answer ready. It rang like a silver bugle:

> Now that it has pleased God to take from this life Alfonso my brother, so long as King Henry may live I shall not take over the government, nor call myself Queen, but will make every effort to the end that King Henry, while he lives, may govern this realm better than he has done.[60]

---

[57]Palencia, *Crónica de Enrique IV*, I, 261 (Dc II, Lb I, Cp IV); del Val, *Isabel*, pp. 65-67; Miller, *Henry IV*, pp. 228-229.

[58]*Crónica incompleta de los Reyes Catolicos (1469-1476), según un manuscrito anónimo de la época*, ed. Julio Puyol (Madrid, 1934), pp. 88-89.

[59]Del Val, *Isabel*, p. 64.

[60]Valera, *Hazañas*, p. 139. Third person of indirect quotation changed to first person in the translation.

Henry is my brother, the King of Castile and León, and I should not please God if I were to commit so grave an act of disrespect [as you propose].[61]

Carrillo was furious; he remained bitterly angry over Isabel's decision for the next two months. But Villena swiftly, smoothly adapted himself to it. Despite Henry's periodic outbursts of stubbornness, Villena was confident that most of the time he could still manipulate him; sadly, the future was to show that his confidence in this regard was not misplaced. He also seems to have still thought he could manipulate Isabel. Soon he was having it said that Isabel had taken her epochal decision on his advice.[62] It is hardly likely; for the past year he had been pushing her brother on exactly the opposite course, and nothing had changed but her own advent. But it was probably Villena who now reopened the channels of communication to Henry, which he had so often used before. While Carrillo alternately raged and sulked, threatening periodically to depart from the area altogether, negotiations began August 17 at a little place called Castronuño. Henry was promised peace and undisturbed possession of his throne if he would formally recognize Isabel as his successor. The necessary price was the renunciation of little Juana.[63]

Henry had renounced his dubious daughter once before, under heavy pressure; but he had always been most reluctant to do so, and when the negotiations began at Castronuño, he still was. On August 15 he summoned his queen to join him in Madrid, saying that he wished to consult with her before making any decision on the matter of the succession.[64]

Queen Juana had been held hostage by Archbishop Fonseca of Sevilla ever since Segovia had been betrayed to Henry's enemies and she was captured in it. Fonseca had held her at an isolated castle in Alaejos, on the north Castilian plain not far from Song of the High Towers. When the mid-August summons arrived, she had been cooped up in Alaejos for almost a year, without contact of any kind with Henry. And she was six and a half months pregnant by one of her guardsmen.

She had covered her changing appearance with voluminous dresses; no one knew her condition but some of her attendants at the castle, and her paramour and a few of his friends. (Fonseca was busy stirring up trouble elsewhere in the kingdom.) But she could not face the king while pregnant with a child which could not possibly be his. Desperate, she had herself let down in

---

[61]"Libre de las dones," by an anonymous Franciscan, a chaplain to Adrian of Utrecht, reprinted in Vicente Rodriguez Valencia, *Isabel la Católica en la Opinion de Españoles y Extranjeros* (Valladolid, 1970), I, 314. Third person of indirect quotation changed to first person in the translation.

[62]Palencia, *Crónica de Enrique IV*, I, 261 (Dc II, Lb I, Cp IV).

[63]Del Val, *Isabel*, pp. 68-70; Miller, *Henry IV*, pp. 229-230.

[64]Del Val, *Isabel*, p. 72.

the middle of the night from her tower room in the castle by a basket suspended from a rope, planning to flee to the castle of the Mendozas at Buitrago, nearly a hundred miles away across the high Guadarrama Mountains; the Mendozas held her daughter and she hoped they would hide her until she came to term. The rope ran out. In the blackness, the maids who were letting her down could not see the ground. They let go the rope. But it had been too short. The basket crashed down; the queen's leg was broken and her face lacerated. The escape party below, near panic, threw her over a mule and fled. Bleeding, terrified, in great pain, she was in no condition to cross a mountain range. She sought refuge in, of all places, the great hall of Beltrán de la Cueva at Cuéllar, just forty miles away from Alaejos over the plain. Beltrán was carousing there with some of his boon companions. Informed that the queen, badly injured and pregnant, was at his door begging his help, he dismissed her with an ugly gibe, refusing her admittance.[65]

Somehow Juana finally reached Buitrago, but the secret was out; Beltrán's roistering guests told the story near and far, with unholy glee. It cast a thick new cloud on the legitimacy of her daughter, and held Henry up to still more public mockery. He no longer felt that he owed anything to Juana or her daughter. By August 25 he had sent word to the negotiators at Castronuño that he was ready to accept Isabel's terms, provided only that some way could be found to annul his marriage to Juana.[66]

Pope Paul II, who had always been cooperative with Henry, might have been willing to issue the annulment, but the contending parties could not wait the months required for a royal annulment proceeding in Rome. However, a solution to the problem was soon found. Since Henry's first marriage (to Princess Blanca of Navarra) had been annulled for non-consummation, the dispensation for his marriage to Juana had been only conditionally granted by Pope Nicholas V. The condition was that the three Spanish bishops who were to execute the dispensation should be satisfied that Henry had been impotent only with Blanca, not with all women. For thirteen years no one had ever questioned that this dispensation had been duly executed. But the three bishops assigned to execute it had been Sánchez of Ciudad Rodrigo (long dead), Fonseca, and Carrillo. The two survivors—both habitual traitors, committed opponents of Henry—promptly declared that they had never been satisfied as to the condition. Ergo—presto!—the marriage was invalid, and little Juana disinherited.[67]

We may imagine Isabel's disgust at these sordid proceedings, but she was

---

[65]Enríquez, Crónica, BAE LXX, 178-179 (Cp CXVII); Palencia, *Crónica de Enrique IV*, I, 258-260 (Dc II Lb I Cp III); Pulgar, *Crónica de los Reyes Católicos*, pp. 16-17; Menéndez Pidal, *Historia de España*, XV, 287; Miller, *Henry IV*, pp. 230-232.

[66]Menéndez Pidal, *Historia de España*, XV, 288; Miller, *Henry IV*, pp. 232-233.

[67]Del Val, *Isabel*, pp. 85-87; Miller, *Henry IV*, pp. 233-235.

in no position to complain about them. There was very good reason to believe little Juana to be in fact illegitimate, and no hope for peace in Castile in the foreseeable future if she were maintained as the heir. How Henry justified removing her from the succession was his problem. Isabel was a profoundly charitable woman; but in matters of state her mind was relentlessly logical, as tough and supple as a leather breastplate. Six years at Henry's court, watching Villena and Carrillo at work, had left her with no illusions about human nature in public affairs. She would not be a rebel, would not raise her hand against her anointed sovereign, unworthy though he was. But she would not let him and his political and personal legacy destroy her country and herself.

And so they came, the party of the rebel League and the party of the discredited king, still full of themselves and their ambitions, still scheming and plotting for better positions from which to continue the pillage of a prostrate kingdom and a suffering people, to a small wooded plain where the Alberche River winds between the rocky bulks of the Sierra de Gredos and the Guadarramas, midway between Avila and Madrid. It had been a place of assembly even in ancient times; four weathered stone bulls stood there, roughly sculpted in distant pagan antiquity, older than Julius Caesar. They gave the place its name of Toros de Guisando.[68]

On September 19, with retinues of thousands, Henry and Isabel met where the four bulls stood. Both of them were mounted; they greeted each other from their saddles. Bishop Antonio de Veneriis of León, the Papal legate, absolved those present of all past oaths which might conflict with those they were about to swear. Isabel, with all her following, swore loyalty to Henry. Henry forgave them for rebellion and all their other acts against him, and formally proclaimed Isabel his successor, with Castile's traditional title for the royal heir, Princess of the Asturias. All present swore loyalty to her as the heir. It was specified that she should never be forced to marry against her will; but Henry must also agree to her marriage. Upon Bible and crucifix they repeated their oaths.[69]

---

[68]The four bulls are still there today, though without their legs and worn down until they look more like pigs, in the midst of an untended field marked only by a small sign by the road.

[69]The Pact of Toros de Guisando was thoroughly reported by contemporary chroniclers and has been exhaustively studied by modern historians. The best contemporary accounts are Enríquez, *Crónica*, BAE LXX, 179 (Cp CXVIII); Palencia, *Crónica de Enrique IV*, I, 262-265 (Dc II Lb I Cp IV); Valera, *Hazañas*, pp. 143-147; Pulgar, *Crónica de los Reyes Católicos*, pp. 14-16; and the anonymous incomplete chronicle edited by Julio Puyol, pp. 64-68. Some of Palencia's details are suspect, notably his statement that Henry explicitly admitted that little Juana had been conceived in adultery. The full text of the Pact appears in Cuartero y Huerta, *Toros de Guisando*, pp. 119-123 and del Val, *Isabel*, pp. 365-372. Though the original has disappeared, we have two early copies and a notarized statement describing the proceedings. For description and analysis, including refutations of attempts by modern

For the first, but far from the last time in her splendid life, Isabel the Catholic had triumphed against all odds, over her enemies and over all who sought to use and control her.

But she was still alone—and that could not and need not continue much longer. There was hardly anyone holding power in Castile whom she could trust. In the past she had been a pawn on the matrimonial chessboard. But now she was Princess of the Asturias, heir to the throne of Castile; and she had a guarantee, sworn by the most solemn oaths, that she would not be married without her consent. The princess could make her choice of a prince.

Away to the northeast, in Aragon, King Juan II had reached the age of seventy. For three years he had been totally blind from cataracts. But the dream of his life would not fade from his mental vision: the union of the two Spanish kingdoms, Castile and Aragon, to make a far greater nation than either could ever be alone, united by their common crusading heritage. He had but one living son, Fernando, by his second wife, dark-eyed, brilliant, devoted Juana Enríquez, dead tragically this very year of cancer of the breast. Fernando was sixteen, just a year younger than Isabel. He was all that Juan of Aragon had ever hoped for in a son. From the moment he had first heard of young Alfonso's death in July, Juan had thought of nothing but how to bring about Fernando's marriage to Isabel.[70]

Though he had many connections in Castile, he also had powerful enemies in both factions there. Villena was the most dangerous of them. But Juan II of Aragon was older and even more experienced than the Machiavellian Marqués. He believed he could defeat him, and gain the union so long sought. There is no reason to suppose that he had as yet any real understanding of the quality of Isabel. But his own wife had borne more than a little resemblance to her in intelligence and courage; Juan II, at least, was capable of appreciating what Isabel was when he did come to know her. And in many ways their interests coincided.

But he could not go into so great an enterprise blind. His skilled Jewish doctors had told him that cataracts could be cleared by surgery. But this was long before anesthetics and antiseptics. An operation—especially one like this, with knives plunging into the eyes, could drive a man mad with pain and terror. A post-operative infection could kill him. His wife had not let Juan try it; she feared too much to lose him. But now she was dead, and his time had come.

historians to cast doubt on the authenticity of the Pact (for example, Jaime Vicens Vives, *Historia crítica de la vida y reinado de Fernando II de Aragon* [Zaragoza, 1962], pp. 236-242) see Luis Suárez Fernández, "En Torno al Pacto de los Toros de Guisando," *Hispania* XXIII (1963), 345-365; Juan Torres Fontes, "La Contratación de Guisando," *Anuario de Estudios Medievales* II (1965), 399-428; del Val, *Isabel*, pp. 76-91; Miller, *Henry IV*, pp. 235-238.
[70]Miller, *Henry IV*, pp. 96-97, 227, 241.

On September 12, just seven days before the Pact of Toros de Guisando—of whose terms he was already well aware—the iron-souled King of Aragon put himself under the knife. He survived; the operation was a success; he could see again.[71] Now at last Princess Isabel had an ally who was fully a match in experience and guile for any of her enemies.

[71]Valera, *Hazañas*, pp. 136-137; Palencia, *Crónica de Enrique IV*, I, 241 (Dc I, Lb X, Cp VI); Menéndez Pidal, *Historia de España*, XV, 452.

3
A Prince Comes
(September 1468-December 1474)

Loyalty and honor had become the rarest of qualities among the high nobles of Castile during the tragic reign of Henry IV. The ink was scarcely dry on the official record of the solemn pledges of Toros de Guisando, sworn upon Bible and crucifix, when the grandees were plotting how to twist and break them to their own advantage.

Villena, as usual, had entry to every camp. He could still pose as Isabel's defender, since he pretended to have been the architect of the Pact of Toros de Guisando; he had long cultivated Portugal as a counterweight to Aragon; he had cooperated closely for years with Archbishop Carrillo, though Carrillo was much more pro-Aragon than Villena generally was; he had always been on very good terms with King Louis XI of France, to whom he had betrayed his own king at the Bidassoa in 1463; he cultivated Queen Juana and her supporters, the Mendozas, with much success whenever it served his purpose. He had even worked with Aragon from time to time, as when he joined the League of Tudela against King Henry after being dismissed from the King's service in 1463, though the fact that much of his vast estate as Marqués of Villena was also claimed by the royal family of Aragon made them always a threat to him.

Trading busily with all these factions, the least of Villena's concerns were Isabel's interests or the King's. Before a month had passed after the Pact of Toros de Guisando, Villena had cobbled together a new secret agreement with the Mendozas, the Velascos, the Marqués de Santillana, the Count of Plasencia, and Bishop Fonseca of Sevilla. The Mendozas, with whom the pregnant Queen Juana and her daughter had finally obtained refuge, had refused to accept the Pact of Toros de Guisando, but were satisfied by Villena's latest deal: Isabel would marry King Afonso of Portugal (whom she had firmly and wisely rejected four and a half years before on the banks of the Tagus); Crown Prince John (Joao) of Portugal would be betrothed to little Juana; the first-born son of either marriage would be heir to Castile.[1] That growing chaos in Castile would

[1] Diego Enríquez del Castillo, "Crónica del Rey don Enrique IV," *Crónicas de los Reyes de Castilla*, ed. Cayetano Rosell, Biblioteca de Autores Españoles, Vol. LXX (Madrid, 1878), p. 180 (chapter 121) (hereinafter cited as Enríquez, Crónica, BAE,

be the obvious consequence of such blurring of the rightful lines of succession seemed to bother none of the deal-makers; they may even have desired exactly that, for their own further aggrandizement.

They sent Pedro de Velasco to explain it all to Isabel after the agreement was made. Henry (whom they had also told about it after the fact) declared it to be his royal will. (He, who had been Villena's target, was now his helpless puppet, and would remain so for the rest of his life.) Isabel reminded Velasco of the provision in the Pact of Toros de Guisando that she was not to be married without her consent. He looked in astonishment at a princess so naive as still to believe that a man's word was his bond in politics. The matter had been decided, Velasco told her icily. She would do as she was told or be locked up in a castle.[2]

Isabel was still only seventeen years old. She had long observed the moral squalor at the Castilian court; she knew how thinly the velvet gloves covered the iron hands of its most skillful political operators. But knowledge of evil is not the same thing as beholding its naked face. This may well have been Isabel's first experience of that—the first explicit, merciless threat addressed to her personally. It is not for nothing that castle dungeons are laden with nightmarish legend. Men—and women—could be held in them for years, never seeing the sun. They could go mad in them. So it was to be, one day, with Isabel's own daughter, Juana "la loca."

Isabel the Catholic was a woman of magnificent courage. It is only at this point in all her life that we see her, confronting deadly menace, in tears. (She was to weep much for her children, but never again in public for herself.) For a moment, the steady blue-green eyes dimmed. Her face flushed crimson. But somehow she kept her voice firm and steady.

"God is my refuge," she said. "I call upon Him to keep me free from so great a shame and to guard me from such cruel injury."[3]

LXX); Ramón Menéndez Pidal, director, *Historia de España*, Volume XV: "Los Trastámaras de Castilla y Aragon en el Siglo XV," by Luis Suaréz Fernández, Angel Canellas López, and Jaime Vicens Vives (Madrid, 1986), p. 289.

[2]Alonso de Palencia, *Crónica de Enrique IV*, Volume I (Biblioteca de Autores Españoles, Vol. 257, Madrid, 1973), p. 270 (Decada [Dc] II, Libro [Lb] I, Capitulo [Cp] VII); Mosén Diego de Valera, *Memorial de diversas hazañas; crónica de Enrique IV*, ed. Juan de Mata Carriazo (Madrid, 1941), pp. 149-150 (hereinafter cited as Valera, *Hazañas*).

[3]Palencia, *loc. cit.*; Valera, *Hazañas*, p. 150. Indirect quotation in Palencia is changed to direct. Palencia was not only one of the principal historians of the reigns of Henry IV and Isabel, but was at court at this time working closely with her and with Carrillo, and was soon to play a critical role in bringing Prince Fernando into Castile to marry her. His description of Isabel's reactions and appearance in this meeting is so detailed and specific as to suggest either that he was an eyewitness (unlikely but possible) or had a report of it from Velasco himself. The thrust of Isabel's response is confirmed by Valera.

She was confident she would never call upon Him for aid in vain. For it had not been in vain that she had called upon Him when Pedro Girón, the Master of Calatrava, was riding through the Pass of the Overthrow of the Infidel Dogs on his way to ravish her two years before—but never arrived.

This time, as it turned out, there was no need of a thunderbolt from Heaven. Isabel was no longer friendless and alone. From the moment that sight was restored to his old eyes after his cataract operations, King Juan II of Aragon had begun a long-distance duel with Villena, using the Spanish Machiavelli's own weapons. King Juan's most skilled, trusted—and ruthless—envoy, Pierres de Peralta, Constable of Navarra, arrived at the Castilian court at Ocaña near Madrid in the middle of November. Peralta had waded the Tagus River at a difficult ford with a strong current to meet Isabel secretly and let her know of the total commitment of the King of Aragon to making it possible for her to marry his son Fernando. King Juan's keen eye had already spotted the principal weakness in Villena's new coalition: the adherence of the Mendozas. His instructions to Peralta ordered him to set to work at once to suborn them.[4]

In this task, Peralta was aided by the fact that Queen Juana too was resisting the double marriage proposal. She was in her last month of an adulterous pregnancy which had brought scandal and disgrace upon both the Castilian royal house and her own family in Portugal. Henry wanted nothing more to do with her. If she went to Portugal with her six-year-old daughter following the little girl's betrothal to Portuguese Prince John, she might never be allowed to come back—might be forced into a convent, or even a dungeon. If the Mendozas lost her, they would lose a major asset in the political game.[5] They began to ask themselves how much they would really gain, after all, from Villena's deal. Perhaps, as Peralta kept telling them, they could get more from Juan. And it seems likely that Isabel's firmness impressed them. She had shown that Villena could not bend her to his will. It might be better to be on her side.

Meanwhile the immediate threat to Isabel was averted by Archbishop Carrillo, now transformed into her partisan because of his long-standing connections with the cause of Aragon and his estrangement from Villena after the Pact of Toros de Guisando. Villena had brought the court to Ocaña, which he owned; but Carrillo owned the town of Yepes just seven miles away, and came there to stay while the court was in Ocaña. Carrillo was not welcome at

---

[4]Palencia, *Crónica de Enrique IV*, I, 270 (Dc II Lb I Cp VII); instructions for Pierres de Peralta, November 1, 1468, and letter from Peralta in 1469, in Antonio Paz y Melia, *El Cronista Alonso de Palencia; su vida y sus obras* (Madrid, 1914), pp. 79-81; Menéndez Pidal, *Historia de España*, XV, 290.

[5]Enríquez, Crónica, BAE, LXX, 181 (Cp CXXII); Isabel del Val, *Isabel la Católica, Princesa* (Valladolid, 1974), p. 87n.

court, but could not be kept out of Yepes without a massive use of force which the belligerent archbishop would be certain to reciprocate. He assembled at Yepes a strong contingent of well-armed cavalry and let Villena know that if any attempt was made to imprison Isabel, he would use them at once for her rescue.[6]

It was check, but far from checkmate; both sides were balanced in a perilous and almost certainly short-lived equilibrium. Isabel could be protected for the moment; but she could not go on much longer being a princess alone. She must marry someone. If not Afonso of Portugal, who?

One other prospective bridegroom was proposed besides Fernando: Charles, Duke of Guyenne, brother of King Louis XI of France, and his heir because after sixteen years of marriage the French king had not yet had a son, and by ancient law a woman could not rule in France. But Louis' wife had married him at twelve; she had at least another fifteen child-bearing years, and in fact was to provide the longed-for male heir just two years later.[7] In that case Charles would remain no more than another French duke. Isabel had, if possible, even less interest in or intention of marrying him than of marrying fat old Afonso of Portugal. Her mind's eye was fixed on Fernando.

She had never seen the Crown Prince of Aragon, who bore the title King of Sicily, since Sicily and southern Italy were dominions of Aragon. She knew that he was a year younger than she, but not that he was well-formed though rather small in stature, with large dark almond-shaped eyes, pale skin, and hair of a dark reddish-brown, full and flowing.[8] He was quick, decisive, and brave. From his parents—indefatigable, far-seeing King Juan II and splendidly competent, devoted Juana Enríquez—Prince Fernando had acquired unusual intelligence and practical capacity, stability and strength. Though he was committed to the Catholic Faith and attended Mass frequently, he lacked Isabel's highly developed moral sense; but he knew how to respect goodness, especially among those personally close to him, even when not fully sharing it.

For the future of Spain, this marriage was desirable above all. Aragon and Castile had always been drawn to each other; there had never been a sense of deep division between them. Three hundred and fifty years before, Queen Urraca of Castile had married King Alfonso the Battler of Aragon—a union generally welcomed at first in both countries, though eventually broken up for lack of a proper Papal dispensation and in the absence of any children. Fifty-six years before, the brother of the King of Castile, Fernando of Antequera, had

---

[6]Townsend Miller, *Henry IV of Castile* (Philadelphia, 1972), pp. 239-240; del Val, *Isabel*, pp. 130-131.

[7]Paul Murray Kendall, *Louis XI* (New York, 1971), pp. 75, 385.

[8]For a personal description of Fernando in his youth, see *Crónica incompleta de los Reyes Católicos (1469-1476), según un manuscrito anónimo de la época*, ed. Julio Puyol (Madrid, 1934), pp. 87-88 (hereinafter cited as Puyol, ed., *Crónica incompleta.*)

been chosen king of Aragon when its royal line died out. King Juan II of Aragon was the second son of Fernando of Antequera; he and his brothers retained great estates in Castile. No natural frontier separated the two countries. Aragon contained a region and people ethnically and linguistically distinct from the rest of Spain—Catalonia—and ruled distant southern Italy and Sicily as well; but the heart of the kingdom, around Zaragoza, was as Spanish as Castile and spoke a language almost identical. Though superficially it might have appeared that Castile could just as well have united with Portugal on its west as with Aragon on its east, in fact there had always been a greater difference on the Portuguese side, linguistically and geographically and above all in attitudes. When in the previous century Castilian King Juan I married Portuguese Queen Beatriz, Portugal had risen in a massive popular revolt against the "foreign" king and decisively defeated him at the Battle of Aljubarrota in 1385. The union of Castile and Aragon would be much easier and more natural than a union of Castile and Portugal. It would provide the foundations of a great nation—if that nation could be properly governed and kept in order, as neither Aragon nor Castile had been for almost all of the fifteenth century thus far.

Isabel was far too intelligent to fail to see the opportunity. She and Fernando, married, of almost the same age, beginning and remaining as equals, had the best chance anyone was ever likely to have of achieving a peaceful union of their two countries. They would need each other too much for either to seek a dominant role. Married to any other king or prince, Isabel would be unable to govern Castile effectively; after sixty years of neglect and disorder it desperately needed firm and comprehensive rule, and that could not be a part-time job. But she could not rule it alone even if she were left alone to rule it. Her clash with Velasco had shown that. She must have a husband, as nearly as possible her political equal, who would champion her cause as well as his own, in the council chamber and on the battlefield.

But for Isabel the Catholic, there was more. She well knew what Catholic marriage is, supernaturally as well as naturally. She knew that it is a genuine, profound personal as well as political union, even when both partners are monarchs. She knew that the husband must be the head of the family, whatever his political status or that of his wife, and that no broader responsibilities can eclipse the responsibility of the parents in a family to their children. She knew that sacramental marriages are registered in Heaven and that God will judge every husband and wife in substantial part on how well they respond to the graces provided by that sacrament. It was her duty, even as a princess and a queen-to-be, to choose as her husband the eligible king or prince with whom she had the best reason to believe that a successful marriage by Catholic standards could be attained. She knew—and always insisted—that, whatever political consequences might accompany and follow it, any valid marriage must ultimately be the free choice of both partners. Isabel the Catholic was not the kind of person to have demanded liberty to marry as a key condition of the Pact of Toros de Guisando purely or primarily for the fulfillment of political ambitions. Most of all she wanted that liberty so that she could make a good marriage that would be pleasing to God.

Personal judgment and political advantage combined to favor Fernando in her eyes. She had rejected all other suitors; she accepted Fernando, under the circumstances, very quickly. The Pact of Toros de Guisando had freed her for marriage in September. The attempt by Villena and Velasco and their confederates to bind her again probably occurred in November—about the time, or very shortly before the arrival of Peralta, the envoy of Juan of Aragon. At least by Christmas, probably earlier, a marriage agreement for Isabel and Fernando was actually being drafted by both parties (or their representatives). It provided that both of them must consent to any measures taken or appointments made in the government of Castile, and that Fernando would reside there and not leave without his wife's consent. Fernando signed the draft agreement and sent it on to his father, who gave it initial approval on January 12, 1469.[9] By January Peralta's persuasions and Isabel's example had brought most of the Mendozas, the Bishop of Sigüenza, the Marqués of Santillana, and even Pedro Velasco out of Villena's camp and into Isabel's; that month they all secretly swore to recognize her as heir, "cost what it might," and left the court, dropping their opposition to the Aragonese marriage.[10]

One major obstacle dogged the whole undertaking: lack of a Papal dispensation. Isabel and Fernando were second cousins; their paternal grandfathers had been brothers. The degrees of relationship within which the Church prohibited marriage without a Papal dispensation were then (and remained until quite recent times) very broad; most of the royal families of Europe fell within them, so that almost every royal marriage required a dispensation. The necessary dispensation often became a political prize to be bargained or even paid for; so it was in this case. Popes of the fifteenth century tended to be hostile to Aragon because of its extensive territorial claims in Italy; even though Aragon's claims were based on the Sicilian revolt against the Angevin kings and the rebels' decision to place themselves under the rule and protection of the crown of Aragon in 1282, the Spanish Aragonese were still widely seen as foreign invaders. Pope Paul II, reigning since 1464, had been particularly hostile to Aragon and friendly to Castile; consequently he favored the Portuguese marriage for Isabel, for which later (when that marriage was no longer feasible) he granted a dispensation. He had not even replied to most of Juan II's messages and requests for a dispensation for the marriage of

---

[9]Diego Clemencín, *Elógio de la Reina Católica Doña Isabel* (Madrid, 1821), pp. 577-581.

[10]Menéndez Pidal, *Historia de España*, XV, 290.

Fernando and Isabel.[11]

However, on January 4 Bishop Juan Arias of Segovia, a friend of the Aragonese cause, announced that he had in his possession a dispensation from the previous Pope, Pius II, executed shortly before his death in 1464, which permitted Fernando to marry anyone related to him in the third prohibited degree (which was the degree that included Isabel) within the next five years, and commissioned the Bishops of Segovia and Cartagena to fill in the name of any prospective bride to whom it applied, during that period. The bishop of Cartagena in 1464 having died, only Bishop Arias remained; and he filled in Isabel's name. Such a dispensation, if authentic, would have rendered unnecessary all Juan II's previous pleas for a dispensation from Pope Paul II. It was almost certainly spurious.[12] There is no specific evidence of who concocted it, but one seems to feel the practiced and by no means always scrupulous hands of Juan II and Peralta (or perhaps Carrillo). There is no reason to believe that Isabel questioned its authenticity at the time; indeed, it may well have been her insistence on the canonically required dispensation (which Paul II refused to grant) that made the forgery necessary.

It seemed to remove the last barrier. Juan II approved the draft marriage agreement, despite its strict provisions maintaining the separate self-governing rights and financial integrity of Castile.[13] On January 30 a second envoy from Aragon, Juan Ferrer, wrote triumphantly to his master that Isabel had told him that no one should have her but Fernando: "He it shall be and never any other."[14] Probably at this time, and if not then assuredly not long afterward, Isabel wrote to Fernando, sending the letter by a special messenger to whom the detailed arrangements to be made were entrusted orally in case a written explanation should be lost or stolen. In her short but moving letter, she asked that Fernando give faith to the message and "tell me what you now wish me to do, so that I may do it."[15]

Princess Isabel at seventeen had pledged her troth; and when Isabel the Catholic made a promise, it would be kept even though the sky should fall.

On March 5 Fernando signed the final draft of the marriage treaty; on March 12 his father approved it, with a cautious new clause requiring that Isabel must be fully at liberty for the marriage to take place. Early in April the first meeting of the *cortes* (parliamentary assembly) of Castile to be held in four

---

[11]Miller, *Henry IV*, pp. 241-242. The bull of dispensation for the marriage of Isabel with King Afonso V of Portugal was dated June 23, 1469 (Antonio de la Torre and Luis Suárez Fernández, eds., *Documentos referentes a las relaciones con Portugal durante el reinado de los Reyes Católicos* [Valladolid, 1958-63], I, 66-67).

[12]Del Val, *Isabel*, pp. 193-195.

[13]*Ibid.*, p. 155.

[14]Juan Ferrer to Juan II of Aragon, January 30, 1469, in Paz y Melia, *Palencia*, p. 85.

[15]Jaime Vicens Vives, *Historia crítica de la vida y reinado de Fernando II de Aragón* (Zaragoza, 1962), p. 247.

years convened at Ocaña, where court was still being held. Only ten cities were represented, and accounts differ on how many of them swore allegiance to Isabel (some cities, such as Baeza, had already so sworn the preceding fall). But there was clearly strong sentiment in her favor, despite the court's coldness toward her. At the same time, Villena was putting together a new confederation of nobles, and finalized a treaty of alliance with Portugal. It provided that Afonso would marry Isabel, whether she liked it or not, and that if she and her partisans resisted, the Portuguese would provide 2,000 knights and 5,000 infantry to overcome that resistance. Part of the price for the new confederation was the marriage of Villena's son Diego to Juana de Luna, of the still powerful family of Alvaro de Luna, and the turning over of the Villena estates to Diego. The former Marqués of Villena retained the office of Master of Santiago, the most powerful and lucrative in Spain, and is therefore henceforth rightly called only by this name or by his given name of Juan Pacheco.[16]

So the precarious equilibrium of forces still endured; and Pacheco (formerly Villena) developed a typically devious plan for breaking it in his favor. Its design shows that he still greatly underestimated and misunderstood Isabel—not surprisingly, in view of the almost total difference in their characters. He proposed to take advantage of what he saw as her naiveté and rashness, while profiting from the respect she had gained for keeping her word. He knew the envoys from Aragon had been frequently in touch with her about marriage to Fernando, and that she inclined toward it. He does not appear to have known that the marriage negotiations had in fact already been concluded. (Indeed, even as Pacheco was working out his latest plot, Fernando had promised her as a wedding gift a magnificent gold necklace left to him by his mother, adorned by seven splendid rubies along with eight gray pearls.) Therefore Pacheco proposed to Henry (who promptly agreed) that they go to Andalusia to try to restore peace to that restive region and submission of its nobles to the tenuous royal authority, while leaving Isabel at Ocaña with a pledge to remain there and do "nothing new" about her marriage while the King was away in the south. Villena expected her to flee Ocaña as soon as she was sure that her chief enemies were gone, and to seek a commitment from Aragon for marriage to Fernando; he could then accuse her of breaking her promise and the Pact of Toros de Guisando as well, which forbade her from marrying without Henry's consent, hopefully rouse public opinion against her, and gain a legal basis for imprisoning her as Velasco had threatened the preceding fall.[17]

---

[16]Menéndez Pidal, *Historia de España*, XV, 291-292, 295; del Val, *Isabel*, pp. 159, 252, 388-396, 440-449; Miller, *Henry IV*, pp. 244-245.

[17]Palencia, *Crónica de Enrique IV*, I, 273-275 (Dc II Lb I Cp VIII); Valera, *Hazañas*, p. 154.

Isabel regarded the Pact of Toros de Guisando as still in effect so far as her status as heir was concerned, but considered its provisions regarding her marriage to have been abrogated by their blatant violation when Villena's coalition, in Henry's name, had attempted to force her into marriage with Afonso of Portugal by threatening to imprison her. As for doing "nothing new" about her marriage, she could promise that with a clear conscience, because everything necessary had already been done. The only promise she would violate would be that of staying at Ocaña—something she felt no obligation to do when her life and liberty were threatened.

So she watched the royal party ride away from Ocaña toward the south on May 7[18] with a determination soon to escape their control once and for all, relying on the justice of her cause and the help of Juan II of Aragon to maintain her position in Castile. She lost no time. Before the month was over she was riding north; Juan II had word of it before May 30.[19]

Meanwhile, in the south, Pacheco's latest confederation had dissolved like a sand castle in the face of the scorn and contempt of most of the Andalusian nobles, who had finally learned how utterly untrustworthy this man and all his promises were. The royal party managed to get into the old Moorish capital of Córdoba on May 26, from which was optimistically proclaimed the pacification of Andalusia. The hollowness of that claim became apparent when the city of Antequera refused to allow the King to enter it at all, while Sevilla declared it would admit the King only if he left his evil genius Pacheco outside. The two premier noblemen in Castilian territory south of Sevilla, the Duke of Medina Sidonia and the Marqués of Cadiz, gave full support to Sevilla and its *alcaide* (commander), whom Pacheco had told Henry to remove; in the end, the battered royal court had to withdraw to the little town of Alcalá de Guadaira. Struggling to mend his fences, Pacheco regained the support of the powerful Count of Plasencia, but only on condition that the royal army would take the city of Trujillo for him. The *alcaide* in Trujillo, the redoubtable Gracián de Sesé, had other ideas; he refused to deliver the city, and held out firmly. All through the tremendous events of the late summer of 1469, leading up to the marriage of Isabel and Fernando, the royal army was encamped immovably at the fruitless siege of Trujillo.[20]

Isabel, after leaving Ocaña, tried first to gain entry to Arévalo, where she lived as a child when it belonged to her mother, and whose *alcaide* had been her partisan. But now Arévalo belonged to the Count of Plasencia, with whom Pacheco had made his latest league; when she approached, she found that the Count had ordered the arrest of the friendly *alcaide*, and she had to turn away.

[18]Palencia, *Crónica de Enrique IV*, I, 274 (Dc II Lb I Cp VIII).
[19]P. Tarsicio de Azcona, *Isabel la Católica* (Madrid, 1964), pp. 145-146.
[20]Enríquez, Crónica, BAE, LXX, 185-187 (Cp 132-136); Valera, *Hazañas*, pp. 158-159.

She rode on to her birthplace, Song of the High Towers, whose people welcomed her, and there she stayed through most of June and July; but despite the King and Pacheco being tied up in the south, she was not safe. Her emissary Palencia the historian went to Aragon, where he conferred with Juan II and Fernando, urging that the final arrangements be completed and the marriage take place as soon as possible; but the important city of Gerona in northern Catalonia had just been betrayed to the French, so Aragon could provide no military support for Isabel. Fernando had to go to Valencia to redeem the precious necklace he was to give to Isabel (it had been pawned to help raise money for the war in Catalonia); he did not leave until June 29, and the journey and the arrangements in Valencia required three weeks. Meanwhile Archbishop Fonseca of Sevilla, a strong Portuguese partisan and long Isabel's enemy, was on his estate at Coca, just 35 miles away from Song of the High Towers. Worse still, Isabel's two closest friends, Beatriz de Bobadilla and Mencia de la Torre, after counselling her against marrying Fernando, had actually gone to Coca. She could not believe they would betray her, and so far as we know they did not; but the fact remained that they were not at her side in this critical hour, but in the establishment of her foe.[21]

The purpose of Isabel's flight from Ocaña was to fulfill the condition set by Juan II of Aragon in her marriage agreement with Fernando, that she be fully at liberty for the marriage to take place. She was now at liberty, but her liberty was precarious. The French ambassador, the Cardinal of Albi, came to her to urge marriage to the French heir, the Duke of Guyenne; Fonseca held his hand until it was clear that she was not going to accept this proposal. (Evidently neither he nor anyone else on Pacheco's side knew, even yet, that a final marriage agreement between Fernando and Isabel had been signed.) But Fonseca's spies were very active, and he sent a steady stream of reports to Pacheco.[22] It was probably at this time (August) that they finally began to suspect strongly that a definite agreement had been made for Isabel's marriage to Fernando. This meant that now, for them, everything depended on preventing Isabel and Fernando from meeting and marrying—just as for Isabel everything now depended on her being able to meet and marry Fernando. She could expect no justice in Castile as it now was; and though the people generally loved and sympathized with her, they alone could not defend her.

A royal proclamation was therefore sent to Song of the High Towers condemning Isabel and ordering her arrest. No one in the town where she was

---

[21]Palencia, *Crónica de Enrique IV*, I, 277-278, 284 (Dc II Lb I Cp X and Lb II Cp I); Enríquez, Crónica, BAE LXX, 185 (Cp 131); Lorenzo Galíndez de Carvajal, Cronica de Enrique IV, in Juan Torres Fontes, *Estudio sobre la "Crónica de Enrique IV"* (Murcia, 1946), pp. 350-351; del Val, *Isabel*, p. 162.

[22]Enríquez, Crónica de Enrique IV, BAE, LXX, 185 (ch. 131); Palencia, *Crónica de Enrique IV*, I, 281-282 (Dc II Lb II Cp I).

born would lift a finger to do that; but they were afraid, for they had no strong defenses and no soldiers who could stand for a moment against the heavily armed and armored cavalry of the great nobles. It would take Fonseca very little time to assemble such a cavalry force and cross the 35 miles of flat Castilian plain from Coca; indeed, he was now on the verge of doing exactly that, having realized that none could predict when the King and Pacheco would return and that he should wait no longer for them. Isabel wrote at once asking for aid from Carrillo and from Fadrique Enríquez, Admiral of Castile, who was related to the royal family of Aragon and had always been their partisan. They responded instantly. Admiral Fadrique, an old man, sent his son Alonso with 200 horsemen. Carrillo came in person with three hundred.[23]

Alonso Carrillo, Archbishop of Toledo, is far from an inspirational figure. He prostituted his high and holy office; he was designing, greedy, ruthless; had it not been for Isabel, he and Villena/Pacheco would probably have destroyed the Castilian state. But even men far gone in evil are sometimes given a moment for genuine glory. This was Carrillo's moment. He should never have been a priest, much less an archbishop; but he was a man of action who knew exactly what to do in a crisis like this. He collected his horsemen posthaste and led them thundering into Salamanca at a pace so punishing, in the blazing midsummer sun on the high plains of Castile, as to leave the road behind him strewn with exhausted men and horses. Pacheco's wife, in Salamanca, sought to delay or divert him. She might as well have tried to delay or divert a whirlwind. With a magnificent outburst of scorn against her husband and all his works, Carrillo was off in another cloud of dust, to meet at the little village of Cabezas del Pozo with Alonso Fadriguez's band. Together their five hundred horsemen rode into Song of the High Towers, pennons whipping in the wind and lances gleaming in the sunlight. Fonseca was indeed on the march, with 400 cavalry; but they had beaten him by three days with a force larger than his. Isabel was safe. Carrillo brought her the ruby and pearl necklace which was Fernando's marriage gift, and a letter from Fernando expressing profound regret that he could not bring it himself, in view of the critical situation of the war in Catalonia.[24]

Characteristically, Isabel's first action after being rescued was to go to help her two friends who were in Archbishop Fonseca's power, even though they had gone to his stronghold voluntarily, deserting her. With her newly arrived cavalry escort she rode to Coca to assure herself of their safety. (Fonseca prudently stayed well away.) Whether they left with her then, we are not told; but soon afterward Beatriz de Bobadilla married Andrés de Cabrera,

---

[23]Palencia, *Crónica de Enrique IV*, I, 282-283 (Dc II Lb II Cp I); Valera, *Hazañas*, pp. 159-160; Puyol, ed., *Crónica incompleta*, pp. 76-79.
[24]Palencia, *Crónica de Enrique IV*, I, 283-284 (Dc II Lb II Cp I); Miller, *Henry IV*, p. 251.

who had previously been in the other camp, and eventually brought him over to Isabel's side, where he was to give her long and faithful service.[25]

The next step was to provide Isabel with the best possible protection while Juan II and Fernando were informed of her narrow escape and the necessity of her marriage to Fernando at the earliest feasible moment. The best protection for Isabel until he came would be provided by a large walled city whose people would join her guard in defending her to the death. They thought first of Avila, whose mighty medieval walls still stand, immune to surprise attack on its high open plain, only forty miles south of her childhood home at Arévalo; its people never wavered in their loyalty to her, but Avila was at this time beset by plague, and they had to look elsewhere. They settled on Valladolid, only a little farther away in the opposite direction (north), where lived Juan de Vivero, a leading nobleman married to Carrillo's niece. On August 30 Isabel and her hard-riding escort arrived at Valladolid, where they were greeted with great enthusiasm. On hearing of her rescue and arrival there, in mid-September, Pacheco and his minions finally raised the siege of Trujillo and prepared to start north.[26]

Isabel lost no time. She drafted a circular letter to all the cities of the realm justifying her actions since leaving Ocaña and explaining how beneficial her marriage to Fernando would be for Castile and for all Spain, and had it copied and dispatched September 8. A few days later she sent two of her most trusted envoys to Aragon with instructions to make every effort to bring Fernando back with them just as soon as possible. The envoys were Gutierre de Cárdenas, nephew of her old teacher Gonzalo Chacón, and Alonso Palencia the historian.[27]

The Castilian countryside between Valladolid and the Aragon border was a patchwork of estates of noblemen and bishops, most of whose loyalties (such as they were) might change at any moment with sufficient inducement. Pacheco was fully alive to the danger now, and his tentacles could appear anywhere. Cárdenas and Palencia left Valladolid in the middle of the night under the full moon of September (it was less conspicuous than travelling openly by day or by night with flaring torches). The next night they reached Burgo de Osma, whose Bishop Pedro de Montoya had been a friend of Carrillo but had just changed sides. Cárdenas, well known as a counsellor of Isabel, decided to hide; Palencia, a priest, went to see Bishop Montoya, telling him with remarkable cleverness that he was going to Aragon to get the ancient dispensation of Pope Calixtus III for Fernando's marriage to Isabel, given a dozen years before when both were little children, and obviously no longer valid; he even promised to show it to him on his return, and the bishop obligingly provided him with a letter of

[25]Palencia, *Crónica de Enrique IV*, I, 284 (Dc II Lb II Cp I).

[26]*Ibid.*, I, 287 (Dc II Lb II Cp II); Enriquez, Crónica de Enrique IV, BAE, LXX, 190 (Cp 136); del Val, *Isabel*, pp. 151-152.

[27]Menéndez Pidal, *Historia de España*, XV, 296.

recommendation. Thinking Palencia on a fool's errand, the bishop did not try to detain him, but burst out into abuse of Aragon and the prospective marriage of Fernando and Isabel and declared that he and the Count of Medinaceli, who had estates along the frontier, would fight to prevent Fernando from getting through. Armed with this valuable though alarming intelligence, Cárdenas and Palencia pressed on the next day to Gómara with a guide who did not know who Cárdenas was, while sending off by a courier a warning to Isabel and Carrillo with the suggestion that another troop of 300 horsemen be ready to come to Burgo de Osma when needed.[28]

Arriving safely in Zaragoza, capital of Aragon, the envoys met Fernando in a chapel in the Church of San Francisco in that city on September 25. He knew they were on the way and was eagerly awaiting them. They explained Isabel's vulnerability, and the new danger posed by the attitude of Bishop Montoya and the likelihood that Fernando, entering Castile, would be captured near the frontier unless he was leading an army, which beleaguered Aragon could not then spare. They proposed, therefore, that he should come in disguise. Fernando accepted this dangerous but romantic project with enthusiasm—so much enthusiasm that his counsellor Pedro Vaca had to press him hard to persuade him to seek the permission of King Juan II first.[29]

Indeed, that permission was needed. Juan II was 71 years old and Fernando was his only son and heir. For Fernando to be captured, injured, or killed, unprotected, in some rocky defile of northeastern Castile, would be a disaster that would probably destroy his father's life work in building up his kingdom—not to speak of the disaster to him personally.

But King Juan II of Aragon was the man who had undergone a double cataract operation without anesthetics at the age of seventy to do his duty. Within minutes or, at most, a few hours of receiving Fernando's letter explaining the plan for him to enter Castile in disguise and begging his consent,[30] his father replied, in the form of a letter of instructions to his messenger Felip Climent:

---

[28]Palencia, *Crónica de Enrique IV*, I, 288-291 (Dc II Lb II Cp III). Rarely does a historian have the opportunity to participate in so dramatic a way in the making of history; and Palencia takes full advantage of it in his exciting and detailed account of his mission to Aragon in September and October 1469.

[29]Del Val, *Isabel*, pp. 176-178; Fernando to Ximen Pérez de Calatayud, Sept. 22, 1469, *ibid.*, pp. 460-461.

[30]In his powerful, profoundly moving account of this dramatic moment, Townsend Miller (*Henry IV*, p. 253), makes one error when he says: "How long he flinched away from it [the decision on whether to give permission to Fernando], how long he hesitated, there is no means of ascertaining." Since we know that Cárdenas and Palencia arrived in Zaragoza on September 25 and Juan II's letter granting permission is dated the 29th, it is clear that he must have answered his son's letter within a few hours at most of receiving it, since at least two or three days would certainly have been required to transmit it.

Tell him first of all that I have received his letter, and would say to him with good reason the words of Santa Susana: "I have trials on every side." For I have no other son and no other good in this world in my old age but he; and in him, as my health falters after the happy days of my reign, lies the welfare and succession of all these kingdoms.

And the mere suggestion that the King of Sicily [Fernando] go alone with three or four men to Valladolid, particularly with the little security that he says he has from the Count of Medina, makes it harder and more difficult than I can express. But on the other hand, I see that events are proceeding so quickly, and the letters and messages coming in are so peremptory, that I cannot wish by any excuse or pretext to lose all that we have worked for. To understand and discuss and weigh these issues, after the counsel and aid of Our Lord, I need counsel, but have none here; not one man of my council has remained with me, neither can I communicate with them ... So I have decided to send my secretary with my decision, and it is this: that the King of Sicily [Fernando] take counsel with the archbishop [of Zaragoza] his brother [an illegitimate son of Juan], and with others in secret counsel, and discuss this matter carefully with them ... and if they counsel him to go, then I tell him to go in the name of Our Lord God, and give him Our Lord's blessing and mine, and pray that Our Lord in His grace and mercy may guide and direct him, and bring him back before my eyes flourishing and happy, as in my old age I long for. And in this case, because the journey of the King of Sicily must be most secret, in order to hide it, I advise that he go to Calatayud with the appearance of intending to stay there ... and from there take to the road.[31]

Fernando received the message; at sunset October 5 he took to the road.[32]

Contrary to his father's recommendation, he appears not to have stopped at Calatayud; indeed, he apparently did not stop anywhere for more than a few minutes (with one exception) in the next fifty-five hours. His party consisted of four of his squires—the brothers Ramón and Gaspar Espés, Guillén Sánchez, and Pedro Núñez Cabeza de Vaca (whose son was to be the famous lone explorer of Texas)—a guide, Pedro de Auñón; and a teen-aged boy named Juan, known as *el andarín* ("the pacer") because he could walk for long distances three times as fast as normal. Fernando was disguised as their mule-driver. (They were not mounted, probably to avoid drawing attention to themselves.) Meanwhile, a day or two ahead of Fernando, Palencia and several envoys from Aragon and their attendants were travelling openly toward the frontier, the only official-appearing party. While in Zaragoza, Cárdenas had remained for the most part in hiding; now he travelled alone to rendezvous with Fernando's party at Berdejo at the foot of the Pass of Bigornia at the frontier. Palencia's party took a different route, crossing the frontier at Monteagudo

---

[31]Instructions from Juan II to Felip Climent, Sept. 29, 1469, in Paz y Melia, *Palencia*, pp. 91-92.
[32]Del Val, *Isabel*, p. 180.

his advisors repeatedly did so. Royal marriages without dispensations had nearly always been publicly condemned by previous Popes. Later, in defending her conduct in response to King Henry's charges against her, Isabel publicly declared that she was entirely clear in her conscience about it. For one as careful about such matters as she, this strongly suggests some more specific assurance than the suspect word of Bishop Arias and the Aragonese. If Bishop Veneris privately dispensed her and Fernando, on authority given him by the Pope for use once he was certain that the marriage would take place, this would fully explain Isabel's statement. In the end, a formal and valid dispensation was given by the new Pope Sixtus IV shortly after Paul II's death in 1471.[43]

The wedding itself also took place at Juan Vivero's house, apparently shortly after noon. Two thousand people were present at the nuptial Mass. Afterwards the whole city of Valladolid gave itself over to public celebration, with fireworks, dancing, and feasting for the rest of the day and evening and all through the ensuing week. That night their marriage was consummated.[44]

It seems they hoped, and even in the first flush of the enthusiasm of their triumph expected, that Henry would accept the marriage as a *fait accompli* and not make it the focus of continuing strife. In all probability that is just what Henry would have done, left to himself. But Henry was never left to himself; Pacheco now dominated him totally, and it was Pacheco who had been outmaneuvered and made a laughingstock by Isabel's escape and marriage to Fernando. Pacheco had her measure now; he knew she was as formidable an opponent as he had ever faced in a lifetime of intrigue and power politics, now strengthened by the unstinting support of her vigorous young husband and her wily, relentless father-in-law.[45] Though he had spent all his adult life offering political deals in every direction, Pacheco made only the slightest gestures of this kind toward Isabel and Fernando, so long as he lived. He wanted them imprisoned, or out of the kingdom. He could not achieve either goal so long as Isabel's right of succession to the throne of Castile was recognized. Therefore he committed himself once and for all to the cause of pathetic little seven-year-old Juana, inducing Henry—whether gladly or resignedly we cannot say, for on the delicate and difficult question of her paternity Henry always said as little as possible—to take it up again.

So Henry made no answer to any of the communications from Isabel and Fernando, except to say that he would discuss them with his advisors (read Pacheco). He made no other response, even when in March 1470 Isabel and Fernando proposed arbitration by a commission consisting of the Spanish superiors of the four greatest religious orders in the country: the Dominicans, the Franciscans, the Carthusians, and the Hieronymites. In that same month

[43]Del Val, *Isabel*, pp. 195-198.
[44]*Ibid.*, pp. 186-191; Palencia, *Crónica de Enrique IV*, I, 297 (Dc II Lb II Cp V).
[45]Menéndez Pidal, ed., *Historia de España*, XV, 298; del Val, *Isabel*, pp. 213-214.

they moved their residence from fractious Valladolid to the smaller but safer Dueñas, where Fernando had stayed on his arrival from Aragon, and where Carrillo's men were in charge.[46]

But already there was friction with the proud archbishop, who had expected the prince and princess to do whatever he told them, and was very annoyed when they did not always do so. In the spring, in a flare of the fierce anger for which he was notorious, he threatened to do to Isabel what he had done to Henry; in the fall he walked out on them for a time, and they moved to Medina del Rioseco (Medina of the Dry River) under the protection of Fernando's close relative, Admiral Fadrique.[47]

Meanwhile Isabel was pregnant; she announced her pregnancy and gave thanks to God for it in February, and on October 2 gave birth to a healthy daughter. Her supporters had hoped for a son, whose sex would have helped his claims and his mother's to prevail over Juana's.[48] But Isabel and Fernando gave no sign of disappointment, and took the greatest care to protect the little girl—who was given her mother's name—from all the manifold dangers of a country near anarchy.

Toward the end of October Pacheco arranged a formal ceremony at an isolated spot called Valdelozoya, declaring the Pact of Toros de Guisando null and void because of Isabel's defiance of Henry's will regarding her marriage; reinstating little Juana as heir; and announcing her betrothal to Charles, Duke of Guyenne in France, who had once been proposed for Isabel's hand. Through his representative the Cardinal of Albi, Charles was hailed as Prince of the Asturias, the usual title for the heir to the throne of Castile. Throughout the betrothal negotiations Pacheco had urged Duke Charles to send troops to Castile as soon as they were concluded, to force Isabel and Fernando out. Now he offered the Duke the city of Avila (which was firmly committed to Isabel) as a further inducement to send the troops.[49] But Duke Charles was no longer heir to the throne of France, since a son had finally been born to French King Louis XI in June of that year, and soon began intriguing with Louis' great enemy, the Duke of Burgundy, seeking to marry his daughter, who was at least of marriageable age, and the richest heiress in Europe. Within a few months it was evident that Duke Charles had lost whatever interest in Castile he might ever have had. A year and a half later he suddenly died, amid rumors of

[46]Enríquez, Crónica de Enrique IV, BAE, LXX, 199-201 (Cp 144); Vicens Vives, Fernando, p. 272.

[47]Vicens Vives, Fernando, pp. 269, 272, 287-288.

[48]Ibid., p. 269; del Val, Isabel, p. 215; Chronicle of Valladolid, Colección de Documentos Inéditos para la historia de España (CODOIN), XIII, 81.

[49]Chronicle of Valladolid, CODOIN XIII, 82-84; de la Torre and Suárez Fernández, eds., Documentos referentes a los relaciones con Portugal, I, 67-70; del Val, Isabel, pp. 227-228; Vicens Vives, Fernando, p. 288.

poisoning by King Louis.[50]

Though spared foreign invasion, Castile was now victimized by the consequences of a nearly paralyzed government which was both distrusted and scorned by most of the nobles and the people. Law and order had almost disappeared over vast areas; noblemen took sides between Isabel and Henry, though often with no real loyalty to either, but only as an excuse for pillage. They fought private wars with one another, laying siege to cities and capturing them with no fear of being curbed by royal authority. Famine stalked the land, as it became more and more difficult to ship agricultural produce safely from one part of the country to another. The coinage was clipped and adulterated, declining rapidly in value. Though some nobles profited from the disorder, the people suffered severely and increasingly.[51]

Isabel and Fernando saw what was happening and shared the sorrow of the people they hoped to rule, but they did not yet have the authority and the means to stop it. Yet we may well imagine, as the ugly news flowed into their little court at Dueñas and at Medina of the Dry River, how they must have planned together—in intervals between their most pressing immediate concerns—how in the future, as king and queen, they would stop it, cure it, take the necessary decisive action to restore justice that would banish from the country the presence and fear of such destructive tumult for the foreseeable future. We presume they must have planned it, because as soon as they were able, that is exactly what they did, with scarcely any delay or wasted effort.[52]

Meanwhile the tragic succession controversy continued, maintained by the enduring malevolence of Pacheco. Soon after the ceremony at Valdelozoya, Henry had circulated a decree to the kingdom condemning Isabel for marrying against his will and without a valid Papal dispensation and insisting once again that little Juana was his legitimate successor.[53] In March 1471 Isabel replied. It was one of her finest documents: measured, thoughtful, respectful, brilliantly argued—and with a core of steel. It was Isabel the Catholic's gage of battle.

> Rather than accepting our just appeal, certain foreigners, hateful to our nation, have been brought in, and steps taken against us and against the legitimate right of succession belonging to us, which Your Highness, of your own free will, in reason and justice [swore] to me the Princess publicly, when I was in your power in the field of Guisando, in the presence of the legate of our most Holy Father, and with his authority; and likewise swore our very reverend fathers in Christ the Archbishops of Toledo

---

[50]Del Val, *Isabel*, pp. 231-232.

[51]Menéndez Pidal, *Historia de España*, XV, 300-303.

[52]On this point, see particularly Townsend Miller, *The Castles and the Crown* (New York, 1963), pp. 84-85.

[53]Decree of King Henry IV of Castile revoking the oath to Isabel and recognizing Juana as his successor, October 1470, in *Memorias de Don Enrique IV de Castilla*, Volume II: La Colección diplomática (Madrid, 1913), pp. 619-621.

[Carrillo] and Sevilla [Fonseca] and the Master of Santiago [Villena/Pacheco] ... Because we continue to desire to serve, respect, and obey you as king and lord and a true father, for which we expect to give an accounting before Our Lord God in Heaven, Who knows truly both public and private intentions, and to your people in this land, and even to foreigners, we have decided to write this letter to Your Grace ... And if it should happen, most excellent lord, that it should not please Your Highness to do this in as kindly a spirit as we ask for it, then we ask what in justice you cannot deny us: that before struggles begin which would be difficult to stop after they start and could result in great offenses to God and irreparable damage to your realms, and even extend to a great part of Christendom, that Your Grace should hear us and command that justice be done ... We beg your royal lordship and, if necessary, demand with that Almighty God Who is a just judge among emperors and kings and great lords, that you may not deny us the justice we ask for, which you cannot and ought not deny to the least in your realms. This we beg and demand of Your Grace, once and for all, with as much insistence as we can and as much reverence as we ought. We intend to publish it in your realms and beyond; for if this is not well received, then in defense of our just cause we shall do all that is permitted to all by divine and human law, and we shall be without blame before God and before the world.[54]

Henry still made no reply. But in the Basque provinces to the north, the people and their leaders knew exactly what Isabel had meant when she spoke of "certain foreigners, hateful to our nation." She meant the French, an immediate threat to the Spanish Basques on their borders, whose lands they were eager to add to their dominions. Pacheco had already sought, by means of the ephemeral betrothal of the Duke of Guyenne to Juana, to bring a French army into Castile to drive out Isabel and Fernando. In May the Basques rose for Isabel, defeating her old enemy Velasco in a combat at Munguía. Henry called a meeting of the *cortes* of Castile in Segovia, but only ten cities sent delegates; the *cortes* never formally convened, to say nothing of giving the failing monarch the support against Isabel that he (or, rather, Pacheco) had hoped for. In that same spring of 1471, Pacheco tried to bring pressure from Rome against Carrillo—precisely the wrong thing to do with that stormy prelate, who promptly forgot his grievances against Isabel and Fernando in a new and ringing avowal of their cause, so convincing that in the fall they left Medina of the Dry River to take up residence on his property at Alcalá de Henares, near Madrid. With all these setbacks, the cautious Pacheco drew back from open war against the young prince and princess, at almost the very moment of the advent of a new Pope who was to look much more kindly upon their cause.[55]

Francisco della Rovere, Pope Sixtus IV, was elected August 9, 1471

---

[54]Enríquez, Crónica de Enrique IV, BAE, LXX, 200 (Cp 144).

[55]Menéndez Pidal, *Historia de España*, XV, 305; del Val, *Isabel*, pp. 233-234, 282; Vicens Vives, *Fernando*, p. 295.

following the sudden death of Pope Paul II. Della Rovere had been the general of the Franciscan order. He came from Liguria, in northeastern Italy, and was predisposed by that background to see the French in the north as a greater potential danger to Italy than the Aragonese in the south; more importantly, he brought a fresh perspective for judging the political issues before the Papacy, one of which was the choice of whom to favor in Spain. When Paul II became Pope in 1464, Isabel was only thirteen years old; few if any in Rome even knew who she was. But now she was the leading claimant to the succession in Castile. Favorable reports of her goodness and piety had assuredly come to Rome already, at least from the Papal legate Bishop Antonio de Veneriis of León (known as her partisan); if the theory that he granted a private dispensation for her marriage to Fernando be true, such reports had made their mark even on Paul II. But Paul II had not wished publicly to change his long-standing policy of support for Henry IV of Castile against Aragon. The new Pope was willing and even eager to do so. He acted with remarkable speed for the Papacy. On the first of December, less than five months after his election, he issued the formal public dispensation validating Isabel's marriage that set forever to rest the strongest argument Pacheco and his supporters had against her succession to the throne. Late that same month, as part of a program which involved sending five cardinals to different parts of Europe to rouse support for a new crusade against the advancing Turks, Pope Sixtus IV directed Cardinal Rodrigo Borja (called Borgia in Italy) to go to his native Spain to try to help stabilize the political situation in Castile so that it might give more effective support to the crusade.[56]

During the first year of his pontificate Sixtus IV—whose real abilities have been somewhat overshadowed in most histories by the financial and moral scandals involving his relatives and his poor judgments of the volatile political situation in Renaissance Italy—also made the position of the Church very clear on an issue barely noticed at the time, but soon to become of great importance and a major concern during the reign of Isabel: the treatment of pagan natives in newly discovered parts of the world. During the course of the fifteenth century the Canary Islands off the coast of Africa were being slowly conquered and settled by a motley assortment of Spanish, Portuguese, and Italian adventurers. The natives resisted; wars were fought against them, which were sometimes called crusades because the natives were not Christian. But neither were they Muslim; they had simply never been evangelized. In the bull *Pastoris aeterni* issued June 26, 1472, Pope Sixtus IV explicitly called upon the Christian powers involved (of which Castile was emerging as the principal) to make a major effort to convert the Canary Islanders, along with the blacks of the

---

[56]Menéndez Pidal, *Historia de España*, XV, 306; Ludwig von Pastor, *The History of the Popes from the Close of the Middle Ages* (St. Louis, 1914), IV, 204-210, 219-222.

Guinea coast of Africa which the Portuguese had explored under Prince Henry the Navigator.[57] Isabel and Fernando were to take this Papal bull as their standard and guide in dealing with the legal and religious condition of native pagan peoples, notably in America after its discovery.

While awaiting the arrival of Cardinal Borja, Isabel and Fernando took advantage of the improving circumstances to strengthen their political position. In January 1472 they were able to move from Alcalá de Henares to Simancas, very near Valladolid, where they had been married, in the high plains of Castile that had always been the heartland of their strength. In February the large and well-defended town of Sepúlveda, on the north slope of the Guadarramas just thirty miles from King Henry IV's principal residence of Segovia, closed its gates to the King, declared for Isabel and Fernando, and called them to its aid. Fernando came, and secured it. In April Isabel made peace between Toledo and Avila, two important cities that both supported her, but were fighting each other. Fernando then went to Aragon, to help his father complete his victory over the ten-year insurrection in Catalonia, sealed by the capitulation of the Catalan metropolis of Barcelona in October.[58]

Meanwhile Cardinal Borja had arrived at Valencia. Very soon after Barcelona was secured, Bishop Mendoza of Sigüenza—a member of one of Castile's most powerful families, which had never fully committed itself to any of the contenders in the struggle over the Castilian kingship and succession—arrived there, to be sumptuously welcomed by the Cardinal (famous for his love of display) and by Fernando.[59] The Cardinal was no moral credit to the Church (as was to become sadly evident when he became Pope Alexander VI, the infamous "Borgia Pope"), but he was an excellent negotiator; he knew Spain and he knew Pacheco and how little reliance could ever be placed on him. He also knew, as Juan II of Aragon had known from the beginning, that the Mendozas were the key to any realistic final settlement of the civil strife in Castile. Pope Sixtus had decided—possibly at Borja's suggestion, possibly at Juan II's—to give a cardinal's hat to Bishop Mendoza. Borja brought Mendoza the news of the Pope's decision in his favor. It would mortally offend Carrillo; but mortal offense was a state which that pugnacious prelate had assumed so often that yet one more might well be risked.

Early in November Cardinal Borja and Cardinal-to-be Mendoza left Valencia for Madrid together. In Madrid they met with Henry IV; the Cardinal persuaded him to agree to settle the succession question together with a four-

[57]Antonio Rumeu de Armas, *La politica indigenista de Isabel la Católica* (Valladolid, 1969), pp. 39-40, 151-157 (for the text of the bull).

[58]Menéndez Pidal, *Historia de España*, XV, 306-307; Vicens Vives, *Fernando*, pp. 293-295, 311; Isabel to the city of Toledo, April 5, 1472, in Eloy Benito Ruano, *Toledo en el siglo XV; vida politica* (Madrid, 1961), p. 266; Miller, *Henry IV*, p. 262.

[59]Vicens Vives, *Fernando*, pp. 319-320.

man commission consisting of Pacheco, Mendoza, Carrillo, and Admiral Fadrique.[60] This gave Isabel a three-to-one advantage, if Carrillo remained loyal to her, as for a time he did; but mere numerical advantage never seemed to be enough in any proceeding to which Pacheco was a party. He now had a wide-open opportunity to promote division between the ambitious Mendoza and the jealous Carrillo, which in all likelihood he proceeded to do, while Isabel—with good reason—was reluctant to give her full trust to either. In May 1473, however, Isabel's most inveterate episcopal enemy died: Bishop Fonseca of Sevilla, who had tried to capture her at Song of the High Towers when Carrillo and Fadrique had saved her.[61]

That spring there was renewed war between France and Aragon. There had been a rising in Roussillon, a region just north of the Pyrenees which had long been contested between the two countries, in favor of Juan II, who had had to let the French occupy it while he was hard pressed by the Catalan rebellion. After his triumph in Barcelona he marched into Roussillon and retook it, whereupon the ambitious French King Louis XI sent a large army to besiege its capital of Perpignan. Despite his age (he was now 75, a very old man by the standards of that time) Juan II was resolved to remain in the beleaguered city in personal command of its defense. Fernando set off to his aid at the beginning of May. On April 29 Isabel wrote to her father-in-law, to whom she owed so much, a letter full of love and zeal:

> I felt such great anxiety on hearing the news of the invasion of the French into your kingdom, that if matters here had permitted, I would not have been able to endure not to go with the prince my lord to rescue Your Majesty, because certainly it would be less onerous for me to travel with him than to remain behind. Thinking of where and how Your Highness is, Our Lord and His Blessed Mother give me consolation and hope that He will guide you on your way and to a return crowned with glorious victory for the efforts of Your Excellency. God knows what great pleasure I would take in the relief of your royal person.[62]

If Juan II had received this letter in Perpignan and answered it (we have no record that he did), he might well have said: "Thank you very much, my dear, but no one needs to rescue *me*!" On June 12 Fernando left Barcelona at the head of a relieving army, marching north across the Pyrenees toward Perpignan. But the lion-hearted old king was worth an army in himself. On June 10 his defenders sharply repulsed a French assault on the city; on the 21st they sallied and smashed the besiegers, who retreated in disorder. When Fernando arrived a week later, the campaign was already won.[63]

---

[60]*Ibid.*, pp. 331-332, 556-558.

[61]Lorenzo Galíndez de Carvajal, "Anales Breves," CODOIN XVIII, 252.

[62]Isabel to Juan II of Aragon, April 29, 1473, in Paz y Melia, *Palencia*, p. 129.

[63]*Ibid.*, pp. 133-135 (letter from the Duke of Alba describing the battle of June 21);

However, there was always the possibility that Louis XI would try again (as in fact he did, the following year). Fernando stayed through the summer to help his father prepare defenses against a renewed invasion. When finally he came back southward, he fell severely ill in Tortosa of a fever, which continued to recur throughout September and October and early November. He did not rejoin Isabel until December 18, by which time momentous events were unfolding in Castile.[64]

Isabel was therefore entirely on her own for seven critical months, from May to December 1473. When Fernando departed to go to the aid of his father, it must have been already clear that Cardinal Borja's hoped-for settlement of the succession controversy had not been attained, though having gained the support of new Cardinal Mendoza was of substantial help to Isabel's cause. Borja had done all he could; by July he was back in Valencia and in September he set sail for Rome. Isabel still did not fully trust either Mendoza or Carrillo. The experience of her whole life, since Henry IV first called her to court when she was eleven years old, had not encouraged her to trust readily. She trusted her husband and her father-in-law, but they were now far away and out of touch; she trusted Gonzalo Chacón and Gutierre de Cárdenas, but there was not much they could do for her in this situation.

There was one other person, besides Chacón, whom Isabel had trusted from her childhood; though once she had let her down, she had never betrayed her. That was her closest friend, Beatriz de Bobadilla. Some time before, Beatriz had married Andrés de Cabrera, a staunch supporter of Henry IV. But Cabrera, at least from the time of his marriage, had never done anything to hurt Isabel. Loyalty to the king was, for him, simple civic duty. Recognizing and valuing this straightforward loyalty of Cabrera's, Henry had made him commander of the *alcázar* (castle) of Madrid, one of the most important strongholds of the realm, where Henry often resided. But Pacheco had not let Cabrera keep it; that devious magnate tended to feel uneasy in the presence of an incorruptible man, and he could hardly fail to know of the special bond between Isabel and Cabrera's wife. In September 1472 Pacheco prevailed on the pliant Henry to give the keeping of the Alcázar of Madrid to him, while appointing Cabrera commander of the King's favorite city, Segovia. Then Pacheco began to put obstacles in the way of Cabrera taking over in Segovia, finally persuading the King to divide the usual office of *alcaide*, so that Cabrera was left responsible for order in and defense of the city and its walls, while Pacheco controlled the castle, where the royal treasure was kept. The distinction was particularly significant because the Alcázar of Segovia had

Menéndez Pidal, *Historia de España*, XV, 267; Vicens Vives, *Fernando*, p. 340.
    [64]Fernando's instructions to Pero Minguez Cabeza de Vaca, November 10, 1473, in Paz y Melia, *Palencia*, pp. 142-143; Vicens Vives, *Fernando*, p. 352; Menéndez Pidal, *Historia de España*, XV, 310.

always been one of the most impregnable as well as one of the most spectacular fortresses in all Spain, situated at the point of a great mass of rock rising above the Castilian plain upon which the city of Segovia is built, surrounded on three sides by sheer cliffs and approachable only by a narrow tongue of land cut by a very deep moat.[65]

The end of Lent and Holy Week in troubled Castile in that year of 1473 saw a recurrence, striking like evil lightning here and there across the country, of a long-standing plague: rioting caused by fear and hatred between "old" and "new" Christians. The "new" Christians were usually called *conversos*—a word which, at least in fifteenth-century Spanish usage, cannot be properly translated simply by its English cognate "converts," for it was applied to anyone whose forebears had converted to Christianity during any of the past four or five generations. The centuries of Muslim occupation of Spain (reviewed in the first chapter of this book) had not made Muslims of the majority of the native population, but large numbers did become Muslims or immigrated from other Islamic countries; also, many Jews immigrated and some were native. The majority, though not all of these Muslims and Jews converted to Christianity at the time of the Christian reconquest or at various times afterward. Many of these *conversos* were exemplary Christians; Cabrera himself was one of them.[66] But others were suspect; and still others were secret traitors, criminals, blasphemers and even satanists. There was no reliable way of finding out in which category any *converso* belonged. His enemies were always ready to suspect the worst, and so were mobs in cities and towns when they had been excited. On March 21 Miguel Lucas, whom Henry had made Constable of Castile (though he had long since ceased to perform the duties of the office) and who was known as a special friend of the *conversos*, was horribly murdered in his home city of Jaén.[67] During Holy Week, ferocious rioting against *conversos* swept Córdoba, once the Muslim capital of Spain.[68]

There was a large *converso* community in Segovia, which had once had a substantial Jewish population and still had some practicing Jews. Since Cabrera himself was a *converso*, Pacheco saw his opportunity to remove him and take over the whole city. In May his agents incited a riot of the "old Christians" to seize control of Segovia. But knowledge of his plans leaked out; Cardinal Borja, far away in Guadalajara, heard of them three days before the stroke was scheduled. He warned Henry, who warned Cabrera, who armed the *conversos*

[65]Del Val, *Isabel*, pp. 318-319; Vicens Vives, *Fernando*, pp. 356-358; personal observations of the Alcázar of Segovia by the writer.

[66]Palencia, *Crónica de Enrique IV*, Volume II (Bibloteca de Autores Españoles, Vol. 258, Madrid, 1975), p. 93 (Dc III Lb VIII Cp I).

[67]Galíndez de Carvajal, "Anales Breves," CODOIN XVIII, 251-252; Menéndez Pidal, *Historia de España*, XV, 307-308. See the terrible, unforgettable description in Miller, *Henry IV*, p. 263.

[68]Palencia, *Crónica de Enrique IV*, II, 85-88 (Dc III Lb VII Cp IX).

and took command in person. There was a wild street fight with swinging swords, whistling arrows and crashing stones which ended with Pacheco's chosen mob leader, Diego de Tapia, dead along with many of his followers. But too many of the survivors knew of Pacheco's involvement for him to dare to appear again in the city. Reluctantly he gave up the command of the Alcázar to Cabrera; and Cabrera, whose own life might have been forfeit had he been in Segovia unwarned at the time of the uprising, now for the first time fully grasped the extent of Pacheco's malevolence.[69]

He wasted no time in acting on his new awareness. Isabel was at Aranda de Duero, fifty miles northeast of Segovia—a long day's horseback ride. With Beatriz as his emissary, by June 15 Cabrera had concerted a written agreement with Isabel by which she agreed to come to Segovia whenever Cabrera should ask her to do so, under his guarantee of her safety, and to remain there indefinitely. They would both serve Henry loyally so long as he should live, but her right to the succession would be recognized and attempts by Pacheco to seize or injure her or her supporters would be met, if necessary, by force.[70]

Pacheco and Henry were occupied all that summer with a futile meeting of the *cortes* of Castile at Santa Maria de Nieva, where the delegates insisted on the revocation of some of his enormous grants to already rich and powerful noblemen (read Pacheco) before they voted any taxes, and called angrily for greater efforts to restore law and order in the kingdom. In October Isabel was formally recognized by the Basque province of Vizcaya as its legitimate ruler, after she swore to respect its ancient *fueros* (rights of self-government) and to repeat her oath later under the legendary tree of Guernica. Meanwhile Cabrera was canvassing among the principal grandees for support for his plan of peace and reconciliation between Isabel and Henry. The Count of Benavente, one of the most powerful nobles, who had previously leaned to Henry's side, was won over. Cardinal Mendoza was favorable. But Carrillo was opposed (he tended toward a visceral rejection of all peace proposals). By November, Isabel informed Fernando and Juan II of Cabrera's plan; they were impressed, and Fernando, now at last recovered from his fevers, set out for Castile.[71]

December by the thin cold flow of the Duero River, some twenty miles

---

[69]Enríquez, Crónica de Enrique IV, BAE, LXX, 214-215 (Cp 161). The rousing and vivid account of the street battle in Segovia and its antecedents in William Thomas Walsh, *Isabella of Spain, the Last Crusader* (New York, 1930), pp. 86-87, is unfortunately marred by a serious chronological error, placing it in the year 1474 instead of 1473, and in bringing Fernando to the scene, when at the time he was in Zaragoza.

[70]*Memorias de Enrique IV*, II, 693-697; del Val, *Isabel*, pp. 319-320.

[71]Menéndez Pidal, *Historia de España*, XV, 310 and XVII (1), "La España de los Reyes Católicos," by Luis Suárez Fernández and Juan de Mata Carriazo (Madrid, 1983), p. 109; del Val, *Isabel*, pp. 320-321.

downstream from Burgo de Osma where, four years before, Fernando had knocked at the city gate at one o'clock in the morning after his long walk from Aragon disguised as a mule driver. There is no palace in Aranda de Duero, not even a relatively modest royal dwelling such as that at Song of the High Towers where Isabel was born. In an unpretentious building—perhaps a convent—Isabel awaits the return of her husband, whom she has not seen for seven months. She holds no pompous court; access to her is not difficult. She may not trust the grandees, but she has always trusted the people, as they trust her.

But surely she has a guard; from it, a challenge rings out into the night. A woman, dressed as a farm girl, has ridden a donkey up to the door.[72] She asks admittance—asks to see the princess. Something about the visitor restrains the guards from driving her away. Isabel is called. She comes to the door. She beholds the visitor. She would know her anywhere.

"Beatriz!"

She brings word from her husband that the time is close at hand when, in accordance with the June agreement, Isabel should go to Segovia and take up her residence there, with Henry. Pacheco has gone to Peñafiel, further downstream on the Duero and, like it, fifty miles from Segovia, to spend Christmas there with his wife. Isabel must come to Segovia while Pacheco is in Peñafiel, too far away to interfere. Because of Pacheco's spies, the utmost secrecy must be maintained until she actually arrives in Segovia. Isabel tells Beatriz that she must discuss this momentous decision personally with Fernando before taking it. But he will arrive soon. They too will spend Christmas together, there in Aranda. If he agrees, then she will come, on the Feast of the Holy Innocents, three days after Christmas.[73]

Fernando came, and it seems he must have advised Isabel to make a direct appeal to Carrillo for a renewal of his active support (better her than him, for he and Carrillo had never been on good terms). For we are told that when Isabel came to Segovia, Carrillo came with her. Henry, his evil genius for once not at his side, embraced Isabel "with much love"—this tragic man who had known no love in all his life, whose mother died when he was born, whose father never seems to have loved anybody, whose two wives despised him, whose pretended friends mocked him obscenely behind his back. Isabel returned his love unstintingly, forgiving in her heart all the wrongs he had done

---

[72]Enríquez, "Cronica de Enrique IV," BAE, LXX, 217 (Cp 164).

[73]Palencia, *Crónica de Enrique IV*, II, 112 (Dc III Lb VIII Cp X); del Val, *Isabel*, pp. 321-322. Walsh, *Isabel*, pp. 81-83, erroneously places Isabel's coming to Segovia, her reconciliation with Henry IV, and Pacheco's last plot against her person in the winter of 1472-73, during Cardinal Borja's visit to Spain, rather than in the winter of 1473-74 when these things actually happened.

her; she even danced for him while he sang and played his beloved mandolin.[74]
But she had not forgotten why she had come; that first evening, after they had
talked long and amicably about inconsequential matters, she told Henry, just
before they retired:

> My lord, I have come for two things: first, to see Your Highness as
> father and lord and elder brother, as duty to our common blood requires;
> second, to beg that you may be pleased, if any anger against me remains, to
> set it aside, and then for what my letters asked you, that you be willing to
> maintain and uphold what you promised and commanded, when you swore
> me as princess and your legitimate successor, because this will serve God,
> while any other course will assuredly lead to great evils, since by God's will
> the succession to these realms belongs by right and justice to me after the
> days of Your Highness, which may God extend for many years.[75]

In this Renaissance age which gave its name to devious diplomacy, Isabel
the Catholic was always straightforward and direct.

Henry told her that he would answer her later, after they had celebrated
the twelve days of Christmas. But at the final banquet, on Epiphany, he
collapsed from a burning pain in his side, which the doctors could not diagnose;
it may have been a perforating ulcer, or kidney disease, or both. So there was
no royal pronouncement on the succession.[76] But Isabel remained at Segovia,
under Cabrera's protection. When Pacheco returned from Peñafiel, horrified
to find out what had happened in his absence, he tried a last plot, to imprison
Isabel and Fernando and Carrillo and kill the Cabreras. It was torpedoed when
he made the mistake of trying to enlist Cardinal Mendoza in its support, only to
have him denounce the plot to the king in no uncertain terms.[77] In May the
Mendoza family formally recognized Isabel and Fernando as the future rulers
of Castile, along with their erstwhile foe Pedro Velasco, Count of Haro.[78] A
February letter from Isabel in Segovia to one of her new adherents, the Count
of Luna, reveals the princess on the threshold of becoming a queen.

> Count, kinsman, I have seen your letter that Anton Rodríguez de
> Vaeza gave me, and I hear you well spoken of, and how you intend to serve
> me and take my part with the Master of Santiago [Pacheco] in all that
> relates to my affairs. Have no doubt of my high regard for you and my
> awareness of the good will you have to please and serve me, and I am sure
> that this, like all matters that come into your hands, will go well. . . . I will

---

[74]Enríquez, "Crónica de Enrique IV," BAE, LXX, 217 (Cp 164); Archbishop
Carrillo to Juan II of Aragon, early 1474, in Paz y Melia, *Palencia*, pp. 156-157.

[75]Enríquez, "Crónica de Enrique IV," BAE, LXX, 217-218 (Cp 164).

[76]*Ibid.*, p. 218; Miller, *Henry IV*, pp. 264-266.

[77]Fernando del Pulgar, *Crónica de los Reyes Católicos*, ed. Juan de Mata Carriazo
(Madrid, 1943), I, 55-57 (ch. 16); del Val, *Isabel*, p. 326.

[78]Palencia, *Crónica de Enrique IV*, II, 124 (Dc III Lb IX Cp V).

entrust this task to you as a gentleman and a person in whom I have great confidence.[79]

It was already very clear to most of those who knew her, what kind of queen Isabel would be. The better men welcomed it, the worse feared or grew angry. Carrillo, knowing now that he could never dominate her, wrote to Juan II of Aragon that he now considered himself free of all obligations toward Isabel and Fernando; he would act toward them solely as he thought best (and for Carrillo, that meant best for himself). He reopened contact with Pacheco with a view to renewing the old alliance between them, as in the days of the rebellion against Henry IV in the name of Isabel's little brother Alfonso.[80]

But Pacheco did not care to cross swords with Isabel again so soon. He went south, to Trujillo in Extremadura ("Extremely Hard"), the city whose defiance at the time of Isabel's escape from Ocaña had delayed him just long enough to make possible her marriage to Fernando. He might not be able to stop Isabel, but at least he could finally take Trujillo. The Machiavelli of Spain had grown old and gaunt; all but one of his teeth had fallen out. But still he was determined to take Trujillo, where Gracián de Sesé, who had commanded its castle against him in 1469, was still *alcaide*. All through the torrid Extremaduran summer Pacheco maneuvered and schemed and threatened and wheedled to induce Gracián to let him have the city. An abscess formed in his throat; his doctors lanced it; but the abscess returned and worsened. On October 3, sinking, wracked by fever, with one eye gone blind, he held a final conference with Gracián in a room with the curtains drawn so that the commander could not see how sick he was. Pacheco made his bargain; he got the city. The next day he died. His last words were: "Has the castle surrendered?"[81]

Henry too was sinking fast. Fernando had returned to Aragon in August, where his father once more needed him, as the French had renewed their attack on Roussillon.[82] In November Isabel wrote to him: Henry might die at any moment, or become incapacitated; she needed her husband very much; would he please come? He prepared at once to return to Castile; but then his father summoned him to bring an army to the defense of the beleaguered city of Elna in Roussillon, and he had to tell Isabel that he would be delayed at least until Christmas. His letter giving her this bad news is his first to her that has been preserved. It reveals much of the best in Fernando, and helps to show why Isabel loved him, as well as how much he loved her:

[79]Isabel to Conde de Luna, February 14, 1474, in del Val, *Isabel*, pp. 509-510.
[80]Del Val, *Isabel*, p. 342; Menéndez Pidal, *Historia de España*, XV, 313.
[81]Palencia, *Crónica de Enrique IV*, II, 139 (Dc III Lb X Cp I); Diego de Valera, *Hazañas*, p. 277; Gutierre de Cárdenas to Fernando, October 20, 1474, in Paz y Melia, *Palencia*, pp. 164-170; Miller, *Henry IV*, pp. 268-269; Walsh, *Isabel*, p. 89.
[82]Vicens Vives, *Fernando*, p. 383.

I do not know why Our Lord gave me so much good with so little pleasure in it, since in three years I have not been with you seven months. Now I must tell you that I have to go to induce these people to do their duty. But all this cannot happen before Christmas, and if in this time you could arrange it so that the King calls me for the oath, within the hour I could be on my way [to you], but otherwise I would have no excuse for my lord the King. Although I do my best, nevertheless this unfortunate predicament puts me in such a mood that I don't know whether I am coming or going. I beg you to work at this, or at least to write to the Archbishop and Cardinal. I do not mean to imply that this is your task, or that I do not think that for me there is no higher duty than fulfilling your wishes. . . . I beg, my lady, that you would pardon me the annoyance and trouble I do not know how to describe, with all the delay in my coming. Awaiting your answer, I ask to be now and to the end, your slave.[83]

Death came for Henry just after midnight, December 13, 1474. Wild tales float through later history and legend of a last testament, of dying declarations about his choice of a successor and the paternity of little Juana, but the truth is far more likely to be as stated by the contemporary chronicler Valera who, after describing the ring of people surrounding Henry's deathbed and shouting questions at him, says simply: "He gave no response." They laid Henry's body on some old boards and lit a few candles around it. We are told it was too wasted to embalm.[84]

Isabel, at 23, was Queen of Castile. No one is ever likely to describe that glorious moment better than Townsend Miller:

Chill dawn was coming in Segovia, and as young Isabel rose to greet it, as she drew her martened robe around her and leaned from her casement and watched the tall square towers grow gray, grow faintly pink, then as at last the sun burst forth above the snowy mountains and scattered gold and diamonds across the wakening city at her feet, a new day, too, was breaking for the kingdom, a day which was triumphantly to free it from the rue and fraction we have sought to chronicle and bring it on—healed, rectified and welded—to might, to majesty, to sway of half the globe, to unimaginable splendor.[85]

---

[83]Rodríguez Valencia, ed., *Isabel la Católica en la Opinion de Españoles* III, 74. The honorific *vuestra señoría* ("your ladyship") which Fernando uses in this letter to address Isabel, as was then customary even in intimate written communication among royalty, is here translated simply as "you." The writer greatly appreciates the assistance offered by Dr. Maria Barone, chairman of the Department of Languages at Christendom College, in the accurate translation of this extremely difficult text.

[84]Valera, *Hazañas*, pp. 292-294; Miller, *Henry IV*, pp. 274-275.

[85]Miller, *Henry IV*, p. 275.

4
Rally to the Queen
(December 1474-February 1477)

That glorious dawn of December 13, 1474 broke on a landscape full of menace, threats and traps for the young queen. Fernando was far away, in Aragon. Pacheco was dead, but his son, bearing his old title of the Marqués of Villena, was very much alive and had gained custody of 13-year-old Juana, who could still be legally regarded as the dead king's daughter. Archbishop Carrillo had been sulking for two years, ever since Mendoza and not he was made Cardinal of Spain. The country was at the edge of chaos: the private armies of the great lords fought each other from the Bay of Biscay to the Rock of Gibraltar; bands of robbers had actually seized castles and were using them as bases to prey on anyone who had anything to steal and was not protected by a strong wall. Not since Urraca 350 years ago had Castile had a reigning queen, and her precedent was hardly an encouraging one. In Castile Isabel could count on nothing and no one not within range of her own eyes.

But here, in Segovia, she had the keys of the kingdom: the principal palace of her father and her half-brother and predecessor; the royal treasure, guarded in the impregnable castle by faithful Andrés de Cabrera and her beloved Beatriz; the people of the city, among whom she had lived for a full year, and who were passionately devoted to her. By her side was Gutierre de Cárdenas, who would go anywhere and do anything for her, who would lay down his life for her if need be. In Segovia, if nowhere else, her word was law.

She moved instantly to take full advantage of it, declaring that she would be crowned in Segovia that very day.

Ceremonies of the magnitude of Isabel's coronation—whose splendor is vividly described by several contemporary historians—are not arranged in an hour or two. Isabel must have made her decision within minutes of learning of King Henry's death, and the planning and preparation must have proceeded from that moment at an almost frantic pace. Before noon on the 13th all was ready. Mounted on a white horse, clad in a magnificent gown glowing with jewels, Isabel was brought under a richly brocaded canopy from the castle to a platform erected in the central square of Segovia. Gutierre de Cárdenas rode before her carrying the naked sword, pointing straight up to the zenith of the sky, which was the ancient symbol of the reigning monarch's judicial power of life and death. Isabel seated herself on an improvised throne upon the platform and was hailed by a mighty roar of approval from Segovia's people. Then she went to the church of San Miguel, offered a prayer, and laid her new royal pendon upon the high altar.[1]

Within the week the official announcements of her succession to the throne and her coronation, with their requirements of loyal obedience, were going out all over the kingdom, from great Sevilla in the far south to Zamora near the Portuguese border in the west and to Murcia upon the Mediterranean in the southeast.[2] On December 21 Cardinal Mendoza arrived to swear allegiance, along with his good friend Rodrigo Pimentel, Count of Benavente; just a day later, undoubtedly furious at having been beaten to the scene by his ecclesiastical rival, came Archbishop Carrillo to do likewise.[3] But it was Fernando whom Isabel wanted most. He had set out instantly for Castile upon hearing the news of King Henry's death. In the early evening of January 2, 1475 he arrived at Segovia, greeted with royal ceremony (undoubtedly by Isabel's order), going first to the cathedral, and then to the palace where Isabel received him "with profound love." That night they presided together at a great banquet.[4]

But all was not well between them. At this most critical moment of their life together so far, Fernando's masculine pride had been stung by the glowing accounts of his wife's coronation which he had received while on his way from Aragon, particularly one incautiously sent to him by Gutierre de Cárdenas describing how he had carried the naked sword of royal authority before Isabel.

[1]Alonso de Palencia, *Crónica de Enrique IV*, Volume II (Biblioteca de Autores Españoles, Vol. 258, Madrid, 1975), pp. 154-155 (Decada [Dc] II, Libro [Lb] X, Capitulo [Cp] X); Mosén Diego de Valera, *Crónica de los Reyes Católicos*, ed. Juan de Mata Carriazo (Madrid, 1927), pp. 3-4; Fernando del Pulgar, *Crónica de los Reyes Católicos*, ed. Juan de Mata Carriazo (Madrid, 1943), I, 64-65 (chapters [ch.] XX-XXI); Andrés Bernáldez, *Memorias del reinado de los Reyes Católicos*, ed. Manuel Gómez Moreno and Juan de Mata Carriazo (Madrid, 1962), pp. 26-27 (ch. X); William Thomas Walsh, *Isabella of Spain, the Last Crusader* (New York, 1930), pp. 92-94; William H. Prescott, *The Reign of Ferdinand and Isabella the Catholic* (Philadelphia, 1893), I, 235-236.
[2]Isabel to the Council of Sevilla, Dec. 20, 1474, in *El Tumbo de los Reyes Católicos del Concejo de Sevilla*, ed. Juan de Mata Carriazo, Volume I (Sevilla, 1968), pp. 1-2; Isabel to the city of Zamora, December 16, 1474, in José Fernández Domínguez Valencia, *La Guerra civil a la muerte de Enrique IV; Zamora-Toro-Castronuño* (Zamora, 1929), pp. 12-13; Isabel to the city of Murcia, December 16, 1474, in Juan Torres Fontes, *Don Pedro Fajardo, adelantado mayor del reino de Murcia* (Madrid, 1953), pp. 237-238.
[3]Chronicle of Valladolid, *Colección de documentos inéditos para la historia de España* (hereinafter cited as CODOIN), XIII (Madrid, 1848), p. 88.
[4]*Ibid.*, pp. 88-89; *Crónica incompleta de los Reyes Católicos (1469-1476), según un manuscrito anónimo de la época*, ed. Julio Puyol (Madrid, 1934), pp. 132-134.

Aragon followed the "Salic law" of France: a woman could not reign, nor could the royal title pass through her alone; she could never be more than the consort of her husband. That law had never been adopted by Castile: it was still remembered how the only son of founding King Pelayo at the dawn of the Reconquest, killed by a bear, had died without issue in the year 739, so that the succession had passed through his daughter Ermesinda.[5] Isabel's marriage agreement with Fernando had spelled out very clearly her independent royal rights; but it seems that Fernando had not expected her to assert them quite so openly, or perhaps not quite so quickly. He thought she was taking too much on herself. In one angry moment he actually threatened to leave her and go back to Aragon.[6]

The blow to Isabel must have been staggering. At the supreme moment of her life thus far—a moment of danger, but also of immense opportunity—her husband not only did not share her joy, but had turned against her for the first time. But she had learned courage and self-possession in a very hard school, from the time she was first brought to the Castilian court as a virtual orphan at the age of eleven. She did not lash back. She gave no visible sign of distress. She treated the question of Fernando's royal rights in Castile as one that had been raised by others, that should now be settled once and for all on terms fully acceptable to both of them. She told Fernando solemnly that "by the grace of God, you and I conform to each other in such a way that no difference can be."[7] In fact he had just created a grave difference; but she healed it, through her love willing such a union into existence. She reminded Fernando that if no son should be born to them or survive them, and their heir should be a daughter such as Princess Isabel their first-born, who married a foreign prince, only the full legal recognition of Isabel's royal rights in Castile would guarantee the rights of their daughter in that situation. Within less than two weeks, with the aid of Mendoza and Carrillo, a new agreement on the exercise of royal authority in Castile had been drawn up. Known as the Declaration of Segovia, it provided that Isabel's and Fernando's authority would be absolutely equal when they were apart and always exercised jointly when they were together, with both their names appearing on official documents, Fernando's first. Fernando accepted these arrangements without demur.[8]

Not only was the rift healed with surpassing swiftness and smoothness, but throughout the full thirty years of the joint rule of Isabel and Fernando, nothing like it ever appeared again. Though they almost always agreed on policy

---

[5]Pulgar, *Crónica*, I, 71 (ch. XXII).

[6]Palencia, *Crónica*, II, 161-162, 167 (Dc III Lb I Cp I, V).

[7]Pulgar, *Crónica*, I, 72 (ch. XXII).

[8]*Ibid.*, I, 72-73; Ramón Menéndez Pidal, director, *Historia de España*, Volume XVII: "España de los Reyes Católicos," ed. Luis Suárez Fernández and Manuel Fernández Alvarez (Madrid, 1969), Part 1, p. 98.

decisions, inevitably there were exceptions, moments of divergence; but never again was there a clash on how their royal authority was to be shared. The reconciliation following this potentially disastrous confrontation of January 1475 actually strengthened their union; and since Fernando originally provoked the clash while Isabel never breathed a word of criticism of him, the credit for this outcome would seem to be all hers. Henceforth, a contemporary chronicler tells us, there was between Isabel and Fernando "neither division nor anger"; they ate together as they slept together, discussing the work and problems of the day at the breakfast table, keeping no secrets from each other, never working at cross purposes.[9] All history shows no closer partnership of a ruling couple. Deservedly they celebrated the closeness of their partnership, and all Spain joined in its celebration. The slogan of their unity, *"tanto monta, monta tanto, Isabel como Fernando"*[10] and its symbol, the yoke and the arrows,[11] were imprinted upon the minds and hearts of the Spanish people as they were inscribed upon the enduring stone of the hundreds of public buildings erected during their reign, many of which still stand today.

In this same month of January they jointly designated the chief ministers of Castile: Cardinal Mendoza as Chancellor, with Juan Manrique, Count of Castañeda, his chief assistant; Pedro de Velasco, Count of Haro, as Constable of Castile; Gonzalo Chacón as Treasurer, with Gutierre de Cárdenas as his assistant.[12] The choices are fascinating in their balance of wisdom, caution, and boldness. Isabel's personal experiences in a girlhood and early youth full of betrayal would have drawn her to rely mostly on a few old friends of proven loyalty, and she knew she could never do without them; but her luminous intelligence would have told her that narrow favoritism can be a fatal error in a reigning monarch. She may have been beginning to trust Cardinal Mendoza, though one doubts that any such trust on her part had yet gone very deep; but Mendoza had already proved himself much more reliable than Carrillo, and she had to have one of them on her side. So she appointed Mendoza Chancellor—and very likely set the loyal Juan Manrique to watch him. Velasco, now Count of Haro, had been the very man who had once threatened her with imprisonment for insisting on her rights under the Pact of Toros de Guisando. But that was six years ago; after her marriage to Fernando he had come over to her side, and in any case, the actual military command in Castile would be Fernando's. The most dangerous post of all, given the state of public morality

---

[9]Puyol, ed., *Crónica incompleta*, pp. 145-146.

[10]"Isabel amounts to Fernando, Fernando amounts to Isabel" gives roughly the sense of this famous, essentially untranslatable phrase.

[11]In accordance with Spanish orthographic customs of the time, Isabel's name was written with an initial Y, while Fernando's initial was F. The yoke—*yugo* in Spanish—stood for Isabel because of its initial "y," and the arrows—*flechas* in Spanish—stood for Fernando because of the initial "f."

[12]Pulgar, *Crónica*, I, 67 (ch. XXI).

in Castile after seventy years of misgovernment and lawlessness, was the treasury. Corruption there would be fatal. There was no man in Castile, save her husband—not even Cabrera—whom Isabel trusted as she trusted her old teacher, Gonzalo Chacón, and his nephew Gutierre de Cárdenas. So to them went the post where the danger of betrayal was greatest.

Almost immediately, wherever the new officials were free to exercise their authority in the name of the Queen, justice began to be done, so that "the men and citizens and workers, and all the common people, desiring peace, were most happy, and gave thanks to God that the time had come in which it pleased Him to have mercy on these kingdoms, with the justice which the King and the Queen began to execute."[13]

But of all the men principally responsible for bringing Castile to its disastrous state at the end of Henry's reign, only Pacheco was dead; and his son, the second Marqués of Villena, was eager to move to the center of the stage and prove himself "a chip off the old block." Deceit, disloyalty, and betrayal had become a way of life to these men; it was as though they could imagine no other way to act. They had their personal agendas; they began to make demands. Archbishop Carrillo saw that, as matters now stood, Cardinal Mendoza was almost sure to supplant him as primate of Spain; he was determined to prevent that at all costs. The Count of Plasencia demanded confirmation of his title to Arévalo, Isabel's childhood home and her mother's estate, which she would assuredly never give him. Villena wanted the Mastership of Santiago his father had held, and would accept nothing less; furthermore, he demanded that Juana be given the title of Princess of Castile. When Isabel inevitably refused both demands, Villena turned to King Afonso of Portugal. Afonso felt left out by the course of recent events in Castile; though he cared nothing for his sister, ex-Queen Juana, who had so disgraced the family, he may have had some shreds of family feeling for little Juana, now 13, of whose maternal descent at least there could be no doubt. Villena assured him that Isabel and Fernando lacked both men and money to repel an invasion. That was certainly true at the moment; their opponents in Castile could already put almost as many men in the field as their supporters, and a Portuguese army could tip the balance decisively in favor of rebellion. And the treasury was almost bare; it had been systematically looted throughout the twenty years of Henry's reign.[14]

Before the end of February, barely two months from Isabel's coronation, Afonso sent letters to many of the leading noblemen of Castile declaring that

---

[13]*Ibid.* For an account, with supporting documents, of how justice was re-established in Toledo in early March 1475, see Eloy Benito Ruano, *Toledo en el siglo XV: vida política* (Madrid, 1961), pp. 281-285.

[14]Bernáldez, *Memorias*, p. 29 (ch. XI); Palencia, *Crónica*, II, 169-171 (Dc III, Lb I, Cp VI, VII); Pulgar, *Crónica*, I, 79, 84-85 (ch. XXV, XXVII).

young Juana was the rightful queen and that he intended to marry her and call upon them for support. Isabel at once sent an ambassador, Dr. Andrés de Villalón, to urge King Afonso at least not to make war until negotiations could be attempted and her case for rightful title to the throne of Castile fully presented to him.[15] But the King of Portugal had made up his mind. He had Villena's support, and Plasencia's, and that of many of the other fractious noblemen of distracted Castile; and when Carrillo ostentatiously departed from Isabel's court at Segovia about February 20,[16] Afonso was confident that the Archbishop would soon join him as well. On March 15 Isabel ordered a general mobilization of the realm to repel invasion; on April 1 she levied a special tax of 30 million maravedís (about $150,000) for the same purpose; on April 3 she and Fernando presided at a splendid tournament in Valladolid, attended by representatives of most of the great noble families who supported her. Isabel appeared with her crown, dressed in green brocade with ornaments of silver and gold in floral design, and forty ladies-in-waiting.[17] Never personally ostentatious, Isabel knew the value—especially for her people—of a brave and brilliant show in moments of danger and decision, of which this was most evidently one.

As the shadow of war swept toward her, she offered this prayer, which she repeated again and again, in public and in private, during the course of the struggle:

> Thou, Lord, Who knowest the secrets of the heart, knowest of me that not by an unjust way, not with cunning nor with tyranny, but believing truly that these realms belong to me by right from the king my father, I have acquired them, that what the kings my forebears gained by so much bloodshed may not go to an alien successor. And Thou, Lord, in Whose hands is the rule of kingdoms, Who hast put me by Thy Providence into royal estate, I beg humbly to hear now the prayer of Thy servant, and show forth the truth, and manifest Thy will with Thy marvellous works; so that if I am not in the right, I may not sin through ignorance, and if I am in the right, that Thou mayest give me wisdom and strength so that with the aid of Thine arm I may be able to carry on and to prevail, and bring peace to these realms, which until now have suffered so much evil and destruction.[18]

Many a Christian and a Catholic leader all down through the last two

---

[15]Menéndez Pidal, *Historia de España*, XVII (1), 114. For Villalón's instructions, see Antonio de la Torre and Luis Suárez Fernández, eds. *Documentos referentes a las relaciones con Portugal durante el reinado de los Reyes Católicos* (Valladolid, 1958-63), I, 73-75.

[16]Puyol, ed., *Crónica incompleta*, p. 155.

[17]Menéndez Pidal, *Historia de España*, XVII (1), 114; Torres Fontes, *Fajardo*, pp. 240-243; MS decree, Simancas Archives, Registro General del Sello, 1475-III, folio 307; Chronicle of Valladolid, CODOIN XIII, 92-94. Townsend Miller estimates the value of the maravedí as about half a cent (*Henry IV of Castile* [Philadelphia, 1972], p. 277).

[18]Pulgar, *Crónica*, I, 101 (ch. XXXI).

thousand years, confident in the justice of his cause, has prayed for God's help, which on occasion has been granted. But very few of those leaders ever asked, as Isabel the Catholic at this critical moment asked, again and again, for all Spain to hear, not only for God to help if her cause was just, but for Him to tell her if it was not.

By the end of April Isabel and Fernando at Valladolid were receiving reports of Portuguese troops massing on the frontier at Arronches,[19] near the headwaters of the Guadiana River facing Extremadura. That province was thinly populated and deeply divided; its people could offer no significant opposition to the coming invasion. From Arronches, King Afonso of Portugal could quickly lead his army across rolling country to the Tagus River above Alcántara. He would then have a choice of two equally feasible and advantageous routes: one going straight east up the Tagus toward the ancient capital of Spain, Toledo, and beyond it to Madrid; the other going northeast up the Alagon River, a tributary to the Tagus, then across a low and easy watershed to the Tormes River, a tributary to the Duero, which led directly to Salamanca and the high plains of Castile, all while keeping within convenient supporting distance of Portugal. Isabel and Fernando still had no army; they would have to raise one while the enemy was actually on the march. And Isabel was pregnant again; a full five years after her first conception, the second had come, at a moment that could not have been worse for her.

They wisely decided to make Valladolid and Toledo their main bases, the former being on the Duero and the latter on the Tagus, each blocking one of the prospective main lines of advance for the invaders. Fernando would stay at Valladolid and Isabel would go to Toledo. On the way from Valladolid to Toledo she would leave their daughter, Princess Isabel, now four and a half years old, in what seemed the safest of all keeps, the Alcázar of Segovia under the care of her friend Beatriz de Bobadilla and its governor Cabrera, her husband.[20] Fernando would set to work at once, and Isabel as soon as she had arrived at Toledo, to raise troops to meet the invaders.

With feelings that may well be imagined, but which no contemporary has recorded, on May 2 Isabel left her little daughter in the care of her dearest friend at Segovia.[21] Duty called—a queen's duty, the duty of the heir to twenty-four generations of the longest crusade; a wife's duty, to her husband who was making a supreme effort to save her kingdom and counted on her to do her part; a mother's duty, for though she could not know it yet, she was carrying in her womb a son who could one day be king of Castile if his mother could remain

[19]Menéndez Pidal, *Historia de España*, XVII (1), 124.
[20]Palencia, *Crónica*, II, 187 (Dc III Lb II Cp III); Pulgar, *Crónica*, I, 103-104 (ch. XXXIII).
[21]Vicente Rodríguez Valencia, *Isabel la Católica en la Opinion de Españoles y Extranjeros*, Volume III (Valladolid, 1970), p. 78n.

its queen. She put spurs to her horse and rode south, up and over the mighty Guadarrama Mountains, then down into the lower plain where Madrid lay—and Alcalá de Henares, the favorite residence of Archbishop Carrillo, where he was then staying. Beyond Madrid rose Toledo, like some enchanted ship on its impregnable crag. Its people greeted her with abounding enthusiasm. The very day that she probably arrived there—May 10—the Portuguese army crossed the border, waving gold and silver crosses and singing hymns, the better to proclaim the righteousness of their cause to make young Juana Queen of Castile.[22]

Isabel's first task was to persuade Carrillo, if possible, not to join the invaders. Her advisors debated whether she should go to him or summon him to her.[23] Isabel well knew the importance of ceremony on many occasions, but was never one to stand on it. Firmly, decisively, she cut the knot.

> Because I have great confidence in God, I have little hope in any service and little fear in any disservice that the Archbishop can do to the king my lord and to me. . . . Because he is my subject, and has been in my service and in my company as a friend, I wish to go to him as a friend, because I think that seeing me will change his will and enable him to draw back from this new course he desires to take. And solely to satisfy the opinion of the people, who think that he has served the king my lord and me, I wish to show the greatest diligence to leave nothing undone that I could do; I do not wish to live with the accusing thought that if I had gone to him in person, he would have drawn back from this wrong course that he desires to take.[24]

Accompanied by Constable Velasco, Count of Haro, Isabel rode for Alcalá. The Count went ahead to see Carrillo. He expounded at length on the Archbishop's many services to Isabel and Fernando, how honorable it would be for him to remain loyal, and how shameful and scandalous it would be to abandon the young couple he had married. Finally he told him that Isabel had come in person and was waiting to see him. When Haro had finished, Carrillo seemed impressed. But as he retired for further thought on the matter, Villena's minions pressed their counsel upon him, no doubt feeding once more his jealousy of Cardinal Mendoza.[25]

It may have been Alonso Carrillo's last crossroads. He came back to the antechamber where Haro was waiting, and announced his decision.

"Tell the Queen," he said shortly, in a tone of cold insult that cut like a

[22]Palencia, *Crónica*, II, 184 (Dc III Lb II Cp I); Fernando to Juan II of Aragon, May 11, 1475, in Antonio Paz y Melia, *El cronista Alonso de Palencia* (Madrid, 1914), pp. 180-182; Antonio Rumeu de Armas, *Itinerario de los Reyes Católicos, 1474-1516* (Madrid, 1974), p. 43.
[23]Pulgar, *Crónica*, I, 104-105 (ch. XXXIII).
[24]*Ibid.*, I, 105 (ch. XXXIII).
[25]*Ibid.*, I, 105-113 (ch. XXXIII).

whip, "that she may be sure that if she comes here, entering Alcalá by one gate, I will at once go out the other!"[26]

Isabel was just coming out from Mass when Haro reported to her. A blunt and outspoken man (as she would have remembered from the time he threatened her with the castle dungeon when she was seventeen), he made no attempt to spare her feelings, giving the Archbishop's reply unexpurgated. Her reaction was so uncharacteristic that the contemporary historian Bernáldez makes special comment upon it.[27] All who knew Isabel spoke admiringly of her calmness, her remarkable self-control, her almost complete lack of temper. She was to show these qualities time and again under the most pressing circumstances throughout her life. But this time, for just an instant, she flared up in white-hot anger. She grasped her lovely red-gold hair in both hands as though she would tear it out by the roots. Was she thinking of all this man had done, not just to help her when it suited him, but to harm her and hers when he had the power and they had none? Was she thinking of her long-dead brother on that platform outside the walls of Avila, shamed before his people and before all history by the disgusting ceremony of the deposition of King Henry in which Carrillo had forced him to take part? Was she thinking of how he had prostituted his holy office—this archbishop who thought it was a reform to promise to say Mass three times a year?[28]

As quickly as the gust of rage had come, it passed. Her face, as Bernáldez memorably puts it, "recovered patience." She said: "My Lord Jesus Christ, I put all my affairs in your hands, and from You alone I ask protection and help."[29]

So full had Isabel's days been, since departing from Valladolid April 30, that either she had not yet found time to write to Fernando, or had not been able to put her letters in the hands of trustworthy messengers who would bring them to him quickly. It says a great deal about the quality of the marriage of this husband and wife, who just four months before had faced what might have been a disastrous quarrel or even a separation, that even in a maximum political and military crisis like this they definitely expected to maintain regular and frequent communication by letter. It says even more that Fernando would remind Isabel of that expectation in the way he did. When by May 16 he had received no letter from her—though she had left him less than three weeks previously—he dashed off his second personal letter to her that has been preserved, writing from Tordesillas near Valladolid to her in Toledo.

This letter can be translated—with extreme difficulty. But it cannot be

---

[26]Bernáldez, *Memorias*, p. 29 (ch. XI). Indirect quotation in the original changed to direct.

[27]*Ibid.*, pp. 29-30 (ch. XI).

[28]Walsh, *Isabella*, p. 88.

[29]Bernáldez, *Memorias*, p. 30 (ch. XI).

fully understood; it is too intimate for that. Across five hundred years, coming out of a marital relationship so close and yet so little known in its inner essence, we can only begin to guess what the allusions and connotations might mean, what double-entendres lurk in its intensely private humor. The one thing we may be sure of is that it does not mean what it superficially appears to say, but very much the reverse, and that it was balm for Isabel's heart after her slashing rejection by Archbishop Carrillo.

> At least it is now very clear which of us feels more sympathy for the other, according as you write to me and give me happiness by letting me know how you are. I cannot sleep, for so many messengers come without letters. It is not because of decreasing supplies of paper nor because you do not know how to write, but because of decreasing love and of pride. So then, you are in Toledo and I am in little villages! Still, some day you will return to your first love. Whether or not you do, you ought to write to me so as not to be a murderer, and let me know how you are. . . . The princess [little Isabel] must not be forgotten, for God does not forget her; neither does her father, who kisses your hands and is your servant.[30]

On May 23, still in Toledo, Isabel wrote to Pedro Fajardo, Adelantado of Murcia, the southeastern province bordering the Mediterranean where the Marqués of Villena had great estates, directing Fajardo to make war upon Villena and all his family who marched with him. The vigorous direct language, the strong moral tone, and the ringing denunciation of the evils of conspiracy, disloyalty, and treason which she had known all too well since she was eleven years old, sound exactly like Isabel. There is every reason to believe that she wrote this letter herself, needing no scribe or secretary to compose it.

> Don Diego López Pacheco, Marqués of Villena, and Don Rodrigo Girón, Master of Calatrava, and Don Juan Girón his brother, Count of Ureña, setting aside the fear of God and of our justice, and the fidelity they ought to have and guard for the commmon good and the peace of these realms and the citizenship which they hold, thinking by clever and perverse ways to carry out their evil plans and to increase tyrannically their power by breaking up and degrading the royal crown of these realms, are rebelling against the king my lord and against me, making leagues and conspiracies and joining with others wishing to insult our royal persons if they can, and alienate my legitimate rights of succession to a private person who has no right to them, and in order to become more powerful have betrayed these kingdoms to the king of Portugal, who has entered into my kingdoms scandalously and totally against my will. Those gentlemen, having committed and given cause for breaking relationships, are and ought to be considered our enemies and the enemies of our country, and thus it can and ought to be done, and is my will and decree, that war be made against them.[31]

---

[30]Rodríguez Valencia, *Isabel*, III, 79. Walsh (*Isabella*, pp. 258-259) dates this letter to 1485, but recent research cited by Rodríguez Valencia (*op. cit.*, III, 77-78) shows it to have been written May 16, 1475—ten years earlier.

[31]Isabel to Fajardo, May 23, 1475, in Torres Fontes, *Fajardo*, p. 266.

The next day she sent essentially the same letter to the city council of Sevilla, and appointed the greatest nobleman of the south, Enrique de Guzmán, Duke of Medina Sidonia, captain-general of Andalusia to carry the war to Portugal by counterattacking across its border in the south in response to its invasion in the north.[32] On the day following, May 25, the invaders reached Plasencia on the Alagon River—which meant that they were committing themselves to the northern invasion route, toward Fernando and away from Isabel—and paused there for a ceremony proclaiming Juana Queen of Castile and King Afonso of Portugal her consort. Four days later their marriage was celebrated, though without a Papal dispensation, obviously required when an uncle was marrying his niece—a lack which Afonso's party had to admit openly.[33]

News of Afonso's arrival at Plasencia would have arrived at Toledo by May 27. On that date Isabel appointed the Count of Cifuentes and Juan de Ribera co-governors of Toledo, arranging the structure of authority in the city to the best of her ability so that it would hold firm in her support. The next day she left Toledo, riding northwest toward Avila.[34] Now that she knew the invaders were marching northeast toward the high plains of Castile, Avila would be a better base than Toledo for intercepting them, closer to their line of march. Avila had always been faithful to her; it was strongly defended and in desolate country where a besieging force could find little support. There she would rally her people.

The road from Toledo to Avila traverses a low broad gap between the Gredos Mountains and the Guadarramas, going directly past the Bulls of Guisando and the meadow in which they stood, which held so many memories for Isabel. This gap is not so rugged as other crossings of these mountains, but the climb from the lower southern plain to the higher northern one beyond the pass is still punishingly steep in places. We know nothing of Isabel's journey beyond its beginning and its end—neither who was in her party, nor how fast she moved. But with the enemy on the march and the gage of battle flung down with the proclamation of Juana as Queen, Isabel would not have been Isabel if she had not pushed herself to the utmost. We may picture her urging her horse on up the long slope from the valley of the Alberche to San Martín de Valdeiglesias, deep into the night or early in the morning, inspiring her companions with her dash and courage, her inexhaustibility.

But Isabel was not inexhaustible; Isabel was human; for once the fire of her dedication consumed her judgment, and she drove herself too far. On May 31, at the little town of Cebreros where the fields of the country round the Bulls

---

[32]*Tumbo de Sevilla*, I, 40-42, 45-48.
[33]Pulgar, *Crónica*, I, 120 (ch. XXXVII); Puyol, ed., *Crónica incompleta*, pp. 182-186.
[34]Benito Ruano, *Toledo*, pp. 288-291; Palencia, *Crónica*, II, 189 (Dc III Lb II Cp IV).

of Guisando give way to the rockbound moonscape of the Avila plain, she slipped fainting from her saddle, gushing blood.

Her baby was dead. He had been a son.[35]

The next four days are a blank. Was there a doctor in tiny Cebreros? Probably not. Was Isabel able to travel again in a few hours or a day, to complete her journey to Avila? We do not know. Only on June 5 does she re-emerge in Avila, writing a letter reminding Toledo of its commitment to send troops quickly to Fernando to fight against the invaders.[36] During the next two and a half weeks she continued writing occasional letters from Avila, and before long must have been raising troops again, since before the end of the month we find a substantial force from Avila on the march with her to join the main army around Valladolid. Meanwhile Fernando had gone to Zamora and Toro downstream on the Duero near the Portuguese border, finding Toro betrayed to Afonso, but Zamora apparently secure. King Afonso advanced from Plasencia to Arévalo, only 35 miles away from Isabel at Avila; but not a village or a man would join him in this region where Isabel had spent her childhood, and he had no desire whatsoever to lay siege to Avila with its formidable walls.[37]

Meanwhile, from all over northern Castile, volunteer troops of both high and low estate poured into the area of Valladolid, to which Fernando had returned June 9. Many were untrained and poorly equipped, but they were full of enthusiasm; Fernando at once set to work training them.[38] On June 19 he left for Burgos, the historic capital of Castile, where the ambitious Stúñiga family dominated and Iñigo de Stúñiga had seized the citadel of Burgos shortly after Afonso's invasion. But the people of the city were for the most part strong supporters of Isabel and Fernando; the Stúñigas and their adherents were isolated in the citadel. Quickly assuring himself that matters in Burgos were in good hands, Fernando returned to Valladolid within two or three days, though not before writing a letter to Isabel describing conditions in Burgos, with special emphasis on the loyalty of most of the people of the city. His letter contains no mention or hint of their recent loss; it is impossible to say whether this is because Isabel had not yet told her husband about it, or because it was too painful for him to mention. But the tone of his letter is much less playful than its predecessor.[39]

By June 22, Isabel was ready and able to travel again. It is surely no accident or coincidence that the first place to which she went, on leaving Avila,

[35]Chronicle of Valladolid, CODOIN XIII, 96-97.

[36]Benito Ruano, *Toledo*, pp. 291-292.

[37]Menéndez Pidal, *Historia de España*, XVII (1), 130-132.

[38]*Ibid.*, p. 132; Pulgar, *Crónica*, I, 132 (ch. XLII); Puyol, ed., *Crónica incompleta*, pp. 194-195; Valera, *Crónica*, pp. 22, 25.

[39]Rumeu de Armas, *Itinerario*, p. 44; Menéndez Pidal, *Historia de España*, XVII (1), 130-131; Rodríguez Valencia, *Isabel*, III, 87-88.

was Segovia.[40] She could not stop long—a day or two at the most—for the army mustering at Valladolid needed to see their queen, and she would be bringing troops that must join them as soon as possible. But at least she could see Beatriz, with whom she could share her sorrow for her irreplaceable loss, and above all little Isabel, dearer now than ever, offering a different kind of consolation. From Segovia, at the head of a large contingent of both cavalry and foot soldiers which she had raised there and at Avila, the Queen rode on to Medina del Campo, where she reviewed the troops brought by the Duke of Alba. On July 9 she and Fernando met again at the bridge of San Miguel del Pino on the way from Medina del Campo to Tordesillas, to plan an advance on Toro with the whole army, now totalling more than 40,000 men.[41]

Their army now had the numerical advantage, but it was not equipped for siege warfare—and a siege would certainly be needed to take Toro—nor had there been time to develop any reliable arrangements for its supply. It would have to move and win very quickly, because without a good supply system it could not stay in the field for long. New forces were still arriving, but others were delayed on the way, and there was the inevitable confusion about where and when to encamp, and where and when to march and ride. Castile had not put a people's army into the field since the spontaneous rally to Henry IV after he was proclaimed deposed at Avila in 1468, and that had not lasted long nor accomplished much; no one present, including Fernando and Isabel, had any experience in handling such a force. The strain and stress is evident in Fernando's letter to Isabel from camp at Tordesillas July 14, all about the horsemen and the noblemen and the foot soldiers who have come and have not come, and what is to be done with them all. He had planned to meet Isabel again the next day, and now he cannot do so. "God knows how it weighs upon me that I cannot see you tomorrow," he writes, "but I swear by your life and mine that I never loved you so much."[42]

Her people loved her too. We are told how she rode among them in the camps, as they prepared for the march on Toro, "with cheerful face" despite all she had recently undergone, addressing personally and thanking one after another, from the greatest nobles to the roughest foot soldiers, with gracious words and promises of reward for what each was contributing. She longed to accompany them to Toro, but finally allowed herself to be persuaded (surely Fernando had a hand in this) not to risk herself at the actual scene of prospective battle. On July 16 the army marched out from Tordesillas toward Toro, leaving Isabel behind there to fling herself down upon her knees and

---

[40]Rumeu de Armas, *Itinerario*, p. 44.

[41]Menéndez Pidal, *Historia de España*, XVII (1), 132-133; Chronicle of Valladolid, CODOIN XIII, 98-99; Pulgar, *Crónica*, I, 134 (ch. XLIII); Palencia, *Crónica*, II, 206 (Dc III Lb III Cp II); Puyol, ed., *Crónica incompleta*, p. 214n.

[42]Rodríguez Valencia, *Isabel*, III, 93-94.

spend long hours in prayer for its success.[43]

It is twenty miles from Tordesillas to Toro. Twenty miles further down the Duero River stands the larger city of Zamora, the last town on the Duero before the Portuguese border. Zamora's governor, Francisco de Valdés, was personally loyal to Isabel and Fernando and had been confirmed by Fernando in his position two months before; but the *alcaide* of its citadel was a relative of Villena and had suborned a leading citizen of the town, Juan de Porres. On July 16, the very day Fernando marched with his army, the conspirators opened the gates of Zamora to King Afonso and the Portuguese before Valdés could stop them. Now the task facing the improvised army was doubled; they must take both Toro and Zamora. Worse still, the smaller but fortified town of Castronuño on the southerly bend of the Duero midway between Tordesillas and Toro had also been seized by the Portuguese at approximately the same time that Zamora was delivered to them. Even if Toro could be taken, it was most unlikely that it could be held while strong enemy garrisons remained on both sides of it, upstream and downstream on the Duero.[44]

The direct route from Tordesillas to Toro did not follow the Duero, which bent south to Castronuño, but cut straight across country; and any plan that might have been entertained of keeping close to the river now had to be abandoned because of the enemy possession of Castronuño. But the main road was dry and barren, and it was the hottest part of the summer. The troops suffered severely from lack of water, accentuated by the enormous quantities of dust stirred up from the arid surface by the passage of forty-two thousand men, several thousand of whom were mounted. It took them four full days to march the twenty miles to Toro.[45] Around the city some food was available, and plenty of water from the river, but the army obviously could not stay there long, and Toro was strongly defended. Fernando issued a challenge to Afonso to settle the issue between them by personal combat. It was splendid chivalry, and Afonso had no choice but to accept—on paper; however, he set no date for the duel, and no one could really have expected there to be one between the fat 50-year-old Portuguese king and the lean, athletic Fernando, 23. Some tentative negotiations were begun, but quickly foundered on the rock of Afonso's insistence that any agreement be guaranteed by an exchange of hostages—Juana for Queen Isabel. Fernando told him he would never agree to that, and there was nothing more to be said.[46]

Stymied, the leaders of the army—which included many of the fractious

---

[43]Puyol, ed., *Crónica incompleta*, pp. 216-218.

[44]Palencia, *Crónica*, II, 208-209 (Dc III Lb III Cp III).

[45]Puyol, ed., *Crónica incompleta*, p. 230; Chronicle of Valladolid, CODOIN XIII, 100.

[46]Palencia, *Crónica*, II, 214-215 (Dc III Lb III CpV); Pulgar, *Crónica*, I, 136-139 (ch. XLIII).

nobles so accustomed to having their own way and feuding with their peers, and a large contingent of Basques who did not particularly like any of the Castilian leaders despite accepting the same sovereign—fell to quarrelling. Fernando found himself unable to restore harmony, especially in the absence of a plan of action, which he did not seem to have. He may well have asked himself whether, after all and despite convention, he should have left Isabel behind at Tordesillas. Perhaps only she could have kept these men in the field; for while there is some question of the extent of their enthusiasm for Fernando, there is no question of the extent of their enthusiasm for Isabel. But she was not there; the lack of supplies pressed them hard; they had brought no siege artillery; and therefore, on July 24, after only four days before Toro, Fernando decided to return, empty-handed.[47]

Despite collapsing discipline, the march back took only two days where the march out had taken four. Isabel seems to have had no warning of it. When the first outriders of the retreat reached Tordesillas in the evening of the 25th, she rode out to meet them with an escort of cavalry whom she ordered to turn them back at lance-point. But she soon learned the sad truth, as the army straggled back into its former camp at Tordesillas with hangdog looks, not even having fought a battle, simply a failure.[48]

Isabel could scarcely believe such a thing had happened. That evening she called the leaders of the army into council, in Fernando's presence. She was careful to declare her continued love and respect for him. But she excoriated the commanders for giving up too soon, with a passion far more effective for being so controlled and articulate: "One must first give battle to be able to proclaim victory; he who begins nothing, finishes nothing. Where will we go and what will we attempt that is good, when with so many people and so many resources we bring forth so cold a triumph? . . . . Those who do not recognize opportunity when it comes, find misfortune when they do not look for it." Fernando's answer held a wisdom that, for once, matched and even exceeded hers; we may hear his father's voice in it: "Prudence is the god of battles. We submit ourselves, above all, to the Most High Judge, without Whom, as St. John says, nothing is done. Perhaps He did not wish that these people perish in this hour, but wishes that we seek final victory with greater work, care, and diligence."[49]

---

[47]Palencia, *Crónica*, II, 215 (Dc III Lb III Cp VI); Puyol, ed., *Crónica incompleta*, pp. 232-237; Chronicle of Valladolid, CODOIN XIII, 100-101.

[48]Rumeu de Armas, *Itinerario*, p. 45; Puyol, ed., *Crónica incompleta*, p. 238.

[49]Puyol, ed., *Crónica incompleta*, pp. 238-247; Palencia, *Crónica*, II, 215 (Dc III Lb III Cp VI). The long speeches attributed to both Isabel and Fernando on this occasion by the anonymous contemporary chronicler edited by Puyol are in many places too stilted to be accurate, especially with their appropriate classical references to Hannibal and Xerxes, which it is very hard to imagine two such practical people as Isabel and Fernando making at a late-night post-mortem on a failed campaign in a war on which

To that goal they both now committed themselves, with everything they had. An offer from Afonso, conveyed through Cardinal Mendoza to Isabel, to make peace on the basis of the cession to him of Toro, Zamora, and the whole province of Galicia north of Portugal, was flatly and immediately rejected. Afonso was still at Arévalo, where he was being urged to march northeast to Burgos where his ally Iñigo de Stúñiga still held the citadel, but he could not make up his mind to go, and remained inactive, giving Isabel and Fernando priceless time. Carrillo had joined him with 500 lances, but no other reinforcement. There was almost no public support in Castile for Juana's claims; those backing Afonso were almost all doing so for reasons of personal gain. Other than his strongholds near the border—most notably Toro and Zamora—Afonso's principal remaining advantage was money, which enabled him to train, equip, and arm his troops better than those of Isabel and Fernando. Cardinal Mendoza as Chancellor, and the Royal Council of Castile, recommended a drastic action, almost unprecedented in the history of Castile, to overcome that advantage: the Church to provide half of all its silver and gold as a loan to the state to create a better army, to be repaid in three years. Isabel was reluctant, but relevant Scriptural precedents were cited to her; in August the loan was approved. There is no record of any resistance from the Church, except for the few prelates like Carrillo who were openly enlisted on the side of the invaders; and Isabel made sure the loan was paid back on time and in full.[50]

Early in September, with the citadel at Burgos hard pressed by Isabel's fighting men in the city and appealing with increasing desperation for help from Afonso, the Portuguese king and his Castilian supporters, with Villena and Carrillo much in evidence among them, at last moved out of Arévalo in the direction of Burgos. They had about 120 miles to go, across country which had always been the heartland of Isabel's strength; there would be no significant local support until Afonso had actually reached Burgos and penetrated to the citadel. Furthermore, Fernando was already at Burgos, ready to give Afonso a very warm reception if he should get that far. It was obviously necessary to bypass Valladolid, where Isabel was staying with a substantial force; Afonso therefore decided to march to Peñafiel some thirty miles east of Valladolid. He swept aside the first attempts to oppose him. On September 12 Isabel left Valladolid with Cardinal Mendoza and the Count of Benavente to go north to Palencia, within striking distance of Afonso's route from Peñafiel to Burgos; there is no record that this time anyone suggested she stay away from the action. On the 14th the Count of Benavente with just 150 horsemen left Isabel at Palencia to ride to the little town of Baltanás north of Peñafiel and throw

---

their crowns and even their lives might depend. But some passages, such as those quoted here, have a more authentic ring; and Palencia confirms Isabel's passionate rejection of the defeat and her direct challenge to Fernando as to why it happened.

[50]Pulgar, *Crónica*, I, 143-149 (ch. XLV, XLVI).

himself in the path of the enemy. In all probability he had been at that evening conference in Tordesillas when Isabel told her commanders what she thought of their retreat from Toro; perhaps he remembered her words "he who begins nothing, finishes nothing." He vowed that this time there would be no weakness and no retreat.[51]

Baltanás was a small town, hardly fortified. In the middle of the night of September 17 King Afonso, Villena and Carrillo came up to it, and prepared for all-out attack at dawn on the 18th. All day long the battle raged. Carrillo, wearing his familiar bloodstained armor, was in the thick of the fight. Benavente and his men were outnumbered at least forty to one.[52] (Were there, among his heroic 150 that day, the fathers of any of the five hundred who marched with Hernán Cortes in 1519 to overthrow the Satanic empire of Aztec Mexico against odds of ten thousand to one?) Twice the vastly superior attacking force fought their way into the narrow twisting rocky streets of the little town; twice they were driven out again. Finally, in the evening, with the defenders' casualties mounting, the minions of Afonso and Villena and Carrillo pushed in to stay. Benavente and his men made their last stand in a street so small that it was little more than an alley, where the enemy's superiority in numbers counted for less. By then, surely most of their crossbow bolts had been fired off and their arquebus ammunition (if they had any) long since expended; it remained for them to show, as the *conquistadores* were later to show from the jungles of the Amazon to the far Pacific shore, "why swords are forged in Spain." Twilight fell on the ringing clash of steel on steel, until at last Benavente and his men could fight no more, and the survivors had to surrender.[53]

Spaniards admire nothing more than this kind of heroism, save only sanctity. As fast as the news could spread, the Count of Benavente's stand at Baltanás became the talk of the whole country. When he was first captured, his life was threatened by his furious and frustrated foes, but they soon realized that in all probability their own men would not obey an order to kill him. Isabel had learned of his great fight while it was actually in progress; Palencia is only

---

[51]Palencia, *Crónica*, II, 231 (Dc III Lb IV [XXIV], Cp II); Chronicle of Valladolid, CODOIN XIII, 102-103; Menéndez Pidal, *Historia de España*, XVII (1), 141-142; Rumeu de Armas, *Itinerario*, p. 46.

[52]When he originally invaded Castile early in May 1475, Afonso brought about 12,000 men with him from Portugal (Menéndez Pidal, *Historia de España*, XVII [1], 125), and probably picked up two or three thousand more in Castile. We do not know how many went all the way to Arévalo with him, and clearly he would have left a substantial garrison there. Still, it is reasonable to assume that he had 6,000 men at Baltanás.

[53]All the chroniclers wax eloquent on the Count of Benavente and his men at the Battle of Baltanás—Palencia, *Crónica*, II, 232 (Dc III Lb IV [XXIV], Cp II); Pulgar, *Crónica*, I, 159-160 (ch. L); Valera, *Crónica*, p. 43; Puyol, ed., *Crónica incompleta*, pp. 269-270.

eighteen miles from Baltanás, less than three hours' ride for a good horseman. She sent cavalry to his aid. They did not arrive in time to prevent his capture, but at dawn of the following day they were all around the fringes of the Afonso's army, taunting the King of Portugal, daring his men to fight them. They did not dare; they turned back—back not only to Arévalo, but all the way to Zamora almost on the Portuguese border.[54]

Historians confess themselves puzzled by this instant retreat of a numerically superior army immediately after prevailing over a much weaker opposing force, though giving some possible reasons—Fernando's strengthening of the defenses of Burgos; Isabel's rallying the troops at Palencia; the failure to pick up any new support for Afonso's cause in this countryside. All these could well have been contributing factors. But the essential explanation lies in Napoleon's maxim: "In war the moral is to the material as three is to one." In all probability Afonso retreated from Baltanás for almost exactly the same reason that in World War II Japanese Admiral Kurita, with victory in his grasp, retreated from the coast of Samar in the Battle of Leyte Gulf in 1944, after sinking four American ships and pursuing the others present in a long chase with enormous odds in his favor, because he could not believe that three American destroyers would have charged his entire fleet, including the largest battleship ever built, if they did not have overwhelming support just over the horizon.[55] But those three American destroyers were unsupported, as was the Count of Benavente at Baltanás. Fortune favors the brave.

The tide had turned; increasingly, everyone in Castile realized it. King Afonso stayed shut up in Zamora, gaining very few additional adherents to his cause, though during the fall the small fortified town of Cantalapiedra, just ten miles west of Isabel's birthplace, Song of the High Towers, was betrayed to him. To balance Cantalapiedra, Ocaña of evil memory was taken for Isabel in November by two local noblemen.[56] About the time of the recapture of Ocaña, Francisco de Valdés, who had been governor of Zamora when that city was betrayed, and who by not resisting its captors had won their favor, got in touch with Isabel to tell her that he was prepared to deliver Zamora, with the King of Portrugal in it, to her and Fernando. But the utmost speed was necessary. The only feasible entry point was the single bridge over the Duero River at Zamora. The commander at the bridge, Pedro de Mazariegos, was cooperating with Valdés, but might be replaced at any moment, since Afonso was actually in the city and alert to the possibility of such an action as Valdés and Mazariegos were planning. Fernando must come at once.[57]

[54]Pulgar, *Crónica*, I, 160 (ch. L); Valera, *Crónica*, p. 43.
[55]Samuel Eliot Morison, *History of United States Naval Operations in World War II*, Volume XII: "Leyte" (Boston, 1958), pp. 242-300.
[56]Valera, *Crónica*, p. 45; Pulgar, *Crónica*, I, 161-162 (ch. LI).
[57]Pulgar, *Crónica*, I, 167 (ch. LII).

Fernando had remained in Burgos since going there in August to direct the siege of its citadel and defend it against attack by Afonso should it come. Isabel worked out a plan whereby he would pretend to be sick, leave by night and ride the 75 miles to Valladolid, where she would secretly assemble a cavalry force and some carefully chosen assistants to go with him. Fernando left Burgos for the two-day ride with just three companions, including Rodrigo de Ulloa, who had been commander of the citadel at Zamora and had remained entirely loyal, though his brother Juan was a traitor. At Valladolid Isabel had 600 horsemen ready, and a star-studded entourage for her husband, including Gutierre de Cárdenas and the now-famous Count of Benavente, who had been ransomed from Afonso in October at the price of three castles.[58]

Rumors of their plan preceded them to Zamora, for there were now too many people in the secret. On December 3 King Afonso told Valdés to change the guard at the bridge. Valdés told him he would do it the next day. But during the night Valdés blocked the bridge with stones on the side facing the city, and at dawn December 4 he stood upon the parapet to proclaim in a thunderous voice: "Castile! Castile for King Fernando and Queen Isabel his wife!" He followed this with a discharge of cannon and the primitive firearms known as *espingardas*. The people of Zamora took arms against King Afonso and his minions; there was an all-day struggle, as at Baltanás, and throughout it Valdés' stone barricade held.[59]

It is sixty miles from Valladolid to Zamora; all that day and night Fernando's six hundred rode like the wind, and King Afonso knew they were coming. When night fell, ending the fruitless battle at the bridge, the King of Portugal took counsel with Carrillo. Valdés and the Zamorans had proved very formidable on their own; reinforced, they could be irresistible. The city could not be effectively defended with the bridge open. One also suspects that neither the King nor the Archbishop was eager to come to grips in narrow stone streets for a second time with the Count of Benavente. That night they and their men evacuated Zamora (except for its citadel) and moved the twenty miles upriver to Toro. When Fernando arrived the next morning he was welcomed with unrestrained enthusiasm by the liberated populace of Zamora.[60]

Just four and a half months before, Isabel had told her retreating *caballeros*: "Those who do not recognize opportunity when it comes, find misfortune when they do not look for it." This time—under her guidance throughout, for the information from Zamora came first to her and the plan to take it was hers—they had recognized their opportunity and had prevailed.

---

[58]*Ibid.*, I, 167-168 (ch. LIII); Palencia, *Crónica*, II, 245-246 (Dc III Lb III [XXIV] Cp VIII); Valera, *Crónica*, pp. 47-48.

[59]Pulgar, *Crónica*, I, 168-170 (ch. LIII).

[60]*Ibid.*, I, 170-172 (ch. LIII); Palencia, *Crónica*, II, 248-249 (Dc III Lb IV [XXIV] Cp IX, X); Valera, *Crónica*, p. 49; Menéndez Pidal, *Historia de España*, XVII (1), 148-149.

It was now obviously necessary for Fernando to remain in Zamora, where his position was strong—because of the support of the people of the city—and yet exposed, since Zamora lay between Portuguese-held Toro and the Portuguese frontier, and its citadel was still in the hands of the rebels. Though the party of King Afonso and Carrillo and Villena still held several scattered small posts in northwestern Castile, the only other major city where they had a foothold was Burgos, where their men still held the citadel. But they were battered and exhausted by prolonged heavy fighting, and at the beginning of January the rebel commander there, Iñigo de Stúñiga, opened negotiations for surrender with Constable Velasco, Count of Haro.[61]

Haro sent word to Isabel in Valladolid, and she promptly set out for Burgos, eighty miles away over the high plains of Castile. So famous are those plains for their summer heat that foreigners often forget how cold they can be in the dead of winter. But Isabel would never be stopped by weather. She set off, either on January 8 or 12, depending on whether we follow the Chronicle of Valladolid or Palencia the historian. Whichever day she left, the trip took substantially longer than usual for her; it must have been a bone-chilling ride. Finally she arrived at Burgos at one o'clock in the morning of the 18th in the middle of a heavy snowstorm—to be received, despite the hour and the weather, with fervent enthusiasm including dancing and singing by the children of the city.[62]

Ten days later the citadel surrendered to her. With an extraordinary combination of magnanimity and wisdom, Isabel pardoned all its defenders, and even settled a substantial income on the rebel commander; but she deprived him and his family once and for all of command or control in Burgos. The loyal Diego de Ribera was appointed *alcaide* in their stead. Despite this deprivation, the Stúñiga family appreciated her forbearance; it was one of the most powerful in Castile, with some members fighting for her and the others for the opposing side, but all Stúñigas now withdrew support from Afonso and the rebels and gave it to Isabel.[63]

It had been evident at least since the recapture of Zamora that Afonso of Portugal now had no hope of prevailing unless heavily reinforced. It was equally obvious that no significant reinforcements could any longer be expected from rebels in Castile. But for months Afonso's remarkably able son John (spelled Joao in Portuguese) had been raising money and troops in Portugal. By late January he had assembled no less than 2,500 horse and 15,000 foot, and

[61]Menéndez Pidal, *Historia de España*, XVII (1), 150.

[62]Palencia, *Crónica*, II, 259 (Dc III Lb V [XXV] Cp III); Chronicle of Valladolid, CODOIN XIII, 110-112.

[63]Menéndez Pidal, *Historia de España*, XVII (1), 150-151; Pulgar, *Crónica*, I, 179-180 (ch. LV); Chronicle of Valladolid, CODOIN XIII, 112-113; Isabel to the Council of Sevilla, January 30, 1476, *Tumbo de Sevilla* I, 129-130.

with this formidable force crossed the frontier in the desolate country south of the confluence of the Duero and the Turones, marching for Zamora. But to reach it he had to cross the Tormes River near Ledesma—and the *alcaide* of Ledesma was a man we have heard of before: Gracián de Sesé, the tough Extremaduran who had held Trujillo against Villena and the royal army throughout the crucial weeks when Fernando was coming from Aragon to marry Isabel in 1468. He liked Villena's son no better than his father, and was whole-heartedly enlisted in Isabel's cause. Gracián's cannon commanded the only bridge, so that the Portuguese army had to cross the icy, rocky stream by fords in which horses slipped and fell and wagons were destroyed. Attacked by the Portuguese in Ledesma after they finally passed the fords, Gracián made a tremendous defense, which cost the Portuguese heavily. Finally forced back by numbers, he razed defenses as he abandoned them, and destroyed the food supplies so large an army badly needed in the middle of the winter. The contrast to Afonso's initially unopposed invasion of the year before could hardly have been greater. Prince John pressed on, but Gracián's fierce resistance and scorched-earth policy left him no choice but to go directly to Toro, where at least he could feed his men. He arrived there February 9 to join his father.[64]

After resting for several days, the united Portuguese and rebel army attempted an attack eastward toward Song of the High Towers and Medina del Campo. Both places were well defended and gave them a hot reception, so they turned back westward, toward Zamora once again, where Fernando was. On February 19 the Portuguese and rebel army arrived, directly across the Duero River from Zamora with his cannon commanding the single bridge. That same day Isabel, coming from Valladolid, arrived in Tordesillas, where she had been the previous year when their first army marched on Toro from the east. From there she launched an immediate attack on the Portuguese-held outpost of Fuentesauco south of Toro by a force of a thousand cavalry under the command of Pedro Manrique, Count of Treviño, who had brought the cavalry escort to Fernando when he reached El Burgo de Osma on his way to marry Isabel. The town was seized without difficulty, increasing the pressure on the invaders and once again testifying to Isabel's remarkable and unexpected military skill. Meanwhile in Zamora, the walls were strong and well defended and the Portuguese cannon proved ineffective, while from their position on the other side of the river the Portuguese could not press the defenders closely.[65]

Perhaps it was time to parley. The two monarchs confronting each other at Zamora agreed to talk—but secretly, at night, in boats on the Duero River

---

[64]Palencia, *Crónica*, II, 264-265 (Dc III Lb V [XXV] Cp VI, VII); Menéndez Pidal, *Historia de España*, XVII (1), 150-151.
[65]Palencia, *Crónica*, II, 267 (Dc III Lb V [XXV] Cp VII); Pulgar, *Crónica*, I, 195-198 (ch. LX); Chronicle of Valladolid, CODOIN XIII, 115; Rumeu de Armas, *Itinerario*, p. 51.

which separated the two camps. This method was hardly practicable; the river was in spate from melting snow and nearly swamped Afonso's boat on the first attempt. The second failed even more ludicrously. In the excitement of the siege nobody was attending to Zamora's church clock, which had become two hours fast. The meeting of the two kings was scheduled for one o'clock in the morning; when the errant clock struck three, Fernando concluded that he was late and did not get into his boat at all. One suspects that he had never been particularly eager to do so. Shortly afterward Afonso asked him for a 15-day truce. Fernando replied: "Not an hour!"[66]

Before dawn March 1 Afonso's army broke camp to march back to Toro. The moment his watchmen from the city towers reported them gone, Fernando marshalled his men for pursuit. It took a long time to get them across the one narrow bridge over the Duero that the Portuguese had been blocking, but it was finally done. All through the day the pursuing Castilians gained, until finally, five miles from Toro, King Afonso, Prince John, Archbishop Carrillo, and all their forces turned to fight. Late in a lowering winter afternoon under a cold rain, the trumpets on both sides sounded the attack, and the decisive battle was joined. The numbers on both sides were approximately equal.[67]

There was a tremendous clash all along the line—thundering of cannon, shivering of lances, clang of steel on armor, wild neighing of horses, many-throated bellows of "Fernando!" and "Afonso!" Both kings were in the thick of the melee, and so—likewise on opposite sides—were the Cardinal and the primate of Spain. For the last time, Alonso Carrillo appears before us in his bloodstained armor; for the first and last time, so does Cardinal Mendoza. (The fighting bishop was a long-established tradition of the Reconquest of Spain from the infidel Muslims, but their participation in battles between Christians was scandalous.) For a full hour the furious combat seemed locked in place; neither side would give way. Then, next to the river, the army of Castile began to press forward against the Portuguese foot soldiers along the bank; while on the other wing, next to the hills, Prince John of Portugal was advancing successfully against the Castilian cavalry. A foggy twilight descended, the rain froze into sleet, and commanders began losing touch with their men as the surge of combat forced them apart. But Fernando saw the point of greatest

---

[66]Palencia, *Crónica*, II, 268 (Dc III Lb V [XXV] Cp VIII); Pulgar, *Crónica*, I, 199-207 (ch. LXI-LXIII).

[67]Extensive accounts of the Battle of Toro appear in all major sources: Palencia, *Crónica*, II, 269-272 (Dc III Lb V [XXV] Cp VIII); Pulgar, *Crónica*, I, 207-215 (ch. LXIV); Valera, *Crónica*, pp. 68-77; Bernáldez, *Memorias*, pp. 57-59 (ch. XXIII); Chronicle of Valladolid, CODOIN XIII, 116-119. For Fernando's own personal account, see his letter to Sevilla, March 2, 1476, *Tumbo de Sevilla*, I, 132-134. Good English summaries are provided in Townsend Miller, *The Castles and the Crown* (New York, 1963), pp. 93-96; Walsh, *Isabella*, pp. 121-125; and Prescott, *Ferdinand and Isabella*, I, 249-255.

danger. He rode among the fleeing Castilian cavalry with his sword swinging in the gray dusk, crying: "Take heart, all you who have courage! Go forth upon the enemy to win glorious victory!"[68] "Fernando! Fernando! Fernando!" came the reply.[69] The Castilian cavalry re-formed and counter-charged—not against Prince John, who was no longer at their front, but against the hard-beset center and river wing of the Portuguese army. It crumpled under the shock. Many Portuguese soldiers were driven into the river and killed there; all the next day their bodies were floating downstream past Zamora. A tide of desperate fugitives carried King Afonso away into the roaring night. He could not see where he was; there were no torches, moon or stars. Only about twenty men stayed with him, pressing away from the fatal river, skirting the hills. For hours they wandered in the dark. Morning found them at Castronuño, the Portuguese-held outpost fifteen miles southeast of the battlefield.

On a hill to the north Prince John rallied his victorious wing, lighting fires and blowing trumpets in the hope that his missing father would see or hear them, insisting to all who would listen that he was holding possession of the battlefield. Meanwhile, down near the edge of the river where the battle had actually been won, Fernando was attempting to collect his scattered men and organize a pursuit. But the night was pitch-black; the Castilian army had left Zamora so quickly that morning that it had almost no food, camping gear, or material for torches; the men were exhausted, staggering, groping in the Stygian gloom. To keep them there in that condition was dangerous and unnecessary; to try to pursue the fugitives would soon cause the pursuers to become as lost as their quarry. The greater part of the enemy had been routed; Prince John's wing was in no position to advance. About midnight both sides abandoned the field. Fernando went back to Zamora; Prince John went on to Toro.

Despite periodic attempts by "revisionist" historians to assert that Fernando did not really win the Battle of Toro (also known as the Battle of Peleagonzalo), there is no rational basis for calling it anything but a decisive victory for him and for Isabel.[70] It permanently shifted the initiative. Though the war dragged on for three years more, Afonso never made another major offensive move. Prince John returned to Portugal in April, leaving Toro closely blockaded.[71] The citadels of Zamora and of Madrid, which Afonso's partisans still held at the time of the battle, both surrendered to Isabel and Fernando within a few weeks.[72] Carrillo left the King of Portugal, never to return to his

---

[68]Palencia, *Crónica*, II, 271 (Dc III Lb V [XXV] Cp VIII).

[69]Pulgar, *Crónica*, I, 215 (ch. LXIV).

[70]See Luis Suárez Fernández's excellent summary of the overwhelming arguments for this conclusion, in Menéndez Pidal, *Historia de España*, XVII (1), 156-157.

[71]Palencia, *Crónica*, II, 282 (Dc III Lb VI [XXVI] Cp II).

[72]The citadel of Zamora surrendered to Fernando on March 19 (Chronicle of Valladolid, CODOIN XIII, 121) and Madrid during April (Pulgar, *Crónica*, I, 227-230 [ch. LXIX]).

side.[73] When Afonso found out where he was the morning after the battle, he went sadly back to Toro and shut himself up there for three months, then departed for France to try to persuade its King Louis XI to take over his war.[74]

In Tordesillas, twenty miles east of Toro, Isabel waited through much of that dark night for news. Messengers sent as Fernando left Zamora must have already told her that the two armies were pressing toward battle; we may imagine the prayers she offered during the passage of the long slow hours. In his supreme moment of victory Fernando did not forget her. Just as soon as he was sure of the Portuguese retreat, well before he decided to return to Zamora, he sent Iñigo López de Albornoz as a special messenger to bring her the glorious tidings. "Avoiding many dangers" on the way, as Palencia tells us—he had to skirt Toro and Castronuño, taking back roads by torchlight, avoiding knots of lost enemy soldiers who would be only too glad to get their hands on one of their victorious foes—Albornoz reached Tordesillas probably about daybreak, and gave her a full report. Once again, a chronicler speaks of her joy as "impossible to describe."[75] Pulgar, her secretary, who in all probability was with her in Tordesillas, tells us what she did:

> The Queen, who was in Tordesillas, knew the victory that the King had won, and how the King of Portugal had fled to Castronuño. She called upon all the clergy of the town to join in a great procession, in which she went barefoot from the royal palace where she was, to the monastery of St. Paul which is outside the town, giving thanks to God with great devotion, for the victory which He had given to the King her husband and to their people.[76]

We also have Isabel's own words describing that glorious morning and its news. No letter she ever wrote is truer to her character than this one. It rings like a silver trumpet.

> At this very hour the news has come that yesterday, Friday the first of March, the Adversary of Portugal with his army that had held the bridge [at Zamora] departed, and then the king my lord went out with his army that was in Zamora, coming to a place a league and a half from Toro, an hour and a half before nightfall, and the Portuguese were struck by the king my lord and his men. They had to turn and fight, and they fought a furious battle, in which by the grace of the Lord our God and of his Blessed

---

[73]He left March 25, on an unsuccessful mission to prevent the citadel of Madrid from falling to Isabel (Palencia, *Crónica*, II, 283 [Dc III Lb VI (XXVI) Cp III]; Isabel to Beltrán de la Cueva, March 26, 1476, in Antonio Rodríguez Villa, *Bosquejo biográfico de Don Beltrán de la Cueva, Primer Duque de Alburquerque* [Madrid, 1881], pp. 124-125).

[74]Menéndez Pidal, *Historia de España*, XVII (1), 163-165. Afonso left Toro on June 13 (*Palencia, Crónica*, II, 297 [Dc III Lb VI (XXVI) Cp X]).

[75]Palencia, *Crónica*, II, 272 (Dc III Lb V [XXV] Cp IX).

[76]Pulgar, *Crónica*, I, 218 (ch. LXV).

Mother the king my lord triumphed and wrecked that Adversary and his army, in which many Portuguese died and others were routed, fleeing to Toro, and the king my lord remained on the field, going up to Toro in pursuit. I make this known to you by Juan Romero, my page, because you should give many thanks to Our Lord for so marvellous a happening, and find in it the pleasure and consolation that it rightly deserves. From Tordesillas, on the second day of March in the year 1476. I, the Queen.[77]

The victory at Toro did not end the war (it was to last three more years), but made it impossible for Portugal and its rebel allies to win the war, though they could still hope to gain something with the aid of a massive French intervention. Isabel and Fernando were confident they could prevent any such intervention; their defenses on the French frontier, notably the great fortress of Fuenterrabía by the sea just beyond the Castilian bank of the Bidasoa River, were very strong, and seemingly indestructible old Juan II of Aragon, now 78, was fully a match for the wily King Louis XI of France both in war and at the negotiating table. Military effort was still needed, but it need no longer consume the royal couple. Without further delay, they could and should set their hands to the task of "bringing these our kingdoms to peace and justice, rewarding the good and castigating the evil."[78]

The principal initiative they undertook for this purpose during the spring and summer of 1476 was the establishment of what amounted to a national police force: the Holy Brotherhood (Santa Hermandad). The idea and occasional practice of designating and supporting local troops of armed men to punish and suppress crime went back in Spanish history for more than a century. However, in the tumultuous years of Henry IV's reign the brotherhoods had generally become indistinguishable from the private armies of the often rebellious nobles and bishops. Isabel proposed to revive, strengthen, and reorganize the brotherhoods under royal ordinances giving them a status and financing of their own, independently of the local nobles and bishops (though usually with their cooperation). They would be given the task of restoring law and order to the many parts of the land where criminals had long operated with virtual impunity. It appears that this program had been originally suggested the previous year to Fernando by Juan de Ortega, Archpriest of Palenzuela, when Fernando came to Burgos to see to the siege of the rebel-held citadel there, and that it had been suggested to Isabel by Alonso de Quintanilla, an Asturian and long-time associate of Cabrera, an excellent administrator who had planned her quick coronation at Segovia and organized the supply train for the army in the war of the succession.[79]

---

[77]Isabel to the city of Murcia, March 2, 1476, in Torres Fontes, *Fajardo*, pp. 276-277.

[78]Isabel to city of Sevilla, June 12, 1476, *Tumbo de Sevilla* I, 194.

[79]Marvin Lunenfeld, *The Council of the Santa Hermandad* (Coral Gables FL, 1970), pp. 18-22; Menéndez Pidal, *Historia de España*, XVII (1), 232, 234; Rafael Fuertes

The proposal was endorsed by the *cortes*—Castile's loosely constructed parliament—which met at Song of the High Towers during April, the month following the victory of Toro, to swear allegiance to Princess Isabel as the heir. The endorsement was in the form of a petition that a reorganized Santa Hermandad be created to police the realm. The delegates almost certainly knew that this was Isabel's desire. The petition quickly received the royal assent and was published as an ordinance April 27. The jurisdiction of the local brotherhoods was strictly limited to crimes: murder, assault, robbery, arson, and false imprisonment. But there was so much of this crime that everyone knew that punishing and preventing it would give the brotherhoods a great deal to do. Financing arrangements were made at subsequent meetings of Isabel's ministers and local representatives at Madrigal again in May, and at Chigales near Valladolid in June.[80]

Still, as Isabel knew very well, there could be a very broad gap between a royal decree and a functioning institution in long-misgoverned Castile. The money for the Holy Brotherhood must actually be raised and disbursed; the local organizations must actually be formed and the *alcaides* and members actually designated. When the local magnates realized that she was in full earnest about this and intended to supervise closely the formation of the brotherhoods and make sure they really did their work, protests came thick and fast. The great nobles were not used to so much direct application of royal power inside their own territories, and they did not want to pay the costs.

These objections came to a head at the first general assembly of the Holy Brotherhood, convened July 25 at Dueñas near Valladolid. Isabel was present, but not Fernando; though Fernando favored the Holy Brotherhood and later urged its extension into Aragon, it was primarily a Castilian institution and Isabel was its chief initial sponsor. Leading ministers and officials were present, along with representatives of eight Castilian cities which would play an essential role in the establishment of the Brotherhood: Avila, Burgos, Medina del Campo, Olmedo, Palencia, Salamanca, Segovia, and Zamora.[81]

Strong objections were made to the cost of the brotherhoods, to the

Arias, *Alfonso de Quintanilla, Contador Mayor de los Reyes Católicos* (Oviedo, 1909), I, 117-119, 131-132. For graphic descriptions of the ravages of crime in Castile at this time, see Pulgar, *Crónica*, I, 230-231 (ch. LXX) and Puyol, ed., *Crónica incompleta*, pp. 305-306.

[80]Lunenfeld, *Santa Hermandad*, pp. 30-31; Menéndez Pidal, *Historia de España*, XVII (1), 232-243.

[81]Lunenfeld, *Santa Hermandad*, pp. 32-33; Rumeu de Armas, *Itinerario*, p. 55. Lunenfeld's account is in error in placing Fernando at this assembly in Dueñas. On the contrary, he was then in the Basque province of Vizcaya, having arrived at Bilbao on July 20; on the 30th he took oath to uphold the Basque *fueros* (local self-governing rights) under the famous tree of Guernica (Rumeu de Armas, *loc. cit.*; Menéndez Pidal, *Historia de España*, XVII [1], 197).

requirement of service by so many local captains, and to the intrusion of what amounted to a new governmental entity. Quintanilla answered all these objections with fiery eloquence in a long speech in which he vividly contrasted the deathless heroism of the Reconquest, the longest crusade, with the present inability of the Castilians to protect their own people from crime. Now they were called upon to conquer or reconquer only their own land, their own towns and cities and fields and homesteads, from the plague of bandits that infested them. How could they quibble about cost, Quintanilla demanded, when surely any of them would give half his wealth if he could be confident that the other half, and the persons of his children and parents and other relatives, would be dependably protected? With crime unpunished and unchecked, Castilians could have neither liberty nor self-respect. Their King and Queen were calling upon them to act. Would they hang back?[82]

Quintanilla's speech carried the day. With the single concession of limiting its legal term of existence to two years, rather than making it immediately permanent as Isabel had wished,[83] the Holy Brotherhood was accepted and firmly established. (Once the two years had run their course, no one seriously wished to abolish it.) It was to be organized nation-wide on a provincial basis, with towns and cities electing delegates to Brotherhood provincial assemblies which in turn would choose delegates to the national assembly. It was to be financed by assessments based solely on population in the local area supporting a brotherhood. All the people would benefit from the suppression of crime; all must therefore be included in the assessment of the costs. Since past assessments had almost always been levied on noblemen according to the size, wealth, and legal privileges of their estates, this assessment based solely on population was a major innovation in Spain.[84]

The Holy Brotherhood, thus approved, went into action immediately. The Santa Hermandad of Avila quickly organized an assault on the notorious thieves' castle at Las Navas in the mountains near Avila, and took it; soon all Spain felt the effects of the pacification, recovering from the long siege of lawlessness as though from a nightmare.[85] Wherever they were functioning, we hear of no more significant opposition to the brotherhoods; but great efforts had to be made to convince the magnates of Andalusia in the south, notably the powerful Duke of Medina Sidonia, to accept them. However, before the end of

---

[82]The text of Quintanilla's speech, as rendered by Pulgar, is in his *Crónica*, I, 233-239 (ch. LXX).

[83]That it was Isabel's intention from the beginning to make the Holy Brotherhood permanent, denied by Lunenfeld (*Santa Hermandad*, p. 31) is stated explicitly in Pulgar's rendering of Quintanilla's speech (*Crónica*, I, 238 [ch. LXX]).

[84]Menéndez Pidal, *Historia de España*, XVII (1), 243, 245; Lunenfeld, *Santa Hermandad*, pp. 34-35.

[85]Palencia, *Crónica*, II, 313-314 (Dc III Lb VII [XXVII] Cp VII); Puyol, ed., *Crónica incompleta*, pp. 308-309.

November the Duke of Medina Sidonia had begun to praise the idea, and on January 15, 1477 the Holy Brotherhood was established in Sevilla by royal order.[86]

Isabel remained in Dueñas only long enough to convene the assembly of the Holy Brotherood, to hear Quintanilla's great speech (undoubtedly with pride and satisfaction in him, for he had been one of her most trusted officials from the beginning of her reign), and to be sure that his counsel would be followed. On July 28 she returned to Tordesillas. After all, there was still a state of war with Portugal, and the Portuguese and rebel troops still held Toro, just twenty miles away. It was her obligation to keep watch on it, especially while Fernando was away to the north, in the Basque provinces. He had gone there in June after a stay in Burgos during which he was engaged in the difficult task of making enough concessions of favors and titles to win back the adherence of rebel nobles now genuinely seeking reconciliation, without offending the long-time supporters of him and Isabel who expected to profit from the disgrace of the rebels. Four brief letters he wrote to Isabel from Burgos and the Basque city of Vitoria during June testify to these efforts, but not much can be learned from them because of their quick, allusive manner of writing. Fernando and Isabel worked so closely together and understood each other so well that he was able to make his meaning clear to her without making it clear for posterity.[87]

So now, at the end of July, Fernando was far away, and Isabel on watch at Tordesillas. The blistering Spanish summer gripped the high plains of Castile. On the first day of August a courier rode hard into Tordesillas on a lathered horse that had been driven to the utmost. He brought urgent news for the Queen. There had been a revolt in Segovia two days before. Beatriz de Bobadilla and her husband Cabrera, the governor of Segovia, were at Tordesillas with Isabel; they had left Segovia in charge of Beatriz's father Pedro. Alfonso Maldonado, a former mayor of Segovia, resenting the elevation of Pedro de Bobadilla, had seized the impregnable entrance tower of the city's famous royal castle, the Alcázar, stabbing its guard and taking Pedro de Bobadilla prisoner and hostage. The first report could tell Isabel nothing definite about what had happened to her six-year-old daughter who had been in Pedro's care, nor whether any opposition to Maldonado's revolt remained in the city or in the Alcázar.[88]

[86]MS letter from the Duke of Medina Sidonia, late November 1476, in Simancas Archives, Registro General de Sello, 1476-XI, folio 791; Isabel and Fernando to Sevilla, January 15, 1477, *Tumbo de Sevilla* I, 274-285. Lunenfeld, *Santa Hermandad*, pp. 38-39, states incorrectly that the Brotherhood was not established in Sevilla until the summer of 1477.

[87]Rumeu de Armas, *Itinerario*, pp. 54-55. Fernando's letters are printed in Rodriguez Valencia, *Isabel*, III, 105-108.

[88]Palencia, *Crónica*, II, 305 (Dc III Lb VII [XXVII] Cp III).

The historian Palencia (who was present) tells us that not a muscle moved in Isabel's face when she received this appalling report. But she sprang instantly into action. Her blue-green gaze swept the court. If she took counsel, it was for a few minutes only. She waited for nothing and no one, not even Beatriz and Cabrera, for whom she left word to follow her with thirty cavalry. Within an hour she was off to the southward with only two companions: the Count of Benavente and Cardinal Mendoza. Just before leaving, she received a second report from Segovia. Maldonado had not captured little Isabel after all. The princess and her attendants had taken refuge in one tower in the Alcázar, while Maldonado and his supporters held another; the Alcázar was divided between the two factions, as was the city. But at least her daughter was safe for the moment; Palencia tells us that on hearing this, Isabel's face lit up with joy.[89]

It is about 65 miles from Tordesillas to Segovia via Olmedo, the most direct route. Isabel left Tordesillas with her two companions late in the afternoon.[90] Across the high plains they galloped, unprotected, unescorted, their straining horses casting ever-longer shadows in the reddening light: the 25-year-old Queen like some legendary Valkyrie, her red-gold hair glinting in the sunset; the dark, almost swarthy Cardinal, no longer a young man, striving manfully to keep up; and the peerless warrior count who had held Baltanás for the Queen an entire day against odds of forty to one. They alone could tame Segovia and save the princess; they needed no one else.

At Olmedo, about a third of the way to Segovia, they stopped to eat and drink, and rest briefly; surely the halt was for the Cardinal's sake, and Isabel must have secretly begrudged every minute of the delay, for Olmedo was only 25 miles from Tordesillas and she was fully capable of covering the entire 65 miles non-stop with the life of her only child at stake. At midnight they were on their way again;[91] there must have been some moonlight to enable them to keep to their route. We would give much to know what they said to one another during the halt at Olmedo, or if they exchanged any words during the long post-midnight ride.

They did not stop again. When the sun rose over the peaks of the Guadarrama Mountains ahead, they were ascending the valley of the Eresma River. As the morning advanced, they caught their first glimpse of the Alcázar of Segovia gleaming in burnished splendor atop its gigantic rock far across the rolling, rising foothills before them. At noon they drew rein at the gates of the city. A delegation was there to meet them—a delegation of the rebels. They told Isabel that they, "the people," held some of the city, but not all; she was welcome to enter, but only by one of the gates they controlled—and not

---

[89]*Ibid.*, pp. 305-306; Pulgar, *Crónica*, I, 267-269 (ch. LXXVIII).
[90]Palencia, *Crónica*, II, 306 (Dc III Lb VII [XXVII] Cp III).
[91]*Ibid.*

accompanied by Cabrera or Beatriz or the Count of Benavente.[92]

Isabel looked down upon them from her panting horse, her color high, her eyes flashing, and her clear voice rang:

> Tell those cavaliers and citizens of Segovia that *I am Queen of Castile*, and this city is mine, for the king my father left it to me; and to enter what is mine no laws nor conditions may be laid down for me. I shall enter the city by whatever gate I choose; I shall enter with the Count of Benavente, and all others whom I need for my service. Say to them also that they should all come to me, and obey my orders, like loyal subjects, and stop making tumults and scandals in my city, lest they suffer harm in their persons and in their property.[93]

The deputation fell silent, abashed; Isabel and the Cardinal and the Count rode through the nearest gate. The whole length of the city of Segovia had to be traversed to reach the Alcázar, which could only be entered on one side, by a single gate; throngs of belligerent people fell back respectfully to make way as the three appeared. No one, not even Maldonado and his men, dared shut the lone gate of the Alcázar in the Queen's face, though the place is almost overwhelming in its impregnability even today: a single small bridge crossing a moat so deep that it might better be called a gorge, to the one door opening in a towering turret-crowned wall of stone. Once inside, Isabel hurried to the tower where a band of devoted men had joined Princess Isabel's attendants as her volunteer bodyguard.[94] The chroniclers, whose vivid descriptions of these events do so much to make them come alive, fail us at this point; none of them so much as mentions the reunion of mother and daughter. Rarely do we hear of Isabel's tears; but surely she would not have been human if she had not shed them then, as the little princess clung to her in the flood of love and relief that flowed from three days of terror.

When Isabel emerged from the tower where she had found her daughter, she could hear shouting from the direction of the gate. An enormous crowd had gathered there, mostly sympathizers with the rebels. They were roaring out their hatred of Cabrera and their demands for his removal as governor, even for his execution. The Cardinal and the Count looked at the mob, the moat, and the wall, and urged Isabel to bar the gate and resist their entry with the loyal men inside the Alcázar. But she knew better. These were her people, whom she loved and who loved her; they would not fight her. The evildoers among them could not stand against her face to face. With a serene and magnificent confidence, she ordered the lone gate opened and the entire crowd invited in.[95]

She asked them what they wanted. They repeated their demand to

---

[92]*Ibid.*; Pulgar, *Crónica*, II, 269-270 (ch. LXXVIII).
[93]Pulgar, *Crónica*, I, 270 (ch. LXXVIII). Emphasis added.
[94]*Ibid.*
[95]*Ibid.*, I, 270-271.

constantly on Isabel's mind; repeatedly, in Segovia, she discussed with her commanders and councillors various plans for taking it, but she would not order a general assault, for the city was well defended and strongly held, and she knew that many of its inhabitants were secretly loyal to her and she wanted to save their lives if at all possible.[105] Then in September, a man appeared who truly seemed to come in answer to the prayers she had made again and again for Toro and its people: a poor shepherd named Bartolomé, who knew of a narrow, rugged path between the Duero River and Toro's city wall which gave access to one of the gates, but was only very lightly guarded. On the night of September 18 seventy vigorous and agile young men went up the path with the shepherd, who cheerfully answered the occasional desultory challenge. They came right up to the gate undetected, and chopped it down with axes. Constable Velasco himself was behind them with several hundred men; they burst into the city through the shattered gate with trumpets blaring. A friend of the shepherd called out Isabel's supporters in the city. After a sharp fight in the plaza the Portuguese were driven out; at dawn the city was in the hands of Isabel's partisans and the Portuguese held only the citadel.[106]

A week later Isabel, leaving Segovia with the princess for the first time since her rescue, came to Toro to thank the victors and most especially the shepherd Bartolomé, marvelling at how he had done what so many more experienced men had been unable to do, and gave thanks to God for him, along with granting him a substantial reward. She visited her soldiers who were attempting to dig a mine under the moat protecting the citadel, speaking personally with many of them. Throughout her stay in Toro she made a point of attending personally to the needs of her troops, whose devotion to her—already keen—consequently became even stronger. The citadel in Toro was commanded by the widow of Juan de Ulloa, the former governor who had helped betray Toro to the Portuguese. Isabel sent word that she would gladly pardon her. On October 20 the citadel surrendered and the victory was complete.[107]

But Isabel's happiness could never be complete unless her family was present. At the end of the month they were reunited at last—the first time all three of them had been together since the war began. Returning from his long sojourn in the north, Fernando arrived at Toro on October 30, joining the Queen there; five days later Princess Isabel was brought to Toro as well.[108]

---

[105]Puyol, ed., *Crónica incompleta*, p. 312.

[106]*Ibid.*, pp. 313-315; Pulgar, *Crónica*, I, 281-286 (ch. LXXXII); Palencia, *Crónica*, II, 317-319 (Dc III Lb VII [XXVII] Cp IX); Valera, *Crónica*, pp. 93-95. For Isabel's own brief account of these events see her letter to Murcia from Segovia, September 19, 1476, in Torres Fontes, *Fajardo*, p. 288.

[107]Puyol, ed., *Crónica incompleta*, pp. 315-317; Pulgar, *Crónica*, I, 285-286 (ch. LXXXII); Palencia, *Crónica*, II, 319-320 (Dc III Lb VII [XXVII], Cp IX).

[108]Chronicle of Valladolid, CODOIN XIII, 124-125; Puyol, ed., *Crónica incompleta*,

There at Toro, upon the scene of their humiliation in the summer of 1475, within distant view of the battlefield where the tide had turned in February 1476, now having won the decisive victory through the intervention of a humble shepherd, Isabel and Fernando rejoiced together in November 1476, with their cherished daughter at their side.

But a queen—especially a queen like Isabel—has little time for rest and family joy. Just two weeks after the Princess arrived in Toro, word came of the death from a sudden and virulent cancer of Rodrigo Manrique, Count of Paredes, one of the noble family of Manrique which had been most loyal to Isabel from the beginning, whose claim to be Master of the crusading Order of Santiago had been recognized by the Queen, though not fully accepted because of the rebellion. The Mastership of Santiago was the richest and most powerful office in Castile, next to the crown itself. (It will be recalled that it had been the chief objective of the greedy ambition of the first Marqués of Villena.) His son still claimed it, and many others aspired to it. At the moment when peace seemed about to return to long-distracted Castile, Isabel and Fernando could not afford to risk that peace in a welter of competing claims for this coveted office. The moment old Juan II got the news of the death of the Count of Paredes, he sent off a special emissary to his son to urge him to take the office himself, at least for the time being, to prevent fighting over it. (Though originally conceived as a celibate military order, the Order of Santiago had long had a dispensation from celibacy for its Master and some others within it.) A meeting of the order was called at Uclés to choose a successor to the Count of Paredes. Fernando was in the field, besieging the Portuguese garrison at Castronuño on the Duero between Toro and Tordesillas; but he came personally to take Princess Isabel to Medina del Campo, leaving her there under the guard of the redoubtable and utterly trustworthy Gutierre de Cárdenas. Meanwhile, on December 5, Queen Isabel set spurs to her horse to ride to the meeting at Uclés, no less than 170 miles away.[109]

It was too far for the kind of furious ride that Isabel had made to save her daughter, nor was the urgency so great; it was and is notorious that large meetings anywhere, and especially in Spain, rarely start on time. But it was essential that she arrive before the formal electoral session began; the ambitious nobles were unlikely to bow to any will but hers, or even to any message of hers not delivered in person. On the 5th she rode only as far as Tordesillas, and on the 6th to her childhood home at Arévalo, where she spent the night. But when she reached the Guadarrama Mountains on the 8th she was riding harder, crossing her chosen pass by torchlight. By the 10th she was in

---

pp. 318-320; Rumeu de Armas, *Itinerario*, p. 58.

[109]Palencia, *Crónica*, III, 11-13 (Lb XXVIII Cp I); Valera, *Crónica*, p. 98; Chronicle of Valladolid, CODOIN XIII, 125; Menéndez Pidal, *Historia de España*, XVII (1), 253-255.

Ocaña of evil memory, arriving late at night in a tempest of rain and wind; she left at dawn of the 11th, arriving in Uclés at five o'clock in the afternoon. The Order had not yet been formally convoked; in fact, she had arrived even before the chief contender for the Mastership, Alonso de Cárdenas (whom Isabel actually favored for the office, but did not wish for him to assume it at this time).[110]

Three days later, on December 14, the electoral session convened. Isabel explained that she and Fernando had already written to the Pope about their plans for the Order of Santiago, and had his oral agreement that it would be best for Fernando to act as its administrator for the time being; a Papal bull authorizing this was on its way. The order needed reform; once the reform had been well launched, normal electoral procedure for choosing the Master would be reinstated. Isabel was careful to praise Cárdenas highly; very likely he knew that she intended eventually to confirm him as Master. The electoral assembly made no significant protest; the election was suspended until the Papal bull should arrive, and when it did Fernando would be—and was—approved as administrator of the order. On January 2, 1477 Fernando joined Isabel at Ocaña. Once again, Isabel's swift action and personal presence had carried the day and averted a major new danger of civil strife.[111]

Castile was now secure; the war of the succession was won. Isabel and Fernando had won it together; but at the critical moments, the hours of decision, everywhere but on the battlefield itself, the guiding intelligence and, above all, the driving will had been Isabel's. Now, as she had begun with a prayer this war forced upon her by her enemies, she would end it not only with prayers of thanksgiving, but with a permanent endowment of prayer and worship by which God's favor to her and Fernando and Castile would be remembered forever. So in February, after making solemn thanksgiving for the victory in the enormous, magnificent cathedral of Toledo, she founded and endowed in that city a new Franciscan monastery, San Juan de los Reyes (St. John of the Kings), and commissioned the building of its great church. San Juan de los Reyes remains one of the most beautiful churches in all of Spain, covered inside and out with a florescence of stone carved at its peaks and edges into shapes almost as delicate as lace. The main church building was completed by 1492, but work on the exquisite cloisters was still going forward when Isabel died. She followed its progress throughout her life with the greatest care, continuing to support and endow it. Probably most precious of all to her in this church was the frequent repetition of the theme of the coats of arms of Castile and Aragon combined with the entwined symbols of Isabel and Fernando, the

---

[110]Chronicle of Valladolid, CODOIN XIII, 125-126; Pulgar, *Crónica*, I, 287-288 (ch. LXXXIII).

[111]Pulgar, *Crónica*, II, 287-288 (ch. LXXXIII); Palencia, *Crónica*, III, 12-13 (Lb XXVIII Cp I); Rumeu de Armas, *Itinerario*, p. 60.

yoke and the arrows. San Juan de los Reyes commemorated and offered up to God not only their victory, but their love.[112]

―――――――――――――
[112]Pulgar, *Crónica*, I, 289-290 (ch. LXXXIV); Jerónimo Münzer, *Viaje por España y Portugal, 1494-1495*, tr. José López Toro (Madrid, 1951), pp. 103-104; Walsh, *Isabella*, pp. 143-146; Ian Robertson, ed., *Blue Guide to Spain: the Mainland*, 3rd ed. (London, 1975), pp. 281-282.

5
The Queen's Justice
(March 1477-December 1481)

Isabel and Fernando celebrated Palm Sunday of the year 1477 in Madrid, to which they had come from Toledo at the beginning of March. Messengers were coming from and going to the King and Queen from all over Castile and Aragon, and from foreign lands; an ambassador from England visited them in Madrid that month, making a great impression for impeturbability when he carried on unshaken with his flowery speech of greeting after the platform on which he was standing collapsed. Most important of all was the Papal nuncio, Nicolás Franco, just arrived from Rome, who talked at length with Isabel and was deeply impressed both by her piety and by her ability. Pope Sixtus IV had never before obtained a really adequate report on Isabel; though Cardinal Borgia had favored her in the dispute with Henry and Pacheco years before, he was too wrapped up in himself to be a good source of information about the character of anyone else—not to speak of the great difference between his character and Isabel's. Franco's visit marked a watershed in Isabel's relations with the Papacy; from this point on, she enjoyed the consistent favor of Rome.[1]

The war of the succession was essentially won, but because formal peace had not yet been made, the possibility remained that the conflict might flare up again, particularly close to the Portuguese border where any restive nobleman could expect to obtain help from efficient Prince John, who governed the realm in the prolonged absence of his feckless father. The Holy Brotherhood was making solid progress in Castile, but also encountering substantial opposition from the aristocrats. The impact of the victory of Toro and Isabel's dramatic and decisive action in defying the mob at Segovia and during the convocation of the Order of Santiago at Uclés had done much to bring the heartland of Castile to admiring obedience. But on the fringes of the realm, in the wild green valleys of Galicia to the northwest, the rolling brown hills of sun-raked Extremadura

---

[1]Ramón Menéndez Pidal, director, *Historia de España*, Volume XVII: "España de los Reyes Católicos," ed. Luis Suárez Fernández and Manuel Fernández Alvarez (Madrid, 1969), Part I, p. 221; Alonso de Palencia, *Crónica de Enrique IV*, Volume III (Biblioteca de Autores Españoles, Vol. 273, Madrid, 1975), pp. 26-27 (Libro [Lb] XXVIII, Capitulo [Cp] VIII); Antonio Rumeu de Armas, *Itinerario de los Reyes Católicos, 1474-1516* (Madrid, 1974), p. 61.

along the Portuguese border to the southwest, and in lush Andalusia fronting the Moorish kingdom of Granada in the south, the Queen was known only by distant rumor and report; few in those regions had taken her measure. All continued to suffer from constant, almost unchecked feuding and crime.

Now that she had met and mastered the maximum crisis arising so soon after her succession, Isabel's primary duty was to restore order in her kingdom. After so long a period of neglect, the restoration and preservation of order required the visible, convincing administration of justice by the Queen personally—incorruptible, inescapable justice that would leave open no window of opportunity for the conniving aristocrats to continue their favorite games of power and privilege, in which Pacheco had been the supreme expert. The establishment of justice in her kingdom was the necessary foundation for everything else Isabel intended to accomplish: full recovery from the disasters of Henry's reign; fairer and more efficient government; the victorious completion of the long crusade; above all, the reform of the church. It was no less necessary for the attainment of a goal that had not yet risen above her mental horizon: expansion into a new world beyond the mighty ocean to the westward.

In view of her actions soon afterward, we may presume that during Holy Week in Madrid, Isabel's thoughts and prayers for her country were concentrated on this restoration and extension of justice and her need for God's help in achieving it. When news arrived that during the very night-watch of the Resurrection, on Easter Eve, April 5, Muslims from Granada had taken and sacked Cieza in the province of Murcia, killing or capturing all of its inhabitants,[2] surely she saw it as clear proof of the urgency of her next task. For she could never forget the enemy to the south, the enemy that had shadowed her land and her people for seven hundred and sixty-seven years, whom twenty-four generations of her forebears had fought to the death. By comparison with the longest war in history, her recent struggle with the Portuguese and the rebels was a mere skirmish. She would lift the immemorial shadow; she would end the long crusade in triumph. But first, to make it possible, there must be unity through justice in the land.

She and Fernando met with the Royal Council of Castile to discuss and decide on the best course of action to take in the areas where disorder was still rampant. The cautious Councillors urged both King and Queen to stay out of Extremadura on the Portuguese border, probably the most disorderly of the troubled areas. Nowhere in Extremadura was it now safe for them to go, the Councillors declared. Its principal stronghold, Trujillo, was in the hands of the Marqués of Villena whose loyalty was, to say the least, dubious. If a successful attack were made on a city in which the King or Queen was staying, the effect

---

[2]Menéndez Pidal, *Historia de España*, XVII (1), 424-425.

would be devastating. In any case, Fernando was needed to make sure that the war with Portugal did not start up again, and to reduce the four remaining Portuguese fortresses in Castilian territory, in the comparatively small towns of Castronuño, Cubillas, Siete Iglesias, and Cantalapiedra. Let him do that, while Isabel went to Toledo, where she would be perfectly safe, gain more information, and seek out loyal men to do her bidding in Extremadura and Andalusia.[3]

Isabel was within a week of her twenty-sixth birthday. She was young, strong, confident, full of energy, riding the crest of a wave of victory. She knew the magnitude of her undertaking, but was challenged rather than daunted. She knew her duty, and that the Council's proposal would never discharge it. Above all, she trusted in God's help, which had never failed her when she needed it most. She replied to the Council:

> I have always heard it said that blood, like a good schoolmistress, goes naturally to heal those parts of the body that are troubled. Every day the King my lord and I hear of war among our subjects that the Portuguese make as enemies and our own Castilians as tyrants. Not to support our people as we should would not be right for a king, but the inhumanity of a tyrant. It seems to me that the King my lord ought to go to the lands beyond the mountain pass, where the enemy makes war from Castronuño and other fortresses, and lay siege to them if possible, as you suggested; and I ought to go to Extremadura, to provide what is necessary there. It is true that there will be some difficulties in my going there, as you have said; but in all human affairs some things are certain and others doubtful, and it is clear to me that all are in the hands of God, Who asks of us good will and great diligence. Upon Him I fix my hope as I go forth. And it does not seem good to me that the King my lord should be in continuous labor and danger, while I stand apart from it; because kings who govern well ought not to flee their duty.[4]

On April 17 she and Fernando set off together from Madrid. It was a Thursday; they rode slowly together through the bloom of spring under the glorious snow-crowned Guadarramas until two days later they reached the little village of Casarrubios, which had rarely if ever played host to a king and queen. They ate their evening meal there Saturday night and stayed all through the following day, after Sunday Mass (one wonders where—there was certainly nothing like a palace in Casarrubios, nor any great aristocrat in residence). On Monday morning they parted, with obvious reluctance. Fernando rode west, to cross the mountains and begin his campaign against the four fortresses; Isabel went south, heading for the shrine of the Blessed Virgin Mary at Guadalupe,

---

[3]Fernando del Pulgar, *Crónica de los Reyes Católicos*, ed. Juan de Mata Carriazo (Madrid, 1943), I, 290-293 (Chapter LXXXIV).
[4]*Ibid.*, p. 293 (ch. LXXXIV).

where she had often gone to prepare herself for great missions.[5]

She had already made arrangements to have the body of her predecessor sovereign, Henry IV, taken from its temporary sepulcher and given proper and permanent burial near the shrine—one of the few, perhaps the only one that had ever attracted Henry's uncertain devotion. It was done while she was there, where she remained sixteen days. From there she sent a messenger to Trujillo in Extremadura to say that she intended to enter its castle. That castle had been the property of the Marqués of Villena ever since his father Pacheco died while securing its keys three months before Isabel became queen; its commander refused to admit her.[6] It must have been as though the ghost of Pacheco, the ogre of her childhood, walked again. But this was a different Isabel from the girl Pacheco had persecuted and betrayed. This was the Queen of Castile, the crusader. Her response flashed out like the naked sky-pointing sword of justice Gutierre de Cárdenas had carried before her at her coronation:

> Must I suffer my subject to presume to lay down the law to me, or fear the resistance he thinks of making? Shall I refrain from going to my city, intending to do service there to God and to my own, because of the obstacle this commander thinks to put in my way? Surely no good king would do it, and neither will I.[7]

Then she called for troops from Andalusia to assault the castle if it did not yield to her. Messengers hurried to Villena to tell him what she had said and done. The Marqués had not fared well in the war. He knew now that he had no choice but to make his peace with Isabel, as indeed he had already agreed to do the preceding September. He disavowed the bellicosity of his commander and on June 24 ordered the gates opened to the Queen. The ghost of Pacheco was laid.[8]

The castle of Trujillo was a symbol of Isabel's triumph. Its lesson was well heeded; no one else in Extremadura now dreamed of defying her. From Trujillo she went to Cáceres, where she reorganized the local government and brought complete peace to the town after years of division and strife. She ordered most of the castles built in Extremadura during recent years, which had mostly become dens of robbers, to be razed. Meanwhile in the north, Fernando had taken from the Portuguese three of his four objectives—Cantalapiedra, Siete Iglesias, and Cubillas—and was pressing hard on the fourth, Castronuño.[9]

---

[5]Chronicle of Valladolid, *Colección de documentos inéditos para la historia de España* (hereinafter cited as CODOIN), XIII (Madrid, 1848), pp. 127-128.

[6]Menéndez Pidal, *Historia de España*, XVII (1), 262; Pulgar, *Crónica*, I, 304-305 (ch. LXXXVII).

[7]Pulgar, *Crónica*, I, 305 (ch. LXXXVII).

[8]*Ibid.*, I, 305-306 (ch. LXXVII); Chronicle of Valladolid, CODOIN XIII, 129.

[9]Pulgar, *Crónica*, I, 308-309 (ch. LXXXVIII); Mosén Diego de Valera, *Crónica de los Reyes Católicos*, ed. Juan de Mata Carriazo (Madrid, 1927), p. 122; Menéndez Pidal,

Now it was time for Isabel to move on to the largest city in the realm of Castile, the ancient and famous metropolis of Sevilla on the Guadalquivir River, lush, rich, and corrupt. All along her way, as she approached the city, she was hailed with ceremony and fiestas; if there was one thing the people of Sevilla knew how to do, it was to celebrate. The climactic ceremony and celebration occurred when she arrived at the city itself, on July 24, the eve of the feast of Spain's national patron, Santiago: the Apostle St. James the Greater. At three-thirty in the afternoon she reached Sevilla's sumptuous palace, the Alcázar, with its intricate Moorish-style decoration and its artful construction to keep out much of the suffocating heat of high summer.[10]

The next day, Friday, was the great feast; but Isabel did not delay. She set up her judgment seat, draped with cloth of gold, in the main hall of the Alcázar, with its slim red pillars, half-dome arches and soaring extravaganza of delicately wrought stone under an orange ceiling carved like a cloud. On one side, below her, she seated selected aristocrats, bishops and abbots; on the other side, learned men and members of her Council. In front of her stood officers of the court and mace-bearers. Secretaries recorded the pleas made and the disposition of the cases. Each litigant was brought to face her personally. In many cases she delivered summary judgment on the spot. Others, involving complex or uncertain issues of law or fact, she referred to a selected Councillor or scholar with orders to investigate further and report back to her. Sevilla had not known disinterested justice for decades. Everything and everyone had had a price. Now, at a single stroke, all that was ended. Isabel was relentless. She spared no one whom she considered guilty. No less than four thousand malefactors, or those who feared being accused as such, fled the city rather than face her.[11]

The historian Palencia was shocked by her severity; but his comments suggest that his shock derived at least as much from an unpleasant astonishment that a woman could do such things, as from any fundamental objection to what she was actually doing. Pulgar tells us, on the other hand, that for the justice she administered she was "much loved by the good, and feared by the evil." After some weeks of this, she graciously consented to a petition by the Bishop of Cádiz, Alonso de Solís, to grant a general pardon, with two exceptions: heretics were not included (she knew there were many in the city, most of them not yet discovered), and those who had robbed or defrauded

Historia de España, XVII (1), 264; Rumeu de Armas, Itinerario, p. 63; Townsend Miller, The Castles and the Crown (New York, 1963), pp. 98-99.

[10]Pulgar, Crónica, I, 309-310 (ch. LXXXIX); Chronicle of Valladolid, CODOIN XIII, 131-132.

[11]Pulgar, Crónica, I, 310-311, 316 (ch. LXXXIX); Andrés Bernáldez, Memorias del reinado de los Reyes Católicos, ed. Manuel Gómez Moreno and Juan de Mata Carriazo (Madrid, 1962), p. 68 (ch. XXIX).

others were still required to give back what they had taken. A lesson in justice had been taught that would not soon be forgotten, in Sevilla or anywhere that men heard what she had done there.[12]

While Isabel was handing down justice from her judgment seat in the great hall of the Alcázar of Sevilla, she was also wrestling with what she feared might be an even more intractable problem of a political nature, concerning the whole of Andalusia: the bitter, long-lasting feud between the two principal noblemen of the region—Enrique de Guzmán, Duke of Medina Sidonia; and Rodrigo Ponce de León, Marqués of Cádiz. The seats of the two potentates, at the very southern tip of Spain, were a scant thirty miles apart; but the great prize of Andalusia was rich Sevilla, and there the Duke had been successful, forcing out his rival. The Duke spared no effort to convince Isabel of the perfidy of the Marqués; and indeed, in Andalusia in recent years there had been more than enough perfidy to go around. (There is evidence that both men had been involved in secret treasonable dealings with Portugal during the war, intended to obtain for them a share in the lucrative trade with the Guinea coast of Africa that the Portuguese had developed from the time of Prince Henry the Navigator.) Isabel read and listened to the reports, reminded the Duke that her chief immediate concern was the firm establishment of law and order in Andalusia, but took no immediate action. In striking contrast to her summary judgments in the great hall of the Alcázar, she was moving with marked caution in this matter, for she had not previously known either nobleman; though both had supported her in the war of the succession, they had done so without much enthusiasm or effort. In any case, she did not want to take sides between them; she wanted them both on her side. If the long war of the reconquest was to be resumed against Moorish Granada, she would very much need both of them for it.[13]

In the end it was the Marqués of Cádiz who cut the knot. Young (only 34), red-haired and red-bearded, brash and impetuous, he was also a military commander of great natural ability, an expert in the construction of fortresses, and a man of genuine vision. He had played the game of power and money because a major nobleman could not survive in the Andalusia of his youth without doing so; but his real thirst was for glory, especially in battle against the Moors. In 1462, at the age of only 19, he been one of the leaders in the final

---

[12]Pulgar, *Crónica*, I, 310-316 (ch. LXXXIX); Palencia, *Crónica*, III, 48-51 (Lb XXXIX Cp IX-X). Palencia also argued that Isabel unduly favored the Duke of Medina Sidonia. In view of her scrupulous even-handedness between him and his rival, the Marqués of Cádiz, and the manner in which she rejected the Duke's charges against the Marqués after the latter's personal visit to her, Palencia's view can hardly have substance.

[13]Pulgar, *Crónica*, I, 317-319 (ch. XC); Menéndez Pidal, *Historia de España*, XVII (1), 275; Miller, *Castles and Crown*, p. 100; John W. Blake, *West Africa; Quest for God and Gold, 1454-1478*, 2nd ed. (London, 1977), pp. 48-50.

reconquest of Gibraltar. Everything he heard of Isabel appealed to the generous side of his nature. So he set out, probably in early September, from his principal residence of Jerez de la Frontera between Cádiz and Sevilla, rode up to the Alcázar in Sevilla, dismounted, and though it was late evening, strode unescorted right to the door of the Queen's chamber, telling the astonished guards that he had come to kiss the Queen's hand.[14]

Isabel seems to have enjoyed this; perhaps she remembered her dramatic night meetings with Fernando when he first arrived in Castile. She gathered a bevy of ladies-in-waiting about her to avoid any scandal, hastily rustled up a couple of counsellors, and commanded that the door be opened to the bold visitor.[15] He kissed her hand, and said to her:

> See me here, most powerful Queen, in your hands . . . I do not wish to anger you, my lady, not even defending my life, but if you have guarded your ears from my enemies as a just prince should do, I will undertake to show you my innocence, and to make Your Royal Ladyship pleased with me. . . . I do not come to speak words, but to show works; neither do I wish to assault your royal ears by condemning anyone, but to save myself with the truth, which always saves the innocent. Send your request then, my lady, to receive your fortresses of Jerez and Alcalá, which my enemies have told you are difficult to take with many men and much time, and if my patrimony is needed for your service, from this your chamber I hand it over, as I hand over my person.[16]

It was a magnificent gesture, of a kind that had a particular appeal to Isabel. Surely she must have smiled, with a radiance not often seen since she left Fernando at the foot of the Guadarramas to plunge into the seething southland. She answered the suppliant:

> Marqués, it is true that I have had some negative reports about you, but the confidence that you have shown in appearing before me signals your answer to the charges. Granted that you deserved punishment, your placing yourself in my hands in this way would obligate me to treat you well. Deliver then my fortresses of Jerez and Alcalá that you hold, and I will investigate the disputes between you and the Duke of Medina, and I will decide what is just, guarding your honor in all things.[17]

They talked animatedly until two o'clock in the morning. When at last the Marqués knelt before her to take his leave, Isabel commanded that he be shown to the door and to his horse by six servants carrying torches.[18]

---

[14]Pulgar, *Crónica*, I, 319 (ch. XC); Eduardo Ponce de Leon y Freyre, *El Marqués de Cádiz, 1443-1492* (Madrid, 1949), pp. 11-41.

[15]Pulgar, *Crónica*, I, 319 (ch. XC).

[16]*Ibid.*, I, 319-320 (ch. XC).

[17]*Ibid.*, II, 320-321 (ch. XC).

[18]Historia de los Hechos del Marqués de Cádiz, CODOIN CVI (Madrid, 1893), p. 189.

After this, the Duke of Medina Sidonia had no choice but to follow suit, to match the generosity and loyalty of the Marqués. He too expressed his willingness to turn over his castles to Isabel as she might have need of them. By October, pacts had been signed with both men defining which castles they would give up and which they would keep, their privileges had been confirmed, and the likelihood of clashes between them had been sharply reduced by Isabel's order that they both stay out of Sevilla until she gave them permission to go back to it.[19]

On September 13 the victorious Fernando arrived at Sevilla, receiving the same kind of ceremonial and enthusiastic welcome as Isabel; for him as for her, it required hours to get through the narrow streets of the city with their cheering crowds from the entrance gate in the walls to the Alcázar. They seem to have been even more than usually well pleased with each other; and indeed both had accomplished a great deal since they parted in June. By the end of the month they had conceived their second child, the first and only son to be born to them and live. On October 1 the last Portuguese fortress in Castile (Castronuño) surrendered; on the 3rd, in a festive mood, Isabel and Fernando boarded a galley for a trip down the Guadalquivir River from Sevilla to San Lucar de Barrameda fifty miles downstream, at its mouth. The trip took all day one way; San Lucar de Barrameda was a possession of the Duke of Medina Sidonia, who entertained them that night in high style. But before the galley stopped at San Lucar, Isabel suggested that they sail out into the open Atlantic, rolling to the far horizon at the mouth of the river. The galley did not actually undertake this; perhaps it was too near nightfall.[20] But for the first time, Isabel's attention had been drawn to the vast western ocean, one of the supreme mysteries of the ages, on which the best remembered of all her subjects was to find his destiny and change the world.

Some sixty years before, Prince Henry "the Navigator" of Portugal, a nation which unlike Castile fronted the open Atlantic for the whole length of its seacoast, had begun sponsoring exploration of the African coast to the southward and searches for islands in the Atlantic. The unknown then began on Portugal's doorstep. No one since the Vikings had ever sailed far out into the open ocean, and the Vikings only in the distant subarctic waters of the far north. Muslim-ruled Morocco extended about 250 miles south from the Straits of Gibraltar, then faded away into the limitless expanses of the Sahara Desert. By coasting another hundred miles along the desert, the mariner reached the point where the closest of the seven large islands of the Canary archipelago, which had been known to the ancients and where Europeans of the fourteenth century had made a few ephemeral landings, lay just fifty miles offshore.

[19]Menéndez Pidal, *Historia de España*, XVII (1), 276-278.
[20]*Ibid.*, pp. 226, 276-277; Chronicle of Valladolid, CODOIN XIII, 132-133.

Westward from the Canaries no man had sailed; southward along the desert coast of Africa the ocean bottom sloped so gently that ships staying near the land were in constant danger of going aground on a waterless shore where shipwreck meant death. Red sand cliffs, easily undermined by the ocean, were frequently collapsing into it under the burning sun, making it appear that the sea was boiling. In the midst of this kingdom of desolation a long low hook of land clawed out into the shallow sea: Cape Bojador. Here, winds and currents together swung westward, straight out into the open ocean. Sailors standing well out from the coast to avoid its shoals and reefs risked being swept away into the endless, unknown sea. There was a legend that no ship could pass beyond Cape Bojador and return.[21]

Prince Henry had been Isabel's great-uncle (he died when she was nine years old), and had more than a little of her spirit. He had no patience with legends that stood in the way of achievement. The Moors—hereditary enemies of the long crusade of the Reconquest—ruled all of North Africa, down to the great desert. But beyond it there could be a way around the enemy's domain, a route to "the Indies" and the storied Orient where Marco Polo had gone and where a Christian king, "Prester John," was reputed to reign. Maps, derived ultimately from classical times when the Phoenicians appear to have sailed at least once around Africa, indicated that such a voyage was possible. Along the way he could expect to find men—not Moors, impervious to conversion—who could be evangelized for Christianity. The causes of missionary and crusader joined in Prince Henry with his duty to serve his country by increasing its trade, prosperity, and influence in the world. He saw the seas west and south of Africa as the road of destiny for Portugal and for Christendom.[22]

For twelve years, beginning in 1421, Prince Henry of Portugal therefore sent out a ship each year with instructions to round Cape Bojador. When each expedition returned with the increasingly familiar excuses for failure, he resolutely proceeded to equip another to try again in the following year. In

---

[21]Ernle Bradford, *A Wind from the North; the Life of Henry the Navigator* (New York, 1960), pp. 103-106; Ian Cameron, *Lodestone and Evening Star* (New York, 1966), pp. 100-102.

[22]Bailey W. Diffie and George D. Winius, *Foundations of the Portuguese Empire, 1415-1480* (Minneapolis MN, 1977), pp. 74-76. Though Prince Henry's motives for undertaking the epochal exploration of the western coast of Africa have been much debated, the above reflects the clearly stated testimony of two contemporary witnesses, Gomes Eanes de Azurara in his *Chronicle of Guinea* and Duarte Pacheco Pereira in his *Esmeralda in Situ Orbis* (both quoted by Diffie in the cited pages). Eanes de Azurara knew Prince Henry personally, and Pacheco Pereira knew many who had known him; later historians, lacking such personal knowledge, have no sound basis for rejecting their testimony. While Azurara and Pereira do not say explicitly that Henry intended to reach India, the bull *Inter Caetera* issued by Pope Calixtus III in 1456, during Henry's lifetime, granted jurisdiction to the Order of Christ which he headed, "all the way to the Indies" (Blake, *West Africa; Quest for God and Gold*, p. 23).

1434 a bold captain named Gil Eanes finally rounded the cape. The sea was calm, with light winds and a morning mist. Beyond the cape Eanes found a place to land. In a hollow sheltered from the barren, burning sands he spied a row of little plants with tiny starlike flowers which the Portuguese called the rose of St. Mary. He dug some of them up, to bring home to prove that life could exist beyond the dreaded promontory.[23] Meanwhile, other Portuguese captains had discovered the islands of Madeira and the Azores, farther out in the Atlantic than the Canaries.[24]

By the time Prince Henry died in 1460, his explorers had reached Sierra Leone below the westernmost bulge of Africa, where the coast begins to trend eastward. They had passed well beyond the desert, finding gold and trees, elephants and people. They called these habitable lands Guinea. The people were black. The Portuguese seized some of them and brought them to Portugal as slaves. (Most of them were baptized; many were set free and accepted into Portuguese society after a few years' service if they had learned Portuguese well.)[25]

After a pause following Henry's death, exploration of the African coast was resumed by order of King Afonso under the direction of a merchant named Fernando Gomes, to whom the king gave a five-year monopoly of the Guinea trade in return for his guarantee that his men and ships would achieve a further 100-league advance along the coast every year. By the time of Isabel's coronation in 1474, the Portuguese mariners sailing for Gomes had come to the great bend of the African coast where the Gulf of Guinea ends, marked by the sky-piercing volcanic peak of Mount Cameroon, and had sailed on southward, crossing the equator. Prince John of Portugal, nineteen years old in 1474, was in that year given charge of the great project of exploration. How much farther his seamen would have to go to reach the end of the continent, no man knew.[26]

Exciting reports of readily available wealth in gold and ivory and exotic products of this previously unknown land spread quickly throughout Europe. Italians in particular, who had long been active in trade with the East and whose countryman Marco Polo had journeyed all the way to the China Sea two centuries before, flocked to Portugal. They formed colonies in its ports and launched voyages to Africa themselves when they could gain the royal favor and permission. Italian trade with Portugal expanded rapidly. In August 1476, just a year before Isabel came to Sevilla, a Genoese fleet was approaching Portugal with valuable cargoes of gum mastic, from which popular medicines were made, which was extracted from trees on the Genoese-ruled island of Chios in the Aegean Sea. For reasons not entirely clear, this Genoese fleet flew the flag of

[23]Cameron, *Lodestone and Evening Star*, pp. 110-112.
[24]Diffie and Winius, *Foundations of the Portuguese Empire*, pp. 58-62.
[25]*Ibid.*, pp. 77-82.
[26]*Ibid.*, pp. 146-147.

Burgundy, with which France was at war. France was allied with Portugal in the war against Castile, and a combined French-Portuguese fleet was based in Lagos, then the principal port on the south coast of Portugal. The Burgundian flag gave its French commodore an excuse to seize the valuable merchant vessels. They were escorted by a heavily armed ship and a battle followed, six miles off Lagos. Three of the Genoese ships were sunk. From one of them a tall red-haired young man of exactly Isabel's age (25) flung himself into the sea to escape the sinking ship. He found and grasped an oar. By pushing the oar ahead of him and resting on it when he became too tired to keep swimming, he eventually reached shore—his first landing anywhere on the Iberian peninsula. His name, as spelled in the records of his native Genoa, was Cristoforo Colombo.[27]

By the time Isabel was crowned, Spanish mariners were also sailing to Guinea, despite an absolute Portuguese prohibition on such voyages enforced by the death penalty if the trespassers were caught. During the war of the succession Spanish sailors had been encouraged to sail to Guinea, after Fernando and Isabel formally laid claim to it in August 1475. But the Portuguese knew these waters much better than the Spanish, and were easily able to defend them; the Castilian mariners were unable to effect any substantial penetration.[28]

However, the Portuguese preoccupation with Guinea and the newly discovered Atlantic islands of Madeira and the Azores had caused them to neglect the Canary Islands, where Castile had established a strong foothold. Before Isabel came to reign, four of these seven large islands—Lanzarote, Fuerteventura, Ferro, and Gomera—had been conquered and occupied by Castilians, despite resistance from the warlike but backward natives, the Guanches. The other three—La Palma, Grand Canary, and Tenerife with its fantastic 12,000-foot peak of Teide—remained in the hands of the natives.[29]

Castile had no historic memory of slavery; it had faded away with the fall of the Roman empire, and never been seen there since. Though the Portuguese had embraced it, at least to a limited extent, under the new conditions resulting from African exploration, Isabel and Fernando would not. In March 1476 they had ordered the release of 120 blacks seized for sale as slaves by an expedition to Guinea commanded by Gonzalo de Stúñiga.[30] The difficulty of voyaging to

---

[27]Samuel Eliot Morison, *Admiral of the Ocean Sea* (Boston, 1942), pp. 23-24. For a review of the irrefutable evidence that establishes (despite all 19th and 20th century claims to the contrary) that Columbus was born into a devoutly Catholic family and grew up in Genoa, see *ibid.*, pp. 7-14. Columbus had no formal education and was only minimally literate in 1476. Portuguese was the first language he learned to write, and he always wrote Spanish in the Portuguese manner (*ibid.*, pp. 15-17).

[28]Blake, *West Africa; Quest for God and Gold*, pp. 41-52.

[29]Diffie and Winius, *Foundations of the Portuguese Empire*, pp. 92-95.

[30]Palencia, *Crónica*, II, 261 (Lb XXV, Cp IV).

the unfamiliar coasts of Guinea and coming back safely made such journeys a rarity; but contact with the Canary Islands was becoming close and frequent, and the enslavement of their native people was beginning. Isabel's primary concern was for the conversion of these natives, who had been entirely pagan. On September 28, 1477, from Sevilla, just five days before their trip down the Guadalquivir and view of the ocean that led to the Canaries and beyond, Isabel and Fernando issued this uncompromising condemnation of what had been done to these Canarian natives:

> Know that we have heard that some persons have brought some natives of the Canary Islands and, by the will of the lord of those islands and other persons, have sold them and divided them out among themselves as slaves, though some are Christians, and others on the way to converting to our Holy Catholic Faith. This is a great disservice to God and to us and is detrimental to our Holy Catholic Faith, and it would be a great burden on our consciences to consent to it, because it would lead to no one wishing to convert to the Holy Faith.[31]

The language and emphasis is so characteristically Isabeline that we may be confident this decree was essentially hers. It went on to prescribe severe fines and confiscation of goods for anyone found guilty of enslaving the natives of the Canaries, particularly those who had become Christians or whose conversion was likely. Isabel would maintain this special emphasis and concern throughout her life, extending the same protection to natives in newly discovered lands much more distant from Spain than the Canary Islands.

On October 15 Isabel and Fernando confirmed Diego de Herrera, who claimed title to the entire archipelago from the reign of Isabel's father, as governor of the four conquered islands, provided that he would henceforth obey Castilian law; but he had to cede to the monarchs all claim to the three unconquered islands.[32] They began keeping a close watch on how well Herrera discharged his duties and respected his obligations. Three days later Dr. Andrés de Villalón, one of Isabel's most trusted advisors, and Dr. Nuño Ramires de Zamora were commissioned to gather full information on the condition of the natives of the Canary Islands, particularly those living on the island of Gomera, and to make sure that they were well and justly treated.[33]

Isabel and Fernando spent most of the month of October 1477 in Jérez de la Frontera with the Marqués of Cádiz. The Papal nuncio Nicolás Franco accompanied them there, before taking his leave in early November to return to

---

[31]Decree of Fernando and Isabel, September 28, 1477, in Antonio Rumeu de Armas, *La Politica Indigenista de Isabel la Católica* (Valladolid, 1969), p. 164.

[32]Roger B. Merriman, *The Rise of the Spanish Empire in the Old World and the New*, Volume I (New York, 1918), p. 158.

[33]Rumeu de Armas, *Politica Indigenista de Isabel*, pp. 166-167.

Rome.[34] Though the Queen had made peace between the greatest feuding nobles of Andalusia, the Marqués of Cádiz and the Duke of Medina Sidonia, not all the local lords were yet prepared to accept full royal authority without a fight. Fernán Arias de Saavedra was holding the castle at Utrera just southeast of Sevilla, refusing to admit the King or the Queen even when they came from Jérez in person to demand entry. Therefore a siege of Utrera was undertaken, beginning November 9. When Fernando and Isabel returned to Sevilla after a few days at Utrera, the ever-reliable Gutierre de Cárdenas was left in charge of the siege.[35]

It was now time to settle the question of the leadership of the great and rich crusading Order of Santiago, which Henry IV had placed in the unworthy hands of Pacheco as Master. After Pacheco's death just before Isabel came to the throne, the order had been led by Rodrigo Manrique, Count of Paredes. Upon his untimely death late the previous year, Isabel had ridden hard to the general assembly of the order at Uclés to prevail upon them by her presence to make Fernando temporary administrator of the order. At that time Alonso de Cárdenas, Gutierre's uncle, had been the leading candidate for the new Master of Santiago. Isabel trusted him, as he trusted her; he took her word that eventually he would gain the position. Now she determined to have him made Master, despite the jealousy of other great lords, notably the Count of Benavente, hero of Baltanás and Segovia. On November 30, at another assembly at Azuaga, Alonso de Cárdenas was formally designated Master of Santiago, with the full personal support of Fernando and despite the vocal criticism of the Count of Benavente—who, with some of the other ambitious nobles, had attempted unsuccessfully to persuade Fernando to disregard Isabel's wishes in this matter.[36]

Isabel and Fernando spent a quiet midwinter at Sevilla, remaining there together throughout December and January. On February 6, 1478 Fernando rode north for Madrid, while Isabel remained in Sevilla, which is at its best in late winter and early spring, to guard her health for the sake of the unborn child in her womb. The siege of Utrera was still going on; however, the rebels had now seized another castle, at Membrilla, from which they robbed and ravaged the countryside, committing many atrocities. Profoundly distressed and angered, Isabel decided that the campaign against them must be pressed harder. Fernando had departed, and she would not risk her new baby by the

---

[34]Safe-conduct for Nicolás Franco from Fernando and Isabel, Nov. 5, 1477, in Luis Suárez Fernández, *Politica Internacional de Isabel la Católica*, Volume I (Valladolid, 1965), pp. 352-353.
[35]Chronicle of Valladolid, CODOIN XIII, 133; Palencia, *Crónica*, III, 64-66 (Lb XXX, Cp VI); Pulgar, *Crónica*, I, 323 (ch. XCI); Menéndez Pidal, *Historia de España*, XVII (1), 279.
[36]Chronicle of Valladolid, CODOIN XIII, 134; Palencia, *Crónica*, III, 68-70 (Lb XXX, Cp VIII); Menéndez Pidal, *Historia de España*, XVII (1), 283.

kind of hard riding in the field which had brought on her miscarriage at Cebreros two and a half years before. So she called on her gallant new friend, the Marqués of Cádiz—very much a man of war who believed in pushing matters rapidly to a conclusion. On March 29 he stormed Utrera, taking it in a single assault. His orders were to execute as traitors all found in arms within. (We are not told whether those were standing orders from Fernando, or specifically from Isabel—but we know she hated wanton rebellion for the sake of plunder, which had almost destroyed her country and had been the cause of so much suffering by the innocent.) On the request of the Marqués, Isabel spared eleven whom he deemed less guilty; the rest were put to death.[37]

For her own part, Isabel was always willing to forgive; but as Queen, she never forgot the responsibility for justice symbolized by that naked sword Gutierre de Cárdenas had carried before her at her coronation. Safety and peace could never be restored in long-disordered and misgoverned Castile, unless and until all men knew that she would administer justice with uncompromising, unhesitating firmness.

Fernando shared her determination in this regard, and that spring applied it in particular to the long-hallowed pilgrimage to the great shrine of Santiago de Compostela, where all Spaniards believed their national patron St. James the Apostle was buried. Upon arriving at Toledo from Madrid May 3, he issued a decree in both Spanish and Latin, in Isabel's name as well as his own, placing all pilgrims to Santiago de Compostela under special royal protection. Anyone harming them would be prosecuted to the fullest extent of the law.[38]

Fernando stayed in Toledo only two days and then rode away to the southward, to be with Isabel at the birth of their child, expected in late June or early July. He arrived back in Sevilla May 13.[39]

On June 30, at quarter of eleven in the morning, the child was born—a son. He was named Juan. Isabel favored that name not only because it had been her father's (though she had no personal memory of her father), but especially because of the deep personal devotion she had to St. John the Evangelist, to whom she had dedicated the splendid new church in Toledo as memorial and thanksgiving for victory in the war of the succession. Three days of universal public celebration in Sevilla followed the birth of the heir to the throne. Ten days later baby Prince Juan was baptized by Cardinal Mendoza in the church of Santa Maria la Mayor in Sevilla, in a splendid ceremony glowing with silver and gold and brocade, with all the priests in black velvet vestments.

---

[37]Rumeu de Armas, *Itinerario*, pp. 66-69; Chronicle of Valladolid, CODOIN XIII, 135-136; Palencia, *Crónica*, III, 71 (Lb XXX, Cp IX); Bernáldez, *Memorias*, pp. 70-71 (ch. XXXI); Menéndez Pidal, *Historia de España*, XVII (1), 283.

[38]MS decree, Simancas Archives, Estado Castilla leg 1-2 parte, folios 113 (Spanish) and 114 (Latin).

[39]Rumeu de Armas, *Itinerario*, p. 71.

The Duchess of Medina Sidonia stood as godmother for the prince; the Count of Benavente arrived with nine maidens all dressed in silk with pearls and scarves of scarlet and white. A month later, Sunday, August 9, an equally splendid ceremony of the presentation of the new prince to God was held in the cathedral of Sevilla. Fernando and Isabel wore cloth of gold; Isabel rode a white horse through the streets to the cathedral, rapturously hailed by the people.[40]

It all testified not only to the importance of the birth of the heir and the Spanish love of display, but also to the now unquestioned authority of Isabel and Fernando and the newly achieved unity of Castile. But for Isabel, surely, there was much more than that, for she was a loving mother and this was only her second living child in nine years of marriage; and now she, like the Blessed Virgin Mary before her, could offer her first-born son to God.

Meanwhile an old enemy had been stirring: Archbishop Carrillo. Despite his pardon and the apparent settlement with him two years before, he was still refusing to accept the fullness of royal authority, excommunicating royal officials when they attempted to check any of the uses he made of his lands and castles. On July 6 Isabel and Fernando asked the Pope to annul these excommunications; on September 17 they sequestered all the rental income of the Diocese of Toledo and ordered their commander at Toledo, the unshakably loyal Gómez Manrique, to keep an even closer watch on the Archbishop. On September 28 Carrillo was ordered to appear at court immediately, on pain of losing his Castilian citizenship.[41]

It appears that he came; but then, in a last spasm of resentment, the man who had long fancied himself the king-maker of Castile reopened communication with King Afonso of Portugal, urging him to renew his invasion, telling him that widespread discontent among the nobles over the limitations placed on their authority by Isabel and Fernando (and particularly by the Holy Brotherhood) would bring more support to his banners in Castile this time. Specifically, Carrillo asked Afonso to attack Toledo, where he had contrived a plot to kill Gómez Manrique. Carrillo had never been very good at security, and Manrique and Isabel very soon found out about this. Manrique clapped the conspirators at Toledo into jail, planted the royal standard in the main square of the old fortress-city, and vowed to defend it to the death if anyone should attack it. No more was needed; never in the history of Spain had virtually impregnable Toledo been taken by assault without betrayal from within.[42]

[40]Chronicle of Valladolid, CODOIN XIII, 136-138; Bernáldez, *Memorias*, pp. 73-75 (ch. XXXII, XXXIII). For Isabel's own report on the birth of her son, see her letter to the Council of Sevilla, July 1, 1478, in *El Tumbo de los Reyes Católicos del Concejo de Sevilla*, ed. Juan de Mata Carriazo, Volume II (Sevilla, 1968), p. 222.

[41]Menéndez Pidal, *Historia de España*, XVII (1), 310.

[42]Pulgar, *Crónica*, I, 341-351 (ch. XCVIII).

This final treason—plotting to deliver the ancient capital of Spain to the enemy after assassinating its commander—was the end of the road for the self-willed, unprincipled archbishop. Isabel had not forgotten that he had saved her life at Song of the High Towers, nor that he had solemnized her marriage; she did not execute or imprison him. But she asked the Pope to deprive him of his archdiocese, and took away all his lands and castles, except for the minimum necessary to support him in retirement. She circulated a letter throughout the kingdom explaining why: "He treated with the King of Portugal to bring him into these kingdoms, and launched new wars within them, in great disservice to God and to us, and broke the oath that he had sworn with great solemnity to remain always in our service."[43] On January 7, 1479 Carrillo, weary of the struggle and knowing he was beaten, surrendered completely. During the rest of the month he turned over to the Queen's representatives, one by one, no less than nine castles in central Spain, leaving in his possession only Alcalá, to which he retired. Pope Sixtus IV did not, for whatever reason, agree to Isabel's request to remove Carrillo as Archbishop of Toledo; he continued to hold that office until his death in 1482, but gave Isabel and the kingdom no more trouble.[44] The little girl who had stood beside him so long ago at the baptism of Henry IV's dubious daughter Juana in 1462, then just being introduced to all the evils of that court and time, had vanquished him as she had vanquished them.

On October 22, 1478 Isabel and Fernando made solemn entry into Córdoba. They remained together in that second city of Andalusia for a full month to settle quarrels among its nobles, administer justice, and assure peace and good order, just as they had done at Sevilla. Indeed, the problems in the two cities were almost identical. Both had become battlegrounds for a pair of feuding nobles: the Duke of Medina Sidonia and the Marqués of Cádiz in Sevilla; the Count of Cabra and Alfonso de Aguilar, lord of Montilla, for Córdoba. Isabel and Fernando adjudicated their conflicting claims and ordered both to stay out of the city until passions had cooled, while severely punishing official corruption and violent crime, both of which had become as common in Córdoba as they had been at Sevilla.[45] The Count of Cabra in particular, like the Marqués of Cádiz, became Isabel's devoted adherent.

With Isabel in Córdoba was her new confessor, the Hieronymite friar Hernando de Talavera. Fray Hernando was known for his purity and simplicity of mind and heart, for total honesty, and for the profundity of his religious commitment, though he was of a *converso* family. He helped Isabel prepare a

---

[43]*Ibid.*, I, 353 (ch. XCIX).

[44]Menéndez Pidal, *Historia de España*, XVII (1), 311; J. H. Elliott, *Imperial Spain, 1469-1716* (New York, 1963), p. 101.

[45]Pulgar, *Crónica*, I, 338-339 (ch. XCVII); Chronicle of Valladolid, CODOIN, XIII, 139; Rumeu de Armas, *Itinerario*, p. 73.

decree against corruption, banning the receipt of gifts by public officials, especially judges, from any litigant who had a personal interest in their proceedings.[46] She had complete confidence in him, most especially from the time she made her first confession to him:

> It was customary for her and her confessor to kneel together at her royal seat. Fray Hernando came and seated himself there in order to hear her confession. The Queen said: "We are both to kneel." The new confessor replied: "No, my lady; I am to be seated and Your Highness on your knees, because this is the tribunal of God, and I am His representative." The Queen fell silent, and he absolved her from her sins. Afterwards she said: "This is the confessor I have been looking for." From this point on she accorded him the greatest respect and reverence, not only in the tribunal of God, but in ordinary affairs.[47]

On November 23 Fernando left Córdoba to go to Trujillo to see first-hand how the campaigning against the remnants of the rebellion and the Portuguese war was proceeding along the Portuguese border in Extremadura. (He found it was going very well.) Isabel remained in Córdoba for three more weeks, then joined Fernando at the shrine of Guadalupe for Christmas.[48] At Guadalupe, on January 10, they ratified the treaty of peace with France which had been drawn up and signed at St. Jean de Luz in the Pyrenees the preceding October. It settled nothing—the status of Roussillon, the principal bone of contention, was referred to a four-man arbitration commission with a prearranged 2-2 deadlock—but it pledged alliance and non-aggression, and marked the tacit but unmistakable formal abandonment of Afonso of Portugal by Louis XI of France.[49]

Louis' negotiators had hoped to drive a wedge between Juan II of Aragon, now 81, and Fernando—who very much wanted the peace for Castile's sake—by refusing to hand over Roussillon, the land north of the Pyrenees which the old man had so stoutly fought for and still vigorously claimed.[50] But the diplomat did not live who could drive a wedge between Juan II of Aragon and his beloved son. Juan consented to the treaty, with full confidence that his son would never forget or abandon Roussillon—and in fact he did not, and ultimately regained it. In January, after the feast of Epiphany, King Juan had

---

[46]Pulgar, *Crónica*, I, 339-340 (ch. XCVII); Jesús Suberbiola Martínez, *Real Patronato de Granada; El arzobispo Talavera, la Iglesia y el Estado Moderno* (Granada, 1982), p. 35.

[47]José de Sigüenza, *Historia de la Orden de San Gerónimo*, Volume II (*Nueva Biblioteca de Autores Españoles*, Volume 12) (Madrid, 1909), p. 295.

[48]Rumeu de Armas, *Itinerario*, pp. 73-74; Menéndez Pidal, *Historia de España*, XVII (1), 310, 312; Chronicle of Valladolid, CODOIN XIII, 139-140.

[49]Menéndez Pidal, *Historia de España*, XVII (1), 214-215. For the Latin text of the treaty, see Suárez Fernández, *Política Internacional de Isabel*, I, 383-415.

[50]Pulgar, *Crónica*, I, 364-366 (ch. CIII).

intended to travel up the Ebro River to meet his son, but in his palace at Barcelona, in the midwinter chill, his years overtook him at last. On January 19 he died, after receiving viaticum. He left a last letter for his son urging him always to serve justice, defend the faith, keep the peace in his kingdoms, and practice humility. As it had been during much of Juan's long reign, his treasury was so empty when he died that there was not enough money available to bury him properly, until his officials sold the jeweled collar of the Order of the Golden Fleece that he had worn as King of Aragon.[51]

Isabel had joined Fernando at Trujillo when the news of Juan II's death arrived. They had barely time to mourn him before being caught up in a new crisis and a new opportunity. Almost simultaneously, at the end of January or the beginning of February, they received disturbing demands from the Countess of Medellín and Alonso de Monroy who claimed to be Master of the crusading order of Alcántara, and a message from Isabel's Portuguese aunt Beatriz proposing private negotiations between her and Isabel to end Portugal's war with Castile.[52]

The Countess of Medellín was an illegitimate daughter of Isabel's old nemesis Pacheco, the first Marqués of Villena, and most definitely her father's daughter. Her husband was dead and she claimed that her son, the titular Count of Medellín, was insane. She demanded life tenure of Medellín castle and confirmation in the possession of the city and castle of Mérida which her men had recently seized. Monroy demanded recognition by Isabel and Fernando of his claim to be Master of Alcántara and to control the castles in Extremadura from which he had been making war and ravaging the countryside. Both Monroy and the Countess clearly implied that if their demands were not met, they would seek aid from the Portuguese.[53]

This was precisely the kind of fundamental lawlessness that Isabel and Fernando had punished at the siege of Utrera by executing all but eleven of the men captured when it was stormed the previous year. Nevertheless at first they replied gently, explaining that they had no authority to dispose of Medellín and Mérida, which belonged by law to the Order of Santiago (Pacheco had, in effect, embezzled them from the order when he was its Master), and that the Pope had approved Juan de Stúñiga as Master of Alcántara so that, if someone else was to be given that office in his stead, only the Pope could do so. Wholly unimpressed by this measured response, Monroy and the Countess carried out

---

[51]Menéndez Pidal, *Historia de España*, Volume XV: "Los Trastámaras de Castilla y Aragon en el siglo XV," by Luis Suárez Fernández, Angel Canellas López, and Jaime Vicens Vives (Madrid, 1964), p. 484. Fernando's last letter to his father, written from Trujillo in Extremadura three days after his death, before the news had reached him, shows that no hint that his father was about to die had come to him (Antonio Paz y Melia, *El Cronista Alonso de Palencia; su vida y sus obras* [Madrid, 1914], pp. 308-310).

[52]Menéndez Pidal, *Historia de España*, XVII (1), 313, 315.

[53]Pulgar, *Crónica*, I, 361-363 (ch. CII).

their threat and offered their obedience to the King of Portugal. He accepted, but demanded Mérida as security. Isabel and Fernando alerted the whole realm that Monroy and the Countess of Medellín were rebels under sentence of imprisonment and the loss of all their estates, warning that no one should give them aid of any kind.[54]

By this time a Portuguese army was on the march, for King Afonso had sent the Bishop of Evora in Portugal—another of the bellicose bishops of the age—in command of a substantial force to secure Mérida which the Countess of Medellín had promised him. The new Master of Santiago, Alfonso de Cárdenas, hurried to intercept the invaders. At Albuera near Mérida he challenged them to battle on February 24. After hard fighting during which Cárdenas received two wounds, he and his men prevailed, and captured the Bishop of Evora. Promptly notified of the victory (Trujillo, where they were staying, is not far from Mérida), the Catholic Kings gave thanks to God; Isabel went to her room for prayers of thanksgiving and to shed tears for the brave men who had suffered death or wounds fighting for her cause and the cause of the nation. She gave Cárdenas principal credit for the victory.[55]

Despite this victory, the disorder in Extremadura was now so great that Isabel's advisors did not believe it safe for her to remain there. They advised her to withdraw to Talavera or even to Toledo, out of harm's way.[56] Isabel would have none of it:

> Since I have already come to this region, surely I do not intend to leave it, neither to flee danger nor to avoid work, nor to give glory to the enemy, nor pain to my subjects. For those reasons, I have decided to stay here, until I see that we make war to the finish, or treat for peace.[57]

She was as good as her word. She and Fernando stayed in Extremadura, first at Trujillo and then at Cáceres. At her orders, the Master of Santiago pressed close sieges of Medellín and Mérida—where the Portuguese remnants were now shut up along with the Castilian rebels—all through the spring and summer of 1479, while she herself began peace negotiations with her aunt Beatriz of Portugal at Alcántara on March 20. Beatriz genuinely wanted peace, and so did Portugal's Prince John. King Afonso was much more doubtful, and kept hoping for some sudden last-minute reversal of his military fortunes. But as the months wore on, even he could see that the one unexpected reinforcement he had received, that of the Countess of Medellín and Monroy,

---

[54]*Ibid.*; Isabel and Fernando to the Council of Sevilla, Feb. 21, 1479, *Tumbo de Sevilla*, II, 314-315.

[55]Pulgar, *Crónica*, I, 370-377 (ch. CVI-CVII); Bernáldez, *Memorias*, p. 82; Menéndez Pidal, *Historia de España*, XVII (1) 314-315.

[56]Pulgar, *Crónica*, II, 381-382 (ch. CX).

[57]*Ibid.*, I, 382 (ch. CX).

had been effectively contained, and that all prospect for dismembering Castile had vanished. On September 4 he finally agreed to the Treaty of Alcáçoba, by which Portugal abandoned the claim that Juana was the rightful Queen of Castile and recognized Castile's title to the Canary Islands in return for a money payment, with Castile in turn recognizing Portugal's title to the African coast. A typical document of its kind for this time, this treaty sealed the peace it proclaimed by a marriage agreement between nine-year-old Princess Isabel and four-year-old Crown Prince Afonso of Portugal, while dubious Juana was to enter a convent immediately and take irrevocable vows to the religious life after her required year of novitiate (unless she chose to wait for Isabel's son to grow up and to marry him—a grotesque prospect, Juana then being seventeen and Prince Juan one, which Isabel must have proposed only in the near-certainty that it would not be accepted).[58]

Juana was not consulted in all this. She had no religious vocation; but if she remained free to marry, her claim could be picked up at any time in the future by any ambitious suitor. Surely Isabel at least felt pity and offered a prayer for the tragic, oft-abandoned waif for whom, at age 11, she had stood as godmother; but that era could see no other way than this to neutralize the danger to the peace of Spain that this 17-year-old girl, if available for marriage, would present for at least the next thirty years. In fact she lived to be 68, outliving Isabel by 26 years; Afonso made her a sort of honorary Portuguese princess before she took her religious vows, and all the rest of her life she signed herself *Yo la Reina* (I, the Queen), though no one was ever quite sure which country she was claiming to be queen of.[59]

Eight days after the Treaty of Alcáçoba was signed, the rebellion in Extremadura finally collapsed. Mérida surrendered to Isabel, and two days later, Medellín as well. On September 30 Isabel ordered the release of all those imprisoned because of the war with Portugal.[60]

In June, assured that the military situation in Extremadura was well in hand and that Isabel was making good progress in the peace negotiations with Portugal, Fernando had gone to Aragon to make the arrangements and conduct the ceremonies for his formal assumption of kingship there and in its provinces of Catalonia and Valencia, along with negotiating a treaty with Navarra which was now independent. This occupied him throughout the summer. Not until

---

[58]*Ibid.*, pp. 382-388 (ch. CX); Chronicle of Valladolid, CODOIN XIII, 142; Menéndez Pidal, *Historia de España*, XVII (1), 315-321, 325-327. For the full text of the Treaty of Alcáçoba (also known as the Treaty of Trujillo), see Antonio de la Torre and Luis Suárez Fernández, eds., *Documents referentes a las relaciones con Portugal durante el reinado de los Reyes Católicos* (Valladolid, 1958-63), I, 245-284.

[59]William H. Prescott, *History of the Reign of Ferdinand and Isabella the Catholic* (Philadelphia, 1893), I, 262n; Miller, *Castles and Crown*, p. 106.

[60]Chronicle of Valladolid, CODOIN XIII, 143; Isabel to the Council of Sevilla, Sept. 30, 1479, *Tumbo de Sevilla* III, 3-5.

October, when he knew that Isabel was expecting their third child in less than a month, was he able to take his leave of Valencia and start back to rejoin her at Toledo. He arrived there in high style on the 23rd, bringing an elephant in his train. On November 6 their child was born: a daughter. Isabel, her devotion to St. John the Evangelist as strong as ever, named her Juana. The history of Isabel's daughter Juana was to be even more tragic than that of her ill-starred namesake who was forced into the convent by the Treaty of Alcáçoba.[61]

Isabel and Fernando came to Toledo at this time because a *cortes* of the realm of Castile had been summoned to meet there. The *cortes* was a centuries-old institution in several of the ancient realms of Spain—Aragon, Catalonia, Valencia, and Navarra all had one as well as Castile, and so did Portugal—and its traditional organization followed the pattern of medieval parliaments in most parts of Europe. There were three houses: the higher clergy, the great landowners, and the representatives of cities and towns. Tradition required the assent of the *cortes* for major changes in the nature of the government and the administration of justice, and for the imposition of new taxes. The *cortes* also offered a forum for the discussion of any question of public policy which any member (though usually a group of members was needed to undertake such discussion) wished to raise. The *cortes* of Castile had not met since 1476 when it convened at Song of the High Towers, and the attendance at that meeting had been poor due to the difficulties created by the war of the succession. Now the country was at peace, the costs of the war had been great and must be paid, and it was known that the King and Queen would propose major changes and new programs. Attendance at this *cortes* was excellent, though the delegates were rather slow in arriving; not until January 1480 did they formally convene, in the Dominican Church of St. Peter the Martyr. They continued to meet through the month of May. Seventeen cities were represented by two delegates each: from Old Castile, north of the Guadarrama Mountains, Burgos, Avila, Segovia, Soria, and Valladolid; from León over to the Portuguese frontier, León, Toro, Zamora, and Salamanca; from New Castile in the center of Spain, Madrid, Toledo, Guadalajara, and Cuenca; from Andalusia and the south, Sevilla, Córdoba, Jaén, and Murcia. Learned counselors and ambitious noblemen from

---

[61]Chronicle of Valladolid, CODOIN XIII, 143-144; Menéndez Pidal, *Historia de España*, XVII (2), 12; Rumeu de Armas, *Itinerario*, pp. 81-82. Much confusion for later historians has been caused by an entry at this point in the Chronicle of Valladolid stating that Princess Isabel began her journey to Portugal on October 30, 1479. No other source supports that date; the Treaty of Alcáçoba called for the Princess to go to Portugal once Henry IV's purported daughter Juana had made her final vows, but not before; we know she did leave for Portugal the next year, after Juana had made her vows, and that Isabel sent her very reluctantly even then, as might be imagined, since she was only ten years old. It is very difficult to imagine Princess Isabel being sent away at this time; since her actual departure came almost exactly a year later, it is very likely that we have a simple copyist's error in the year in the Chronicle of Valladolid.

each city were on hand to advise and seek to influence the delegates. Next to the King and Queen themselves, the two most respected voices at the *cortes* of Toledo were Cardinal Mendoza and Isabel's holy and incorruptible confessor, Fray Hernando de Talavera.[62]

The most critical problem facing the *cortes* and the realm was the severe shortage of public funds arising from the massive alienation of royal lands during the chaotic and desperate reign of Henry IV. That deeply disturbed and fiscally irresponsible monarch had, partly due to the combination of pressure and deceit regularly practiced on him by most of those around him, partly due to his almost compulsive efforts to buy friendship with gifts of land and money, and partly due to sheer caprice, alienated the greater part of the royal domain, from whose income the reigning monarch of Castile was supposed to support the government in normal times. Not only had Henry given away or been forced to concede vast estates and lucrative incomes; still more royal estates and incomes had been converted to private holdings during the rebellion of Isabel's late brother Alfonso by noblemen shamelessly taking advantage of his minority. If the aristocrats were to retain all the land titles and income they now claimed, the government of Castile was and would remain bankrupt unless heavy, indeed unprecedented new taxes were levied—which only the *cortes* could do.[63]

It was a problem too difficult and complex to admit of any easy solution, with almost unlimited opportunities for more fraud and deceit and confusion and self-aggrandizement in any attempt to solve it. But in fact it was solved—quickly, completely, with almost no resistance or evasion. It is impossible not to see and feel Isabel's guiding spirit in the remarkable straightforwardness, simplicity, and moral soundness of the measures adopted as the solution, though the one detailed account of this *cortes* of Toledo that we have, by the chronicler Pulgar, gives much of the credit to Cardinal Mendoza.[64] Isabel herself, who in her humility never sought personal praise for her achievements, often pointed with pride to the success of the settlement, but seems to have been content to let others have the credit.

Once the magnitude of the problem was clear, Fernando and Isabel wrote to all the great landowners who had received additional lands from the Crown during the reign of Henry IV—which was most of them—to come to Toledo for the *cortes* if at all possible. Whether present or not, they were required to furnish a written statement of how and why they had obtained their new lands and rents—in other words, what they had done to earn them. With this

---

[62]Pulgar, *Crónica*, I, 415-417 (ch. CXV); Menéndez Pidal, *Historia de España*, XVII (1), 357-361.
    [63]Pulgar, *Crónica*, I, 416-418 (ch. CXV); Menéndez Pidal, *Historia de España*, XVII (1), 359, 363-364.
    [64]Pulgar, *Crónica*, I, 418-419 (ch. CXV).

information in hand, Fray Hernando de Talavera was made chairman of a commission to decide which of these properties should be returned to the Crown. He was to base his decision primarily on the justification, if any, for their having been granted. If the grant had been made because of genuine services the grantee performed for Henry, such as defending him against his many enemies, it was allowed to stand. (Isabel assumed throughout—as indeed she had always assumed, from the day her brother died—that Henry, whatever his inadequacies and failures, was the legitimate King of Castile and that no one had the right to rebel against him.) If no such justification for the grant could be found (as in the majority of cases it could not be), then the land was subject to repossession. Whether or not it was actually repossessed depended on what the recipient (or his progenitor) had done with it—whether he had contributed substantially to the lawlessness and scandal which had swept Castile in Henry's reign, and/or during the recent rebellion and invasion. Loyal support of Henry and Isabel was rewarded by permission to retain a greater amount of the land granted without good reason. But nearly all the noblemen lost at least a quarter or a third of their lands—Isabel's old teacher Gonzalo Chacón was the only major exception; he actually found himself with more land when the *cortes* ended. Even some of Isabel's strongest supporters—men such as the Marqués of Cádiz and Beltrán de la Cueva—lost more than half of what they had. All the greater malefactors lost the majority of their lands; but no one was deprived of everything.[65]

Before the final settlement was announced, Isabel took care, by a decree of April 20, 1480, to preserve all lands and rents held by the Church, insuring that they would not be a part of any redistribution.[66] Though, as we shall see, she had very strong views on the need for reform in the Church and was prepared to go far in pressing for it, she would never deprive the Church in Spain of the funds necessary to carry on its work.

Few monarchs, however powerful, of any time and country could have brought about so massive a land reform as this of 1480 in Castile without vocal and probably violent opposition and at least a major threat of civil war. But in just five years of reigning, Isabel's prestige and moral authority had risen so high that nothing of the kind occurred. Instead, almost everyone involved actually seemed to take pride in what they had done, in at long last behaving like statesmen. Some 30 million maravedís in rents came back to the Crown from the coffers of the aristocrats. Isabel insisted that two-thirds of the first year's new income be used to compensate those who had suffered with particular severity from the war with Portugal—notably the widows and orphans of those who had died in defense of the kingdom—and the plunder, rapine, and mayhem

[65]Pulgar, *Crónica*, I, 418-421 (ch. CXV); Menéndez Pidal, *Historia de España*, XVII (1), 364-366.
[66]MS decree, Simancas Archives, Diversos de Castilla, leg. 5, folio 79.

that had ravaged the land until the Holy Brotherhood could be organized in each locality to put it down. To assure that no such evils came again, she had already declared that the Brotherhood would continue in existence; now she and the *cortes* also decreed that no one was allowed to build a new castle without royal permission.[67]

The *cortes* also enacted—evidently at Isabel's suggestion—many important administrative reforms. The membership of the Royal Council was set at eleven: a bishop-president, four *oidores* (judges), three *alcaldes* (city governors), a treasurer, and two officials known as "advocates of the poor." Members had to be appointed or reappointed each year. The Council normally met at least three hours every day, and a two-thirds vote was required for approval of any action. *Veedores* were commissioned to go on a regular basis to observe how cities and towns were being governed, whether there was law and order and justice there; as needed, *corregidores* would then be sent to correct any misgovernment which the local authorities had not taken action to terminate. Limitations were placed on the practice of passing on municipal offices by inheritance. The value of the maravedí was fixed in terms of gold, and the number of mints was reduced from the 150 during Henry's reign—virtually legalized counterfeiting—to a manageable and tightly supervised five. Cattle and merchandise were allowed to pass freely in trade between Castile and Aragon for the first time, a harbinger of the full economic union between the two countries that was to bring so much prosperity to Spain in the years to come, when it was the leading power in the world.[68]

In addition to all the work of legislation and administrative reform, there was, as ever, the enforcement of law, the dispensing of justice and of royal favor, and the splendid ceremonies by which the Spanish have always set great store. The *cortes* formally swore allegiance to little Prince Juan as the heir to the throne. At the request of Master of Santiago Alonso de Cárdenas, there was a solemn blessing of the pendons of the Order of Santiago at the great cathedral in Toledo, climaxed when Cárdenas knelt before the King and Queen to receive their accolade: "Master, God give you good campaigns against the Moors, enemies of our holy Catholic faith."[69] (Despite everything else she had on her mind and that she had had to do in her reign thus far, Isabel never forgot the long crusade—nor did many of the best of her commanders.) Fernando's soldiers took the castles of Cantalapiedra and Castronuño, long held by the

---

[67]Pulgar, *Crónica*, I, 423-424 (ch. CXV); Isabel and Fernando to the Council of Sevilla, Dec. 24, 1479, *Tumbo de Sevilla* III, 15-17; Miller, *Castles and the Crown*, pp. 107-108.

[68]Pulgar, *Crónica*, I, 423-424 (ch. CXV); *Tumbo de Sevilla*, III, 316-317; Menéndez Pidal, *Historia de España*, XVII (1), 361-363, 366-372; Miller, *Castles and the Crown*, pp. 108-109.

[69]Pulgar, *Crónica*, I, 425-427 (ch. CXVI).

Portuguese during the war of the succession and consequently suffering particularly from war damage and impoverishment, which had been seized by robber gangs.[70]   Isabel's old friends Andrés de Cabrera and Beatriz de Bobadilla were presented for special honor by the *cortes* in their new capacity as Marqués and Marquesa of Moya.[71] And the Count of Treviño, though a very early supporter of Isabel and Fernando, was given a peremptory order in April to release his mother whom he had unjustly imprisoned and robbed, and who had appealed to Isabel for rescue and justice—an order which, despite earlier prevarication, the Count now obeyed.[72]

There now remained only one part of Isabel's kingdom still in serious disorder, where crime was rampant and rebellion endemic: the wild and thinly populated northwestern province of Galicia, the most mountainous and inaccessible part of Castile. Before this, Isabel and Fernando had had neither time nor resources to spare for distant Galicia; now it was time for Galicia as well to feel the firm grip of the Queen's justice. On August 3 an energetic and hard-hitting knight, Fernando de Acuña, was appointed governor of Galicia. He took up his duties immediately and with exemplary rigor; by November he had destroyed no less than 46 castles and towers held by criminals or rebels, executed the worst of them, and caused some 1,500 of them to flee the country. There was a good deal more to be done, for the steep hills and narrow valleys of this province were almost made to order for outlaws; but by the end of the following year (1481) Acuña had fully pacified it.[73]

The pacification of Galicia was the last major operation to discharge Isabel's fundamental duty as head of state in Castile: to provide for all her people that protection against crime and foreign invasion which has always been the primary responsibility of government among civilized men. In all of Castile as it was at her coronation, she never again faced any serious threat from invasion or crime during all the rest of her life and reign. She was now free to turn her attention to the two great causes closest to her heart, where major new initiatives were required: the reform of the Church, and the resumption of the long crusade. (With them was to come, though she did not know it yet except for the foreshadowing she seems to have felt for a moment when she sailed with Fernando from Sevilla down the Guadalquivir River to the edge of the open ocean in October 1477, a third undertaking, which the world calls her greatest—the opening up of a new world beyond the seas.) It was totally characteristic of Isabel that she should begin with what she always saw as

---

[70]Valera, *Crónica*, p. 125.

[71]Pulgar, *Crónica*, I, 427-428 (ch. CXVI).

[72]MS letters from Fernando and Isabel, April 1480, Simancas Archives, Registro General de Sello 1480-IV, folio 141.

[73]Pulgar, *Crónica*, II, 430-434 (ch. CXVIII); Valera, *Crónica*, pp. 102-104; Menéndez Pidal, *Historia de España*, XVII (1), 342.

the most important of these undertakings, Church reform.

The Church was still united in 1480, but corruption of many kinds had penetrated it deeply, and seemed ineradicable. Throughout almost the whole of the fourteenth century and on into the fifteenth, the prestige and authority of the Papacy had been sapped by its transfer from Rome to Avignon under threat of force, and the double and then triple schism which followed the final return of the legitimate Popes to Rome in 1378 and was not ended until the Council of Constance in 1415. Doctrine was not involved in the schism, but heresies had grown out of it, notably those of Wyclif in England and Hus in Bohemia. The settlement of the schism by a council had bred the theory that a council was in some way superior to the Pope and could elect its own pope if a majority of its members disagreed with the reigning pontiff. Though the last conciliar antipope had abandoned his pretensions in 1449, two years before Isabel was born, the Popes of her age feared nothing more than a new council which would challenge them and divide Christendom once again. Since councils tended to be dominated by powerful bishops working closely with the kings and leading nobles of their country, the Popes sought tighter control over the bishops. But Popes were also temporal heads of the Papal state in central Italy, and as such immersed in Italian politics, never more complex and dissolute than in this age which formed Niccolò Machiavelli.[74]

The reigning Pope Sixtus IV was impressed by Isabel and had been generally a friend to her. Though persuaded on bad advice to give King Afonso of Portugal a dispensation to marry Juana (for which he had apologized, and which he had revoked in 1478),[75] he had never recognized Juana's claim to be Queen of Castile. But Sixtus IV was no reformer. Particularly after the bloody Pazzi conspiracy in April 1478, when during Mass in the Cathedral of Florence and in the presence of the Pope's nephew Cardinal Raffaelo Riario, Giuliano de Medici was cut down and Lorenzo de Medici barely escaped the assassins, he shrank from the bloody maelstrom of Italian politics.[76] He sought protection in his family and friends, who monopolized most of his episcopal appointments.

Among these were episcopal appointments in Spain. Absentee bishops and bishops with multiple sees were one of the worst of the corruptions of the late medieval Church. (Both practices were later outlawed by the Council of Trent.) Effective Church reform required at least some support from the bishop, which could hardly be given if he was never to be found in his diocese. But Pope Sixtus' appointments, especially after the Pazzi conspiracy, were compounding the problem. In September 1478 the Cardinal Bishop of

---

[74]He was eleven years old in 1480.

[75]Menéndez Pidal, *Historia de España*, XVII (1), 226.

[76]Ludwig von Pastor, *The History of the Popes from the Close of the Middle Ages*, Volume IV (St. Louis, 1914), pp. 300-319; Christopher Hibbert, *The House of Medici: its Rise and Fall* (New York, 1974, 1980), pp. 128-143.

Tarazona in Aragon, Pedro Ferriz, died in Rome, where he had lived for many years. The Pope proposed to replace him with Ferriz's nephew, also a long-time resident in Rome. In 1479 Cardinal Antonio de Véneris, Bishop of Cuenca, also died in Rome after residing there for many years. Perhaps because he had given indispensable aid to Isabel at Toros de Guisando and at the time of her marriage, she does not seem ever to have protested his absence; but she was much distressed when the Pope proposed to appoint for that diocese his much-criticized nephew Rafaello Riario, a cardinal at 19 and a witness to the Pazzi attack who was widely though unjustly suspected of guilty knowledge of it. It was, to say the least, unlikely that young, ostentatious Cardinal Riario would ever quit Rome for hot, dusty little Cuenca in the harsh brown hills just east of Madrid. Then in the summer of 1480 just after the *cortes* of Toledo had adjourned, Bishop Rodrigo de Vergara of León—an authentic Spaniard and a resident—died. León was one of the major dioceses in Castile and Isabel most definitely did not want it to pass to a stranger or an exile.[77]

The usual arrangement for the appointment of bishops, then and long afterward in the Catholic countries of Europe, was that they should be nominated by the king or queen, and either confirmed or rejected by the Pope. Nothing Isabel or Fernando ever said or did suggests the slightest doubt of, or casts any aspersion on the Pope's authority to appoint bishops. But since bishops were so intimately involved in the public life of every European nation in that age—Carrillo and Mendoza were not unusual, but typical examples—most monarchs of the time reserved the right to try, judge, and expel from their kingdom any bishop they regarded as particularly undesirable politically. Isabel and Fernando also took this position, which received full support from the *cortes* of Toledo. But their interests were different. Fernando's chief concern, then and later, seems to have been for the maintenance of good order and close and effective cooperation between Church and state. Reform, for him, was secondary. (His own record in the matter of episcopal appointments was far from spotless, since in 1478 he had pressed successfully for the appointment of his illegitimate eight-year-old son as Archbishop of Zaragoza. Appointing children as bishops was another great abuse of the age—it did not happen very often, but every instance gave scandal, and few more than this one.) But for Isabel, reform was primary. She supported Fernando's policy regarding royal confirmation of episcopal appointments because she saw it as an essential element in bringing about the necessary and difficult reform.[78]

---

[77]Menéndez Pidal, *Historia de España*, XVII (1), 373-379.

[78]*Ibid.*, XVII (1), 226, 373-374, 377. The Papal Chancery in Rome announced the formal appointment of Fernando's illegitimate son as Archbishop of Zaragoza on August 14, 1478, when he was eight years old. Therefore, though he was probably born after Fernando's marriage to Isabel October 19, 1469, he was almost certainly

But Fernando never resisted his wife's policy of vigorously supporting Church reform. He and Isabel signalled its concrete beginning June 17, 1480, when they signed a decree at Toledo taking the Cistercian abbeys of Spain under their special protection for the purpose of carrying out the reform of their religious life that some of their own abbots had requested, giving the full support of their royal authority to these reforming abbots and their visitors sent out to Cistercian monasteries to "correct and castigate the superiors, monks and nuns who may have need of it."[79]

Neither side in the dispute over episcopal appointments in Spain was disposed to be unyielding. Isabel in particular never wished to be a committed adversary of the Vicar of Christ on any issue, and Pope Sixtus IV—particularly after receiving the glowing reports on her from Nicolás Franco—did not wish to be her adversary either. She and the Pope agreed on the new Bishop of León. Isabel accepted Riario as Bishop of Osma (one of Spain's less important sees), while Cardinal Rodrigo Borgia (no moral credit to the Church, but at least a Spaniard) took over Tarazona in addition to his existing see of Cartagena. What Isabel gained was the Pope's approval for the first of her personally selected reformers, Alonso de Burgos, to be Bishop of Cuenca. Fray Alonso de Burgos had accompanied Isabel almost from the moment of her coronation; he was a man without influence in Rome, without high family connections, with nothing to recommend him but his fervent dedication to the purification of the Church.   Luis Suárez Fernández truly says: "This appointment may be considered the beginning of a total renovation in the church leadership of Castile."[80]

The two months following the close of the *cortes* of Toledo May 28 were a time of high drama in the eastern Mediterranean. During two centuries the Muslim empire of the Ottoman Turks had been built up there, until it became one of the great powers of the world. Twenty-seven years before, Ottoman Sultan Mohammed II the Conqueror had taken Constantinople, the capital of the late Roman empire and long the greatest city in Christendom, making it his own capital under the name of Istanbul. Constantinople's Hagia Sophia, the Church of the Holy Wisdom, the greatest in Christendom, had become a mosque. The Crusader kingdom in the Holy Land was long gone. Despite frequent calls by the Popes for a revival of the Crusades, no serious attempt of this kind had been made since the Crusade of Varna failed nine years before the fall of Constantinople. But one Christian outpost remained within sight of

---

conceived before it. Though Fernando was not always faithful to his marriage vows, the evidence indicates that his lapses into infidelity were rare and brief, and that despite them he never ceased to love and honor his wife.

[79]The decree is printed in José García Oro, *La Reforma de los Religiosos españoles en tiempo de los Reyes Católicos* (Valladolid, 1969), pp. 419-420.

[80]Menéndez Pidal, *Historia de España.*, XVII (1), 380-381.

the Turkish coast, manned by members of a celibate crusading military order founded 350 years before in Jerusalem: the Knights of St. John of the Hospital, now known as the Knights of Rhodes for the island which was their base. Mohammed the Conqueror had sent a mighty host to take Rhodes, outnumbering the defenders nearly forty to one. Still they held out, under their dauntless Grand Master Pierre d'Aubusson. Nearly half the defending knights were killed, and the majority of the survivors were wounded. In a final desperate battle July 27, d'Aubusson led his men personally in a magnificent stand in a breach in the wall, under huge floating banners of the Holy Cross, St. John the Baptist, and Our Lady. D'Aubusson fell badly wounded, but the men around him held firm, and it was the attackers who broke. Within ten days the Turks withdrew from Rhodes.[81]

But the furious and frustrated Mohammed the Conqueror had in the meantime launched a powerful military expedition against southern Italy. It landed on the coast of Apulia July 29, just before the Turkish retreat from Rhodes, and assaulted the Italian city of Otranto, taking it by surprise and successfully storming it August 11. Twenty-two thousand of Otranto's people fell into Turkish hands. Twelve thousand were killed, many after refusing offers to spare their lives if they converted to Islam; the rest were sold into slavery. The Archbishop of Otranto stood fast at the altar of his cathedral; the Turks sawed him in two, along with deliberately killing every cleric in the city.[82] The anguished Pope Sixtus IV called desperately for help:

> If the faithful, especially the Italians, wish to preserve their lands, their houses, their wives, their children, their liberty, and their lives, if they wish to maintain that Faith into which they have been baptized and through which we are regenerated, let them at last trust in our word; let them take up their arms and fight.[83]

Spain responded at once; a great expedition to regain Otranto began to be prepared, with many volunteers and much enthusiasm.[84] The storming of Otranto and the ensuing massacre was a warning to all Christendom of the magnitude of the danger that had arisen because of the Turkish conquests. Turkish ships and men could go anywhere in the Mediterranean, seize any port, and wreak similar devastation. Though they had not yet reached Spain, it would be very easy for them to do so, for the Muslim-ruled land of Granada in the south had two major Mediterranean ports of its own, Málaga and Almería, which they could use as bases. Castile had just endured four years of war

---

[81]Eric Brockman, *The Two Sieges of Rhodes, 1480-1522* (London, 1969), pp. 58-90.

[82]Bernáldez, *Memorias*, pp. 103-106 (ch. XLV); Von Pastor, *History of the Popes*, IV, 333-334.

[83]Von Pastor, *History of the Popes*, IV, 335-336.

[84]Pulgar, *Crónica*, I, 435-438 (ch. CXIX).

because of the Portuguese invasion and the accompanying rebellion; but at least the Portuguese and the rebels did not inflict mass martyrdom. The Turks did. Any Castilian or Aragonese port could become an Otranto. And there were tens of thousands in Spain, outside Granada, who might well rise to greet invading, slaughtering Turks as liberators: the false *conversos*.

Conversos, it will be recalled, were those Spanish Christians who had converted from Islam or Judaism, or were descended from converted Muslims or Jews one or two or three generations back. Many of these conversions were genuine; or if the original conversion was not, the living descendant of the original convert had always been or had become a sincere, believing Catholic. But conversion of Muslims or Jews in Spain to Christianity, at least for the preceding century, had often been stimulated by ambition and greed—only Christians were allowed to hold high public office, and obviously only they could hold positions in the Church, which were very influential—or by fear, particularly when there was large-scale mob violence against non-Christians. Canon law, while condemning forced baptism, then held that even a forced baptism was valid, leaving—like voluntary or infant baptism—an ineffaceable mark upon the soul. But most of the baptisms of the *conversos* were not forced; it was their motives that were suspect.[85]

There is convincing, indeed overwhelming evidence—which even the most critical modern historians have acknowledged—that tens of thousands of false *conversos*, who did not believe in the Christianity they professed and by all indications never had believed in it, continued to live secretly by the teachings and rites of their former religion. Many had risen high in society, and even in the Church; some were priests who mocked the Mass as they said it. While most of the reports of *conversos* engaging in Satanic rites and crucifying children were probably false, it would be rash to say that all of them were; for the worst passions in human nature feed on the kind of situation in which the false *conversos* found themselves.[86] No one can excuse the pogroms, the threats, and the forced baptisms which drove some of the *conversos* so unwillingly into the Church; but by no means all of them, and probably only a minority, entered in this way. The rest chose to do so, and there was no one to ascertain what their motives might have been—or those of their descendants. Nor can the restrictions which made life so difficult for those who continued to profess their original faith be fully justified; but in fairness it must be pointed out that such restrictions on religious minorities were universal in that age, most certainly

---

[85]Bernáldez, *Memorias*, pp. 94-95 (ch. XLIII); Edward Peters, *Inquisition* (New York, 1988), pp. 77-83.

[86]Henry Charles Lea, *A History of the Inquisition of Spain* (New York, 1906), I, 145-147; William Thomas Walsh, *Isabella of Spain, the Last Crusader* (New York, 1930), pp. 195-203; Henry Kamen, *Inquisition and Society in Spain* (Bloomington IN, 1985), p. 28; Menéndez Pidal, *Historia de España*, XVII (2), 210-212.

found in Muslim as well as Christian countries—and to a substantial degree in modern Israel as well. Two wrongs do not make a right, but they assuredly can create severe problems and dangers for a state.

Every false *converso* in Spain was a potential traitor, a man capable of, and very possibly inclined to opening the gates to the likes of the Turkish mass killers of Otranto, welcoming the invader into the land to kill his countrymen and saw bishops in two. And by the same token, every *converso*—and there were now millions of them, including Hernando de Talavera, Isabel's saintly confessor; Alonso de Burgos, her choice as reforming Bishop of Cuenca; and Andrés de Cabrera, the husband of her dearest friend[87]—was open to the suspicion of infidelity and treason, his reputation and career forever in jeopardy of a false accusation to this effect. The danger was greatest in the south, particularly in Sevilla, the most populous city in Spain, not reconquered until 1250, where at least half of the population had been non-Christian. Particularly after the horror of Otranto, the danger simply could not be ignored.

From the time of her first visit to Sevilla in the summer of 1477, Isabel had been warned of these dangers and shown the evidence for them. She had discussed the problem with Nicolás Franco, the Papal legate, in the fall of 1477. In Sevilla she had been exposed to the ferociously anti-semitic preaching of Fray Alonso de Espina, including a harangue about the alleged Jewish crucifixion of a child on Good Friday 1478. It does not seem to have impressed her much, for all she did then was to encourage Cardinal Mendoza to prepare a new catechism for the better instruction of the Catholics of Sevilla, with particular emphasis on the sacraments. But on November 1, 1478, at the request of the Bishop of Osma, Pope Sixtus IV issued a bull authorizing Isabel and Fernando to set up an Inquisition in Spain, if they thought it necessary.[88]

At that time, they did not think it necessary. It was probably the catastrophe at Otranto that changed their minds.

On September 27, 1480 Isabel nominated Miguel de Morillo and Juan de San Martín to head an inquisition in Sevilla. On October 9 she formally presented their nominations as Inquisitors to the City Council of Sevilla. Further letters from her in November and December directed the Council to give full cooperation and support to the two friars. Many were questioned; many suspects fled, others were imprisoned, though many were also cleared of suspicions which proved baseless. On February 6, 1481 the first executions occurred, of six convicted of falsely professing Christianity, whom the inquisitors turned over to the secular authorities to be burned at the stake, then the

---

[87]Suberbiola Martínez, *Real Patronato de Granada*, p. 35; William Thomas Walsh, *Characters of the Inquisition* (London, 1940), pp. 135, 155.

[88]Pulgar, *Crónica*, I, 334-335 (ch. XCVI); Bernáldez, *Memorias*, pp. 95-96 (ch. XLIII); Lea, *Inquisition*, I, 148-160; Menéndez Pidal, *Historia de España*, XVII (2), 211-212; Bernardino Llorca, *La Inquisición en España* (Barcelona, 1936), pp. 73-74.

standard punishment for heresy. A few days later three of the richest men in the city suffered the same fate. During the remainder of the year, 14 more found guilty by the Inquisition were executed by burning in Sevilla.[89]

The Inquisition is the centerpiece of the "black legend" of Spanish history. Some aspects of its work are undoubtedly very offensive to the modern reader (though it is necessary always to keep in mind that, regardless of our sensibilities, we live in the bloodiest century in all history, in which millions of victims of Nazi and Communist totalitarianism died in almost inconceivable agony while the sympathizers and appeasers and frightened subjects of each kept silent). But at least the historian has a duty to put the Spanish Inquisition in perspective—rarely though this may be done. It did not engage in mass murder; the contemporary historian Pulgar estimates the total number of those burned to death because of its findings during Isabel's reign (or most of it) as no more than 2,000, an average of about 100 a year.[90] Some 15,000 were found guilty of false profession of Christianity,[91] but were reconciled with the Church in the public ceremony known as the *auto-de-fe*, meaning "act of faith"—that is, public confession of their error and reconciliation with the faith they had previously rejected. Because on that same occasion the few (usually those who had been found guilty twice) deemed irreconcilable were burned, the term *auto-de-fe* has come to mean, for those who know no Spanish, "burning at the stake," but the number reconciled was always much larger than the number burned. (However, those reconciled did suffer substantial penalties in addition to their often lengthy period of public penance—almost always large fines, and often a period of imprisonment.)[92] But a large majority of all those questioned by the Inquisition were completely cleared—as were St. Ignatius of Loyola and St. Teresa of Avila, and all so-called witches whose cases were brought before the Inquisition in the next century. For them, the Inquisition was a shield against calumny.

The Inquisition had no jurisdiction over practicing Jews and Muslims—only over professed Christians who were in fact still Jews or Muslims, though concealing it.[93] After its initial abuses were eliminated following the appointment of Tomás de Torquemada as Inquisitor-General for Castile in 1483,[94] the inquisitorial tribunals were generally very fair; many Spaniards preferred to have their cases heard before them rather than other courts.

---

[89]Letters of Isabel to the Council of Sevilla, October 9, November 9, and December 27, 1480, *Tumbo de Sevilla* III, 113-115, 129-132; Bernáldez, *Memorias*, pp. 99-101 (ch. XLIV); Menéndez Pidal, *Historia de España*, XVII (2), 212-214.

[90]Pulgar, *Crónica*, I, 336 (ch. XCVI).

[91]*Ibid.*

[92]*Ibid.*, I, 335-337 (ch. XCVI); Bernáldez, *Memorias*, pp. 101-103 (ch. XLIV).

[93]Lea, *Inquisition*, I, 145.

[94]For the date of Torquemada's appointment (which is not known precisely), see Llorca, *Inquisición*, pp. 106-107.

Those questioned were not allowed to face their accusers, because of the danger of blood feuds and revenge-seeking if their identity were known; but no one could be confined even briefly without the prior testimony of three witnesses against him, and the first thing that was done when a man was called before the Inquisition was to ask him to make a list of all his personal enemies, whose testimony was immediately thrown out. No anonymous testimony or denunciation was permitted. The accused had a defense attorney, often two, although they were assigned by the Inquisition.[95]

The Inquisition was a Church court, because by Catholic belief only the Church has the right to decide whether a man is or is not a Christian; therefore it did not execute the death penalty on its own authority, but turned the most guilty over to the state (the "secular arm") for the punishment reserved for heretics and traitors. These two crimes were regarded similarly, though heresy was deemed even worse, as treason against God. Every government in Europe in the fifteenth century punished both treason and heresy by an exceedingly painful death. Then and long afterward, the punishment for treason in England was hanging, drawing, and quartering. In this ghastly procedure, the traitor was hanged, but cut down before he was dead; his intestines were drawn out, and he was cut into four pieces—all while still alive. Let us by all means condemn such punishments, but not attribute them to some imaginary unique evil of Spain.

The modern world regards heresy as not a crime, but a joke. But the vast majority of the immense slaughters of men, women, and children by totalitarian regimes in our twentieth century have been carried out by men who bitterly hated Christianity and never hesitated to say so. They would not have been free to operate in a time which would have taken them at their word and knew the cost and consequences of such hatred, which many of those condemned by the Inquisition also nourished. Hitler was an apostate Catholic, Stalin an apostate Orthodox seminarian. Between them, they took at least 25 million lives —beside which the grand total of executions by referral from the Inquisition over its entire 300-year history is hardly measurable by comparison. Tomás de Torquemada would have known how to deal—and to deal early—with Hitler and Stalin.

Isabel saw the Inquisition as clearly necessary to preserve the security and promote the spiritual and social unity of Spain. The enduring cause of the reconquest had defined Spain by its Catholic faith in a way matched by no other country, unless by Ireland and Poland, whose nationality has been largely defined by persecutions of their people's Catholic faith. Because of this history, in all three of these countries up until the last few years, to reject the Catholic faith has been to all intents and purposes to reject the nationality. Isabel could

---

[95]*Ibid.*, pp. 171-176, 196-199, 203-205; Menéndez Pidal, *Historia de España*, XVII (2), 232-235; Walsh, *Characters of the Inquisition*, pp. 162-169.

trust no Spaniard not a Catholic, and particularly none who pretended to be Catholic but were not. Neither could her people. Such deceivers must be exposed, then reconciled if possible, or forced to flee, or if stubborn and beyond reclamation in their evil, executed. She did not flinch from ordering their execution, regarding it as her duty, as an essential part of the administration of justice to which she had devoted most of her immense energies and unyielding resolve since the victory at Toro. And justice was also the shield of the innocent. Those falsely accused of hidden heresy, of not being genuine Christians, deserved and would receive full vindication from a court uniquely competent to determine whether such accusations were true, whose judgments were accepted as definitive by the great majority of the nation.

These considerations were Isabel's justification for establishing the Inquisition. The initiative for its establishment and the determination for its retention were hers. Her admirers must face it; while the critics of the Spanish Inquisition, if they have any awareness of Isabel's character, should ask themselves how a woman so good, so honest, and so just could have brought such an institution into being if it were as evil as is commonly thought. And the Spanish Inquisition succeeded; it accomplished the task Isabel had set for it. Except in the kingdom of Granada after its conquest—a separate and special problem—there was no major anti-Christian revolt or treason in Spain during Isabel's reign or for sixty years after her death; and whenever there was a religious dispute involving accusations of heresy or occult practices, the Inquisition was available to settle it, and did, before it became a threat to the Church or to the country.

This is not to justify burnings at the stake, or torture. The Church permitted both, and so did Isabel; they should not have. But these were common evils of the age, against which almost no one even protested. And there is evidence that torture was very rarely used by the Inquisition during Torquemada's years (1483-1498) as Inquisitor-General.[96] Far from the ogre of legend, Torquemada was a just and devout man and a careful administrator, who took his responsibilities to the accused as well as to the accusers very seriously, and seems to have been the architect of most of the procedures that kept the inquisitorial tribunals fair and almost universally respected. He was one of Isabel's best appointments.[97]

The fall of 1480, which saw the establishment of the Inquisition in its first city, Sevilla, was also the time for Henry IV's dubious daughter to take her permanent religious vows, the signal for red-haired, ten-year-old Princess Isabel to leave her mother and go to the castle of Moura in Portugal where she would be cared for by her Aunt Beatriz until she was old enough to marry Portuguese

---

[96]Llorca, *Inquisición*, p. 218.
[97]*Ibid.*, pp. 121-124; Walsh, *Isabel*, pp. 270-273.

Crown Prince Afonso, who was also to live at this same castle. This harsh requirement had been insisted upon by Beatriz and King Afonso in negotiating the Treaty of Alcáçoba. In effect, the children were to be held hostages for the maintenance of peace between Castile and Portugal. We may well imagine how little Queen Isabel liked it, and it is almost painfully obvious in the manner in which she contrived to prolong her daughter's journey so that she would remain within the borders of her mother's realm as long as possible; the little girl and her escort took more than two months to travel the 150 miles from Medina del Campo to Moura.[98] But marriage to a prince was the destiny of every princess, and little Isabel was only a year younger than her mother had been when she was brought, no more willingly, to the dissolute court of Henry IV.

Still, Isabel's heart surely ached when her daughter crossed the border of what had been until so very recently an enemy country, to be held indefinitely in an isolated castle, with no way of knowing when she would see her mother again. Isabel must have rejoiced at the better prospect that opened for her daughter when, in August 1481, King Afonso died and was succeeded by his upstanding son John, who had always regarded the war with Castile as a mistake. Portugal could now be a friendly neighbor, without need of holding hostages from the royal families to guarantee its treaties. The news of John's accession to the Portuguese throne came to the Queen when she and Fernando and little Prince Juan were in Barcelona meeting with the *cortes* of Catalonia, so that it might swear allegiance to Isabel as co-regent and Prince Juan as heir, just as the *cortes* of Aragon had done in May.[99] Isabel must have known enough about John to know not only that he was trustworthy, but also that he adored his son. He would not allow him to remain indefinitely confined in the castle of Moura; and if he were released, so would her daughter be.

On September 10 Mohammed the Conqueror, the Sultan of the Turks under whom both Constantinople and Otranto had been taken, suddenly died, substantially lessening the immediate threat of further Turkish aggression and enabling the prompt recovery of Otranto by Ferdinand of Naples, a relative of Isabel's Fernando, with the aid of the substantial Spanish forces which had been gathered for that purpose.[100] This created an opportunity to take up Castile's ancient cause of reconquest by resuming military pressure on the kingdom of Granada in the south of Spain. The Marqués of Cádiz lost no time in doing so. The very next

---

[98]Chronicle of Valladolid, CODOIN XIII, 145; Bernáldez, *Memorias*, p. 93 (ch. XLII); de la Torre and Fernández,, eds., *Documentos referentes a las relaciones con Portugal*, II, 100-108 (Instrucciones para la entrada en tercería de la infanta Isabel, Nov. 3, 1480) and II, 145-152 (entrega de Isabel en tercería y de Manuel en rehenes, Jan. 11, 1481); Menéndez Pidal, *Historia de España*, XVII (1), 350-352.
[99]Pulgar, *Crónica*, I, 444-446, 451 (chs. CXXII, CXXIV); Menéndez Pidal, *Historia de España*, XVII (1), 349; (2), 13, 50.
[100]Pulgar, *Crónica*, I, 447 (ch. CXXIII).

month after the Sultan's death he led a raid all the way to Ronda, the city of the kingdom of Granada nearest the Castilian frontier. Neither Ronda nor any other major fortress was taken, but considerable damage was done.[101]

On November 7, 1481 Isabel, Fernando and Prince Juan left Barcelona to go to Valencia, which had its own *cortes* which was also to swear allegiance to Isabel as co-regent and Prince Juan as heir. They arrived in Valencia on the 25th of the month and remained there through Christmas.[102] Isabel was pregnant again, just two years after the birth of Princess Juana. Both her domains and Fernando's were entirely orderly and loyal, presenting a totally different picture from that of their turbulent past. She had saved her throne in the war of the succession; she had successfully and almost completely imposed justice on a once lawless land. Now she must decide where next, and how best, to use her country's renewed strength.

Before she could make that decision, it was made for her. On the pitch-black night of December 26, the day after Christmas, in the midst of a howling storm, the Moors of Granada struck the Christian frontier fortress of Zahara, just fifty miles from Sevilla and of the greatest strategic importance, with a surprise attack. Zahara was believed to be impregnable; but the screaming, scimitar-swinging attackers carried it in their first rush and put every man in the fortress to the sword, except for a very few who leaped from the parapets to flee through the roaring night.[103] The raid to Ronda by the Marqués of Cádiz had been, by comparison, a small flesh wound; this was a body blow, a thrust to the vitals. The ancient enemy had flung down the gage of battle. The 759-year-old war of the reconquest had resumed—that seemingly eternal war that was already old in the time of Isabel's first direct royal ancestor twenty-four generations back.

But now she had the means; she had always had the will; she was resolved to win that longest war at last, once and for all, forever.

---

[101]Bernáldez, *Memorias*, pp. 109-110 (ch. XLVIII).

[102]Rumeu de Armas, *Itinerario*, pp. 97-98.

[103]*Ibid.*, p. 98; Pulgar, *Crónica*, II, 3-4 (ch. CXXVI); Bernáldez, *Memorias*, p. 114 (ch. LI).

6
Crusade Resumed
(December 1481-June 1486)

The mountain-girt kingdom of Granada, the last great stronghold of the conquering Moors in Spain, held between 300,000 and 500,000 people at Christmastide of 1481[1]—a large majority Muslim, some Jewish, and few Christians. The forebears of many of the Muslim inhabitants had come there from other parts of Spain as they were reconquered (notably by King St. Ferdinand of Castile and King James the Conqueror of Aragon in the thirteenth century) rather than live under Christian rule. They were the most irreconcilable of the Muslims in Spain. They had broad and fertile fields, notably in the famous *vega* of Granada, their capital; they had rich mineral deposits in the high mountains around Granada. Though relatively small in area, the kingdom was well-defended and formidable. It was in close touch with Muslim North Africa (Morocco and Algeria) by sea from the commodious ports of Málaga and Almeria. Along the coast the country was so rugged as to preclude any amphibious assault and effective attack northward; a military approach to Granada from the north or the east was almost as impracticable for the same reason. The only feasible route was from the west, where the mountains dwindled to hills which, though still often steep and rugged, were penetrated by valleys through which armies could move easily unless artificially impeded.

Zahara fortress crowned a large, abruptly rising rock in the middle of one of the most important valleys giving access to and from the kingdom of Granada from the west, that of the Guadalete River. (It was on this same Guadalete River that the Spanish Christian army of 711, the year of the Muslim invasion across the Straits of Gibraltar, had made its stand and been destroyed, so completely that the body of its commander, King Rodrigo, was never found.) To this day, as one stands on Zahara's scored and weathered parapets, a magnificent, commanding view sweeps miles upon miles of the way to Granada

---

[1] Joseph F. O'Callaghan estimates 300,000 (*A History of Medieval Spain* [Ithaca NY, 1975], p. 605). However, Granada regularly fielded an army of over 100,000 men (Ramón Menéndez Pidal, director, *Historia de España*, Volume XVII: "España de los Reyes Católicos," ed. Luis Suárez Fernández and Manuel Fernández Alvarez [Madrid, 1969], Part 1, p. 400) and normally no more than 20 per cent of a population bears arms except in a desperate emergency.

to the east, and Sevilla to the west. Every part of the valley is in plain sight. No army, hardly a squad could pass through the valley by Zahara unseen, unless by night without lights—impractical for more than a few men. The ancient keep still stands, a timeless sentinel, upon the highest point of the rock. The climb is arduous even by full daylight.[2] It is hard to imagine hundreds of men making it successfully in the middle of the night and a furious storm; but that is what the Muslim attackers of December 26, 1481 had done. By securing Zahara they had not only made it impossible for the Castilians even to think of attacking Granada via the Guadalete valley without first reducing this almost impregnable fortress, but they had also obtained a formidable base for ravaging the peaceful Andalusian countryside to the west, down the Guadalete to the town and vineyards of Jérez de la Frontera, which gave its name to sherry—and was the principal residence of the Marqués of Cádiz.

From the beginning, the Marqués of Cádiz regarded the resumed crusade against Granada as not only his sovereign's, but his personal war. The tall and charming redhead who had so unexpectedly visited Isabel in her chamber late at night at Sevilla in 1478, was now on fire with a resolve as passionate as hers, to bring the longest war in history to an end in complete victory for the Christian cause. Before January ended he had sent off a long letter to the King and Queen proposing vigorous offensive action against Granada; on February 17, from Medina del Campo in the north, they responded with complete approval and the firm statement of their intention, with God's help, to make full-scale war against the Moors.[3] They had already conveyed the same intention to Diego de Valera, old warrior and historian, who on February 10 had sent them comprehensive recommendations for a truly national war effort,[4] and to the Council of Sevilla on February 12. Their letter to Sevilla, in particular, breathed a resolve so massive and primordial as to go far beyond even Isabel herself, calling up the deathless determination of those twenty-four generations of crusaders of the Reconquest who were her ancestors:

> For the loss of Zahara of which you write us, we have deep anger and grief
> . . . for the Christians who died there. For although the city and fortress

---

[2]The foregoing is based on personal observations by the author.

[3]Fernando and Isabel to the Marqués of Cádiz, Feb. 17, 1482, in Miguel Angel Ladero Quesada, *Los Mudejares de Castilla en Tiempos de Isabel I* (Valladolid, 1969), p. 94. Unfortunately the letter from the Marqués of Cádiz is lost, so we do not know for certain whether he proposed in it the capture of Alhama which he so spectacularly carried out later that month. However, the historian Palencia tells us that Fernando knew well in advance that an attack on Alhama was under consideration (Alonso de Palencia, *Crónica de Enrique IV*, Volume III [Biblioteca de Autores Españoles, Vol. 273, Madrid, 1975], p. 89 [Guerra de Granada, Libro II]), so it is probable that the Marqués of Cádiz did inform him of it.

[4]Diego de Valera to King Fernando, Feb. 10, 1482, *Epístolas de Mosén Diego de Valera* (Madrid, 1878), pp. 55-59.

may be recovered, as we hope in God that they may be recovered soon, the death of the Christians cannot be remedied. . . . But let this be clear: we intend to make war upon the Moors throughout the land, and in such a way that we hope in God that we may not only quickly recover this city which we have lost, but gain others so that Our Lord may be served and his Holy Faith exalted, and that we may thus render Him great service.[5]

The heart of the kingdom of Granada was the beautiful, verdant *vega*, stretching from the city of Granada itself at the foot of its mighty mountains to dark rocky Loja thirty miles downstream on the Genil River, which there runs almost due west. Southwest across the *vega*, at the edge of the mountains to the south, lay Alhama, 25 miles from the capital. It was far from the Castilian frontier and readily accessible from Granada. No Christian warrior, except an occasional unhappy prisoner, had been seen around Alhama for generations. Its people felt secure; consequently, they did not keep careful watch, as a bold reconnaissance by Ortega de Prado, a young nobleman from León, established.[6]

The Marqués of Cádiz struck. In one of the most daring operations of this or any war, he thrust with some five thousand men—half cavalry, half infantry—through the wild mountain tangle south of Alhama in two days of forced marching, conducted so skillfully that the Moors never detected the attacking host, though they were slicing almost through the center of the kingdom of Granada. They arrived in the last hour of the night of February 27-28. A group of picked men put up their scaling ladders in the darkness and swarmed over the city wall. Not one of them was seen until the first light of dawn revealed them inside the city, where they promptly opened the gates to their whole army.[7]

The trapped inhabitants fought desperately, but against so complete a surprise they had no chance; we are told that no less than 800 of them were killed, at small cost to the Spanish, while virtually all the rest of the population was captured.[8] The position of the town was naturally very strong, for it stood where a precipitous gorge opened out upon the *vega*, and from its frowning battlements no assault force could be concealed from defenders who were looking for it (as the Moors had not been). The Marqués of Cádiz knew that in a very few days he would face a massive counterattack from nearby Granada.

---

[5] Fernando and Isabel to the Council of Sevilla, Feb. 12, 1482, in *El Tumbo de los Reyes Católicos del Concejo de Sevilla*, ed. Juan de Mata Carriazo, Volume III (Sevilla, 1969), p. 193.

[6] Palencia, *Crónica*, III, 89 (Guerra de Granada, Lb II).

[7] *Ibid.*; Fernando del Pulgar, *Crónica de los Reyes Católicos*, ed. Juan de Mata Carriazo (Madrid, 1943), II, 5-10 (chapter CXXVII); Historia de los Hechos del Marqués de Cádiz, in *Colección de documentos inéditos para la historia de España* (hereinafter cited as CODOIN), CVI (Madrid, 1893), pp. 200-202.

[8] Andrés Bernáldez, *Memorias del reinado de los Reyes Católicos*, ed. Manuel Gómez Moreno and Juan de Mata Carriazo (Madrid, 1962), p. 116 (ch. LII).

On March 3 he sent off messages requesting immediate aid from his sovereigns (who were still far to the north, in Medina del Campo) and from his old enemy the Duke of Medina Sidonia, who was much closer with a substantial army that had not been involved in the original operation.[9]

The courier bearing such a message to his king and queen would drive himself and his horses to the utmost. We may hear his pounding hoofbeats up the storied route of heroes: past Archidona on the frontier, under its bald mountain topped by an ancient watchtower and fortress; past crag-girt Jaén just beyond the high sierra north of Granada; through the Pass of the Overthrow of the Infidel Dogs; across the dead-flat, rusty prairie of La Mancha; past Madrid huddled under the icy March winds off the Guadarramas; through the Gate of the Lion in that towering range; on past the glorious castle of Segovia to Medina del Campo on its fertile but still winter-bound plain. The message delivered, Fernando and Isabel responded March 10, in another letter to the Council of Sevilla:

> Knowing how well and advantageously it will serve God and us to hold and sustain that city [Alhama] for the conquest of the kingdom of Granada, we intend to make and prosecute that endeavor with all our force and power. We are sending to those frontiers more horsemen than you can supply, and I the King intend to go quickly to those regions to take charge of the supply of that city, and of the war to be made and pressed against the Moors.[10]

Fernando was as good as his word. Just four days later he was riding south almost as furiously as the messenger had ridden north, without his regular escort and with only a few companions. There was certainly need for haste. On the very day he and Isabel despatched their letter of March 10 to Sevilla, the Moors under Muley Abul-Hassan, King of Granada, had launched a massive counterattack on Alhama with no less than 50,000 troops. For hours they strove in vain to scale its walls. But the Marqués of Cádiz inspired the defenders; they rushed to every threatened point, the Moors on their scaling ladders could find no foothold, and after losing some two thousand men they drew off. Abul-Hassan now settled down for a regular siege. His men cut off most of the flow of the river running by the walls which supplied Alhama's only water. Every drop of the little that remained had to be scooped up under showers of Moorish arrows. Still the defenders held out, and on March 31 the Duke of Medina Sidonia arrived with a strong relieving force. He and his old enemy, the Marqués of Cádiz, embraced at the city gate and swore undying friendship for the future.[11]

---

[9]Menéndez Pidal, *Historia de España*, XVII (1), 445-449.

[10]Fernando and Isabel to the Council of Sevilla, March 10, 1482, *Tumbo de Sevilla*, III, 194.

[11]Palencia, *Crónica*, III, 90-91 (Guerra de Granada, Lb II); Bernáldez, *Memorias*,

Meanwhile Fernando had reached Córdoba, and was calling up more troops and beginning to sign contracts for the supply and support of the powerful artillery that would be needed to take the fortified Moorish towns.[12] On March 26 Isabel followed him south, after making careful arrangements for the proper governance of the heartland of Castile in her absence, which she obviously expected would be long. He had made the journey in just nine days; she took twenty-seven. There were the great holy days to be celebrated; she timed her journey to be in Toledo from Good Friday through Easter (April 5-7 that year).[13] And she was pregnant again, in her seventh month; this pregnancy seemed especially burdensome, for a reason she was soon to discover. But the climax of the longest crusade had begun; she could not stay away.

Close to her thirty-first birthday (April 22) Isabel arrived in Córdoba, just as Fernando was setting out for Alhama with 18,000 troops and large quantities of supplies, to drive off a second large Moorish force attempting to retake the city. He arrived at Alhama April 29. Its reinforced garrison was placed under the command of one of Andalusia's most redoubtable captains, Luis Fernández Portocarrero. Three of its mosques were converted into churches.[14] By May 6 Fernando was back in Córdoba, where he and Isabel levied a financial assessment upon all of Castile south of Toledo to help pay for the coming campaign against Granada. They ordered ships brought up to guard the Straits of Gibraltar and the waters of the Mediterranean immediately east of the Straits to prevent reinforcement of the Moors of Granada by their co-religionists in Africa.[15] And they held councils of war in which new military enterprises were proposed.

Fernando wanted to march directly on Loja, the anchor of the frontier, the most powerful fortress in the Moorish kingdom other than Granada itself, and try to take it. The Marqués of Cádiz advised against this very ambitious undertaking, but the Master of Santiago, Alonso de Cárdenas, and his nephew Gutierre, Isabel's most loyal retainer, favored it. Isabel, who took part in most of these discussions, is not recorded as expressing a strong view on the attempt to take Loja, but she flared up when some began to speak of withdrawing from Alhama, because of the cost and trouble of maintaining a garrison indefinitely

---

pp. 118-119 (ch. LIII); Pulgar, *Crónica*, II, 11-16 (ch. CXXVII-CXXVIII); Hechos del Marqués de Cádiz, CODOIN CVI, 203-204; Menéndez Pidal, *Historia de España*, XVII (1), 447-448.

[12]Antonio Rumeu de Armas, *Itinerario de los Reyes Católicos, 1474-1516* (Madrid, 1974), p. 101; Fernando to the Council of Sevilla, April 1 and 6, 1482, *Tumbo de Sevilla*, III, 195-196; Ladero Quesada, *Conquista de Granada*, p. 124.

[13]Rumeu de Armas, *Itinerario*, p. 102; Pulgar, *Crónica*, II, 19-20 (ch. CXXX).

[14]Rumeu de Armas, *Itinerario*, p. 103; Palencia, *Crónica*, III, 93 (Guerra de Granada, Lb II); Pulgar, *Crónica*, II, 23-24 (ch. CXXXII); Hechos del Marqués de Cádiz, CODOIN CVI, 206-207; Menéndez Pidal, *Historia de España*, XVII (1), 460.

[15]Rumeu de Armas, *Itinerario*, p. 103; Pulgar, *Crónica*, II, 24-27 (ch. CXXXIII).

in such an exposed position. All wars bring cost and trouble, she declared; she and Fernando were resolved to reconquer the entire kingdom of Granada, and Alhama was the first fruit of this great undertaking. It would be weakness, if not cowardice, to abandon it.[16]

The preparations for the grand assault on Loja went forward; by the end of June an army of 8,000 horse and 10,000 foot had been assembled. The Marqués of Cádiz continued to advise against the plan, since Loja was so strongly held; he said that even Málaga, the second city of the Moorish kingdom located south on the coast, would be easier to take and should be attacked in preference to Loja. But Fernando would not change the objective. Isabel may well have been torn between the two commanders in whose judgment she had such confidence—Cárdenas the Master of Santiago and Ponce de León the Marqués of Cádiz—who were at odds on this decision. By the end of June she had more intimate matters to deal with. On June 29 she went into labor. That evening another daughter, Maria, was born. But the labor continued. It went on for no less than thirty-five hours after Maria's birth. Forty hours or more of labor was an ordeal that often killed women, right down to the twentieth century. We know of nothing in her life that tested Isabel's physical strength like this. She endured; she survived. Maria's twin did not. When the agony ended at dawn July 1, the second girl baby was finally delivered, dead.[17]

The army was ready to depart, but Fernando would not leave until Isabel's life-and-death struggle was over. Limp, exhausted, her normally ruddy cheeks pale as cobwebs, she bade him farewell in the blue blaze of an Andalusian summer morning. The army marched out of Córdoba on its way to Loja. A week later Princess Maria was baptized in the cathedral of Córdoba by its bishop, Alonso de Burgos, the vigorous reformer who had long been one of Isabel's favorite priests.[18]

On July 9 the Christian army arrived before Loja. The long high ridge and rough broken country north, east and west of the heavily fortified city posed formidable problems for any army attempting to besiege it; there was not room for nearly the full number of the Spanish troops in any campground close enough to the city to meet the needs of a besieging force. Several small camps therefore had to be made instead of one big one, and they were not closely in touch with one another. The wily old Moorish commander in Loja, Ali Atar, knew just how to exploit this situation; he pretended to attack at various points until he enticed a substantial number of Christian troops to pursue, then cut in

[16]Pulgar, *Crónica*, II, 22-23 (ch. CXXXII); Hechos del Marqués de Cádiz, CODOIN CVI, 209-210.

[17]Palencia, *Crónica*, III, 94 (Guerra de Granada, Lb II); Mosén Diego de Valera, *Crónica de los Reyes Católicos*, ed. Juan de Mata Carriazo (Madrid, 1927), pp. 148-149 (ch. XLVIII).

[18]Chronicle of Valladolid, CODOIN XIII (Madrid, 1848), pp. 148-150.

behind them to attack one of the camps. After four days of this, Fernando had to admit that the Marqués of Cádiz had been right, and ordered a withdrawal. Ali Atar promptly attacked the confused and dispirited Castilians; as his Moors appeared unexpectedly charging down from the heights, much of the Christian army panicked. Fernando rushed among them shouting "Hold, *caballeros*, hold!" But he could not stop the rout. The Marqués of Cádiz saw the danger. Rallying sixty brave knights, he counter-charged and reached his king, lancing down a Moor who was about to kill him. Fernando's horse was killed under him, but his life was saved. Many of the great nobles of Castile were wounded, and the young Master of Calatrava was slain.[19]

Not until five days later did Isabel receive news of the disaster. (It may be that at first no one quite had the courage to tell her.) It was less than three weeks after her great ordeal. But she showed neither anger nor distress, in words or expression, and immediately turned her attention to a new expedition to resupply Alhama.[20] Isabel the Catholic always knew how to persevere.

So did Luis Portocarrero in Alhama. With a fighting speech he persuaded his men, shaken by the news of the defeat at Loja, to stand firm. They repelled a third massive Moorish attack, and on August 22 Fernando arrived, leading a large relief expedition.[21] Meanwhile the Moors were demonstrating an ancient, ironic human failing (one from which Isabel was singularly free): inability to stand success. Scarcely was their great victory at Loja won when the partisans of Abu Abdallah (whom the Spanish called Boabdil), the young prince long pushed for the succession by Muley Abul-Hassan's favorite wife Zoraya, rose in Granada against the aging king, charging him with insufficient vigor in supporting the defense of Loja, where he had not made an appearance. Boabdil was acclaimed king of Granada; but his father escaped, and took up his rule in Málaga.[22] The kingdom of Granada was divided; the ancient Roman maxim of "divide and conquer" was about to prove itself once again.

That winter Fernando and Isabel returned to the north, leaving Córdoba early in October and arriving at Madrid in November.[23] It was a quiet winter for them, though they continued to press preparations for a new campaign against Granada in 1483.[24] Archbishop Carrillo had just died, and they asked the Pope to appoint Cardinal Mendoza to the primatial see of Toledo in his

---

[19]Pulgar, *Crónica*, II, 27-31 (ch. CXXXIV, CXXXV); Bernáldez, *Memorias*, p. 124 (ch. LVIII); Valera, *Crónica*, pp. 153-154 (ch. XLVII).

[20]Pulgar, *Crónica*, II, 31-32 (ch. CXXXV); Fernando and Isabel to the Council of Sevilla, July 20, 1482, *Tumbo de Sevilla*, III, 224-225.

[21]Pulgar, *Crónica*, II, 32-37 (ch. CXXXVI); Rumeu de Armas, *Itinerario*, p. 105; Menéndez Pidal, *Historia de España*, XVII (1), 478-479.

[22]Palencia, *Crónica*, III, 97 (Guerra de Granada, Lb II).

[23]Rumeu de Armas, *Itinerario*, pp. 106-107.

[24]Isabel to the Council of Sevilla, Feb. 27, 1483, *Tumbo de Sevilla* III, 349-354.

place; he soon did so.[25] But as the winter drew to an end, probably on or very close to Easter (it fell on March 30 that year) even worse news than the defeat of Loja came to the royal couple at Madrid. The flower of Andalusian chivalry, led by the Marqués of Cádiz and the Master of Santiago, had blundered into a devastating ambush in a wild tangle of hills and ravines in a desolate region called the Ajarquía northwest of Málaga. A full four thousand had gone in; less than half of them had come out.

The Castilian nobles had been made overconfident by the gratifying reports coming in ever since the end of the preceding summer on the civil war between Abul-Hassan and his son Boabdil. When a defector from the kingdom of Granada named Bernaldino de Osuna proposed a raid into an area of rich grassland and orchards near Málaga which the Moors believed secure, which had been extensively developed for silk culture and cattle raising, the ever-optimistic Master of Santiago was enthusiastic, along with the *alcaide* of Antequera. They knew that Abul-Hassan—whom everyone now called *el rey viejo*, "the old king"—was most unlikely to come out from the protection of the walls of Málaga to challenge them in the field. The threat from his son Boabdil—whom the Castilians called *el rey chico*, "the little king"—was too great, and the old king's eyesight was failing. The terrain of the planned approach through Ajarquía was very difficult, but defector Bernaldino offered to provide guides, and assured the nobles that with their help the transit would not be a serious problem. The Marqués of Cádiz was doubtful; he, who had used harshly broken country to such good advantage in the approach to Alhama, knew better than any of the others its hazards as well as its opportunities for a major military operation. But he had never been in the Ajarquía, and eventually accepted Bernaldino's glib promises.

None of them seems to have been aware that another member of the royal family of Granada, this one neither old nor little—Abdallah called El Zagal, "the Valiant," Abul-Hassan's younger brother—was in the area, ready to take a hand.

The raid was launched at daybreak March 19. Speed was essential, as in any raid, to get through the rough country and on to the objective before strong forces could be gathered to stop it; but the attackers lingered to loot and burn villages, heedless of the signal fires on the mountain-tops and the messengers riding hard to Málaga with news of their advance. They even waited to assemble transport for their booty back to their home estates. By the afternoon of the 20th, more than thirty hours later, they had covered no more than ten miles, and were still among the precipitous hills and arroyos of the Ajarquía. The guides were confused; some detachments were virtually lost. More and

---

[25]Fernando and Isabel to Pope Sixtus IV, Dec. 3, 1482, in Luis Suárez Fernández, *Politica Internacional de Isabel la Católica*, Volume II (Valladolid, 1966), pp. 208-214.

more Moorish missiles were being flung from the heights upon the Castilians. They decided to withdraw.

It was too late. The country through which they were now passing was so full of steep slopes and gorges that much of the time it was literally impossible to ride; the proud nobles had to dismount and lead their frightened horses by hand. The sun set; dusk fell; they were not nearly out of the labyrinth. When full night cloaked the Ajarquía, El Zagal struck.

Wild Moorish yells resounded from the high ground, re-echoing eerily in the dark canyons. Stones, spears, and arrows rained down upon the milling, bewildered Castilians at the bottom of them. They lost all sense of direction and all touch with their guides, who themselves obviously did not know the country nearly as well as its inhabitants. The darkness made it difficult to impossible to climb out of the ravines and escape. At sunset most of the Castilians had been headed upstream, away from the coast where Málaga was, and as they blundered forward more and more of them came into glens and box canyons, from which there was no escape except by the way they had come. By midnight most of the Castilian force had given way to stark panic. Crazed knights tried to climb sheer rock walls and fell to their deaths. Others hunkered down paralyzed amid the rocks, ready to surrender to the first Moor they saw. The historian Palencia tells us that sons abandoned fathers to their fate, and brothers abandoned brothers; chiefs abandoned their men, while the survivors plundered their own dead. The Master of Santiago with 250 men huddled all the rest of the night at the bottom of a canyon, with the Moors hurling missiles at them; they could not see their targets, but neither could the targets see the missiles coming. Only the Marqués of Cádiz lost neither his head nor his heart. He was wounded and a horse was killed under him, but he never gave up. With a band of fifty who stayed with him all through the night, he climbed to the top of a ridge where he and they were safe from the foe. But no one else would follow him; he was even separated from his own brothers, two of whom were killed while the third was taken prisoner.

The next day El Zagal completed the rout; the shattered Castilians were limping out, hiding, wandering lost and grubbing roots to appease their hunger, every man for himself, fair game for any of their foes. Castilian knights were captured by their Moorish pursuers almost up to the gates of Antequera. The Marqués of Cádiz made his way to safety with his fifty men, though no one knew where they were for several days. The Master of Santiago escaped as well, more by luck than by his own efforts. The Count of Cifuentes was captured and held for high ransom, along with some four hundred other noblemen. Nearly every great family in Andalusia named one of its own among the dead of Ajarquía, over eight hundred in all. In addition to the 400 noble captives, there were more than a thousand others, who if they could not be ransomed would be enslaved. It was the greatest Moorish victory of the war.[26]

Fernando was in Astorga far to the north, pacifying troubled Galicia; Isabel had to bear the blow alone. Never did her faith, her courage, her fundamental stability and inner strength show to better advantage. All during the first two weeks of April her letters flowed out to shocked, mourning Andalusia, where many of the principal public office-holders were missing in the disaster. On April 3 she directed that "for the duration of the absence of the Asistente" of Sevilla (that was the Count of Cifuentes, now a prisoner of the Moors), "so that there would be no innovation," all the subordinate officers he had appointed would remain in place.[27] On April 13 she directed that since Juan de Pineda, chief secretary of the *cabildo* (popular assembly) of Sevilla, had disappeared in the disaster and no one knew whether he was alive or dead, his son Pedro should assume his office.[28] She was ready to help in ransoming the captives, but firmly directed that the ransom be paid only in money, not in tangible goods of any kind which could be useful to the enemy in the war.[29] On April 10, writing to the Council of Sevilla, she gave them broader counsel. No document of Isabel's in all her life expressed more wisdom and goodness:

> From the letters of the Master of Santiago and the Marqués of Cádiz and the Governor-General and Don Alfonso de Aguilar, I know all about what happened with the Moors, which has greatly distressed me. But this is nothing new in war. In such matters we are in the hands of Our Lord. We may not and ought not do otherwise than give thanks to Him for everything. Truly, since this was done in service to Our Lord and for the exaltation of our Holy Faith, that is consolation for whatever death or loss may result from it. It pleases me to give the offices of those who died there [in the Ajarquía] to their sons or nearest relatives, because it is right for those who have lost fathers or relatives in this struggle to have the offices they held. But since some of these offices, according to the law of the Cortes of Toledo [in 1480] may not be so provided [to avoid concentrating too much power and wealth in a few noble families], and since that law may not be revoked for any reason, yet this situation is special, the King my lord is coming; he will be here this week, God willing, having pacified Galicia in our service. He and I will maintain the law [of the Cortes of Toledo] in effect, but suspend it in this case. I do not suspend it now, because the presence of His Majesty is necessary to give authority and deliberation to how this law is handled, and then to provide the offices as is needful. And

---

[26]This account of the disaster at Ajarquía is a collation and harmonization of the extensive descriptions of this event in all the principal chronicles, aided by the similar effort of Juan de Mata Carriazo in Menéndez Pidal, *Historia de España* XVII (1), 489-493. The original sources are: Bernáldez, *Memorias*, pp. 126-130 (ch. LX); Palencia, *Crónica*, III, 100-102 (Guerra de Granada, Lb III); Pulgar, *Crónica*, II, 63-69 (ch. CXLVI); Valera, *Crónica*, pp. 161-165 (ch. LI); Hechos del Marqués de Cádiz, CODOIN CVI, 218-224.

[27]Isabel to Council of Sevilla, April 3, 1483, *Tumbo de Sevilla*, III, 312.

[28]Fernando and Isabel to Council of Sevilla, April 13, 1483, *ibid.*, pp. 343-345.

[29]Pulgar, *Crónica*, II, 80-81 (ch. CXLIX).

I send to you Rodrigo de Ayala, friend of my dearest and much-loved son
the Prince, who has represented me for a long time in speaking with you. I
ask you to give him full faith and credit. I the Queen.[30]

Isabel was firm and unshaken, but the Moors were drunk with victory.
Boabdil, now ruling in Granada, was very much disinclined to let El Zagal
occupy the limelight of military fame alone. He decided to show what he could
do. (Since he had never been in a real battle, some had been wondering about
that.) He led an army north from Loja through the mountains to Lucena in
Castilian territory, hoping to take advantage of the shock effect of Ajarquía.
But it had not been Boabdil who won that battle; nor had the Count of Cabra,
whose domain he had now entered, fought in it. The Count of Cabra was a
competent general; Boabdil was not. Their armies met in country as familiar to
the Castilian defenders as Ajarquía had been to the Moors, if not as
geographically difficult. Though heavily outnumbered, the Count of Cabra
achieved total victory by surprise attack. Well over a thousand Moors were
killed. Just as Fernando had done at the Battle of Loja, Boabdil rushed among
his fleeing men trying unsuccessfully to rally them. But he lacked Fernando's
relentless fighting spirit, and had no Marqués of Cádiz to come to his rescue.
As his men scattered, Boabdil flung himself off his horse and tried to hide in a
briar patch. But his elaborately decorated, snow-white clothing made
concealment very difficult. Up came a foot soldier from Lucena, the town he
was trying to capture, named Martin Hurtado, waving a dagger in his hand.
Boabdil defended himself; Martin called for help, and his comrades gathered.
It then occurred to someone that this richly dressed prisoner might be
important, so they brought him to the Count. Weeping profusely, Boabdil
admitted that he was indeed the King of Granada.[31]

Boabdil was captured April 21; a week later, probably immediately upon
receipt of the news, Fernando departed for the south. Isabel could not
accompany him because she was completing the negotiation of a new treaty
with Portugal. Sufficient trust had now been re-established with this former
enemy so that neither Portuguese King John II nor Isabel any longer felt it
necessary for their own beloved children to be held hostage to each other's
good behavior. Portuguese Crown Prince Afonso and Princess Isabel of Castile,
intended to marry but too young to do so yet (Princess Isabel was 13, Afonso
eight), had been confined for two years in the castle of Moura. They were
under the loving care of Queen Isabel's aunt Beatriz, but that did not make the
separation much easier for either parent to bear, particularly since the records

---

[30]Isabel to Council of Sevilla, April 6, 1483 *Tumbo de Sevilla*, III, 319-320.
[31]Bernáldez, *Memorias*, pp. 131-134 (ch. LXI); Pulgar, *Crónica*, II, 70-72 (ch.
CXLVII); Palencia, *Crónica*, III, 103-105 (Guerra de Granada, Lb III); Agustín G. de
Amezúa de Mayo, *La batalla de Lucena y el verdadero retrato de Boabdil* (Madrid,
1915).

make it very clear how much King John of Portugal loved his son, and Queen Isabel of Castile her daughter. The solution was to annul the marriage treaty of September 1479, while leaving open the expectation that it would be renegotiated later, either for Princess Isabel and Prince Afonso when he was older, or for Afonso and Princess Juana, who was a year younger than the Prince. The treaties were signed May 15, and the prince and princess released May 24.[32]

Our sources do not tell us when and where Isabel met her daughter, whom she had not seen for more than two years. At the time of her release the Queen was in Burgos, the capital of Old Castile, while Moura was hundreds of miles away in southern Portugal. It would have been a long journey. But surely it was made as quickly as possible, and before the end of June Isabel and her daughter were reunited in Santo Domingo de la Calzada east of Burgos, where Isabel spent the summer.[33]

Abul-Hassan, upon hearing of Boabdil's capture, returned to Granada and resumed his rule over its whole kingdom. At the end of June, after Fernando had led a great military sweep through Granadan territory to Alhama and back, Abul-Hassan offered a truce to the Spanish monarchs. Fernando wrote to Isabel at Santo Domingo de la Calzada, asking her opinion of the offer. She recommended against accepting it, unless Abul-Hassan should be willing to give over several Granadan cities as security for keeping it (he was not). Boabdil's mother Zoraya—presumably no longer Abul-Hassan's favorite wife, but still a leading figure in the harem—offered a large ransom for her son. Fernando called Boabdil to meet him at Córdoba in August to discuss the truce offer. Boabdil swore he would be Fernando's faithful vassal if he were released. Asked his opinion, the Marqués of Cádiz favored Boabdil's release, saying it would keep the enemy divided. Isabel said she favored it if the liberation of a substantial number of Christian captives were made part of the ransom. Fernando thereupon made a treaty with Boabdil, releasing him and promising to support him against his father in return for a large ransom payment, the release of 400 Christian captives, and an oath of vassalage to him and Isabel. Fernando also promised Boabdil not to interfere with the practice of Islam in Granada and not to attack cities giving allegiance to Boabdil. Boabdil was released September 2 and returned to Granada.[34]

---

[32]Palencia, *Crónica*, III, 106 (Guerra de Granada, Lb III); "Acuerdo para anular los conciertos matrimoniales entre Isabel y Alfonso y suspender las tercerias," May 15, 1483, *Documentos referentes a las relaciones con Portugal durante el reinado de los Reyes Católicos*, ed. Antonio de la Torre and Luis Suárez Fernández (Valladolid, 1958-63), II, 262-268; Menéndez Pidal, *Historia de España*, XVII (2), 53; Elaine Sanceau, *The Perfect Prince* (Barcelos, Portugal, 1959), pp. 150-163, 172-173.
[33]Rumeu de Armas, *Itinerario*, p. 113.
[34]Pulgar, *Crónica*, II, 74-91 (ch. CXLVIII-CL); Menéndez Pidal, *Historia de España*, XVII (1), 509-515.

On September 17 a large raiding party of Moors made a substantial incursion into Christian territory between Zahara and Sevilla, raiding the fields around El Coronil and Utrera. The Marqués of Cádiz rushed up from Jerez de la Frontera to repel them, but when he arrived they had already been defeated at Utrera by Luis Portocarrero, relieved as commander at Alhama by Fernando in June. Nearly a thousand of the raiders were killed; the Marqués of Cádiz led the pursuit which harried them back to the frontier. It was a victory comparable to the Count of Cabra's at Lucena. Meanwhile Fernando had gone back north to rejoin Isabel, who was now at Vitoria in the Basque country. He brought the Count of Cabra with him, who was richly honored for his victory at Lucena and capture of Boabdil.[35]

The year 1483 was drawing toward its end, and the Marqués of Cádiz was feeling unlucky. For all his courage, he had barely survived the disaster at Ajarquía in March; he had missed the Battle of Lucena and the capture of Boabdil in April; he had accompanied Fernando in his march through Granadan territory to Alhama in June, but the Moors had then refused to come out and fight; now he had arrived too late for the Battle of Utrera. This was not nearly a good enough record to satisfy his martial spirit. So in October he undertook the recapture of Zahara, using virtually the same tactics he had employed the previous year to take Alhama. He approached the town stealthily at night with about two thousand men. At daybreak he ordered a diversionary assault on the city gate while personally leading thirty picked men up the walls on scaling ladders at a hidden corner. Incredible as it may seem that the Moors, who had captured Zahara because they had surprised its Christian defenders, would not have kept better watch, they did not detect the ladders or the men on them until they had entered the town and opened the gate. Scaling a well-defended city wall by a ladder was one of the most perilous operations in medieval and early modern warfare; to picture Spain's best general on top of one staggers the imagination. One firm push by an alert defender would have flung him to his death on the rocks below, depriving Isabel of her most capable commander. But the fiery redhead loved it, and within an hour his triumph was complete.[36]

Fernando and Isabel in Vitoria heard the news with joy and intense admiration for the Marqués de Cádiz. They compared him to Fernán González, one of the greatest heroes of the Reconquest, the central figure in a cycle of ballads that were known all over Spain. They gave him Zahara as his personal possession, and the next year they made him a Duke, the highest title of nobility, in a document which gave his recapture of Zahara as the principal

---

[35]Bernáldez, *Memorias*, pp. 145-148 (ch. LXVII); Pulgar, *Crónica*, II, 92-94 (ch. CLI); Palencia, *Crónica*, III, 115-116 (Guerra de Granada, Lb III).

[36]Bernáldez, *Memorias*, pp. 149-150 (ch. LXVIII); Hechos del Marqués de Cádiz, CODOIN CVI, 228-229; Menéndez Pidal, *Historia de España* XVII (1), 536.

158 ISABEL OF SPAIN

reason for granting him this great honor.[37]

When the twelve days of Christmas had passed, Fernando and Isabel left Vitoria for Tarazona in Aragon in the new year 1484, accompanied by Princess Isabel. The *cortes* of Aragon was meeting in Tarazona in February; they came to preside over the session and ask for funds both for the war on Granada and to recover Roussillon for Aragon from France. Louis XI, the wily "spider king" of France, had died the previous summer; his successor, Charles VIII, was only thirteen years old. Fernando's father, Juan II, had always maintained and sought to enforce his claim to Roussillon. But the *cortes*, convening February 12, resisted voting money for either purpose, while making demands of its own which tended to grow if any were granted; and the deputies from Catalonia, the area adjacent to Roussillon, were not even in attendance.[38] Six weeks passed with no progress made. The campaign season in Andalusia was at hand. Isabel, who had been absent from Andalusia for a year and a half, grew increasingly impatient. Without a substantial grant of funds from the *cortes* of Aragon, she and Fernando did not have the means to conduct both wars at once. (It did not occur to either of them to levy a war tax without the approval of the *cortes*. Neither Aragon nor Castile were royal absolutisms, no matter how many modern histories may say so.) They would have to choose. For Isabel, there was only one choice. The 762-year crusade of the Reconquest must be won, and won now.

Fernando did not agree. The Moors of Granada could be fought any time. The 1484 campaign against them could be foregone. But the opportunity to seize Roussillon from a young, untried French king who might not even have the capacity to rule might never come again. So Fernando held out for war against Roussillon—one of the few occasions, after the disagreement immediately following Isabel's coronation, when there was a public rift between the two of them.[39]

Isabel loved her husband very much, and submitted to him on all matters within the family; but this issue touched the heart of her understanding of her duty as Queen of Castile. Twenty-four generations of crusading forebears spoke through her as she took her stand:

> This is so just and so holy an enterprise that among all those of
> Christian princes there was none more honorable or more worthy, none

---

[37]Hechos del Marqués de Cádiz, CODOIN CVI, 231-234; decree of Fernando and Isabel naming Rodrigo Ponce de León Duke of Cádiz, August 16, 1484, Simancas Archives, Registro General de Sello, 1484-VII, folio 2.
[38]Pulgar, *Crónica*, II, 102-107 (ch. CLV); Palencia, *Crónica*, III, 117 (Guerra de Granada, Lb IV); Rumeu de Armas, *Itinerario*, p. 121; Menéndez Pidal, *Historia de España*, XVII (2), 59; Paul M. Kendall, *Louis XI, the Universal Spider* (New York, 1971), pp. 353-355, 369-374.
[39]Pulgar, *Crónica*, II, 113-115 (ch. CLVIII).

more likely to gain the aid of God and the love of the people. . . . Two years ago the war with the Moors began, in which great efforts were made and great preparations undertaken on land and sea, at immense cost. In view of all this, it appears unwise to lose all by beginning another war with the French.[40]

Whatever his decision, hers was made. She would go south, leaving some Castilian troops with Fernando, but using all the other resources of Castile to fight the long crusade. He would do as he thought best with the resources of Aragon. On March 24 she departed, reaching Toledo once again, as had become her custom, on Good Friday and staying through Easter Sunday (April 18 that year). She celebrated her thirty-third birthday on the road; early in May she rode through the Pass of the Overthrow of the Infidel Dogs, turning aside to visit the famous battlefield of Las Navas de Tolosa close to its southern entrance, where her ancestor King Alfonso VIII had repelled the last attempt of the Moors to break out of Andalusia and regain central Spain from the Christians in the year 1212. On May 15 she arrived in Córdoba, accompanied now by her children Juan, Juana, and Maria. The day before, Fernando had left Tarazona to follow her south, thereby tacitly acknowledging her decision to be correct. The *cortes* of Aragon had provided nothing; the projected war against Roussillon had been given up. On May 29, to her great joy, he joined her at Córdoba. The will of Isabel the crusader had prevailed.[41]

Once jointly committed, Isabel and Fernando now held nothing back from the struggle for Granada. They spent the next year and a half continuously in Andalusia, conducting fall as well as spring campaigns for the first time in both 1484 and 1485. French artillery experts were called in to speed the construction of the giant cannon of that day, known as lombards, which fired massive, roughly shaped balls of stone or marble (less frequently, of iron), some of them more than two feet in diameter and weighing as much as 165 pounds. No stone wall could withstand bombardment by such missiles for long; it was cannon such as these, in the hands of the Muslim Turks, that had finally smashed through the 40-foot-thick walls of Constantinople in 1453, unbreached in more than a thousand years. Beginning in the spring of 1484, the lombards became the key to the war against Granada; they were the decisive and irresistible weapon, once brought to the scene of action. It was not easy to transport these monsters over the primitive roads of southern Spain, but it was done under Isabel's constant prodding. While Fernando commanded in the field, it was her task to see that the army was kept supplied and the artillery kept moving. She

---

[40]*Ibid.* Indirect discourse converted to direct.

[41]Rumeu de Armas, *Itinerario*, pp. 122-124; Palencia, *Crónica*, III, 120-121 (Guerra de Granada, Lb IV); Pulgar, *Crónica*, II, 118 (ch. CLIX); Menéndez Pidal, *Historia de España*, XVII (1), 554.

discharged that duty as if she had been doing it all her life.[42]

The selection of the first major military objective for 1484 was made by the Marqués of Cádiz,[43] but it bears the personal stamp of Isabel as well—this relentlessly confident woman who would never accept defeat. The objective chosen was the town of Alora up the valley of the Guadalhorce River which flows into the sea very close to Málaga. It was near the wild broken country in which the disaster of Ajarquía had occurred; indeed, Alora was the first major town in the fertile valley of the Guadalhorce after it opened up out of the Ajarquía tangle. It would have been wholly characteristic of Isabel to have determined to wipe out the disgrace of the Christian defeat in Ajarquía by an equally stunning victory at the next major enemy strong point beyond its site.

This was certainly a vastly different operation from that of Ajarquía. The Castilian army consisted of no less than 30,000 men, supplied by an enormous number of ox-drawn carts assembled by Isabel. Other carts bore the immense weight of the lombards and their balls. On June 11 this overwhelming force reached Alora. By Isabel's orders a fully equipped field hospital was immediately set up in six large tents, with doctors, medicines, bandages, and attendants all supplied in advance and all medical care for the soldiers to be at her expense (a novelty in those days).[44] When the giant lombards opened fire, the effect was shattering in every sense of the word; Bernáldez tells us that "at their first firing [they] demolished a great part of the city and fortress."[45] Several of its towers fell; attempts to build a new wall behind the smashed portions were fruitless. Many of the defenders fled the city; the women and children, unable to flee, gave heart-rending cries and wails as the terrible bombardment continued, and their men pressed the garrison commander to surrender. On June 20 he did so. Down came the green banners with the Muslim crescent; up rose the red-and-gold banners of Fernando and Isabel, and the pennant of the crusade upon the highest remaining tower. Hard-bitten Luis Portocarrero was put in charge of the garrison left to defend Alora against any Moorish counterattack.[46]

Fernando immediately rode east, to ravage the *vega* right up to within sight of Granada, from which Abul-Hassan did not dare emerge, and to

[42]Ladero Quesada, *Conquista de Granada*, pp. 117-125; Pulgar, *Crónica*, II, 124-126 (ch. CLX); Townsend Miller, *The Castles and the Crown; Spain, 1451-1555* (New York, 1963), pp. 122-123.

[43]Hechos del Marqués de Cádiz, CODOIN, CVI, 240; Valera, *Crónica*, pp. 180-181 (ch. LVII).

[44]Pulgar *Crónica*, II, 120-121 (ch. CLX); Menéndez Pidal, *Historia de España*, XVII (1), 557.

[45]Bernáldez, *Memorias*, p. 152 (ch. LXXI).

[46]Pulgar, *Crónica*, II, 122-123 (ch. CLX); Palencia, *Crónica*, III, 122 (Guerra de Granada, Lb IV).

resupply Alhama once again.[47] The first fall campaign was then decided upon, with the main objective being Setenil near the frontier in the region of recaptured Zahara.[48] Setenil had never been taken by Christians; the Muslims had ruled it since the original Muslim invasion of Spain by Tariq, 773 years before. New roads had to be built to bring the lombards through rough country to Setenil, but they were quickly built under Isabel's constant urging. Once again it was she who organized the supply train, making sure the great army lacked for nothing essential; once again she set up her special, splendidly equipped field hospital. Once again the lombards overwhelmed the defense; Setenil surrendered September 21, ten days after it first came under attack.[49] Isabel came south from Córdoba to Écija, nearly halfway to the Granadan frontier, to celebrate the victory there with her husband. From Écija they made their way west across the broad Andalusian plain to beautiful Sevilla, where they intended to spend the winter together. They rejected all proposals for peace from Abul-Hassan, though accompanied by offers of large quantities of gold. For Isabel and Fernando were both now utterly resolved to accept nothing less than the total restoration of Christian rule in Spain by the reconquest of the entire kingdom of Granada.[50]

In August Pope Sixtus IV had died after a long and active pontificate of thirteen years. He had always been Isabel's friend; in February 1483 he had written her a warm and appreciative letter speaking in glowing terms of her love for the Faith, her orthodoxy, piety, and constancy.[51] He and she had agreed on nominating a bishop—Archbishop Manrique of Sevilla—to hear appeals from the procedures of the Inquisition, as a check on abuses. Pope Sixtus had approved, though somewhat reluctantly, the establishment of the Inquisition in Aragon in 1482, and in the fall of 1483 he had approved Torquemada provisionally as head of the Inquisition for all of Spain.[52] The new Pope, Innocent VIII (formerly Cardinal Cibò) was a well-meaning, good-natured but not particularly talented prelate very much under the influence of the powerful

---

[47]Pulgar, *Crónica*, II, 124-126 (ch. CLX).

[48]*Ibid.*, II, 126 (ch. CLX); Fernando and Isabel to the Council of Sevilla, August 8, 1484, *Tumbo de Sevilla* III, 495-496.

[49]Bernáldez, *Memorias*, pp. 154-155 (ch. LXXIV); Pulgar, *Crónica*, II, 127-128 (ch. CLXI); Palencia, *Crónica*, III, 132 (Guerra de Granada, Lb IV); Menéndez Pidal, *Historia de España*, XVII (1) 564-566.

[50]Pulgar, *Crónica*, III, 128-129 (ch. CLXI); Palencia, *Crónica*, III, 133 (Guerra de Granada, Lb IV).

[51]Pope Sixtus IV to Isabel, Feb. 23, 1483, in Vicente Rodríguez Valencia, *Isabel la Católica en la Opinion de Españoles y Extranjeros* [hereinafter cited as IOEE] (Valladolid, 1970), I, 51; Ludwig von Pastor, *History of the Popes* (St. Louis, 1914), IV, 386-388.

[52]Bull of Pope Sixtus IV, April 18, 1482, in Henry C. Lea, *A History of the Inquisition of Spain* (New York, 1906), I, 587-590; Menéndez Pidal, *Historia de España*, XVII (2), 220; Bernardino Llorca, *La Inquisición en España* (Barcelona, 1936), pp. 106-107.

Cardinal Giuliano della Rovere, whose failure to support the ambitious Spanish Cardinal Rodrigo Borgia had cost Borgia the election as Pope which he ardently desired.[53]   Probably on Torquemada's advice, Isabel wrote the new Pope in October asking him to authorize increases in the clerical staff of the Inquisition and greater freedom of action for them.   In November the Inquisition began operating in Valencia for the first time, and Fernando gave full vigorous support to the Inquisitors in Aragon despite protests against its in the *cortes* of Aragon, then meeting.[54]

There was a general assembly of the Inquisition at Sevilla in late November under the chairmanship of Torquemada. Soon afterward, evidently at least in part as a result of its deliberations, Torquemada promulgated a detailed set of instructions on just and proper Inquisitorial procedure.   In December Fernando dismissed Marimón, first Inquisitor for Catalonia, for harshness and injustice, replacing him with two chief Inquisitors who could check each other. All these developments clearly indicate that Isabel and Fernando intended to supervise the work of the Inquisition very closely and prevent any major abuse of its great powers. In this they had the full support of Torquemada. The new Pope appeared well satisfied with these actions, though Isabel had been initially concerned that he had would intervene in individual cases brought to his attention (as his predecessor had sometimes done), which Isabel thought improper at least until the Inquisition's arguments were heard in Rome.[55]

In January 1485 the *auto-de-fe* (act of faith) ceremony of reconciliation of first-offender heretics discovered by the Inquisition was held at Sevilla, followed by the burning at the stake of 19 relapsed or unrepentant heretics. This brought to about 500 the total number burned in Sevilla since the Inquisition was launched there in 1480. In all probability this was much the largest number of persons executed for heresy anywhere in Spain during these first years of the Inquisition's existence, since Sevilla held the largest concentration of *conversos* in Spain and the dangers the Inquisition was founded to deal with were most acute there. The next month Torquemada was confirmed by Pope Innocent VIII as the permanent Grand Inquisitor for all Spain.[56]

Fernando was still haunted by his defeat at Loja, where he had been so nearly killed. In January 1485 Ortega de Prado, who had organized the surprise attacks on Alhama and Zahara, presented him with a proposal to take Loja by

[53]Von Pastor, *History of the Popes*, V, 233-243.

[54]Menéndez Pidal, *Historia de España*, XVII (2), 224-229.

[55]Llorca, *Inquisición*, pp. 110-113; Lea, *Inquisition*, I, 571-575; Menéndez Pidal, *Historia de España*, XVII (2), 231; Isabel to the Church in Sevilla, Sept. 20, 1484, *Tumbo de Sevilla* III, 517-519.

[56]Palencia, *Crónica*, III, 139 (Guerra de Granada, Lb V); Menéndez Pidal, *Historia de España*, XVII (2), 223.

the same means. He tentatively agreed, with Isabel's approval, and led an army toward it; but he ordered it carefully scouted first. Alhama had been unprepared and the garrison at Zahara culpably careless, but Fernando's scouts found neither situation existing in bristling Loja, anchor of the central Genil valley which was the heartland of Granada. The city was closely guarded and firmly held. Cold rains beat down on the Christian army, which would make an attack even more hazardous. Wisely, though surely with some bitterness, Fernando called a retreat.[57]

But otherwise it was a happy winter for Isabel and her family; they were all there with her in Sevilla. So was her oldest and best friend, Beatriz, and her husband Andrés Cabrera; in January Beatriz bore her second child, a healthy daughter. Princess Isabel, at fourteen, was now old enough to accompany her father and mother on many more of their incessant activities; and we may well imagine that Queen Isabel, who had been deprived of any direct contact with her oldest daughter for two years, kept Princess Isabel as close by her as she possibly could. They went hawking together; when the Duke of Medina Sidonia (perhaps to show that he could be as charming as his old rival the Duke of Cádiz) held a magnificent feast in the woods of his ducal estate, Princess Isabel was a guest of honor along with the King and Queen. We are specifically told how much the fourteen-year-old princess enjoyed this occasion; it is good to know, for in her short life she had already experienced much sadness and deprivation, and was to know much more before it was over, all too soon.[58]

A shadow fell upon this family joy at the end of February when plague broke out in Sevilla. Severe contagious disease was as deadly as it was unpredictable in the fifteenth century. Doctors could do little or nothing for its victims; the connection between sanitation and health was unknown, unsuspected. A sudden visitation of pestilence could carry off the entire royal family. The best protection was to scatter. So the royal family left Sevilla, and after another splendid entertainment (this time by the Duke of Cádiz, not to be outdone, at his estate at Marchena east of Sevilla) Isabel went on to Córdoba with Princesses Isabel and Maria, while Juan was sent to the isolated castle of Almodóvar and Juana to Carmona. Fernando remained with her throughout March; it was then that their last child was conceived.[59]

In Córdoba they had an unexpected guest: Boabdil. The attempt to keep the Moorish realm divided through his agency had ended, at least for the time being, in failure. Expelled by the redoubtable El Zagal from his last stronghold, the coastal city of Almería far to the west, Boabdil had fled to the Christians, begging refuge in Córdoba. Isabel was never one to turn away a helpless

[57]Palencia, *Crónica*, III, 138-139 (Guerra de Granada, Lb V).
[58]*Ibid.*; Chronicle of Valladolid, CODOIN XIII, 156.
[59]Palencia, *Crónica*, III, 140 (Guerra de Granada, Lb V); Pulgar, *Crónica*, II, 146 (ch. CLXIX); Rumeu de Armas, *Itinerario*, p. 129.

suppliant, especially one who had sworn loyalty and friendship to her (though she was surely realistic enough to doubt Boabdil's commitment to his oaths). Boabdil was given the refuge he asked.[60]

But the main concern of Isabel and Fernando that Easter season of 1485 was the build-up for the spring campaign: the assembling of hundreds of the giant lombards, which had begun months before; the gathering of the men, the largest army so far, numbering at least 30,000 and possibly much more; and the gathering of the commanders—the Duke of Cádiz, the Duke of Medina Sidonia, Alonso Cárdenas the Master of Santiago, the Count of Cabra, and a new leader, two years younger in Isabel, destined to become the greatest captain of Europe, Gonzalo de Córdoba.[61]

Just at this moment, when she was totally occupied with her duties of seeing to the supply of the army and encouraging and inspiring its commanders, Isabel received word that a restive nobleman, Rodrigo Osorio, Count of Lemos, had attacked Ponferrada castle in Galicia far to the north, laying siege to it. This reminder of the perpetual internecine warfare of the nobles in the reign of Henry IV, with all its painful memories, stirred Isabel to a fierce anger which burned visibly behind her calm and controlled mask of disciplined royalty. Much as her heart was in the climactic struggle of the seven-century war of the Reconquest, she almost left it to go to Galicia to give Lemos a lesson in person. Finally concluding, reluctantly, that she must not leave Córdoba then, she sent strongly worded letters to the loyal noblemen of Galicia to bring an end to this aristocratic brigandage at once. Hearing by mid-April that Ponferrada castle had fallen to the predatory Count, she ordered it besieged and retaken without delay, and sent a letter directly to the Count ordering him to submit and establish the Holy Brotherhood in his domain to enforce law and order there.[62]

Within a day of Isabel's despatch of her letter to the Count of Lemos, the Christian army marched out of Córdoba, with Isabel working even harder to keep it supplied as it moved southward toward Alora in the valley of the Guadalhorce, captured the preceding year. Its first objective was the town of Benamaquis, whose people had taken an oath of allegiance to Fernando and Isabel the year before and broken it, along with torturing and killing Christian captives. It was decided to make an example of the town, which was burned to

---

[60]Palencia, *Crónica*, III, 141 (Guerra de Granada, Lb V).

[61]*Ibid.*, III, 140; Pulgar, *Crónica*, II, 146-151 (ch. CLXIX); Bernáldez, *Memorias*, pp. 155-156 (ch. LXXV); Menéndez Pidal, *Historia de España*, XVII (1) 578, 584. The name of Gonzalo de Córdoba is still often seen in its older (and outmoded) spelling of Gonsalvo.

[62]Palencia, *Crónica*, III, 148-149 (Guerra de Granada, Lb V); powers from Isabel and Fernando to Fernando de Acuña and Alonso de Quintanilla, April 11, 1485, in Simancas Archives, Estado Castillo, Legajo 1-2, folios 23, 53-54, 62; Isabel and Fernando to Count of Lemos, April 14, 1485, in Simancas Archives, Registro General de Sello, 1485-IV, folios 209 and 314.

the ground; at Fernando's orders, twenty out of every hundred men of military age in the town were slain. This severity was unusual in the Granadan war, despite the passions surrounding it; however it may be judged, it is significant that actions of this kind remained relatively rare, both before and after the punishment of Benamaquis.[63]

Beyond Alora and Benamaquis were Cártama on the Guadalhorce and Coín a few miles south of the river. Both were taken before the end of April, overwhelmed in hours by the smashing blows of the lombards. Fernando gave their people generous terms, on condition that their Christian captives were well treated; there were no more reprisals such as those at Benamaquis, and Fernando acted vigorously against those who took or tried to take personal vengeance on Muslims in Coín. The Christian army was now placed squarely between Málaga, the great port which was the second city of the kingdom of Granada, and Ronda, a substantial and well-fortified Moorish city in the east near the old frontier with Castile. The army could attack either Málaga or Ronda, or neither, simply raiding the *vega*. Isabel, writing to Fernando, made it very clear how strongly she felt that a campaign so well begun should aim at further major victories. El Zagal was in personal command at Málaga, which was very strongly defended; Fernando skilfully feinted in that direction, to draw some of the troops from the Ronda garrison to reinforce Málaga, and then turned on Ronda with the whole army.[64]

Ronda lies in an arid plain, topping two beetling cliffs that drop into a deep but narrow gorge spanned by an ancient stone bridge. A stream runs through the bottom of the gorge, but is inaccessible from the city itself due to the remarkable depth of the gorge.[65] The waters of an abundant spring outside the walls were led into Ronda by a hidden, underground passage; but the Duke of Cádiz knew where and what it was and blocked it at the outset of the siege. That alone would have sufficed for ultimate victory, for only a very few other limited sources of water were available to Ronda's defenders; but the lombards settled the matter sooner. In four days they broke down all the outer defenses, driving the Moors into the central city, which was then bombarded in its turn. A great ball of fire was flung into it as well. It was all over in ten days. The Moors asked for terms, and Fernando was generous: all who wished to leave the city for Granada or Africa were allowed to go, with whatever possessions they could carry, provided they left within fifteen days; those remaining were granted full pardon and all their possessions if they would swear loyalty to Fernando and

[63]Pulgar, *Crónica*, II, 153-154 (ch. CLXX); Palencia, *Crónica*, III, 142 (Guerra de Granada, Lb V).

[64]Pulgar, *Crónica*, II, 154-164 (ch. CLXX-CLXXI); Palencia, *Crónica*, III, 142-143 (Guerra de Granada, Lb V); Valera, *Crónica*, pp. 188-189 (ch. LX).

[65]This description is based on personal observations by the writer.

Isabel. Most chose to leave. On Pentecost Sunday Fernando entered the city.[66]

About 400 Christian captives were liberated at Ronda. They went to Córdoba to give their personal thanks to Isabel. She received them with Princess Isabel at her side. They kissed the hands of the Queen and Princess with reverence and went in procession to the cathedral; afterwards Queen Isabel asked them all to eat with her, and gave them money. The captives included about forty women, and a Moor who was baptized. The chains with which they had been held captive were sent by Isabel's order to the church of San Juan de los Reyes which she had built in Toledo to commemorate the victory in the Battle of Toro that won her War of the Succession with Portugal. They were hung upon its outside walls, where they remain to this day.[67]

Isabel granted Ronda to a gentleman of her house, Antonio de Fonseca, and had its chief mosque converted into the Church of St. Mary of the Incarnation. Other mosques in Ronda were made into churches of the Holy Spirit, the Apostle St. James, the Apostle St. John the Evangelist, and St. Sebastian. She contributed substantial funds to beautify them all. On June 2 the feast of Corpus Christi was celebrated in Ronda for the first time since the original Muslim conquest more than seven centuries before; the presiding bishop, Luis de Sona, had been designated for Málaga as soon as it should be reconquered. A great fiesta followed, with music and song; it was continued the following day on the estates of the Duke of Cádiz at Arcos de la Frontera. The Moors were then still departing in accordance with the surrender terms; when some of them were harassed by the Spanish, robbing their goods and seizing their women, Isabel intervened personally to punish the offenders and return the stolen goods. Fernando ordered the walls of Ronda rebuilt, with some lombard balls fired during the siege to be placed on top of them as mementoes of the great victory.[68]

He then marched back to the Guadalhorce River where the campaign had begun, securing all the coast west of Málaga (now the world-famous fashionable strand of the Costa del Sol, whose best-known resort is Torremolinos). He approached Málaga; but El Zagal was still there with a formidable force, the Spanish army had suffered the attrition inevitable in any substantial campaign, and Fernando decided he was not yet strong enough to assault this heavily defended city. El Zagal made no move to expose himself, but he was still dangerous. After Fernando and his army had returned to Córdoba, El Zagal led a force of a thousand past Alhama. The overconfident Spanish garrison attacked him with less than 200 men, and lost half of them. Meanwhile the

---

[66]Pulgar, *Crónica*, II, 165-172 (ch. CLXXII); Palencia, *Crónica*, III, 144-146 (Guerra de Granada, Lb V); Bernáldez, *Memorias*, pp. 157-160 (ch. LXXV).

[67]Bernáldez, *Memorias*, p. 161 (ch. LXXV); Pulgar, *Crónica*, II, 188 (ch. CLXXV).

[68]Bernáldez, *Memorias*., pp. 161-163 (ch. LXXV); Pulgar, *Crónica*, II, 174, 190 (ch. CLXXII, CLXXVI).

plague had ceased its ravages in Spanish Andalusia, so all Isabel's children rejoined her in Córdoba, where they welcomed Fernando's return in a manner befitting his triumphs, with another round of great public celebrations and joy unconstrained. A full report was made to Pope Innocent VIII on all that had been accomplished.[69]

The contemporary historian Pulgar memorably sums up the spirit which animated the brilliant Ronda campaign of the spring of 1485—a spirit developed primarily by the character and leadership of Isabel:

> You may well believe from all that is recorded in this chronicle, that the great lords and knights and captains who served the King and Queen in this campaign had a special love of service to God and to them. This showed itself in the full obedience they gave to the commands given them, because from this obedience of each one individually came the grand concord of all of them together; and from this concord came good understanding and wisdom to deal with whatever happened. Giving themselves to their work, and giving good example to others willing to work, the glorious outcome was attained that we have described.[70]

As they had been the year before, Isabel and Fernando were resolved on a fall campaign in 1485. Though some advised against it, the Duke of Cádiz was strongly in favor, and on July 31 the summons went out to Sevilla and many other cities to bring up men and supplies to assemble at Écija on August 30 to march once more against the hereditary foe.[71] Early in September the Count of Cabra decided to cross the frontier mountains for a bold attack on the strong fortress of Moclín, just fifteen miles northwest of Granada, even closer to it than Alhama; but he walked into a trap set by El Zagal and was badly defeated, losing nearly a thousand men. El Zagal ordered many of the bodies decapitated. The defeat was shocking, particularly after such great success earlier in the year. Fernando reprimanded the Count of Cabra for his recklessness, and he and Isabel promptly left Córdoba to go to Baena, about 25 miles northwest of Moclín over the mountains, to be closer to the scene of action.[72]

Cardinal Mendoza urged that the fall campaign be called off, except for resupplying Alhama, but Isabel would not hear of this. Some new conquest must be made; but it should be more easily attainable than Moclín, the goal of

---

[69]Pulgar, *Crónica*, II, 178-179, 185-189 (ch. CLXXIV-CLXXVI); Palencia, *Crónica*, III, 150-151 (Guerra de Granada, Lb V).

[70]Pulgar, *Crónica*, II, 188 (ch. CLXXV).

[71]Pulgar, *Crónica*, II, 192 (ch. CLXXVIII); Palencia, *Crónica*, III, 151 (Guerra de Granada, Lb V); Isabel and Fernando to the Council of Sevilla, July 31, 1485, *Tumbo de Sevilla*, IV, 28-30.

[72]Pulgar, *Crónica*, II, 193-194 (ch. CLXXVIII); Palencia, *Crónica*, III, 152-153 (Guerra de Granada, Lb V); Menéndez Pidal, *Historia de España*, XVII (1), 613; Rumeu de Armas, *Itinerario*, p. 134.

the Count of Cabra's overambitious venture. The frontier post of Cambil, on the northern slope of the boundary mountains just fifteen miles from the Spanish city of Jaén, was selected as the objective. Fernando laid siege to Cambil September 16, while Isabel—now six months pregnant—came to Jaén with Princess Isabel and Prince Juan and Cardinal Mendoza, and remained there throughout the campaign. Cambil, embedded in rugged mountains, was well fortified and quite strongly held. To take it, the lombards would have to be brought up; but the mountain roads in the region of Cambil were in no condition to permit their passage. Cambil was so close to Jaén that Isabel, without entering a combat zone, could still observe the problem personally. She supervised the search from a better route; when it was found, with the aid of a shepherd, she assembled no less than six thousand men to build a new road to convey the lombards to Cambil. Once they had arrived, it was all over; the fortress surrendered in 24 hours, the Christian army entering on September 23.[73]

During that month of September the "old king," Muley Abul-Hassan, died in Granada.[74] Of much more concern to Isabel would have been the assassination by a group of *conversos* of Peter Arbues, one of the chief Inquisitors of Aragon, while he was praying before the Blessed Sacrament. As he fell to the floor under the slashing of the assassins' knives, Arbues cried out: "Praised be Jesus Christ; I die for his Holy Faith!" Mortally wounded, he lived 24 hours, praising Christ, without a word against his murderers.[75] Peter Arbues and his work did not come under Isabel's direct jurisdiction, since he was in Aragon; but she surely would have believed him a martyr, as did the Catholic Church, which later canonized him.

Within two weeks of the triumphant entry into Cambil, Fernando and Isabel headed north, leaving Andalusia after the longest continuous stay in one area in their entire reign. Isabel's time for childbirth was approaching; she had decided to await it in Alcalá de Henares in central Spain, near Madrid. It turned out to be a very fortunate choice, for that year in Castile it rained almost every day in November and December, causing unprecedented flooding; but Alcalá was in high country and unaffected. Surrounded by her whole family, with Cardinal Mendoza in personal attendance, Isabel gave birth to the last of her children there on December 15, 1485: Catherine, whom the family always called Catalina.[76]

It was well that the three older children could not see, as they stood round

---

[73]Pulgar, *Crónica*, II, 195-200 (ch. CLXXVIII-CLXXIX); Palencia, *Crónica*, III, 153-154 (Guerra de Granada, Lb V).

[74]Bernáldez, *Memorias*, pp. 165-166 (ch. LXXVII).

[75]For a full critical account of the background, circumstances, and consequences of this much discussed event, see Llorca, *Inquisición en España*, pp. 139-154.

[76]Pulgar, *Crónica*, II, 203-204, 209-210 (ch. CLXXXI-CLXXXII).

their mother's bed to behold the tiny squalling form of their newborn sister, what lay ahead for them: Isabel, now fifteen; Juan, now seven; Juana, now six. (Maria, age three, would only slightly have understood the occasion.) All but Maria were marked for tragedy; only Catalina was marked for heroism. If she were not a history-maker to match her mother, it was only because no other woman since the Blessed Virgin Mary ever matched her mother as a history-maker. For Catalina was to be "Catherine of Aragon," the pure and dauntless wife of Henry VIII of England, heroine of history's most famous divorce, which split the English-speaking peoples (with the sole exception of the Irish) from the Roman Catholic Church for nearly five hundred years and still counting.

The royal family spent more than two months at Alcalá de Henares with the new baby. Just over a month after Catalina's birth, on January 20, at the special request of Fray Antonio Marchena, head of the Franciscan monastery of La Rábida at Palos on the south coast of Spain and a noted astronomer and cosmographer, they received in audience a Genoese sailor they had never met before, who was called in Spanish Cristóbal Colón, and signed his name in Latin Christopher Columbus.[77]

Columbus and Isabel were of exactly the same age, and very similar in appearance and character, though he lacked her calmness and unfailing good judgment in dealing with people. Both had strikingly fair skin and blue eyes. Columbus' hair had originally been close to the red-gold color of Isabel's, but had been bleached almost white by sun and sea. Both were tall, strong in their bodily constitution, brilliant in their minds, highly articulate, with a commanding presence and striking personal attractions. Far more significant than any of this, both were profound, devoutly believing Catholics.[78] Of this epochal meeting we have only Bernáldez's infuriatingly brief and vague account, written many years later on we know not what authority:

> And so Colón came to the court of King Fernando and Queen Isabel, and told them what he had imagined, to which they did not give much credit, and he talked with them and told them that what he said was true, and showed them his world map, arousing in them a desire to know those lands [of which he spoke].[79]

But subsequent history makes it clear that a spark was struck between

[77]Paolo Taviani, *Christopher Columbus; the Grand Design* (London, 1985), pp. 169-172; Juan Manzano Manzano, *Cristóbal Colón; siete años decisivos de su vida, 1485-1492* (Madrid, 1964), pp. 55-60.

[78]Samuel Eliot Morison, *Admiral of the Ocean Sea* (Boston, 1942), pp. 86-87; Robert H. Fuson, tr. & ed., *The Log of Christopher Columbus* (Camden ME, 1987), pp. 16-17. It is no part of the purpose of this biography to enter the thorny tangle of controversy over Columbus' alleged Jewish ancestry. Most historians at least agree that, whatever his ancestry, he himself was a totally committed Catholic.

[79]Bernáldez, *Memorias*, p. 270 (ch. CXVIII).

Isabel and Columbus on that cold January day in Alcalá de Henares, kindling a fire which the Queen never allowed to go out. She knew virtually nothing of navigation and seamanship; she could not herself judge Columbus' claims and his project. In the midst of the final struggle for the age-old goal of reconquering all Spain from the infidel, she had little time and money to spend then on an enterprise to open up a new route to Asia over the unknown western ocean. What impressed her was the man—for she was a superlative judge of men. This was a man like none she had met before, a man with a vision and a mission, overmastering, overwhelming, who had an absolute confidence that he could triumph over all odds if only given the opportunity to begin. Isabel knew and well understood that kind of confidence; all her life she had had it herself, and had achieved her goals against odds as great in her own world as any this poetic mariner would encounter in his uncharted seas.

Before coming to Spain in the early spring of the preceding year,[80] Columbus had presented his project—to reach Asia, specifically Japan (Cipangu) by sailing westward around the world—to King John II of Portugal and his court, Portugal having been Europe's leader at sea since the days of Prince Henry the Navigator. But King John and his scientific and maritime experts had rejected Columbus' proposal, for the very good reason that his estimate of the size of the earth was absurdly small (indeed, it was the smallest purportedly scientific estimate of the size of the earth ever made).[81] It had to be, to give his enterprise any prospect of success. No ship known or imaginable to the fifteenth century—not even the best of all its exploring vessels, the caravel as improved and put into use by Prince Henry—could have come close to crossing the enormous waste of waters that would have stretched from Spain to Japan had America not been in the way. Every man aboard would have died of starvation before they had gone much more than half the distance.

But Columbus felt his mission as a divine calling. He had taken to himself the prophecy of the ancient Roman writer Seneca, in his *Medea*: "An age will come after many years when the Ocean will loose the chains of things, and a huge land lie revealed; when Tiphys will disclose new worlds and Thule no more be the ultimate."[82] He would go where no man had ever gone before; he would pull aside the curtain that had enclosed the known world from the beginning of history, the unbroken horizon of the River Oceanus that none before him had ever dared to pierce. Not for him the coasting along known or even unknown shores, the gradual progress of the Portuguese caravels around Africa toward India. He would strike direct into the blue, span the ocean and reach the goal. He would become Admiral of the Ocean Sea, bringing untold glory to the country and its sovereign who had the vision and the courage to launch him.

---

[80]Manzano, *Cristóbal Colón*, pp. 37-38.
[81]Morison, *Admiral of the Ocean Sea*, pp. 65-69.
[82]*Ibid.*, p. 54.

Above all, he would give glory to God by his achievement, and win for Him thousands and even millions of souls in the far lands beyond where the Gospel had ever penetrated.[83]

Columbus' conviction that those far lands were there and could be reached derived not only or even primarily from his inaccurate geography or that of the Florentine scholar Toscanelli who endorsed his project, but from his own observations of the trade winds blowing from east to west in the latitude of the Canary Islands and the prevailing westerlies blowing in the opposite direction to the northward, together with the reports he had gathered of strange plants, unfamiliar carved wooden objects, and even two bodies of men of non-European race, that had washed ashore on the coasts of islands in the open Atlantic—Porto Santo near Madeira, and the Azores.[84]

Columbus' audacity, his perseverance, his constancy, and his obvious competence in his profession all would have contributed to the ineffaceable impression he made upon Isabel. Fernando gave no indication of special interest, but Isabel acted immediately. She directed her treasurer, Alonso de Quintanilla, to provide for Columbus' personal maintenance; she introduced Columbus to Cardinal Mendoza; and she set up a special commission, headed by her own saintly confessor, Fray Hernando de Talavera, to consider his project. But government commissions, then as now, moved very slowly; this one, with a much lower priority for the busy men who composed it than anything to do with the war of reconquest against Granada, did not even meet for the first time until the last months of the year 1486.[85]

On February 22 Isabel and Fernando left Alcalá de Henares. They went first to Madrid, where Fray Marchena of La Rábida came personally to speak with them about Columbus and his mission, urging them to give it active support.[86] Then they went on to Medina del Campo via familiar Segovia, with its treasury of memories good and bad for Isabel. Arriving at Medina on March 10, Isabel at once took in hand the continuing problem of the Count of Lemos in Galicia; she officially proclaimed him a rebel and sent the Count of Benavente, hero of the War of the Succession, against him.[87] Meanwhile,

---

[83]John S. Collis, *Christopher Columbus* (London, 1976), pp. 45-49.

[84]Taviani, *Columbus*, pp. 127-163, 383-388, 393-427; Morison, *Admiral of the Ocean Sea*, pp. 54-65, 78. The elaborate hypothesis of the nineteenth-century French writer Henri Vignaud, that Columbus never intended to reach Asia but only undiscovered Atlantic islands, and that the Toscanelli letters were forged later, has been repeatedly and decisively refuted by Morison, Taviani, and other respected historians they cite; yet still it lives on in some quarters because of the seemingly indestructible popularity of "debunking," almost for its own sake, among both professional historians and popular writers.

[85]Manzano, *Cristóbal Colón*, pp. 67-79; Morison, *Admiral of the Ocean Sea*, pp. 87-88.

[86]Rumeo de Armas, *Itinerario*, p. 137; Taviani, *Columbus*, p. 172.

[87]Pulgar, *Crónica*, II, 211-212 (ch. CLXXXIII); Rumeu de Armas, *Itinerario*, p. 138.

Boabdil had finally gained some success in Granada; early in March there had been a rising in his favor, perhaps stimulated by the harshness of the rule of the fierce warrior El Zagal, in full control since Abul-Hassan died; after a two months' struggle the two agreed to divide the kingdom, though with El Zagal retaining the title of emir. Boabdil got the western portion, facing Castile, and went to Loja to rule from there.[88]

On April 4 Isabel and Fernando left Medina del Campo together, travelling south. They made their first stop at Isabel's birthplace, Song of the High Towers. They directed their journey so as to spend Isabel's thirty-fifth birthday at the shrine of Our Lady at Guadalupe, always a particular favorite of theirs. On April 28 they returned to Córdoba, ready for the spring campaign, which was launched on May 19.[89]

The largest Spanish army so far assembled in the war against Granada, consisting of 12,000 cavalry, 40,000 infantry, 60,000 animals and 2,000 carts which Isabel had collected to bear the artillery, had gathered at the Yeguas River. They were joined for the first time by substantial numbers of fighting men from other nations of Christendom, who had heard of their crusade and wanted to be a part of it. Anthony Woodville, Lord Scales, brother of a past and uncle of a future Queen of England, had come with 300 men, including 100 bearing the famous English longbow.[90]   Isabel wrote a short letter of fond farewell to Fernando, which has been preserved; she tells him tenderly that she kisses his hand a hundred thousand times for all the care he has taken of her, and promises unceasing prayers that God may help him to victory and guard him from danger.[91]

The objective of this mighty crusading host was Loja, the great dark fortress against its long rock ridge which had defied so many Christian assaults, where Fernando had had his closest brush with death. Some still thought Loja too strongly defended and dangerous to attack, but Fernando and the Duke of Cádiz were sure its time had come at last. The whole army knew that Isabel back in Córdoba was praying night and day for their success; knowing her holiness, they were immensely confident in the power of her prayers. Never had her prestige among them stood so high; her constant care for the wounded, her fine and firm hand upon their supply line, keeping them equipped with all they needed wherever they might go, were now known and honored by every soldier.[92]

[88]Ladero Quesada, *Conquista de Granada*, p. 42.

[89]Rumeu de Armas, *Itinerario*, pp. 138-139; Palencia, *Crónica*, III, 160, 162 (Guerra de Granada, Lb VI); Isabel and Fernando to the Council of Sevilla, May 12, 1486, *Tumbo de Sevilla*, IV, 106-108.

[90]Pulgar, *Crónica*, II, 213-214 (ch. CLXXXIV); Menéndez Pidal, *Historia de España*, XVII (1), 642-644.

[91]Isabel to Fernando, May 18, 1486, in Rodríguez Valencia, IOEE III, 115.

[92]Palencia, *Crónica*, III, 166 (Guerra de Granada, Lb VI); Pulgar, *Crónica*, II, 215

As soon as the Christian army arrived before Loja, the defenders sallied; a pitched battle raged for eight hours on May 24, inflicting nearly a thousand casualties on the Christians. The foreign crusaders were in the thick of the fight; Lord Scales was wounded. But when it was over, the sally had failed; the Christian army had not yielded an inch. Isabel gave thanks to God for the victory, glorying in the heroism of her crusaders, in another letter to Fernando May 30. Now the lombards were brought up. Four days later their irresistible bombardment began. Through a full day and two nights the giant stone and marble and iron missiles hammered down the walls of Loja. Then the Moors surrendered on the now customary terms, with all who wished to do so allowed to leave with whatever property they could take with them. Boabdil came out with hanging head, full of shame, and flung himself down to kiss Fernando's feet. In Córdoba, Queen Isabel and Princess Isabel went together to the cathedral to give thanks for the victory.[93]

The Christian army now marched up the Genil River toward Granada, taking Illora on the way; but their next major objective was Moclín, where El Zagal had inflicted the severe defeat on the Count of Cabra the preceding year. Shortly after Loja was secured, Fernando had written Isabel, asking her for the first time to come to the war zone. She agreed at once, while doing her best to console the wounded in Córdoba who did not want her to leave them. She came with Princess Isabel, a splendid escort, and her most trusted counsellors, including Gonzalo Chacón and Gutierre de Cárdenas, and Diego Hurtado de Mendoza, the Archbishop of Sevilla.[94] At Archidona, which had been the last Castilian town before reaching the old Granadan frontier near Loja, the Duke of Cádiz met her; he had prepared a great feast in an open field. Isabel said to him: "It seems, Marqués [he still preferred his old title despite having been given a greater one], that the fields from which you come are full of joy. You have merited great honor, and the king my lord and I will give you great rewards." She wore a brocaded dress, with ornaments of silver and gold, as they dined at the Spanish dinner hour in the early afternoon; then she went on to captured Loja, which the Duke showed her.[95]

The next day, June 11, she met Fernando at Illora at the head of his army,

(ch. CLXXXV); Historia de los Hechos del Marqués de Cádiz, CODOIN CVI, 251-253.

[93]Pulgar, *Crónica*, II, 220-226 (ch. CLXXXVI-CLXXXVII); Palencia, *Crónica*, III, 164-166 (Guerra de Granada, Lb VI); Bernáldez, *Memorias*, pp. 167-168 (ch. LXXIX); Menéndez Pidal, *Historia de España*, XVII (1), 648-650. For Fernando's own crisp account of the reduction of Loja, see his letter to the Council of Sevilla, May 29, 1486, *Tumbo de Sevilla*, IV, 119-120; Isabel's letter to him of May 30 is in Rodríguez Valencia, IOEE III, 116-117.

[94]Pulgar, *Crónica*, II, 231-232 (ch. CLXXXIX); Valera, *Crónica*, pp. 206-207 (ch. LXVIII).

[95]Hechos del Marqués de Cádiz, CODOIN CVI, 257-258.

greeted by a grand chorus of musical instruments; on June 13 they moved on to Moclín, where a tent was set up for Isabel on a high hill overlooking the town, its fortress still held by the enemy, and the countryside all the way to Granada in the distance. Moclín fortress (much of which remains quite well preserved today) crowns a huge hummock of rock with massive protuberances that make natural redoubts. The view from it, or from any of the hills in the area, is magnificent, especially to the south, where sharp-pointed ridges and circling foothills gradually drop away to the beautiful green-and-yellow *vega* rolling like sea waves across the broad valley of the Genil to Granada in the distance, under its mighty sierra.[96] It was as though the whole kingdom Isabel the crusader had come to reconquer was laid out at her feet. From this vantage point, for the first time she could actually watch what she may well have thought of as her lombards, for whose transportation and supply she had taken such care, brought up to do their work. They hammered the walls; when the walls proved unusually resistant, the decisive blow was inflicted by a primitive shell—a huge stone hollowed out and filled with powder, apparently discharged by a fuse. The Moors then surrendered on the now-familiar terms.[97] On June 23 the small town of Montefrío offered to surrender specifically to Isabel; she came the next day to accept it.[98]

At the end of June Isabel returned to Córdoba, where she rejoined her younger children (Princess Isabel had accompanied her all the way on the journey to Loja and Moclín) and prepared a splendid reception for her husband when he arrived a few days later with the Duke of Cádiz.[99] On June 30, Pope Innocent VIII delivered his personal congratulations to the Castilian ambassador in Rome for the great victory at Loja.[100]

The kingdom of Granada had lost nearly half its territory—all that was readily accessible from Castile. Spanish troops now held strong points within sight of its two principal cities, Granada and Málaga. The war was not over; every Moor now knew that the survival of their kingdom was at stake, and though they had surrendered many cities, they were not yet ready to surrender their country. Years of struggle remained. But end of the longest crusade was in sight. While Isabel the Catholic lived, it would not fail.

---

[96]Based on personal observations by the writer.

[97]Hechos del Marqués de Cádiz, CODOIN CVI, 259; Pulgar, *Crónica*, II, 234-235 (ch. CXC); Valera, *Crónica*, p. 208 (ch. LXVIII); Jerónimo Münzer, *Viaje por España y Portugal, 1494-1495*, tr. José López Toro (Madrid, 1951), p. 55.

[98]Chronicle of Valladolid, CODOIN XIII, 163; Hechos del Marqués de Cádiz, CODOIN CVI, 260.

[99]Hechos del Marqués de Cádiz, CODOIN CVI, 260-261.

[100]Pope Innocent VIII to the Count of Tendilla, June 30, 1486, in Rodríguez Valencia, IOEE I, 55-56.

7
Crusade Triumphant
(July 1486-January 1492)

The costs of the campaign which had culminated in the victories of Loja and Moclín had been exceptionally great; there were no nearly sufficient resources for any major new military effort against the Moors in 1486. Isabel stayed at Jaén until her friend Beatriz de Bobadilla (now the Marquesa de Moya) gave birth on July 16 to a son. Then she and Fernando departed for the north, leaving their children in Jaén under the care of Beatriz and her husband, Andrés de Cabrera. They went to wild, green Galicia in the northwestern corner of Spain, at the request of the Count of Benavente. For the rebellion of the Count of Lemos continued despite the best efforts of the Count of Benavente, and only Isabel in person could quench it. And she had never, during all of her reign, visited Galicia, the most remote and difficult of access of all her domains; only there had her reforms not taken root, so that commands from afar were no substitute for her personal presence.[1]

At the end of August the royal couple arrived at Ponferrada castle, which the Count of Lemos still held against their will. Upon their arrival he submitted unconditionally, asking their pardon, while berating the Count of Benavente. Isabel paid no attention to Lemos' complaints about his fellow Count. She pardoned Lemos, while ordering him to stay out of Galicia for some time, to pay for an indefinite period the costs of the troops she would now maintain there to keep the peace, and to make restitution to all he had robbed. She kept the title to Ponferrada castle in her hands, while providing to Lemos' two daughters an income equivalent to their share in it. This problem settled once and for all, in the middle of September Isabel and Fernando went on to Santiago de Compostela, the most famous shrine in Spain. They prayed at its chapel and gave it rich donations, while Isabel sat in judgment on local troublemakers, condemning some but pardoning many. Four months later they

---

[1]Fernando del Pulgar, *Crónica de los Reyes Católicos*, ed. Juan de Mata Carriazo (Madrid, 1943), II, 243 (chapter CXCIII), 245 (ch. CXCV); Alonso de Palencia, *Crónica de Enrique IV*, Volume III (Biblioteca de Autores Españoles, Vol. 273, Madrid, 1975), pp. 169-170 (Guerra de Granada, Libro VI); Chronicle of Valladolid, in *Colección de documentos inéditos para la historia de España* (CODOIN), XIII (Madrid, 1848), pp. 163-164.

gave special new instructions for keeping the pilgrimage route to Santiago open and protected. During October, passing through some of the wildest regions of Galicia, they went on to the distant, isolated seaport of La Coruña, with Isabel administering justice and making special provisions for the maintenance and protection of the Church there. On November 2, coming back southward into the plains of León, they reached Salamanca, where they settled down for the winter, turning over the more complex legal issues and cases Isabel had felt she should not settle on the spot, to the learned jurists of the famous university there.[2]

At Salamanca that winter, Fray Hernando de Talavera's commission met to consider the strange project of the red-haired Genoese sea-captain Cristóbal Colón, Latinized as Columbus. Hernando de Talavera was a holy priest and a genuine statesman; Isabel was later to nominate him as bishop of Granada as soon as it had at last been reconquered from the infidel. But he knew little if anything of geography and navigation. Nor were there many in Spain who did. Except for their conquest and colonization, one by one, of the Canary Islands (originally discovered by Italians and first settled by Frenchmen), Spain had not been active in maritime ventures, far surpassed in that area by both the Portuguese and the Italians. Whatever intellectual resources Castile could bring to bear on Columbus' project were probably concentrated at the University of Salamanca, but we know almost nothing about the members of Talavera's commission; we have only two of their names—Rodrigo Maldonado, a writer and diplomat, and Andrés de Villalón, mentioned by Columbus in two letters many years later. Columbus was there to explain his plans and his theories; but if the maritime experts of King John II of Portugal had known too much to accept his largely erroneous geography, Talavera's commission knew too little. They seem to have had almost no idea what Columbus was talking about. Their discussions with him bore no fruit during the three months Isabel and Fernando were in Salamanca, and we have no hint of whether Isabel saw or communicated personally with Columbus during that period.[3]

Isabel and Fernando left Salamanca for Andalusia late in January 1487. Already preparing for the 1487 campaign against Granada, they sent for the Duke of Cádiz to meet them to discuss it as soon as they should arrive in Córdoba. They arrived March 2, to be reunited with their children there. Columbus came as well, with the royal party or shortly after it. The very next

---

[2]Antonio Rumeu de Armas, *Itinerario de los Reyes Católicos, 1474-1516* (Madrid, 1974), pp. 143-145; Pulgar, *Crónica*, II, 246-248 (ch. CXCV); Palencia, *Crónica*, III, 170, 173-174 (Guerra de Granada, Lb VI); Ramón Menéndez Pidal, director, *Historia de España*, Volume XVII: "España de los Reyes Católicos," ed. Luis Suárez Fernández and Manuel Fernández Alvarez (Madrid, 1969), Part 2, p. 156.

[3]Juan Manzano Manzano, *Cristóbal Colón; siete años decisivos de su vida, 1485-1492* (Madrid, 1964), pp. 70-80; Taviani, *Columbus*, p. 442.

day the Duke of Cádiz came in with trumpets sounding. Riding to the palace where Isabel and Fernando were staying, he saw them watching him from a window. He went in and knelt before them; they raised him up, seated him on a richly decorated chair, and talked for three hours about the coming campaign. Their discussions continued regularly for the next twelve days.[4]

All were agreed that the port city of Málaga, second only to Granada in population and strength of fortifications in the entire Moorish kingdom, was the logical and inevitable primary objective for the 1487 campaign. It lay exposed to Christian attack from both the north and the west, thanks to the victories they had won earlier in the war. Málaga could be blockaded from the sea, but unless the attackers had a naval base nearby, the blockade would be porous. Isabel was present at the conference at which it was decided to seize nearby Vélez Málaga first. It would provide the needed naval base close by, and its defenses were not nearly as formidable as those of Málaga itself. Since Isabel's instinct was always to push on quickly to the greater and higher goal, and her opinions carried great weight even in a military council, evidently this time she was convinced by the arguments for the more cautious policy. It was probably the Duke of Cádiz who convinced her; she had great faith in his ability and judgment as a commander, and this was the course he recommended.[5]

They had much to do that year; the campaign began exceptionally early. On April 7 Fernando left Córdoba with an army of 20,000 horse and 50,000 foot.[6] He had been with Isabel continuously ever since the fall of Loja the previous June, and seems to have found it harder than ever to part from her, as is attested by his brief but passionate letter to her April 8, bemoaning only a single night alone away from her and already speaking of the great joy which will be theirs when they meet again.[7] Holy Thursday fell on April 12 that year; the army built a wooden church in the field for Holy Week, adorning the altar with rich cloths, and a solemn Mass of the Last Supper was said by Juan Bermúdez, who had been a priest in the Canary Islands. Heavy rains fell, making it difficult to bring up the essential artillery, but on Easter Monday, April 16, the siege of Vélez Málaga began. The next day Fernando repulsed an afternoon sally of 2,000 Moors personally, sword in hand.[8]

---

[4]Chronicle of Valladolid, CODOIN XIII, 165-166; Isabel and Fernando to the Council of Sevilla (Salamanca, Jan. 10, 1487), in *El Tumbo de los Reyes Católicos del Concejo de Sevilla*, ed. Juan de Mata Carriazo, Volume IV (Sevilla, 1968), pp. 175-176; Hechos del Marqués de Cádiz, CODOIN CVI (Madrid, 1893), pp. 264-265; Taviani, *Columbus*, p. 468.

[5]Pulgar, *Crónica*, II, 260-261 (ch. CXCVIII); Hechos del Marqués de Cádiz, CODOIN CVI, 267-268.

[6]Pulgar, *Crónica*, p. 260 (ch. CXCVIII).

[7]Fernando to Isabel, April 8, 1487, in Vicente Rodríguez Valencia, *Isabel la Católica en la Opinion de Españoles y Extranjeros* (IOEE) (Valladolid, 1970), III, 124.

[8]Hechos del Marqués de Cádiz, CODOIN, CVI, 268, 275; Pulgar, *Crónica*, pp. 262-

In the face of this threat El Zagal and Boabdil temporarily buried their differences in Granada, and El Zagal set out from there with a large force to relieve Vélez Málaga.[9] Reports of his coming flew ahead of him, reaching Isabel in Córdoba as quickly as they reached Fernando before Vélez Málaga. Isabel instantly called up all men in Andalusia between twenty and sixty to take arms as foot soldiers and militia, and prepared to lead them personally to Fernando's rescue, while Cardinal Mendoza set to work assembling more cavalry.[10]

El Zagal's goal was to destroy the indispensable siege artillery, which could not be quickly moved; but before he could get to it, Fernando sent the Duke of Cádiz and Gutierre de Cárdenas out to make a surprise night counterattack on his force before it had even reached the siege lines. They struck on the night of April 25; when dawn showed the Christian army still pressing on up the mountain slopes after them, the Moors fled, dropping their weapons.[11] El Zagal's prestige, previously high despite the Moorish reverses, suffered a drastic drop; before the month was over there was an uprising against him in Granada, and he was driven out of the city and forced to take refuge in Almería, the only remaining Moorish seaport besides threatened Málaga. Boabdil took over in Granada, maintaining an appearance of friendliness with Isabel and Fernando despite the war, justifying himself to them by arguing that his people would not allow him to make peace, though he himself wished to do so, and that they should not attack the Granada area until he had consolidated his control. (They were not planning to do so in 1487 in any case, since Málaga was their principal objective that year.) Boabdil then sent the mayor of Granada to Vélez Málaga to negotiate a new treaty for him with Isabel and Fernando. It guaranteed Boabdil extensive lands in the eastern part of the kingdom of Granada and houses and income in the city of Granada for him and for his chief followers, in return for his delivery of city and kingdom to Isabel and Fernando. The treaty provided for them to cooperate with Boabdil against El Zagal, and gave Isabel and Fernando reason to hope that the upcoming Málaga campaign might bring a victorious end to the entire war.[12]

---

266 (ch. CXCVIII, CXCIX); Chronicle of Valladolid, CODOIN XIII, 167.

[9]Palencia (*Crónica*, III, 180 [Guerra de Granada, Lb VII]) gives El Zagal 1,000 horse and 20,000 foot; Mosén Diego de Valera, *Crónica de los Reyes Católicos*, ed. Juan de Mata Carriazo (Madrid, 1927), pp. 224-226, gives him twice that number.

[10]Pulgar, *Crónica*, II, 276 (ch. CCI).

[11]*Ibid.*, II, 271-276 (ch. CCI).

[12]*Ibid.*, II, 277-278 (ch. CCI); Andrés Bernáldez, *Memorias del reinado de los Reyes Católicos*, ed. Manuel Gómez Moreno and Juan de Mata Carriazo (Madrid, 1962), pp. 174-175 (ch. LXXXII); Palencia, *Crónica*, III, 180 (Guerra de Granada, Lb VII); Chronicle of Valladolid, CODOIN XIII, 168; letter of Boabdil to Isabel (Granada, April 29, 1487), in Miguel Garrido Atienza, *Las Capitulaciones para la Entrega de Granada* (Granada, 1910), pp. 169-170; Miguel Angel Ladero Quesada, *Castilla y la conquista del Reino de Granada* (Granada, 1967), pp. 49-50.

There was now no hope of relief for the Moors in Vélez Málaga. When the inevitable cannonade began the very day of El Zagal's defeat, the defenders at once sued for peace. Fernando granted it to them on the usual terms—the city and all Christian captives to be delivered up; the defenders allowed to choose whether to stay or go and, if they went, to take with them anything they could carry.[13]

On April 28 the Christian army entered Vélez Málaga under the flag of the Crusade, with trumpets blowing and the cry: "Castile, Castile for King Don Fernando and for Queen Doña Isabel, our lord and lady!" The chief mosque in the town was proclaimed the Church of St. Mary of the Incarnation. The next day there was a victory parade, featuring 75 liberated Christian captives who came before the king in procession with many priests and friars, singing "*Te Deum laudamus*" and kissing Fernando's hand. He immediately sent them on to Isabel at Córdoba. She received them in another procession, with her daughter Princess Isabel beside them, greeting each one individually and giving each a gold florin.[14]

Meanwhile Fernando wasted no time in moving on Málaga from newly taken Vélez Málaga. On May 7 the siege of Málaga began, with the whole army encamped at the edge of its suburbs and the artillery being brought in by sea. Málaga's fortifications were immense; though ancient, they were in good condition, and the crowning castle, known as the Alcazaba, had no less than eighty towers on its walls. Fernando sent the city a summons to surrender; its commander, Hamet Zeli, fired back with: "I have not been entrusted with this city to surrender it, as the king asks, but rather to defend it." El Zagal had selected Hamet Zeli for this post, and of the two contenders for the Moorish crown he was clearly the more aggressive and resolute, despite the failure of his attempt to relieve Vélez Málaga. Furthermore, a substantial group of fanatical Muslim warriors known as *gomeres* had come over from North Africa to join the garrison, resolved to fight to the death if necessary to prevent the Christians from capturing the city.[15]

Hard fighting began immediately. The Christians fortified their camps, while the navy pressed a close blockade. More of the huge lombards were brought in, with their stone ammunition. A separate siege was mounted of the great fortress called Gibralfaro castle, a few miles away from Málaga, but it held out no less strongly despite the fact that the Duke of Cádiz was personally in charge of its siege. Moorish sallies inflicted heavy casualties on the Christians.

[13]Bernáldez, *Memorias*, p. 176 (ch. LXXXII); Pulgar, *Crónica*, II, 278-280 (ch. CCII).
[14]Bernáldez, *Memorias*, p. 176-177 (ch. LXXXII); Pulgar, *Crónica*, II, 278-279 (ch. CCII); Valera, *Crónica*, p. 233.
[15]Pulgar, *Crónica*, II, 281-284 (ch. CCIII, CCIV); Chronicle of Valladolid, CODOIN XIII, 169.

During the first week, no significant progress was made. This was nothing like the much easier sieges of Loja and Moclín the previous year, and Vélez Málaga this year. The soldiers and even some of the noblemen, frustrated and depressed, began to spread discouraging rumors. Plagues were spreading, new Moorish rescue expeditions forming, the defenses were impregnable. Then, on May 15, came the most discouraging rumor of all: their heroine Queen had decided the undertaking was too much for them. She had written to Fernando asking him to raise the siege. The Moors heard this report almost as soon as the Castilian soldiers, and rejoiced.[16] They knew by now only too well what manner of adversary they faced in this unique woman crusader, a kind of monster in their eyes, for in their society women were hidden behind their veils and took no part (or, at least, never openly) in affairs of state, to say nothing of warfare. But hers was the relentless, driving will behind six long years of the war against their kingdom of Granada, that would never give up until their last foothold on the soil of Spain was wrenched away from them. Behind Isabel the Catholic rode the ghosts of vanished King Roderick of the Battle of the Guadalete River 776 years before, of Pelayo who stood at his last redoubt at Covadonga 765 years before crying "This little mountain shall be the salvation of Spain!", of the 24 generations of her royal forebears who had been engaged in the longest crusade. Had it been her idea to bring up to Málaga from Algeciras some of the ancient cannon used by Alfonso XI the Avenger 150 years before, to take Gibraltar?[17] If this woman would retreat and thereby give the Moorish garrison of Málaga a reprieve, they had done well indeed.

Fernando heard these rumors, both from his own and the enemy's camp. He knew what they meant, knew how powerful was the impact on their military operations of his wife's personality and commitment, both in legend and in reality. It says much for Fernando—whose personality most historians have not found attractive, and which did have dark corners—that not only did he not resent that impact, he welcomed it and never stood in the way of magnifying it. Most men, especially in that age, would have wanted to keep for themselves the glory of the capture of the second largest city remaining in enemy hands in Spain, rather than sharing it with their wife. But Fernando loved Isabel—no one who reads his letters to her, especially the one sent at the beginning of this campaign (already mentioned) can doubt that; he admired her as much as he loved her, knowing what she had already done and how much more she could do, and being honest and realistic enough to recognize it; he never hesitated to call upon her when he truly needed her, as she never hesitated to call upon him likewise. He called upon her now. On May 15 Fernando wrote Isabel asking her to come in person to disprove the rumors, hearten their army, and

---

[16]Pulgar, *Crónica*, II, 295-296 (ch. CCVII).
[17]*Ibid.*, II, 292 (ch. CCV).

dishearten the Moors. Gutierre de Cárdenas wrote to her at the same time, to the same effect.[18]

Six days later Isabel was in the camp before Málaga. She brought with her Princess Isabel, Beatriz, Gutierre de Cárdenas' wife Teresa, Cardinal Mendoza, her confessor Hernando de Talavera, and many other clerics and ladies. She was received with surpassing enthusiasm; everyone wanted to come at once to "kiss her hand," so much so that she had to remind the eager soldiers to be sure to leave sufficient men at the lines on guard duty. Word of her coming spread like wildfire; within a few weeks, noble volunteers began arriving from as far away as Catalonia, at the other end of Spain, because they heard that Isabel had come to camp and announced that she would stay there until Málaga was gained. That same word had long since gone out to the Moors. In the ensuing days she visited many of the strong points along the besieging lines, often guided by her husband or by the Duke of Cádiz.[19]

Oak-hearted Hamet Zeli was publicly unmoved, but clearly undermined; shortly after Isabel's arrival, he felt it necessary to issue an order that anyone proposing the surrender of Málaga be killed or mutilated, and the penalty was enforced in the ensuing days. The besieged in Málaga could not reasonably expect help from their fractured countrymen, though many nevertheless clung to the hope of it; El Zagal was now based far away in Guadix, on the other side of the high mountains behind Granada, and Boabdil was clearly not about to move outside the sheltering walls of that city when his grip on it was so insecure and he wished Isabel and Fernando to continue to think that he was personally well disposed toward them.[20] Isabel's continued presence, with her promise to stay until Málaga fell, hung like the legendary sword of Damocles over the heads of its hard-pressed defenders.

The fanatical *gomeres* from Africa saw only one solution: to kill her, and Fernando with her.

Abraham Algerbi of Tunisia volunteered to be the assassin, claiming he was acting at the command of an angel of God. He and several others showed themselves at a Spanish outpost early on a June evening. Algerbi let himself be captured, and was brought before the Duke of Cádiz. He was a little old man, who did not seem to the Duke to be dangerous; he said he had a message that God had commanded him to deliver only to the King and Queen, that Málaga would fall in seven somethings, but he would not say whether they were hours, days, weeks, or months. The Duke informed Isabel and Fernando, and was told

[18]Pulgar, *Crónica*, II, 296 (ch. CCVII); Valera, *Crónica*, p. 247; Hechos de Marqués de Cádiz, CODOIN CVI, 281.

[19]Bernáldez, *Memorias*, pp. 182-183 (ch. LXXXIII); Pulgar, *Crónica*, II, 296-297 (ch. CCVII); Valera, *Crónica*, pp. 247-248; Hechos de Marqués de Cádiz, CODOIN CVI, 281-283.

[20]Pulgar, *Crónica*, II, 298, 302, 307-308 (ch. CCVII, CCIX, CCXII).

they would see the Moor. But when Algerbi's guards finally brought him to the neighborhood of the royal tent, Fernando, exhausted by his labors that day, had fallen asleep, and Isabel, always careful never to exclude her husband in matters of state, said she would not see Algerbi until Fernando had awakened, and refused to wake him up.

At Isabel's suggestion, Algerbi was taken to the tent shared by her old friend Beatriz and Philippa, wife of Alvaro of Portugal, son of the Duke of Bragança who was cousin to King John II of Portugal. Philippa was absent for the moment when the guard brought Algerbi in; Beatriz and Alvaro were playing cards. Also in the tent were the royal treasurer, Rodrigo López of Toledo, and Fray Juan de Belalcázar. Beatriz and Alvaro were richly dressed, and Algerbi, who spoke no Spanish, assumed they were the King and Queen. His chest was heaving and his eyes rolling. Beatriz thought he looked frightened; she called for some food to be brought to him, and water to drink (knowing that devout Muslims would take no alcoholic beverage). Then, from beneath his long flowing robe, Algerbi whipped out a scimitar, the wickedly curved sword of the Moors, and swung it in a whistling cut at Beatriz.

Beatriz de Bobadilla, Marquesa de Moya, lithe and dark-eyed, had been at Isabel's side, almost her shadow, for thirty years, ever since they had been little girls together on the meadows of Arévalo. She was intelligent and quick-witted; she had been in life-and-death situations before, in the deadly intrigues during the reign of Henry IV, and when she governed turbulent Segovia at her husband's side. Her alertness and lightning-fast reactions saved her life that night, and would have done credit to the Duke of Cádiz himself. Somehow she saw the slashing scimitar out of the corner of her eye and threw herself flat on the floor; it sliced into her clothing but never touched her body. Algerbi turned to swing at Alvaro, who seems to have been as slow as Beatriz was fast; he took a near-mortal wound in the head. Beatriz got up and dived for the entrance to the tent. Algerbi swung at her again, but wildly; his scimitar caught in the tent cloth. Beatriz emerged unharmed into the night air, shouting for Isabel; the guard rushed into the tent, where they found the impeturbable friar Juan de Belalcázar had dropped the assassin to the ground with a tackle from behind, and Treasurer López had already struck him with his sword. The guard dispatched him instantly. A moment later Fernando rushed up, wrapped in a sheet, and Isabel at his side. They gave thanks to God for Beatriz's escape—and for their own.[21]

---

[21]The attempted assassination of Isabel and Fernando by Abraham Algerbi before Málaga in June 1487, one of the most dramatic moments of the war against Granada, is recounted at length by all the major historians of that war. The account given in the text is a collation and harmonization of these accounts, found in Pulgar, *Crónica*, II, 314-316 (ch. CCXVI); Palencia, *Crónica*, III, 188-189 (Guerra de Granada, Lb VII); Valera, *Crónica*, pp. 258-259; Bernáldez, *Memorias*, p. 185 (ch. LXXXIV); and Peter

In all probability Fernando, at least, did not forget this shocking proof of the malignity of their enemy. Though there is no proof that it influenced the exceptionally harsh surrender terms he ultimately imposed upon Málaga, humanly speaking it may well have done so.

On June 22 the besiegers held a council of war. The participants told Fernando that the siege was going well; after a temporary shortage of powder and shot, there were now some 25 of the giant stone cannon-balls available for each lombard, and plenty of powder. Reinforcements of soldiers were steadily coming in. The Duke of Cádiz urged that they press forward, though with caution. One breach had been made in the walls of the city; there should be others before a general assault was launched. Isabel agreed. The besiegers held the initiative, and there were no more rumors of retreat.[22]

A month passed. Hunger gripped Málaga now; Hamet Zeli, tough fighting man though he was, had neglected to plan and prepare for a long siege without relief. On July 29 the Duke of Cádiz reported that the Moors in Málaga were dying of hunger, coming out to surrender in increasing numbers; he estimated that the city could not hold out much more than two weeks longer. On August 3 Treasurer López took a key tower on the walls, from which he opened a breach and was contacted by some of the Moors who wanted to surrender. Others were calling for negotiations. Hamet Zeli and the *gomeres* still fiercely rejected all thought of capitulation, and the commander even threatened to kill everyone in the city but the fighting men; this only caused more, including fighting men, to come out and give themselves up. But when at last Ali Dordux, a rich man of Málaga, undertook formal negotiations on his own authority, he found Fernando only reluctantly willing even to promise the defenders their lives. The Duke of Cádiz supported him in calling for harsh punishment of the Moors of Málaga, so that Moorish fortresses in the future would not hold out to the last.[23]

By August 14 the defenders were at their last extremity, and Ali Dordux and his supporters seized the Alcazaba, expelling the raging Hamet Zeli, who still would not hear of negotiation, but whom most would no longer follow. But Fernando was now almost equally implacable; he indicated that all the inhabitants would be enslaved or held to ransom. A threat to kill all the Christian captives if he did not grant better terms was met with the steely response that in that case he would kill them all. Wailing, starving, desperate,

Martyr de Anglería to Cardinal Arcimboldi of Milan, Oct. 29, 1488, *Documentos inéditos para la Historia de España* (DIHE), published by the Duke of Alba et al, Volume IX (Madrid, 1955), pp. 98-99.

[22]Valera, *Crónica*, p. 260; Pulgar, *Crónica*, II, 303-306, 311-312 (ch. CCXI, CCXIV).

[23]Valera, *Crónica*, pp. 264-265; Pulgar, *Crónica*, II, 321-322 (ch. CCXIX); Bernáldez, *Memorias*, pp. 189-192 (ch. LXXXIV, LXXXV); Hechos de Marqués de Cádiz, CODOIN CVI, 287.

left with no other choice, the Moors surrendered Málaga on August 18. Fifteen thousand people were still in the city when it surrendered. Isabel and Fernando chose Fray Juan de Belalcázar (the priest who had brought down the assassin) to plant the cross, the royal banner, and the pennant of Santiago on the highest tower of the Alcazaba.[24]

Harsh and unyielding in negotiation over Málaga, Fernando and Isabel were relatively merciful in victory. Large quantities of food were brought into the city the moment the gates were opened. Ali Dordux and eight of his relatives were given their freedom and full pardons. All who could pay the relatively small ransom of 36 ducats within sixteen months were allowed to escape slavery, and some of the others were exchanged for Christian prisoners. Isabel took many of the women into her personal service.[25]

The ancient diocese of Málaga, which had existed in Roman times but had not been functional for more than seven hundred years, was restored, and Pope Innocent VIII accepted Isabel's nomination of Pedro de Toledo, a highly regarded canon of Sevilla, to be its bishop.[26]

Eleven days after the surrender of Málaga, Christopher Columbus was summoned to the conquered city and given the bad news that Hernando de Talavera's commission had decided not to recommend or support his projected voyage across the western sea, which it regarded as impossible. However, Isabel and Fernando did not reject Columbus completely, but urged him not to lose hope and to await a time when they were less preoccupied with the great war against Granada.[27] The climactic struggle of the longest crusade was not a good time for Columbus to be presenting to the Spanish court so strange and apparently visionary a venture; but something about Columbus still appealed to Isabel, and she would not abandon him.

Portugal was less distracted. In this same month of August King John II sent one of his best captains, Bartolomeu Dias, south along the coast of Africa with the usual instructions, first given in the time of his great-uncle Prince Henry the Navigator, to go beyond the farthest south of the last explorer of that coast, Diogo Cao who had passed the mouth of the Congo River and sailed all the way to Walvis Bay in Namibia (Southwest Africa). Less than a thousand miles further south—though no man knew it yet—the long southward reach of the Dark Continent ended at last, and the ocean gateway to the fabulous Orient, that Columbus wished to seek in the west, lay open. On December 8 Dias passed Walvis Bay. In January, after many days battling a furious storm

---

[24]Palencia, *Crónica*, III, 193-196 (Guerra de Granada, Lb VII); Pulgar, *Crónica*, II, 327-331 (ch. CCXXII); Valera, *Crónica*, pp. 266-269, 271.
   [25]Palencia, *Crónica*, III, 196 (Guerra de Granada, Lb VII); Pulgar, *Crónica*, II, 335-336 (ch. CCXXIII); Valera, *Crónica*, p. 268.
   [26]Palencia, *Crónica*, III, 198 (Guerra de Granada, Lb VII).
   [27]Taviani, *Columbus*, pp. 186, 443; Manzano, *Cristóbal Colón*, pp. 105, 108-110.

beyond the sight of land, he came back north to find the coastline trending a little north of east. He had rounded the Cape of Good Hope without knowing it; he sighted it only on his return voyage, after his men had forced him to turn back in March at the coast of Natal in South Africa. In December 1488 Dias returned to Lisbon; Columbus' brother Bartholomew was there at his arrival, and actually had an opportunity to examine his navigation chart.[28]

There was unrest in Aragon that fall and winter; Fernando went to Zaragoza in November with Queen Isabel, their daughter Princess Isabel, and Prince Juan. The Inquisition and the Holy Brotherhood were established there, to apply in that kingdom the medicine so effectively applied earlier, at Isabel's urging, in Castile. In December Pope Innocent VIII, assuredly with Isabel's encouragement and probably at her suggestion, gave her confessor Hernando de Talavera, Bishop of Avila, and the bishops of Córdoba, Segovia, and León instructions and full powers to reform the Benedictine, Cistercian, and Augustinian monasteries in long-troubled Galicia.[29]

In January, still at Zaragoza, Isabel and Fernando wrote to the Duke of Cádiz that because of pestilence in Córdoba and the exhaustion of their commanders and troops, there would be no major campaign against Granada in 1488. We do not know the full explanation for this highly uncharacteristic lapse in perseverance by the crusading royal couple. Perhaps it was a product of Fernando's desire to stay longer in his native Aragon until he was sure it was well in hand, perhaps a rare moment of discouragement in Isabel herself. Whatever the cause of the lapse in will, it was fleeting, and vanished utterly when the Duke of Cádiz wrote back at once emphatically counselling against any such reprieve for the enemy. A year without a campaign, he explained to his sovereigns, would give the Moors time to recover their strength. Pestilences were usually short-lived, he reminded them; the one now raging in Córdoba should be gone when the spring campaigning season had arrived. Castile still had sufficient resources for a campaign, and so did he personally. He promised 50,000 *fanegas* of wheat and 50,000 of barley for the army from his own stock, along with a substantial gift of gold, silver, and jewels for the campaign, which he likened to a "holy pilgrimage." Isabel was moved to tears by the Duke's generosity and ardor; she and Fernando told their court "that all the emperors and Christian kings have not raised up a more knightly *caballero* than we have in the Marqués of Cádiz" and resolved then and there on a 1488 campaign

---

[28]Bailey W. Diffie and George D. Winius, *Foundations of the Portuguese Empire, 1415-1580* (Minneapolis MN, 1977), pp. 156, 160-161; Taviani, *Columbus*, p. 189.
    [29]Rumeu de Armas, *Itinerario*, p. 156; Pulgar, *Crónica*, II, 337-340 (ch. CCXXIV); Pope Innocent VIII to the Bishps of Avila, Córdoba, Segovia, and León (Rome, Dec. 11, 1487), in José García Oro, *La Reforma de los Religiosos Españoles en tiempo de los Reyes Católicos* (Valladolid, 1969), pp. 143-147.

against Granada. However, it would not be conducted on the western and northern approaches to Granada, as all their other campaigns had been, but rather on the eastern side, in the region of Almería where the dangerous El Zagal ruled. The Christian army would assemble at Lorca on May 5.[30]

From Aragon, Isabel and Fernando went with their whole family and Cardinal Mendoza to Valencia, historically a separate kingdom in Spain, where they called a *cortes*, restored the rule of law where it had been challenged, and obtained 75,000 pounds for the upcoming campaign against Granada.[31] Back in Zaragoza, Peter Martyr de Anglería, an Italian scholar who had recently moved to Spain because the unity and good order of the Spanish realm contrasted so strikingly with the internecine strife and lawlessness of Renaissance Italy, wrote to a friend back in Italy that Isabel and Fernando were so close as almost to be animated by a single spirit and to think with a single mind.[32]

On April 26 Isabel and Fernando, with Prince Juan and Princess Isabel, arrived at Murcia, the capital of the province adjoining the Moorish kingdom of Granada to the east. They were welcomed at Murcia with the greatest enthusiasm, but Prince Juan soon came down with fever and dysentery there. In mid-May the Duke of Cádiz arrived at Lorca with a splendidly arrayed army under a banner proclaiming "Hope in the Faith." At the end of May Fernando took command of 4,000 horse and 15,000 foot to march on Vera, a town close to the coast and just over the mountainous border of the kingdom of Granada. The Duke of Cádiz kept Isabel regularly informed by letter on the progress of the campaign. On June 10 Vera surrendered; in his third letter to Isabel the Duke gave thanks to God for their many victories.[33] She replied:

> Your splendid works and loyal services have brought me great glory and pleasure. The wish and desire you have to serve the King my lord and me is apparent from your work and the signal good you have done. You deserve great rewards and will receive them, through the life-time of the King my lord and me. I would be especially pleased and well-served if you would write to me at length on the events of each passing day.[34]

Fernando proceeded from Vera to Almería, but was unable to take that large and well-defended city with the limited forces at his disposal for this campaign. He was no more successful against equally well-defended Baza, and

[30]Hechos de Marqués de Cádiz, CODOIN CVI, 291-294.

[31]Pulgar, *Crónica*, II, 341-342 (ch. CCXXV); Manuel Ballesteros Gaibrois, *Valencia y los Reyes Católicos* (Valencia, 1943), p. 14.

[32]Peter Martyr de Anglería to Pomponio Leto (Zaragoza, March 23, 1488), DIHE IX, 10.

[33]Chronicle of Valladolid, CODOIN XIII, 174; Rodolfo Bosque Carceller, *Murcia y los Reyes Católicos* (Murcia, 1953), pp. 154-155; Hechos de Marqués de Cádiz, CODOIN CVI, 296-298, 301-304; Palencia, *Crónica*, III, 205 (Guerra de Granada, Lb VIII).

[34]Hechos del Marqués de Cádiz, CODOIN CVI, 300.

the Moors were beginning to counter-attack in force against isolated strongholds held by the Christians. On July 16 Fernando rejoined Isabel in Murcia; the 1488 campaign against Granada at an end.[35]

On August 1 the royal family departed for Valladolid,[36] and on that day Peter Martyr de Anglería reviewed Isabel's character and achievements for Cardinal Ascanio Visconti:

> In my judgment, this woman cannot be compared with any of the queens honored by antiquity; she is brave, lofty and worthy of praise in her undertakings. . . . She gives an admirable example of honesty and modesty, something very rare in one unconstrained; she is endowed with a prudence beyond the limits of the imaginable. She rules by right much greater and more powerful realms than her husband. In all of them she has brought good order; but she rules in such a way that she always seems to act in full accord with her husband, since all decrees and documents are published with the signature of both. . . .
>
> United in consummate prudence, little by little they drew innumerable cities out of the jaws of the wolves, from the hands of the nobles—who, with the compliance of King Henry, had usurped the greater part of the realms of Castile—thus forming a unified body politic from many bits and pieces. To a degree never known until then, they established peace and harmony in both parts of Spain, so that no region, even if secure, could boast of ever having had greater security. They banished rioting and civil tumults which had seethed everywhere, not only in the villages but also in the cities. They freed the highways from the ambushes of thieves and the violence of highwaymen. They restored shattered justice and strengthened wavering faith, giving them solid support and removing all corruption.[37]

The glowing tributes paid to Isabel by Peter Martyr de Anglería for his international audience show how Spain, once looked down upon by most of Europe as a kind of backward poor relation, was emerging as a world power. Practical testimony to that was given by the eagerness with which sovereigns and their diplomats were now seeking marriage treaties with Isabel's and Fernando's children, even the youngest. Princess Isabel had already been promised to Prince Afonso of Portugal, but in this year 1488 preliminary agreements were made for the marriage (years hence, when they would be old enough) of Princess Juana to Prince Philip of Burgundy, heir to the Low Countries and the Holy Roman Empire, and of Princess Catherine to Arthur, eldest son of the new king of the new dynasty now ruling England, Henry VII Tudor. Early in 1489 the agreement that Catherine would marry Prince Arthur was adopted in permanent form as part of the Treaty of Medina del Campo,

---

[35]Rumeu de Armas, *Itinerario*, pp. 160-161; Pulgar, *Crónica*, II, 350-351 (ch. CCXXVII); Palencia, *Crónica*, III, 209-212 (Guerra de Granada, Lb VIII).

[36]Rumeu de Armas, *Itinerario*, p. 161.

[37]Peter Martyr de Anglería to Cardinal Ascanio Visconti, August 1, 1488, DIHE IX, 40-41.

which created a defensive alliance between Spain and England, with neither party to make peace or alliance with the common enemy, France, without the approval of the other.[38]

Meanwhile, Christopher Columbus had heard from his brother in Lisbon of the return of Bartholomew Dias from the epochal voyage during which he had at last rounded the southern tip of Africa, opening the gateway to the Orient that Prince Henry the Navigator had begun seeking some seventy years before. After his rejection by the Talavera commission, Columbus had hoped for a reconsideration soon, since Isabel had told him not to lose hope; then he sought an opportunity to present his "grand design" once more to King John II of Portugal. But there had been no suggestion of any immediate further interest by Isabel and Fernando in his project, and Dias' success made it virtually certain that the next great Portuguese expedition would be to follow his route all the way to India. So Columbus turned his thoughts and dreams to France, and began planning to go there to appeal to the French court of young King Charles VIII. But Fray Marchena, the prior of La Rábida monastery in Palos where Columbus had arrived late in 1485, a rejected and almost penniless wanderer, still believed in him, as he had ever since first talking with him. He urged him to seek out a noble patron who might revive his interest at court. The Duke of Medina Sidonia was not interested, but the almost equally wealthy and influential Duke of Medinaceli was. Medinaceli wrote to Isabel and Fernando requesting them to reconsider Columbus' project, along with offering to supply himself, if necessary, the three ships Columbus was asking for.[39]

The letter from the Duke of Medinaceli arrived soon after Isabel and Fernando had returned to Córdoba April 13 to launch the 1489 campaign against Granada. Thereupon Cardinal Mendoza took Columbus' side, along with one of Isabel's most trusted and long-serving officials, Alonso de Quintanilla, and Rev. Diego de Deza, a former professor of theology at the University of Salamanca who was now tutor to Prince Juan. On May 12 Columbus was recalled to court, and Isabel and Fernando sent out a letter commanding that he and his party be given food, lodging and maintenance, without cost to him, as he made his way to Córdoba.[40]

Leaving Córdoba May 18, probably before Columbus could reach it in

[38]Pulgar, Crónica, II, 357-360 (ch. CCXXXI); indenture agreement between Spanish ambassador De Puebla and English commissioner Richard, Bishop of Exeter, July 7, 1488, in G. A. Bergenroth, ed., Calendar of Letters, Despatches, and State Papers relating to the Negotiations between England and Spain, Volume I: Henry VII, 1485-1509 (London, 1862), p. 5; Treaty of Medina del Campo, ibid., pp. 20-24.

[39]Taviani, Columbus, pp. 191-192, 474-480.

[40]Ibid., pp. 192-194, 480-483; Rumeu de Armas, Itinerario, p. 166; Isabel and Fernando to the Councils, ministers and public officials of the realm, May 12, 1489, in El Tumbo de los Reyes Católicos del Concejo de Sevilla, ed. Juan de Mata Carriazo, Volume V (Sevilla, 1971), p. 7.

answer to their summons, Isabel and Fernando moved with their children to the mountain-girt city of Jaén north of Granada, to launch from there an expedition against the Muslim stronghold of Baza in the eastern part of the kingdom of Granada, where El Zagal ruled. It promised to be a very difficult enterprise. Baza was well prepared and provisioned for attack and a long siege. Guadix, another heavily defended Moorish fortress, was only twenty miles away. New roads would have to be built through rugged rocky mountains to supply the besieging army. Isabel and Fernando had committed a substantial amount of their own income to pay the costs of this campaign; knowing this, the long-burdened people of Castilian Andalusia accepted new and heavier taxes for 1489 with surprisingly little complaint. As usual, Isabel took charge of supporting the army from the rear, in Jaén, while Fernando, after his banners were blessed in Jaén cathedral, went forth against Baza at the head of his army, with 12,000 horse and 50,000 foot.[41]

Early in June the Christian army reached the area of Baza, a city situated on a relatively small plain at the foot of snow-capped mountains. Much of the plain was covered with thick fruit tree orchards. The orchards proved to be full of hidden fortifications—moats, stone walls, redoubts—while the poor visiblity in what was almost a forest was a constant invitation to ambush. Entangled in this maze, Fernando retreated just in time to avoid serious danger of the entrapment of much of his army, and settled down to a long siege, beginning at a great distance from his objective.[42]

Baza was defended by some 20,000 Moors under Hassan the Old, a hardened veteran in the mold of Hamet Zeli who had commanded at Málaga. With immense effort, the besiegers began building walls of circumvallation, which when completed would surround the beleaguered city and cut off all its communication with the surrounding country. But the lombards, Fernando's siege artillery, though brought up over the roads Isabel had built, could not be brought through the fortified maze of orchards in the plain to get close enough to Baza's walls to knock them down.[43]

Some time that summer Isabel, still at Jaén, formally received Columbus in audience and promised him that, once the kingdom of Granada was reconquered for Christian Spain, his project would receive immediate reconsideration, with a strong prospect for its approval. Unfortunately we

---

[41]Rumeu de Armas, *Itinerario*, pp. 166-167; Palencia, *Crónica*, III, 216-217, 222 (Guerra de Granada, Lb IX); Pulgar, *Crónica*, II, 363-364 (ch. CCXXXIII); Menéndez Pidal, *Historia de España*, XVII(2), 756.

[42]Fernando to Diego de Torres from camp before Baza, June 20, 1489, in Ballesteros Gaibrois, *Valencia y los Reyes Católicos*, pp. 96-97; Peter Martyr de Anglería to Cardinal Ascanio Visconti from camp before Baza, DIHE IX, 115-117; Palencia, *Crónica*, III, 222-223 (Guerra de Granada, Lb IX).

[43]Bernáldez, *Memorias*, pp. 207-208 (ch. XCII); Palencia, *Crónica*, III, 223 (Guerra de Granada, Lb IX).

know nothing else about this vital interview. Its very occurence has to be deduced from chronologically confused recapitulations in much later histories; there are no contemporary accounts of it or references to it. As we shall see, Isabel's promise in the summer of 1489 did not mark a final favorable decision on Columbus' project; it was to be rejected yet again before final acceptance came. But this interview with Isabel gave Columbus real hope; and she did guarantee his personal maintenance at court until a final decision should be made, directing her treasurer Alonso de Quintanilla to provide for him.[44]

From then until the final victory over Granada, Columbus remained most of the time close to Isabel's side. Neither of them then believed that the war would last two and a half years more. The general expectation at this time was that Baza would soon fall, and El Zagal shortly after it, whereupon Boabdil would readily hand over Granada. But the prolongation of the war gave Columbus and Isabel many opportunities to come to know each other better; and there are indications in their later years that they had an understanding and appreciation of each other's character that could only have flowed from considerable personal contact which was possible only at this period.

Also that summer, in July, two Franciscan friars arrived from Jerusalem, where they had been discharging the traditional responsibility of their order for the care of the Holy Places. They bore a message to Fernando and Isabel from the Burji Mameluke Sultan of Egypt, al-Ashraf Saif ud-Din Qa'it Bay, who also ruled Palestine and Syria, and had just won a major victory over the Ottoman Turks. Sultan Qa'it Bay demanded that the Spanish Christians stop their war against Granada, and threatened that if they did not stop it, he would not only send much aid to Granada, but also take reprisals against Christians in Palestine, Syria, and Egypt, and might even destroy the Holy Sepulcher (as an earlier ruler of Egypt, the mad Caliph al-Hakim, had done early in the eleventh century, thereby providing a justification for the First Crusade). But Fernando was no man to be intimidated by threats, especially from an infidel. He fired back with a hard-hitting summary of the history of the Reconquest and claim of the absolute right of his people to regain the whole of their ancestral homeland from its Muslim conquerors; he reminded Qa'it Bay of the money from pilgrims he would lose if he destroyed the Church of the Holy Sepulcher; and he declared that for every Christian the Sultan might kill to try to stop the war in Granada, he would kill one Granadan Muslim.[45]

On July 27 Isabel issued a sharp order to the officials of Sevilla to round up knights and office-holders who had not responded to her call-up for the 1489 campaign; they were to come to camp at once or lose their offices and revenues. The same demand was made and penalty threatened for those who had come to

---

[44]Taviani, *Columbus*, p. 193; Manzano, *Cristóbal Colón*, pp. 193-196.

[45]Palencia, *Crónica*, III, 221-222 (Guerra de Granada, Lb IX); Taviani, *Columbus*, p. 193; John B. Glubb, *Soldiers of Fortune* (London, 1973), pp. 378-379.

camp, but had left without permission.[46] The need for such a missive showed all too clearly the erosion of morale due to the inability of the Castilian army to make any progress toward Baza in two full months of siege and battle. They had still not penetrated the fortified orchards. Even the usually optimistic Duke of Cádiz had let it be known that in his opinion it would take no less than fifteen months to reduce Baza. Difficulties in supplying the army would multiply in the rains of autumn and the snows of winter. The military problem was much more intractable than that of the siege of Málaga, which had been difficult enough. Some of Fernando's counsellors recommended that the siege be abandoned and the army retreat to Jaén.[47]

Fernando wavered. First he agreed to give up the siege; then he listened to other counsellors (notably Gutierre de Cárdenas, faithful as always to the will of his royal mistress) who still urged its continuation, telling him that, however time-consuming and costly it might be, the orchards must be and could be cut down and all the defenses within them destroyed, opening the way to the city. Fernando could not make up his mind. Finally, in a moment vividly revealing where the real strength of their partnership lay, he sent a message by post-riders to Isabel, asking her what he should do.[48]

The post-riders brought Fernando's message across sixty miles of mountain trails to Isabel in just ten hours. She answered almost as quickly: they must persevere; if they did, God would give them the victory. They had beaten these enemies before; surely they could do it again. They should cut down the orchards, however long it took and however hard it might be. She would personally guarantee all the material support they needed; and she and her ladies would offer the constant prayers that were even more necessary for their success. Soon she would come herself and join them, to be at their side in all their efforts, until they triumphed.[49]

News that their beloved and inspiring Queen was so totally committed to their victory rallied the flagging spirits of the besiegers as nothing else could have done. They began at once the herculean task of felling the far-flung orchards and taking the Moorish fortifications hidden within them. Gutierre de Cárdenas took charge of destroying the orchards, knowing that Isabel particularly wanted this done. In the thickest of them, it took four thousand men a full day to advance just ten paces. But they pressed on, and the Moors

---

[46]Isabel to the Asistente of Sevilla (Jaén, July 27, 1489), *Tumbo de Sevilla*, V, 9-10.

[47]Palencia, *Crónica*, III, 225-226 (Guerra de Granada, Lb IX); Pulgar, *Crónica*, II, 375-381 (ch. CCXXXVI-CCXXXVII).

[48]Pulgar, *Crónica*, II, 380-383 (ch. CXXXVII); Palencia, *Crónica*, III, 225-226 (Guerra de Granada, Lb IX).

[49]Pulgar, *Crónica*, II, 383 (ch. CCXXXVII); Peter Martyr de Anglería to Cardinal Ascanio Visconti and Cardinal Arcimboldi of Milan, (Jaén, April 12, 1489), DIHE IX, 118-124.

could not hold them back.[50]

So passed August, and September. With the coming of fall, which at that altitude usually brought much cold rain and then early snow, the Moors hoped for relief; but none came. The besiegers pressed on, and though late September had been rainy, the whole month of October was cool but clear, and this highly unusual weather continued into November. The besiegers' walls of circumvallation now entirely surrounded Baza. Neither El Zagal in Almería nor Boabdil in Granada made any move to send assistance; perhaps they remembered too well the debacle of the relieving force El Zagal had led to Málaga two years before. But Christian knights were coming in from all over Europe to fight on the side of the crusading Queen of Castile. Under Isabel's personal supervision, all necessary supplies were brought with great effort by land and sea. She collected grain from all over Spain, saw that it was properly milled, and sent it on to the camps around Baza on the backs of no less than 14,000 pack animals. Some of the fertile ground where the orchards had stood was sown in November with winter wheat, to supply the army in the spring if they were still needed there then.[51]

The costs of the siege of Baza—much the longest siege of the war against Granada, and the most massive military operation of such length since the days of Alfonso XI the Avenger 150 years before—were enormous. No one, not even Isabel, had expected the siege to go on so long or to be so difficult. The higher taxes levied in Andalusia for 1489 had been paid almost in full and with little complaint, but they now proved to be not enough. The noblemen of Castile gave substantial gifts from their own goods and revenues to carry on the war; but this also was not enough. So Isabel pawned her jewels for loans totalling 60,000 gold florins, or more than 9,300,000 maravedís.[52] On October 27, at Fernando's request, she set out for Baza herself, as she had earlier promised to do, taking with her Princess Isabel, Beatriz, Teresa Enríquez the wife of Gutierre de Cárdenas, and Cardinal Mendoza. Isabel departed from Ubeda, a town east of Jaén, where she left Prince Juan and his younger sisters. In a letter she wrote that day, from Ubeda to Sevilla to call up more supplies, a phrase appears that flashes like a sunbeam on a sword-blade. The siege of Baza, Isabel writes, "has to be continued and *it will continue.*"[53]

---

[50]Pulgar, *Crónica*, II, 383-387 (ch. CCXXXVIII).

[51]Palencia, *Crónica*, III, 227-233 (Guerra de Granada, Lb IX); Pulgar, *Crónica*, II, 408-411 (ch. CCXLVI-CCXLVII); Bernáldez, *Memorias*, p. 209 (ch. XCII).

[52]Pulgar, *Crónica*, II, 411-412 (ch. CCXLVII); Manzano, *Cristóbal Colón*, p. 196. The later legend that Isabel pawned her jewels to help finance Columbus' voyage arises from her offer to provide part of a loan for this purpose in this way; but she did not actually have to do it. The total cost of outfitting Columbus' expedition was, in any case, less than one-seventh of the value of the jewels Isabel pawned to meet the costs of the siege of Baza.

[53]Isabel to the Council of Sevilla (Ubeda, Oct. 27, 1489), *Tumbo de Sevilla*, V, 68

Fernando, with the Duke of Cádiz and several other grandees, met his wife and her party on the road and brought them into camp November 7. Once again, as at the seige of Málaga, her arrival occasioned a veritable explosion of joy and confidence. The Moors watched in astonishment as she was greeted with bugles, trumpets, sackbuts, flageolets, and kettle-drums. Almost all bickering among the besiegers ceased. Three days later she rode out with a large escort, approaching the walls of Baza. Three hundred Moors rose to the challenge; they attacked and were beaten back. The Duke of Cádiz then proposed a truce of a few hours. The Moors granted it, and formed up their army to stand in respect as Isabel and her escort rode back atop a ridge to their camp.[54]

The Moors of Baza well knew that Isabel's arrival meant their defeat. Within a week of her arrival, their spokesman Yahia el-Nayer had written to Fernando asking to begin surrender negotiations. Fernando replied on November 15 accepting the offer and designating Gutierre de Cárdenas as his chief negotiator.[55]

Hassan the Old came in person to parley. Cárdenas told him what was now obvious to all: that the Queen would never relent until the city was taken, that her army had come to stay until it surrendered. He urged Hassan to seek the capitulation, not only of Baza, but of Guadix and Almería as well, indeed of all the territory of eastern Granada held by El Zagal. Hassan said he would go personally to El Zagal and recommend a general capitulation. El Zagal agreed to it. Baza was surrendered on the usual terms. On December 4, in a snowstorm, Hassan was standing in the plaza of the city he had defended so long, to turn it over to its new rulers. Isabel and Fernando entered to receive his surrender. As always, she let him go first. The siege had lasted six months and twenty days and had cost 20,000 lives. Five hundred and ten Christian captives in Baza were set free. It was the climactic and hardest conflict of the war to reconquer Granada; and more than any other conflict in that war, it was Isabel's triumph.[56]

On December 10 El Zagal signed the general capitulation.[57] For a time Isabel and Fernando thought the long war was over at last. Boabdil, whom they

---

(emphasis added); Pulgar, *Crónica*, II, 417-418 (ch. CCXLIX-CCL).

[54]Rumeu de Armas, *Itinerario*, pp. 171-172; Pulgar, *Crónica*, II, 418-419 (ch. CCL); Peter Martyr de Anglería to Cardinal Ascanio Visconti (Baza, Dec. 7, 1489), DIHE IX, 133.

[55]Fernando to Yahia el-Nayer (camp before Baza, Nov. 15, 1489), in Garrido Atienza, *Entrega de Granada*, pp. 181-182.

[56]Pulgar, *Crónica*, II, 419-429 (ch. CCLI-CCLIII); Palencia, *Crónica*, III, 235-238 (Guerra de Granada, Lb IX); Bernáldez, *Memorias*, pp. 209-210 (ch. XCII); Peter Martyr de Anglería to Cardinal Arcimboldi of Milan (Jaén, Jan. 4, 1490), DIHE IX, 139.

[57]The text is in Garrido Atienza, *Entrega de Granada*, pp. 182-183.

had captured, released, and aided, had repeatedly declared himself their vassal. They now wrote telling him that, with El Zagal's capitulation, the time had come for him to deliver up Granada. But he temporized, saying that his people would not permit him to do that yet. He could do no more than offer a two years' truce. Isabel and Fernando replied that they would refrain from demanding immediate and complete control of the government of Granada, but that he would have to allow a Christian garrison in the city and the collection of the arms held by its people. To this demand, Boabdil made no immediate response.[58]

Through continuing snowstorms, Fernando went to Almería to accept El Zagal's surrender in person on December 23, 1489. Tall, light-skinned, solemn, the Moorish chieftain and pretender-king was clad all in black except for his white turban. He hailed Fernando as "king-conqueror." Isabel joined her husband in Almería on Christmas Eve with Princess Isabel, Cardinal Mendoza and many others. El Zagal received her with equal honor. Almería's chief mosque was consecrated as a church, and Christmas Mass was said there. It was the first time Christmas had been publicly celebrated in Almería in seven hundred and seventy-eight years. On December 30 Isabel and Fernando received in person the surrender of Guadix. Of the whole kingdom of Granada, only the city itself and its immediate surroundings now remained under Moorish control—and it no longer had any outlet to the sea whence its only hope of help from other Muslims must now come. As for El Zagal, the next year he departed for Africa, never to return.[59]

For some time Isabel and Fernando continued to hope that they could gain effective control of Granada from Boabdil without further fighting; in a letter written January 18, 1490 they said he had agreed to deliver up the city to them.[60] But Boabdil, neither a man of war nor a man of his word, as ever followed the path of least resistance. His people demanded that he not submit to the Christians; very well, he would not do it. There still remained in many of his people the fanatic tenacity responsible for the fact that in the fourteen hundred years Islam has existed, only one country they conquered—Spain—has ever been taken from them. There can have been few kings less fitted than Boabdil to challenge that tenacity. But for a time he continued to hold out the hope to Isabel and Fernando that he would find a way to bring peace despite the contrary will of his people. It was not until May that Fernando finally issued

---

[58]Boabdil to Governor Abulcásim et al, Dec. 16, 1489, in *ibid.*, pp. 188-189; Boabdil to Isabel and Fernando (Zafar, Jan. 22, 1490), *ibid.*, pp. 200-201; Pulgar, *Crónica*, II, 434-435 (ch. CCLV).

[59]Rumeu de Armas, *Itinerario*, pp. 172-173; Palencia, *Crónica*, III, 238-239 (Guerra de Granada, Lb IX); Pulgar, *Crónica*, II, 431-433 (ch. CCLIII-CCLIV); Menéndez Pidal, *Historia de España*, XVII(1), 798-800.

[60]Isabel and Fernando to the Council of Sevilla (Écija, Jan. 18, 1490), *Tumbo de Sevilla*, V, 98-99.

a formal demand for the immediate submission of Granada; when Boabdil refused it, the war was renewed, though with a much smaller army than in the past because, until May, the Catholic sovereigns had not been sure they would have to use it.[61]

In this interlude, flush with the victory of Baza and still with the hope of peace with Granada, Isabel and Fernando completed the final negotiation of a marriage treaty with Portugal. On the Sunday after Easter the betrothal of Princess Isabel to Crown Prince Afonso of Portugal was joyously celebrated at Sevilla. As was customary in royal betrothals of that time, only one of the betrothed was present, in this case the princess. But her whole family was with her, and she had received the prince's portrait; she had known him from the time they lived together under Beatriz's care in Portugal as hostages for the fulfillment of the terms ending the war of the succession. The prince was the only son of John II of Portugal and the apple of his eye. He was five years younger than the princess, fifteen to her twenty; but in those days of early maturing, such a difference was not a serious barrier. There is every indication that both young people were delighted with the marriage their parents had arranged, and it could confidently be expected to bring a permanent end to any lingering hostility between Spain and Portugal deriving from the war of the succession and to lay the foundation for a close and enduring alliance between the two Iberian nations.[62] Isabel's letter to King John II of Portugal on May 10 made it very clear that these were her expectations:

> Most serene Lord Brother, I thank you for what you wrote me by Ruy de Sande and for the great love you bear for the Princess my daughter, and for the pleasure you have found in this marriage of the Prince your son and my daughter. I value this more highly than I can express. I hope in Our Lord that this will be as much to your service and good and satisfaction as it is for all of us, for the satisfaction and the growth of love on our part could not be greater; we all feel thus. And in the Princess you have a very obedient daughter who will always make good use of whatever you do for her. Call upon us, lord, to make use of and request from our realms and all our possessions as though they were yours. Because I spoke at greater length with your ambassadors, I conclude by asking Your Serenity to give heed to them as proper. May Our Lord keep your royal person in His holy guard.[63]

---

[61]Boabdil to Fernando and Isabel, January 22, 1490, in Garrido Atienza, *Entrega de Granada*, pp. 200-201; Bernáldez, *Memorias*, p. 216 (ch. XCVI).

[62]Bernáldez, *Memorias*, p. 215 (ch. XCV); Elaine Sanceau, *The Perfect Prince* (Barcelos, Portugal, 1959), pp. 317-320. For the text of the marriage treaty see Antonio de la Torre and Luis Suárez Fernández, eds., *Documentos referentes a las relaciones con Portugal durante el reinado de los Reyes Católicos* (Valladolid, 1958-63), II, 368-385.

[63]Isabel to King John II of Portugal, May 10, 1490, in Luis Suárez Fernández, ed., *Política internacional de Isabel la Católica* (Valladolid, 1969), III, 190.

The military campaign of 1490 was brief, little more than a demonstration of Isabel's and Fernando's determination to continue the struggle. It lasted less than a month, beginning in mid-May. Queen and Princess Isabel stayed at Moclín; Prince Juan, now eleven, for the first time accompanied his father to camp. By June 12 the royal family was back in Córdoba.[64] In the fierce heat of July Isabel—normally in excellent health—fell ill with a severe fever which seems to have continued, at least intermittently, for several weeks. During this time Boabdil sallied from Granada to take and destroy the castle of Alhendín and besiege the heroically defended fortress of Salobreña. He was soon driven away from both places, and Fernando again raided the countryside around Granada.[65]

The fervent prayers for Isabel's recovery of health which were offered all over Spain testify to the love her people had for her. Isabel gave thanks for these prayers in a notable letter to Diego de Torres in Valencia in September:

> We have seen your letter and have heard much about the desire you have shown to keep our health in mind, and your diligence in asking God for the welfare of the king my lord and for our convalescence. We make known to you that through the blessing of Our Lord the fever has gone and we are well disposed, and with your aid will soon be recovered. May you in your prayers asking God for our health give thanks to Him for the improvement which has occurred, and ask that all we do may be for His service. We are sending you also a list of things needed by the illustrious Princess of Portugal, our most beloved daughter, charging you to work diligently in our service to provide them and to tell us beforehand what you will be able to do.[66]

Meanwhile Isabel and Fernando had taken an extraordinary action which was to have a far broader significance than anyone realized at the time. The Canary Islands, the only Spanish territory in Africa except for the Spanish outposts in Morocco just across the Straits of Gibraltar, were still in process of conquest, and in 1487 there had been a general uprising of the native Guanches on the island of Gomera, in the course of which Fernán Peraza, the governor, had been killed by the rebels. The Spanish military commander in the islands, Pedro de Vera, was a harsh and cruel man operating far from royal supervision and fully supported by Peraza's vengeful widow Beatriz. Most of the inhabitants of the island were killed or sold into slavery, including all the children and virtually everyone but the elderly and a small group which had

---

[64]Rumeu de Armas, *Itinerario*, pp. 179-180; Pulgar, *Crónica*, II, 441-444 (ch. CCLIX).
[65]Bernáldez, *Memorias*, pp. 218-219 (ch. XCVII); Pulgar, *Crónica*, II, 445-450 (ch. CCLX, CCLXI); Peter Martyr de Anglería to Cardinal Archbishop Arcimboldi of Milan, dated January 21, 1490 but apparently actually written in August, DIHE IX, 148-150.
[66]Ballesteros Gaibrois, *Valencia y los Reyes Católicos*, pp. 67-68.

fought with the Spaniards. The Christian Gomerans—many had been converted before the uprising—were treated exactly the same as the others. To his everlasting credit, the newly appointed Bishop of the Canary Islands, the Franciscan Miguel López de la Serna, came to court and protested vigorously. By the summer of 1489 the visible proof of the Bishop's reports began to arrive in the ports of Spain: Vera's pathetic victims being offered on the slave market, with the Widow Peraza taking her share of the proceeds of each sale. Isabel and Fernando, maximally committed to the gruelling siege of Baza, could barely begin to investigate the situation then; but by the summer of 1490 they had learned more than enough about it.[67]

On August 27 they issued a blistering order, applying to the Canary Islands and also to the whole of Spain, which was a virtual charter of human rights for the oppressed Christian natives. The order recognized the guilt of many of the men of Gomera for the uprising and the murder of Peraza. But, it declared, these women and boys and girls had been Christians before the men committed their crimes; most of them had nothing to do with the uprising and the murder, and no one even claimed they had. They had not been charged with any crime, let alone found guilty, yet they had been enslaved. As Christians, they were citizens of Castile with the full rights of any citizen. Consequently they could not justly "be held captive, nor sold, nor held in slavery." By explicit royal command, any Christian Gomeran so victimized could go before any royal official or notary public and claim full liberty at once, with the right to be transported back to Gomera. Furthermore, there must be an exact accounting of the price paid for these illegally enslaved people; the money received for them must be returned by the slave-sellers to the buyers; and Pedro de Vera and the Widow Peraza must post a bond of 5,000,000 maravedis as security that the required repayments would in fact be made. As a flood of documents through the ensuing year and more bear witness, these orders were carried out to the letter.[68]

It was the last time anyone tried to enslave Christians in the Canary Islands. Before the new decade ended, Isabel was to apply exactly the same standards and procedure to the non-Christian Indian captives brought to Spain from the New World by Christopher Columbus—a man she profoundly admired and trusted, who had done her probably the greatest service any subject ever provided for his sovereign, opening up the New World and making Spain the greatest power in the world, but who would face the same God as she on Judgment Day, and must live as he would be judged, by God's law before which all men, women, and children, Canarians and Indians included, are equal.

In November Isabel and Fernando escorted their oldest daughter from

[67]Antonio Rumeu de Armas, *La Politica Indigenista de Isabel la Católica* (Valladolid, 1969), pp. 67-70; Menéndez Pidal, *Historia de España*, XVII(2), 315-316.
[68]Rumeu de Armas, *Politica indigenista de Isabel*, pp. 236-268.

Sevilla on the first two days of her journey to the Portuguese border. Arriving there on the 22nd, she was met by a large delegation joined by the King and Prince of Portugal in person, the prince breaking the usual marriage protocol in his eagerness to see his bride for the first time since he was a child. He took the reins of her horse to lead it into Portugal. At the end of the month they were married at Evora; the celebrations continued a full thirty days. When the feasting was done, Andrés Bernáldez the contemporary historian gently tells us, "the Princess dwelt in peace with her husband."[69]

Princess Isabel, oldest daughter of the great Queen, is little more than a wraith in history. Her slender, red-haired, self-effacing figure seems to float, dreamlike, always in the background of the great events that surged around her. The one letter of hers that we have, written to her prospective father-in-law on the morrow of her engagement, is too short and stilted to reveal anything, if indeed she wrote it at all.[70] It was she, at six years of age, whom Isabel had ridden sixty-five miles across the torrid high plains of Castile to rescue in the castle at Segovia in the summer of 1476. During the long war against Granada she was never far from her mother's side. This glorious marriage to the Prince of Portugal was her hour, her moment in the sun.

It was all too brief. Not eight months after Princess Isabel's marriage, on July 12, 1491, just after sunset near Santarem on the River Tagus, Prince Afonso mounted a wild black horse and rode furiously through the twilight with one young companion. In the gathering darkness his galloping horse put his foot in a hole and crashed to the ground, with the prince underneath. His companion rushed to get help. The prince was taken, unconscious, to a fisherman's hut upon the banks of the nearby river. There he lay, pale and still, barely breathing, for all that night and a long day following, with his mother the Queen of Portugal and his wife the Princess of Spain clinging to his hands. At last the King came and led them away, blinded by tears, so that the priests could give the last anointing to his only son. Prince Afonso died the second night. He was just sixteen years old.[71]

Princess Isabel bore that cross to her grave. For Isabel the Queen, now in her fortieth year, the sudden, totally unexpected death of her oldest daughter's beloved young husband was the first of many crosses her Lord and Savior was to ask her to bear.

But no hint of this coming shadow appeared on Isabel's horizon as she set out on April 11, 1491, eight days after Easter, with Fernando and Prince Juan

---

[69]Bernáldez, *Memorias*, p. 222 (ch. XCIX); Pulgar, *Crónica*, II, 440-441 (ch. CCLVIII); Rumeu de Armas, *Itinerario*, p. 182; Sanceau, *Perfect Prince*, pp. 325-333.

[70]Princess Isabel to John II of Portugal, May 7, 1490, in Suárez Fernández, *Política internacional de Isabel*, III, 189.

[71]Chronicle of Valladolid, CODOIN XIII, 277-278; Menéndez Pidal, *Historia de España* XVII (1), 164; Sanceau, *Perfect Prince*, pp. 337-343.

and all her other daughters and probably as many as 80,000 men—the greatest army in the history of Christian Spain—to take Granada at last and complete the 769-year war of the Reconquest.[72] The general headquarters for the Christian army was built in stone and called Santa Fe, "Holy Faith."[73] It was to be completed, and all necessary supplies brought up, by July. "Within one month and a half," Isabel wrote to her ambassador in England late in May, "it will be finished, with the help of God, and no further danger need be feared."[74] In June she joined Fernando at the advanced camp at Gozco, an assemblage of tents in the open field, with Prince Juan and Princess Juana; the irreplaceable Duke of Cádiz and her soldiers greeted her with all their usual enthusiasm and confidence. On June 18 the Duke fought a major battle actually before the Queen's eyes—the first and only battle she ever personally witnessed. She and Juana watched it from the window of a house in a little village called Las Zubias, praying throughout that God would aid the Christian soldiers. Isabel's army was victorious; the Moors were routed. Congratulated upon his success, the Duke of Cádiz credited it entirely to God and to Queen Isabel.[75]

Late in the evening of July 14, Isabel was saying her night prayers in her tent at Gozco, as she always did before going to sleep. A candle burning in her tent fell against its cloth, baked dry and flammable by the fierce heat of Andalusia in mid-summer. The tent caught fire, and the conflagration quickly spread to other tents nearby. Seizing her dispatch-case, Isabel rushed to Fernando's tent; then they hurried to see to the safety of their children. The fire did much damage and caused substantial though temporary confusion; Isabel lost almost everything that had been in her tent except the dispatch-case, including her entire wardrobe. The wife of one of Isabel's favorite young noblemen, Gonzalo de Córdoba, later to be known as "the great captain" and one of history's most famous generals, quickly made good her queen's loss by a

---

[72]Bernáldez, *Memorias*, pp. 223-226 (ch. C-CI); Menéndez Pidal, *Historia de España*, XVII (1), 803-804. The estimate of 80,000 for the total size of the Spanish Christian army comes from Peter Martyr de Anglería in a letter to Cardinal Ascanio Visconti (DIHE IX, 156-157) which bears the date June 24, 1490 but from internal evidence clearly belongs to the year 1491 and probably to June 24 of that year. Bernáldez gives a lower estimate, but he wrote many years later, while Peter Martyr's testimony is contemporary.

[73]Although a letter from Peter Martyr de Anglería to Cardinal Ascanio Visconti written October 31, 1491 (DIHE IX, 166-168) implies that the stone buildings of the Santa Fe camp were constructed after the July 14 fire in the tent encampment at Gozco and as proof of Isabel's determination to persevere in the siege despite the accident, other evidence shows that the construction of the Santa Fe camp in stone began as early as April 30. See Bernáldez, *Memorias*, pp. 225-226 (ch. CI) and the modern synthesis of the evidence by Juan de Mata Carriazo in Menéndez Pidal, *Historia de España*, XVII (1), 810-813, 820-821.

[74]Isabel to Dr. de Puebla, May 26, 1491, Bergenroth, *Calendar of State Papers*, I, 36 and Suárez Fernández, *Política internacional de Isabel*, III, 245.

[75]Bernáldez, *Memorias*, pp. 226-228 (ch. CI); Rumeu de Armas, *Itinerario*, p. 187.

generous gift of her own clothing.[76]

Prince Afonso had died of the fall from his horse just the day before the fire. Some time during the ensuing week Queen Isabel received the appalling news; she and her whole court went into mourning. In August the widowed Princess Isabel returned to Spain and rejoined her parents, in deepest mourning, inconsolable. She insisted she would never remarry, and would wear only coarse wool for the rest of her life. Another of Queen Isabel's daughters—it must have been either Maria or Catalina, but our informant does not say which—lay seriously ill, indeed in danger of death, from an undiagnosed illness accompanied by a high fever. But Isabel's public demeanor never changed; she always presented "a serene face" to those around her. The siege of Granada was pressed relentlessly, and by September it was clear that the end was near; surrender negotiations had begun.[77]

Boabdil was making his usual plea, that he wanted peace and was willing to submit to Isabel and Fernando, but his bellicose people and nobles would not let him. He was now at last ready to set a specific date for surrender, but wanted it put as far into the future as possible to give him time to accustom his people to the prospect. He asked for six months. Gonzalo de Córdoba, Isabel's chief negotiator (whom she trusted absolutely, and who spoke fluent Arabic), pressed the Christian advantage. Letter after letter flew back and forth between Boabdil's vizier Bulcacin al Muleh and Yusuf Aben Comixa the mayor of Granada, and Fernando de Zafra, secretary to the Catholic sovereigns (most of these letters have survived, but to the despair of historians they are undated, though clearly written from September to November of 1491). Despite the fury of his amazonian mother, Boabdil finally gave way completely. On November 25, as the first snows began to fall upon the Sierra Nevada, Boabdil agreed to hand over Granada to Isabel and Fernando within 65 days, by the end of January. The Muslim inhabitants of the city and the surrounding area would be allowed to continue to practice their religion and to live according to their ancestral customs, with full freedom to emigrate with all their property or to remain as subjects to the Crown of Castile.[78]

[76]Bernáldez, *Memorias*, pp. 228-229 (ch. CI); Peter Martyr de Anglería to Cardinal Ascanio Visconti, October 31, 1491, DIHE IX, 165-166; Hernando Pérez de Pulgar, "Breve Parte de las Hazañas del Gran Capitán," in *Crónicas del Gran Capitán*, ed. Antonio Rodríguez Villa, Nueva Biblioteca de Autores Españoles X (Madrid, 1908), 575-576.

[77]Peter Martyr de Anglería to Cardinal Ascanio Visconti, October 31, 1491, DIHE IX, 166-167; Bernáldez, *Memorias*, p. 229 (ch. CI); Jerónimo Münzer, *Viaje por España y Portugal, 1494-1495*, tr. José López Toro (Madrid, 1951), p. 11; Menéndez Pidal, *Historia de España*, XVII (1), 840, 842-843. Münzer, in his reference to Princess Isabel's insistence that she would never remarry, confuses her with her sister by calling her "Juana," but the context makes it clear that Princess Isabel is meant.

[78]For the full text of the capitulation agreements, see Miguel Angel Ladero Quesada, *Los Mudejares de Castilla en tiempo de Isabel I* (Valladolid, 1969), pp. 165-

Once these agreements were signed, Isabel recalled Columbus, who had gone back to the La Rábida monastery near Palos. Columbus' long-time supporters from that monastic community, Fray Marchena and Fray Juan Pérez, had continued to speak in his favor to the Queen, no doubt with increasing urgency as the moment approached for which she had so often told him he must wait before a final decision was made on his project for sailing westward across the ocean to the Orient: victory in the long war against the Moors of Granada. She sent him his travelling expenses. Probably during the Christmas season of 1491 he arrived, weary and travel-stained, at the stone-built camp of Santa Fe.[79]

Now that he had made up his mind to surrender, Boabdil decided that he no longer really wanted to wait until the end of January to do it; his hold on the restive, sullen and bewildered city of Granada was too tenuous. So he asked that the surrender date be moved up to January 2, 1492, and that a body of Christian troops be brought up secretly the night before to guard against any uprising. They were commanded by Gutierre de Cárdenas. At dawn January 2 the gates of the famous palace and fortress of the Alhambra, the age-old stronghold of the Moorish kings overlooking Granada, were opened to Cárdenas and his men; Boabdil came in person to turn it over to them with a document formally attesting his surrender. The very first action of the victors was to set up an altar inside the Alhambra and say Mass—the first time a Mass had been said there, as several contemporary observers pointed out, in 780 years. Three cannon shots were fired as a signal that the Alhambra was now safely in Christian hands; thereupon the bulk of the army began its march from the camp at Santa Fe with Isabel and Fernando at their head.

They arrived at about three o'clock in the afternoon. All—even Princess Isabel—had put off the mourning dress which they had worn since August in memory of Prince Afonso of Portugal and his tragic death; jewels, brocade, armor, and lances glowed in the golden light of a cool clear winter day under the Sierra Nevada and the ochre battlements of the Alhambra. Fernando rode ahead, with Isabel behind him, and Prince Juan, Princesses Isabel and Juana, and Cardinal Mendoza with her. Boabdil came forth to meet them, with the symbolic keys to the Alhambra and the city in his hand; he delivered them to Fernando, and made his submission. Fernando turned, and gave the keys to Isabel. She gave them to Prince Juan, and he passed them on to the Count of Tendilla whom Isabel and Fernando had appointed governor of Granada, while

---

182; for the voluminous correspondence between Aben Comixa and Bulcacin el Muleh for the Moors and Zafra, see Garrido Atienza, *Entrega de Granada*, pp. 207-230; for the anger of Boabdil's mother, see Hernando de Baeza, "Las Cosas que pasaron entre los reyes de Granada," in Emilio Lafuente y Alcántara, ed., *Relaciones de algunos sucesos de los últimas tiempos del Reino de Granada* (Madrid, 1868), pp. 42-44.
[79]Taviani, *Columbus*, pp. 193-194; Manzano, *Cristóbal Colón*, pp. 232-240, 248-249.

Hernando de Talavera, Isabel's confessor, had been named its bishop.

The royal family then entered the Alhambra at the head of their army. They were greeted at once by a procession of Christians who had been captives and slaves of the Moors, carrying an image of the Blessed Virgin Mary; Isabel received them "with great reverence," and ordered them taken immediately to Santa Fe. Hernando de Talavera climbed to the Alhambra's high tower of Vela to place a cross upon it, while the army chanted *Ave Cruz, spes unica*! ("Hail to the Cross, our only hope!") The royal standard and the pendon of Santiago, patron of Christian Spain, were then also planted high above the captured stronghold, whose rule henceforth by the Catholic sovereigns of Spain was proclaimed by all present in re-echoing cries of triumph. Trumpets sounded; cannon fired; all fell to their knees to give thanks to God, singing the *Te Deum laudamus.*[80]

Those who were there tell us that tears of joy filled every eye—and, we may be sure, none more than the lovely, commanding blue-green eyes of Isabel, which had been fixed upon this goal ever since she first learned what it meant to be a Princess of Castile, heir to twenty-four generations of the longest crusade. Climaxing full seven hundred and seventy years of struggle beginning at the Battle of Covadonga in 722, she and her husband had at last brought that crusade to total victory. Spain was reconquered—Christian once again from sea to sea, from the mountains of the Pyrenees to the Rock of Gibraltar and all that lay between. The power of the age-old invader was destroyed forever. The Cross stood over the Alhambra, against the sky, the gate of Heaven.

---

[80]There are many accounts of the surrender of Granada, one of the most impressive and dramatic episodes in the history of Christendom. Several are collected in Garrido Atienza, *Entrega de Granada*, pp. 313-326; see also Bernáldez, *Memorias*, pp. 230-232, and Alonso de Santa Cruz, *Crónica de los reyes católicos*, ed. Juan de Mata Carriazo, Volume I (Sevilla, 1951), pp. 46-47. The account in the text follows the brilliant and exhaustive reconstruction of the precise sequence of events by Maria del Carmen Pescador del Hoyo, "Cómo fué de verdad la toma de Granada," *Al-Andalus* XX (1955), 283-344, which also contains a valuable, previously unpublished account of the surrender of Granada by an otherwise unknown Cifuentes in a letter from Granada to Bishop Alonso de Valdivieso of León on January 8, 1492.

8
Columbus Sails
(January 1492-September 1493)

With Granada secured and the long crusade of 770 years ended in triumph, Isabel could now turn once again to the poor but increasingly impatient suppliant awaiting her, the tall red-haired sea captain convinced that he could accomplish a voyage that no man had dreamed of before him. As we have seen, she recalled him to court in December 1491. The court was still at Santa Fe; it would be weeks, more likely months, before the former enemy capital was ready to serve as a royal residence and seat of court. The crush of business in the immediate aftermath of a ten years' war was almost overwhelming. But Columbus had been waiting for almost seven of those years; he had been promised a prompt reconsideration of his case; he should get it.

The report of the advisory commission of experts back in 1487 had been unfavorable; no attempt was made to seek another review of this kind. The Duke of Medinaceli had become something of a patron of Columbus, though we do not hear of any direct intervention by him in 1492; Cardinal Mendoza, the primate of Spain, perhaps influenced by the long-lasting and strongly committed support of Columbus by the Franciscan friars of La Rábida monastery in Palos, was very favorable to him,[1] and Isabel had always been personally impressed by him.

But the Royal Council, now consulted on the project for the first time, was unfavorable. Like so many others in Spain who had reviewed his plans, most of its members did not really understand what Columbus was talking about; world geography and long-range voyaging were not within their horizons. What they did understand, as leading noblemen of the realm, was the presumptuous audacity of this Italian foreigner in demanding (if he was successful) to become an hereditary admiral of Castile, governing all lands he discovered. Throughout its history Castile had had only a single admiral. Fadrique Enríquez, Fernando's uncle, now held that distinguished office. To ennoble this penniless adventurer if he found a stray island or two in the middle of the ocean seemed positively subversive of social order. We have it on the authority of the

---

[1]Alonso de Santa Cruz, *Crónica de los Reyes Católicos*, ed. Juan de Mata Carriazo, Volume I (Sevilla, 1951), pp. 64-65, (chapter VIII).

discoverer's son that this is the main reason the Royal Council flatly turned Columbus down in January 1492. Isabel rarely overrode the advice of her Council except on matters very close and important to her. Her initial response was to accept their verdict, unwelcome to her instincts though it was. Columbus was informed that his cause in Spain was lost. As soon as he could—probably within two or three days—he departed, with only a mule, for France.[2]

Columbus' friends at court obviously knew of his departure, and that Isabel had always been favorably inclined toward him. Up to this point Fernando had shown little or no interest in him. But the arguments for supporting his venture were so strong, particularly at this dramatic and decisive hour in Spanish history, and the reaction of the Royal Council so patently narrow-minded, that Columbus' friends resolved on immediate and strongly-worded appeals to both Catholic sovereigns. Luis de Santángel, a *converso* with Genoese connections who was keeper of the Queen's privy purse, appealed to her, along with Isabel's oldest friend, Beatriz de Bobadilla; Juan Cabrero, grand chamberlain and long-time favorite of Fernando, appealed to him, as did Father Diego de Deza, Prince Juan's tutor. No doubt they all used the common-sense arguments attributed by Fernando Columbus to Santángel: the amount of money the navigator asks for is comparatively small, the potential benefits are enormous, he will get nothing if he finds nothing, but what if he succeeds and another country reaps the benefit? Hernando de Talavera, the recently nominated Archbishop of Granada who had been head of the commission which originally recommended against supporting Columbus' project, was persuaded; he added his voice to those urging that Columbus be recalled and given what he asked. Santángel offered to lend a substantial part of the required money himself, and then or soon afterward proposed that two ships for the expedition be obtained by transmuting a fine levied on the small Andalusian port of Palos into a requirement that the town supply two ships to Columbus at its expense. Isabel and Fernando seem to have made the decision together, though Isabel—given her character and long history of special interest in Columbus—probably took the lead in urging it. Columbus was recalled, while actually on the road some six miles out from Santa Fe. We would give much for a description of the scene when the royal messenger, doubtless riding a dashing charger, drew rein on the dusty track before the plodding mariner with his mule to tell him that his royal mistress and master had changed their minds, and would now send him out upon his epochal journey after all.[3]

---

[2]Ferdinand Columbus, *The Life of the Admiral Christopher Columbus*, tr. & ed. Benjamin Keen (New Brunswick NJ, 1959), pp. 41-42; Samuel Eliot Morison, *Admiral of the Ocean Sea* (Boston, 1942), pp. 100-102; Juan Manzano Manzano, *Cristóbal Colón; siete años decisivos de su vida, 1485-1492* (Madrid, 1964), pp. 256-260.
[3]Fernando Columbus, *Life of Christopher Columbus*, pp. 43-44; Peter Martyr de Anglería to the Archbishop of Granada, September 13, 1493, *Documentos inéditos para*

There remained only the work of the secretaries, which like so many bureaucratic undertakings then and now consumed much more time than was necessary by any reasonable standard. Probably no more than the month of January had been required for the Royal Council to meet and reject Columbus' project; for Columbus to decide to leave for France, and set out upon the road; for Isabel to receive Santángel and Hernando de Talavera and Fernando to receive Cabrero and Deza, and for the king and queen to decide that the project should now be supported, with at least a good idea of how it might be financed. It took no less than three full months—until the end of April—for Secretary Juan de Coloma and his clerical staff thereupon to get all the required documents drafted, polished, written in fair copies, and assembled for Columbus to take with him.

First came the Capitulations of Santa Fe, signed by Isabel and Fernando April 17, formally commissioning Columbus' expedition of discovery and naming him Admiral of the Ocean Sea from the time of his first discovery of new lands, with the right to govern them as viceroy and to keep for himself one-tenth of all valuables and merchandise found there.[4] On April 30 several supporting documents were added granting Columbus the authority and authorizations he would need, including the order to the town of Palos to provide him with two caravels for his fleet of three ships. Much the most interesting and significant of these documents of April 30 were his official credentials to the monarchs of the Orient—to the Great Khan of Cathay; to Prester John; to the successor of Tamerlane; and to others whose names could be inserted in blank spaces left for the purpose.[5]

These documents reveal inescapably the utter ignorance with which history's most important voyage was launched, and the intellectual chaos of the assumptions on which Columbus' project was based. For there had not been a Grand Khan in Cathay (China) for 124 years, since the last one was overthrown by the Ming dynasty in 1368; Shah Rukh, the successor of Tamerlane in Iran, had been dead for 45 years; Prester John was a legend whose only tenuous link with reality was the half-barbarous black Christian king of Ethiopia, whose kingdom had been cut off from the sea by the Muslims for eight hundred years;

---

la Historia de España (hereinafter cited as DIHE), published by the Duke of Alba et al, Volume IX (Madrid, 1955), p. 242; Manzano, *Cristóbal Colón*, pp. 263-277; Paolo Taviani, *Christopher Columbus; the Grand Design* (London, 1985), pp. 199-201, 494, 497-500.

[4]Decree of Isabel and Fernando, April 17, 1492 (Santa Fe de Granada), in Samuel Eliot Morison, ed., *Journals and Other Documents on the Life and Voyages of Christopher Columbus* (New York, 1963), pp. 27-28 (English translation).

[5]*Ibid.*, pp. 29-35 (seven documents all signed by Isabel and Fernando on April 30, 1492 in Granada, in English translation); Santa Cruz, *Crónica*, I, 65-67 (ch. VIII); Manzano, *Cristóbal Colón*, pp. 281-314; Morison, *Admiral of the Ocean Sea*, pp. 104-108.

and not a man then lived in eastern Asia who could read a word of the Latin in which the letters of Isabel and Fernando were written. Columbus really did not have any idea where he was going or what he would find or do there if he should reach his goal. Yet these letters establish beyond the shadow of a reasonable doubt that the Orient *was* Columbus' objective, however unrealistic, and that the later historians who have attempted to deny that clear and evident fact have no basis for their skepticism.

The human consequences of the last-minute decision of Isabel and Fernando to support Columbus are so great as to be far beyond calculation. Even in the strictly material sense, they are awesome. It has been calculated that for every maravedi the Spanish Court, aided by Santángel's loan, invested in Columbus' expedition, during the next hundred years they received back, in gold and silver alone, a profit of 1,733,000.[6]

Isabel's final decision to sponsor Columbus' enterprise—in which she was belatedly but fully supported by Fernando—was based not on geographic knowledge or any economic calculation. By such standards the decision was evidently wrong. But in human terms it was overwhelmingly right. For Columbus was a man born and driven to discover a new world, and such a discovery was bound to bring transcendent glory, power, and wealth to whatever nation made it. In fact, it made Isabel's Spain the world's greatest power for a century and a half, and the savior of Catholic Europe. Isabel, and the others who believed in Columbus, could see in him a history-maker, a man capable of opening up spiritual and material opportunities never known before. It was the man to whom they ultimately gave their blessing, far more than to his project. Because it had so often happened to her, Isabel above all understood how and why it is that fortune favors the brave.

Columbus' expedition could never have reached the Orient. Yet even in 1492 there was a way to reach the Orient, by a commercially feasible route—a way which might well have forestalled him. The Portuguese were following that way, around the coast of Africa. Just over three years before Columbus finally received Isabel's and Fernando's endorsement, the Portuguese navigator Bartolomeu Dias had opened up that route to the Orient by rounding the southern tip of the Dark Continent. Just one more voyage under a resolute and persevering commander would have brought Portugal to India and achieved all that Columbus hoped to accomplish by his project. At the normal pace Portuguese exploration had followed since the able and enterprising John II had become king of Portugal, that voyage would have been undertaken in 1492. But King John II was prostrated by the tragic death of his beloved only son, Crown Prince Afonso, the year before—almost as prostrated as Afonso's widow, Queen Isabel's daughter and namesake. John II never sent another

---

[6]Taviani, *Columbus*, p. 500.

expedition towards India, though he began preparations for one shortly before he died in 1495; these preparations ceased at his death.[7] Not until 1497—five years after Columbus sailed—did Vasco da Gama set out for India.[8] Da Gama reached India in 1498, returning the next year; but by then the New World was already beginning to match the allure of the Orient.

With the conquest of Granada, the kingdom of Castile had obtained several hundred thousand new citizens.[9] Only a small minority were Christians; over the long centuries of the Reconquista, particularly since the early thirteenth century when the Christian frontier advanced into Andalusia, the Christian inhabitants of the kingdom of Granada had tended to leave it while Muslims and Jews from the territories reconquered by the Christians had come into it. The terms of the surrender of Granada guaranteed the Muslims the right to practice their faith, and most of them had remained behind to take advantage of it—only about 40,000 Muslims left.[10] Jews had no such guarantee. They had long been tolerated in Christian as well as in Muslim Spain, but popular antagonism toward them was strong. In the cities (where most of them lived), they were largely restricted to ghettoes, though the segregation laws (like most segregation laws, particularly those not based on an instantly detectable distinction of race) were by no means always strictly enforced. Since coming to the throne of Castile, Isabel had protected the Jews of Castile to the best of her ability, as a long series of her decrees and letters from 1483 to 1489 clearly attests.[11] But the investigations of the Inquisition since its establishment in 1480 had uncovered numerous examples of professed Jews inducing and pressuring conversos to abandon their Christian faith and return to Judaism; and one particular investigation, begun in December 1490 and concluded eleven months later with five spectacular executions at Avila, had raised popular hostility to Jews to fever heat.

Three of those executed at Avila November 16, 1491 were conversos, but the other two were professed Jews charged with collaborating with and encouraging them in crucifying a four-year-old Christian boy (later known as

---

[7]Elaine Sanceau, The Perfect Prince; a Biography of the King Dom Joao II (Barcelos, Portugal, 1959), pp. 353-355, 381-382.

[8]The best account of Vasco da Gama's history-making voyage is Vincent Jones, Sail the Indian Sea (London, 1978).

[9]The prewar population of Granada is estimated at 300,000 to 500,000 (see Chapter 6, Note 1).

[10]Jerónimo Münzer, Viaje por España y Portugal, 1494-1495, tr. José López Toro (Madrid, 1951), p. 44.

[11]No less than ten are specifically cited in a single paragraph in Ramón Menéndez Pidal, director, Historia de España, Volume XVII: "España de los Reyes Católicos," ed. Luis Suárez Fernández and Manuel Fernández Alvarez (Madrid, 1969), Part 2, pp. 251 and 262-263.

the Holy Child of La Guardia). The boy's heart was then said to have then been cut out and used with two stolen consecrated Hosts in a ritual of black magic against the Christians. Before the executions, two independent judicial panels had reviewed and confirmed the Inquisition's findings. Torture had been used once in the interrogation, but only with one of the accused, and in a relatively mild form (not the rack). Though no extant source makes any explicit connection between this case and the action of Isabel and Fernando four months later in expelling all Jews from Spain, there is strong reason to suspect that it was a precipitating factor in that decision, which was certainly recommended by the Inquisition.[12]

Whether the charges were true, no man can now say. Ritual murder of Christian children was part of anti-Semitic legend, and some of the specific cases in which it was charged have been shown to be historically fraudulent; but it would be rash to deny that it could have happened, and there is no specific evidence to contradict the Inquisition's findings in this case—suspect though they must be because of the use of torture, however limited. In view of the number and horror of Christian atrocities against Jews over the ages, it would be strange if there had never been any Jewish atrocities against Christians. For both Christians and Jews are sons of Adam.

The decree ordering the expulsion of the Jews, and contemporary chroniclers commenting on it, give as the primary reason for its issuance the activity of professed Jews in trying to persuade *conversos* who had been Jews, or whose ancestors had been Jews, to leave the Catholic Church and return to Judaism. But there were undoubtedly other reasons. Spain was now unified for the first time in nearly eight hundred years; Isabel and Fernando believed this new unity must be preserved at all costs, and the Inquisition had proved some Jews were a real threat to it. Public anger, particularly after the Inquisition's public revelation of the case of the Holy Child of La Guardia, was so great that it might be impossible to keep it under control and protect innocent Jews. So the decision was made to remove from Spain all Jews who would not accept baptism. They were given four months—from March 31 to July 31—to consider their choice and to liquidate their property if their decision was to retain their faith and go. They could take anything with them they wished, with the important exception of gold and silver, which no one without special royal license was allowed to remove from the country. (This prohibition was, of course, widely evaded.) They were allowed to convey money to other countries by letters of credit and exchange, if they were in a position to acquire them.[13]

---

[12]*Ibid.*, pp. 250, 252; William Thomas Walsh, *Isabella of Spain, the Last Crusader* (New York, 1930), pp. 342-368.

[13]The text of the decree expelling the Jews is in Santa Cruz, *Crónica*, I, 54-59 (ch. VI). See also Andrés Bernáldez, *Memorias del reinado de los Reyes Católicos*, ed. Manuel Gómez Moreno and Juan de Mata Carriazo (Madrid, 1962), pp. 251-252 (ch.

During the four-month period of decision and departure all Jews were specifically declared to be under royal protection, and it appears that there were comparatively few robberies of Jews departing from Spain. Some did accept baptism, notably Abraham Senior, chief rabbi of Castile and a prominent figure in that country's government, but a large majority refused. The contemporary historian Bernáldez estimates that 35,000 Jewish households—about 170,000 people—left Spain because of this decree. More than half of them went to Portugal, where King John II allowed them to stay no more than eight months, shipping most of them on to the Kingdom of Fez in Morocco, where they were abominably treated: robbed, raped, slain, and even dismembered to find gold they had allegedly hidden inside their bodies. When some pathetic refugees from these horrors in Fez tried to return to Spain, they were told they could come back only if they accepted baptism.[14]

Historians for centuries have denounced the expulsion of the Jews from Spain by Isabel and Fernando, coloring it with the "black legend" of an imagined unique evil of Spaniards and with blatant anti-Catholic prejudice, as though no one but Catholics ever mistreated Jews. (Anti-Semitism has been an ugly constant in the world's history ever since Nebuchadnezzar of Babylon; pogroms against Jews in the ancient world, untouched by Christianity, fully matched the worst any Christians were ever to do to them, while Hitler, the ultimate anti-Semite, rejected Christianity altogether.) The expulsion was certainly not ordered because of hatred for Jews; as we have seen, Isabel had done her best to protect them since she first became Queen of Castile. She particularly valued *converso* priests, notably Alonso de Burgos whom she made Bishop of Cuenca, and her confessor, Hernando de Talavera; her best friend Beatriz de Bobadilla married a *converso*. She gave professed Jews, like Abraham Senior, important positions in her government. The decree of expulsion was issued for reasons of state, which seemed compelling, and for the protection of threatened souls, as Isabel undoubtedly regarded the *conversos* so weak in their Christian faith that Jewish friends could entice them away from it. The measures taken to protect the Jews as they emigrated show that the decree of expulsion was not marked by pettiness or spite.

Yet still it was unjust. Isabel knew that a reigning King or Queen is called above all to dispense justice, by the authority given to that King or Queen by God Himself. (Had not His Son said to Pilate at his judgment seat: "You would have no power if it had not been given to you from above?")[15] That was

CX); Peter Martyr de Anglería to Cardinal Arcimboldi, March 11, 1492 (Granada), DIHE IX, 171-173; Menéndez Pidal, *Historia de España*, XVII (2), 254-257.

[14]Santa Cruz, *Crónica*, I, 58-59 (ch. VI); Bernáldez, *Memorias*, pp. 255, 258-262 (ch. CX, CXIII); Chronicle of Valladolid, in *Colección de documentos inéditos para la historia de España* (hereinafter cited as CODOIN), XIII (Madrid, 1848), p. 195.

[15]John 19:11.

why Gutierre de Cárdenas had carried that symbolic sword before Isabel as she rode to her coronation Mass in Segovia. That was why her supreme task, once she had secured her right to the succession, had been to bring justice to all Castile. That was why she had established the Inquisition, to find out who was truly guilty and who was truly innocent of betrayal of and blasphemy against the Christian Faith. But here, on this one occasion, she put justice aside, washed her hands like Pilate, and ordered innocent citizens, whom it was her duty to protect, out of her country. Certainly not all those expelled were innocent. But the majority—comprising most of the women and all of the children—must have been.

Isabel the Catholic was not perfect. Like all the saints, she would have been shocked and angered to be told by some overzealous flatterer that she could do no wrong. We will soon see her blaming her own sins for her husband's brush with death in an assassination attempt. This once, in decreeing the expulsion of the Jews from her domains, she evaded her clear public duty. So far as we know, she was not ever to evade it again. It is our misfortune—not hers, for she is beyond misfortune now—if the special sensitivity every just man must have to this particular issue in our murderous century causes us to give this judgmental and moral lapse of hers more weight than it is due.

While still in Granada, at about the time that the decree for the expulsion of the Jews was issued, Isabel encountered a man who would be a decisive influence on Spain throughout the rest of her life and well beyond it: Gonzalo Ximénes de Cisneros, who had taken the name of Francisco in religion.[16] Oldest of three sons of a minor official in the little town of Torrelaguna, Cisneros had studied at the University of Salamanca—the best in Spain—and at Rome, gaining a reputation in both places for exceptional intellectual and teaching ability. Returning from Rome about 1465, Ximénes brought a Papal appointment called a *letra expectativa*, which entitled him to the next vacant pastoral appointment in his home diocese of Toledo. But the man who had to honor his *letra expectativa* was Archbishop Alonso Carrillo, then at the height of his ill-used power (1465 was the year that he and his henchmen ceremonially kicked the effigy of King Henry IV all over a platform at Avila). Cisneros asked for the parish of Uceda near his home town of Torrelaguna. Carrillo had someone else in mind for the appointment. Cisneros refused to give way, and Carrillo—who respected Papal authority only when it suited him—flung him into prison for six years. There Cisneros learned to meditate, and to value and practice the ascetic life. Finally released from jail, he was appointed chaplain at Sigüenza by Bishop (later Cardinal) Mendoza, Carrillo's rival and Cisneros' continuing patron. At Sigüenza Ximénes learned Hebrew and Aramaic, and

---
[16]Peter Martyr de Anglería to Fernando Alvarez, first secretary to King Fernando, April 5, 1492 (Granada), DIHE IX, 196-198.

became vicar-general of the diocese.[17]

But it was the contemplative and ascetic life Cisneros wanted. So he joined the Observantine Franciscans, strictest of their order, at their monastery which Isabel had founded at San Juan de los Reyes in Toledo. He asked repeatedly to be allowed to live as a hermit, and was sent for three years to the small isolated Franciscan community at Castañar, where much of his desire was fulfilled. Later he went to a similar community at Salzeda. From these distant retreats he was brought back to court by Cardinal Mendoza, who knew that Isabel would soon need a new confessor now that Hernando de Talavera had been made Archbishop of Granada, and believed that Cisneros was the kind of priest she wanted and needed. So indeed he was; meeting him, she was deeply impressed, and made him her confessor (though she continued to seek Hernando de Talavera's spiritual guidance frequently by letter).[18] In the words of Peter Martyr de Anglería, who was at her court at the time:

> The Queen—because she fears God and respects Him—appears to have found what she so ardently desired: a man able to discern with full tranquillity her inmost thoughts, when sometimes she casually incurs a fault; and this has made her extraordinarily content. . . . This man is called Francisco Ximénez, a Franciscan, formerly a well-favored cleric at the cathedral of Sigüenza. He passed from full liberty to a very ascetic life in solitude, apart. . . . In wisdom he is an Augustine; in austerity, a Jerome; in zeal for intractable souls, an Ambrose. Fleeing from the affairs of men, his chosen place was the deep woods. He went barefoot through the silent glades, clothed in sackcloth, sleeping on straw. Secretly he mortified his body with vigils and the discipline. . . . Attentive only to the contemplation of the divine, he sustained himself on vile food, and even this in very small quantity. Many of the friars of his order attest that on many occasions they have seen him caught up in ecstasy, as we read of St. Paul.[19]

This was the man whom Isabel would choose to reform the Church in Spain, finally and decisively, and so thoroughly that for centuries those who in the name of reform sought to overthrow and destroy the Church, could find no following in Spain.

On May 12, with all his documents in hand, Columbus left Granada (where Isabel and Fernando still held court) to go to Palos and fit out his expedition. After spending several days with his old friends the Franciscans of La Rábida monastery, he came into Palos May 23 to read in its *plaza* the royal order to supply him with two caravels and the royal authorization for his

---

[17]Reginald Merton, *Cardinal Ximenes and the Making of Spain* (London, 1934), pp. 1-6.

[18]*Ibid.*, pp. 6-12.

[19]Peter Martyr de Anglería to the Count of Tendilla, May 29, 1492 (Valladolid), DIHE IX, 200-201.

command and to hire seamen.[20]

Palos was then a little town of only about 600 inhabitants, not counting transient seamen. It fronted the Rio Tinto, the eastern of two branches of an estuary edged with salt marshes in western Andalusia near the Portuguese border. With its sister towns of Moguer (also on the Rio Tinto) and Huelva on the Rio Odiel, the other branch of the estuary, Palos—the land around it being dry and infertile—looked primarily to the sea for its living; many of its permanent residents were fishermen. The people of Palos knew Columbus because of his long periods of residence at La Rábida monastery just below their town, near the point where the two branches of the estuary joined. They regarded him as a dreamer. All they knew of his project—all he would tell them—was that he intended to seek islands in the Atlantic. There were islands in the Atlantic—the Canaries, Madeira, the Azores—but they had been discovered long ago. Many seamen, including some from Palos, had sailed to and among and around these islands in the fifty years since the last Azores were discovered. No new islands had been found in all that half century; these men knew the sea well enough to feel quite sure that no more were there. How could this crackpot foreigner find them where so many good captains had failed? No one wanted to sign up for his crew. It appears that the only crewmen Columbus obtained during the first two weeks after coming to Palos were four criminals whom he released from jail to join his expedition by the royal authority given him for this specific purpose. At the beginning of June he had to write to court to report this humiliating rejection, and wait for someone to find a way to help him. It must have galled his proud spirit.[21]

Again and again, throughout Columbus' seven years of residence in Spain, the Franciscan friars of La Rábida—particularly Antonio Marchena and Juan Pérez—had rescued him and his cause when all seemed lost, most recently when the Royal Council recommended the rejection of his entire project in January and Isabel temporarily confirmed its verdict. Now the friars rescued his enterprise once more, the more readily since this time the trouble was on their home ground. Everybody in Palos knew the good friars of La Rábida, only two and a half miles away from their village; and the friars knew everyone in Palos. They were trusted as Columbus was not. But their personal recommendation of him and his project still would not be enough; the villagers' trust of the friars did not necessarily imply confidence in their judgment on maritime questions. Shrewdly realizing this, Fray Marchena and Fray Pérez decided they must enlist

---

[20]Fernando Columbus, *Life of Christopher Columbus*, p. 44; official record of the reading of the royal decree in Palos, appended to the official copy of the decree, in Morison, *Journals and Other Documents of Columbus*, p. 33 (English translation); Morison, *Admiral of the Ocean Sea*, pp. 108-112; Antonio Rumeu de Armas, *Itinerario de los Reyes Católicos, 1474-1516* (Madrid, 1974), pp. 193-194.
[21]Manzano, *Cristóbal Colón*, pp. 340-341, 355-364.

the support of the town's leading native-born mariner, much admired for his skill and success, whose brother was also a sea captain and who had numerous relatives scattered through the town and neighborhood. This mariner was named Martín Alonso Pinzón.

Doubtless the friars would have acted even sooner to enlist Pinzón's aid, but he had just taken a shipment of sardines to Rome. He returned about June 20, and Fray Marchena immediately introduced him to Columbus. The two men told Pinzón the whole truth about Columbus' project—that he intended to reach the Orient. Pinzón must have had a bold and adventurous spirit; his imagination (and avarice) were fired, and he gave full support to the expedition. By June 23 he had announced that he not only believed the enterprise feasible and promising, but would join it himself as a captain under Columbus, with his brother Vicente Yáñez as the other captain. The attitude of Palos toward Columbus changed at once; its seamen, and others in the region, now flocked to join the expedition, with Pinzón in a position to tell Columbus which ones were truly best at their trade.[22]

The chronology of these events makes their true character very clear. When Columbus arrived in Palos, Martín Alonso Pinzón was in Rome; when Martín Alonso returned, he was persuaded to join the expedition and then gave it his full support. He deserves credit for obtaining the crew and to a considerable extent for fitting out the three famous vessels—nothing else. The truth has been clouded by a legal claim filed 23 years later by relatives and friends of Pinzón that Martín Alonso was equally or more responsible than Columbus for the whole project of crossing the Atlantic. In support of this claim, sworn testimony was taken from many witnesses (mostly members of the crew of the ship Martín Alonso had commanded, responding to leading questions); but the claim is most unlikely to have any foundation in fact. There is no reason to suppose that Pinzón knew anything of Columbus' project before he came back from Rome. If he had favored it, surely he would have been called upon earlier to help engage the crew; if he had opposed it, why did he suddenly change his mind? The theory that gives Pinzón any credit for conceiving and planning the greatest voyage in history founders in absurdity when one encounters the assertion that during his visit to Rome in June 1492 Martín Alonso went to the Vatican Library to study the geography of voyaging to the Orient, preparatory to making the voyage. With all due respect to Martín Alonso, a brave and capable seaman, the vision of his leaving his cargo of sardines to do research in the Vatican Library stretches credulity to the breaking point. How would he have known what books to ask for? Could he read Latin? There is no evidence of it. He would have been most unlikely to

---

[22]Manzano, *Cristóbal Colón*, pp. 364-365, 368-372, 378; Taviani, *Columbus*, pp. 204-205; Morison, *Admiral of the Ocean Sea*, pp. 136-137.

find books on global geography in Spanish in the Vatican library, even presuming that he was literate enough to understand them—which most Spanish sea captains were not.[23]

Now that the necessary seamen had been found, it only remained to acquire and prepare the ships—the three most famous ships in history, whose names (even in this time of declining educational standards) every school child in the Western hemisphere still knows: *Niña*, *Pinta*, and *Santa María*. It is not clear how they came to be customarily named in this order, from the smallest to the largest, but it is very appropriate: for *Santa María* was wrecked on the coast of Haiti, *Pinta* lost its rudder three days out from Spain and under Martín Alonso Pinzón deserted Columbus when he needed her most, but *Niña* under Columbus' personal command came triumphantly through two mighty storms in the winter Atlantic and later was the only ship of a squadron of four to survive a West Indian hurricane—"a vessel to sing about," Admiral Samuel Eliot Morison says, "one of the greatest little ships in the world's history."[24]

Niña was a caravel, of that unique design developed specifically for exploration by Portugal's great Prince Henry the Navigator. She could carry 60 hogsheads (tuns) of wine and was 67 feet long and 21 feet wide, drawing less than seven feet of water;[25] her crew numbered about twenty. She belonged to Juan Niño of Moguer, a village up the Rio Tinto from Palos and even smaller than Palos. Her official name was *Santa Clara*, but following a common Spanish custom she was generally called by the feminine form of the name of her owner, which had the additional attraction in this case of meaning "little girl" in colloquial Spanish. Juan Niño sailed with her as master; her captain was Vicente Yáñez Pinzón, a much more attractive and loyal character than his brother Martín Alonso, and later a great explorer in his own right, the discoverer of the Amazon River in Brazil. *Niña* was originally three-masted, carrying the triangular sails of the "lateen rig," useful for beating to windward; but Columbus had her refitted to square rig in the Canary Islands to take fullest advantage of the trade winds in that latitude that would blow steadily from astern as they made their ocean crossing.[26] Recent research has revealed that when re-rigged *Niña* received a fourth mast, a counter-mizzen, significantly adding to her stability and good sailing.[27] Storage space for sails for all four

---

[23]Manzano, *Cristóbal Colón*, pp. 365-368; Taviani, *Columbus*, pp. 503-505; and Morison, *Admiral of the Ocean Sea*, pp. 137-138, all take the tale of Martín Alonso Pinzón researching in the Vatican Library much more seriously, in the opinion of this writer, than it deserves, though none of them fully accepts it as it was propounded in the hearings of 1515.

[24]Morison, *Admiral of the Ocean Sea*, pp. 113, 114.

[25]Robert H. Fuson, ed., *The Log of Christopher Columbus* (Camden ME, 1987), p. 40.

[26]Morison, *Admiral of the Ocean Sea.*, pp. 114-117, 139.

[27]Eugene Lyon, "Fifteenth-Century Manuscript Yields First Look at *Niña*,"

masts was in short supply on so small a vessel, and Columbus took barely enough; as we shall see, he returned under literally his last sail.

Pinta was also a caravel, a little larger than *Niña*, with a crew of about thirty. *Santa Maria* was a *nao* or ship, not a caravel, built in Galicia rather than in the Palos area; Columbus chartered her from her master, Juan de la Cosa, who sailed with him but disappointed him. She is described as "somewhat, but not very much" bigger than the two caravels, and carried about forty men. Columbus' crews as a whole therefore numbered 90, including four foreigners (a Genoese, a Venetian, an Italian from Calabria, and a Portuguese), ten from Galicia of the *Santa Maria*'s original crew, and a few from other parts of Spain; but at least two-thirds of them were Andalusians, and many from the immediate area—from Palos, Moguer, and Huelva. Except for the Genoese Columbus himself (though he now said he thought of himself as a Spaniard), this was almost entirely a Spanish undertaking, manned by ordinary Spanish seamen with no special standards for selection other than the Pinzón brothers' personal knowledge of them.[28]

The day selected for departure reflected the profound Catholic faith of the people from whom Columbus' crew was drawn and the particular charism of the Catholic community of Palos. August 2, 1492 was the fiesta of Our Lady of Angels, patroness of the Franciscan monastery of La Rábida which had played so central a role in the Columbus story, and protector of the people of Palos, Moguer and Huelva especially when in danger at sea, as had been officially proclaimed by Pope Eugenius IV fifty-five years before. It was a day of thanksgiving for Our Lady's favors, and like all Spanish fiestas, a day of special celebration. Columbus scheduled his departure for the day following the fiesta, so that his men could join in thanksgiving and prayer with their families and relatives on the feast-day especially dear to them and to their people. He made his own farewell at La Rábida to the Franciscan brothers who had helped him so much, and probably to his son Diego who had often lived there with them.[29] At first light the next morning, Friday, August 3, half an hour before sunrise, Columbus' three ships weighed anchor and ghosted down the shallow bay against the flooding tide with only a vagrant land breeze behind them, until they crossed the bar at the bay's mouth at eight o'clock in the morning and squared away southward. By sunset they had sailed 45 miles. As night fell and the little copper lamp that illuminated the compass card in the binnacle was lit, Columbus called to his helmsman: *"Sur cuarta del sudoeste"*—"South and by West," the course for the Canary Islands.[30]

National Geographic, November 1986, pp. 601-605.
[28]Morison, *Admiral of the Ocean Sea*, pp. 117-122, 141-143.
[29]Manzano, *Cristóbal Colón*, pp. 397-400.
[30]*The Log of Christopher Columbus*, ed. Fuson, Introduction and entry for August 3, 1492, pp. 52-54 (hereinafter cited as Columbus' Log, ed. Fuson, with date of entry and

Three days later came the first crisis of the voyage: the rudder of *Pinta* became unshipped in heavy seas. It could not be properly repaired except in port. Martín Alonso jury-rigged the rudder with ropes, but the next day they broke and the work had to be done again. Still, thanks to strong and steady winds, the three ships made a fast passage, and on August 9 were in sight of the principal island in the archipelago, Grand Canary. By now *Pinta*, perhaps more battered by waves because of the difficulties with her rudder, was leaking badly, and Columbus considered replacing her with another ship. To increase prospects of finding one, he told Martín Alonso to go to the harbor of Las Palmas, the principal town of the Canary Islands, while he sailed west to Gomera to see if there might be a suitable ship there.[31]

Arriving at Gomera August 12, Columbus heard that Beatriz de Peraza, the young widow who was mistress of four of the Canary Islands including Gomera (there were seven altogether, two still unconquered while Grand Canary was ruled directly by the government of Castile) was expected momentarily from Grand Canary with a 40-ton ship Columbus hoped to charter. This was the same Widow Peraza who had been the object of Isabel's wrath three years before for enslaving so many of the Christian natives of Gomera. When she had not arrived by August 24, Columbus sailed to Grand Canary where he had *Pinta*'s rudder repaired (Martín Alonso had made no progress on repairs until Columbus arrived) and re-rigged *Niña* as described earlier. By August 31 both these tasks had been completed, and all three ships sailed again to Gomera, where their supplies were replenished; Columbus says he was expecting his transatlantic voyage to require just three weeks, but took on wood and water for four weeks as a safety margin (the voyage actually required 36 days). This time, on Gomera, he finally met the Widow Peraza. Later tradition says he fell in love with her; we may hope not, for her record by no means suggests that she was lovable, though she is reputed to have been beautiful. At such a moment it is most unlikely that Columbus would have been thinking of anything but his mission. He certainly did not dally; on September 6, shortly before noon, his three ships hoisted sail at their anchorage off Gomera and set course due west into the unknown.[32]

---

page reference); Morison, *Admiral of the Ocean Sea*, pp. 158-159, 187-189. The log of Columbus, one of the most important and rivetingly dramatic original sources in all of recorded history, has been preserved for us only in a copy, partly verbatim and partly paraphrased and summarized, by the great Spanish Dominican historian and advocate of the Indians, Bartolomé de Las Casas. That both the original Log, which Columbus gave to Queen Isabel, and the one complete copy known to have been made, which was given to his son Fernando, could have been allowed to disappear, staggers the imagination. But both are lost. We have only Las Casas' partial copy.

[31]Columbus' Log, ed. Fuson, August 6-9, 1492, pp. 54-56; Morison, *Admiral of the Ocean Sea*, pp. 160-161.

[32]Columbus' Log, ed. Fuson, August 9, 1492 (covering events up to September 6),

In all probability, by the day Columbus departed from Gomera no word had yet reached the distant Canary Islands of the momentous events which had occurred in Rome the previous month. Pope Innocent VIII had died July 25. As soon as his illness was reported to be mortal, ambitious prelates were spinning webs of intrigue all over the city of St. Peter. The conclave began August 6, with 23 cardinals present in the Sistine Chapel. The first three ballots were inconclusive: Cardinals Caraffa and Costa, two of the best and most upright members of the College, received a substantial number of votes, but neither approached the two-thirds required. In the background, two cardinals fired by a devouring ambition were maneuvering with consummate skill—Rodrigo Borgia, by origin a Spaniard from Valencia, but who had lived in Italy for most of his adult life; and Ascanio Sforza of Milan, brother of Ludovico "the Black" who ruled that city while keeping his hapless young nephew, the rightful Duke, in prison. Neither Borgia nor Sforza had sufficient votes to prevail. But Sforza was a much younger man than his rival, and they soon made an agreement by which Sforza would give his votes to Borgia in return for a promise of appointment as Papal Vice-Chancellor, which would make him an excellent prospect to be the next Pope after Borgia. All the day and night of August 10 Sforza and Borgia were lining up votes by promising offices, dioceses, and revenues (the practice of "pluralism"—bishops holding several dioceses—was unfortunately widespread in the Church at this period, particularly in Italy). By late evening the Borgia-Sforza alliance lacked only one vote to elect Borgia. That last vote was obtained from the senile, 96-year-old Cardinal Gherardo.[33]

Borgia took Alexander VI as his Papal name. His election was well received by the Roman people and in Italy generally. He was a man of known ability in leadership and administration, charming and impressive in person and highly energetic, with a reputation for lavish generosity and joviality which the pleasure-loving Renaissance Italians particularly appreciated, and for patronage of literature and the arts which reassured the intellectuals.[34]

He also had (by two different women) seven illegitimate children, all born after he had taken holy orders, and he had taken a strong personal interest in the preferential advancement of the last four; while everyone in Rome knew the new, third mistress with whom the 61-year-old Pope openly cohabited: the beautiful Giulia Farnese, the 19-year-old wife of Orsino Orsini.[35]

Queen Isabel had known her countryman Rodrigo Borgia for twenty

---

pp. 57-61; Morison, *Admiral of the Ocean Sea*, pp. 161-165.

[33]Ludwig von Pastor, *The History of the Popes from the Close of the Middle Ages*, Volume V, 2nd ed. (St. Louis, 1914), pp. 376-385.

[34]*Ibid.*, pp. 390-397.

[35]Von Pastor, *History of the Popes*, V, 399-418; E. R. Chamberlin, *The Fall of the House of Borgia* (New York, 1974), pp. 33-42.

years. He had intervened to help her during the troubled and dangerous last years of the reign of her half-brother Henry IV. He had always shown her respect. He wrote twice to her about the time of his consecration—formally announcing his elevation to the pontificate on August 24 and declaring his intention to appoint his son Caesar to succeed him as Archbishop of Valencia, while praising her as a "zealous defender of the Holy See" on August 26.[36] But such flattery could not deceive Isabel; she saw the new Pope for what he really was. She had grown up in the shadow of Archbishop Carrillo of Toledo, a man very similar to Rodrigo Borgia in both immorality and greed, who had helped her when it suited him and betrayed her likewise. After years of struggle she had beaten Carrillo, supplanted him, forced him into submission. But she could not do anything like that with a man, however unworthy, who had become the successor of Peter, the Vicar of Christ.

Isabel the Catholic was appalled to her very soul. While most of the world was celebrating the choice of liberal Alexander VI as Pope, her warnings were ringing like alarm bells in the night. In the most prophetic moments of her life, she foresaw much of the incomparable train of disasters heralded by this man's accession to the highest office in Christendom. The chronicler Santa Cruz tells us:

> The Catholic Kings [Isabel and Fernando] deeply regretted the death of Pope Innocent, and they were not at all pleased by the election of Rodrigo Borgia, as much because he was known to be very ambitious and greedy, as because he had two sons of ill fame, who were not good Christians, for whom he had already obtained much as a Cardinal, and could be expected to obtain much more as Pope. Therefore she expected nothing good to come of his election, and it gave her deep discontent.[37]

Writing to the Count of Tendilla September 23 from Zaragoza, where Isabel and Fernando then held court, Peter Martyr de Anglería spoke of the distress reflected on the faces of Isabel and Fernando as they contemplated the election of this Pope, of their shame at his boasting about his "sons in sacrilege," of their fear that the hour would soon come of the "pillaging of the tiara of St. Peter."[38] In a letter just four days later to the man chiefly responsible for Borgia's election, Cardinal Ascanio Sforza, Peter Martyr's rolling, florid Renaissance Latin prose suddenly gives way to a blunt directness that sounds so much like Isabel that we can almost hear her telling the Cardinal of Milan what she really thought of what he had done:

---

[36]Pope Alexander VI to Queen Isabel, August 24 and 26, 1492 (Rome), in Luis Suárez Fernández, *Política Internacional de Isabel la Católica*, Volume III (Valladolid, 1969), pp. 299-303.

[37]Santa Cruz, *Crónica*, I, 69 (ch. IX).

[38]Peter Martyr de Anglería to the Count of Tendilla, September 23, 1492 (Zaragoza), DIHE IX, 216; Rumeu de Armas, *Itinerario*, p. 197.

You must understand, most illustrious prince, that the death of Pope Innocent and the pontificate falling upon Alexander has aroused the utmost disgust in my king and queen, whose subject he was. They regard his ambition, lewdness, and grave weakness for his sons as pushing the Christian religion toward ruin. And you are not free from censure for having contributed to his election, as it is said, with many votes.[39]

Meanwhile, out in the midst of the Atlantic, Columbus with his three ships and ninety men was making his world-historic crossing. The weather was almost perfect—"like April in Andalusia," Columbus says, "smooth as the river of Sevilla."[40] For ten days the trade winds blew steadily from the northeast, ideal sailing. After September 18 the winds became variable; the little fleet had entered the "Sargasso Sea," where a pelagic weed often seems to fill the ocean, though actually offering no obstacle to a ship's passage. Columbus' men became restive as they sailed farther and farther from their home shores, into a sea they all realized to be utterly unknown.[41] There is no record that Columbus told them even now what his real objective was, but he made it repeatedly clear that he expected to find land soon. They were not so sure. He had ceased to trust Martín Alonso, shrewdly and correctly observing that "he is a skilled mariner, but he wants the rewards and honors of this enterprise for himself. He is always running ahead of the fleet, seeking to be the first to sight land."[42] On September 25 Martín Alonso claimed to have sighted land, but it was only a cloud on the horizon. Columbus and his men kept trying to identify the birds that flew near or alighted on their ships and to deduce from their real or imagined species whether land was near. The officers and men worried about temporary divergences between the direction of the compass and the North Star, though Columbus understood that this was because Polaris did not actually stand at true north.[43]

By October 1 they had come almost 1,800 miles. Columbus quoted approximately this figure to his men, though he believed they had actually travelled more than 2,100 miles, but concealed this for fear of frightening the men. Now the winds picked up again; during the next week they sailed over a hundred miles a day. On October 6 Columbus had a surrealistic discussion with Martín Alonso on whether they had missed Japan and should change course for China. Reality displaced these fantasies the following day when, after another false sighting of land, Columbus observed large flocks of birds of kinds they had not seen before, flying southwest. These really were land birds and there was

---

[39]Peter Martyr de Anglería to Cardinal Ascanio Sforza, September 27, 1492 (Zaragoza), DIHE IX, 218.

[40]Columbus' Log, ed. Fuson, September 16 and 18, 1492, pp. 63-64.

[41]*Ibid.*, September 8-24, 1492, pp. 62-66.

[42]*Ibid.*, September 24, 1492, p. 67.

[43]*Ibid.*, September 25-30, 1492, pp. 67-70.

land (Turks Island in the Bahamas) about three hundred miles to the southwest. Columbus knew that the Portuguese had discovered the Azores Islands by following the flight of birds. He altered course to west-southwest, insuring that (if he kept going) he would reach the Caribbean islands rather than the coast of Florida.[44]

But Columbus' men had lost faith in the portent of birds, having seen so many throughout the voyage, which had now lasted a full month out of sight of land. They were becoming increasingly frightened and angry. No voyage they had ever heard of—indeed, none in the whole history of the world up to that point—had covered such a distance out of sight of land. In fact, they had come a full three thousand miles.[45] Most of the time the wind, often strong, had been from astern or close to astern. How were they ever going to get back, beating against it? Columbus knew that further north the prevailing winds were from the west, and planned to go north to catch the westerlies before he returned. But his men knew nothing of world geography; all they knew was what they had seen, that in these strange and empty seas the winds almost always blew from the east or the northeast.

Though partisans of the Pinzóns later claimed that they were determined to sail on while Columbus wished to turn back, this is no more likely than that Martín Alonso helped devise the plan to reach the Orient by sailing west. It is inconceivable that Columbus could ever have been turned back from his lifelong goal except by irresistible force. Morison believes that a conference of the captains was held on October 9, when there was little wind and the seas were calm, and that the Pinzóns urged Columbus to turn back, but that he persuaded them to agree to follow him for three days more.[46] The next day the wind picked up substantially, driving the ships well over a hundred miles, and the men of the *Santa Maria* came to the verge of open mutiny. Columbus tells us in his Log how he answered them, in words so true to his character that they cannot be false to history:

> They [the crew] could stand it no longer. They grumbled and complained of the long voyage, and I reproached them for their lack of spirit, telling them that, for better or worse, they had to complete the enterprise on which the Catholic Sovereigns [Isabel and Fernando] had sent them. I cheered them on as best I could, telling them of all the honors and rewards they were about to receive. I also told the men that it was useless to complain, for I had started out to find the Indies and would continue until I had accomplished that mission, with the help of Our Lord.[47]

On the next day, October 11, signs of nearby land were picked up from

---

[44]*Ibid.*, October 1-7, pp. 70-71.
[45]Morison, *Admiral of the Ocean Sea*, p. 221.
[46] *Ibid.*, pp. 220-221.
[47]Columbus' Log, ed. Fuson, October 10, 1492, p. 72.

the sea—floating plants which were not seaweed, and a carved stick. The wind was blowing almost a gale and the following sea was heavy. At the daily vespers prayer, Columbus tells us, "a special thanksgiving was offered to God for giving us renewed hope through the many signs of land He has provided."[48] The sun set, but Columbus kept up all the sail his ships would carry, while doubling the lookouts. Through the whistling dark, at ten o'clock in the evening, Columbus says: "I thought I saw a light to the west. It looked like a little wax candle bobbing up and down. . . . It was such an uncertain thing that I did not feel it was adequate proof of land."[49] The wind had not abated; the white sails strained against their halyards, the dark hulls swooped over the waves. Let Admiral Morison, one of America's greatest historians, describe that climactic moment as only he can:

> His [Columbus'] ships rush on, pitching, rolling, and throwing spray, white foam at their bows and wakes reflecting the moon. *Pinta* is perhaps half a mile in the lead, *Santa Maria* on her port quarter, *Niña* on the other side. Now one, now another forges ahead. With the fourth glass of the night watch, the last sands are running out of an era that began with the dawn of history. Not since the birth of Christ has there been a night so full of meaning for the human race.
> At 2:00 a.m. 12 October, Rodrigo de Triana, lookout on *Pinta*, sees something like a white cliff shining in the moonlight and sings out *"Tierra! tierra!* Land! land!"[50]

Columbus shortened sail, turned to take the wind abeam, and stood safely off the unknown shore for the rest of the night. At dawn he and the two Pinzón captains came ashore. They unfurled the banners of Isabel and Fernando, displaying a large green cross with the letters F and Y for the Catholic sovereigns on the left and right sides of the cross. Columbus, now having earned his title of Admiral of the Ocean Sea, took possession of the island for Isabel and Fernando and the Spain they ruled, and named it San Salvador, the island of the Savior. Soon afterward the natives began to appear, naked except for loincloths, brown-skinned, wondering but friendly. The New World had

---

[48]Columbus' Log, ed. Fuson, October 11, 1492, p. 73; Morison, *Admiral of the Ocean Sea*, p. 223.
    [49]Columbus' Log, ed. Fuson, October 11, 1492, pp. 73-74. As he himself here indicates, Columbus doubted that what he saw was real. Writing *Admiral of the Ocean Sea* in 1941, Morison gave his firm opinion that it was an illusion (p. 225); writing again of the great voyage 33 years later in his last book (*The European Discovery of America: the Southern Voyages, 1492-1616* [Boston, 1974], p. 62), he says it might well have been a large fire lit by the Indians on the island Columbus was approaching. Just before midnight the moon rose, a little past full, the constellation Orion following it up the curve of the night sky. It was over the helmsman's left shoulder, still in the eastern sky, casting its silver beams ahead of the ships into the unknown ahead (Morison, *Admiral of the Ocean Sea*, pp. 224-225).
    [50]Morison, *European Discovery of America: Southern Voyages*, p. 62.

been found by the man Queen Isabel the Catholic had chosen.[51]

Where were they? The argument has gone on for centuries. Somewhere in the Bahama Islands, certainly; the question is: which island? At first glance it seems hard to believe that the knowledge of the exact location of the most important geographical discovery in the history of the world could have been lost. But the Bahama Islands were devoid of natural resources, essentially valueless except for the use which might be cruelly made of their peaceful and defenseless inhabitants for forced labor; between that and the ravages of European diseases to which they had no natural resistance, the entire native population of the Bahamas was wiped out within a generation of Columbus' arrival, and the trickle of new settlers—American, African, and European—who slowly replaced them over the years had no knowledge of where Columbus arrived. Once they had discovered the greater and richer islands not far away to the southward, the Spanish had almost no interest in the Bahamas; knowledge of the location of Columbus' San Salvador (in the native tongue Guanahaní) was preserved for perhaps forty years, then forgotten.

Historians did not begin addressing themselves to the problem in a methodical way until the pioneering work of the Spaniard Navarrete in the eighteenth century; and since navigational considerations were vital to solving it, erudite naval officers soon involved themselves in the debate. Over the past two centuries no less than nine different islands have been proposed as Columbus' first landing place. Admiral Morison pronounced authoritatively for Watling's Island, which was actually renamed San Salvador in respect for his judgment, and many then regarded the case as closed; but it was not. A brilliant reinterpretation of the evidence by Joseph Judge and Luis and Ethel Marden, working with the help of computers, published in 1986 and aided by a careful re-translation of Columbus' Log by Eugene Lyon, has provided almost conclusive evidence that Columbus' landfall was made on Samaná Cay, some sixty miles southeast of Watling's Island. After staying there for two days, according to this remarkable new study, Columbus took his three ships to Acklins Island, Crooked Island, Long Island, back to Fortune Island adjoining Crooked Island, and then south to Cuba.[52]

On October 28 Columbus arrived at Bariay Bay on the verdant coast of Cuba, with level fertile land and streams of pure water, and mountains inland. The beauty of the land deeply impressed him. Its inhabitants were of the same race and language and timidity as those of the Bahamas. The Indians he had brought with him from the Bahamas could therefore talk with those of Cuba and alleviate some of their fear of the strangers, though two-way communica-

[51]Columbus' Log, ed. Fuson, October 11-12, 1492, pp. 75-76; Morison, *Admiral of the Ocean Sea*, pp. 133-134.

[52]Joseph Judge, "The Island of Landfall," and Luis Marden, "Tracking Columbus Across the Atlantic," *National Geographic*, November 1986, pp. 566-599.

tion was still impossible. Cuba was big enough so that Columbus could readily think it part of the continent of Asia; indeed, he continued to believe that, against mounting evidence, at least until the last of his four voyages, and probably to his dying day. For the next three weeks he expected to arrive in China and get into contact with the Great Khan at almost any moment.[53] But by mid-November he had to face the fact that all he had so far found was a beautiful land with few if any precious metals and a very primitive people. He liked the people, finding them good and trusting. He saw no evidence that they had any strong religion of their own. His Log entry for November 6 contains a passage addressed directly to Isabel and Fernando, showing his profound interest in the conversion of these people he had discovered:

> I have to say, Most Serene Princes, that if devout religious persons knew the Indian language well, all these people would soon become Christians. Thus I pray to Our Lord that Your Highnesses will appoint persons of great diligence in order to bring to the Church such great numbers of peoples, and that they will convert these peoples, just as they have destroyed those who would not confess the Father, Son, and Holy Spirit [probably a reference to the defeat of the Muslims by the completion of the Reconquest of Spain]. And after your days, for we are all mortal, you will leave your realms in a very tranquil state, free from heresy and wickedness, and you will be well received before the Eternal Creator, Whom may it please to grant you a long life and a great increase of larger realms and dominions, and the will and disposition to spread the holy Christian religion, as you have done up until this time. Amen.[54]

This passage shows the aspect of Columbus' character that probably appealed most to Queen Isabel, since in this he was most like her.

But Columbus felt he had to gain some immediate, tangible return from the new lands he had discovered, to justify his enterprise and merit the continuing confidence of Isabel and Fernando. Though he never says so, it appears from his Log that by the middle of November he had concluded that he was unlikely to reach Japan or China on this voyage, and that he must now search for precious metals on islands east of Cuba with the aid of the Indians, who were constantly being asked in sign language for directions to islands where gold was to be found. They had little interest in gold nor understanding of the Spaniards' passion for it, and responded simply by giving him directions to the two largest islands other than Cuba that they knew: Great Inagua, which they called "Babeque," and Hispaniola (as Columbus was to name it), today divided between Haiti and the Dominican Republic, which the Indians called "Bohío."[55]

Sailing east against the trades was difficult, particularly away from the land, and Columbus' attempts to reach Great Inagua Island were unsuccessful

[53]Morison, *Admiral of the Ocean Sea*, pp. 254-261.
[54]Columbus' Log, ed. Fuson, November 6, 1492, p. 105.
[55]Morison, *Admiral of the Ocean Sea*, pp. 262-263.

for this reason. But *Pinta* was a better sailer than *Santa Maria*, and on November 21, when Columbus gave up his attempt to reach Great Inagua, Martín Alonso Pinzón defied his commander and beat on toward it in *Pinta*, determined to get to the gold (though in fact there was no gold on Great Inagua). This was mutiny, as Columbus stated in his Log entry for that day, but he wisely made no attempt to pursue the rebel captain, though he remained in sight throughout that day and the next due to the difficulty of making headway against the wind.[56]

Martín Alonso Pinzón's desertion of Columbus on November 21, 1492 was accompanied by a decisive moment of choice rarely if ever mentioned in later accounts of the great voyage. The choice was made by Martín Alonso's brother, Vicente Yáñez. If he had followed Martín Alonso that day he would almost certainly have doomed the Columbus expedition, and there is good reason to believe that not one man of it would have returned alive to Spain. *Santa Maria* was not the right kind of ship for exploring unknown coasts, as was shown by the fact that she was eventually wrecked. Without *Niña*, Columbus would have been marooned on Hispaniola after the wreck, and would probably have died as did all the men he later had to leave behind there. Only Columbus, the greatest seaman of his age and probably of any age, knew how to get home by the westerlies farther north in the unknown western Atlantic. Without him to guide them, the two caravels would probably not have been able to return. Martín Alonso forgot or ignored that, in his pride; his brother did not. He may also have understood better his obligation of loyalty. Whatever his reasons, the fidelity of Vicente Yáñez Pinzón that November day in 1492 saved the expedition that discovered America, as well as probably saving his own life and the lives of all his men. More often than the cynical believe, loyalty brings its own reward.

On November 24 Columbus, now with only *Santa Maria* and *Niña*, returned to the coast of Cuba at Puerto Cayo Moa. Above it, on the hillsides, he saw a great quantity of pines which would be ideal for ship timber and masts; and he made a new mast and yard for *Niña* there. On the 26th he set sail again, following the northeastern coast of Cuba; he reached its end December 4. The next day, across a broad sea passage to the eastward, he saw the loom of another island, and had crossed to it by the time the sun set.[57] This was Hispaniola, Little Spain, "the Spanish Isle"—and in Hispaniola, though it was no El Dorado, there were significant quantities of gold.

Meanwhile, without any way of knowing what their great captain was doing in and beyond the Sea of Darkness, Isabel and Fernando had left

---

[56]*Ibid.*, pp. 268-271; Columbus' Log, ed. Fuson, November 21-22, 1492, p. 113.
[57]Columbus' Log, ed. Fuson, November 24-December 5, 1492, pp. 115-125.

Zaragoza and arrived in Barcelona in the latter part of October. In addition to the blow of the election of Alexander VI as Pope, they had endured a major personal loss in the death of their peerless comrade and champion in the great victorious war against Granada, the Duke of Cádiz, on August 28, still in the year of his triumph, at little more than forty. The whole court put on mourning for him. Since he left no legitimate children, many of his possessions were forfeited to the crown, including the city of Cádiz itself, to become under royal administration a great emporium for trade with the New World just discovered.[58]

One of the reasons Isabel and Fernando had gone to Barcelona was to conduct negotiations with France for the quick return of the Catalan province of Roussillon north of the Pyrenées, much fought over in the past, but promised in the name of the young French King Charles VIII to be returned to Spain. The French were dragging their feet; the new Pope, still trying to ingratiate himself with Isabel and Fernando whose disapproval of him he must have known (if for no other reason than the frankness of Peter Martyr de Anglería in writing to his Chancellor, Cardinal Sforza, telling him of it), ordered Charles VIII to turn Roussillon over to Spain on pain of excommunication.[59] Unsure (with reason) that even this would induce Charles (or his advisors) to keep their promises, Fernando was conducting negotiations in Barcelona for a general treaty with new benefits for France.[60] Isabel's role in these negotiations was probably very small; they were an Aragonese affair, and she had always tended to defer almost entirely to her husband in matters pertaining strictly or primarily to his kingdom.

On December 7, the vigil of the great Feast of the Immaculate Conception—when Columbus was sailing away from the first great harbor he had found on the island of Hispaniola, Puerto San Nicolas (named for the patron saint of children on whose day he discovered it, which still bears this name in its French form)[61]—Fernando had just completed four hours of judging cases brought to him by the citizens of Barcelona. It was about noon of a very cloudy day. He was descending a short flight of marble stairs from his judgment seat near the gate of the old royal palace. Seeming to come out of nowhere, a poorly dressed man of about sixty ran up to him, pulled a cutlass from his cape, and swung it at Fernando's neck as though to cut off his head. Whether because he saw his attacker at the last moment, or by pure fortunate chance,

---

[58]Bernáldez, *Memorias*, pp. 236-240 (ch. CIV); Santa Cruz, *Crónica*, I, 100 (ch. XVII); Rumeu de Armas, *Itinerario*, p. 198.
[59]Bernáldez, *Memorias*, pp. 264-265 (ch. CXV); Santa Cruz, *Crónica*, I, 69-70 (ch. IX).
[60]This was the Treaty of Barcelona, finalized the following month, January 1493.
[61]Columbus' Log, ed. Fuson, December 6-7, 1492, pp. 127-130; Morison, *Admiral of the Ocean Sea*, p. 282.

Fernando turned his head a split second before the blow struck, so that part of its force fell on the side of his head rather than fully upon the neck, and part of it on a thick gold collar he was wearing. Nevertheless a deep wound was inflicted; in an instant Fernando was covered with blood. Crying treason, he called on the Blessed Virgin Mary for help. His guards rushed up and wounded the attacker, but Fernando told them not to kill him. Going into the palace, he fainted briefly, but then recovered consciousness and declared firmly that, with God's help, he would live. Doctors assembled from all over Barcelona declared the wound dangerous, but not necessarily mortal. He suffered much pain, bearing it all, as he said, "for his sins."

Word of the attempted assassination flew through the city, with all the wild rumors that inevitably accompany such a report. When Isabel heard it, her first thought was that a general uprising was underway. The house where she and Fernando were staying had a postern gate opening on the sea; she called up a ship to come there and put Prince Juan aboard it so that he would be completely safe. This was the Queen acting, quick and decisive as ever; then the loving wife supplanted the Queen. She broke down in tears and even cries (not since before her coronation have we seen Isabel in tears). She ran to the palace, crying out as she asked if her husband was alive. Assured that he was, and that there was reason to hope that the wound was not mortal, "she rejoiced as though he had been raised from the dead." But for nine days his life remained in danger. During all those days she was almost constantly at his bedside, except for the time when she and all the children went on foot to the great shrine of the Blessed Virgin Mary at Montserrat to pray for his recovery. Often with a high fever, Fernando did not wish to eat; it was Isabel who coaxed him to do so, feeding him with her own hands.[62]

The external evidence regarding this event alone would show us how much Isabel loved her husband, but we have more—the second longest surviving personal letter she ever wrote, written to her former confessor, Archbishop Hernando de Talavera, on this occasion. This document is absolutely essential to understanding Isabel the Catholic. It shows her to us with all her guards down, all the dignified reserve which so many witnesses report in her gone. We see the soul of a selfless woman in love—and of a saint.

> Since we see that kings may die by accident like other men, we
> should be prepared to die well. And I say this because, although I have

---

[62]This account is based on a collation of the five descriptions we have of the near-assassination of Fernando and his subsequent recovery: Bernáldez, *Memorias*, pp. 265-267 (ch. CXVI); Santa Cruz, *Crónica*, I, 72-74 (ch. X); Peter Martyr de Anglería to the Count of Tendilla, December 8 and 23, 1492 (Barcelona), DIHE IX, 226-227, 229-230; same to the Archbishop of Granada, December 14, 1492 (Barcelona), DIHE IX, 227-228. The quotation about Isabel's rejoicing "as though he had been raised from the dead" is from Santa Cruz, I, 74.

never doubted it, and grandeur and prosperity made me think of it more, and fear, yet there is a great difference between believing this and thinking on it, and experiencing it. Since the King my lord has seen death close at hand, I have experienced it more often and more deeply than if I faced it myself from another cause, nor could I feel as I did even if my soul should leave my body. I cannot exaggerate what I suffer. Before I taste death again, which I pray God may not be in such a way, I should like to be in a different position than I am now, especially in meeting my obligations. I beg you and charge you for Our Lord's sake to tell me if there is anything I can do to make return for the many good things done for me . . . and to make restitution and satisfaction to those I have wronged, in whatever manner you prescribe. Please send me a memorandum about this, for it will be the greatest relief in the world for me to have it. . . .

The wound was so great—as Dr. Guadalupe said, for I could not bear to look at it—that it was four inches deep and long; my heart trembles to speak of how great our fear was, but God in his mercy decreed that it should be in a place where it would not be mortal, leaving nerves and spine untouched. . . . After the seventh day came a surge of fever worse than all that had gone before. It lasted a day and a night which I can only say, with St. Gregory in the office of Holy Saturday, that it was a night of hell. . . .

[But] God in His goodness took pity on all of us, so that when Herrera left to bring you another letter from me, my lord was already quite well, as I said, and as he has remained, thanks and praise be to Our Lord. He is up and walking about, and tomorrow please God he will ride to the city to take up residence in another house. Our pleasure at seeing him up is as great as was our sadness before, as though we had been raised from the dead. I do not know how we shall thank God for so great a favor. Only great virtue would suffice. What shall I do, since I have none? This was one of the pains I felt, to see the King suffer what I deserved to suffer. While not deserving it, he paid for my sins, he destroyed them all for me; I pray God that from now on I shall serve Him as I should.[63]

Nor did Isabel, amid her suffering, forget what Christ had commanded about loving our enemies. It was almost immediately established that the attacker, Juan de Colmeñares, was hopelessly insane. Consequently Fernando and Isabel both wished to spare his life, but the Royal Council argued that the stability of the realm required his execution; if he were not memorably punished, others not insane might attempt what he had attempted. Isabel was a woman who combined fire and love and iron and sanctity in her unique spirit, but she had no trace of sentimentality; she saw the force of the Council's argument—far stronger than our modern sentimentalists are ever inclined to admit—and she accepted it. But there was no cruelty in her, no desire for revenge. In her letter to Archbishop Hernando de Talavera she explained at length how she had insisted that Juan de Colmeñares be given the opportunity to make a good confession, which she says he did; and we learn from another

---

[63]Isabel to Hernando de Talavera, Archbishop of Granada, December 30, 1492 (Barcelona), in Vicente Rodríguez Valencia, *Isabel la Católica en la Opinion de Españoles y Extranjeros*, Volume III (Valladolid, 1970), pp. 31-33.

source that she arranged for him to be killed quickly and painlessly before, on December 12, five days after the assassination attempt, his body was put through the repulsive ceremonial dismemberment which the law of almost every European country then required for treason (called "hanging, drawing, and quartering" in England), which was supposed to be carried out while the victim was still alive.[64]

By the beginning of January Fernando was almost entirely recovered from his brush with death, and ready to put the finishing touches on a major treaty with France, known as the Treaty of Barcelona. Final agreement on its terms was reached in Barcelona on January 8; the treaty was ratified by Charles VIII of France on January 18 and by Fernando and Isabel on the 19th. It purported to establish an alliance between long-time enemies France and Spain. In fact it did nothing of the sort, and it is most unlikely that either side expected it to. The French were planning an invasion of Italy to make good the ancient claim of their royal dynasty to the kingdom of Naples at the far end of the Italian peninsula. Confident in their ability to divide and conquer Italians, their chief concern was intervention against them by an outside power. They hoped to keep Spain from intervening by concessions, and knew that it had long been a prime goal of Fernando to regain the trans-Pyrenean province of Roussillon, which his father Juan had been forced to turn over to France as security for a large loan from France to provide him with the money to put down a rebellion in Catalonia. Juan during the rest of his lifetime, and after him Fernando, had made repeated but unsuccessful efforts to regain Roussillon. It was Fernando's goal to get it back by appearing to be willing to let France take Naples, without actually committing himself in writing to non-intervention in Italy. A highly skilled diplomat, Fernando achieved his goal. The Treaty of Barcelona committed France to restore Roussillon to Spain and to recognize Spanish rule over the Italian island of Sardinia, but made no mention of Naples. But it did include a specific provision that France would not attack the Pope and that the Spanish were free to defend him if he was attacked.[65]

On December 7, the day Fernando was attacked, Columbus found a broad deep harbor on the north coast of Hispaniola which he called Port Conception, since it was discovered on the vigil of the feast of the Immaculate Conception. Threatening weather and contrary winds confined Columbus in

---

[64]*Ibid.*, pp. 33-34; Santa Cruz, *Crónica*, I, 74-75 (ch. X); Menéndez Pidal, *Historia de España*, XVII (2), 337.

[65]For the text of the treaty, see Suárez Fernández, *Política Internacional de Isabel*, III, 368-383; there is an English summary in G. A. Bergenroth, ed., *Calendar of Letters, Despatches and State Papers relating to the Negotiations between England and Spain*, Volume I: "Henry VII, 1485-1509" (London, 1862), p. 43. See also Menéndez Pidal, *Historia de España*, XVII (2), 194-195, 343-345, 353.

Port Conception for a full week, during which his men were able to explore the countryside and he had numerous opportunities for personal contact with the Indians. He still could not communicate with them directly, being limited to sign language and whatever the Indians from the Bahamas (whose language was very similar to that of the Indians living in this part of Hispaniola) could tell them about their experiences with the Spaniards. Columbus' persistent belief that he was very near to China and its long-gone "Grand Khan," and his burning desire for gold and the natives' desire to play up to it without really understanding it, compounded the mistakes and misunderstandings inevitable in such a situation. But the Indians, after initial fear, continued to give a generous welcome to the "men from heaven" (as the Bahaman Indians always described the Spaniards), and Columbus was entranced with this new land he had found, even more than he had been with Cuba.[66]

> As to the country, the best in Castile in beauty and fertility cannot compare with this. This land is as different from that surrounding Córdoba as day is from night.
> All the land around the village is cultivated, and a river flows thorugh the middle of the valley. It is very large and wide and could irrigate all the lands around. All the trees are green and full of fruit, and the plants are in flower and very tall. The roads are wide and good, and the breezes are like those in Castile in the month of April. The nightingales and other small birds sing as they do in Spain in the same month, and it is the greatest pleasure in the world.[67]

Observing the remarkably unwarlike character of these Indians, along with their friendliness and desire to please, on December 16 Columbus wrote in his journal words that will forever cast a shadow on the otherwise admirable character of the greatest mariner and discoverer in the history of mankind:

> All that is needed here is to build a town and order the Indians to do your [the sovereigns'] bidding. I, with the people I have with me, who are not many in number, could go through all these islands without any opposition. I have already seen three of my sailors go ashore where there is a great number of Indians, and the Indians have all fled without anyone wishing to do them any harm. They have no arms and are naked, and have no knowledge of arms and are very timid. A thousand of them would not face three Christians, and so they are suitable to be governed and made to work and sow and do everything else that shall be necessary, to build villages and be taught to wear clothing and to observe our customs.[68]

The Dominican friar Bartolomé de las Casas, missionary, historian, and advocate of the Indians, a great admirer of Columbus whose father had sailed

---

[66]Columbus' Log, ed. Fuson, December 7-13, 1492, pp. 130-134.

[67]*Ibid.*, December 13, 1492, p. 134.

[68]*Ibid.*, December 16, 1492, p. 138.

with him and who remembered, as a boy, his return from the first voyage, and who alone preserved his Log for posterity, breaks in at this point in his transcript of the Log with words that remind the historical relativist that it was not only a later age that could see the evil in that statement by Columbus:

> Note here, that the natural, simple and kind gentleness and humble condition of the Indians, and want of arms or protection, gave the Spaniards the insolence to hold them of little account, and to impose on them the harshest tasks that they could, and to become glutted with oppression and destruction. And sure it is that here the Admiral enlarged himself in speech more than he should, and that what he here conceived and set forth from his lips, was the beginning of the ill usage he [and many others] afterwards inflicted upon them.[69]

Isabel, as we shall see, throughout the remainder of her life did all she could to protect her native American subjects, as did her grandson Charles V, King of Spain and Holy Roman Emperor. Between them they prevented legal enslavement of the Indians; nor was the African slave trade to America significant in their time. But Spanish treatment of the Indians all too often followed Columbus' ugly recommendations of December 16, 1492, as Las Casas in his long, unsparing *History of the Indies* amply proves (despite considerable exaggerations). Millions of Indians were soon converted, as Columbus so often said he desired, but most of these early converts came into the Church in Mexico thanks to the intervention of Our Lady of Guadalupe; many others who should have been converted were not. No significant number of conversions were ever made in the Caribbean, and it was fifty years after the conquest of Peru before they began in quantity in South America. The Indians of the Caribbean were wiped out to the last man—the majority of them dying, to be sure, of European diseases to which they had no natural resistance, but far too many as a result of oppression, forced labor, and war. The rich fair island of Hispaniola which Columbus discovered has had, beginning in 1493, as grim a history as any land on the face of the earth, extending all the way to yesterday's brutal dictatorship of the Duvaliers in Haiti.

But it was not only Hispaniola that Columbus' great discovery opened up, it was everything from Point Barrow, Alaska to Cape Horn—a new world. It brought rescue and liberation for the fifteen million Indians of Mexico under the Satanic rule of the human-sacrificing Aztec emperors;[70] it offered new homelands for the peoples of Europe, including the United States of America which was to lead mankind's ultimately successful resistance to the bloodiest despotisms in all history: Hitler's Germany and Stalin's Soviet Union.

During the beautiful days of December it seemed to Columbus that his

---

[69]Las Casas as quoted in Morison, *Admiral of the Ocean Sea*, p. 291.
[70]See my *Our Lady of Guadalupe and the Conquest of Darkness* (Front Royal VA, 1983).

stopping at Puerto Rico, of which some of the Indians had told him. But when they indicated that it lay to the southeast, while his route back to Spain lay to the northeast, he decided to sail for Spain.[77]

Beating against the trade wind, Columbus with his two surviving ships fought his way northeast until they had left the tropics behind. He passed with fortunate ease through the belt of variable winds later known as the "horse latitudes" (from the ships carrying horses which had to throw them overboard when they were becalmed so long that they ran out of water for them) and on February 1 he first picked up the westerlies he had been seeking.[78] The next night he tried to obtain a star sight on Polaris with his quadrant and astrolabe from the heaving deck of little *Niña* (Columbus had not set foot on *Pinta* since its return; he had no desire to spend any time with Martín Alonso). He could not catch Polaris because of the motion, but the naked eye of "perhaps . . . the greatest dead-reckoning sailor who ever lived"[79] was almost as good as a quadrant or astrolabe; he estimated his latitude within 175 miles of the correct figure, even without the instruments.[80]

On February 6 they picked up a strong westerly wind which drove them nearly 200 miles in 24 hours, the fastest sailing of the entire voyage. For the next three days the winds were lighter; then during the 24 hours of February 10-11 the caravels again made 150 miles.[81] But on the 12th they were struck by one of the terrible winter storms that have been the curse of the North Atlantic—Nicholas Monserrat's "cruel sea"—from that day to this. All day the wind blew at full gale. "If the caravel had not been very sound and well equipped, I fear we would have been lost," Columbus says, adding that every mile's progress was made "with great difficulty and in constant danger."[82] All that night *Niña* ran before the howling wind under bare poles (no sail set). The next day the force of the wind abated somewhat, but the sea was worse. That night the gale returned and the waves rose even higher, breaking over the ship, which was now driven helplessly before the storm. During that fearful night the lights of *Pinta* vanished from sight, and at dawn she was nowhere to be seen. Columbus had no way of knowing whether she had survived or gone down.[83]

In the wild gray morning, Columbus tells us, "the wind became stronger and the crossing waves more terrible; I carried only a low mainsail, so that the ship might escape some of the waves breaking over her and not sink."[84] For six hours the ordeal continued with no sign of relief. Columbus called his men

---

[77]Columbus' Log, ed. Fuson, January 13-16, 1493, pp. 171-178.
[78]Morison, *Admiral of the Ocean Sea*, pp. 317-318; but see Note 70, above.
[79]Fuson, ed., *Log of Columbus*, p. 29.
[80]Morison, *Admiral of the Ocean Sea*, p. 319.
[81]*Ibid.*, pp. 320-322.
[82]Columbus' Log, ed. Fuson, February 12, 1493, p. 184.
[83]*Ibid.*, February 13-14, 1493.
[84]*Ibid.*, February 14, 1493.

together and they vowed a pilgrimage to the great shrine of Our Lady of Guadalupe in Spain if they were spared, with their representative to be chosen by lot; and Columbus was chosen.[85] This shrine in central Spain was a favorite of Isabel and Fernando; they had spent a full two weeks there in June 1492.[86] Columbus fulfilled the vow on his way across Spain after his return. When the Blessed Virgin Mary first appeared in the New World, to the Indian convert Juan Diego in Mexico in 1531, she named herself to him as Our Lady of Guadalupe.[87]

Still the tempest continued, and all the men now vowed if they were spared to go in procession in only their shirts to give thanks in a church dedicated to the Blessed Virgin Mary on the first land they reached. Columbus feared very much for his two sons in Spain if they were left fatherless, and that the knowledge of his epochal discovery would be lost (for it is most unlikely he believed that Martín Alonso Pinzón in *Pinta*, a ship little bigger than his own, could survive a storm that would sink him). So, during that day of shrieking wind and crashing wave, he wrote a brief account of his discoveries, rolled it in waxed cloth, tied it securely, put it in a barrel, and cast it overboard. None of his men knew what was in it, and the barrel has never been found.[88]

After sunset on the 14th the skies began to clear, though the seas were still high, and the next morning land was sighted.[89] It was the island of Santa Maria, southernmost of the Azores, discovered and settled by Portugal. Columbus approached the island and anchored, for he and his men were in much need of food and water. The first of the inhabitants with whom he spoke told him "they had never seen such a storm as that which has prevailed for the past fifteen days, and they wondered how we had escaped."[90] The Azoreans came down to the shore and gave him some of the needed supplies. The next day half of Columbus' crew went ashore to fulfill their vow of a pilgrimage in their shirts to a shrine of Our Lady to give thanks for their deliverance. They were seized by the acting governor of the island, who tried to capture Columbus as well, but the Admiral was armed and ready, and the Portuguese then had no ship at the island. After three days Columbus' sailors were released, and the following day *Niña* departed with a fair wind for Spain.[91]

Columbus was now back in waters he knew well from the years he had lived in Portugal and sailed from it. But his ordeal was not yet over. He had eight hundred miles more to go, and this winter of 1493 was one of the worst of

[85]*Ibid.*, p. 185.
[86]Rumeu de Armas, *Itinerario*, pp. 194-195.
[87]See my *Our Lady of Guadalupe*, pp. 104-105.
[88]Columbus' Log, ed. Fuson, February 14, 1493, pp. 185-186.
[89]*Ibid.*, February 15, 1493, pp. 186-187.
[90]*Ibid.*, February 18, 1493, p. 187.
[91]*Ibid.*, February 19-23, 1493, pp. 188-191.

the century. On February 27 *Niña* was once more facing "contrary winds, great waves, and a high sea."[92] This time she appears to have been closer to the storm center. In the evening of March 2 a cold front of the storm overtook *Niña* with a violent squall which stripped every sail she was carrying off her masts. All through the day of March 3 she hurtled eastward under bare poles before a roaring northwest wind. The squall line of the cold front was parallel to her course and the wind was close to hurricane force. Columbus' superb dead reckoning, and signs visible even in the tempest, warned him that he was approaching land.[93] Just after sunset "the waves came from two directions, and the wind appeared to raise the ship in the air, with the water from the sky and the lightning in every direction."[94] But the wind was tearing at the clouds as well as the waters, so that occasionally the full moon shone through. Between the moon and the lightning, at seven o'clock land was sighted dead ahead, high enough to mean cliffs.[95] A rockbound lee shore in a near-hurricane for a ship driven before the wind means certain death if its course cannot be changed.

There is no more dramatic moment in all of maritime history. They had one sail left. Columbus and his men must get it up the mast without its being shredded as the others had been, and wear ship at a right angle to take the gale abeam. They must do it quickly, for the cliffs were close ahead. They must do it in the dark, except for the bursts of unearthly brilliance from the cloud-wracked moon and the lightning bolts. We may visualize Vicente Yáñez Pinzón and Columbus side by side on the thundering deck, directing the men at the halyards in the raising of the sail; then, as the wild wind caught it with a snap that set hearts racing, the Admiral going back to stand above the helmsman. The helmsman of a caravel could not see forward, and only a little of the sky; he steered by feel, and by orders from above.[96] The slightest error in turning into the monster waves rolling up from behind would swamp the ship and sink it like a stone. They could not do it in trough or on crest, but only on the upward roll, when there was moonlight or lightning to show them their opportunity.

The sail was drawing hard, adding its pressure to the pull on the helm. The tall Admiral, his once red hair bleached white by sun and strain, stood with feet braced, waiting for his moment. So far as he knew, his ship and men and they alone bore the secret of the greatest geographical discovery of all time. Their lives and its fate depended on what would happen in the next few minutes. Then his voice would have rung out:

"Helm a-lee! Ease her round to course south-southwest!"

---

[92]*Ibid.*, February 27, 1493, p. 192.

[93]*Ibid.*, March 3, 1493, p. 192; Morison, *Admiral of the Ocean Sea*, p. 338.

[94]Columbus' Log, ed. Fuson, March 4, 1493, p. 192.

[95]Morison, *Admiral of the Ocean Sea*, p. 338.

[96]*Ibid.*, p. 127. For the seamanship involved in Columbus' turn and its dangers, see *ibid.*, pp. 132, 338-339.

Niña made the turn flawlessly, and squared away on her new course. "God protected us until daylight," Columbus says, "but it was with infinite labor and fright."[97]

The Admiral of the Ocean Sea, the discoverer of America, had not let storm and death cheat him of his victory.

At sunrise Columbus saw where he was: off the Rock of Sintra at the mouth of the Tagus River, the entrance to Lisbon, the capital of Portugal. The fishermen of Cascais, the first town on the river mouth, could not imagine how the little ship they saw sailing in had escaped the fury of the tempest; spontaneously they offered prayers of thanksgiving.[98]

Columbus passed a tense nine days in Portugal, in the power of the king who had rejected his enterprise and had once warred against Queen Isabel; but John II was an honorable man. He praised Columbus, entertained him lavishly, and let him go, though the Portuguese chronicler Ruy de Pina tells us that at one point he publicly beat his breast, saying "O man of little comprehension! Why did I let slip an enterprise of such great importance?"[99] He did put in a claim to Columbus' discoveries on the grounds that the Treaty of Alcáçoba, which had provided for the marriage of his son Afonso and Princess Isabel which ended so tragically, gave him title to all oceanic discoveries beyond the Canaries, not just those made down the coast of Africa.[100]

Allowed to leave Portugal in peace, Columbus sailed the *Niña* on the last leg of his incomparable voyage, and on March 15 entered the Rio Tinto on the flood tide at noon to anchor at Palos, whence he had departed seven and a half months before. By a coincidence no novelist would dare invent, *Pinta* followed *Niña* into Palos on the same tide, arriving just an hour or two later. Martín Alonso, not having stopped at the Azores, had reached the little port of Bayona near Vigo in Galicia in northern Spain in the latter part of February. From there he wrote to Isabel and Fernando at Barcelona asking permission to come and tell them about the great discovery, but they replied that they would wait to hear the news from their Admiral. Martín Alonso therefore proceeded disconsolately to Palos, only to find Columbus arrived just before him.[101] As Morison caustically puts it, "without waiting for *Pinta*'s sails to be furled, without reporting to the flagship, or so much as hailing [his brother] Vicente Yáñez, Martín Alonso Pinzón had hismelf rowed ashore, went to his country house near Palos, crawled into bed, and died."[102]

Columbus had already sent a brief account of his discoveries, written on

[97]Columbus' Log, ed. Fuson, March 4, 1493, p. 192.
[98]*Ibid.*
[99]Morison, *Admiral of the Ocean Sea*, p. 346.
[100]*Ibid.*, p. 344.
[101]*Ibid.*, pp. 350-352.
[102]*Ibid.*, p. 352.

Niña in February, to Isabel and Fernando from Lisbon.[103] He now sent them another copy, with a formal request to be allowed to come to report to them in Barcelona. He stayed at familiar La Rábida while waiting for their answer, giving thanks to Our Lady at two of her shrines in the area. There were celebrations in Palos and Moguer and Huelva—nobody but Martín Alonso Pinzón seems to have felt bitter at this moment about the great voyage—and immense enthusiasm wherever the news of the discoveries was received.[104] It spread with amazing speed; just four days after his arrival in Palos the Duke of Medinaceli was writing from Cogullado north of Madrid to Cardinal Mendoza that Columbus "has found everything he looked for, the whole of it"—the information had reached him from Lisbon.[105] Before the end of March the news had reached Florence, and was very soon all over Italy.[106] On March 30 Isabel and Fernando replied to Columbus' letter, expressing their great pleasure at his success, promising him continued aid and favor, and urging him to come to court as quickly as possible, so that a second expedition to America might be more promptly dispatched.[107]

The next day was Palm Sunday; Columbus spent Holy Week in Sevilla with the ten Indian captives he had brought with him on *Niña*, where the boy Bartolomé de Las Casas caught a never-forgotten glimpse of them.[108] He was received everywhere with the greatest honor, but clearly he came to Holy Week in Sevilla above all to give thanks to God, through participating in its glorious pageantry commemorating the death and resurrection of Christ which still commands the admiration and attendance of Catholics throughout the world. By Easter he had the royal invitation, and immediately drafted a set of recommendations for the colonization of Hispaniola that were a model of statesmanship. He urged that 2,000 settlers be sent to found three or four towns in Hispaniola, each with a church and a number of priests and friars sufficient for the needs of the settlers and for missionary work as well. Only settlers who would build houses and be licensed by the governor should be allowed to collect gold, and for only part of each year, with all to be handed

---

[103]The text of the letter, transmitted on March 4, 1492 from Lisbon, appears in Morison, *Journals and Other Documents on Columbus*, pp. 182-186 (English translation). The superscription of the letter indicates that it was sent to Luis de Santángel, Keeper of the Privy Purse, whose last-minute intervention at Santa Fe in January 1492 had finally persuaded Isabel to endorse and authorize Columbus' voyage, "contained in another for their Highnesses"—presumably a copy of Columbus' letter on his discoveries to Isabel and Fernando. Only the copy sent to Santángel is extant.

[104]Morison, *Admiral of the Ocean Sea*, pp. 322-323, 353-354.

[105]Duke of Medinaceli to Cardinal Mendoza, March 19, 1493 (Cogullado), in Morison, *Journals and Other Documents on Columbus*, p. 20.

[106]Columbus, *Admiral of the Ocean Sea*, pp. 367, 375-376.

[107]Isabel and Fernando to Columbus, March 30, 1493 (Barcelona), in *ibid.*, p. 355.

[108]*Ibid.*, p. 354.

over to a designated treasurer and half reserved for the crown.[109]

It might have actually been done—by a man of sterling honor with the power of instant decision and the charism of command over men, such as the late Duke of Cádiz, Gutierre de Cárdenas, or Gonzalo de Córdoba. Tragically, Columbus was to show all too soon that he was not such a man. He had magnificent courage and immense talent, but not of this kind.

Columbus reached Barcelona in mid-April and was given a splendid reception, the climax of his life. He brought six of his Indians with him; they were soon baptized, with Isabel, Fernando, and Prince Juan as their sponsors.[110] The second expedition to America was given royal authorization and ordered to depart as soon as possible from Cádiz, with Archdeacon (later Archbishop) Juan de Fonseca of Sevilla in charge of providing the ships and supplies for it. All Columbus' promised titles and privileges were confirmed, including rule of the Indies (as the Spanish then and ever afterward called America, taking their cue from Columbus). The royal instructions for the second expedition specified its purposes as conversion of the Indians, establishment of a trading colony, and the exploration of Cuba. Columbus was given full authority over everyone sailing in the second expedition, and authorized to designate an official to remain in charge of Hispaniola while he went exploring.[111]

It was accepted international law in Europe at this time that the Pope could grant sovereignty over any land not inhabited and ruled by Christians to any Christian king who applied for it. Portugal had already obtained Papal grants of sovereignty over the coast of Africa all the way to the lands of the fabulous Prester John. Even before Columbus reached Barcelona, reacting immediately to the first news reports of his discoveries, Isabel and Fernando had made a similar application to Pope Alexander VI for the lands their Admiral had discovered and that he and his successors would discover to the west and southwest, across the Atlantic. The Pope, eager to obtain Spanish support against the growing French menace to Italy and to allay the known displeasure of Isabel and Fernando with his election, gave them what they asked for, almost by return mail. Because of his lack of knowledge of what had been found, and apparently also the lack of a specifically worded proposal from Isabel and Fernando, the bull *Inter caetera* which the Pope issued on this matter May 3 was so vaguely phrased as to be almost meaningless, merely recognizing Spanish sovereignty over "certain very distant islands and even mainlands

---

[109]*Ibid.*, pp. 355-356.

[110]Bernáldez, *Memorias*, p. 278 (ch. CXVIII); Santa Cruz, *Crónica*, I, 90-91 (ch. XIV).

[111]Instructions of the Catholic Sovereigns to Admiral Cristóbal Colón, May 29, 1493 (Barcelona), in Antonio Rumeu de Armas, *La Politica Indigenista de Isabel la Católica* (Valladolid, 1969), pp. 301-302; Bernáldez, *Memorias*, p. 278 (ch. CXVIII); Santa Cruz, *Crónica*, I, 96-97 (ch. XVI).

hitherto undiscovered by others." After consultation with Columbus, Isabel and Fernando dispatched a new ambassador to Rome. He arrived May 25, and just over a month later the Pope issued a revision of *Inter caetera*, backdating it to May 4, which drew a line of demarcation one hundred leagues west of the Azores. Placing the line there was almost certainly Columbus' idea. All non-Christian lands which could be conquered to the west of it were to belong to Spain; all to the east, to Portugal. Any Spanish or Portuguese who ventured without permission into the lands and seas thereby assigned to the other would incur excommunication.[112]

Expansively as geographic horizons were opening up, no one yet thought to ask whether the line extended all the way around the world, over the poles and along the opposite meridian on the other side of the globe, though this was to become a burning question within twenty-five years' time.

In June Columbus left Barcelona on the return journey to Sevilla, stopping on the way to fulfill his vow taken during the first great storm of the return voyage, by praying at the shrine of Our Lady of Guadalupe. To reach it by the usual pilgrimage route, he would have passed through the town of Trujillo, where he might have been seen by the strapping 13-year-old Francisco Pizarro, who was to be the worst and most faithless of all the *conquistadores*, the tyrant of Peru. Leaving the shrine, heading south for Sevilla, Columbus would have passed through or near the smaller town of Medellín, where he might have been seen by a thin and sickly eight-year-old boy named Hernán Cortés, who was to become the greatest and best of all the *conquistadores*, the Christian liberator of Mexico.[113]

Arriving at Sevilla, Columbus began engaging men for his second voyage. The first voyage, rather surprisingly in view of Columbus' genuine devotion to his Faith and his Church, had included no priest. This time several priests and religious would sail with him, headed by a Catalan friar named Buil, to whom Pope Alexander VI had given full Power to administer the Church in the newly discovered lands.[114]

Isabel and Fernando continued to hold court at Barcelona during the spring and summer of 1493, because Roussillon had not yet been delivered up by the French. The original Treaty of Barcelona had not mentioned Naples, which the French intended to conquer; the French now wanted some explicit guarantee that Spain would not help Naples if it was attacked. On August 25 a guarantee was finally made, though with an escape clause; Fernando promised

---

[112]Santa Cruz, *Crónica*, I, 94-95 (ch. XV); instructions from Isabel and Fernando to Diego López de Haro as ambassador to Rome, May 3, 1493 (Barcelona), Suárez Fernández, *Política internacional de Isabel*, III, 394-414; Morison, *Admiral of the Ocean Sea*, pp. 367-371.
[113]Morison, *European Discovery of America: Southern Voyages*, pp. 99-100.
[114]Santa Cruz, *Crónica*, I, 97-98 (ch. XVI).

not to aid Naples against an attempt by Charles VIII of France to assert whatever rights he might have there (leaving open the possibility that Fernando might conclude that in truth he had no such rights). But the people of Roussillon were agitating for an end to French rule, and the carefully planned French invasion of Italy was to begin in just a few months. The French could wait no longer. On September 15 they ceremonially transferred control of Roussillon to Spain at the provincial capital at Perpignan during a heavy rainstorm.[115] It was yet another victory for Isabel and Fernando: in less than two calendar years they had reconquered Granada, annexed Hispaniola, secured their claim to all the lands west of it they could discover, and regained this long-lost province north of the Pyrenees.

On September 25, at the beginning of autumn, Columbus set sail once again for America with a veritable armada of 17 ships and some 1,500 men, departing from the now royal port of Cádiz all bedecked in flags and colors, with cannon firing and trumpets and harps playing.[116] Most people were not yet quite sure just what had been discovered, but everyone sensed that history had been made, that their world would never be the same again. As Peter Martyr d'Anglería said in a letter that month: "Now—O happy event!—under the auspices of my Kings [Isabel and Fernando], there is becoming known that which from the beginning of creation had been hidden from us."[117]

---

[115]Menéndez Pidal, *Historia de España*, XVII (2), 196-198; Bishop of Albi to Isabel and Fernando, May 3, 1493 (Claira), Suárez Fernández, *Política internacional de Isabel*, III, 388-389.

[116]Santa Cruz, *Crónica*, I, 98 (ch. XVI); Morison, *European Discovery of America: Southern Voyages*, pp. 100-101.

[117]Peter Martyr d'Anglería to Cardinal Ascanio Sforza, Sep. 13, 1493 (Barcelona), DIHE IX, 244.

9
Isabel at the Summit
(October 1493-October 1497)

In 1493 Queen Isabel was forty-two years old. No longer young, no longer with limitless energy, she had begun to put on weight; but her face remained beautiful, dignified yet inviting, making her look younger than her years.[1] Piety and wisdom she had always had, from her youth; now not only her countrymen, but the whole world knew it. Said the German physician Hieronymus Münzer, after travelling through her kingdom and then seeing her in Madrid in January 1495:

> So great is her knowledge of the arts of peace and war, so keen her penetration, that she seems to have all the virtues in the highest grade that the female sex permits. She is exceedingly religious, and spends so much on the ornamentation of the churches, that the results are incredible. She shows for the Observant religious an admirable reverence, and founds their monasteries. During the conquest of Granada she was always with the army at the side of the king, and much happened according to her advice. She sits in the tribunal of judgment with the King, hearing the cases and the pleas, and resolving them with a settlement or a definitive sentence. I believe that the Omnipotent sent this most serene lady from Heaven to languishing Spain, so that with her king the public good might be restored to it. What else? She is very religious, very pious, and very gentle.[2]

Isabel—with Fernando always by her side, in full equal partnership—had brought law and order, justice, and peace to Spain; completed the longest crusade with total victory; sent out the expedition that discovered the New World, and watched it return in glory. Along with maintaining and following up these triumphs, she now turned her hand to undertakings no less demanding, and even closer to her heart: the purification and renewal of the Church, and providing for the royal future of her children. In the performance of these tasks she reached her summit of greatness, both temporally and spiritually; she experienced the sweetest joy of her life, and the deepest sorrow; she climbed Sinai, and she climbed Calvary. In the world's eyes then, she succeeded in the

---

[1]Hieronymus Münzer, *Viaje por España y Portugal, 1494-1495*, tr. José López Toro (Madrid, 1951), p. 112.
[2]*Ibid.*

first task, and failed in the second; but history has shown that in the end, beyond the grave, she triumphed in both. For victory was Isabel's way.

All her life Isabel had been vividly aware of the corruption and subversion of the Church in Spain, and in much of Christendom. She had been given many ugly lessons in it by the late Archbishop Carrillo of Toledo; she had even had to watch, without public protest, while her husband installed his six-year-old illegitimate son (conceived shortly before their marriage) as Archbishop of Zaragoza, the capital of Aragon. She had established the Inquisition to root out the enemies hidden inside the Church, and the Inquisition had done that with considerable success; but those hidden enemies were only a part, and not the greatest part of the problem in the Church. As ever, the Church's heaviest cross was not anti-Christians but bad Christians. Isabel knew how often men and women without a real religious vocation were shunted into monasteries and convents, to get them out of the way or even as a special kind of preferment; she knew that many genuine vocations were lost in the kind of religious communities created by such practices.   In Cardinal Mendoza, who had occupied the primatial see of Spain since Carrillo's death in 1482, she had an old friend whom she could trust; but he was one of Spain's wealthiest men, essentially a political rather than a religious figure, not hostile to Church reform, but not one to push it. The new Pope was the last man to promote reform on his own, as Isabel well knew; with remarkable frankness, she asked Papal Nuncio Francisco des Prats early in November to urge the Pope to change his way of life and not to give so much favor to his sons.[3]

Full Church reform would require a different kind of primate; Isabel could do nothing about that while Cardinal Mendoza lived. Nevertheless, she refused simply to wait. Reigning monarchs in the fifteenth century had much more authority over the Church in their country than Catholics of the last two centuries would expect any government to have; the Protestant and the French revolutions were still in the future, and though there had been many clashes between royal and Papal authority, they were always in the context of a shared Catholic commitment. The Church might resist a king or queen, but could never ignore them. A king or queen might resist the Church, but could never ignore it. Major changes required the cooperation of both Church and monarch. In the past, reform had been the work of monks (who usually started it), bishops, and the Pope; but a king or queen could launch it as well. And that is what Isabel did, with the great church reform in Spain.

It did not begin, as is usually believed, when the great Cardinal Cisneros became Archbishop of Toledo in 1495, though he was essential to its fulfillment; it began with Isabel herself, and Fernando cooperating with her unhesitatingly.

---

[3]Francisco des Prats to Pope Alexander VI, November 5, 1493, in Vicente Rodriguez Valencia, *Isabel la Católica en la Opinion de Españoles y Extranjeros*, Volume I (Valladolid, 1970), pp. 45-47.

In March 1493 Pope Alexander VI (undoubtedly on Isabel's request) had authorized Isabel and Fernando to nominate persons to reform convents.[4] The reformers, called Visitors, were selected. A series of letters in December 1493 to the Bishop, Councillors and Visitors of Barcelona, and to Juan Daza—some signed by Isabel alone, others by both her and Fernando, but evidently speaking with her voice—launched the reform in selected convents in Aragon and Catalonia. Surely these are Isabel's words in their December 11 letter to Daza:

> The reformation of the nuns must be carried out in the service of God and well done, so we have begun it, for this is a great service for Our Lord, and we will not relax our efforts until it is brought to completion. To this end we command you to heed us and pursue this task with great diligence and write us often about how it is going.[5]

"We will not relax our efforts until it is brought to completion"—it was the theme of Isabel's whole life: of securing the succession, restoring justice, conquering Granada, discovering America.

The goal of the reform was simply to require the religious communities in Spain to live up to the rule of their order. Many of them were not doing that, and had not done it for a long time, their superiors unconcerned or feeling unable to act because of pressure from lay sponsors of the monasteries and convents. Now, Isabel told Daza and the lieutenant-general of Catalonia, those who brought scandal to convents—as by letting in unauthorized persons (presumably men) at night—were to be punished; superiors who would not cooperate with the reform visitations and deal decisively with abuses which those visitations uncovered, were to be removed.[6]

By the spring of 1494, Isabel was ready to begin reform of the Benedictine monasteries and convents. A letter of April 18 from Isabel and Fernando cited the Pope's authorization to them and the Benedictine prior at Valladolid to launch that reform, and announced that reformer Visitors for the Benedictine monasteries and convents would soon be selected, and would control the appointment of successors for abbots and abbesses who died.[7]

That same spring a new brief from Pope Alexander authorized Isabel and Fernando to proceed to the reform of Franciscan monasteries.[8] The next month Isabel named her new confessor, the ascetic Ximénes de Cisneros, now

---

[4]Pope Alexander VI to Isabel and Fernando, March 27, 1493 (Rome), in José García Oro, *La Reforma de los Religiosos Españoles en tiempo de los Reyes Católicos* (Valladolid, 1969), pp. 150-151.

[5]Isabel and Fernando to Juan Daza, December 11, 1493 (Zaragoza), *ibid.*, p. 256.

[6]Isabel to Daza, December 20, 1493 (Zaragoza) and April 5, 1494 (Medina del Campo), *ibid.*, pp. 262, 279.

[7]Letter from Isabel and Fernando, April 18, 1494, *ibid.*, p. 453.

[8]Brief of Pope Alexander VI, June 18, 1494 (Rome), in Luis Suárez Fernández, ed., *Politica Internacional de Isabel la Católica*, Volume IV (Valladolid, 1971), pp. 205-206.

the Franciscan Provincial for Castile, as Visitor and reformer of all Franciscans in Castile, and with Fernando she ordered their officials to give full support to Cisneros.[9] He went immediately into action in the tough-minded manner which all Spain came to know so well in the years ahead.[10] In October Cardinal Mendoza fell ill, and on January 11, 1495 he died.[11] There is good reason to believe that Isabel had already resolved upon Cisneros as his successor.

Spain during these years was profoundly peaceful and orderly—the fruit of Isabel's dedication to justice throughout the two decades of her reign thus far. This is made very clear by the detailed and almost idyllic report of the German doctor, Hieronymus Münzer, who journeyed through much of the Iberian peninsula from September 1494 to February 1495 and found prosperity and contentment everywhere. He travelled well over a thousand miles, from Barcelona down through Valencia, over to Granada and Sevilla, up through Portugal to Santiago de Compostela, and then back to the center of Castile at Toledo and Madrid, without the slightest indication of concern about his physical safety or the reception he would receive anywhere, and with almost nothing but praise for the people, the cities, and especially the churches that he visited.[12] Beyond the great task of religious reform, Isabel could now follow with care and without distraction those events abroad which were of particular importance to Spain. In 1494, these were the French invasion of Italy and the second expedition of Columbus to "the Indies."

Spanish involvement in Italy dated back more than two centuries, to the sequel of one of the most ferocious massacres in European history, known by the deceivingly gentle name of "Sicilian Vespers." When the massacre took place, Sicily had for seven centuries been the footstool of a long and and varied succession of conquerors from distant lands who had nothing in common other than being totally foreign to Sicily: the Arabs, the Normans, the Germans, and the French. It is said that the origin of the Mafia goes back to somewhere in those seven ravaging centuries which Sicily endured. Finally the oppressed rose up, and at the vesper bell on Monday evening, March 30, 1282, the people of Sicily's capital, Palermo, seized and slew every Frenchman (their current rulers)

---

[9]Isabel and Fernando to Cisneros, July 20, 1494 (Segovia), and general directive to their officials the same day, in García Oro, *Reforma*, pp. 457-458.

[10]Ramón Menéndez Pidal, director, *Historia de España*, Volume XVII: "España de los Reyes Católicos," ed. Luis Suárez Fernández and Manuel Fernández Alvarez (Madrid, 1969), Part 2, p. 271.

[11]Peter Martyr de Anglería to the Count of Tendilla, October 27, 1494 (Alcalá de Henares), *Documentos inéditos para la Historia de España* (hereinafter cited as DIHE), published by the Duke of Alba et al, Volume IX (Madrid, 1955), p. 262; Lorenzo Galíndez Carvajal, "Anales breves del reinado de los Reyes Católicos," in *Colección de documentos inéditos para la historia de España* (hereinafter cited as CODOIN), XVIII (Madrid, 1851), pp. 285-286.

[12]Münzer, *Viaje, passim.*

they could lay their hands on—which was almost all of them who were in Palermo. However, their French ruler, Charles of Anjou, was not in Sicily at the time, but in Naples, for he also ruled southern Italy. To protect themselves from his vengeance, the Sicilian leaders called on the king of Aragon and Catalonia in Spain, Pedro III the Great, offering to accept him or one of his sons as their ruler. He agreed. In time and after much conflict, the title of the royal house of Aragon to Sicily was accepted. Fernando had been officially King of Sicily, even while his father Juan II lived, when he married Isabel.

The other half of Charles of Anjou's French-ruled Italian kingdom, Naples and the "boot" and "toe" of Italy south of it, had remained more or less under the rule of his increasingly disorganized successors until 1435, when their line ran out with the death of Queen Joanna II without issue. In the course of a luridly dissipated life, which would have made Boccaccio or even Machiavelli blush, Joanna had "adopted" no less than three princes as her successor. One was Alfonso V "the Magnanimous," King of Aragon and uncle of Isabel's Fernando. Alfonso V fell in love with Italy and its Renaissance, abandoned his homeland, and won the kingdom of Naples by the sword. He died there without legitimate heirs, leaving his Spanish domains and Sicily to Juan II and the kingdom of Naples to his bastard son Fernando, called Ferrante, the Italian version of the name. Joanna II's other two "adopted heirs" were French Angevin princes; their claims passed ultimately to the kings of France, Louis XI and his son Charles VIII, who was reigning in 1494—young (24), romantic, unintelligent, and shockingly ugly, yet sovereign of what had been the strongest and richest kingdom in Europe before Isabel brought Spain up to match it. The petty Italian states had played at war so long they had forgotten how to fight a real one. They were incapable of withstanding the highly developed French cavalry and artillery. The French proposed simply to march through the whole length of Italy and take Naples on the basis of Charles' dubious hereditary claim. The death of Ferrante on January 25, 1494 gave them their opportunity. On March 17 Charles announced his intention of invading Italy to occupy the kingdom of Naples (after which he vaguely promised to launch a crusade), despite the Pope's condemnation of his plans.[13]

Within three days of Charles' announcement, Pope Alexander VI wrote to Fernando and Isabel asking their help in protecting Roman territory from the invaders; Fernando replied cautiously, refraining from giving a guarantee, but pointing out that there was language in Spain's Treaty of Barcelona with France which permitted him either party to intervene in defense of Rome if its security

---

[13]Menéndez Pidal, *Historia de España*, XVII (2), 355-357; *The Cambridge Modern History*, Volume I (New York, 1902), pp. 105-109; Ludwig von Pastor, *The History of the Popes from the Close of the Middle Ages*, Volume V, 2nd ed. (St. Louis, 1914), p. 425.

was threatened.[14] On August 25, 1493, in a follow-up to that treaty, by which the French had thought to secure Spanish neutrality when they invaded Italy, Fernando had cleverly agreed to recognize only such rights as Charles "might have" in southern Italy.[15] The Pope had never recognized the French king's claims there, and now it appeared most unlikely that he ever would recognize them; hence Fernando could reasonably do likewise. It would have required a veritable scholarly commission on genealogy and the laws of succession to extract from the sordidly tangled history of the late Joanna II a solid argument as to who the rightful claimant might be. Under such circumstances the real issue was whether one of the two nations now the greatest powers in Europe, France and Spain, would dominate rich and vulnerable Italy. Neither one intended to let the other do it. But France was in the field first.

On April 18 the Pope sent his son, Cardinal Juan Borgia, to crown Ferrante's son Alfonso II King of Naples. Five days later Cardinal Giuliano della Rovere (the future Pope Julius II), the Pope's greatest enemy in the College of Cardinals, put the fortress of Ostia at the mouth of the Tiber (which he controlled) in a state of defense, and fled to France. There he gave his blessing to the impending French invasion and called for the deposition of Pope Alexander VI on the grounds that he was elected by simony. On June 24 the Pope refused passage through Papal territory to Charles' army, until such time (date unspecified) as he determined Charles had any right to the kingdom of Naples. On June 28 Cardinal Ascanio Sforza, whose support had been essential to Alexander's tainted election, also abandoned him for the French. On September 3 Charles crossed the border into Savoy with an army of about 40,000 men, much artillery, and a strong supporting fleet.[16]

The Pope immediately made two "anguished appeals for help" to Spain[17]—indeed, he really had nowhere else to turn. The Italian states were virtually helpless in the face of the potent invader; Turin, Pavia, and Piacenza opened their gates to the French without a fight.[18] Emperor Maximilian—his strength scattered in far-flung and often chimerical ventures throughout much of Europe—had at the time no capability to intervene significantly in Italy. England was far away and unconcerned. In his desperation the Pope even tried to get money from the Sultan of the Ottoman Turks, on the grounds that if the

---

[14]Pope Alexander VI to Fernando and Isabel, March 20, 1494 (Rome), in Suárez Fernández, *Politica internacional de Isabel*, IV, 189-90; Menéndez Pidal, *Historia de España*, XVII (2), 357.

[15]Menéndez Pidal, *Historia de España*, XVII (2), 196-198; see Chapter 8, above.

[16]Von Pastor, *History of the Popes*, V, 423-427, 431-432; Menéndez Pidal, *Historia de España*, XVII (2), 358-361.

[17]Menéndez Pidal, *Historia de España*, XVII (2), 362; Pope Alexander VI to Fernando and Isabel, September 19 and 28, 1494 (Rome), in Suárez Fernández, *Politica internacional de Isabel*, IV, 220-222.

[18]Von Pastor, *History of the Popes*, V, 434-435.

French conquered Rome they might get possession of the Sultan's fugitive brother Jem who was living there.[19]

In response to the Pope's September requests, on October 6 Fernando made his first formal offer of military aid to the Pope, and ordered a naval fleet to Sicily. Help was on the way.[20]

Because the Spanish interest in Italy was historically Aragonese, this was more Fernando's concern than Isabel's; we hear little of her direct involvement in the far-flung, long-lasting Italian wars that followed. But we may be sure that she followed them closely: it was one of her most trusted retainers, Gonzalo de Córdoba, who was made the commander of the Spanish expeditionary force sent to the aid of Naples and the Pope; her dealings with the Pope regarding the Church and reform were often influenced by the continuing crisis in Italy; and the alliances and diplomatic realignments resulting from the French invasion played a central role in the marriage negotiations for Isabel's son Juan and her daughters Juana and Catalina (Catherine).

As far back as November 1493, in instructions to Francisco de Rojas as ambassador to Emperor Maximilian, Isabel and Fernando had proposed a double Habsburg marriage for their children, with Prince Juan to marry the Emperor's daughter Margaret and Juana to marry the Emperor's only son and heir, Archduke Philip the Handsome.[21] Now that Isabel and Fernando and the Emperor had an ambitious and dangerous common enemy in the French, to add to the attraction of Spain's sudden rise to great power status, the prospects for this double marriage were substantially improved.[22] But it would still be an extraordinary diplomatic achievement, if attained; rarely did any royal house tie itself to another more than once in a generation.

Meanwhile, on March 7 Isabel and Spain had received their first news of Columbus' second expedition from across the Atlantic. Captain Antonio de Torres sailed triumphantly into Cádiz with no less than twelve of his admiral's 17 ships after an open ocean passage of just 25 days; the February weather in the North Atlantic in 1494 was much better than it had been the preceding year. Torres brought 30,000 ducats' worth of gold from Hispaniola, American spices, 26 Indians, 60 parrots, the majority of the men of the expedition (many of them sick from unfamiliar germs and change of climate and diet), and a memorandum from Columbus asking for the immediate despatch of at least two caravels loaded with food and medicine. Columbus explained that he had

---

[19]*Ibid.*, V, 428-430.

[20]Peter Martyr de Anglería to the Bishops of Braga and Pamplona, October 31, 1494 (Alcalá de Henares), DIHE IX, 264-265; Menéndez Pidal, *Historia de España*, XVII (2), 363.

[21]Menéndez Pidal, *Historia de España*, XVII (2), 355, 373.

[22]Peter Martyr de Anglería to Juan Borromeo, Conde del Lago Verbano, October 20, 1494 (Alcalá de Henares), DIHE IX, 260-261.

sent the 26 Indians to Spain so that they might learn Spanish and consequently be able to act as interpreters for the instruction of their people in Christianity. He had established what he intended to be a permanent colony on the north coast of Hispaniola, named Isabela for the Queen.[23]

Torres sent Columbus' written report on his voyage and discoveries to Isabel and Fernando, along with the memorandum requesting aid; but only the memorandum has been preserved. However, we fortunately have a long letter from Dr. Diego Alvarez Chanca of Sevilla, who had attended Princess Isabel and consequently was well known to the Queen, giving a circumstantial account of Columbus' second expedition and its discoveries up to Captain Torres' departure. Except for one severe thunderstorm, the weather had been excellent during the westward crossing, as it had been on the first crossing in 1492. Land was sighted at dawn November 3, 1493—an island well south of Hispaniola, in what were later to be called the Lesser Antilles. That day being a Sunday, Columbus called the island Dominica—a name it still bears. Keeping his large fleet carefully together, Columbus sailed north along the Antillean island chain, encountering the cannibalistic Caribs. They were particularly numerous and dangerous on the island of Guadalupe, which Columbus named for the great shrine of the Blessed Virgin Mary in Spain to which he and Queen Isabel were especially devoted. Passing through the Virgin Islands, Columbus reached Puerto Rico and then Hispaniola. At nightfall November 27 he came to the site of the fort of La Navidad where he had left his men. But the firing of signal guns brought no response, and he soon learned from the Indians that all his men were dead. Guacanagarí, the chief who had befriended Columbus on his first voyage, indicated that another chief named Caonabo and his men, who lived in the gold country, were responsible. Columbus believed Guacanagarí; many of the officers and men with him did not. (Investigation in later years proved that discipline among the Spanish at La Navidad had collapsed, with most of them leaving the fort, scattering inland in small parties seeking gold and women, and provoking Caonabo and his people until they killed them all; but no one could be sure of all this at the time, due to the still very limited ability of the Spanish to communicate with the Indians.) Columbus then founded Isabela on January 2, 1494, about 75 miles east of the site of La Navidad along the north coast of Hispaniola. Four days later, on the feast of Epiphany, Fray Buil celebrated the first Mass in America. Isabela was founded at this place (quite unsuitable, as was later learned) because it was close to the gold-bearing area. During January the gold was collected that Torres brought back to Spain.[24]

[23]Samuel Eliot Morison, *Admiral of the Ocean Sea* (Boston, 1942), pp. 433-436; Columbus to Isabel and Fernando, January 30, 1494 (Isabela), in Cecil Jane, ed. *Select Documents Illustrating the Four Voyages of Columbus* (London, 1930), I, 74-112.

[24]Dr. Diego Alvarez Chanca to the City of Sevilla, sent with Torres in February 1494, in Jane, ed., *Documents illustrating the Voyages of Columbus*, I, 20-72; Morison,

Isabel and Fernando replied to Columbus with great approval on April 13: "Rely upon it that we consider ourselves well served and obliged by you, so that we shall confer upon you favors, honors and advancement as your great services require and deserve."[25] They at once ordered three caravels to sail in support of Columbus, one more than he had requested; commanded by his brother Bartholomew, they arrived at Isabela June 21.[26] Bartholomew found that his brother had left the colony two months before, and already serious trouble was brewing.

Christopher Columbus was the greatest mariner of his age, a visionary, a genius; his personality and career sum up all that is denoted and connoted by the word "explorer." But he had none of the particular talents required for administration, and for leading men anywhere but at sea. Though his pride prevented him from ever admitting that, his first love was always exploration. Given a choice between governing on land and sailing away across new horizons, Columbus always chose to sail away. That is what he did in April 1494. After establishing a fort in the gold country and sending 250 of its garrison of 400 men out under the command of Pedro Margarit with vague orders to explore and "live off the country," and turning the responsibility of governing over to a five-man council of which his brother Diego was chairman, he set off to explore the south coast of Cuba. On his first voyage he had explored only its north coast; the south coast was unknown.[27]

During the ensuing six weeks, with the fair trade winds behind him, Columbus explored almost all the long south coast of Cuba, and also discovered the island of Jamaica. But he did not quite reach the end of Cuba, turning back on June 13, just fifty miles short of it. Thus he continued to believe Cuba to be a peninsula of Asia, though his curious action in requiring all the men with him to swear, on the day they turned back, that Cuba was part of a continent and not an island, suggests that his belief was not entirely free from doubt. The return journey had to be made by beating constantly against the trade winds—extraordinarily difficult sailing which required more than three months.[28]

Admiral of the Ocean Sea, pp. 401-433.

[25]Morison, *Admiral of the Ocean Sea*, p. 436.

[26]*Ibid.*, pp. 481-482.

[27]*Ibid.*, pp. 437-447, 483; Ferdinand Columbus, *The Life of the Admiral Christopher Columbus*, tr. & ed. Benjamin Keen (New Brunswick NJ, 1959), pp. 128-130; Michele de Cuneo to Hieronymo Annari, October 15, 1495 (Savona), in Samuel Eliot Morison, ed., *Journals and Other Documents on the Life and Voyages of Christopher Columbus* (New York, 1963), pp. 214-215, 221-222; Andrés Bernáldez, *Memorias del reinado de los Reyes Católicos*, ed. Manuel Gómez Moreno and Juan de Mata Carriazo (Madrid, 1962), pp. 307-308 (chapter CXXIII).

[28]Morison, *Admiral of the Ocean Sea*, pp. 447-479; Bernáldez, *Memorias*, pp. 308-332 (ch. CXXIII-CXXXI); Cuneo to Annari, October 15, 1495, in Morison, ed. *Journals and Other Documents on Columbus*, pp. 222-225.

That meant Columbus had left his charge in Hispaniola untended for five full months, which proved more than time enough for disaster. Margarit and his 250 men, whom Columbus had thoughtlessly turned loose on a peaceful countryside, seized and extorted food, women, and gold wherever they went. Not only had Columbus permitted this to happen by the vagueness of his orders, but he had also given the untested Margarit full viceregal powers in his absence, in the previously unexplored areas Margarit was penetrating. So when Diego Columbus tried to bring Margarit to heel, he could claim that the Admiral's brother had no power over him. However, Margarit and his men now thought they had gained plunder enough, and wanted to return to Spain with it. The three caravels Bartholomew Columbus had brought from Spain were available. Margarit and his supporters simply seized the ships, in defiance of both the Columbus brothers, and sailed for Spain. They were accompanied by none other than Fray Buil, a Catalan like Margarit, who had supported his fellow-countryman but totally neglected the mission on which his sovereigns had sent him—he never converted a single Indian.[29] The reform of the Church which Isabel had launched the previous year in Catalonia had obviously not reached Fray Buil.

In August, about the time Margarit and Fray Buil left Hispaniola in their stolen ships, with Columbus still beating his way back along the south coast of Cuba, Isabel and Fernando wrote Columbus again. Their April letter had been carried by Bartholomew, though his brother the Admiral had not yet seen it or him; now this August letter was to be carried by Captain Torres, who was about to return to Hispaniola with four caravels carrying more Spanish food. (Most of the Spanish could not adapt quickly to the foods native to America; without receiving the kind of food to which they were accustomed most of the time, many of them sickened and died.) In their August letter, Isabel and Fernando urged Columbus to come home as soon as possible. They also wanted more information on what had happened to the Spanish left behind and killed at La Navidad, and on the new islands he had discovered; they urged him to send a caravel back to Spain each month with news and requests for whatever help he might need.[30] It seems almost as though Isabel had sensed her Admiral of the Ocean Sea might have taken on more than he could handle.

In this August letter, Isabel and Fernando also sent Columbus a copy of the Treaty of Tordesillas with Portugal which had been signed June 7. This treaty supplemented and modified Pope Alexander's bull *Inter caetera* of the preceding year, which had drawn the demarcation line between Spanish and Portuguese seas and shores 100 leagues west of the Azores Islands. The Treaty of Tordesillas moved the line to 370 leagues west of the Azores, and provided

[29]Morison, *Admiral of the Ocean Sea*, pp. 483-484.
[30]*Ibid.*, p. 485; Alonso de Santa Cruz, *Crónica de los Reyes Católicos*, ed. Juan de Mata Carriazo, Volume I (Sevilla, 1951), pp. 111-114 (ch. XXI).

assurance that Portugal would now accept it. No reason for moving the line, or for the odd figure of 370 leagues, is given in any document that has come down to us. If it was coincidence that the whole coast of Brazil, in the supposedly yet undiscovered South American continent, lay on the Portuguese side of the new line, it was certainly a very fortunate coincidence for Portugal.[31] Nevertheless, all the rest of America (except Newfoundland) still lay on the Spanish side of the redrawn line, and no other European power had yet made or planned any voyages to America. The eastern approaches to Asia, as Columbus still believed his discoveries to be—the New World, as we now know it was—remained in the hands of Spain, as much of it as she could find and hold. That, supplementing her own substantial resources and peerless fighting men, was enough to make Spain the greatest power in Christendom and in the world for the next 150 years.

The autumn of 1494 in Italy was the season for the triumphal and virtually unopposed southward march of the invading French. By October 23 the splendidly bannered and equipped French army, unblooded except for a brief and farcical encounter with one-tenth their number of Neapolitans near Genoa, had secured all of northern Italy and were marching on Florence. In that beautiful, highly cultured, ostentatiously wealthy but unwarlike city an extraordinary figure had appeared like a latter-day Elijah: Girolamo Savonarola. He preached the rising wrath of God against his sinful city—where, indeed, the corruption of the Church exceeded that in Spain and public morality was virtually nonexistent, as the writings of Machiavelli (then 25) were to testify. Not without reason, Savonarola blamed the ruling Medici family for the political corruption in Florence and Pope Alexander VI for the religious corruption. At this point he had not yet publicly defied the Pope, but he had defied the Medici, and he and his followers were prevailing. Savonarola welcomed Charles VIII and his French army as God's host sent to cleanse Florence and punish it for its sins. All this made Piero de Medici, weak son of Lorenzo the Magnificent who had died two years before, even less able than he would otherwise have been to offer any serious resistance to the invaders. On October 26 he agreed to surrender to them all the fortified cities under Florentine rule; on October 29 another small Neapolitan army which had tentatively approached the French retreated precipitately without a battle; on November 9 Piero de Medici was overthrown and Savonarola came to Pisa to welcome the French; on November 17 Charles VIII was welcomed in Florence with his army.[32]

---

[31]Santa Cruz, *Crónica*, I, 108-110 (ch. XX); Morison, *Admiral of the Ocean Sea*, p. 485; Elaine Sanceau, *The Perfect Prince; a Biography of the King Dom Joao II* (Barcelos, Portugal, 1959), pp. 370-380.
[32]Von Pastor, *History of the Popes*, V, 188-212, 437-439; Menéndez Pidal, *Historia de*

Much encouraged by this latest bloodless victory, Charles VIII issued a manifesto November 22 claiming that his long-range objective was to overthrow the Turkish empire and liberate the Holy Land, and that he desired to gain control of the kingdom of Naples only to accomplish this, and demanding that the Pope grant his army free passage through the Papal states, supplying his troops on the way.   The demand was given a very sharp edge by his announcement in the manifesto that he would force his way through even if the Pope denied him permission.[33] For good measure, Charles repeated his earlier threat to sponsor a council aimed at deposing the Pope (despite precedents over many centuries showing that no one on earth had power to depose a Pope).[34] At the same time Charles learned of the Pope's earlier request for financial help from the Turks, and broadcast this all over Christendom. Pope Alexander responded with a formal appeal for help to the traditional defender of the Papacy from military danger, the Holy Roman Emperor; but, as already noted, Maximilian was not at this time in a position to give it.[35]

Fernando and Isabel were. On December 1 instructions to a new Spanish ambassador in Rome, Antonio de Fonseca, authorized him to deny that the Treaty of Barcelona had been anything more than a purely defensive alliance; to declare that the Pope had a right to recover Rome's port of Ostia from Cardinal della Rovere's rebels who had seized it, and to offer Spanish aid for this purpose; and, if the Pope showed signs of wavering, to tell him that if the sons and brothers of Ferrante were rejected as kings of Naples, Fernando might well advance his own claim to it and incorporate it into his existing Sicilian domain.[36]

This was no mere diplomatic ploy or bluff. By Christmas, Fernando and Isabel had assembled much of the expeditionary force they had promised the Pope in October. A powerful fleet was gathering at the port of Cartagena to carry an army of between 2,000 and 2,500 men to Italy. Manuel Ponce de León, brother of the late Duke of Cádiz who had held the principal military command in the war against Granada, was originally designated commander; but before the army departed he was replaced by Gonzalo de Córdoba, who had himself fought brilliantly in the Granadan war and was highly esteemed by Queen Isabel.[37]

España, XVII (2), 363.

[33]Von Pastor, *History of the Popes*, V, 440-441.

[34]See my *The Building of Christendom* (Front Royal VA, 1987), *passim*, for examples and explanation of these precedents.

[35]Menéndez Pidal, *Historia de España*, XVII (2), 367; von Pastor, *History of the Popes*, V, 444-445.

[36]Menéndez Pidal, *Historia de España*, XVII (2), 366-367.

[37]Santa Cruz, *Crónica*, I, 122 (ch. XXIII); Menéndez Pidal, *Historia de España*, pp. 367, 374; William H. Prescott, *History of the Reign of Ferdinand and Isabella the Catholic* (Philadelphia, 1893), II, 277-278.

Once again, Isabel's unerring judgment of men was confirmed. Gonzalo de Córdoba in Italy became one of the premier generals in history, ever afterwards known as "the great captain." But his campaigns and triumphs proved more than his own military genius. They first displayed on the European stage what remained a pre-eminent fact in the history of Europe for the next century and a half: that Spanish infantry and cavalry, their military tradition formed by the reign of Isabel and the splendid reconquest of Granada, were man for man the best soldiers in Christendom.

Preparing so large an overseas expedition was, however, a prolonged and difficult undertaking, inevitably beset by delays; Gonzalo de Córdoba and his men did not actually arrive in Sicily and cross the Straits of Messina into Italy until May.[38] Long before that, Charles and his army had taken both Rome and Naples.

On Christmas day 1494 Pope Alexander VI reluctantly concluded that he lacked the military means to defend Rome against the French. With a Spanish bodyguard he took temporary refuge in the Vatican, outside the walls of Rome. On December 31 Charles VIII made triumphal entry into the city of St. Peter, with great pageantry and pomp, and rebel Cardinals Giuliano della Rovere, Ascanio Sforza, Giovanni Colonna, and Giovanni Battista Savelli riding in his van. On January 7, 1495 the Pope, with his two cardinal sons Juan and Cesare, withdrew by the ancient escape tunnel to the famous Papal stronghold of Castel sant'Angelo. Despite threats, which included twice bringing up his potent artillery, the French king did not quite dare open fire on the Pope, who in turn had no way to get out of the castle. This deadlock produced an agreement on January 15 providing that the Pope's son Cesare would go with the French to Naples, effectively a hostage; that the fugitive Turkish prince Jem who was the Pope's bargaining counter with the Sultan would be turned over to the French; that Cardinal della Rovere would retain Ostia and all his other possessions, and that those who had supported France against the Pope would be given amnesty; but that Rome would be turned back to the Pope, who would keep all his lands and territories, while Charles would profess religious obedience to him and guarantee his personal liberty and safety. On January 19 Charles made public obeisance to the Pope, even after the Pope had refused to respond directly to his formal request to be recognized as King of Naples.[39]

At this dramatic juncture—and surely influenced by it—the preliminary agreements for the double Habsburg marriage for the children of Isabel and Fernando were signed at Antwerp: Prince Juan to marry Emperor Maximilian's daughter Margaret, and Princess Juana to marry his son Philip.

---

[38]Menéndez Pidal, *Historia de España*, XVII (2), 388-391.
[39]Von Pastor, *History of the Popes*, V, 448-460; Menéndez Pidal, *Historia de España*, XVII (2), 368.

Confirmation by Maximilian and Philip was still required.[40]

Whatever one may think of Rodrigo Borgia, Pope Alexander VI, he was at least in one way a true Spaniard: he had remarkable courage. He gained considerably more than he lost by the agreement with the French king January 15, and had not compromised his position on Naples. But the reigning king of Naples, Alfonso II, for all his Spanish name, was three generations removed from Spain. He gave way to panic, abdicating his throne January 21 and fleeing to Sicily, crying out, it is said, even in his sleep: "I hear the French coming!" His son Ferrante II was young and more spirited; he resolved to stay and fight, but had neither the means nor the experience to do so effectively.[41]

Charles VIII left Rome January 28 for his march on Naples, taking Cesare Borgia and the Turkish prince Jem with him. He seized three villas belonging to the Pope that day, in violation of his promises of the 15th. Camping that night at Velletri, twenty miles south of Rome, he called the Spanish ambassador Antonio de Fonseca to review with him the terms of the Treaty of Barcelona. Fonseca pointed to no less than seven provisions of the Treaty which he accused the King of violating. "Observe, señor," said the Spanish ambassador bluntly, "how Your Highness signed all these provisions and promised to abide by them, then did not honor but violated them. Speaking for the King of Spain my lord I tell you, that he will now honor them no more than you do, so they count for nothing." And Fonseca took the copy of the treaty he was holding, ceremoniously tore it into small pieces, and flung it at Charles' feet. Livid with rage, the King of France snarled: "Stay where you are, or you will be killed!" and sent him to Rome under guard.[42]

But the efficiency of the French guards obviously left much to be desired, for that very night Cesare Borgia made his escape. Both he and the ambassador were soon safely ensconced in Castel sant'Angelo under the Pope's protection. A month later the French lost their other personal trophy of the January 15 settlement when Prince Jem suddenly died, apparently of overeating.[43]

Charles pushed on southward, taking the Neapolitan border fortresses at the first assault, and making another triumphal entry—this time into Naples—on February 22. Ferrante II now fled to Sicily as his father had done, though he did not abdicate, and the French occupied the whole kingdom of

---

[40]The marriage capitulations were dated January 20, 1495 at Antwerp; their text is found in Suárez Fernández, *Política internacional de Isabel*, IV, 284-299. See also Menéndez Pidal, *Historia de España*, XVII (2), 380.

[41]Von Pastor, *History of the Popes*, V, 461-462; Menéndez Pidal, *Historia de España*, XVII (2), 370.

[42]Bernáldez, *Memorias*, pp. 350-352 (ch. CXXXIX); von Pastor, *History of the Popes*, V, 462; Menéndez Pidal, *Historia de España*, XVII (2), 369-370.

[43]Von Pastor, *History of the Popes*, V, 462, 465.

Naples in southern Italy, establishing garrisons throughout its territory.[44] But the French were in a very dangerous situation strategically, for both the Pope and Fernando had made it very clear that they would never accept French rule of Naples; the Papal states barred the Italian peninsula to the north; Sicily across the Straits of Messina provided an ideal base for a Spanish counter-invasion from the south; and the Spanish were bringing up a fleet fully equal to the French to contest control of the seas. The French king and army could be cut off and destroyed if they simply remained where they were. The weak link in the chain being formed around Naples was the Papal state, which had no real army; but Pope Alexander moved decisively to strengthen his position by forming the Holy League with Emperor Maximilian, Spain, and the north Italian states of Venice and Milan against the French invaders. The League was finalized March 31, announced to Charles by the Venetian ambassador April 5, and formally proclaimed on Palm Sunday, April 12.[45]

Charles was furious, but had no choice now but retreat if he were to avoid being trapped in southern Italy. To salve his dignity he had himself crowned King of Naples in an empty ceremony May 12, then took the road to the north May 20 with half his army, leaving the rest to try to hold the kingdom of Naples. Just six days later Gonzalo de Córdoba and his army landed at Reggio di Calabria at the foot of Italy, determined to drive them out.[46]

Charles' retreat was very different from his advance; those who had hailed him when he came spurned him as he left. The doors that had initially been opened to him were now all closed. The Pope would not even see him as he passed through Rome.[47] Savonarola met him at Poggibonzi near Siena, but only to berate him for not having reformed the Church as the honest but naive prophet-friar had genuinely believed Charles intended to do.[48] The French had to fight a major battle at Fornovo near Parma July 6 in which the Italians, Germans, and Bohemians, though weakly commanded and poorly trained, gave the French a stiff fight and seized most of their baggage train, with the plunder of Italy and Charles' own helmet, sword, and royal seal.[49] Ferrante II returned to Naples, the French garrison having been unable to keep its turbulent and

---

[44]*Ibid.*, V, 463-464.

[45]*Ibid.*, V, 466-467; Menéndez Pidal, *Historia de España*, XVII (2), 385; Bernáldez, *Memorias*, p. 359 (ch. CXLII). For the full text of the treaty establishing the Holy League, signed in Venice March 31, 1495, see Suárez Fernández, *Política internacional de Isabel*, IV, 327-347.

[46]Von Pastor, *History of the Popes*, V, 468; Menéndez Pidal, *Historia de España*, XVII (2), 386, 388, 390-391.

[47]Pope Alexander VI to Fernando and Isabel, June 1, 1495 (Civitavecchia), in Suárez Fernández, *Política internacional de Isabel*, IV, 375-376; von Pastor, *History of the Popes*, V, 470-471.

[48]Von Pastor, *History of the Popes*, V, 472.

[49]*Ibid.*, V, 472-474; Menéndez Pidal, *Historia de España*, XVII (2), 387; Bernáldez, *Memorias*, pp. 362-363 (ch. CXLIII).

unsinkable populace, the famous *lazzaroni,* under control; on August 5 Pope Alexander threatened King Charles with excommunication if he did not stop all French military operations in the kingdom of Naples within nine days.[50]

It was hard to believe less than a year had elapsed since the great invasion began at the border of Savoy September 3, 1494—at first carrying all before it, but ending in this harried and ignominious retreat of the invaders to France. Rather like Isabel's old acquaintance Archbishop Carrillo, Rodrigo Borgia was a scandal as Pope, but he knew how to fight; and the Spain that Isabel had built had proved strong enough to prevent the French conquest of Italy so long as the Pope held firm.

While Fernando's attention was focussed primarily on these momentous events in Italy, Isabel was making good use of them to take fullest advantage of the opportunity for accomplishing a complete reform of the Church in Spain that the death of Cardinal Mendoza in January had opened up. It has often caused surprise to find Francisco Ximénes de Cisneros, one of the greatest reformers in the entire history of the Catholic Church, a man ascetic and austere as the stony plains around Avila, appointed to the primatial see of Spain and fully supported in his reform by such a Pope as Alexander VI. Though we know Pope Alexander always respected Isabel—indeed, that enduring respect, along with his outstanding personal courage, are among the few but striking redeeming features of Rodrigo Borgia—that does not seem quite enough to account for the unwavering and unhesitating endorsement this Pope gave to Cisneros; nor is it. The mystery is only solved when we remember what was going on in Italy in 1495 when Cisneros was reluctantly assuming his history-making charge. For once, the self-interest of Pope Alexander VI and the Church's interest fully coincided. Alexander's domains, his pontificate, even his life depended on Spanish support. There is every reason to believe that he would gladly have accepted another Alonso Carrillo as Archbishop of Toledo had Isabel demanded his like; but it was Cisneros she would have, and none other. Pope Alexander VI well knew it, and had little choice but to comply.

Fernando did not particularly want Cisneros; he preferred his own illegitimate son, who had been Archbishop of Zaragoza from the age of six and was now a ripe 25, with no visible interest in Church reform. But Isabel's deference to her husband did not go nearly this far; she would not hear of the young man for this position, would not even consider him. (She could also point to the deathbed advice of Cardinal Mendoza that his successor should not be a relative of nobles or royalty, but a religious.) Fernando knew her far too well to protest; this was Castile, after all, where she was reigning Queen, and he had the Italian war to fight. He left the matter entirely in her hands.[51]

---

[50]Menéndez Pidal, *Historia de España,* XVII (2), 393-394, 396; Prescott, *Ferdinand and Isabella,* II, 284-285.

[51]Luis Fernández de Retana, *Cisneros y su siglo* (Madrid, 1929), I, 153; Menéndez

With her superb judgment of men, Isabel knew that Cisneros, in his humility and love of contemplative solitude, would fiercely resist the appointment she intended to press upon him; for the primate of Spain was as much a worldly office as a religious one, and had been ever since the reconquest of Toledo from the Muslims in 1085. Archbishops of Toledo had stood beside the Kings of Castile on many a bloody battlefield; they had often been virtual prime ministers, and even made or broken kings as Carrillo had tried to do. A new thrust and emphasis could be given to the office, but by no means all of its worldly aspects could simply be rejected or ignored. When he joined the Franciscan order Cisneros had intended to leave the world, to be a man of the Church alone. He did not want to come back to the world. It was not even enough to appeal to his sense of duty; he could always say that others were as well or better qualified than he. He must, ultimately, be ordered; and only the Pope had authority to do that. That the reigning Pope was a public sinner did not disturb either Isabel or Cisneros in the slightest regarding his authority as head of the Church. Cisneros would obey him without question regarding a Church appointment. Obedience to proper ecclesiastical authority was one of his monastic vows.

Therefore Isabel did not tell Cisneros what she had in mind, and all the available evidence indicates that in his genuine humility he did not even suspect it. He knew, of course, that a new Archbishop of Toledo must be appointed soon; that office could never be left vacant for long without a dangerous contention for it developing. He recommended a nephew of the late Cardinal Mendoza, Diego Hurtado de Mendoza, presently Archbishop of Sevilla—a worthy man, though not noted as a reformer, quite like his uncle. Isabel probably told Cisneros she would consider his suggestion. But what she had already done, within no more than three weeks of Cardinal Mendoza's death, was to write to the Pope telling him that she was determined to have Cisneros, and no one else. Her letter would have arrived in Rome some time during the first three weeks of February 1495, during the very days of Charles VIII's triumphal march on Naples, while the Pope was staying in Castel sant'Angelo with the Spanish ambassador only a month after he had literally looked into the mouths of the French cannon. At no time in his life and pontificate would Alexander VI have moved so fast to grant any ecclesiastical request from the King or the Queen of Spain. On February 22, just 41 days after Cardinal Mendoza's death, Pope Alexander VI sent to Spain his official brief designating Francisco Ximénes de Cisneros Archbishop of Toledo and primate of Spain.[52]

The scene of Cisneros' reception of that letter is deservedly famous, almost legendary, in Spanish history. Its date is uncertain, but it seems most

---

Pidal, *Historia de España*, XVII (2), 272.

[52]Brief of Pope Alexander VI, February 21, 1495 (Rome), in Suárez Fernández, *Política internacional de Isabel*, IV, 303-304.

likely to have been March 10, the first Sunday in Lent. We have no contemporary account, but it is vividly attested in two sixteenth-century biographies of Cisneros which are solidly based on contemporary documents and memories of persons alive during the great reformer's time. Cisneros was planning to spend Lent at an isolated retreat near Ocaña, and was ready to leave that day. Isabel invited him to *comida* (the Spanish early afternoon meal) before his departure. At some point during or after the meal she told him that she had some letters for him from Rome. One was from the Pope, addressed to Francisco Ximénes, Archbishop-elect of Toledo. Cisneros took one look at this superscription and dropped it on the ground. The Queen bent over and picked it up. For all her enormous respect for Cisneros and the habitual gravity of her presence, we may well imagine the hint of a smile on her lovely face as she did so. "Reverend Father," she asked, "may I open it?" Cisneros responded that he was Her Highness' servant and would do whatever she commanded; but he could not bear to hear the letter read, knowing now what it contained. "My lady," he said, in much distress, "this is not for me." And he fled from her. We are told she was "not offended"; no doubt she had expected exactly this reaction.[53]

Isabel let Cisneros complete his Lenten retreat undisturbed. Soon after Easter, she asked Fernando's uncle Enrique Enríquez and the president of her Council to go to Cisneros to urge him to accept the appointment as Archbishop of Toledo. They actually met him on the road, accompanied only by his little donkey Benitillo, and made their appeal to him by the roadside. He kept insisting that he lacked the sanctity, knowledge, judgment, and eloquence ao lofty a position required (they might have replied that it had been a long time since its occupants were noted for sanctity), and finally said he would not discuss it further but would resume his journey, away from Madrid. Isabel then commanded him to come back to Madrid, a command he felt he must obey. Then she sent her long-time friend and faithful servant Gutierre de Cárdenas to

---

[53]Fernández de Retana, *Cisneros*, I, 158. The 16th-century histories are Alvar Gómez, "De rebus gestis a Francisco Ximenio Cisnerio" (Alcalá de Henares, 1569, unpublished) and Juan de Vallejo, *Memorial de la vida de fray Francisco Jiménez de Cisneros*, ed. A. de la Torre (Madrid, 1913), p. 12. Luis Suárez Fernández, in *Historia de España* ed. Menéndez Pidal, XVII (2), 273, casts doubt on the reality of Cisneros' resistance to the appointment on the grounds that later correspondence from the Pope to and about Cisneros makes no mention of that resistance. But the Pope would not necessarily have been immediately notified of Cisneros' resistance, and in any case would have continued to communicate with him officially as the Archbishop-elect, unless and until the Pope revoked the appointment, which assuredly he had no intention of doing. The Pope's eventual command to Cisneros that he accept the appointment may have been sent orally rather than in writing, or may simply have been lost, as were many important documents of that age. File clerks capable of losing both copies of the log of Columbus' first voyage to America were certainly capable of losing a letter from the Pope.

him. Gutierre actually got down on his knees before the stern old monk (59 years old at this time, with hawklike profile and lean tough body, he was to live to 81, very active and in total possession of his faculties to the end), calling him a saint, and begging him to accept the appointment. Still he would not, until the Pope personally intervened again, commanding him to accept under holy obedience.[54]

Even then, Cisneros laid down conditions: "If he accepted this, the Church would have to be free, for he would have to give a very strict account to God and in no way could he be burdened with hard conditions."[55] Isabel assured him she would gladly comply with any conditions he made. By June 11 Peter Martyr was writing as though his appointment were final, and on September 25 Cisneros took possession of the archdiocese of Toledo *in absentia*, though he did not actually go there in person until two years later. On October 1 he was consecrated at Tarazona in Aragon, where Fernando and Isabel had been staying while the *cortes* of Aragon met there; Isabel presented him, as her gift for the occasion, with a pontifical robe she had sewn herself.[56]

He tested the independence he had demanded immediately, and in a very unusual way. One of the most important lay offices he had to bestow was that of Governor of Cazorla, an area near Jaén which a much earlier Archbishop of Toledo had reconquered from the Moors in the reign of King St. Fernando III, and which had consequently been granted to the archdiocese as its territory in 1231. The incumbent governor was Pedro Hurtado de Mendoza, the late Cardinal's brother and a worthy man. It was universally assumed that Cisneros would immediately confirm him in this office, but he did not do so, even when Isabel strongly recommended the confirmation. It was therefore assumed that Cisneros had some unreasonable grudge against Pedro Hurtado de Mendoza, and there was considerable anger against him, which moved Cisneros not at all. But in his own good time he did in fact confirm the appointment, telling Mendoza that he had been his choice all along, but that the Archbishop of Toledo must be assured of total independence in making appointments. From then on, "it became known in the diocese that the one certain way not to obtain a benefice or other post was to ask him [Cisneros] for it, directly or indirectly."[57]

One problem remained in the transformation from humble, ascetic monk to archbishop. At first Cisneros refused to change the way he lived in any manner. He continued to wear his old friar's habit, which he had sewed and

[54]Fernández de Retana, *Cisneros*, I, 159-160. See Note 53, above, regarding the lack of a written document from Pope Alexander VI to this effect.

[55]*Ibid.*, I, 161.

[56]Peter Martyr de Anglería to Cardinal de Carvajal, June 11, 1495 (Zaragoza), DIHE IX, 300; Menéndez Pidal, *Historia de España*, XVII (2), 274; Fernández de Retana, *Cisneros*, I, 161.

[57]Reginald Merton, *Cardinal Ximenes and the Making of Spain* (London, 1934), p. 64.

mended himself; he would ride no mount but plodding little Benitillo; he refused a bed and slept on a board. Many complained about all this; public splendor was expected of the primate of Spain. On December 15 the Pope ordered Cisneros to meet this expectation and make more use of the trappings of his office. Despite the irony of the luxurious and ostentatious Borgia Pope telling the faithful disciple of the Little Poor Man of Assisi to live with less poverty, in the circumstances of the time Alexander VI was correct. Cisneros complied, but no more than he had to. He did wear the archepiscopal robes in public, but with his friar's habit and his hair shirt always underneath; he had a magnificent bed installed, but never slept on it, keeping his board underneath and pulling it out when he was ready for the little sleep he took.[58]

The prophet Jeremiah has been called "God's iron." The phrase applies equally well to Archbishop Francisco Ximénes de Cisneros, Queen Isabel's choice for primate of Spain. This was the man who would carry on and bring to complete fulfillment the reform of the Church in Spain, purifying it so thoroughly that for more than three hundred years neither Protestant nor secularist—critics and enemies of the Catholic Church who gain their credit and their base from scandals inside the Church—could establish even a foothold in Spain.

The establishment of the Holy League against France, by bringing Emperor Maximilian and the reigning monarchs of Spain formally into alliance, speeded the final negotiations for the double Habsburg marriage. On August 25 the Emperor's daughter Margaret formally renounced her rights to succession to the Habsburg dominions (thereby preserving them for the male Habsburg line),[59] while Princess Juana's succession rights were conserved, meaning that a Habsburg succession to control of Spain was a legal possibility, though it seemed very unlikely at the time since both Prince Juan and Princess Isabel were ahead of Juana in the line of succession to the throne of Castile. On November 5 the betrothal of Archduke Philip and Juana was formally celebrated at Malines near Brussels in Philip's native Flanders, by proxy as was customary for royal betrothals. On April 11, 1496 Philip confirmed the marriage agreement, and on July 1 Emperor Maximilian confirmed it also.[60]

Meanwhile, in October, Charles VIII and his officials had finally succeeded, after much behind-the-scenes negotiation, pressure, and bribery, in

---

[58]*Ibid.*, pp. 65-66; Fernández de Retana, *Cisneros*, I, 178-180; Menéndez Pidal, *Historia de España*, XVII (2), 274. For the text of the Pope's letter to Cisneros (dated December 15, 1495, from Rome) see Fernández de Retana, *op. cit.*, I, 179.

[59]Oath of renunciation at Worms, August 25, 1495, in Suárez Fernández, *Politica internacional de Isabel*, IV, 416-418.

[60]Menéndez Pidal, *Historia de España*, XVII (2), 426-427. For the text of Philip's confirmation, at Brussels, see Suárez Fernández, *Politica internacional de Isabel*, IV, 511-516.

breaking Milan away from the Holy League so that the French army might pass peacefully out of Italy and back to France. After an initial check at Seminara in June due to the military incompetence of his Neapolitan allies, Gonzalo de Córdoba, fighting with Spaniards only and using tactics they had learned from the Moorish light cavalry in the Granadan war, pushed his way up the hilly, rocky Calabrian peninsula over terrain very much like that of the mountains around Granada. After being forced to wait two months during the winter of 1496 due to lack of supplies, by spring he had gained possession of almost all Calabria, climaxed by the capture of the heavily defended town of Laino in May. In July, moving north from Calabria, he laid siege to the still more strongly fortified town of Atella. By the end of the month he had forced its capitulation, which virtually eliminated the French military presence in the kingdom of Naples. The first phase of the Italian war had ended in complete victory for Spain.[61]

Isabel was now involving herself more actively in the Italian war. During the spring of 1496 she and Fernando had written frequently to their ambassador in England, Dr. de Puebla, urging him to make every possible effort to persuade Henry VII, the cautious King of England, to join the Holy League and thereby add to the pressure against France. A treaty for the marriage of Henry's first-born son Arthur, aged nine, and their youngest daughter Catherine, aged ten, was the principal inducement held out to him.[62] Henry was interested and flattered, but characteristically reluctant. On July 10 Isabel wrote Dr. de Puebla herself, telling him he was her ablest ambassador, emphasizing the importance of his mission, and explaining to him what she saw as the fundamental principles at stake:

> If therefore he [King Henry VII] assist the Church, and defend her from the danger in which she now stands, he will have it in his power, with the help of God, to do what he likes with the King of France. He can either make him concede part, if he do not wish to do him more harm, but only to prevent him from taking what belongs to others, and from destroying and setting on fire the whole of Christendom, as he has hitherto done. . . . This business is the business of God and the Church, to defend which all we Christian princes are obliged.[63]

---

[61]Menéndez Pidal, *Historia de España*, XVII (2), 387, 392-393, 398, 405; Prescott, *Ferdinand and Isabella*, II, 279-294; Mary Purcell, *The Great Captain, Gonzalo Fernández de Córdoba* (London, 1962), pp. 106-111.

[62]Fernando and Isabel to Dr. de Puebla, April 14, 1496 (Daroca); Dr. de Puebla to Fernando and Isabel, June 13, 1496 (London); Fernando and Isabel to Dr. de Puebla, June 21, 1496 (Almazán), in G. A. Bergenroth, ed., *Calendar of Letters, Despatches, and State Papers relating to the Negotiations between England and Spain*, Volume I: "Henry VII, 1485-1509" (London, 1862), pp. 89-93, 99, 104-106.

[63]Isabel to Dr. de Puebla, July 10, 1496, in Bergenroth, *Calendar of State Papers*, I, 109.

This letter crossed with one from de Puebla in which he explained that Henry was quite willing to join the Holy League, being very desirous of alliance with both the Holy Roman Empire and Spain, but that he did not want to commit himself to war against France. Probably before either letter was delivered, Henry joined the League on July 18; thereby Isabel's goal was achieved.[64] During this same month a substantial French army was reported assembling on the frontiers of Roussillon and Navarra for a possible invasion of northern Spain in retaliation for the war in Italy. Fernando went to Roussillon to prepare its defenses, and Isabel went to Navarra for the same purpose.[65]

While Isabel was at work on the Navarrese frontier overseeing and inspiring the strengthening of its defenses, Columbus had returned to Spain and was making his way north to see her. The great explorer had fallen on hard times since his return to Hispaniola from the long voyage along the south coast of Cuba in September 1494. At almost the end of this voyage, after reaching the southeastern tip of Hispaniola, he had suddenly collapsed with fever and delirium, and been brought back an invalid to his colony of Isabela. When he recovered from the fever, he found himself crippled for weeks with arthritis.[66]

In this condition he could do little about the near-chaos on the island, and became obsessed with the need to find some way to make a profit from his exploring and colonizing enterprises, since fabled Cathay had not been found, nor any mine of gold (there was some gold in Hispaniola, but it could only be obtained by the slow and laborious method of panning the rivers). He believed that his efforts and the support of his sovereigns deserved a prompt and substantial material return, which so far they had not obtained. So, instead of bringing the mutinous Spaniards to order and halting their depredations upon the Indians, he blamed the natives for everything and sent a force to round them up with horses and hounds. They brought over 1,500 Indians captive to Isabela; Columbus declared them enslaved as war booty. Four hundred of those appearing strongest and healthiest were loaded aboard Torres' four caravels recently arrived from Spain, to be sent back there on their return voyage. The Spanish colonists were then allowed to "take as many as they pleased" as their own slaves. Those left over, many of them nursing mothers, were allowed to go free; but they were now in such a panic that many of them left their babies behind.[67]

The four caravels left February 17, 1495 to return to Spain with their

[64]Dr. de Puebla to Isabel and Fernando, July 11, 1496 (London), in *ibid.*, I, 110-113; von Pastor, *History of the Popes*, V, 484.

[65]Bernáldez, *Memorias*, p. 375 (ch. CLIII); Fernando and Isabel to Dr. de Puebla, July 6, 1496 (Almazán), in Bergenroth, *Calendar of State Papers*, I, 107-108.

[66]Morison, *Admiral of the Ocean Sea*, pp. 479-480, 484.

[67]*Ibid.*, pp. 484-487; Michele de Cuneo to Hieronymo Annari, October 15, 1495 (Savona), in Morison, *Journals and Other Documents on Columbus*, p. 226.

tragic human cargo—the first transatlantic slaving voyage, harbinger of 350 years of this horror to come. Torres tried to make the passage too far to the south, had to come back north to catch the westerlies, and in the end required about six weeks for the journey. As was to become usual on these passages, about half the slaves died on the way.[68] Torres' ships reached Cádiz at the beginning of April. Isabel and Fernando were informed of the arrival of the slaves. In the memorandum accompanying his first report, brought by Torres in March of the preceding year, Columbus had proposed making war on the cannibalistic Caribs, who habitually killed and ate the peaceful Taino Indians who lived in Hispaniola, Cuba, and the islands to the north, and sending Carib prisoners of war to Spain as slaves. (Spanish law, going back to the wars of the Reconquest, permitted the enslavement of non-Christian prisoners taken in war against Christians.) Responding, Isabel and Fernando had neither approved nor condemned the proposal, but taken it under advisement and urged Columbus to do likewise.[69] It is likely that at first they thought the newly arrived Indians were some of the expected Carib prisoners, because on April 12 they approved their sale as slaves.[70]

Only four days later, some hint or suspicion of the truth must have come to them. In a sharp reversal, they suspended their letter and permission of April 12:

> Regarding our letter about selling the Indians that Admiral Columbus sent in the caravels just arrived, because we wish to inform ourselves from counsellors, theologians, and canonists, if in good conscience we may sell them, and cannot make this [decision] until we see the letters that the Admiral has written us, in order to find out why he has sent them here captive, and Torres has these letters, which he has not sent to us, therefore, for sales of these Indians already made, hold the money for a time, during which we may find out if we can sell them or not; those buying them should not make payment, but should know nothing of this; and have Torres make haste to come.[71]

Whatever the letters Torres brought with him may have contained (none of them has survived), they evidently did little to allay the sovereigns' concern about what was happening on Hispaniola. Fray Buil and his mutineers who had returned the previous fall in Columbus' three ships had of course placed the

---

[68]Cuneo letter to Annari, October 15, 1495 (Savona), in Morison, *Journals and Other Documents on Columbus*, pp. 226-227.

[69]Memorandum of Columbus to Fernando and Isabel, January 30, 1494 (Isabela), in Jane, ed., *Documents Illustrating the Voyages of Columbus*, I, 90-92.

[70]Letter of Isabel and Fernando, April 12, 1495 (Madrid), in Antonio Rumeu de Armas, *La Política Indigenista de Isabel la Católica* (Valladolid, 1969), p. 314; Bernáldez, *Memorias*, p. 303 (ch. CXX).

[71]Letter of Isabel and Fernando, April 16, 1495 (Madrid), in Rumeu de Armas, *Política Indigenista de Isabel.*, p. 315.

Admiral's conduct in the worst possible light. It is most unlikely that Buil and the mutineers objected to Columbus' bad treatment of the Indians, in which they had themselves played so active a part; but the arrival of the slaves was a new and serious warning sign of trouble on Hispaniola. Isabel had not reigned 21 stormy years without learning how to read such signs early and well. She decided she could not trust any of the reports she was getting about conditions on Hispaniola, and commissioned Juan Aguado, a former member of her household who had sailed with Columbus on his second voyage and returned with Torres on his first voyage the year before, to investigate and report on the Admiral's conduct as viceroy and governor. On August 5 Aguado sailed from Sevilla.[72]

Meanwhile the spiral of disintegration and destruction was continuing on Hispaniola. Columbus' great slave raid roused the Indians to all-out war; on March 27 a major battle was fought in the broad inland valley called the Vega Real, which the Spaniards won despite great inferiority in numbers by means of their horses, which terrified the Indians. Columbus, now healthy again and in personal command, ranged over the island killing, capturing, and terrorizing the Indians into submission. An annual tribute of four hawk's bells full of gold dust was levied on every Indian man and woman over fourteen on the island. Since the gold could only be obtained by panning, so large a quantity was impossible for most of the Indians to obtain. Columbus later cut the required amount in half, but maintained his insistence on that. Many of the Indians fled or fought, and were pursued into the mountains with horses and dogs. It is reliably estimated that in this and the following year (1495-96) no less than one-third of the native population of Hispaniola died, many of them probably from the white men's diseases to which they had no natural resistance, but a substantial number in the wars and pursuits. In the midst of all this, in June 1495, an early hurricane struck and sank every ship Columbus still had with him except stout little *Niña*.[73]

Aguado's arrival recalled Columbus to his senses. He stopped ravaging the land, came back to Isabela, and did his best to cooperate with Aguado, who seemed to regard his commission as giving him the power to countermand Columbus' orders and even to arrest people without his consent, not simply to gather information. Aguado's hostility made it imperative that Columbus return to Spain to protect his interests; many others on the island were now ready and eager to go as soon as transportation was available. Columbus' last act as governor was to transfer the capital of the colony from Isabela, which had proved unhealthy, infertile and with a poor harbor, to Santo Domingo, the first town planted in the New World that has endured. On March 10 he set sail in

[72]Morison, *Admiral of the Ocean Sea*, p. 493.
[73]*Ibid.*, pp. 488-493.

Niña and a caravel built in Hispaniola and hence named *India* (Aguado kept for himself the ships he had come in), with no less than 225 Spaniards and 30 Indians aboard, an enormous number of passengers for two such small vessels. They gathered extra provisions in the Lesser Antilles before starting across the Atlantic, but winds were light and contrary and they faced starvation before finally arriving at Cádiz June 11.[74]

In July Isabel and Fernando, then at Almazán on the upper Duoro, invited Columbus to join them. Columbus set out from the south with his surviving Indians, baptizing them on the way at the shrine of Our Lady of Guadalupe.[75] (Sad to say, Columbus seemed interested in baptizing Indians only after bringing them to Spain.) He eventually caught up with the court in Burgos, where he reported in late August or early September. The sovereigns had examined the charges against him, calling Fray Buil and Pedro Margarit and some other enemies of his to court to testify. Evidently Isabel and Fernando were not impressed with these witnesses or their testimony. In view of Columbus' extraordinary earlier accomplishments, they dismissed the charges and for the time being confirmed his powers. But in a special instruction they ordered him in the future to take more care for the conversion of the Indians—which, they pointed out, would first of all require peace and good order and more priests in Hispaniola (which suggests they were not happy with Fray Buil's departure thence). They approved sending 500 more colonists to Hispaniola and gave preliminary approval to Columbus' plans for a third voyage, though without issuing implementing directives at that time.[76]

Justice was not done for the Indians, but there was simply no way at this time for Isabel to have ascertained what had really happened on Hispaniola. It was too far away, the events were too confused, and those reporting to her had too many axes of their own to grind. The full truth was not learned until the investigations of Fray Bartolomé de Las Casas many years later, and he sometimes erred in the opposite direction, overemphasizing the perfidy of his countrymen and neglecting the role of Old World diseases in the extermination of the Indians. What Isabel saw in 1496 was one of history's greatest opportunities for her country and her people, which Christopher Columbus and he alone had provided by opening up these vast new lands with all their promise. She was always remarkably loyal to those who had served her well. Columbus would get another chance. He should, in any case, keep on sailing and exploring. But, though superlatively loyal, Isabel was never naive—she had lost all of that quality she might ever have had in her perilous years so long ago as a princess alone. She knew now that Columbus had serious weaknesses as an

---

[74]*Ibid.*, pp. 493-501.
[75]*Ibid.*, pp. 505-507; Bernáldez, *Memorias*, pp. 333-334 (ch. CXXXI).
[76]Santa Cruz, *Crónica*, I, 153-154 (ch. XXXII) and 161-162 (ch. XXXIV); Morison, *Admiral of the Ocean Sea*, pp. 507-508.

administrator. One more major mistake and she would have to remove him from the authority on land which he exercised so poorly.

Church reform was pushed vigorously during 1496 and 1497, with Isabel and Cisneros working closely together in complete harmony, and Fernando willing to put his signature to every directive Isabel produced in support of the reform. This was particularly evident in the case of the convents of Santa Clara and San Francisco in Calatayud in Aragon, where friends of the lax nuns enlisted the mayor of Calatayud, one of its judges, and other Aragonese magistrates to harass the Visitors and even prevent their access to the convents. Writing to officials of Calatayud February 13, 1496, Isabel (the letter is as usual also signed by Fernando, but we know that the reform of the women religious was her special concern) said:

> At the time we passed through your city we heard that you were well disposed toward carrying out the reformation of the convents of Santa Clara and San Francisco, which pleased us, as a good service to God and for the honor of your city and for the good of these convents. Now it seems the opposite is being done. Because of the importunity of some who care little for honor and conscience, and for the respect you have shown to us, it is said that you have impeded the work of the Visitors to these nuns and permit the Franciscans to abandon the true observance of their rule. Some of the nuns of Santa Clara, to block the reformation, present to you directives from the magistrates of Aragon which give the impression of favoring them, so that the Visitor was blocked, the doors of Santa Clara were closed against him, and he was not welcomed at San Francisco nor given lodging as was his right. We are surprised that such things should happen. And because we will not permit that the judicial deputy intervene in this manner, we command that you revoke these directives, proceeding by apostolic authority, and if he will not obey, that you proceed against him for disturbing the visitation.[77]

The mayor was told on the same day, in no uncertain terms, that his directives regarding the visitation of the convents were revoked, by royal and Papal authority; that he ought never to have intervened in this matter in the first place, it being outside his authority and competence; and that he should signify his full assent without delay and make all necessary provisions to see that interference with and disturbance of the visitation of the two convents cease immediately.[78]

Similar action was taken in Zaragoza, where nuns of a convent known as the Sepulcro of Zaragoza were being obstructive, pretending that they had already been investigated and approved, though not by the Visitors designated by the monarchs. The Vicar-General was told not to accept that excuse, and

---

[77]Isabel and Fernando to officials of Calatayud, February 13, 1496 (Tortosa), in García Oro, *Reforma*, pp. 330-331.

[78]Isabel and Fernando to the mayor of Calatayud, February 13, 1496 (Tortosa), *ibid.*, p. 332.

the Sepulcro community was "charged and commanded," in the most vigorous terms, to "comply with and obey everything the Visitors may order" and not to "look for other evasions to postpone what you ought to do, for your honor and honest living, [but] to desire and obtain whatever the Visitors may ask of you, with much rectitude and according to your Augustinian rule, and not oppose it, which, over and above the fact that we will not permit it, would be to fail in your duty."[79]

Monasteries and convents which did reform often experienced reprisals from opponents of the reform. Isabel took care, to the best of her ability, to see that they were protected. Some communities, on the other hand, were so determined to avoid facing the Visitors, with the iron Archbishop behind them, that they left the country, going to Italy or even to Muslim North Africa. At the end of December Pope Alexander VI renewed his commission to Cisneros to reform both the Franciscan and Dominican orders in Spain.[80]

Not only was Cisneros essential to the reform of the priests and religious and utterly dedicated in pursuit of it, but he was also much involved in improving the Spanish episcopate. In February 1497 he consecrated the new Bishop of Burgos, the holy Dominican friar Juan Pascual, in the presence of Isabel and Fernando, and remained there to celebrate the gorgeous marriage of Prince Juan and Archduchess Margaret on Palm Sunday (see below). Not until September 1497, more than a two years after he accepted his appointment, did he make formal personal entry into the archdiocese of Toledo to take possession of it. He was received with overwhelming enthusiasm and respect; he might set a higher standard of life and commitment than most were accustomed to, but he was a man of the people, Spanish to the marrow of his bones, a living saint—the people of Toledo felt honored simply to be near him. At once he launched within the archdiocese the reform he was sponsoring everywhere else, beginning with the chapter of Toledo cathedral, whose members were not even living in community; Cisneros demanded that they do so, and follow a more reflective and devotional way of life. Their resistance to the great Franciscan reformer was no more effective than anyone else's had been.[81]

---

[79]Isabel and Fernando to the religious of the Sepulcro of Zaragoza, February 25, 1496 (Tortosa), *ibid.*, p. 340; same to the Vicar-General of Zaragoza (same date and place), *ibid.*, pp. 338-339.

[80]Letter of Isabel and Fernando to the abbot of Veruela, June 14, 1496 (Almazán), *ibid.*, pp. 343-344, directing the abbot to assure the full support and protection of the convent of Trasobares which had fully reformed; letter of Pope Alexander VI to Cisneros and Diego de Deza, December 26, 1496 (Rome), *ibid.*, pp. 171-174; Fernández de Retana, *Cisneros*, I, 145; Menéndez Pidal, *Historia de España*, XVII (2), 276.

[81]Vallejo, *Cisneros*, pp. 14-18; Menéndez Pidal, *Historia de España*, XVII (2), 274-275; Merton, *Cisneros*, pp. 71-73.

By July 1496 all treaties, provisions, confirmations, ratifications, and other necessary advance arrangements for the double Habsburg marriage for Prince Juan and Princess Juana had been made, leaving only the actual transportation of the two brides and the marriage ceremonies themselves to be completed. Juana would go to Flanders, to marry Archduke Philip in his native country, which he in effect already ruled in view of Emperor Maximilian's many commitments elsewhere. She would be conveyed by a splendid fleet then gathering on the north coast of Spain, which in turn would later bring back Archduchess Margaret to marry Prince Juan in Castile. These two magnificent marriages were seen as the crowning achievement of Isabel's reign, the clearest possible indication of how far she had raised her native land, from endemic disorder and weakness which made it an object of international derision and contempt, to the greatest power in Europe. For the Habsburgs controlled the succession to the Holy Roman Empire, the highest temporal office in Christendom. Archduke Philip was Emperor Maximilian's only son; his son and Juana's would someday be the Emperor, while the simultaneous marriage of the only son of Isabel and Fernando with Philip's sister was seen as guaranteeing lasting friendship and alliance between the Empire and Spain.

A word is in order at this point about the Holy Roman Empire. For more than a century, many professional historians have outdone themselves in mocking, downgrading, and distorting the historical significance of the extraordinary political-religious concept it represented. Word-play and the *bon mot* have so much influence in human thought (historians not excepted) that it is almost impossible to exaggerate the intellectual damage done by the famous but fundamentally misleading quip of the highly regarded nineteenth-century historian James Bryce, that this pivotal political institution in medieval and early modern Christendom was "neither holy, nor Roman, nor an empire." Bryce's quip has a superficial plausibility: most of the Emperors were not saints, some were very far from sanctity, and several actively opposed the Pope and much of the Church; the Emperors did not reign in Rome, rarely came there, and stayed only with difficulty and against strong opposition; and the division of Germany and the Low Countries, whence they all came and where they spent most of their reigns from the tenth century onwards, into numerous small self-governing states meant that the Emperors could establish no such central government as was found in France, England, or Spain under Isabel and Fernando. These are facts; but ideas are facts too. The idea of the Holy Roman Empire was profoundly Christian, and central to Christendom; like all great ideas, it had many real and practical consequences. And the idea *was* holy, and Roman, and imperial in the Christian sense. (Christianity properly understood does not permit absolute rule, because the Church must always be present and the Church ought always to be free.)

The Holy Roman Emperor was regarded as the ultimate temporal authority in Christendom.   He was charged with the particular duty of protecting the Church and the Pope, and the general duty of protecting Christendom from its enemies both foreign and domestic—that is to say, from the infidel without and the heretic within. He might not be holy, but his mission was holy. He was not Roman, but his first title was King of the Romans, and his imperial coronation by the Pope (though often long delayed) could take place only in Rome. He was not supposed to be an absolute monarch, but a Christian emperor, and the natural leader of Christendom on its united temporal undertakings, such as a crusade. The idea of the Holy Roman Empire was not substantially affected by human failures and shortcomings and political circumstances that inhibited its full realization in practice.   So long as Christendom remained united in faith, the idea of the Holy Roman Emperor had great power and influence. Even when Christendom was cloven by the Protestant revolution (begun just thirteen years after Isabel's death), the idea and vision of the Holy Roman Emperor remained very important until the end of the Thirty Years War in 1648, when it finally became clear that Europe could never in the foreseeable future be religiously reunited. Only then did the great Christian imperial idea fade.

These points need to be kept clearly in mind in order to grasp how important Isabel—who had all the traditional understanding and respect of the medieval and early modern Catholic for the office of Holy Roman Emperor—regarded a close alliance of her royal house with the Habsburgs, the imperial dynasty; how much it meant for her to be able to look forward to a day when her grandson would inherit that office (as indeed her grandson Charles did, and used it to save Christendom when the Protestant revolution would have destroyed it); and how grateful she was to think that her descendants would never have to go to war against the Holy Roman Empire, but could help uphold its lofty aims (as her great-grandson Philip II did, during a prolonged period of imperial incapacity).   Even wholly secular historians recognize that these Spanish-Habsburg marriages of 1496 and 1497 created a lasting bond which remained a central political fact in Europe until the line of Philip and Juana finally died out in the year 1700. That bond was the creation of Isabel and Fernando.

Along with the two Habsburg marriages, Isabel and Fernando had for some time been negotiating marriages for their other daughters with the King of Portugal and the Crown Prince of England (entitled Prince of Wales). King Manuel of Portugal wanted the widowed Princess Isabel for his wife. King Henry VII of England very much wanted Isabel's youngest daughter Catherine for his son Arthur. These four marriages, taken together, would bring Spain to a level of influence in Europe which no royal dynasty had enjoyed since the fall of the Roman empire.

Though it seems odd to men and women of the twentieth century that the diplomacy of the medieval and early modern age placed such great value on marriage alliances, a family tie through marriage was then universally seen as the only reliable guarantee that treaties and alliances would be honored. To the reader of today it sometimes seems that Isabel was sacrificing her children to these marriages; but for a royal child, especially a princess, marriage was a public as well as a private vocation. They were brought up for it, trained for it, expected it. Isabel had never shrunk from that vocation herself when, in her days as a princess, it lay ahead of her, though with no living parent able to protect her she had insisted on her right to choose her husband from among the kings and princes who sought her hand. She took it for granted that no child of hers would shrink from it either. So far as we know, only Princess Isabel did, and that only after the shatteringly tragic death by accident of her beloved husband the Crown Prince of Portugal, at whose side there is every reason to believe that she had looked forward to ruling.

But Princess Isabel's reluctance did cast a shadow over Isabel's shining expectations in the summer of 1496, as we may see from her sad reference to it in a letter to her ambassador in England on August 18,[82] while the fragmentary but significant accounts we have of Juana's departure from Spain at that time suggest that another and darker shadow was already gathering over her. It is a constant frustration to the historian and biographer of Isabel that so little information is available about her children before they were married. By contrast to our knowledge of Isabel before she was married, our personal information about her children before their marriages consists of mere scraps and flickers. We have conventional, flattering tributes to Juan's goodness and intelligence from Peter Martyr de Anglería, who knew him well but always seems to talk about him as though he were a hundred miles away; Maria and Catherine are little more than wraiths throughout their girlhood. We know that Princess Isabel saw some of the war against Granada, but hear virtually nothing about how she responded to it. Juana also accompanied her mother frequently in those campaigns, but we know even less about how she responded; she was only twelve when Granada surrendered. For Juana before her departure from Spain we have little more of a personal nature than Dr. Hieronymus Münzer's brief but interesting and rather puzzling comment when he saw her at Madrid in January 1495:

> She is very well educated for her age and sex, and can compose in prose and verse. She is fourteen [actually she had just turned fifteen], and is dedicated entirely to letters. Her teacher, an ancient and venerable Dominican friar, eulogized her, and wished that I might hear her speak, but it was not possible for me to wait long enough.[83]

---

[82]Isabel to de Puebla, August 18, 1496 (Laredo), in Bergenroth, *Calendar of State Papers*, I, 115.
[83]Münzer, *Viaje*, p. 112.

Dr. Münzer's comment is puzzling because later in her life, even before she lost her sanity, Juana showed little sign of interest in literature or desire to write and speak, though there can be no doubt that she was highly intelligent and well educated; and no religious with whom she came in contact after her marriage ever came close to "eulogizing" her. The contrast suggests suppressed childhood rebellion, a docile and attractive front with some deep contradiction behind it. She did not even look like the other children. All Isabel's children tended to inherit her coloring and complexion, except Juana; Princess Isabel was red-haired, Juan and Maria were blond, Catherine had honey-colored hair. Only Juana was black-haired and black-eyed, like her father. Theories have been many about the character of the relationship between Juana and her mother and father. The only significant evidence we have about those relationships before her marriage comes from the days surrounding the departure of the great fleet from the little port of Laredo near Santander on the north coast of Spain that was to bear Juana away to Flanders to marry the heir of the Holy Roman Emperor.

The fleet at Laredo consisted of more than 100 ships and may have carried as many as 35,000 people, including 10,000 soldiers.[84] Juana was to travel on one of the biggest ships, called a carrack; there were only two of these sumptuous vessels in the whole fleet. She and her mother had left Almazán on the upper Duoro, in the highest part of the Castilian plain, and travelled for two weeks across rugged mountainous country to reach Laredo August 3. We would give a great deal for some account of that journey and what passed between mother and daughter during it, but we have only the bare itinerary. Fernando had bade farewell to his daughter in early July, before she left Almazán; he had to go to Catalonia to be ready to repel the invasion of Roussillon that the French were said to be planning. Isabel and Juana stayed for two weeks at Laredo, whose meager facilities must have been overwhelmed by the horde boarding the armada in its harbor. The days must have been frantically busy, the nights filled with roistering and clamor.[85]

On August 19, a Friday, Juana went aboard her carrack. She was only sixteen years old, and had never before left Spain (nor had her mother, nor was she ever to do so). The fleet was not yet entirely ready to sail—or perhaps the wind was foul. Isabel spent the next two nights on board with her daughter, while writing personal letters to King Henry VII of England and her ambassador there urging them to treat Juana and her party with the highest honor and give them all possible help should the fleet or any part of it be forced into English harbors by bad weather. Those two nights aboard Juana's carrack

---

[84]Bernáldez, *Memorias*, p. 377 (ch. CLIV); Peter Martyr de Anglería to Cardinal de Carvajal, October 5, 1496 (Burgos), DIHE IX, 319.

[85]Antonio Rumeu de Armas, *Itinerario de los Reyes Católicos, 1474-1516* (Madrid, 1974), pp. 227-228; Menéndez Pidal, *Historia de España*, XVII (2), 428-429.

suggest that Isabel felt that her dark-eyed daughter badly needed some special help which she alone could provide. The chronicler Santa Cruz also tells us that Isabel shed many tears, thinking that she might never see her daughter again.[86]

As matters turned out, it would have been better for everyone if she had not.

We hear nothing of any tears from Juana. On Sunday August 21 Isabel came ashore, probably first of all to attend Mass; we do not know if Juana came with her. Later that day, or possibly at the following dawn, the great fleet set sail and surged out of Laredo harbor into the stormy Bay of Biscay.[87]

There is a final disturbing note. Three days after the departure of the fleet, on August 24, Isabel sent a brief note to a courier named Cartello covering a packet of despatches for England and for the Emperor, which he was to deliver. But first of all he was "to overtake the fleet of the Archduchess, and deliver letters to her chaplain."[88] What letters? Why were they directed to Juana's chaplain? What did they say? We do not know. The peremptory tone of Isabel's instructions to Cartello, and the extraordinary difficulty and expense of the task she gave him—he would have to engage a fast ship and catch up with a fleet having two or three days' head start—suggest that these letters were far from routine. It is hard to avoid the conclusion that something she had seen in her daughter during those last two days on board the carrack had rung a warning bell in Isabel's sensitive, experienced mind and heart, giving her some premonition—perhaps her first—of the monsters of the night that lay in wait for her daughter in the years to come, and that she hoped to ward them off with the spiritual armor that had served her so well since that day when she prayed for deliverance from Pedro Girón. But in all probability we shall never know what messages Cartello carried to Juana's chaplain, nor even if they were actually delivered.

Isabel returned to Burgos, where she learned that her mother, long wrapped in the shades of unreason at Arévalo, had at last died.[89] There is no good time to get such news, but the morrow of Juana's departure and of the despatch of the message to Cartello surely made it one of the worst of times for her to receive it. History shows us no great personality more stable and sound than that of Isabel the Catholic. But her mother had lost her mind, and her daughter was to lose hers.

For a full month Isabel, so deeply worried that she could not hide her

---

[86]Santa Cruz, *Crónica*, I, 155 (ch. XXXII); Isabel to Henry VII of England, August 19, 1496 (Laredo) and to Dr. de Puebla, August 20, 1496 (Laredo), in Bergenroth, *Calendar of State Papers*, I, 119.

[87]Santa Cruz, *Crónica*, I, 155 (ch. XXXII); Menéndez Pidal, *Historia de España*, XVII (2), 429.

[88]Isabel to Cartello, courier, August 24, 1496 (Laredo), in Bergenroth, *Calendar of State Papers*, I, 121.

[89]Santa Cruz, *Crónica*, I, 156 (ch. XXXII).

concern behind the stoical front she usually displayed at court, awaited news of Juana; but no news came. On September 12, in a letter to her ambassador in England concerning the marriage negotiations for Catherine (which were progressing rapidly), she asked particularly for news of Juana and said that if he heard anything about her, he should write at once by the fastest courier. Her distress of mind is evidenced in another way in another letter to that ambassador three days later, in which she urges him to press Henry of England to go to war against France (as a means of putting an end to Charles' designs on Italy) in agitated, bellicose language very unlike her usual calm, thoughtful, morally sensitive and quietly resolute tone.[90]

Finally, near the end of September, Isabel learned that Juana had arrived safely in Flanders. The voyage had been stormy, and the fleet had found it necessary to take refuge in the English harbor of Portland from August 31 to September 2, but they were well received there and only a single caravel was lost. One carrack ran aground on the notorious shoals of the Flemish coast, later to play an important part in the defeat of the Spanish Armada, but Juana's carrack was unharmed. The chronicler Santa Cruz says that since Isabel was so disconsolate, God wished to make her happy by this news—a comment of such personal warmth as to give us an unforgettable glimpse of how much Isabel's subjects loved her.[91]

On October 1 the terms of the English marriage treaty for Catherine and Prince Arthur were agreed upon by the negotiators; Isabel and Fernando confirmed them January 1, 1497 and Henry VII on July 18 of that year.[92] On October 12 Archduke Philip arrived at the Flemish city of Lille, where Juana and his sister Margaret awaited him. It was the first time he and Juana had seen each other. There was apparently an immediate, almost violent physical attraction between them; on the 18th they were wed, so quickly and unceremoniously that the final documents relating to their marriage were not signed until two days later.[93]

For the moment, however, all seemed well with them, though there was

[90]Isabel to de Puebla, September 12, 1496 and September 15, 1496 (Oña), in Bergenroth, *Calendar of State Papers*, I, 123-128.

[91]Santa Cruz, *Crónica*, I, 156 (ch. XXXIV); Menéndez Pidal, *Historia de España*, XVII (2), 429.

[92]Bergenroth, ed., *Calendar of State Papers*, I, 129-130 (text of the treaty, translated); Luis Suárez Fernández, ed., *Política Internacional de Isabel la Católica*, Volume V (Valladolid, 1972), pp. 128-142 (Spanish text of the treaty and the Spanish ratification); J. D. Mackie, *The Earlier Tudors, 1485-1558* (Oxford, 1952), p. 148 (English ratification).

[93]Menéndez Pidal, *Historia de España*, XVII (2), 429; for the marriage documents see Suárez Fernández, *Política internacional de Isabel*, IV, 646-648. See Townsend Miller, *The Castles and the Crown; Spain 1451-1555* (New York, 1963), pp. 182-185, on the nature of their meeting and the attraction between them, although Miller's dates are incorrect.

much friction between the enormous Spanish party waiting to return with Archduchess Margaret to Spain, and their unwilling Flemish hosts— exacerbated by the five-month stay required by the inclement winter weather at sea, during which more than 10,000 of the Spaniards died, poorly treated, poorly housed and unused to the northern winter.[94] During the first year of Juana's marriage, Isabel does not seem to have received any further forewarning of the disasters it was to bring. Instead, she was told that Philip and Juana could not have made a more fortunate marriage, and that Juana was well liked by her new subjects.[95]

The year's triumphs for Isabel and Fernando in marriage negotiations for their children reached a climax in November when Princess Isabel was finally prevailed upon to marry King Manuel of Portugal, after he had been offered her sister Maria in her place but had refused to accept the substitution. The terms of the marriage agreement were similar to those of the princess' first marriage with Afonso of Portugal in 1490, except that—in recognition of Spain's great upsurge in wealth and power during the intervening six years—her dowry was larger. But Princess Isabel insisted as a separate condition that Manuel expel the Jews from Portugal, as her mother had expelled them from Spain. He agreed, and did so before their marriage, which was scheduled for September of the following year.[96]

On December 19, 1496, in recognition of all that Isabel and Fernando had done to uplift the Church and defend the Pope, Alexander VI granted them officially, by Papal bull, the title of the Catholic sovereigns, *los reyes católicos*, by which they have been ever since known in Spain.[97]

Much of Isabel's sadness, and possibly her premonitions as well, had been swept away by the good news of Juana's safe arrival in Flanders and her apparently happy marriage; and it seemed that the shadow cast by Princess Isabel's long and apparently inconsolable widowhood had at last been swept away as well. Nothing but joy and fulfillment now beckoned, as the Catholic sovereigns and devoted parents looked ahead to the climactic wedding of their heir, Prince Juan, and Archduchess Margaret. The somewhat reduced Spanish fleet and escort put to sea from Flanders, with Margaret aboard, in February 1497. Once again it had to seek English ports as protection from bad weather,

---

[94]Bernáldez, *Memorias*, p. 377 (ch. CLIV); Peter Martyr de Anglería to Cardinal de Carvajal, April 29, 1497 (Burgos), DIHE, IX, 331-332.

[95]Santa Cruz, *Crónica*, I, 165 (ch. XXXV).

[96]Menéndez Pidal, *Historia de España*, XVII (2), 412-413; Elaine Sanceau, *Reign of the Fortunate King* (Hamden CT, 1969), pp. 19-20; for the text of the marriage treaty, see Antonio de la Torre and Luis Suárez Fernández, eds., *Documentos referentes a las relaciones con Portugal durante el reinado de los Reyes Católicos* (Valladolid, 1958-63), III, 1-8.

[97]Bull of Pope Alexander VI, December 19, 1496 (Rome), in Rodríguez Valencia, *Isabel en la Opinion*, I, 48.

but this was no problem in view of the eager hospitality of the English king, looking forward to his son's joining the matrimonial parade for the royal progeny of Spain. The story was told and retold of how Archduchess Margaret, with a merry courage in striking contrast to the demeanor of her new sister-in-law, had written a provisional epitaph on her wrist-band in case she went down with her ship: "Here lies the gentle damsel Margaret, who had two husbands, yet died unwed." (She had earlier been betrothed to Charles VIII of France, who rejected her.) On March 8 Margaret arrived at Santander on the north coast of Castile; on the following day Gonzalo de Córdoba "the great captain" took Ostia at the mouth of the Tiber from the enemies of the Pope to restore complete freedom to the Papal states. He had required just 15 days to reduce what was generally believed to be an almost impregnable fortress. The good news was brought swiftly to Spain.[98]

Iñigo Velasco, Constable of Spain, won the honor of leading the escort that went to Santander immediately upon news of Margaret's arrival, to conduct her to Burgos where Isabel and Fernando and Juan were waiting and the wedding was to take place. When they heard that Margaret's party was approaching, Juan and Fernando rode out ten miles to meet them on the road. Isabel remained in Burgos; upon her first sight of Margaret she kissed her and flung her arms around her, then brought her to her own rooms. History and art, chary of realistic descriptions and depictions of Isabel's children at the time of their marriages, have more to offer for Margaret. An anonymous Flemish portrait at Versailles is particularly revealing, matching all we hear of Margaret from the Spanish sources. It shows no stiff courtly pose, no classic beauty, but a piquant, vivacious, delightful face that seems to have to make an effort not to smile. Margaret was small, with long blonde hair that when unbound fell almost to her feet, easy and friendly and natural in her manner, "without artifice." Juan fell instantly and totally in love with her, and so in their own way did everyone else who saw her whom we hear about.[99]

They were married on Palm Sunday, which fell early that year, on March 19. Archbishop Cisneros presided; we may well believe that even his gaunt iron-bound countenance found a smile that day for Princess Margaret and her Prince, the heir to Spain. Admiral Christopher Columbus was a guest of honor. No one could remember such rich, joyous, and magnificent celebrations ever before in Spain. But even at this supreme moment came a touch, a warning,

---

[98]Bernáldez, *Memorias*, pp. 372 (ch. CLII) and 377 (ch. CLIV); Santa Cruz, *Crónica*, I, 164 (ch. XXXV); Menéndez Pidal, *Historia de España*, XVII (2), 432; von Pastor, *History of the Popes*, V, 491; William T. Walsh, *Isabella of Spain, the Last Crusader* (New York, 1930), p. 434.

[99]Santa Cruz, *Crónica*, I, 164-165 (ch. XXXV); Peter Martyr de Anglería to Cardinal de Carvajal, April 29, 1497 (Burgos), DIHE IX, 331-332; Menéndez Pidal, *Historia de España*, XVII (2), 431-432; Walsh, *Isabel*, pp. 433-434.

from the kingdom that knows not joy; in one of the splendid tournaments Alonso de Cárdenas, son of Isabel's ever-faithful Gutierre, was flung from his horse and trampled on the chest, caving in his ribs and killing him within four hours, during which he never regained consciousness. In love and honor especially for his father, the festive court for a time exchanged its cloth of gold for the colors of mourning.[100]

For three months Juan and Margaret lived an idyll, a honeymoon that seemed to have no end. Then the doctors noticed that Juan appeared pale and weak, increasingly listless in sharp contrast to Margaret's bubbling energy. They began to worry. Juan had never been physically strong. The constant round of ceremony was exhausting him; so perhaps was his young and irresistible wife, so full of life and health. The doctors actually went so far as to recommend a temporary separation of the newlyweds.[101]

Isabel would not hear of it. What God had joined together, she reminded them with all the leashed passion of her own nature, man must not put asunder. That had ever been her creed, lived and practiced to the fullest with Fernando. She would defend it absolutely for her son. "I do not wish to call her contumacious or too self-confident," says Peter Martyr woodenly, in one of the few implied criticisms of Isabel he ever makes in his letters;[102] but she understood her son far better than he. If Juan were to be not only Margaret's true love but King of Spain some day, he must learn to find the strength he needed, not be shunted periodically into some gilded cage to regain it.

Soon afterward, during the summer, Margaret told her delighted husband and his parents that she was pregnant.[103]

Meanwhile Isabel and Fernando prepared and issued further instructions to Columbus for his third voyage, requiring him to take priests with him to evangelize the Indians, and appointed his brother Bartholomew governor of the Indies while the Admiral was out exploring.[104] It was an appropriate time for a new venture by Columbus, for 1497 was the year second only in importance to 1492 in the history of European discovery: the year when John Cabot sailed from Bristol for Henry VII of England in May, reached Newfoundland off the coast of North America in June, and returned successfully to Bristol in

---

[100]Santa Cruz, *Crónica*, I, 165 (ch. XXXV); Peter Martyr de Anglería to Cardinal de Carvajal, April 29, 1497 (Burgos), DIHE IX, 331-332; Chronicle of Valladolid, CODOIN XIII (Madrid, 1848), p. 213; Samuel Eliot Morison, *The European Discovery of America: the Southern Voyages, 1492-1616* (New York, 1974), p. 161.

[101]Peter Martyr de Anglería to Cardinal de Carvajal, June 13, 1497 (Medina del Campo), DIHE IX, 334-335.

[102]*Ibid.*

[103]Bernáldez, *Memorias*, p. 378 (ch. CLIV).

[104]Santa Cruz, *Crónica*, I, 167 (ch. XXXVI); Morison, *Admiral of the Ocean Sea*, pp. 509-510.

August;[105] the year when on July 8 Vasco da Gama dropped down the Tagus from Lisbon on the outflowing tide with five ships, three of them bound for India around the Cape of Good Hope to fulfill at last the 80-year-old dream of Prince Henry the Navigator.[106] As Columbus sailing for Spain had opened up the Caribbean Sea just five years before, now da Gama sailing for Portugal would open up the Indian Ocean and bring the riches of its shores flooding back to the country whose king Isabel's oldest daughter was about to marry; while Cabot sailing for England had opened up North America for the country whose heir Isabel's youngest daughter would wed.

Never in all of history have so many horizons expanded so quickly; and in the center of their flowering, in touch with them all, was the form and the spirit of Isabel the Catholic Queen. In the summer of 1497 she stood at the summit.

On September 14 Isabel and Fernando and Princess Isabel set out from Medina del Campo for the wedding of the princess to the King of Portugal. The first day's journey brought them to Madrigal de las Altas Torres, Isabel's birthplace, which surely roused her memories of the days she had spent there as a hunted fugitive, seeking freedom from the Marqués of Villena and his henchmen so that she might marry Fernando, the prince of her choice. From Madrigal they went on to Toro, scene of their decisive victory in the war of the succession—a victory over Portugal, now friend and ally. On the 23rd they arrived in Salamanca, where they stayed five days. The day after they left it on the final leg of their journey to Valencia de Alcántara and Princess Isabel's wedding, Juan and his lovely bride came riding in, to a glorious welcome: large formations of splendidly adorned horsemen, resounding trumpets, people singing at the windows, the streets covered with flowers and sweet-smelling herbs, the doors all hung with green boughs and brilliant banners. On September 30 King Manuel of Portugal came to Valencia de Alcántara and married Princess Isabel.[107]

It is a hundred miles from Salamanca to Valencia de Alcántara over rough and broken country—a long day's ride even for couriers using relays of post horses. Some time during the night of October 2 or the morning of October 3 a courier on a foaming horse galloped into the little town with shocking news: Prince Juan had fallen seriously ill, with a raging, rising fever the doctors could not control. At least one more courier must have come in during the day of the 3rd with news that Juan's condition was steadily

---

[105]Samuel Eliot Morison, *The European Discovery of America: the Northern Voyages, 500-1600* (New York, 1971), pp. 157-189.

[106]Vincent Jones, *Sail the Indian Sea* (London, 1978), pp. 23-34.

[107]Rumeu de Armas, *Itinerario*, pp. 236-237; Isabel and Fernando to Alonso da Silva, September 14, 1497 (Medina del Campo), in Antonio Paz y Melia, *El Cronista Alonso de Palencia* (Madrid, 1914), pp. 336-337; Peter Martyr de Anglería to Cardinal de Carvajal, October 19, 1497 (Villasandino), DIHE IX, 344-345.

worsening.[108]

Isabel was ill in bed; in any case, the days of her magnificent rides were over. But Fernando, though only a year younger, was in better health and still a great horseman. Through the night of the 3rd and the early morning of the 4th he followed the track of the post-riders northward, desperate to reach his son in time to try to inspire in him the will to live. When he arrived at Salamanca, Juan was at death's door. To his father's pleas that he believe recovery to be possible, that he draw upon the resilience of youth, he would only reply that he was reconciled to death, that he felt it approaching, that it was God's will. He prayed that his father would be able to accept it as he had done. Fernando was impressed by his son's spiritual fortitude, but could not endure the agony of that moment. He "melted in tears." So did everyone around him. Peter Martyr, who was there beside him, said days later: "It is impossible for me to speak of this without being overwhelmed by tears." Prince Juan died that day, and the whole court put on sackcloth.[109]

They entombed him at the church at the monastery of Santo Tomás in Avila, where his remains rest to this day. Let Townsend Miller, in his unforgettable poetic prose, describe it:

> Even the foreigner cannot escape a tremor of emotion as he walks down the dusty road to the Convent of Santo Tomás . . . and stands beside the tomb that enshrined the hopes, the whole future, of Spain. White, heavy, still, cruelly alone in the icy transept and with the small figure lost in tons of marble—surely it is one of the world's saddest monuments.[110]

It remained to tell Isabel—and Fernando could not do it, could not face it. In Valencia de Alcántara, she must have been watching the road for every courier; and he sent couriers, several of them, some bearing letters saying Juan was better, others saying he was worse, but none saying that he was dead. Finally he came back himself, five days after Juan's death. When he arrived, and she put to him the inevitable, instant question, he could only say that their son "was well."[111] No chronicler reports how or when or by whom the truth finally came to her. But Andrés Bernáldez tells us what that truth was for her: a "dagger of grief that transfixed the soul of the Queen and lady Isabel."[112]

---

[108]Santa Cruz, *Crónica*, I, 167 (ch. XXXV).

[109]*Ibid.*, pp. 167-168 (ch. XXXV); Peter Martyr de Anglería to Cardinal de Carvajal, October 19, 1497 (Villasandino), DIHE IX, 345-347.

[110]Miller, *Castles and the Crown*, p. 175.

[111]Bernáldez, *Memorias*, p. 379 (ch. CLV); Santa Cruz, *Crónica*, I, 167-168 (ch. XXXV); Peter Martyr de Anglería to Cardinal de Carvajal, October 19, 1497 (Villasandino), DIHE, IX, 346; Rumeu de Armas, *Itinerario*, p. 238.

[112]Bernáldez, *Memorias*, p. 380 (ch. CLV). His original Spanish words were *cuchillo de dolor que traspasó el ánima de la reina doña Isabel*.

10
Isabel on the Cross
(October 1497-July 1500)

Isabel the Catholic Queen, in the forty-seventh year of her life, had received a devastating blow. It must have seemed to her then that nothing else that would ever happen to her could be worse, or as bad, as the loss of her only son, Prince Juan, at the age of eighteen. She and Fernando did their best to put up a brave front, to carry off their unending succession of public appearances with the confident serenity their people had come to expect of them. But their friend and counsellor Peter Martyr tells us that, in this October of 1497, when they were seated near each other in public, they were no longer able to look steadily into each other's faces, as they had often done before.[1] (And this tells us more than the depth of their grief for their lost son; it tells us of their love for each other. It is not every husband and wife, then or now, royal or not, whose glance regularly seeks his spouse's face in public.)

But Prince Juan's death was no isolated, unique tragedy. It was not the sum of his mother's agony, only its beginning. Isabel the triumphant, Isabel the history-maker, Isabel whose will had changed destinies and surmounted oceans, was now on the cross. She had been chosen to share much of the ordeal of her Savior. Other women have suffered as much, themselves and for their families—though mercifully, not many. But no ruling Queen, loving and cherishing her children, has ever suffered so much in so relatively short a time as Isabel was to suffer. Before death released her at last, it was to seem that all she had made and built, publicly and privately, lay in ruins. Darkness eclipsed the noonday sun, and even the stars went out.

Yet Isabel the Catholic endured. She did not blaspheme; she did not despair; she did not even complain, where anyone could hear her. She let the nails be driven into her hands and feet without a whimper. If her agony affected her judgment, the effect was barely discernible, even after five centuries of historians have sifted through the records of her decisions. If her agony affected her faith, it was only to make it stronger.

---

[1]Peter Martyr de Anglería to Archbishop Hernando de Talavera, October 30, 1497 (Alcalá de Henares), *Documents inéditos para la Historia de España* (hereinafter cited as DIHE), published by the Duke of Alba et al, Volume IX (Madrid, 1955), p. 347.

It was her ultimate test—of faith, of hope, of love, of potential sanctity. None could have been harder. She passed it with flying colors. Those who loved her, then and now, trust that it was all made up to her in Paradise.

It had begun at Valencia de Alcántara, where Isabel had seen her oldest daughter married for the second time, and then learned within a few days that she had lost her only son. It continued at Alcalá de Henares, in the highlands east of Madrid, where she and Fernando arrived November 8, under the chill skies of autumn, with Princess Margaret and their daughter Catherine, whom they called Catalina—and Archbishop Cisneros.[2]   The passionate, austere Franciscan monk-prelate who was her confessor knew what Isabel was enduring; he knew how much she needed him, and so for the moment he subordinated all his other duties—as leader of the great reform of the Church in Spain, as Archbishop of Toledo and primate of the realm—to be with her, to do what he could to comfort and console her.

Catalina was eleven years old. Her mother did not bring her older sister Maria with her to Alcalá de Henares; we do not know why. Catalina was beside her mother almost constantly during her first three years on the cross. Time and history were to show Catalina to be by far the strongest of all Isabel's children, the only one much like her. Catalina was to need all that strength, all she learned from her mother in these years about how to endure suffering, when as "Catherine of Aragon," thirty-five years later, she defied King Henry VIII of England and the Protestant revolution alone, unwavering, unyielding, until death.

Isabel and Fernando came to Alcalá de Henares not only to face their grief and seek balm for it, not only to reorder their lives in the wake of the immense tragedy that had struck them, but also to guard a hope that some good might yet be snatched from the jaws of disaster. For Princess Margaret was pregnant. Juan's passionate love, in the last weeks before he died, had borne fruit in her. If the baby were a son, he could legally—and perhaps in some other ways—take Juan's place. He would be the King of Spain that Juan would have been. Even if the baby were a daughter, she would be heiress to Castile, and if she lived to maturity, would be married with that heritage the fundamental consideration in selecting a consort, her scepter borne as her grandmother had borne it. The succession would be safe, would not slip into foreign hands. In either case, Margaret would stay in Spain, would guide her child, would be ready to rule if need be as regent if neither Isabel nor Fernando should live to see her child come of age. So fine a judge of character as Isabel the Catholic surely already sensed in Margaret the potential for the remarkable political ability that, joined with her winsome charm and rare honesty and

[2]Alonso de Santa Cruz, *Crónica de los Reyes Católicos*, ed. Juan de Mata Carriazo, Volume I (Sevilla, 1951), p. 179 (ch. XL); Juan de Vallejo, *Memorial de la vida de Fray Francisco Jiménez de Cisneros*, ed. Antonio de la Torre (Madrid, 1913), p. 21.

directness of manner, was one day to make her an unsurpassed regent of the Netherlands.

Juan was dead. But Margaret had been his. She had much to offer Spain, and her child had everything to offer it.

But on December 14 Margaret miscarried. Her child was barely recognizable as human, though it was determined that it had been a daughter. Just a little more than two months after Juan's death, Isabel and Fernando were dealt another paralyzing blow, engulfed in another wave of sorrow. For the rest of her life, after Margaret's miscarriage, Isabel wore only mourning black, and under it the rough habit of the third order of St. Francis.[3]

For Castile, the succession now passed to Isabel's eldest daughter, who bore her name and had just been married to King Manuel of Portugal after six years of widowhood. But for Aragon the situation was not so clear. The law of Aragon was a modified version of the famous "Salic law" of France. As in France, no woman could legally rule in Aragon, and none ever had. But in Aragon, as not in France, succession could pass through a woman.

In January 1498 Isabel and Fernando wrote to King Manuel, asking him and his wife to come quickly to Spain, where the *cortes* of Castile would swear fealty to them as co-heirs to the throne; then perhaps Aragon, despite its laws, would follow suit. Manuel replied that he would come, but not immediately; he must first reassure his people that Portugal would not be absorbed into the larger political entity of Spain, for the Portuguese had always been vehemently opposed to any such absorption. By March Manuel had set his people's fears at rest, guaranteeing that Portugal would always be ruled only by Portuguese—though in fact this meant only that, in a united Spain and Portugal, no Spanish officials would be sent to Portugal. The *cortes* of Castile convened at Toledo, and on March 29 Manuel and his Queen Isabel set out on from Portugal to attend its meeting.[4]

Isabel and Fernando met their daughter and her husband at their favorite shrine, that of Our Lady of Guadalupe. They all spent Holy Week there together. On April 29 Manuel and young Isabel made solemn entry into Toledo. They pledged the *cortes* to observe all the laws and ancient privileges

[3]Chronicle of Valladolid, in *Colección de documentos inéditos para la historia de España* (hereinafter cited as CODOIN), XIII (Madrid, 1848), p. 216; Andrés Bernáldez, *Memorias del reinado de los Reyes Católicos*, ed. Manuel Gómez Moreno and Juan de Mata Carriazo (Madrid, 1962), p. 378 (ch. CLIV); Santa Cruz, *Crónica*, I, 179 (ch. XL); Peter Martyr de Anglería to the Archbishop of Braga, June 5, 1498 (Alcalá de Henares), DIHE IX, 365-366; Garrett Mattingly, *Catherine of Aragon* (New York, 1941, 1990), p. 20.
[4]Santa Cruz, *Crónica*, I, 179 (ch. XL); Ramón Menéndez Pidal, director, *Historia de España*, Volume XVII: "España de los Reyes Católicos," ed. Luis Suárez Fernández and Manuel Fernández Alvarez (Madrid, 1969), Part 2, p. 476; Elaine Sanceau, *Reign of the Fortunate King* (Hamden CT, 1969), p. 22.

of Castile. The ceremonies of swearing fealty to them as heirs to the throne extended through two full weeks, with all 34 members of the *cortes* who were present along with many great noblemen swearing individually, with much pomp and pageantry.[5] Finally all the protocol was fulfilled, and on May 19 Isabel and Fernando departed for Aragon, where they would meet its *cortes* at Zaragoza.[6] Manuel and young Isabel seem to have travelled separately from Isabel and Fernando, perhaps more slowly, for the new Queen of Portugal was six months pregnant.

The unification of Spain and Portugal for which these proceedings were providing would have been momentous in the history of the world. Their union was not actually accomplished until 1580, when Europe was very different than it had been in 1498, and the enemies of Spain much stronger. A union earlier in the century might well have endured, as the union of 1580 did not, and created the greatest and richest nation on earth. Even separated from Portugal, Spain was fast being recognized as the world's leading power; with Portugal's lucrative monopoly of the trade of Africa added, Spain would have been stronger and wealthier still. But more was at stake than Africa. For just after Portugal's King Manuel and his Queen Isabel graciously received the oaths of allegiance to them as royal heirs from the grandees of Spain, the soaring dream of Prince Henry the Navigator had at last been fulfilled (though no one in Europe would know it until another year had passed). Vasco da Gama had sailed full ten thousand miles around the whole continent of Africa: rounding the Cape of Good Hope November 22, 1497, passing Bartolomeu Dias' farthest east on November 25, overcoming a mutiny December 12, reaching Mozambique and the outliers of Arab civilization March 2, picking up a pilot for India at Melindi in Kenya April 22, at last anchoring off the south Indian city of Calicut May 20.[7] And in that same month of May 1498, truly a landmark in the Age of Discovery, Christopher Columbus sailed from Sevilla on his third voyage, which was finally to bring him to the American mainland, in what is now Venezuela.[8]

Both the Americas and the Orient were simultaneously being opened up by Spaniards and Portuguese. The world's first overseas empires were being created. The succession of young Queen Isabel of Portugal to the thrones of Castile and Aragon would unite them under the rule of a royal couple who gave every indication of being as united in spirit and purpose as Isabel and Fernando had always been.

[5]Menéndez Pidal, *Historia de España*, XVII (2), 476-477; Santa Cruz, *Crónica*, I, 179 (ch. XL); Luis Fernández de Retana, *Cisneros y su siglo*, Volume I (Madrid, 1929), p. 210; Sanceau, *Fortunate King*, pp. 22-23.

[6]Antonio Rumeu de Armas, *Itinerario de los Reyes Católicos, 1474-1516* (Madrid, 1974), p. 243.

[7]Vincent Jones, *Sail the Indian Sea* (London, 1978), pp. 50-73.

[8]Samuel Eliot Morison, *Admiral of the Ocean Sea* (Boston, 1942), pp. 513-517.

But the royal succession laws of Aragon were a real obstacle to such a union. Queen Isabel of Portugal was presented to the *cortes* of Aragon June 14, but there was far from instant acceptance of her as heir. Long legal discussions ensued. Fernando does not seem to have been of much help—in fact, oddly enough, he is hardly mentioned at all in the accounts we have of that critical meeting of the *cortes* of his native kingdom. Isabel of Castile was sorely tried, and probably beginning to be fearful for her daughter. Young Isabel had never been strong, and her own dreadful tragedy, when her beloved young husband Prince Afonso of Portugal was thrown from his horse and killed in 1491 when they had been married less than a year, had shadowed her whole adult life. She was alarmingly thin. Her pregnancy burdened her, and her two long journeys over rough roads—from Portugal to Toledo in April, from Toledo to Zaragoza in late May and early June—had been very tiring.[9] Isabel the Catholic dearly loved all her children, and most probably this daughter especially, the first fruit of her and Fernando's love, so dramatically rescued at Segovia when she was six, so desperately bereaved when she was 21. But her daughter did not look like a woman ready to rule half the world, and Isabel in her unsparing realism probably sensed it. As the debates in the *cortes* of Aragon dragged on interminably, for one of the few times in her life the monumental patience of Isabel the Catholic snapped.

In the hearing of many of the Aragonese grandees, she lashed out: "It would be more glorious and would cost me less to bring these people to the right by force of arms, rather than to suffer their insolence!" Alonso de Fonseca, an Aragonese councillor, answered her in measured terms, with a hint of rebuke: "The Aragonese, my lady, are right to discuss what they promise, because as much as they are careful in examining what they swear to, they will be constant in that to which they swear."[10]

Archbishop Cisneros, who had remained with Isabel in Aragon, led a solemn procession of the Blessed Sacrament through the streets of Zaragoza on Corpus Christi day in June, in which all the royalty present took part. Many in that procession must have prayed for a quick and healing resolution of the controversy, as all prayed publicly for a safe delivery of the child of the King and Queen of Portugal. Finally someone had the idea of postponing the legal decision on the successor until the now fast approaching birth, to see what sex the baby might be. If it were male, Aragonese law would allow Fernando's grandson to inherit the kingdom; presumably his mother could rule in his name, if need be, for some time. Isabel and the *cortes* both accepted this partial and perhaps temporary compromise, and everyone settled down to wait for the

---

[9]Santa Cruz, *Crónica*, I, 179-180 (ch. XL); Menéndez Pidal, *Historia de España*, XVII (2), 477-478; Peter Martyr de Anglería to the Archbishop of Braga, September 1, 1498 (Zaragoza), DIHE IX, 374.

[10]Fernández de Retana, *Cisneros*, I, 213.

birth.[11]

Meanwhile beyond the seas, Vasco da Gama was haggling and maneuvering brilliantly with the bewildered Hindu ruler of Calicut, whose exotic title was the Zamorim, and his Muslim counsellors who would obviously have preferred that none of the far-voyaging Portuguese ever returned home with news of what they had done; and Columbus, after being becalmed for a frightening week in the torrid heat of equatorial waters, had reached the island of Trinidad and then the mainland of South America, of which he formally took possession August 6.[12] Leaving the Spanish Canary Islands, Columbus had written in his journal: "May Our Lord guide me and grant me that which may be for His service and that of the King and Queen, our lords, and to the honor of Christendom; for I believe that no man has yet taken this course and that this sea is altogether unknown."[13] Leaving the Portuguese Cape Verde Islands, he had written: "May That which is Three and One guide me by Its charity and mercy that I may serve It and that I may give Your Highnesses and all Christendom some great delight, as was done by the finding of the Indies, which resounded throughout the world."[14] Now, after sailing along the coast of South America for ten days in mid-August, he concluded that it was in all probability a new continent, an "other world."[15] In his journal he addressed Isabel and Fernando as follows:

> As Your Highnesses know, a short time ago it was not known that there was more land than that described by Ptolemy, and there was no one in my own time who believed that a man could sail from Spain to the Indies. For this reason I spent seven years at your court, and not a few took part in the discussions. But finally only the extraordinary daring of Your Highnesses decreed that the venture be made, against the judgment of all those who said it could not be done. And now the truth appears, and will before long appear in greater measure. And if this is a continent, it is a wonderful thing and will be so regarded by all men of learning, since from it flows so large a river [the Orinoco] as to form a sea of fresh water 48 leagues [in extent].[16]

Young Isabel's pregnancy came to term in the latter part of August. But at some time during that strenuous spring and summer she had given up hope. We are specifically told by Peter Martyr, who was there, and by the chronicler

---

[11]Vallejo, *Cisneros.*, p. 26; Santa Cruz, *Crónica*, I, 179-180 (ch. XL); Peter Martyr de Anglería to the Archbishop of Braga, June 22, 1498 (Zaragoza), DIHE IX, 368-369.
    [12]Jones, *Sail the Indian Sea*, pp. 73-97; Morison, *Admiral of the Ocean Sea*, pp. 524-545.
    [13]Samuel Eliot Morison, ed., *Journals and Other Documents on the Life and Voyages of Christopher Columbus* (New York, 1963), p. 261.
    [14]*Ibid.*, p. 263.
    [15]*Ibid.*, p. 276.
    [16]*Ibid.*, p. 280.

Santa Cruz, that she had become convinced she would die in childbirth. She made a full confession, and took communion which she regarded as viaticum. After that, if she felt she had committed the slightest sin, she was at once on her knees begging absolution. When she went into labor, she persevered just long enough to see the baby born—a son. Within less than an hour of his first cry, she expired.[17]

We are not told what Isabel the Catholic thought of her daughter's premonition of death, but it is clear from her reaction when death came that she herself did not share it—could not contemplate another bereavement within less than a year of the first. Archbishop Cisneros heard the appalling news, and rushed to the chamber where Isabel and Fernando had confined themselves, weeping uncontrollably. The great Queen was on her knees, in such agony that Peter Martyr says she appeared "stupefied." That he did not exaggerate is shown by Cisneros' reaction when he saw her. The iron reformer, the spiritual athlete broke down himself, so completely that far from being able to offer any consolation to Isabel, *she* had to console *him*. Somehow, on seeing his distress, she roused herself to say that "all being mortal, they had begotten a mortal and would not fail to give thanks to God for the period of life that had been granted to her."[18]

King Manuel was almost as desolated; he had truly loved his gentle, slender, often sorrowing young wife. Her body was taken away for burial in Toledo; he waited in Zaragoza for the ceremony of the baptism of his son, the heir to three kingdoms, christened Miguel. But there was little joy for anyone at that baptism; shock and grief were universal. Noblemen and the poor felt it alike, and deeply. They sorrowed not only for the young Queen of Portugal, but even more for their own beloved sovereigns, Isabel and Fernando, in the excruciating ordeal they were enduring.[19]

Worse still, the baby prince, upon whom the whole hoped-for succession and union with Portugal now depended, was weak and sickly, with a low birth weight. "Perhaps his nature can change, as sometimes happens, with good feeding," Peter Martyr says, whistling in the dark. "God grant it!"[20]

A few days after the baptism, King Manuel and his men stole away suddenly and silently, at night, with only a few torches to hold back the shadows, to return to Portugal. Manuel left his newborn son with Isabel and Fernando. But Isabel was seriously ill, confined to bed. The pall lifted only a little when,

---

[17]Peter Martyr de Anglería to the Archbishop of Braga, September 1, 1498 (Zaragoza), DIHE IX, 373-374; Santa Cruz, *Crónica*, I, 180 (ch. XL); Chronicle of Valladolid, CODOIN XIII, 215-216.

[18]Fernández de Retana, *Cisneros*, I, 214-215; Peter Martyr de Anglería to Archbishop of Braga, September 1, 1498 (Zaragoza), DIHE IX, 374.

[19]Santa Cruz, *Crónica*, I, 180 (ch. XL); Vallejo, *Cisneros*, pp. 26-27.

[20]Peter Martyr de Anglería to Cardinal Bernardino de Carvajal, October 4, 1498 (Zaragoza), DIHE IX, 376-377.

on September 22, the fractious *cortes* of Aragon finally agreed to swear fealty to Prince Miguel as heir.[21]

If Miguel lived, he would be the King of Castile, Aragon, and Portugal, lord of the Indian Ocean, emperor of the Americas. But if he did not live, the succession to the throne of Castile would pass to Juana far away in the Netherlands, with the Habsburg Archduke Philip her consort; the succession in Aragon would again be disputed, unless and until Juana had a son (she was now also pregnant with her first child); the union with Portugal would be lost. Even if the unity of Castile and Aragon could be salvaged, the new heirs of Castile and Aragon would be primarily influenced by the German, Dutch, and Flemish environment and interests of the Habsburg family; Spain could well become simply an appendage of their empire.

That would be bad enough, with an immense and unpredictable potential for political disaster and even civil war, for none knew better than Isabel and Fernando the vehement patriotism and national pride of the Spanish, fueled by all the history and traditions of their unique 770-year war of reconquest against the Moors. In all that history, neither Castile nor Aragon had ever been ruled by a foreigner or the wife of a foreigner. But there could be worse, for Isabel as Queen and for Isabel as mother. It had now been more than two years since Juana departed for the Netherlands. Letters from her had been alarmingly few. Though other communications had at first been reassuring about her situation, by now evidence was accumulating under Isabel's discerning eye that all was not well with her daughter and son-in-law in Flanders. Most of Juana's personal staff of Spanish officials and ladies had been dismissed and replaced by Flemings; her own countrymen who remained often did not receive their promised pay and sustenance. When the news of Prince Juan's death came to the Netherlands, Philip had had the temerity to proclaim himself Prince of Castile. Though a vigorous protest by Isabel and Fernando promptly forced him to withdraw the totally unjustified pretension, that he had made it at all was a dangerous sign; if Miguel died he could claim to be Prince of Castile with far more plausibility. There was nothing to indicate that Juana had made any effort to restrain him from attempting to usurp the rights of her sister. Indeed, there was nothing to indicate that she had any influence over Philip at all, although she was reputed to be passionately in love with him. Isabel's second daughter was becoming almost a stranger to her.[22]

So Isabel had sent a special emissary, Tomás de Matienzo, Sub-prior of the monastery of Santa Cruz in Segovia, to Brussels. He arrived in midsummer 1498, spoke three times with Juana, and sent a detailed report to Isabel on August 16. Given the usual time for the transmission of letters in that era, it

---

[21]Santa Cruz, *Crónica*, I, 180-181 (ch. XL); Vallejo, *Cisneros*, p. 27.

[22]Townsend Miller, *The Castles and the Crown; Spain 1451-1555* (New York, 1963), pp. 189-191.

would have come to Isabel in Zaragoza at the worst possible time for her, psychologically—just a few days after her daughter's death. Matienzo said he had asked Juana if she had any message for her parents; she replied that she had none. He asked her why she had not written to them; she replied that she had nothing to say. She made no inquiry of him about her parents, nor did she ask after anyone in Spain. She said she thought he had been sent to be her confessor, and declared she would not accept him as such. On Ascension day in June, when it was usual to confess, she had not done so and he did not know why.[23]

We do not know how Isabel interpreted Matienzo's report, but it can only have been deeply disturbing to her, especially at such a time. Whatever she had seen in Juana that worried her at the time of Juana's departure for the Netherlands in 1496[24] must have caused her even more concern now. It surely played a part, along with the enormous shock of her oldest daughter's death, in her prostration in bed during most of September. Not until October 18 was she well enough to travel, to leave death-haunted Zaragoza and go by easy stages to Ocaña, where the *cortes* of Castile was to meet to swear allegiance to Prince Miguel as the heir.[25] At Ocaña she received new reports from Brussels. On November 11 her ambassador Gómez de Fuensalida gave a much more encouraging report on Juana, at least with reference to her relationship with her husband, which he described as excellent; this was followed by the news of the birth of Juana and Philip's first child, a daughter Eleanor, five days later.[26]

Meanwhile, through all these storms and stresses battering the royal family, Archbishop Cisneros was carrying on resolutely with his sweeping reform of the Church in Spain. Reform of the orders and of the diocesan clergy was now proceeding in tandem. In his own order, the Franciscans, strong resistance had developed. The Franciscan general, Fray Francisco Nanni, known as Samson for his vigor in debate, was hostile to Cisneros, and on November 9, 1497 had prevailed on the Pope to suspend the entire reform of the Franciscan order in Spain pending investigation of alleged abuses. Cisneros had gone to Isabel and told her that a complete suspension of the reform in any order, most especially his own, with no date set for its resumption, would be disastrous for the work so well begun. The faithful and the zealous would lose

---

[23]Tomás de Matienzo to Isabel, August 16, 1498 (Brussels), in Luis Suárez Fernández, ed., *Political Internacional de Isabel la Católica*, Volume V (Valladolid, 1972), pp. 287-288; Miller, *Castles and the Crown*, pp. 192-193.

[24]See Chapter Nine, above.

[25]Santa Cruz, *Crónica*, I, 181 (ch. XL); Rumeu de Armas, *Itinerario*, pp. 246-247.

[26]Letter of Gómez de Fuensalida, November 11, 1498 (Brussels), *Correspondencia de Gutierre Gómez de Fuensalida, Embajador en Alemania, Flandes e Inglaterra*, published by the Duke of Alba (Madrid, 1907), pp. 106-107; Archduke Philip to Princess Maria, November 16, 1498 (Brussels), in Suárez Fernández, *Política Internacional de Isabel*, pp. 338-339.

heart; transgressors of the rules would be confirmed in their pride and confidence that their influence and family connections would prevent their ever being called to account. She wrote to Rome, and on June 4 Pope Alexander VI renewed the authorization for Cisneros to reform the Franciscans in Spain.[27]

The reform of the diocesan clergy was finalized under Cisneros' direction at the Synod of Talavera October 14—just before the partially recovered Isabel left Zaragoza for Ocaña. It provided a virtual blueprint for the reforms finally adopted and made binding on the universal Church by the epochal Council of Trent 65 years later. Priests were to say Mass every Sunday without fail (an obligation that many, probably a majority, had long neglected, strange as it seems to a post-Trent Catholic). Children were to be regularly instructed in the faith every Sunday. The Blessed Sacrament was to be reserved in all major churches and given due reverence: all entering the Church were required to kneel to It after blessing themselves with holy water. Priests were to reside in their parish or in whatever other place they might be assigned. Priests publicly keeping concubines must send them away or face canonical penalties which could include arrest and imprisonment. Parishes must maintain baptismal records and complete registers of all parishioners, with an indication of who had not confessed and communicated at Easter. Immediately following the promulgation of these "constitutions of Talavera," Cisneros set to work himself to prepare the now required catechism for children.[28]

During the years since the conquest of Granada the Inquisition had been less active, corresponding to the decline in the perceived threat to Spain and her Church from the false *conversos*; but in the fall of 1498 its jurisdiction was extended for the first time to Granada, probably due to reports of increasing restiveness there which was to culminate in the uprising of December 1499. Tomás de Torquemada, the incorruptible monk who had directed the Inquisition so well since he brought it to order and justice after its first troubled years, was in failing health; he would die the next year. Diego de Deza, who had tutored Prince Juan and supported Columbus, was appointed to succeed Torquemada as General Inquisitor for Castile; his jurisdiction included the newly established Inquisition in Granada.[29]

Isabel, with her devotion to duty and her always profound interest in the Church, its reform, and its spiritual health, would not have failed to keep informed of these important developments in the Church in Spain and to give them her active support despite her personal suffering. But her reserves of strength and energy, which had once seemed limitless, were now almost

---

[27]Menéndez Pidal, *Historia de España*, XVII (2), 275-276; Fernández de Retana, *Cisneros*, I, 143-145.

[28]Vallejo, *Cisneros*, pp. 22-23; Fernández de Retana, *Cisneros*, I, 272-279.

[29]Jesús Suberbiola Martínez, *Rel Patronato de Granada; El arzobispo Talavera, la Iglesia y el Estado Moderno* (Granada, 1982), pp. 184-185.

exhausted. The recovery which had permitted her to make the grueling journey from Zaragoza to Ocaña in October and November proved only temporary. That she was now primarily responsible for the care of her precious grandson, upon whose life so much depended and whose life was so very fragile, must have added greatly to her burden and undermined her rehabilitation. Ocaña is in the heart of the high plains of Castile, between Madrid and Toledo. The cold fierce winds of winter blowing across the largely barren plateau can challenge the strongest. During the Christmas season Isabel fell ill again, so ill that she seemed at the point of death. Not only were multitudinous prayers offered for her life, but there were even procession of flagellants seeking to take upon themselves the punishment for whatever sins she or Spain might be being punished for. Some time during January 1499 the members of the *cortes* of Castile, which had met at Ocaña December 5 but had not yet acted, swore allegiance to Prince Miguel as heir.[30]

Probably in this same month of January, as she lay prostrate, Isabel received reports of a harsh confrontation in Rome between her ambassadors—Iñigo de Córdoba, brother of the Count of Cabra, and Dr. Felipe Ponce, supported by the ambassadors of Portugal—and Pope Alexander VI. During the preceding summer the Pope had openly aligned himself with France. His son Caesar had resigned his cardinalate, renounced his priesthood, and gone to France as Papal legate bearing a scandalous annulment of the marriage of the new King of France, Louis XII,[31] to crippled, suffering Jeanne de Valois (later canonized), to permit him to marry Anne of Brittany and thereby add her province to his kingdom. Caesar was demanding to marry the daughter of King Fadrique of Naples against her expressed will; Isabel and Fernando had unequivocally refused to join in pressuring or forcing her to marry him. It seemed the Pope would stop at nothing to advance the political career of his ambitious, ruthless son. On December 22, 1498 the Spanish ambassadors accused him of gaining his election by simony and of putting the interests of his illegitimate children ahead of the interests of the Church. The Pope responded by recalling some of the circumstances of Isabel's difficult accession to the throne of Castile. Though up to that time he had always supported her, now he called her a usurper. Soon afterward he threatened to sequester the incomes of all Spanish and Portuguese clergy residing in Rome. King Manuel of Portugal gave Isabel full support, but this sharp clash with the

---

[30]Santa Cruz, *Crónica*, I, 188 (ch. XLIII); Menéndez Pidal, *Historia de España*, XVII (2), 478; Fernández de Retana, *Cisneros*, I, 215; Rumeu de Armas, *Itinerario*, p. 251.

[31]King Charles VIII of France had died April 7, 1498, without issue, from an accidental blow to the head; Louis XII was a distant relative of the house of Orléans, who had married Charles VIII's sister Jeanne.

Pope surely added to her burdens.[32]

Then, probably early in February, Isabel received another letter from that bird of ill omen, Sub-prior Tomás de Matienzo of Santa Cruz, in Brussels, dated January 15. He had passed on her mother's advice to Juana, and she had promised to write her mother a long letter; but without his efforts he was sure she would never write anything to her mother. He had felt called upon to tell Juana "that she had a very hard and obdurate heart, and no piety—as is the truth. She answered that, on the contrary, she had only too soft a heart, and felt so oppressed that she could not think of her mother, and how far she was separated from her for ever, without shedding tears." After this exchange, he felt that Juana's conduct improved; indeed, "she passed New Year's Eve in such humility that he quite forgot all she had done before."[33]

But Isabel could hardly forget it, nor Juana. The Sub-prior had been no model of tact, and by his own confession he had no real idea what was wrong with Juana; but something was evidently very wrong, and the alleged improvement in all probability either temporary or illusory. At this great distance in time we know little better than the Sub-prior what Juana's basic problem was, though theories have been many; but hindsight at least tells us how deep were the shadows creeping up on this Princess of Castile and Archduchess of the Netherlands. Surely Isabel—so close to all her children—saw some of them, and suspected others. But at her distance and with Juana's obvious reluctance to communicate with her, there was almost nothing her mother could do to help. It was yet another cross, superimposed on the daily care and anxiety for the feeble little Prince Miguel, and the new hostility of the Pope.

Yet Isabel the Catholic rallied. She had faced inescapable, overwhelming crises and trials before, even if never any like this. She had the courage of a crusader—the courage of grizzled Raymond of Toulouse and mighty Godfrey of Bouillon at the walls of Jerusalem, the courage of Richard the Lion-hearted. Her country depended on her. The New World depended on her. Even the strongest people around her—Fernando; the iron Archbishop Cisneros himself—depended on her; she had had to rise out of her own overwhelming grief to console them both as the scythe of the Grim Reaper struck. Baby Miguel depended on her for the very breath of life. So much dependence—so much duty. She could not remain ill in bed. And she did not.

---

[32]Ludwig von Pastor, *History of the Popes from the Close of the Middle Ages*, Volume VI (St. Louis, 1898), pp. 60-64; Menéndez Pidal, *Historia de España*, XVII (2), 463, 526-527; instructions of King Manuel of Portugal to his ambassadors in Rome, January 2, 1499 (Lisbon), in Suárez Fernández, *Politica internacional de Isabel*, V, 349-351.

[33]Tomás de Matienzo to Isabel, January 15, 1499 (Brussels), in Suárez Fernández, *Politica internacional de Isabel*, V, 338-339; G. A. Bergenroth, ed., *Calendar of Letters, Despatches, and State Papers relating to the Negotiations between England and Spain*, Volume I: "Henry VII, 1485-1509" (London, 1862), pp. 198-202.

By a transcendent effort of will she mastered her faltering body. In the first week of March 1499, while the winter winds still blasted the high plains of Castile, she was on the road again, though the chronicler Santa Cruz tells us she was still very weak. She reached Madrid on the 8th, took up residence in her palace there, and set to work on negotiations for the English marriage of her youngest daughter Catalina. A treaty of alliance between her and Fernando and their heir Miguel, and Henry VII of England and his heir Arthur, was drawn up and confirmed. Catalina was pledged to marry Arthur, and Isabel promised to send her to England when Arthur became fourteen, in the winter of 1501. We can only imagine what this promise must have cost her. But she regarded it, too, as duty; and, by ample later evidence, so did Catherine. Kings and queens, princes and princesses were not supposed to consider their own feelings in such matters, only the good of their people and the peace among peoples that could be served by alliances sealed by a royal marriage.[34]

Isabel and Fernando stayed in Madrid until the end of May. Their firmness and constancy in reproving the Pope—it should be remembered that they had never disobeyed his legitimate authority, only pointed out publicly the moral and political significance and consequences of his most ill-advised actions—began to bear fruit that spring. Alexander VI was still committed to a pro-French policy: Caesar Borgia married the great heiress Charlotte d'Albret that spring, and the Pope told Louis XII that he recognized his claims to the duchy of Milan. But he made a major effort to mollify Isabel and Fernando and to respond to their criticism of his excessive partiality toward his children. The duchy of Benevento in Italy, whose lands he had taken away from the Church to give to his oldest son (later murdered), he restored to the Church March 20. In May he promised to send his children away from Rome and to make some reforms; though most of his children now preferred to be elsewhere and the reforms proved illusory, at this time he also granted Isabel and Fernando even broader authority to continue the genuine reform they and Cisneros had launched in Spain.[35]

How much that broad authority for reform was needed was clear from the stormy interview, which most likely occurred some time during this year 1499, between Isabel and the new general of the Franciscan order, Gil Delfino, who came to Spain for the express and declared purpose of persuading or bullying Isabel into deposing Archbishop Cisneros as primate of Spain, evidently because of his determination and perseverance in the reform of the Franciscans. After Delfino's lengthy and angry exposition of what a disagreeable man

---

[34]Santa Cruz, *Crónica*, I, 188 (ch. XLIII); Rumeu de Armas, *Itinerario*, p. 252; Fernando and Isabel to Dr. de Puebla, ambassador to England, March 12, 1499 (Madrid), and draft treaty with England, in Bergenroth, *Calendar of State Papers*, I, 203-205; Menéndez Pidal, *Historia de España*, XVII (2), 487.

[35]Von Pastor, *History of the Popes*, VI, 67-68.

Cisneros was, how his holiness was counterfeit, his learning negligible, and his experience sadly lacking, Isabel finally cut him short with: "Father, have you thought what you are saying, or to whom you are speaking?" Carried away with his own eloquence, Delfino shot back with: "Yes, my lady. I am speaking with Queen Isabel, who is dust and ashes like me." Isabel would never take such a reminder amiss, but neither would such petty spite ever move her. Neither she nor Cisneros made any further response to Delfino; the Pope had confirmed their authority; the reform went on undisturbed.[36]

The Catholic sovereigns of Spain kept their fingers on the pulse of discovery, not only in what Columbus had finally identified as a "new world" but also in the Indian Ocean, since if baby Prince Miguel should survive long enough to unite the two Iberian kingdoms, this too would be part of his heritage. Columbus had arrived at Hispaniola's new capital of Santo Domingo August 31, 1498, enthused about his tremendous new discoveries in South America but afflicted by arthritis and inflamed eyes. He was bitterly disappointed to find that his brother Bartholomew had been no better able than he to establish order among the Spaniards on the island, many of whom refused to accept the authority of a foreigner. Francisco Roldán, a power-seeking nobleman whom Columbus had unwisely appointed chief judicial officer for the island, was in full rebellion, holding the southwestern peninsula called Xaragua. Roldán had seized the three caravels Columbus had sent directly to Hispaniola from the Canary Islands in June, while he took the new southwesterly course which had brought him to South America. Most of the Spaniards aboard these three ships joined Roldán, so that his forces now outnumbered the loyal troops. Consequently he was preparing an attack on the principal fortress of the Columbus regime, Concepción de la Vega in the lush central valley. Columbus did not feel strong enough to prevail over Roldán, so felt he had no choice but to negotiate. Meanwhile he dispatched letters to his sovereigns October 18, which sounded vague and confused. He asked for more men and ships to suppress the rebellion, but at the same time talked of colonizing the new lands he had discovered in South America. He asked without apology for the full legalization of a slave trade in Indians, though Isabel had repeatedly made it clear she would never permit that. And he asked that a reliable man be sent to administer justice, which had been the duty assigned to the faithless Roldán.[37]

These letters from Columbus, arriving in Spain before the end of the year 1498, created a bad impression which was supplemented by other critical and negative reports from Hispaniola. This evidence convinced Isabel—when her recovery in March 1499 permitted her to turn her mind decisively to the situation in Hispaniola—that Columbus should not continue as sole governor of

---

[36]Fernández de Retana, *Cisneros*, I, 145-147.
[37]Morison, *Admiral of the Ocean Sea*, pp. 561-567.

the lands he had discovered. He lacked both the personal qualities and the special talents of a good administrator. She liked and admired Columbus and understood how great a service he had rendered her and Spain, but was surely disappointed with the very small spiritual return in Indian conversions thus far, and by Columbus' persistent attempts to enslave those whose souls he claimed to have gone there to save. He had given her an opening by requesting that an official be sent to administer justice. She decided to send a judge who would also have the viceregal power to hear and settle disputes and grievances including those against the Admiral himself, who thereby lost forever his original full authority over the first Spanish colony in the New World. The man appointed to exercise these powers, by royal decrees of May 21 and 29, was Francisco de Bobadilla, a nobleman of fine lineage and reputation—which tragically he was not to honor when he found himself far from home and law, where ruthlessness and cruelty were a great part of the price for gold.[38]

Bobadilla did not leave to take up his duties in Hispaniola for more than a year, until July 1500. During that year the situation on that now bloody island went from bad to worse. Columbus felt he had to pardon Roldán, restore him to his former position as chief justice, and mollify him and the other rebels by granting each Spanish settler a substantial tract of cultivated land with a number of Indians to till it, solely for his own personal support and enrichment. This was the infamous *repartimiento* or *encomienda* system, which Bartolomeu de Las Casas, the "apostle to the Indians," spent his life fighting, and which Isabel's mighty grandson Charles V was to struggle desperately and with only limited success to eliminate. If not quite slavery, the *repartimiento* was certainly serfdom, imposed upon a people who had no custom or tradition of regular hard work on the land and would often die quickly if forced to do it.[39]

By May 30 Isabel felt well enough to travel a long distance again, and she and Fernando set out for the scene of their greatest triumph: Granada. Journeying somewhat more slowly than in the past, probably because of the lingering effects of Isabel's long illness, they arrived July 2. Either then, or while on the road, they heard the electrifying news of another maritime triumph, another quarter of the world opened up to European Christian penetration, commerce, and missions. Vasco da Gama had left Calicut under difficult and dangerous circumstances in late August 1498, almost at the very moment of the death of young Isabel the Queen of Portugal—he seized hostages from the faithless Zamorim just in time to exchange them for many of his men whom that monarch had also seized, and then sailed away pursued by 70 Indian galleys which he only escaped thanks to an opportune thunderstorm. Ever since, da Gama had been making his way back on the extraordinarily long and often

---

[38]*Ibid.*, pp. 569-570; Morison, ed., *Journals and Other Documents of Columbus*, p. 289.

[39]Morison, *Admiral of the Ocean Sea*, pp. 567-568, 570.

difficult route across the Arabian Sea and around Africa, losing men to scurvy, beaching and burning one of his ships, finally doubling the Cape of Good Hope March 20, then all during the spring in a race with death to reach home as more and more of his men perished, including his beloved brother Paul. Vasco had accompanied Paul to the Azores to try to save him; but another of his ships, the *Berrio* commanded by Nicolau Coelho, had gone directly to Lisbon, arriving in June. Their news of reaching India and opening up a practicable trade route with it flew through Europe just as the news of Columbus' initial discovery had flown; everyone recognized immediately an historic moment, passing on with fascination Coelho's account of the wealth and strangeness of India and the unlimited prospects for trade and power in the Indian Ocean. On July 12 King Manuel officially informed Isabel and Fernando that Portuguese ships and men had reached India at last. Vasco da Gama himself returned in August, and was officially welcomed with the greatest honor in Lisbon September 18.[40]

Meanwhile the French were again on the warpath in Italy. King Louis XII, just as predatory as his young predecessor Charles VIII and much more experienced, was not aiming as Charles had at the virtually impossible goal of conquering the whole peninsula, but for the moment only at annexing Milan. The Pope's recognition of his claim to Milan, made on the occasion of his son's marriage to Charlotte d'Albret, gave Louis a substantial advantage. A French army crossed the Alps in July and began taking fortresses in Milanese territory. There was no immediate Spanish intervention; southern Italy, not northern, was of particular interest to Spain. Protecting Milan was primarily the concern of Emperor Maximilian; but as always he was short of cash and troops, and could do little more immediately than offer Duke Lodovico Sforza of Milan asylum in the Tyrol when he fled from the victorious French armies September 1. Five days later the French occupied Milan. Determined not to be left out, Caesar Borgia now attempted the conquest of the Romagna, the rich and fertile region of many cities south of the Po River, curving toward Rome. In November he laid siege to Imola and Forli; the latter city was held by a member of the Sforza ducal family of Milan, Catarina, who resisted fiercely but was eventually overwhelmed.[41]

Though they did not intervene in the French war with Milan, Isabel and Fernando evidently watched these developments closely and with concern. They underlined their determination to honor their alliance with Naples by receiving with ostentatious public honor the Queen Mother of that kingdom

---

[40]Bernáldez, *Memorias*, pp. 383-386 (ch. CLIX); Manuel to Isabel and Fernando, July 12, 1499 (Lisbon), in Suárez Fernández, *Política internacional de Isabel*, V, 394-396; Jones, *Sail the Indian Sea*, pp. 98-108.

[41]Peter Martyr de Anglería to the Count of Tendilla, August 27, 1499 (Madrid), DIHE IX, 393-395; Menéndez Pidal, *Historia de España*, XVII (2), 530-531; von Pastor, *History of the Popes*, VI, 68-72.

(Fernando's sister) and her daughter, when they visited Granada in July. Gonzalo de Córdoba, the brilliant Spanish military commander and personal favorite of Isabel who was already beginning to be known as "the Great Captain," accompanied the royal visitors from Naples and may have suggested their visit. Isabel and Fernando used the occasion to shower praise on Gonzalo for all he had accomplished in Italy at the time of the earlier French invasion by Charles VIII.[42]

The Spanish alliance with England was also firming up during the spring and summer of 1499. On May 19 there was a "proxy marriage" between Prince Arthur of England and Isabel's Catalina—a formal prelude to an actual marriage often used in that age where royalty was involved, rather like a solemn engagement. A full treaty between Spain and England was signed July 10, providing that both countries would assist and defend the other (except for wars involving the Pope, the Holy Roman Emperor, Archduke Philip, and the King of France—the exceptions being so that the cautious Henry VII of England would not be committing himself to fighting at Spain's side in wars with these potentates); providing mutual commercial privileges; and pledging that neither state would harbor rebels against the ruler of the other (this again was for Henry VII's benefit, since there were then no rebels against Isabel and Fernando, while Henry still had remnants of the Yorkists to contend with, including that curious and persistent pretender, Perkin Warbeck). By October young Prince Arthur (still only twelve) was corresponding with Catalina, letters of a genuine childlike innocence; Isabel may well have read them with tears, thinking how soon these children must grow up, though she could hardly have imagined the Via Crucis that her daughter Catherine would ultimately have to walk.[43]

In September, by a coincidence which may have shaken Isabel, three of the principal figures of her triumphant early reign died within a few days of each other: Torquemada, the pillar of the Inquisition; the Count of Benavente, who had fought so bravely for her in the War of the Succession and had ridden at her side in the magnificent rescue from the castle of Segovia of little Isabel, who now lay so young in her tomb at Toledo; and Alonso de Burgos, Bishop of Palencia, the first of the holy bishops Isabel the Catholic had advanced to the episcopate.[44]

By October Archbishop Cisneros had joined Isabel and Fernando in

---

[42]Bernáldez, *Memorias*, p. 386 (ch. CLX); Santa Cruz, *Crónica*, I, 183 (ch. XLI) and 190-191 (ch. XLIV).

[43]Bergenroth, *Calendar of State Papers*, I, 209-212 (including the proxy marriage and treaty documents and a letter from Arthur to Catherine dated October 5, 1499, from Ludlow in England).

[44]Lorenzo Galíndez Carvajal, "Anales breves del reinado de los Reyes Católicos," CODOIN XVIII (Madrid, 1851), p. 295; Santa Cruz, *Crónica*, pp. 194-195 (ch. XLV).

Granada. They had discussions with him, and doubtless also with the Archbishop of Granada, Hernando de Talavera, Isabel's former confessor, on how best to bring about the conversion of the 50,000 Muslims still living in the city and its immediate environs. During the seven years since the conquest of Granada, Archbishop Talavera had been working hard at their evangelization by the traditional methods of the Church: preaching, persuasion, and good example. He had even made a serious effort to learn Arabic so as to preach to the Moors in their own language. The Moors accorded him great respect, and some of them did convert, but the great majority—like most Muslims everywhere, throughout the history of Islam—refused to give up their militant religion.[45]

The terms of the capitulation of Granada in January 1492 had guaranteed that its Moors could continue to practice Islam. However, Spanish tradition put former Christians now professing Islam, and their immediate descendants, in a different position. Catholic teaching declared unequivocally that baptism is irreversible. A baptized man or woman is rendered perpetually a Christian by the fact of his or her baptism, whatever apostasy and false religion might later be professed. Logically and dogmatically this doctrine did not extend to the unbaptized children of apostates, and certainly not to their later descendants, but in practice it tended to include them as well—perhaps by infection from the Muslim doctrine that once a man professed Islam, all his descendants forever would be Muslims for whom the penalty for apostasy was death. Cisneros requested authority to use the Inquisition and the power of the state to bring apostate Christians professing Islam in Granada, and their children, back to the Faith even by force. (The Inquisition, it will be remembered, had jurisdiction over Christians, but not over non-Christians.) On October 31 Isabel and Fernando granted Cisneros and the Inquisition the authority he had asked for, while reiterating that born Muslims (except for the children of the apostates) must not be forced in their profession of religion.[46]

The execution of this decree seems to have caused no problems during the ensuing month of November. On December 1 Isabel and Fernando left Granada for Sevilla, where Isabel spent the winter and spring.[47] All was peaceful in Granada when they left. But within just a few days full rebellion flared up, threatening the whole hard-won victory after ten years of unrelenting war that had completed the great Reconquest.

---

[45]Menéndez Pidal, *Historia de España*, XVII (2), 287-289; Suberbiola Martínez, *Real Patronato de Granada*, pp. 182-183.

[46]Decree of Fernando and Isabel, October 31, 1499 (Granada), in Miguel Angel Ladero Quesada, *Los Mudejares de Castilla en tiempo de Isabel I* (Valladolid, 1969), pp. 226-228; Fernández de Retana, *Cisneros*, I, 229; Suberbiola Martínez, *Real Patronato de Granada*, pp. 186-187.

[47]Rumeu de Armas, *Itinerario*, p. 256.

How and why did it happen? The almost universal conclusion of historians has been that it was due to the adoption by Cisneros of a policy of forcible conversion of born Muslims, unrelated to apostate Christians, in flat violation of the capitulations of 1492. This conclusion is based on the evident belief of many of the Moors living in the former kingdom of Granada that forcible conversion was intended or was actually taking place; on the indubitable fact that one leading Moor, Zegri Azaator, was put in chains for 20 days when he refused to obey Cisneros' order to become a Christian;[48] and, by hindsight, on the mass conversion, beginning in December and quickly completed, of virtually all the Moors remaining in the city of Granada.

But the evidence does not support this conclusion of the historians. The many examples throughout history of the prodigious impact on popular opinion of rumor and propaganda, regardless of its truth or falsity, should warn us at once that because many Muslims in December 1499 thought they were about to be forcibly converted does not necessarily make it so. The chaining of Zegri Azaator proves only that an attempt was made to convert *him* to Christianity by force—not anyone else. Our sources tell us that he was singled out because of his particularly vigorous and outspoken opposition to Cisneros' efforts to convert other Moors by normal methods of evangelization. Indeed, the evidence suggests that Zegri Azaator may have been the only Moor—aside from apostate Christians and their children—whose conversion by force was attempted at this time. The later mass conversion followed the uprising and was conditioned by it; we cannot rightly read it back to reflect a policy adopted before the uprising had occurred.

The initial revolt took place in Albaicín, a suburb of Granada immediately outside its walls, which had a large mosque with 86 columns.[49] The story of the attempt to force the conversion of Zegri—who actually did convert after twenty days in chains, although he claimed a special revelation from Allah was the cause rather than his chaining and imprisonment—had spread quickly through Albaicín. When two of Cisneros' officials, Salcedo and Barrionuevo, came there early in December to arrest the daughter of a Christian apostate, the angry and fearful citizens, crying "Muhammad and liberty!," seized arms, barricaded the streets, closed the gates, and besieged Archbishop Cisneros in his house, which he refused to leave for the safety of the Alhambra. Salcedo and Barrionuevo were killed. At dawn the next day the Count of Tendilla sallied from the Alhambra to rescue Cisneros, though the Moors outnumbered his men thirty to one and blocked his access to Albaicín. The Count called Moorish leaders to a parley, but it proved fruitless. Archbishop Talavera then came into Bib-el-Benut Plaza in Albaicín, heroically carrying his archepiscopal

---

[48]Vallejo, *Cisneros*, p. 34.

[49]Hieronymus Münzer, *Viaje por España y Portugal, 1494-1495,* tr. José López Toro (Madrid, 1951), pp. 40-41.

cross forward into the midst of the angry Moors. They greeted it with showers of stones, though some rememberd how good and patient Talavera had been with them, and knelt to kiss his robe. His clerics had to pull the intrepid Archbishop back.[50]

The Count of Tendilla, who also had a very high reputation among the Moors for integrity and justice, now came into Bib-el-Benut Plaza unarmed and stood in the middle of it to show that he desired peace. Twenty-six Moors gathered around him and kissed his hand with respect. They agreed with him to stop the fighting, and he actually left his wife and children in Albaicín as hostages. A Moorish leader named Cidi-Ceibona soon afterward delivered to the Count four of the murderers of Barrionuevo, who were promptly hanged. There were no more hostilities. The fighting had lasted just three days, and a week later Albaicín formally capitulated.[51]

Though quickly ended, this defiance of Spanish authority had been on a much larger scale than any other resistance by the Moors since the conquest of Granada. It was inevitable that it would be magnified by rumor, fear and hope as the news spread. Since the immediate trigger for the uprising had been the seizure and killing of two men Archbishop Cisneros had sent out to arrest the daughter of a Christian renegade who was a professed Muslim, and since Cisneros was known to have attempted the forcible conversion of Zegri Alaator, it was easy for the Moors to believe that he had adopted a general policy of forced conversion and that this had caused the revolt. Cisneros foresaw that some such report would come to Isabel and Fernando in Sevilla, and realized that it was essential to convey an accurate account of these events to his sovereigns just as soon as possible. But he made an extraordinary blunder. Instead of sending his account to Sevilla by the best horseman available, he entrusted it to a black slave (there were a few now in Spain, due to the slave traffic with West Africa in which the Portuguese had engaged for the past sixty years) who was reputed very fleet of foot. But however fleet of foot, he could hardly have outpaced a horse; and as it turned out, he became drunk on the way and did not arrive in Sevilla for almost a week.[52]

By then "the rumor mill" was in full operation; it was even being said that the entire city of Granada had fallen into the hands of rebels. Fernando, who had never liked Cisneros, was furious. He actually turned on Isabel in public (the only such incident recorded in the history of their life together, though undoubtedly there had been private quarrels) and snarled: "What do you think, Lady, of the situation your Archbishop has put us in? What the kings our forebears won with so much zeal and blood, we have now lost in an hour

---

[50]Santa Cruz, *Crónica*, I, 191-193 (ch. XLIV); Vallejo, *Cisneros*, pp. 36-37.
[51]Fernández de Retana, *Cisneros*, I, 248-249.
[52]Vallejo, *Cisneros*, pp. 37-38.

because of him!"[53]

It is hard to imagine his lashing out at Isabel like this during the past winter, when she lay prostrate at Ocaña from the hammer-blows of grief and loss; but now that she seemed so much recovered, evidently he felt less constraint in hurting her. The cold sarcasm in his phrase "*your* Archbishop" was nothing less than a public personal attack. And Isabel the Catholic was not, would never be again, the woman she had been before the deaths of Juan and his stillborn daughter, and Isabel her daughter. She bore herself courageously and well, but as more than one contemporary commentator tells us, she carried grief and suffering with her all the rest of her life. It made her stronger spiritually, but more vulnerable psychologically. The complete confidence of her youth, that with God's help she could always prevail in just causes, always defeat her enemies, was gone. For death was now her enemy, and only One has defeated death.

Though she would never have acknowledged it in any way that could become public, Isabel now needed help; but she got very little of it in any form that we can see. Instead, her husband and her confessor were now at odds; her confessor had blundered, and her husband had attacked her over him without even waiting for a confirmation of the truth about what had happened in Albaicín. Once again Isabel was called upon for strength and courage, more than any of those around her would ever be asked to provide. Once again, she answered the call.

With her face and voice reflecting the quiet gravity and clear luminous intellect which so impressed almost everyone who saw and heard her, she reminded her husband that he should not give credit to any reports about what had happened in Granada until the whole truth was known from reliable sources. Then she wrote to Cisneros demanding a detailed report immediately. By the time he received her letter, he was fortunately able to tell her that the uprising was over and that full peace had been restored, and he sent the report to her by one of his most trusted friars, Francisco Ruiz. But Fernando was still angry with Cisneros, despite the pacification of Albaicín, as a sharply worded letter from him to the Count of Tendilla on December 22 makes very clear. The letter also criticizes the Count for deferring too much to the Archbishop—who, Fernando says caustically, never saw Moors before he came to Granada and knows nothing about them.[54]

The capitulation of Albaicín was unconditional, containing no promise of amnesty for the rebels. Too severe a punishment for them could cause the revolt to break out again, there or elsewhere. Too light a punishment or no punishment might well have the same effect. The action taken—and very

[53]*Ibid.*, p. 38; Fernández de Retana, *Cisneros*, I, 250.
[54]Vallejo, *Cisneros*, p. 38; Fernando to the Count of Tendilla, December 22, 1499 (Sevilla), in Ladero Quesada, *Mudejares*, pp. 278-279.

swiftly taken—was extraordinary, indeed unique: to remit all punishment for the rebellion in Albaicín for everyone who became a Christian. The idea came from Archbishop Cisneros.[55]

In carrying out this policy, no distinction appears to have been made between the suburb of Albaicín and the main city of Granada, either by the Moors or by the Spanish authorities. The response was immediate and overwhelming. Almost the entire Muslim population of 50,000 in Granada and its environs agreed to convert. (The few who did not presumably left the city, either to go into the still Muslim countryside or to emigrate to North Africa.) On December 18, Albaicín's great mosque with its 86 columns was turned into a Christian church.[56]

The circumstances and available evidence suggest that Cisneros began the administration of baptism in Granada as an alternative to punishment for rebellion on his own authority, obtaining royal consent only after he had begun. The annals of Galíndez de Carvajal state that the mass conversions began December 17. But when he wrote his letter of December 22 to the Count of Tendilla, Fernando does not seem to have heard of the policy, since he says that only those guilty of the murders of Salcedo and Barrionuevo deserve punishment. But two weeks later, on January 3, 1500, Fernando and Isabel signed official instructions to their emissary Enrique Enríquez, departing for Granada, that all Moors in Granada accepting baptism be pardoned for any support they had given to the revolt, while those rejecting baptism would remain liable to punishment. Children of Christian renegades were required to be baptized, but all other baptisms should be voluntary. Evidently at some time between December 22 and January 3 Cisneros sent them word of what he was doing. Then Isabel (however reluctantly) approved it, and Fernando was persuaded to agree also.[57]

Echoes of the discussion and argument surrounding this decision come down to us even in guarded official correspondence. It is clear that Archbishop Talavera did not agree with it, though it is not clear whether he conveyed his disagreement in person or by letter to Isabel during the critical days of the Christmas season of 1499. There is a cautious reference in the instructions to Enríquez to "differences" between the two archbishops on this matter, which Isabel and Fernando will later come to Granada to resolve in person if

---

[55]Peter Martyr de Anglería to the Cardinal of Santa Cruz, July 16, 1500 (Sevilla), DIHE IX, 408-409.

[56]Santa Cruz, *Crónica*, p. 193 (ch. XLIV); "Relacion del caso de Granada," late February 1500, in Ladero Quesada, *Mudejares*, pp. 246-247; Menéndez Pidal, *Historia de España*, XVII (2), 290.

[57]Galíndez de Carvajal, "Anales breves," CODOIN XVIII, 296; Fernando to Count of Tendilla, December 22, 1499 (Sevilla), in Ladero Quesada, *Mudejares*, pp. 278-279; instructions of Isabel and Fernando to Enrique Enríquez, January 3, 1500 (Sevilla), in *ibid.*, pp. 232-235.

necessary. In a later letter, dated March 30, 1500, Archbishop Talavera urges Isabel and Fernando to keep the newly converted Moors of Granada as much as possible apart from the Muslims living elsewhere in the former kingdom—not only, he says significantly, because the newly converted might be wrongly influenced, but also because those not yet converted might be *less* attracted to Christianity. Clearly obtaining conversions by remission of temporal punishment—however deserved the punishment might be—was repellent to Archbishop Talavera. Nevertheless he accepted this procedure, though with grave misgivings. Cisneros was eager to gain and claim his acceptance; in a letter of January 4 he says that the Archbishop of Granada, "who is a holy person," has joined in the work of conversion and approves of it, declaring that soon no one will remain in the kingdom of Granada who is not a Christian.[58]

We know from Isabel's expulsion of the Jews from Spain how anxious she was to bring about full religious unity in her country. For that reason as well as her always strong desire for the salvation of souls, she wanted very much to see the conversion of as many of the Moors as possible, as quickly as possible. But, as she was to show clearly during the next two months, she never favored or approved forced conversion, nor did she break faith with the capitulation agreements made when the Moors surrendered Granada in 1492. No evidence indicates that anyone was ever actually punished for the revolt of Albaicín, except the four murderers of Barrionuevo. None of the 50,000 who were baptized in Granada in December 1499 and January 1500 were directly forced to do so; nor is there any basis for assuming that most of them were even liable to the punishment from which baptism would excuse them, since the majority of the population of Granada had not been involved in the tumults in Albaicín. The mass conversion bears all the marks of one of those sudden, irresistible surges of popular feeling under heavy stress, which again and again in history have caused large numbers people to do what they probably would not have done individually or in small groups. Cisneros welcomed this, believing that whatever the bad faith of many of these sudden converts, their children at least would mostly become loyal Catholics—which turned out to be true. But Talavera was deeply troubled by it, because he wanted conversions to be sincere, and believed that in time he could obtain many more of this kind. Morally and spiritually Talavera's view was admirable, but the history of Islam strongly suggests that it was over-optimistic.

If in fact Isabel learned of Cisneros' new policy of using baptism as a

---

[58]Instructions of Isabel and Fernando to Enrique Enríquez, January 3, 1500 (Sevilla), in Ladero Quesada, *Mudejares*, pp. 233-234; Archbishop Hernando de Talavera to Isabel and Fernando, March 30, 1500 (Granada), *ibid.*, p. 255; Archbishop Cisneros to the dean and chapter of the Church of Toledo, January 4, 1500 (Granada), *ibid.*, p. 235.

shield against punishment for the revolt of Albaicín only after he had already begun employing it—as appears to be the case—she would have been most unlikely to countermand it. She had great confidence in him, or she would not have made him primate. She enormously admired the thorough manner in which he was reforming the Church in Spain—and had every reason to admire it, for Cisneros' reform changed the course of history and probably saved the Catholic Church in Europe, by making the Church in Europe's greatest power impervious to penetration by the coming Protestant revolution. She personally depended on Cisneros more than ever in these years of her greatest travail. She knew that, if frustrated in a matter he regarded as properly within his own domain as primate, he was fully capable of resigning. So his will prevailed. He may have been wrong, but he had a case; he had done nothing directly contravening Catholic doctrine and fundamental justice, except for the chaining of Zegri Azaator and the forced baptism of the children of the Christian renegades. And the fruits were good, at least in this respect: the danger of religious war in Spain in the long run was substantially lessened.

For the moment, however, that danger was increased. For the Moors outside Granada were not making fine moral and doctrinal distinctions among baptism by true conviction, baptism under threat of punishment for rebellion, and baptism by force. The story coming to them was that the Christians had simply forced baptism on the entire population of Granada. Some were prepared to submit to that, but others were not. In the little hidden valleys and occasionally terraced hillsides of the wild mountain region called the Alpujarras, between Granada and the sea—the most Muslim region of all the old kingdom of Granada, which had been the last area outside the city itself to resist in the final months of the war of the Reconquest, where hardly a Christian was to be found—the people rose in almost unanimous rebellion in the middle of January 1500. On the 27th of that month Fernando rode out from Sevilla for Granada with his knights to put down that rebellion—just as he had ridden out again and again during the ten-year war to reconquer the kingdom of Granada for Spain. Isabel, as she had usually but not always done during the war of the reconquest, stayed behind. Once again, as of old, the Catholic sovereigns sent out a call for troops from all over Andalusia and Murcia to join the campaign against the Moors.[59]

The reports Fernando and Isabel had received in Sevilla showed that the main stimulus to the rebellion was the belief that the Muslims of Granada had been forcibly converted and that all the other Muslims in the region were soon to be compelled in the same way. Isabel and Fernando wrote to their secretary Fernando de Zafra, who had worked so effectively in negotiating for the

---

[59]Bernáldez, *Memorias*, pp. 386-387 (ch. CLX); Santa Cruz, *Crónica*, I, 193 (ch. XLIV); Galíndez de Carvajal, "Anales breves," CODOIN XVIII, 296; Menéndez Pidal, *Historia de España*, XVII (2), 291, 294.

surrender of Granada, that they pledged their royal word and by their Holy Faith that they would baptize no Moors by force. On February 18 this policy was proclaimed in an official document, a written pledge by Isabel to the Moors of the region of Ronda and Málaga (who had not rebelled, though they were restive) that under no circumstances would they be made Christians against their will.[60]

The rebel Moors in the Alpujarras never had a chance. Spain—united, orderly, well-governed, victorious—was now a great power. They had only a small mountain hideaway, cut off from the world. Their one attempt to break through to the sea and get aid from North Africa was frustrated by the redoubtable Pedro Fajardo of Murcia with just thirty cavalry and 800 foot soldiers. Early in February Gonzalo de Córdoba and the Count of Tendilla appeared with a strong force before the fortress of Huéjar at the entrance to the Alpujarras. When its defenders refused a demand to surrender, Gonzalo and the Count attacked at once and carried the place by storm. As the laws of war then permitted in such a case, all men of military age found in the city were killed, and it was sacked and burned to the ground. More troops quickly assembled, and by March 1 so many were available that Fernando was able to divide them into three columns—the one already in action, led by Gonzalo de Córdoba and the Count of Tendilla; another led by the Count of Lérin; and the third led by the King himself. Only a week more was required to win complete victory. Fernando stormed the fortified city of Lanjarón, though this time he spared his prisoners; the Count of Lérin took Andarax, the largest town in the Alpujarras, but let his men go so far out of control that they massacred hundreds of women and children in a mosque along with many of the men, an act which the Spanish chroniclers rightly called shameful.[61]

It was all over by March 8, when Fernando made his formal entry into Lanjarón. Organized resistance in the Alpujarras was at an end, and as earlier in Granada, the survivors there were told they would not be punished if they became Christians. Most of them were promptly baptized, and were not punished. But in an extraordinarily bitter letter, Archbishop Talavera of Granada clearly reveals that he still could not fully accept or justify this kind of conversion, or its authorization by Isabel and Fernando.[62]

---

[60]Isabel to Hernando de Zafra, January 27, 1500, in Fernández de Retana, *Cisneros*, I, 254; decree of Isabel, February 18, 1500 (Sevilla), in Ladero Quesada, *Mudejares*, pp. 240-241.

[61]Bernáldez, *Memorias*, pp. 386-387 (ch. CLX); Santa Cruz, *Crónica*, I, 201-203 (ch. XLVII); Hernando de Zafra to Isabel, February 26, 1500 (Granada), in Ladero Quesada, *Mudejares*, p. 243; "Relacion del caso de Granada," late February 1500, *ibid.*, p. 249; Menéndez Pidal, *Historia de España*, XVII (2), 294-295; Fernández de Retana, *Cisneros*, I, 254-255.

[62]Bernáldez, *Memorias*, pp. 386-387 (ch. CLX); Peter Martyr to the Cardinal of Santa Cruz, July 16, 1500 (Sevilla), DIHE IX, 409-411; Archbishop Talavera to Miguel

Just about the time this brief but bloody war ended, confirming the Reconquest, Isabel would have received news of the birth, on February 24, 1500 at Ghent in Flanders, of a healthy son to Juana and Philip, whom they named Charles. He was baptized March 7.[63] Charles was Isabel's second grandson. The first, baby Prince Miguel, she still watched over every day, as though he were her own child. Charles she was never to see, nor to live long enough to know what he had done or showed promise to do. But in good time he was to become almost all she could ever have hoped for in a son: one of Spain's most beloved kings, the champion of the Catholic Faith, the tireless defender of Christian Europe against the infidel Turks without and the Protestant rebels within for forty long years—the man who, more than any other of his time, saved Christendom.

All this was hidden from her eyes, while still she bore her cross.

Explorers were busy in that spring of 1500, though not the two greatest of them, Columbus and da Gama—Columbus bogged down in Hispaniola, still unable to restore order there; da Gama exhausted from the travail of his mighty voyage and still stricken with grief for his brother who had died on it. A second Portuguese expedition for India, including no less than 14 ships and 1,200 men commanded by Pedro Alvarez Cabral, set out from Lisbon March 8; veering far to the west when passing the great bulge of West Africa, on April 22 they reached Brazil and claimed it for Portugal. First ashore was Captain Nicolau Coelho, who had commanded the *Berrio* on da Gama's voyage and brought the first news of it back to Europe. At almost the same moment Vicente Yáñez Pinzón, the skilful and loyal mariner who had so well commanded the *Niña* on Columbus' first voyage, had reached the mouth of the world's greatest river, the Amazon of Brazil, and sailed fifty miles up it; for most of the way the giant stream of fresh water was so vast that no land could be seen on either side. The bond between the two great discoverer nations remained close; on May 20 the marriage agreement between King Manuel of Portugal and Isabel and Fernando's third daughter, Maria, was drawn up; they were to marry before the year was over.[64]

Isabel continued to maintain her concern for the victims of the greed of her subjects overseas, and her unwavering conviction that the aborigines of the New World were fully human and entitled to all the rights of a citizen of Castile. On June 20 she issued another decree ordering the liberation of Indian captives

---

Pérez de Almazán, June 22, 1500, in Ladero Quesada, *Mudejares*, pp. 262-263.

[63]Bishop of Astorga to Isabel and Fernando, March 14 and March 28, 1500 (Ghent), in Antonio Rodríguez Villa, *La Reina Doña Juana la Loca* (Madrid, 1892), pp. 42-45.

[64]Samuel Eliot Morison, *The European Discovery of America: the Southern Voyages* (New York, 1974), pp. 213-214, 219-227; marriage treaty between Portugal and Spain, May 20, 1500, in Antonio de la Torre and Luis Suárez Fernández, eds., *Documentos referentes a las relaciones con Portugal durante el reinado de los Reyes Católicos* (Valladolid, 1958-63), III, 35-43.

in Spain and their return to Hispaniola in the fleet of its new goveror Francisco de Bobadilla, which after many delays was about to depart.[65]

The situation in Italy was disturbing; after considerable difficulty because of a popular outbreak against them, the French had secured a firm hold on Milan and its surrounding territory, captured its Duke Ludovico Sforza, and sent him a prisoner to France. There was every reason to believe that the predatory Louis XII would soon raise again the French claim to Naples which had been the excuse for the earlier French invasion of Italy in 1494. So Gonzalo de Córdoba, fresh from his triumphs over the Moors in the Alpujarras, was sent back to Italy with a large army and fleet; he departed June 5. While the final preparations for the dispatch of Gonzalo's expeditionary force were being made, Isabel and Fernando secured a solid understanding with Jean d'Albret of Navarra, who pledged that the Spanish part of his kingdom would remain entirely loyal to them despite the fact that he himself was French, and that he would marry his little daughter, when she was old enough, to any member of their family whom they selected as her husband.[66]

All that winter and spring, since leaving Granada just before the revolt, Isabel had remained in Sevilla. Now, on June 22, at the beginning of summer, she set out under the hot Andalusian sun to return to Granada.[67] She still had little Prince Miguel with her; it does not appear that he was ever separated from her from the time of his birth. He had always been fragile, and as much depended on him as ever. Upon his frail life rested the whole prospect for the union of Spain and Portugal and their growing overseas domains, for the rule of the Iberian peninsula by a native son without any obligations to foreign nations other than those of his own making. The alternative was rule by Juana. There can have been nothing that Isabel feared more. Whatever Juana's trouble was, Isabel knew now that it was deep-seated and almost inaccessible to help, especially hers. The letters of Sub-prior Matienzo of Santa Cruz had revealed unmistakably a coldness in Juana toward her mother that nothing we ever hear of her other children even suggests.[68] The Spanish royal family had been exceptionally close, exceptionally loving. But Juana was rejecting her family; her unwillingness to write to them, to send them news, even to ask about them, clearly indicated that—along with other problems. And Juana was married to a man who gave no indication of caring anything about Spain—a man to whom,

---

[65]Isabel and Fernando to Pedro de Torres, June 20, 1500 (Sevilla), in Antonio Rumeu de Armas, *La Política indigenista de Isabel la Católica* (Valladolid, 1969), pp. 341-342.

[66]Bernáldez, *Memorias*, p. 393 (ch. CLXIV); Santa Cruz, *Crónica*, I, 204-205 (ch. XLVIII); Menéndez Pidal, *Historia de España*, XVII (2), 529, 532, 536; von Pastor, *History of the Popes*, VI, 74-75.

[67]Galíndez de Carvajal, "Anales breves," CODOIN XVIII, 297.

[68]Matienzo to Isabel, August 16, 1498 and January 15, 1499 (Brussels), in Suárez Fernández, *Política internacional de Isabel*, V, 288-289, 351-356.

by all accounts, she was passionately devoted despite his relative lack of interest in her.

But surely there was more than politics in Isabel's special care for Miguel, in her refusal to be parted from him. He was all that was left to her from her first two beloved children. Juan had died in the flower of his youth, Isabel after seven years of sorrow; Juan's stillborn daughter had been, in Peter Martyr's terrible phrase, little more than "a shapeless mass of meat."[69] Juana was far away, her children being brought up in a foreign court; Catalina was going to England soon, where Isabel could never expect to see her children. Maria, when she married King Manuel, might give Isabel more grandchildren whom she could see, but the family history was not encouraging. For now, perhaps for the rest of her life, she had Miguel, only Miguel. The chroniclers and letter-writers tell us nothing of him after his first few weeks of life, except that he stayed with his grandmother. We can only imagine the pitiless alternations of joy and terror as the feeble infant contended with the shocks and diseases of childhood, took his first faltering steps, spoke his first faltering words, struggled for breath on hot summer days or cold winter nights. So much depended on him. Would he ever be strong enough to bear up under the multitudinous burdens of his destiny?

Isabel arrived at Granada with him on July 3.[70] The trip in the blazing Andalusian summer may have been especially hard on him. On July 20 the little prince breathed his last. Peter Martyr provides us with the heartrending fact that he actually died in his grandparents' arms.[71]

Once again, as at the death of their daughter Isabel, Fernando and Isabel seemed stunned, overwhelmed. They strove desperately to maintain an appearance of serenity of spirit, to show themselves in public with the semblance of a smile. But no one was deceived. Their agony showed; in an unforgettable phrase of Peter Martyr, they looked "as though thrown among thorns."[72]

As though they bore a crown of thorns, as Christ their Lord had done.

Isabel and Fernando wrote at once, by fastest messenger, to Juana and Philip, asking them to come to Spain to receive the oaths of allegiance as heirs to the kingdom.[73] With that Isabel the Catholic, who had already been nearly three years on the cross, must have realized that the worst might be yet to come.

And it was.

---

[69]Peter Martyr de Anglería to the Archbishop of Braga, June 5, 1498 (Alcalá de Henares), DIHE IX, 365.

[70]Rumeu de Armas, *Itinerario*, p. 263.

[71]Peter Martyr de Anglería to Cardinal de Carvajal, July 29, 1500 (Granada), DIHE IX, 411; Chronicle of Valladolid, CODOIN XIII, 216.

[72]Peter Martyr de Anglería to Cardinal de Carvajal, July 29, 1500 (Granada), DIHE IX, 411-412; Santa Cruz, *Crónica*, I, 206-207 (ch. XLIX).

[73]Peter Martyr de Anglería to Cardinal de Carvajal, July 29, 1500 (Granada), DIHE IX, 412.

11
Duty Abides
(July 1500-November 1504)

For Isabel the Catholic, in that dark summer of the year the century changed, the glory and the joy were gone, the future was obscured by towering thunderclouds, and her own power and strength to lead the way to it were fading. Throughout the last four years of her life Isabel was a sick woman, her once splendid health fundamentally and permanently undermined by all that she had endured during her three years on the cross, and by the constant anxiety which gripped her now. Upon her death, the normal rules of monarchical succession would place Juana, with Philip her consort, immediately upon the throne of Castile; Fernando would revert to being only king of Aragon. Deeply distressing as this prospect was, there was no help for it; Isabel must do everything possible to make the best of it. And that, in the shrouded twilight of her once triumphant life, she set herself to do, with all the strength she still had—to do her duty as Queen and mother and Catholic. For through all storm and stress and suffering, so long as life endures, the duty of a Queen and a mother and a Catholic abides. Isabel knew that, and she lived it.

Isabel's letter to Juana and Philip in Flanders, announcing little Prince Miguel's death and their succession as heirs, crossed with a letter from Gutierre Gómez de Fuensalida, her able and clear-thinking ambassador in Brussels—one of the two poles of action in the grim psychological drama now about to unfold. On August 6 Fuensalida had forwarded to her the latest report from Tomás Matienzo, Sub-prior of Santa Cruz, on Juana's spiritual state: Matienzo said Juana had been in grave trouble but was now improved, and Fuensalida added that she had told him she had improved. (Insofar as there was truth in this, it demonstrated that variability which was to continue to be characteristic of Juana's malady, and has misled many later investigators. For the next ten years she was not insane, nor even unbalanced, all or most of the time, but could fall into disorder very quickly.) Fuensalida said that Juana was not really in charge even of her own household, and passed on with approval her request to her parents to send her a strong and honest personal counsellor. The Spanish ambassador noted that in political matters the Archbishop of Besançon, a city located in eastern France with a traditional link to the Dukes of Burgundy and rulers of the Netherlands, had primary influence over Philip.[1]

Shortly after the news that Miguel's death had made Juana and Philip heirs to Spain arrived in Brussels, probably around the middle of August, Philip left for Holland. He did not write to Juana during the first three weeks of his absence; only Princess Margaret came to talk with her about what had happened, full of memories of her own brief stay in Spain, first so joyous and then so tragic. Fuensalida tells us that Margaret asked lovingly after the health of Isabel and Fernando, how they were bearing up under the succession of personal blows. One gets the distinct impression that Margaret was more concerned about them than Juana was. Everyone, Fuensalida said, was talking about the trip to Spain that Juana and Philip must take, to be officially recognized as heirs to Castile. All recognized that the journey must be made; but despite Isabel's and Fernando's urging, no one was in a hurry to make it. The best estimate was that it would be more than a year before the Habsburg royal pair departed from the Netherlands. More than a year indeed it was—thirteen months after the writing of Fuensalida's letters in September and early October 1500.[2]

Isabel and Fernando wrote to Philip and Juana at this time, thanking them for their letters and for the painting of their two children, Eleanor and Charles, which "gave them much pleasure." They expressed the hope that Philip and Juana would be able to bring Prince Charles with them when they came to Spain. Indeed this was critical, for Charles would inherit Spain if he lived (and he did inherit it, at the early age of sixteen) and he needed to live at least long enough in the country he was to rule so that he would not be regarded as a foreigner by its people nor see it as foreign himself. But there is not yet in these letters of Isabel and Fernando any hint of pressure on this vital point; they even say that it might be better to wait until Charles was a little older before bringing him, since they anticipated that Juana and Philip would be making many visits to Spain in the next few years. God had made them their successors, and they loved and were content with them. They should come very soon, without waiting (as Philip had suggested) to send ambassadors first to plan the visit, headed by the Archbishop of Besançon.[3]

With these words and thoughts Isabel carried a torch of hope into night and storm-wind, and it must have seemed to her like a harsh buffet from that wind when Philip coldly replied that she should have written him in Latin rather than in Spanish, that he and Juana certainly could not leave for Spain until

[1]Fuensalida to Isabel and Fernando, August 6, 1500 (Brussels), *Correspondencia de Gutierre Gómez de Fuensalida, Embajador en Alemania, Flandes e Inglaterra*, published by the Duke of Alba (Madrid, 1907), pp. 139-142.

[2]Fuensalida to Isabel and Fernando, September 13, 1500 (Brussels); same to same, October 8, 1500 (Brussels), *ibid.*, pp. 151-155.

[3]Fuensalida to Isabel and Fernando, November 5, 1500 (Brussels), *ibid.*, pp. 157-159.

spring, and that the Archbishop of Besançon and another would go as advance ambassadors (in effect, whether Isabel liked it or not).[4] Soon Philip had an even better excuse for delay: Juana was pregnant again, due to give birth in July, and he and his courtiers believed that she must stay in Flanders until then. Fuensalida protested in vain that it was very early in her pregnancy and that the need for securing the succession was very urgent.[5] In March he penned an outspoken warning letter to Isabel and Fernando, saying that Philip's counsellors in Brussels "have no more desire to go to Spain than to hell," that they feared to lose their influence over the pliable Philip if he stayed long in Spain, and that Philip himself was irresponsible and would cause much pain both to Juana and to her parents.[6]

So it was to be.

On September 23, 1500 Isabel's third daughter, Maria, set out for Portugal to marry the widowed King Manuel, who had been her sister's husband; Isabel and Fernando accompanied Maria for the first week of her journey. Alone among all the marriages of Isabel's children, Maria's was normal and uneventful; her first child was a son, Crown Prince John of Portugal, born June 6, 1502.[7] Fuensalida once mentioned the possibility that Manuel and Maria might displace Juana and Philip for the succession of Spain, if Juana and Philip should not come to Spain to swear and be sworn to as the rightful heirs;[8] but they did eventually come, and the prospect of transferring the succession to Manuel and Maria was never raised again. And on April 8, 1501 Isabel notified King Henry VII of England that her youngest daughter Catherine (whom she always called Catalina), now fifteen, was ready to start for England to marry his son Arthur, Prince of Wales, and would be on her way the next month.[9]

On August 23, 1500 Francisco de Bobadilla, the new governor of Hispaniola whom Isabel had commissioned more than a year before to take over from Columbus and restore order to that distracted island, arrived at Santo Domingo. Upon a hill overlooking the town seven rebel Spaniards, just

---

[4]*Ibid.*, pp. 159-161.

[5]Fuensalida to Isabel and Fernando, February 8, 1501 (Ghent), *ibid.*, p. 171.

[6]Fuensalida to Isabel and Fernando, March 22, 1501 (Bruges), *ibid.*, pp. 181-182.

[7]Lorenzo Galíndez Carvajal, "Anales breves del reinado de los Reyes Católics," in *Colección de documentos inéditos para la historia de España* (hereinafter cited as CODOIN), Vol. XVIII (Madrid, 1851), pp. 298-299; Antonio de la Torre and Luis Suárez Fernández, eds., *Documentos referentes a las relaciones con Portugal durante el reinado de los Reyes Católicos* (Valladolid, 1958-63), III, 105 (announcement of the birth of Crown Prince John—later King John III—of Portugal).

[8]Fuensalida to Isabel and Fernando, February 8, 1501 (Ghent), *Correspondencia de Fuensalida*, pp. 173-174.

[9]Isabel to Henry VII of England, April 8, 1501 (Granada), summarized in G. A. Bergenroth, ed., *Calendar of Letters, Despatches and State Papers relating to the Negotiations between England and Spain*, Volume I: "Henry VII, 1485-1509" (London, 1862), p. 257.

executed by Columbus' order, hung from gallows.   It appears that the
executions were amply justified, but Bobadilla was—or affected to be—shocked
and angered.   He made not even a pretense of a thorough, impartial
investigation, but seized power at once, countermanded all Columbus' standing
orders, and called for his arrest.   When Bobadilla arrived, Columbus was in the
La Vega valley in the northern part of the island.   Never having been shown
Bobadilla's commission, he could not at first believe that his great patroness
Queen Isabel had deprived him of all power and given it to this upstart, who
though he had a creditable record in Spain had never, so far as we know, been
out of that country before.   So at first Columbus attempted to overrule
Bobadilla's decrees appointing officials, remitting financial obligations for
twenty years, and granting permits for gathering gold to many whom Columbus
knew would steal from the Crown's share and from others.   But as soon as
Columbus arrived in Santo Domingo, Bobadilla's men arrested him and put him
in chains.   Bobadilla seized his property, including papers and household goods
as well as gold; most of it was never seen again.   Bobadilla himself never spoke
to Columbus nor sent him any message.   Early in October the great discoverer
was sent back to Spain in the caravel *La Gorda*.   The caravel's captain offered
to remove his shackles, but Columbus proudly refused.   The Queen's deputy
had put them on; only by her direct order should they now be taken off.[10]

The *La Gorda* made a quick passage, docking at Cádiz before the end of
October.   On board Columbus had written a letter describing his ordeal to
Juana de Torres, a friend of Isabel who had been governess of two of her
children.   Juana de Torres passed on the letter to Isabel, then staying at the
Alhambra in Granada.   On December 12 an order came back from the Queen
to strike off Columbus' chains immediately.   The released discoverer and his
two brothers rode at once for Granada, where they were received with honor on
the 17th.   All Columbus' rights and privileges were temporarily restored, at least
on paper.   But investigations continued, and by the summer of 1501 Isabel and
her advisors had concluded that both Columbus and Bobadilla were in the
wrong.   On September 3, 1501 Bobadilla was summarily removed as governor,
to be replaced by Nicholas de Ovando, who was given strongly worded orders to
protect the Indians from robbery, rape, and the many other abuses they had
suffered.   On September 27 Isabel and Fernando decreed that Bobadilla should
restore to Columbus all of his personal wealth and possessions that had been
taken from him, and that Columbus would remain entitled to an eighth of the
profits from all Spanish trade with Hispaniola.   A good friend of Columbus,
Alonso Sánchez de Carvajal, was authorized by the royal letter to oversee the

---

[10]Columbus to Juana de Torres, October 1500, in Samuel Eliot Morison, ed.,
Journals and Other Documents on the Life and Voyages of Christopher Columbus (New
York, 1963), pp. 289-299; Samuel Eliot Morison, *Admiral of the Ocean Sea; a Life of
Christopher Columbus* (Boston, 1942), pp. 570-572.

collection of his eighth portion and payment to him on the spot. But Columbus himself was not restored as governor, nor was he to return to Hispaniola.[11]

Early in October 1500, just as Bobadilla was committing Columbus to the ship that would bring him back to Spain marked as a criminal, a new Moorish rebellion broke out in the mountains northeast of Almería, a region similar to but about fifty miles east of the Alpujarras where the rebellion earlier that year had arisen. By January this second mountain uprising was suppressed, with considerable brutality; all Moorish fighting men captured were killed, though Isabel and Fernando gave explicit orders that the women and children were to be spared, and they were. But this was followed immediately, in that same month, by a larger Moorish revolt in the Sierra Bermeja which overlooks the rugged coast between Málaga and Gibraltar, and slopes down to Ronda in the north. The Moors of Ronda had been assured by Isabel, at the time of the first outbreaks in Granada a year and a half before, that the Spanish authorities would not require their conversion by force. At that time the Moors had trusted these assurances. But the Spanish policy of exiling all Muslims in other areas who would not accept baptism had undercut this trust, so now they too rebelled.[12]

This convinced Isabel and Fernando that they now had no choice but to apply the policy originally devised by Archbishop Cisneros throughout the entire former Moorish kingdom of Granada. On February 11, 1501 they decreed that all Muslims under the authority of the kingdom of Castile must choose conversion or exile by the end of April. It was exactly the same policy—with the same conditions and almost the same time span for decision—that had been applied to all the Jews of Castile in 1492.[13]

On February 17 the Count of Cifuentes arrived at Ronda with 300 horse and 2,000 foot to suppress the rebellion in the Sierra Bermeja. The rebels, now

[11]Morison, *Journals and Other Documents of Columbus*, pp. 299-302 (including an English translation of the text of the decree of September 27, 1501); Isabel and Fernando to Ovando, Sept. 16, 1501 (Granada), in Antonio Rumeu de Armas, *La Politica Indigenista de Isabel la Católica* (Valladolid, 1969), pp. 373-377; Morison, *Admiral of the Ocean Sea*, pp. 576-580.
[12]Galíndez de Carvajal, "Anales Breves," CODOIN XVIII, 299-300; Peter Martyr de Anglería to Cardinal of Santa Cruz, June 9, 1501 (Granada), *Documentos inéditos para la Historia de España* (hereinafter cited as DIHE), published by the Duke of Alba et al, Volume IX (Madrid, 1955), p. 426; agreement between Castilian officials and representatives of the Moors of Nijar, Huebro, Torrillas and Inox, January 17, 1501 (Almería), in Miguel Angel Ladero Quesada, *Los Mudejares de Castilla en Tiempos de Isabel I* (Valladolid, 1969), pp. 300-302; Ramón Menéndez Pidal, director, *Historia de España*, Volume XVII: "España de los Reyes Católicos," ed. Luis Suárez Fernández and Manuel Fernández Alvarez (Madrid, 1969), Part 2, pp. 296-297.
[13]Alonso de Santa Cruz, *Crónica de los Reyes Católicos*, ed. Juan de Mata Carriazo, Volume I (Sevilla, 1952), pp. 243-244 (ch. LVIII); Menéndez Pidal, *Historia de España*, XVII (2), 300.

with little left to lose, resisted desperately. On March 16 they won a signal victory over a Spanish detachment led by the Count of Ureña and his son Pedro Girón, who had let greed overcome vigilance as they robbed captured Moors. The Count and his sons were of the family of the infamous Pedro Girón from whom Isabel had prayed for deliverance in her early youth; but among those caught in the ambush were two young officers who had fought splendidly in the campaigns of the reconquest of Granada and were highly regarded personally by Isabel and Fernando: Alonso de Aguilar and Francisco Ramires. The Count of Cifuentes covered the retreat of the survivors of the ambushed force, and Fernando went immediately in person to take command of the complete suppression of the revolt, which he accomplished by the end of April.[14]

The final chapter in this sad history was written in February 1502, close to the anniversary of the decree requiring all Moors in the kingdom of Castile to accept baptism or leave. This same decree was then applied to the rest of Spain—specifically, Aragon and Valencia.[15] There, as in Castile, most of the resident Moors accepted baptism and became known as "Moriscos." Just over a hundred years later, they were in their turn to be expelled from Spain by King Philip III.

Thus the tenacious resistance to dispossession from their ancestral lands for which Muslims all over the world are famous, combined with the fiercely unremitting zeal of Archbishop Cisneros and the immovable determination of Isabel and Fernando to secure the great reconquest once and for all, produced a tragic but probably unavoidable outcome. Arguments to justify what Isabel and Fernando did to the Moors are much stronger than arguments to justify the expulsion of the Jews in 1492, despite the similarity of the decrees and procedures used, because the events of 1499-1501 had left no doubt that the Moors—especially those who clung to their ancestral religion—were relentless fighters who could be expected to rebel again and again if not removed. Exactly the same logic was used by the Jews of Israel in the twentieth century in expelling the Arab inhabitants of their territories. The justification may well be debated, but it is not without basis.

Meanwhile Italy was still a powder-keg. The French had secured their hold on Milan; King Fadrique, descended on his father's side from Fernando's uncle, ruled in Naples under Spanish protection. But a major new factor had been added to the volatile Italian situation by the death of Prince Miguel and

---

[14]Andrés Bernáldez, *Memorias del reinado de los Reyes Católicos*, ed. Manuel Gómez Moreno and Juan de Mata Carriazo (Madrid, 1962), pp. 396-399 (ch. CLXVI); Santa Cruz, *Crónica*, I, 243-244 (ch. LVIII); Menéndez Pidal, *Historia de España*, XVII (2), 298-299.

[15]Bernáldez, *Memorias*, pp. 472-473 (ch. CXCVI); Santa Cruz, *Crónica*, I, 274 (ch. LXVI). For the text of the final decree ordering expulsion or baptism of the remaining Moors in Spain, dated February 12, 1502, see Ladero Quesada, *Mudejares*, pp. 320-324.

the fact that Philip and Juana were now the heirs to Castile. Philip's mother had been Burgundian French; the Netherlands were generally pro-French; and Philip's own sympathies were strongly pro-French. It behooved Isabel and Fernando to avoid a war with France if at all possible, so as not to force Philip to choose between them. Furthermore, Isabel always hated making war on other Christians. By securing Milan, the new French King Louis XII had made it clear that French ambitions in Italy were still active; and he was a considerably more competent leader and effective diplomat, with much more fixity of purpose, than his young predecessor Charles VIII.

These were probably the principal reasons why Fernando (who seems to have carried on the negotiations himself with comparatively little involvement by Isabel, who had never taken a leading role in making Italian policy, seeing that as primarily Fernando's concern as king of Aragon with its historic connections with Italy) entered into a secret treaty with Louis XII in November 1500 for the partition of the kingdom of Naples. But this agreement, known as the Treaty of Granada (where Fernando and Isabel were residing when it was concluded), was curiously incomplete. It gave the French the city of Naples and Campania surrounding it, and the territory of Abruzzi e Molise on the Adriatic coast north of Naples, while Spain was granted Calabria and Apulia, the "heel" and "toe" at the end of the Italian "boot," where Gonzalo de Córdoba had so effectively campaigned. But for some reason, never elucidated, the treaty made no provision for the province of Basilicata, lying between Apulia and Calabria (the "arch" of the "boot"), other than to grant the French some income from it, with source unspecified. It also made no mention of King Fadrique, whom Fernando simply abandoned. The French renounced their claims—such as they were—to Roussillon and Sardinia.[16]

As pointed out in an earlier chapter, the issue of who was the rightful king of Naples was so clouded and jumbled by the extraordinary political ineptitude and lurid personal life of its last native queen, Joanna, that it was virtually impossible to disentangle, so the abandonment of Fadrique was not quite the callous and greedy act that it has often been called. Nevertheless, Fadrique had worked loyally with the Spanish, and was now simply and abruptly dumped. The need to secure continuing good relations with Philip was at this point overriding in Fernando's and Isabel's thought. However, this does not explain the failure to close the gaps and loopholes in the Treaty of Granada. Perhaps it was impossible for the negotiators to agree on the disposition of all the Neapolitan territory, so the treaty embodied what they could then agree on, leaving the rest to be settled later.

In the following month the Spanish ambassador in France worked out

---

[16]Santa Cruz, *Crónica*, I, 227-228 (ch. LIV); Peter Martyr de Anglería to the Cardinal of Santa Cruz, Feb. 16, 1501 (Granada), DIHE IX, 419-420; Menéndez Pidal, *Historia de España*, XVII (2), 532-533.

specific plans with the French on how the Treaty of Granada should be implemented. These plans provided that France and Spain would begin the conquest of the kingdom of Naples with equal forces at the beginning of May, after informing Pope Alexander VI so that he might invest the kings of both countries with their respective portions, since theoretically the kingdom of Naples had been a fief of the Pope since the early thirteenth century. Meanwhile negotiations began for sealing this new and rather predatory alliance, as was customary with all serious alliances in that period, by a marriage agreement—a promise by both countries that one-year-old Prince Charles would someday wed the infant French Princess Claudia.[17]

On June 1 a French army comprising 12,000 to 15,000 troops departed from Milan, reaching Rome toward the end of the month. On June 25 Pope Alexander VI invested the kings of France and Spain with Neapolitan territory as the Treaty of Granada provided, on the grounds that the King of Naples had been dealing with the Turks, whom the Spanish under Gonzalo de Córdoba had conspicuously fought and defeated on the Greek island of Cephalonia on the day before Christmas, 1500. Caesar Borgia and his Papal army joined the French on their southward march early in July. Late that month the French stormed and sacked the Neapolitan city of Capua, and soon proceeded to overrun the whole of Campania, taking Naples without a fight. In September the hapless King Fadrique surrendered to the French on the sole condition that he receive a French title of nobility. But on the Spanish side of the dividing line, Gonzalo de Córdoba had to lay siege to the city of Taranto where Ferrante, son of Fadrique, was refusing to accept dispossession as tamely as his father, and hoped eventually to be able to play off the French and Spanish against each other. As the course of events was soon to show, that was no vain hope.[18]

On May 21, 1501 Isabel and Fernando had bade farewell to Catalina, their youngest daughter. Together they went down the long slope from the red walls of the Alhambra in Granada, through the streets of the city, and out into the green *vega* beyond, where they gave her their blessing, praying God to grant her a good voyage and a good marriage. They could hardly have escaped, at that moment of parting, racking memories of Juan, of Princess Isabel, and of Juana. It is interesting, and perhaps significant, that Isabel did not accompany Catalina on any part of her journey, as she had done with her daughter Isabel and with Juana. Perhaps she simply could not endure to extend the leavetaking; perhaps

---

[17]Gómez de Fuensalida to Isabel and Fernando, Nov. 22, 1500 (Brussels), *Correspondencia de Fuensalida*, pp. 163-167; Menéndez Pidal, *Historia de España*, XVII (2), 544.

[18]Ludwig von Pastor, *History of the Popes from the Close of the Middle Ages*, Volume VI (St. Louis, 1898), pp. 83-84; Roger B. Merriman, *The Rise of the Spanish Empire in the Old World and the New*, Volume II (New York, 1918), pp. 301-302; Menéndez Pidal, *Historia de España*, XVII (2), 547-549.

she was surer of the mental and physical sturdiness of Catalina, the brightest and strongest of all her children; perhaps her reason partook of a little of both. Others did travel with Catalina on the long journey from the far south to the far north of Spain, where she would embark for England: the Archbishop of Santiago de Compostela; the Count of Cabra and his mother; and Gutierre de Cárdenas, that rock of faithfulness and loyalty upon whom Isabel had leaned since before her reign began.[19]

Garrett Mattingly, the eloquent biographer of Catherine of Aragon, writes movingly of Catalina at this pivotal moment in her life, and of her closeness to her mother:

> From Catherine's infancy her physical likeness to her mother was striking, and as she grew older observers remarked an increasing resemblance of bearing and mind and character, the same gracious dignity, slightly aloof, the same direct, vigorous intelligence, the same basic gravity and moral earnestness. Something of this, no doubt, was conscious imitation, something the trick of heredity, something a peculiar bond of sympathy. Isabella sensed and returned the child's adoration. . . .
> One may doubt that Catherine shared all her mother's reluctance at parting. She was fifteen, an age at which many queens married, and she had trained for marriage as an athlete trains for a race. . . . On May 21, 1501, Catherine set off towards her high, uncertain destiny, alone.[20]

Catalina had been at her mother's side through all her tragedies—a factor in her mental and spiritual development that Mattingly does not mention, but which was undoubtedly profound. She was beautiful, as Isabel had been in her youth, with very white unblemished skin and red-gold hair and steady eyes;[21] she was highly intelligent and deeply devout; and the world was to learn one day that she had in full measure the courage of her mother. An earthquake that still rends Christendom came because Isabel's daughter would not surrender truth and right in her marriage to political expediency—any more than Isabel herself would have done.

But that was far in the future. In this world, Isabel was never to see her beloved youngest daughter again, after she said good-bye to her in the fields outside Granada on that bright blue day in May 1501.

On her way north Catalina stopped at the shrine of Our Lady of Guadalupe, so much beloved of Isabel and Fernando and Columbus. On August 26 she embarked for England at La Coruña, but was forced back by a storm.[22] On September 27 she tried again, leaving this time from the little

---

[19]Isabel to Dr. de Puebla, Spanish ambassador in England, May 21, 1501 (Santa Fe), summarized in Bergenroth, *Calendar of State Papers*, I, 258; Bernáldez, *Memorias*, p. 394 (ch. CLXV); Santa Cruz, *Crónica*, I, 245 (ch. LIX).

[20]Garrett Mattingly, *Catherine of Aragon* (New York, 1941), pp. 20-21.

[21]*Ibid.*, pp. 36-37.

[22]Isabel and Fernando to Dr. de Puebla, July 5, 1501 (Granada), summarized in

Basque port of Laredo whence Juana had departed for her marriage to Philip in Flanders. Catalina's fleet was now guided by an English pilot from Devon named Stephen Brett. He brought them safely through a terrifying thunderstorm off Ushant at the northwestern tip of France, and safely into Plymouth harbor October 2[23]—from which, eighty-seven years later, the mighty fleet of Isabel's great-grandson Philip II, come to liberate the Catholics of the British Isles, was first challenged by Francis Drake, admiral of the queen whose mother Anne Boleyn destroyed Catalina's marriage and England's faith.

Catherine was received with the greatest public enthusiasm in England[24]—she was always to be beloved by the English people—and with much satisfaction by King Henry VII, who wrote to her parents, in a rather stilted third-person style that still seems to convey some genuine feeling (not, unfortunately, to be maintained): "Though they cannot now see the gentle face of their beloved daughter, they may be sure that she has found a second father who will ever watch over her happiness."[25] On November 14 she was married in London to Prince Arthur, who was just her age but seemed much younger. Because Arthur bore the title of Prince of Wales, which King Edward I of England had taken from the Welsh to whom it properly belonged more than two centuries before, the proprieties required that he take his new wife to the Welsh marches. They spent the winter of 1501-02 at bleak Ludlow Castle on the uplands of Shropshire, which must have seemed to Catherine very far indeed from the sunny meadows of Granada.[26]

On July 15 Philip and Juana's third child, a second daughter, was born in Brussels, and named Isabel—one of Juana's few actions showing any feeling for her mother.[27] Deprived of the pregnancy argument for delaying Philip's and Juana's trip to Spain, their counsellors fell back on any others they could think of; snapped the infuriated Ambassador Fuensalida, in a letter to Isabel and Fernando September 20: "Now they say that they will leave at the end of October, others say at the end of November; I do not believe any of it, because they do not speak the truth."[28]

King Louis XII of France had by now invited Philip and Juana to travel to

Bergenroth, *Calendar of State Papers*, I, 259; Galíndez de Carvajal, "Anales breves," CODOIN XVIII, 301; Santa Cruz, *Crónica*, I, 245-246 (ch. LIX).

[23]Galíndez de Carvajal, "Anales breves," CODOIN XVIII, 301; Bernáldez, *Memorias*, p. 394 (ch. CLXV); Bergenroth, *Calendar of State Papers*, I, 262; Mattingly, *Catherine of Aragon*, p. 22.

[24]Mattingly, *Catherine of Aragon*, pp. 29-35.

[25]Henry VII to Fernando and Isabel, Nov. 28, 1501 (Windsor), in Bergenroth, *Calendar of State Papers*, I, 264.

[26]Mattingly, *Catherine of Aragon*, pp. 38-47; J. D. Mackie, *The Earlier Tudors* (Oxford, 1952), p. 173.

[27]Galíndez de Carvajal, "Anales breves," CODOIN XVIII, 301.

[28]Gómez de Fuensalida to Isabel and Fernando, Sept. 20, 1501 (Brussels), *Correspondencia de Fuensalida*, p. 192.

Spain across his dominions, though they had originally planned to go by sea. This looked more appealing as the season grew later, since winter voyages were the most perilous. The last thing Isabel, Fernando, and Fuensalida wanted was for their heirs and their entourage to come to Spain across the territory of their former (and likely future) enemy, being wined and dined and possibly suborned along the way; but in the end they had to agree to it. On November 4 the royal party set out, with all the finery for which the Habsburgs, the Flemings, and especially Philip the Handsome were noted. The cavalcade even brought along its own historian, Antoine de Lalaing, Sieur de Montigny, whose account of the entire grand tour—though containing some fascinating bits of information—is mostly a prolonged and (to the modern reader) paralyzingly boring account of ponderous ceremonies and gorgeous apparel described almost bow by bow and garment by garment.[29]

On December 7 Philip and Juana and their party reached the castle of Blois in the heart of France, where Louis XII was holding court. In addition to lavish entertainment, Louis offered both his royal guests a large sum of money. Philip accepted it, but Juana, now accompanied and advised by the Bishop of Córdoba whom her parents had sent for that purpose in response to her request of the previous year, refused her proffered gift. Six days later the agreement for the marriage of Philip's and Juana's son Charles and Louis' daughter Claudia—long the subject of secret negotiations—was formally announced, to seal a treaty with Philip and his father, Emperor Maximilian, by which Louis recognized Habsburg claims to Bohemia and Hungary in return for an implicit acceptance of French rule over Milan. On December 15 Philip's cavalcade resumed their journey, south toward Spain.[30]

The weather was severe; all the Pyrenean passes were blocked by snow, though it was still possible to enter Spain by the western coastal route, guarded by the great fortress of Fuenterrabía. There the somewhat bedraggled royal party arrived on January 26, 1502, after passing through Bayonne, the last major French city, by boat because most of its streets and bridges were under water. In the initial Spanish welcoming party, as the historian has by now come to expect, was Gutierre de Cárdenas. The formal reception of the heirs to the Castilian throne took place three days later.[31]

It is surprising to find Isabel and Fernando still in the far south, in Sevilla,

[29]*Ibid.*, pp. 191-192; Antoine de Lalaing, "Voyage de Philippe le Beau en Espagne," in Louis P. Gachard, ed., *Collection des Voyages des Souverains des Pays-Bas*, Volume I (Brussels, 1876), p. 129 and *passim*.

[30]Lalaing, "Voyage de Philippe le Beau," in Gachard, *Voyages des Souverains des Pays-Bas*, I, 135-142; Santa Cruz, *Crónica*, I, 253-254 (ch. LXI); Menéndez Pidal, *Historia de España*, XVII (2), 507.

[31]Lalaing, "Voyage de Philippe le Beau," in Gachard, *Voyages des Souverains des Pays-Bas*, I, 146-148; Santa Cruz, *Crónica*, I, 254 (ch. LVIII); Menéndez Pidal, *Historia de España*, XVII (2), 577.

on this critical occasion; the last major Moorish rising had been crushed months before, and they certainly knew Philip and Juana were coming—they had waited long enough for them. They took advantage of their stay in Sevilla to oversee the departure of new Governor Ovando for Hispaniola, with a fleet of 30 ships carrying 2,500 men, and to hear Columbus' proposal for a fourth voyage, which they formally authorized the next month, along with a specific provision forbidding him to enslave any Indians. The chronicler Santa Cruz tells us that Isabel made a point of explaining to Columbus face-to-face why she had felt compelled to remove him as governor, and how highly she continued to value his services. By April 3 his exploring fleet was assembled—four ships and 135 men, 56 of whom are described as "boys." On May 11 he set sail from Cádiz on what was to be his last voyage.[32]

Isabel and Fernando did not leave Sevilla until February 23, and then travelled slowly, taking a route which put them in an obscure town named Zalamea de la Serena for Holy Week, which in previous years they had almost always celebrated at some major city or great shrine. They did visit their favorite shrine of Guadalupe, but not until April (Easter fell on March 27 in 1502). On April 22—Isabel's 51st birthday—they finally arrived in Toledo, where they had already summoned the *cortes* to swear the prescribed oaths to Philip and Juana as heirs. Philip and Juana had been waiting for them at Madrid for almost a month. The long delay may have been a miscalculation, or may have had motives that escaped the historical record. That happens more often than historians like to admit.[33]

Awaiting the arrival of their daughter and son-in-law, Fernando and Isabel were informed that Philip had fallen ill with measles on April 30 at Olías, a village not far from Toledo. Isabel remained at Toledo, but Fernando went to Olías. Then Antoine de Lalaing interrupts his interminable catalogue of etiquette and protocol to record a striking scene:

> Running to meet the King [Fernando], descending from his horse, came Madame his daughter [Juana] from a gallery, and embraced him and kissed him, and gave him the best welcome she could, and led him by the hand to the bedroom of Monsigneur [Philip].[34]

This behavior contrasts so vividly with Juana's previous coolness toward Isabel as to suggest, as Townsend Miller believes, that her aversion to her mother was matched by a great though usually unexpressed devotion to her

---

[32]Morison, *Admiral of the Ocean Sea*, pp. 580-587; Santa Cruz, *Crónica*, I, 278-279 (ch. LXVII).

[33]Antonio Rumeu de Armas, *Itinerario de los Reyes Católicos, 1474-1516* (Madrid, 1974), pp. 278-279; Lalaing, "Voyage de Philippe le Beau," in Gachard, *Voyages des Souverains des Pays-Bas*, I, 171-172.

[34]Lalaing, "Voyage de Philippe le Beau," in Gachard, *Voyages des souverains des Pays-Bas*, I, 173.

father.[35] Here we may see the beginning of that growing and terrible tension between her feelings for her father and for her husband that was to tear Juana apart.

Philip's case of measles was evidently a mild one, for within a week he was fit to travel again, and he and Juana made their ceremonial entry into Toledo May 7. Isabel was there to greet them, and they both went to her room together. They were lodged in a house belonging to Isabel's oldest friend Beatriz de Bobadilla and her husband, now the Marquis and Marquisa de Moya.[36]

The next day was Sunday. Isabel and Fernando and Philip and Juana all went to Mass together; there was a 64-voice choir. After Mass there was a splendid dinner, complete with five-foot-high silver urns, presumably held at or close to the usual Spanish dinner hour of 2 p.m. After dinner, Philip and Juana conducted Fernando and Isabel to their room, and then returned to their own. Did Isabel see hope, or only premonitions of further tragedy, in the demeanor of her disturbed daughter and her vain and frivolous son-in-law during this dinner with them, on the second day of their coming together? (It should be remembered that Isabel had never met Philip until the preceding day.) Was her ever-active, thoughtful but practical mind devising new plans for somehow better enabling them, despite their handicaps, to rule Spain as it ought to be ruled? We do not know. But we can be quite sure that the last thing Isabel expected was the new blow that struck like a thunderbolt that very day. In the coolness of a spring evening in high Toledo, during what is now the pleasant hour of *paseo* in Spain when families go out to walk the streets and meet their friends, a courier on a hard-ridden horse came galloping up to the frowning gate of Spain's most impregnable fortress. He brought appalling news. The scythe of the Grim Reaper had swung again. Prince Arthur of England, Catalina's young husband, was dead.[37]

Isabel and Fernando had five children. Their only son had died within six months of his marriage. Their oldest daughter's first husband had died within a year of his marriage, and she had died within a year of her marriage to her second husband. Their second daughter was going insane. Now their fourth daughter had lost her husband within six months of marriage.

The superstitious would have called it a curse. Isabel knew it was a cross. Knowing that did not make it easier, emotionally, to bear. But it gave her a

---

[35]Townsend Miller, *The Castles and the Crown: Spain 1451-1555* (New York, 1963), *passim.*

[36]Galíndez de Carvajal, "Anales breves," CODOIN XVIII, 304; Santa Cruz, *Crónica*, I, 254 (ch. LXI); Lalaing, "Voyage de Philippe le Beau," in Gachard, *Voyages des souverains des Pays-Bas*, I, 174-176.

[37]Lalaing, "Voyage de Philippe le Bel," in Gachard, *Voyages des souverains des Pays-Bas*, I, 176-177.

reason—a transcendent reason—to live on, to do her duty to the end, to keep on trying to serve her God.

At the castle of Ludlow in Shropshire, both Catherine and Arthur had sickened after a long winter in its cold gray confines. Catherine's strong, vibrant young body eventually fought off the illness. Arthur's pale slender form did not. On April 2 he died in the castle. They buried him in Worcester cathedral, on what one observer called "the foulest cold windy and rainy day I have ever seen," with the mud so deep and viscous that only the strongest oxen could pull the hearse through it on the road from Ludlow. Catherine was still too ill to be there. It was probably fortunate. It does not seem likely that this was a memory she would have wished to have.[38]

Nine days of mourning for Arthur followed in Spain; on May 12 there was a solemn requiem Mass for him at the church of San Juan de los Reyes (St. John of the Kings) in Toledo, which Isabel had built to commemorate her victory in the war of the succession against Portugal (which must have seemed to her now very long ago) and on which she had hung the chains her soldiers had struck off the Christian captives of the Moors during the war for the reconquest of Granada.[39] On that day Isabel wrote to her ambassador in England a letter of such courage as even she never exceeded in her life. She had learned "with profound sorrow" of the death of Prince Arthur. That news had "revived the affliction caused by all their former losses." But—ring of steel, for this woman would not *allow* her heart to break: "The will of God must be obeyed." Then no more thought of herself, only of her suffering, most dearly beloved daughter: "She must be removed, without loss of time, from the unhealthy place where she now is." Could it be that only her mother, a thousand miles away, had yet thought of that? Where was her "second father," Henry VII? "Write and send the fastest messengers by land and by sea."[40]

Within a few days Isabel and Fernando had begun to plan a new proposal to Henry, that would keep the English alliance and most of their daughter's hopes and dreams intact: that Catalina should now marry Arthur's brother Henry, five years her junior, when he was old enough. Meanwhile Ambassador de Puebla was instructed to insist that Henry fulfill his financial obligations to Catherine, at least from her dowry, and to remind him of similar examples from their own sad experience: when Princess Isabel was widowed by the death of Prince Afonso of Portugal, and when Margaret was widowed by the death of

---

[38]Mattingly, *Catherine of Aragon*, pp. 48-49; Bernáldez, *Memorias*, p. 394 (ch. CLXV).

[39]Lalaing, "Voyage de Philippe le Bel," in Gachard, *Voyages des souverains des Pays-Bas*, I, 177.

[40]Isabel and Fernando to Dr. de Puebla, May 12, 1502 (Toledo), in Bergenroth, *Calendar of State Papers*, I, 267-268. The letter is signed by both Isabel and Fernando, but the sentiments are clearly Isabel's and so in all probability was the composition.

their own son Juan, both widows had been properly cared for by their royal fathers-in-law and mothers-in-law.[41]

On May 22 the members of the *cortes* and the assembled grandees of Castile, temporal and religious, stepped forward in the cathedral of Toledo to swear fealty to Juana and Philip her consort as heirs to the kingdom.[42] That was easy enough; but difficulties could be expected from the *cortes* of Aragon, whose law had not previously permitted rule by a woman, a problem that had been evaded, not solved, during the period when it was expected that Queen Isabel of Portugal would be the successor. Fernando called the *cortes* of Aragon to meet July 23; it appears that Isabel expected to go there with him and her daughter and son-in-law, as she had gone to meet the *cortes* of Aragon with her daughter Isabel and King Manuel of Portugal in 1498. But she fell quite seriously ill; as earlier stated, Isabel's health was never again really sound after Prince Miguel's death. Her condition was undoubtedly aggravated by concern for Catalina and probably also by concern about Juana's mental condition. Probably because of Isabel's illness, Fernando waited to leave until July 18, which meant that he was two weeks late arriving at Zaragoza.[43] One could usually afford to be some days late for a major Spanish meeting, which almost never started on time.

On the road, and soon after arriving at Zaragoza, Fernando wrote Isabel two letters, the last we have between them. The love they express and the tone in which Fernando expresses it is almost unchanged from his letters to her twenty-five years before. As then, he mourns in the first letter of this pair because he has not heard from her, and rejoices in the second letter because he has. He is full of concern about her health; in the second letter he underlines "with the health of Your Ladyship please God all will be well."[44] Fernando was a strong man, but almost all of his few extant letters to Isabel show how much he needed and depended on her. It will come as no surprise to anyone who has read these letters, how different a man and a king he was when she was no longer with him.

Early in this troubled summer Columbus, after making his Western

---

[41]Galíndez de Carvajal, "Anales breves," CODOIN XVIII, 305; Mattingly, *Catherine of Aragon*, pp. 50-52; Isabel and Fernando to Dr. de Puebla, May 29, 1502 (Toledo), in Bergenroth, *Calendar of State Papers*, I, 268-269; Isabel to Fernando, Duke of Estrada, July 12, 1502 (Toledo), *ibid.*, pp. 272-274.

[42]Galíndez de Carvajal, "Anales breves," CODOIN XVIII, 304-305; Santa Cruz, *Crónica*, I, 254 (ch. LXI); Lalaing, "Voyage de Philippe le Bel," in Gachard, *Voyages des souverains des Pays-Bas*, I, 178-181.

[43]Vicente Rodríguez Valencia, *Isabel la Católica en la Opinion de Españoles y Extranjeros* (Valladolid, 1970), III, 131-132; Rumeu de Armas, *Itinerario*, pp. 281-282.

[44]Fernando to Isabel, August 1502 (Zaragoza), in Rodríguez Valencia, *Isabel en la Opinion*, III, 139. The other letter from Fernando to Isabel at this time was written at Calatayud on July 30, 1502, *ibid.*, pp. 137-138.

hemisphere landfall at Martinique in the Caribbean June 15, had sailed to Santo Domingo in defiance of the royal orders that he stay away from Hispaniola. He found 28 ships of the 30 that had come with new Governor Ovando ready to sail back to Spain with ex-Governor Bobadilla, a large number of Spaniards who had come to Hispaniola to get rich, and their ill-gotten gains: a considerable quantity of gold including the largest nugget ever found on the island, worth 3,600 pesos and known (with a bit of exaggeration) as the "golden table." Ovando would not allow Columbus into the harbor, since the Queen had not authorized him to come there. Columbus cast his mariner's eye skyward, and saw that a hurricane was making up. He had sailed more than enough in the Caribbean Sea during the past ten years to be able to see a hurricane coming and to learn just how dangerous these West Indian cyclones were. He sent a message to Ovando warning the fleet not to set out, and asking shelter for his four ships. Ovando had never seen a West Indian hurricane, and if Bobadilla had seen one he had apparently forgotten what it was like, or would not heed the despised Columbus even on the weather. The warning from the discoverer of America was scornfully dismissed and his request to enter the harbor summarily denied.[45]

"What man ever born," Columbus cried, "not excepting Job, would not have died of despair when in such weather, seeking safety for my son, brother, shipmates and myself, we were forbidden the land and the harbors that I, by God's will and sweating blood, had won for Spain?"[46]

The hurricane struck. No one now living in North America needs to be told about the danger of West Indian hurricanes. Given names, followed assiduously hour by hour by space satellites, they can still do hundreds of millions of dollars' worth of damage in a few hours, overwhelming all the resources of modern technology. This hurricane of June 30, 1502 was one of the worst. Every ship but one of the 28 in the returning flotilla from Hispaniola went to the bottom of the sea, along with the "golden table," Francisco de Bobadilla who had put Columbus in chains, and most of the greedy gold-hunters who had inflicted robbery and rape on the helpless Indians. Off the thundering coast as darkness fell, Columbus anchored his flagship *Capitana* so well that her anchors held all through the storm. His other three ships were torn loose; but on *Santiago* the Admiral's brother seized command from her terrified and immobilized captain, pointed her seaward into the howling night, and survived with every man aboard. So did *Gallega* and *Vizcaina*. Three days later they rendezvoused at a little harbor known only to Columbus, Puerto Escondido ("hidden port") at the head of Ocoa Bay. Perhaps somone aboard reflected that in such a storm it was better to sail with the Admiral of the Ocean

―――――――――
[45]Santa Cruz, *Crónica*, I, 279-280 (ch. LXVII); Morison, *Admiral of the Ocean Sea*, pp. 589-590.
[46]Morison, *Admiral of the Ocean Sea*, p. 591.

Sea than with a golden table.[47]

On July 14 Columbus' proud survivors sailed from Hispaniola. A month later they raised the Central American mainland at Honduras, where Columbus landed and took formal possession of this previously unknown coast for Spain. Through September he beat southward along the coasts of what are now Nicaragua and Costa Rica, hoping to find a strait which would be a sea approach to civilized Asia. All during the fall and on into the winter he explored the coasts of Panama, where the American continent is in fact at its narrowest—though it does not appear Columbus knew that—in the hope of finding the desired strait. He carried on until Easter of 1503, when his ships were so riddled by the holes made by the teredo or shipworm (previously unknown to European mariners) that he had to sail back toward Hispaniola. He was unable to reach it; on June 25, 1503 he had to beach his last two ships on Jamaica in a sinking condition. He was abandoned there. Even after one of his officers, Diego Méndez, reached Hispaniola by canoe and informed Governor Ovando that Columbus and the rest of his men were on Jamaica, it was ten months before the hostile Ovando would allow Méndez to take a ship to rescue him. By then Isabel's mortal illness was at hand.[48]

On August 4, 1502 Fernando went before the *cortes* of Aragon to urge their recognition of Juana as heir, with Philip as co-heir. He also asked for money to prepare defenses to resist a French attack upon Roussillon, for war between Spain and France had again broken out over the division of the kingdom of Naples. A large new French army was marching south, France had made an alliance with the faithless Caesar Borgia, and Gonzalo de Córdoba was entrenched and ready to fight the French at the key stronghold of Barletta on the Apulian coast directly across the Italian peninsula from Naples.[49]

The Aragonese were traditionally reluctant to grant royal requests without a great deal of argument; not until October was Fernando finally able to summon Juana and Philip to receive oaths of fealty as his successors. But those oaths, given October 27, were a real political triumph for Fernando. The Aragonese dropped their legal opposition to a woman ruler; they accepted Princess Juana as *primogenita sucesora* ("first-born successor"), with Philip to share her authority so long as she lived, and took their oaths accordingly, asking in return only that Philip and Juana swear likewise to maintain the rights, liberties, and privileges of Aragon, which they did. The only limitation on the

---

[47]*Ibid.*, pp. 591-592; Bernáldez, *Memorias*, pp. 473-474 (ch. CXCVII); Santa Cruz, *Crónica*, I, 278, 280 (ch. LXVII); Ferdinand Columbus, *The Life of the Admiral Christopher Columbus*, tr. & ed. Benjamisn Keen (New Brunswick NJ, 1959), pp. 228-229.

[48]Ferdinand Columbus, *Life of Christopher Columbus*, pp. 230-282; Morison, *Admiral of the Ocean Sea*, pp. 592-658.

[49]Menéndez Pidal, *Historia de España*, XVII (2), 558, 564-566, 580; von Pastor, *History of the Popes*, VI, 120-121.

oaths was the provision that if Isabel should die and Fernando remarry and have a son by his second wife, that son would displace Juana in the succession.[50]

During the long delay required to obtain this agreement, however, the problems with Philip and Juana had festered. They remained at Toledo for more than three months after the oaths were sworn to them by the *cortes* of Castile. Isabel was ill, Fernando was in Aragon, and there was no one to maintain a concerted effort to "hispanicize" Philip or keep him in touch with a country still very strange to him. He became increasingly restive, petulant, and exasperated. He suffered from recurring fevers. When his mentor the Archbishop of Besançon suddenly died August 23, Philip thought he might have been poisoned. On August 29 he and Juana left Toledo for Ocaña, Aranjuez, and Alcalá de Henares. In these three places they spent September, wholly out of touch now with both Isabel and Fernando. The observant Peter Martyr, who returned to Toledo in September after a lengthy sojourn in Italy, reports September 20 that Philip wanted to return soon to Flanders, despite all Isabel's efforts to dissuade him. Juana was pregnant again, unfit for a long journey. France and Spain were now openly at war, with the French besieging Gonzalo de Córdoba in Barletta; this made it very risky for either of the heirs to the Spanish throne to travel across France, while the stormy winter weather made a sea journey dangerous. Yet Philip seemed determined to go, and to go soon.[51]

In October Isabel became seriously ill again, perhaps partly due to these mounting stresses. Fernando was so concerned about her that he departed abruptly from Zaragoza and the *cortes* of Aragon to go to her on the very day after its members swore the oaths to Philip and Juana as successors, leaving Philip to preside over the *cortes*. When Fernando arrived at Madrid, where Isabel had gone from Toledo at the end of September, he found her much better. But scarcely had he arrived when the news came that Philip had publicly announced his intention to leave Spain, and written Louis XII asking for his safe-conduct to pass through France. Two days later Philip set out from Zaragoza toward Madrid with a small company, travelling fast. He left Juana behind, ostensibly to preside over the *cortes* which remained more or less in session.[52]

During the second week of November Isabel and Fernando met with Philip in Madrid. They had been so intent on gaining the full endorsement of

---

[50]Lalaing, "Voyage de Philippe le Bel," in Gachard, *Voyages des souverains des Pays-Bas*, I, 244; Menéndez Pidal, *Historia de España*, XVII (2), 580.

[51]Peter Martyr de Anglería to Cardinal of Santa Cruz, Sept. 20, 1502 (Toledo), DIHE X, 34-36; Lalaing, "Voyage de Philippe le Bel," in Gachard, *Voyages des souverains des Pays-Bas*, I, 196-197, 216-219; Menéndez Pidal, *Historia de España*, XVII (2), 566.

[52]Santa Cruz, *Crónica*, I, 255 (ch. LXII); Lalaing, "Voyage de Philippe le Bel," in Gachard, *Voyages des souverains des Pays-Bas*, I, 241-242; Menéndez Pidal, *Historia de España*, XVII (2), 580-581, 585.

the *cortes* of the two realms for the new heirs that they had made insufficient effort to attain the greater objective of preparing Philip to rule Spain. Perhaps no amount of effort would have achieved that end, given Philip's indiscipline and irresponsibility and Juana's inability to help him; but Isabel and Fernando had to try, and there was no chance of real improvement while Philip was in Flanders. The Spanish people had a strong dislike of foreigners—this had been the root of many of Columbus' problems in governing Hispaniola—and neither Castile nor Aragon had ever had a non-Spanish king, or a non-Spanish consort for a ruling queen. The Spanish were strong-willed, touchy about their honor, very brave, sometimes violent—as Isabel knew better than most, from a lifetime's experience with them. She loved them and they loved her; Philip and his Flemings and Frenchmen did not love them and they did not love Philip and his countrymen. The only hope was for him to develop some bond with them and they with him, to gain some significant understanding of and appreciation for the land and people he would rule. Nothing that had happened so far during his ten-month visit had given him such understanding and appreciation. If he left and did not come back until he was king, he would probably never get it.

These were the political stakes. The personal stakes, for Isabel and Fernando, were higher still. Juana's passionate, largely unrequited love for Philip—commented on repeatedly in the letters of Peter Martyr from the Spanish court as they had been in the reports of Ambassador Fuensalida from Brussels[53]—created a psychological situation in which she could have almost no influence over any decision or policy of his on matters of state. She would go where and as he went, as long as he would have her. If Philip rejected the Spanish culture and way of life, so would she—even if it meant going against her father for whom she still seemed to have much affection. But since Philip did not reciprocate her love, she had value for him only as the heiress to Spain, and whatever power and money he could derive through it. Philip was no dissembler; sooner or later Juana, in her saner moments, would see how she was being used, and that would be more than her weakened mind could endure.

A mad king or ruling queen is the nightmare of monarchy. A mad child is the nightmare of every parent. Both nightmares were on the point of becoming reality for Isabel and Fernando. Every possible attempt must be made to avert them. Philip's departure from Spain without Juana would end any immediate hopes of preparing him adequately to rule the country and bring Juana to the brink of disintegration as she realized that she had been abandoned.

Isabel urged upon Philip in person, with all the eloquence and force of which her repeated illnesses had still left her capable, the arguments against his

---

[53]E.g., Peter Martyr to the Cardinal of Santa Cruz, Sept. 20, 1502 (Toledo), DIHE X, 35. See also Santa Cruz, *Crónica*, I, 256-257 (ch. LXII).

immediate departure which she had already given to him in letters: that those who are to be kings must spend much time with their future subjects if they expect to be obeyed when they wear the crown; that he needed to learn more about how government was conducted and justice administered in Spain; that travel across France when France was at war with Spain was risky for the heir to the Spanish throne, even with a French safe-conduct; that Juana was six months pregnant and he should at least stay with her until the child was born, if he loved her. Philip, "hard as diamond" in Peter Martyr's words, was unmoved. He said he had promised his people he would return within a year. He said he had pressing business back in the Netherlands, and would suffer great damage if he did not return quickly. He pointed out that several of his most valued advisors, notably the Archbishop of Besançon, had died in Spain, probably because of the harsh climate and the unfamiliar food. He said that Juana could have her baby in Spain and rejoin him later.[54]

Philip retained enough human feeling—or was it only a sense of appearances?—to call Juana to come from Zaragoza to bid him good-bye. They met at Alcalá de Henares on December 6 and travelled together to Madrid, where they arrived on the 9th. Lalaing, discreet or simply unperceptive, tells us only that they were "poorly lodged." During the ensuing ten days Philip and his counsellors met repeatedly with Isabel and Fernando. The *cortes* of Castile sent a long memorial to Philip begging him to stay. All the old arguments were rehashed; neither side's opinion changed. But now Juana was present. She was—as her mother had undoubtedly foreseen—desperate. She "could do nothing but wail and weep," the chronicler Santa Cruz tells us; she alternately begged and pleaded with Philip not to leave her, and bitterly denounced him. He did not care. On the 19th of December he departed, ceremoniously kissing the hands of Isabel, Fernando and Juana. We may imagine their expressions as they held out their hands to him: Isabel and Fernando grim and tight-lipped, the weight of the heaviest cross they had yet borne beginning to press down upon their shoulders; Juana with her sanity dissolving in her tears. By January 10, 1503 Philip the Handsome was over the border into France. Isabel never saw him again. When Fernando did, it was the beginning of the worst six months of his long life.[55]

---

[54]Santa Cruz, *Crónica*, I, 255-257 (ch. LXII); Peter Martyr de Anglería to the Cardinal of Santa Cruz, Sept. 20, 1502 (Toledo), DIHE X, 35-36; Isabel and Fernando to the Marqués of Villena, Dec. 7, 1502 (Madrid), in Antonio Rodríguez Villa, *La Reina Doña Juana la loca* (Madrid, 1892), pp. 68-69; Lalaing, "Voyage de Philippe le Bel," in Gachard, *Voyages des souverains des Pays-Bas*, I, 242; Menéndez Pidal, *Historia de España*, XVII (2), 581.

[55]Santa Cruz, *Crónica*, I, 256-257 (ch. LXII); Lalaing, "Voyage de Philippe le Bel," in Gachard, *Voyages des souverains des Pays-Bas*, I, 242-250; Peter Martyr de Anglería to Cardinal of Santa Cruz, Jan. 4, 1503 (Madrid), DIHE X, 40-41; Rodríguez Villa, *Juana la loca*, pp. 70-71; Miller, *Castles and the Crown*, pp. 216-217.

As the first effects of this shock began to wear off in the days following Philip's departure, with Juana nursing her sorrow and anger at Alcalá de Henares some distance away, Isabel and Fernando began to think of ways of recovery. They simply could not afford to alienate Philip permanently. However, they knew now they could never really trust him. Therefore they must place their hopes in his and Juana's son, two-year-old Charles, who would ultimately be the sole legitimate ruler of both Spain and the Netherlands, if he outlived his father and if his mother became incapable of ruling. Neither of them had ever seen Charles. If Philip would not accept their guidance, perhaps in time to come Charles would. Child of such parents, he would most certainly need it and very possibly want it. Isabel would probably have remembered how much her own parents had failed to give her, and how much she had obtained from her teacher Gonzalo Chacón. They needed to bring young Charles to Spain.

As a first step in building bridges to both Philip and Charles, they decided to authorize Philip to negotiate for peace between France and Spain, so long as any prospective treaty included a firm guarantee of the already discussed betrothal of Charles with Claudia, or another of the daughters of the King of France. A messenger was sent January 14 to catch up with Philip and his slow-moving party in France and deliver this secret authorization.[56]

Two days later they went to Alcalá de Henares to be with Juana. Isabel stayed there for the next two months, until Juana's child was born. Among those in her party, as he had been so often through the twenty-eight years of her reign, was her stalwart spokesman and champion who had carried the royal sword at her coronation, Gutierre de Cárdenas. A week after their arrival, he died. Three days later Fernando set out for Aragon, leaving Isabel alone with Juana.[57]

Another who accompanied Isabel to Alcalá de Henares, and stayed with her all through those two harrowing months, was the humanist scholar, diplomat, royal advisor and elegant writer of letters, Peter Martyr de Anglería. His letter of March 10, written on the day that Juana's child—a second son, named Fernando for his grandfather—was born, conveys the essence of what Isabel endured that winter far better than any other notice we have from her last years:

> The Queen has taken up the court . . . and removed it to Alcalá de Henares, six leagues from Madrid. She has piled up sorrow upon sorrow. You know that Her Majesty was assisted by two most faithful lords, Treasurers of Castile: Juan Chacón, lord of Cartagena and Commandant of Murcia, and Gutierre de Cárdenas, whom the Queen had raised up from

---

[56]Menéndez Pidal, *Historia de España*, XVII (2), 582.
[57]Rumeu de Armas, *Itinerario*, pp. 288-289; Galíndez de Carvajal, "Anales breves," CODOIN XVIII, 307.

nothing to the peak of the highest responsibilities . . . Both died here, in the short span of a few days. The Queen—although far more strong and upright and prudent than is usual for a woman—feels the blows of a cruel fortune; she passes through her life like a gigantic rock in a sea torn in every direction by the onslaught of the waves, while her husband devotes himself to foreign wars, as the French whet their appetites for his power. Her son-in-law, heartlessly and precipitately abandoning her pregnant daughter, his wife, decided to leave without waiting for the coming birth. With three of her most honorable companions, who had helped greatly in bearing her burdens, dead [Chacón, Cárdenas, and Diego Hurtado de Mendoza who also died during these two months], she nevertheless surmounted her grief and the turbulence of her daughter, who cared nothing at all for kingdoms nor power, without seeming to be affected in the least by whether or not she had to reach for power. Concerned only for her husband, living plunged in despair, thickly frowning, withdrawn day and night, she speaks no word except for hectoring questions, always put in an offensive manner. Her mother promises her freedom to go to her husband once she has given birth and the war with the French has ended, showing her that she could do nothing else, since the French have Spain blocked everywhere by land and by sea. She [Isabel] suggested that the time was near for making an alliance with the French. And she urged and begged her to be calm, but her maternal words were not enough to move her . . . Cursed fruit of the tree, wretched shoot from the earth is this daughter of such a mother! Hardened in heart, not showing any sign of royal dignity or courage! Wherever her obstinate saturnine humor takes her, there she goes, there she plants her feet. This daughter's conduct—to say it in a word—burns her mother's heart. Each day is renewed in the Queen the agony for Prince Juan, and the agony of her concern for the future government of these kingdoms.[58]

Though it spoke the truth about her situation, Isabel would not have liked this letter if she had ever seen it. She would not have blamed Juana, whom she still loved, as Peter Martyr—who loved Isabel—blamed her. Isabel knew the shadow that was engulfing her daughter. She had lived with it now for a long time, watching it grow steadily blacker. It was her heaviest cross, the cross that in the end would kill her. But still she would not have blamed Juana, for she followed One who had prayed: "Father, forgive them, for they know not what they do."

A month later Isabel suffered yet another shock involving her children. Letters from London reported that not only was Henry VII showing little inclination (after an initial appearance of interest) in having Catherine betrothed to his boy son Henry, but that he was now actually hinting that he might wish to marry her himself! Henry VII was 45 years old and Catherine 17. Isabel fired back to her new ambassador in England, Duke Fernando of Estrada:

---

[58]Peter Martyr de Anglería to Cardinal of Santa Cruz, March 10, 1503 (Alcalá de Henares), DIHE X, 47-48.

This would be a very evil thing—one never before seen, the mere mention of which offends the ears. We would not for anything in the world that it should take place. Therefore, if anything be said to you about it, speak of it as a thing not to be endured. You must likewise say very decidedly that on no account would we allow it, or even hear it mentioned, in order that by these means the King of England may lose all hope of bringing it to pass.[59]

At the same time Isabel wrote to Dr. de Puebla, her long-time ambassador in England, sharply rebuking him for allowing such a marriage even to be discussed. To the Duke of Estrada she also wrote that preparations should be made to bring Catherine home until her future in England, if any, was determined; but despite Henry VII's offensive suggestion, negotiations for her betrothal to young Henry should continue. These negotiations bore fruit much sooner than would have been expected in view of this unpleasant passage in April. On June 23 a treaty was signed at Richmond for the marriage of Catherine and the future Henry VIII, now Crown Prince—conditional on obtaining a dispensation from the Pope to allow Henry and Catherine to disregard the Biblical prohibition against marrying a brother's wife. Isabel and Fernando ratified the marriage treaty at Barcelona in September.[60]

On Good Friday, April 5, Philip took advantage of his commission from Fernando and Isabel to sign the Treaty of Lyons with France, which did little more than restore the original incomplete provisions of the Treaty of Granada of November 1500, dividing the kingdom of Naples between France and Spain, but not awarding to either the province of Basilicata which lay between the two Spanish provinces of Apulia and Calabria. The Treaty of Lyons provided for the marriage of Charles and Claudia ten years in the future, and also for Philip to govern the Spanish part of the kingdom of Naples. At the moment Fernando and Isabel did not trust him to govern anything, certainly not hard-won Apulia and Calabria; and this treaty, like its predecessor, contained the seeds of its own ruin. Not only did Fernando repudiate it, but so did Philip's own father the Emperor and his sister Margaret.[61]

So the war in Italy went on, and before April was over Gonzalo de Córdoba accomplished his greatest military achievement. After a Spanish cavalry victory at Seminara on the 21st, Gonzalo faced the main French army under the Duke de Nemours at Cerignola, on a field where the famous Swiss pikemen who fought for the French were thought sure to prevail. But Gonzalo maneuvered brilliantly with his tough Spanish infantry armed with the primitive

[59]Isabel to Duke Fernando of Estrada, April 11, 1503 (Alcalá de Henares), in Bergenroth, *Calendar of State Papers*, I, 295.

[60]Isabel to Dr. de Puebla and to Duke Fernando of Estrada, April 11, 1503 (Alcalá de Henares), in *ibid.*, I, 295-302; text of the treaty signed at Richmond June 23, 1503, *ibid.*, I, 306-307.

[61]Menéndez Pidal, *Historia de España*, XVII (2), 583-584.

firearm known as the arquebus. Thus far in military history the arquebus had been little more than an auxiliary weapon, which made a terrifying noise but was very inaccurate. But the big stolid squares of Swiss pikemen made a target which even arquebuses could not miss, when borne into suitable range. Cerignola was the first battle in history won by infantry gunfire, and it was won decisively. The Duke de Nemours died on the field. Less than three weeks later Gonzalo and his Spanish army entered Naples in triumph.[62]

However, the French still held a number of strong fortresses in the kingdom of Naples, notably Gaeta, and after the repudiation of the Treaty of Lyons, no immediate peace was in sight.[63] Fernando still expected that the French would strike at Roussillon, the Aragonese territory north of the Pyreness which had been a bone of contention between France and Spain throughout his life; he was soon to be proved correct in that expectation. It was impossible for Juana to travel alone across France when France was at war with Spain; for her to travel by sea, along the whole western and northern coast of France which she must pass in order to reach Flanders, entailed too great a risk of capture.

But Juana could no longer heed rational arguments. All her thoughts and emotions were fixed on Philip—an explosive mixture of love, fear, and hatred. She knew of his infidelities, knew that he could now carry them on unconstrained by her presence. In her more lucid moments she knew the truth of what she so passionately wished to deny, that his abandonment of her in Spain, in the face of her parents' pleas and her own, proved that he did not love her. She could only think that she must reach him, return to him regardless of the risks, so that she might try to win him back. It seemed to her that only her mother was restraining her. Her father in fact agreed completely with Isabel that Juana must for the time being be kept in Spain, but was not there to say so; he was in Aragon and Catalonia, preparing to fight for Roussillon. But her mother was constantly with her, at Alcalá de Henares, and it was upon Isabel that Juana poured out the vials of her frustrated, increasingly psychotic rage. As Peter Martyr explained, that rage did not often take the form of storming anger, but rather of bitter sarcasm, of cruel asides intended to cut and to hurt, to inflict some of her own suffering on her mother. At other times Juana would not speak at all, simply sitting in a black and frowning silence. She slept badly, ate little, and went on periodic hunger strikes.[64]

Mother and daughter had a particularly bad encounter June 19. Isabel went to Juana's room in the late afternoon and had a long talk with her. When

---

[62]*Ibid.*, XVII (2), 590-594.

[63]Peter Martyr de Anglería to the Archbishop of Granada and the Count of Tendilla, June 3, 1503 (Segovia), DIHE X, 54-56.

[64]Doctors Soto and Julian to Fernando, June 20, 1503 (Alcalá de Henares), in Rodríguez Villa, *Juana la Loca*, pp. 82-83; Miller, *Castles and the Crown*, pp. 219-220.

Isabel came out, her ladies were shocked and frightened by "the great change in her color and countenance." For four hours she was overcome by chills and fever, in great pain. By eleven o'clock the worst of the attack had passed, though her clothes were soaked with sweat; after midnight she was able to eat a little, and fell into a troubled sleep. Her doctors wrote to Fernando in Barcelona telling him that his wife's health required that she not spend nearly so much time with Juana. Still Isabel would not leave her daughter; when she did finally depart from Alcalá de Henares in mid-July, after a stay of six dreadful months, it appears she took Juana with her. We know they were together again by the beginning of August, when Isabel travelled north with Juana to Segovia, in an attempt to reassure her by bringing her slowly toward the French border that she would truly be allowed to go to Flanders once the war with France was over.[65]

The course of events in Italy had now taken a new turn which was to aid in bringing the Franco-Spanish war to an end. For many centuries the hot summer month of August was much the most unhealthy time of the year in Italy, when malaria was most widely prevalent. In August 1503 both Pope Alexander VI and his son Caesar fell ill with severe fever. The doctors knew nothing to do but the useless and dangerous bleeding; this and the fever together were more than the Pope's aging body (he was 73) could stand. On August 18 he died; Caesar rallied, but remained seriously ill for the rest of the month, during the critical days when the conclave was assembling to elect a new Pope. The Italian cardinals and the ambassadors of Germany, France, Spain, and Venice joined together to force Caesar to withdraw from Rome before the conclave actually began. On September 1 he was carried out of the city on a litter, and immediately joined the French. But it was very soon to be revealed how much his power had depended upon his dead father rather than upon him.[66]

The conclave convened September 16, with 37 cardinals in attendance, 22 of them Italian. It was deeply divided. A deadlock was averted only by electing Cardinal Francesco Piccolomini, a very sick man whom few expected to live long. In fact he died within a month, far too soon for him to make any policy changes. The war between Spain and France went forward; during September a new French army commanded by the Marquis of Mantua marched south from Rome, while another French army under the Marshal de Rieux invaded Roussillon, just as Fernando had been expecting, and laid siege to the fortress

---

[65]Doctors Soto and Julian to Fernando, June 20, 1503 (Alcalá de Henares), in Rodríguez Villa, *Juana la Loca*, p. 82; Rumeu de Armas, *Itinerario*, pp. 294-296; Menéndez Pidal, *Historia de España*, XVII (2), 628.

[66]Von Pastor, *History of the Popes*, VI, 132-136, 185-189. The lurid tales repeated then and since involving poisoning of Pope Alexander VI, or his having drunk poison intended for another, have no historical basis, as von Pastor demonstrates.

of Salses, defended by a small but resolute garrison which refused even to consider surrender.[67]

Fernando hurried north to Roussillon in mid-October, while Isabel, still at Segovia, busied herself at a familiar task, insuring that he and his army received a steady stream of supplies and reinforcements. By the end of the month he was victorious. The French attack had been in fact little more than a diversion. Their forces quickly withdrew before Fernando; Salses was relieved, and the brave garrison was greatly honored.[68] But the chronicler Santa Cruz tells us that Isabel was particularly unhappy with this war of Christians against Christians, and prayed constantly for its ending.[69] We may well believe that another reason for her prayers was so that it might be possible for Juana to return soon to Philip as she so desperately wanted to do, though Isabel could hardly have had much hope that this would help her deeply troubled daughter in the long run.

On November 1 the second conclave in two months elected the formidable Cardinal Giuliano della Rovere as Pope Julius II. The new Pope was known as an inveterate foe of the Borgias and was thought to be friendly toward the French, since he had worked with them against the Borgias. But in fact his overriding goal was to restore the genuine independence of the Papal states, which he set about doing at once. Before the month was over he had ordered Caesar Borgia's arrest, while making it clear to the French that he was not and never would be their puppet or anybody else's.[70] He was not unfriendly toward Spain, and on December 26 granted the dispensation permitting Prince Henry of England to marry Isabel's daughter Catherine despite the fact that she had been his brother's wife.[71] However, for reasons that have never been fully explained, that critical Papal dispensation was not immediately delivered.

The loss of French influence on the Papacy, the victories of Gonzalo de Córdoba, and the French repulse in Roussillon had enough impact on Louis XII to cause him to accept a five months' truce with Spain on November 15, mediated by his wife Anne of Brittany and Philip's sister Margaret, now Duchess of Savoy where Italy and France meet. (Margaret's influence was almost always exerted for the good even in the selfish turmoil of Renaissance politics. She was more than a little like the great woman who had been her

---

[67]*Ibid.*, VI, 192-206; Bernáldez, *Memorias*, p. 476 (ch. CXCVIII); Santa Cruz, *Crónica*, I, 293-294 (ch. LXX); Peter Martyr de Anglería to Cardinal of Santa Cruz, Oct. 14, 1503 (Segovia), DIHE X, 59-61; Menéndez Pidal, *Historia de España*, XVII (2), 599, 604.

[68]Bernáldez, *Memorias*, pp. 477-480 (ch. CXCVIII-CC); Santa Cruz, *Crónica*, I, 294-295 (ch. LXX); Rumeu de Armas, *Itinerario*, p. 298; Menéndez Pidal, *Historia de España*, XVII (2), 601.

[69]Santa Cruz, *Crónica*, I, 295 (ch. LXX).

[70]Von Pastor, *History of the Popes*, VI, 210-217, 236-239.

[71]Bergenroth, *Calendar of State Papers*, I, 322.

mother-in-law, and would have been an outstanding Queen of Spain.) The truce applied everywhere but to the bitterly contested territory of the kingdom of Naples, where the reinforced French and Spanish armies were confronting each other at the Garigliano River, resolved upon battle to see which was better. This was not, therefore, real peace; but to Juana the news of it (which was apparently sent before the truce was publicly announced) came like a rope thrown to a drowning woman. Almost at the same time that she had the news of the truce, a letter came from Philip asking her to rejoin him. To the best of our knowledge, it was the first and only letter Philip had written her since his cold departure in the face of her tears and lamentations eleven months before. Ablaze with passion and hope, Juana declared that she would leave at once to cross France to Flanders, where Philip was.[72]

Some time before—we do not know exactly when; it could have been at any time after mid-August—Isabel had finally separated from her daughter, who had taken up her residence at the castle of La Mota near Medina del Campo while Isabel remained in Segovia. So when this new crisis came, they were some fifty miles apart. Messengers quickly informed the Queen of her daughter's new resolve.[73]

Isabel could not let Juana go so quickly. A truce was not nearly as reliable as a peace; it could be broken at any time, as had often happened. Juana could be caught in France and imprisoned. It would probably be safe to send her to Flanders by sea during a period of truce, but the sea route from Spain to the Netherlands was very dangerous in winter, and no preparations for a voyage had been made.[74] In any case, Juana was not even thinking about going by sea; she was insisting on going by land, across France. At the very least, she must be properly accompanied and guarded. A Princess of Castile and the Netherlands could not simply set off across the chill countryside of northern Castile, heading for the lofty and snow-bound Pyrenees, without a substantial and well equipped escort.

In her younger days Isabel would have been on a horse at once, riding north. Indeed, the route from Segovia to Medina del Campo was almost exactly the same route that she had ridden like a Valkyrie in the opposite direction on that unforgettable day and night twenty-seven years before when the life of her first-born, Princess Isabel, hung in the balance in Segovia's Alcázar. But Isabel the Catholic was long past Valkyrie-rides now. Her doctors discouraged her from travelling at all, and at the pace she now had to move to avoid

---

[72]Bernáldez, *Memorias*, p. 481 (ch. CC); Santa Cruz, *Crónica*, I, 295 (ch. LXXX); Isabel to Gómez de Fuensalida (estimated date January 1504), *Correspondencia de Fuensalida*, p. 195; Menéndez Pidal, *Historia de España*, XVII (2), 601, 606, 628.
[73]Menéndez Pidal, *Historia de España*, XVII (2), 629.
[74]Isabel to Gómez de Fuensalida (estimated date January 1504), *Correspondencia de Fuensalida*, pp. 195-196.

endangering her health, the journey from Segovia to La Mota would take about five days—ten miles a day. What might Juana in her present mood do—where might she go—in five days? Isabel sent Bishop Fonseca of Córdoba to La Mota castle, with instructions to make every effort to persuade Juana to wait until proper plans could be made for a journey to Flanders by sea, probably in the following March. But Isabel knew only too well how little effect persuasion was now likely to have on Juana. Therefore she authorized Bishop Fonseca, if all else failed, to use force to prevent her departure.[75]

The Bishop arrived at La Mota on or about November 21. He found Juana on the point of leaving, though it is not clear if anyone at all was ready to accompany her; we do know that she had no horses. She would listen to no arguments, no alternative plans, no appeals for delay; she was going, she was going at once, and there was nothing more to be said about it. When the Bishop finally saw no choice but to tell her that she would not be allowed to go, she made a run for the gate. He ordered it shut in her face. The Princess of Castile was a prisoner by her mother's order.[76]

What followed was the stuff of nightmare. Juana raged; she screamed; she howled. She gripped and tried to shake the iron bars and the cold stone of the battlements of the fortress, and would not let go. Hour after hour, her face distorted and her knuckles white, she clung to them. Afternoon passed, and twilight. Night fell on the high plains of Castile, which in November become quite cold, and we are told that this night was unusually cold for the season. Still Juana would not move. Her skin blanched, her body shivered, but she did not seem to notice. Her attendants, the Bishop, and priests came to her, begging her at least to take shelter. She would not. The long, hellish night passed—how slowly, only those who were there could truly understand. When the sun rose at last over the far serrated horizon, Juana was still gripping the wall.[77]

Messengers galloped off to Segovia to give Isabel the appalling news. Perhaps even her transcendent courage faltered for a moment at the prospect of going herself to see her daughter on that castle wall. Perhaps she simply thought that she had lost all influence with Juana, that others might reach her where she could not. Whatever the reason, she sent Archbishop Cisneros and Admiral Fadrique Enríquez to La Mota while she remained at Segovia. Cisneros was the holiest man she knew, whose prayers she probably believed had the greatest power; the Admiral had always been a particular defender and partisan of Juana in a court where she was generally and often strongly disliked. The Archbishop and the Admiral came; they saw; they spoke with the madwoman; they departed, totally unable to reach her. All anyone had been

[75]Isabel to Fuensalida (estimated date January 1504), *ibid.*, p. 197.
[76]*Ibid.*
[77]*Ibid.*

able to accomplish with her since the nightmare began was to persuade her, when the second night came on, to leave the open wall and go to a kind of lean-to that the castle guard had set up against the wall, where they kept a fire going to boil water and do a little rough cooking. There she could find some warmth and shelter, but would still remain in contact with the wall she refused to leave. Word of all this came quickly to Isabel. Now she had no choice but to go to La Mota.[78]

On November 26 she set out. Sick in mind and heart and body, she nevertheless covered seventeen miles a day. She sent a messenger ahead to tell Juana she was coming. Juana replied that she wanted nothing to do with her. Isabel pressed on. Late in the afternoon of November 28 she arrived at the gate. The drawbridge dropped. The portcullis opened. Through the gate, toward the dirty guard's kitchen, came the Queen of Castile, Aragon, Sicily and the Indies, the most powerful woman and most successful ruler on the face of the globe in her time. She walked slowly now; her once strong athletic legs were swollen with the beginnings of the dropsy that was so greatly to afflict her in the coming year. Her beautiful red-gold hair now streaked with gray, her large blue-green eyes dimmed with tears, she entered the squat structure. Surely she was offering a prayer with every step she took. Her daughter looked up at her from where she crouched clinging to the stones of the wall, as she had clung for six full days and nights, and loosed upon her mother a torrent of obscene vituperation. "She spoke such words to me," Isabel said later in the saddest letter she ever wrote, to Juana's husband who had spurned her, "as no daughter should say to a mother, which I would never have endured if I had not seen the condition she was in."[79]

Yet once more, she endured. And when Juana's tigerish, insane fury was for the moment spent, Isabel the Catholic drew upon the deepest wells of strength in her own being, and in the Precious Blood of her Lord Who died upon a cross, and spoke to Juana as a mother to a child, a desperately sick child who even in delirium still knows her mother's voice. Her mother was calling her in, out of the cold and the dark. Juana got to her feet, stepped away from the wall, and went with her mother to her room.

"*Yo vine y la metí,*" Isabel said, in her letter to Philip. "I came and put her in."[80]

[78]*Ibid.*; Peter Martyr de Anglería to Cardinal of Santa Cruz, March 10, 1503, (Alcalá de Henares), DIHE X, 47-48.

[79]*Ibid.*; Isabel to Fuensalida (estimated date January 1504), *Correspondencia de Fuensalida*, pp. 195-196; Galíndez de Carvajal, "Anales breves," CODOIN XVIII, 308; Rumeu de Armas, *Itinerario*, pp. 299-300. Isabel's letter to Philip is not extant, but is extensively summarized and paraphrased in her letter to Fuensalida, probably written in January 1504, cited above.

[80]Isabel to Fuensalida (estimated date January 1504), *Correspondencia de Fuensalida*, p. 197.

The dreadful scene was over; but now there could be no reasonable doubt that Juana was insane. For several years her insanity would remain periodic, and no historian at this distance in time can always be sure when during these years she was sane and when she was not,[81] but it was clear that she could never provide stable government for Spain. Nor could Philip, for quite different reasons. Isabel and Fernando must skip a whole generation, and look to little Charles—soon to have his fourth birthday—for the rescue of their country. Charles must be brought to Spain if there was any possible way this could be done. The evidence is strong that this became the final objective of the foreign policy of Isabel and Fernando during the last year of Isabel's life. But in pursuit of that goal, Isabel in her physical decline was unable to do enough, and Fernando tried to do too much. Without her clear vision and firm moral direction, he tended to lose himself in the intricacies of his own diplomacy, mistaking means for ends.

A splendid opportunity was opened up for this new policy just a month after the baleful scene at La Mota, when Gonzalo de Córdoba, Isabel's peerless "Great Captain," won a decisive battle on the Garigliano River, thereby securing Spanish control of the kingdom of Naples. (Just three days after the battle the French agreed to abandon both unconquered Gaeta, and Naples.) There was now no point in nor good prospect for France continuing the war with Spain in southern Italy or renewing it elsewhere. On January 30, 1504 the two kingdoms agreed to a three years' truce, a much more durable arrangement than the previous truce of five months, this one including Naples as its predecessor had not. Meanwhile Isabel and Fernando had written to Ambassador Fuensalida in Brussels telling him to propose to Philip a revision of the Treaty of Lyons which he had negotiated and they had rejected the previous year, providing for the eventual marriage of his son Charles and Princess Claudia of France, with the title of King and Queen of Naples, and Philip to act as regent during their minority, with the promise of the full revenues of the kingdom. But there were two essential conditions: that Philip guarantee the government of Naples by Spanish officials, and that his son Charles should come to Spain soon for an extended stay. After only a brief hesitation, Philip accepted. He would send Prince Charles to Spain with 100,000 ducats to maintain his household, on the sole additional condition that his other son

---

[81]Unfortunately a great many have tried to make these determinations, or to deny that Juana could rightly be described as insane from the time of the confrontation with Isabel at La Mota. But periodic insanity is actually more common than permanent insanity; and Juana's behavior in November 1503 renders untenable any and all of the theories that her insanity was (at least for some time) faked by others or that she was somehow driven into insanity later by her father and her son. It is impossible realistically to imagine any sane person doing what Juana did during those six days at the La Mota castle gate.

Fernando, born in Spain the year before, be sent to the Netherlands.[82]

On March 1 Juana finally departed for Flanders, travelling overland to the port of Laredo, from which, eight years ago in what must have seemed to her a different world, she had left her native land to go to the Netherlands and marry Philip.[83] During the intervening winter months Isabel had written to Philip and to her ambassador Fuensalida about what had happened at La Mota (her letters are our principal sources for those tragic events) explaining that she had concluded that despite all that had happened, Juana should be with her husband since this was her overwhelming desire. However, Juana clearly needed men and women of authority and good presence of mind around her to calm and restrain her, since otherwise her passions could "cause damage and dishonor to her person." Isabel sent two such persons, Monsieur de Melun and Madame de Aloyn, with her daughter.[84] Philip seemed genuinely concerned, having written Isabel in February that he wished he had not left Castile as he did, thanking her for all she had done and regretting the pain it must have caused her, and accepting her recommendations for the care of Juana.[85] But by now Isabel surely knew Philip too well to take much comfort in this. Even if he truly felt these sentiments as he was writing them, he was too shallow and inconstant to be likely to keep to them. When Juana got in his way he would probably thrust her aside again. Madness in the marriage partner is the greatest burden a spouse is ever called upon to bear; few men of his status can ever have been less fit to bear it than Philip the Handsome.

Yet still, in the relative calm that followed the storm of those November days at the La Mota castle wall, with Juana returning to her husband and at least a chance—however slight—that they might find some way of living together, and the good news from Italy and the peace with France and what seemed good reason to hope that her grandson would soon come to Spain, Isabel had a last opportunity to carry on the work of governing and improving Spain as well as discharging the duties of a mother and trying to secure the future of her country. Even during the agony with Juana, she had kept herself informed on the progress of the reform of the Church, making sure that the officious and unsympathetic Gil Delfino, superior-general of the Franciscans,

---

[82]Bernáldez, *Memorias*, pp. 448-451 (ch. CXC); Isabel and Fernando to Gómez de Fuensalida, Jan. 1, 1504 (Medina del Campo) and Fuensalida to Isabel and Fernando, Feb. 5, 1504 (Mons, Hainaut), *Correspondencia de Fuensalida*, pp. 198-199, 204-210; Menéndez Pidal, *Historia de España*, XVII (2), 608-609, 611, 630.

[83]Isabel and Fernando to Gómez de Fuensalida, March 8, 1504 (Medina del Campo), *Correspondencia de Fuensalida*, pp. 212-215; Santa Cruz, *Crónica*, I, 301 (ch. LXXII).

[84]Isabel to Gómez de Fuensalida (estimated date January 1504), *Correspondencia de Fuensalida*, pp. 197-198.

[85]Philip to Isabel, Feb. 10, 1504 (Mons, Hainaut), *ibid.*, pp. 209-210.

did not interfere with it.[86] In a series of letters in January 1504 she ordered the abbesses of Santa Cruz and Santa Inés of Córdoba to submit to the authority of the reforming friar Juan de Quevedo. In February she wrote approvingly to Marcial Boulier, Ultramontane Vicar-General, praising his devotion to reform, and with Fernando she called upon the royal officials at Burgos to support the vicar-provincial of the Trinitarians in reforming the monasteries of that order in the Burgos area.[87] In this vital area her clarity of thought and vigilance were unimpaired; so the great reform, with Cisneros its executor under the Catholic sovereigns, swept onward, cleansing the church in Spain of the evils whose accumulation elsewhere, especially in the Papacy and in Germany, were to bring about the Protestant uprising just thirteen years later—that devastating revolt from which Isabel's and Cisneros' reform spared Spain.

In March, while Juana was at sea, Isabel and Fernando wrote to Philip reminding him of how much they wanted him to send Prince Charles to them soon, asking for a specific date by which they could expect Charles, and expressing pleasure at Philip's February letters and the love and concern they displayed. Isabel told him that she had accompanied Juana on the road for some distance when she departed from Medina del Campo on March 1, and that Juana went to him with her mother's "best blessing." She probably arrived during April, since on May 10 her parents still had no news of her arrival. All was well at least until June 4, when Ambassador Fuensalida wrote that Juana was in good condition and taking great pleasure in Philip and her children.[88]

But it was only a temporary remission of suffering. For some obscure reason Fernando, or one of his diplomats in France, raised the prospect in April that Spain might after all once again recognize the claims of the Spanish dynasty in Naples that would otherwise be repudiated by the proposed treaty assigning that kingdom to Charles and Claudia, with Philip as regent. It was even suggested that Fadrique, the former Neapolitan king now captive in France, be married to Fernando's niece. Word of this strange initiative reached Philip's ears. He became angry, charging Isabel and Fernando with double-dealing. They assured him the proposal was not intended seriously, but it is very hard to understand why it was made at all (as Ambassador Fuensalida rather sharply

[86]Isabel to Gil Delfini, Nov. 6, 1503 (Segovia), in José Garcia Oro, *La Reforma de los Religiosos españoles en tiempo de los Reyes Católicos* (Valladolid, 1969), p. 509.

[87]Isabel to the abbesses of Santa Cruz and Santa Inés in Cordoba, Jan. 11, 1504 (Medina del Campo); Isabel to Fray Juan de Quevedo, Jan. 11, 1504 (Medina del Campo); Isabel and Fernando to their officials in Córdoba, Jan. 27, 1504 (Medina del Campo); Isabel to Marcial Boulier, Feb. 27, 1504 (Medina del Campo); Isabel and Fernando to their officials in Burgos, Feb. 29, 1504 (Medina del Campo), in *ibid.*, pp. 206-207, 513-518.

[88]Isabel and Fernando to Gómez de Fuensalida, March 8 and 26, 1504 and May 10, 1504 (Medina del Campo); Fuensalida to Isabel and Fernando, June 4, 1504 (Brussels), *Correspondencia de Fuensalida*, pp. 212-215, 218-219, 238, 247-248.

pointed out to his master and mistress). Before realizing that this problem had arisen, Isabel and Fernando wrote April 20 again calling for prompt agreement on the time and manner of Charles' coming to Spain, and expressing the hope that little Prince Fernando might stay with them until, or even after Charles' arrival. Now increasingly suspicious, Philip by May 15 had taken alarm at the implication that Charles was to come to Spain before he was formally invested with the kingdom of Naples, with Philip as regent, not afterward as Philip said he had expected. He accused Isabel and Fernando of trying to get possession of both his sons and give him nothing in return.[89]

Before this disturbing news reached them, Isabel and Fernando had left Medina del Campo to spend nearly a month in La Mejorada monastery. So long a stay—longer than they normally spent even at their beloved Guadalupe shrine—suggests some kind of religious retreat, a quest for relief and renewal away from the overwhelming duties they struggled to bear. It may explain the otherwise puzzling long delay in their response to Ambassador Fuensalida's exceedingly important letter of May 15, which they did not answer until July 6. The answer was full of reassurances, excellent arguments, and reasonable proposals for Philip: they intended no change in the arrangements for Naples they had originally offered to him; they could not turn Naples over to him now because the Pope, by long-standing practice, must first invest any occupant of the Neapolitan throne; they were willing to have oaths of loyalty to Philip sworn in Naples immediately, in return for a written guarantee that Charles would arrive in Spain within forty days after they were sworn; Philip should understand that the French were using these fears and red herrings to try to draw him away from them.[90]

But it was all too late. The last chance for reconciliation, for honest and open cooperation with Philip, for sending Charles to Spain, had vanished with the last lingering hope that Juana might be able to live a mostly normal life. In early June, while Isabel and Fernando were staying at the La Mejorada monastery, Juana's madness, fed by her devouring jealousy, broke out again. Philip was flaunting his favorite mistress at court, a girl with long red hair to whom he had become much attached during his long separation from his wife. One day at court Juana flung herself upon this girl "like a fiery serpent," shouting and screaming and grinding her teeth, raining blows upon her, and ordering one of her terrified servants to cut off the girl's hair down to the scalp with scissors. When Philip protested, she flared out against him, heaping him with abuse, which he returned in kind, finally dragging her away. He may have

---

[89]Gómez de Fuensalida to Isabel and Fernando, April 10, 1504 (Ghent); Isabel and Fernando to Fuensalida, April 20, 1504 (Medina del Campo); Fuensalida to Isabel and Fernando, May 15, 1504 (Bruges), *ibid.*, pp. 220-224, 227-229, 238-242.

[90]Isabel and Fernando to Gómez de Fuensalida, July 6, 1504 (Medina del Campo), *ibid.*, pp. 251-256; Rumeu de Armas, *Itinerario*, pp. 305-306.

beaten her, though the chronicler Santa Cruz says only "they even say he put his hands on her." He told her he would never have her with him again. Juana was put to bed, raving, out of her mind.[91]

The report of Juana's latest outbreak came to Isabel and Fernando shortly after they wrote their two letters to Ambassador Fuensalida on July 6, full of calm and reasonable suggestions on how to regain Philip's confidence in their plans for disposing of the Kingdom of Naples. After the terrible scene at La Mota castle the preceding November, this news should not have truly surprised them. But they must have let themselves hope too much that all might yet be well, or at least manageable, once Juana had fulfilled her passionate desire to return to her husband. Peter Martyr tells us in a letter of July 19 that the news prostrated both Isabel and Fernando. Both of them came down almost at once with severe fevers. The doctors told them they must stay apart from each other, which proved as great or greater a trial for them than the illnesses. Each worried constantly about the other, hesitating to believe the doctors' reports and reassurances.[92]

But, as the doctors were telling Isabel, Fernando was rallying. By August 17 he wrote Gonzalo de Córdoba that he was entirely recovered.[93] On August 25 Fernando and Isabel sent their first letter to Fuensalida in direct response to the news of Juana's outbreak of madness in June:

> What is said of the discord and loss of love between the Prince and the Princess grieves us much; we still try to encourage more accord. Try to restore love between them as best you can.[94]

It sounds a sad, almost resigned note. They knew now that in all probability there could never be peace and joy for Juana in this world, nor harmony and trust between her and Philip. They were not yet completely certain that she could not rule at all; but clearly either Philip would rule alone, or there would be almost constant strife between him and Juana.

---

[91]Santa Cruz, *Crónica*, I, 301-302 (ch. LXXII); Peter Martyr de Anglería to the Archbishop of Granada and the Count of Tendilla, June 26, 1504 (Medina del Campo), DIHE X, 83-84. There has been considerable confusion about the date of this famous catastrophe in Juana's life, but it clearly must fall between Fuensalida's letter of June 4 saying she is well and finding great pleasure in Philip and the children, and Peter Martyr's letter of June 26 reporting the event, news of which had by then reached Spain. Since the transmission of news from Flanders to Spain normally took at least two weeks, the assault on Philip's mistress must have happened a very few days after June 4.

[92]Peter Martyr de Anglería to the Archbishop of Granada and the Count of Tendilla, July 19, 1504 (Medina del Campo), DIHE X, 84-85; Santa Cruz, *Crónica*, I, 302 (ch. LXXII).

[93]Menéndez Pidal, *Historia de España*, XVII (2), 633.

[94]Isabel and Fernando to Gómez de Fuensalida, August 25, 1504 (Medina del Campo), *Correspondencia de Fuensalida*, p. 267.

They could take some comfort in the tranquil life of Queen Maria of Portugal, the only one of their children to be spared tragedy; and in the continued good progress of the negotiations for the future remarriage of their daughter Catherine to Prince Henry of England, when he was of age. The dispensation from Pope Julius II permitting Henry to marry his brother's widow had been sent to England and Spain, and would be publicly proclaimed November 1. But Catherine was unhappy; she had lost her color and her appetite, and had fallen ill. She had learned from Juana (of all people) that her mother was unwell, but had few details, and no word directly from her mother or her father. On the very day of Isabel's death Catherine was writing piteously to Fernando that she had heard nothing from him for an entire year, and to Isabel that she could not feel "satisfied or cheerful" until she had a letter from her; she said she had "no other hope or comfort than that which comes from knowing that her mother and father are well." It is very hard to believe that neither Isabel nor Fernando would have written to their daughter in England for an entire year, but quite possible that their letters were being intercepted or delayed in the coils of intrigue that wound through the English court and, unfortunately, among the several Spanish ambassadors as well—notably Dr. de Puebla, who had been in London far too long, more than sixteen years, and was bitterly resentful of the ambassadors more recently sent.[95]

The situation in Italy was deteriorating fast. The French were concentrating troops at Milan; Pisa raised the banner of revolt and called for French assistance against Florence; Fernando ordered Gonzalo de Córdoba to be ready for a renewal of the war at any moment and now began to take active steps toward the restoration of Fadrique, former king of Naples, to his abandoned crown. Philip, seeing all his earlier suspicions confirmed, joined with his father Emperor Maximilian to make a treaty with France, proclaimed at Blois September 22, by which Maximilian and Louis XII would join in an attack on Naples, Philip's son Charles would later marry Princess Claudia of France and inherit Milan and Brittany if Louis XII died without a son, and France and the Empire would ally with Pope Julius II for an attack upon Venice. Spain was left entirely out of this treaty, both in its negotiation and in its terms, though Spain was offered admittance to the alliance created by the treaty within the ensuing four months. Since Spain was not a party to the treaty as originally proclaimed and Philip was now openly hostile, no mention was made of sending Prince Charles to Spain.[96]

---

[95]Duke Fernando of Estrada to Isabel, August 10, 1504 (London); Catherine to King Fernando, November 26, 1504 (Westminster); Catherine to Isabel, November 26, 1504 (Westminster), in Bergenroth, *Calendar of State Papers*, I, 329-330, 340. The earliest letter to or from Dr. de Puebla as Spanish ambassador to England, found and published by Bergenroth, dates from 1488.

[96]Fernando and Isabel to Gómez de Fuensalida, September 10, 1504 (Medina del

It was the greatest diplomatic defeat Spain suffered in Isabel's and Fernando's reign; but Fernando was saved from the consequences that would have resulted from it by discord among the allies, the perfidy of Louis XII, and the awesome military reputation of Gonzalo de Córdoba (Louis felt free to dispose of territory controlled by Gonzalo only on paper at a very safe distance).[97]

By mid-August Fernando had recovered from the fevers and general illness that forced him to his bed the previous month; but Isabel, who had fallen ill at the same time as he, was not improving. Her temperature rose higher in her bouts of fever, so that occasionally she fell into delirium; her veins were disintegrating, so that her circulation was seriously impaired; her legs swelled with dropsy, and she suffered unquenchable thirst. She was almost constantly nauseated and could eat very little. Slowly but steadily her physical strength declined.[98]

Still duty abided; Isabel continued to do all that she could, and probably more than she should have done, to fulfill her duty. All the state letters going out from Medina del Campo, where she lay, during August and the first half of September of 1504 still bore her name as well as Fernando's. There were occasional remissions in the inexorable advance of her diseases. But by the end of September it was clear to the doctors, to her husband, and to those closest to her that she was probably dying. Fernando admitted as much in a letter to Ambassador Fuensalida September 26 which he alone signed. "My most dear and best loved wife," he said, is very ill. Though she has recently shown some improvement, the periodic fevers continue, and he fears much for her. Philip and Juana should be prepared for her death and to assume the succession. It would be better for them to come to Spain by sea rather than by land across hostile France. He promises to keep the kingdom in good order until their arrival.[99]

Many prayers were offered for Isabel's life. At some time during October she was anointed, receiving the sacrament "with great contrition and many

---

Campo); Fuensalida to Fernando and Isabel, September 19, 1504 (Bolduque), *Correspondencia de Fuensalida*, pp. 273-282; Menéndez Pidal, *Historia de España*, XVII (2), 635-636; von Pastor, *History of the Popes*, VI, 257.

[97]Von Pastor, *History of the Popes*, VI, 257-258; *The Cambridge Modern History*, ed. A. W. Ward, G. W. Prothero and Stanley Leathes, Volume I: "The Renaissance," (New York, 1902), pp. 127-128.

[98]Santa Cruz, *Crónica*, I, 302 (ch. LXXII); Peter Martyr de Anglería to the Archbishop of Granada and the Count of Tendilla, Oct. 3, 1504 (Medina del Campo), DIHE X, 85-86.

[99]Fernando to Gómez de Fuensalida, September 26, 1504 (Medina del Campo), *Correspondencia de Fuensalida*, pp. 286-287; Peter Martyr de Anglería to the Archbishop of Granada and the Count of Tendilla, Oct. 3, 1504 (Medina del Campo), DIHE X, 85-86.

tears, humbling asking God to pardon her sins."[100] She made her will, which is dated October 12. The will of Isabel the Catholic is a comprehensive, carefully considered, and highly significant document throughout; but the heart of her life, her reign, and her will is in its ringing opening, its confession of faith, and its humble submission to Divine judgment:

> In the name of God the omnipotent, Father and Son and Holy Spirit, three persons in one divine essence, creator and governor of the universe, of Heaven and Earth and all things visible and invisible, and of the glorious Virgin Mary his mother, Queen of Heaven and of the Angels, our Lady and advocate, and of the most excellent Prince of the Church and of the Angelic Knighthood Saint Michael, and of the glorious heavenly messenger the Archangel Saint Gabriel, and in honor of all the holy men and women of the Court of Heaven, most especially the most holy precursor and herald of Our Savior Jesus Christ St. John the Baptist, and of the most blessed Princes of the Apostles Saint Peter and Saint Paul and all the other apostles most notably Saint John the Evangelist, the beloved disciple of Our Lord Jesus Christ, the eagle, to whom He revealed the most high mysteries and secrets, and gave as special son to His most glorious mother at the time of His holy Passion, entrusting most rightly the Virgin to him most chaste, taking this holy apostle and evangelist as my special advocate in this life and as I await the hour of my death and the most terrible Judgment, most terrible against the powerful, when my soul shall be presented before the royal throne of the Sovereign Judge, most just and most even-handed, who will judge us all according to our merits, at one with his most blessed and worthy brother the Apostle St. James, singular and excellent father and patron of my kingdoms, most marvellously and mercifully given to us by Our Lord as special guardian and protector . . . being infirm in body with the illness God has chosen to send me, but free and sound in mind, believing and confessing firmly all that the Holy Catholic Church of Rome holds, believes, confesses and teaches . . . in which Faith and for which Faith I am prepared to die . . . I ordain this my last will and testament . . .
>
> First of all, I commend my spirit into the hands of Our Lord Jesus Christ, the Uncreated, redeemed by His Most Precious Blood, Who put me by means of the Cross in the hands of His Eternal Father, Whom I confess, and recognizing that I owe to Him all the great and immense benefits I have received which He has given to all mankind, and to me as one small person of His, unworthy and sinful, from His infinite goodness and ineffable generosity in many ways at all times, which I have not tongue to recount nor strength to thank Him for, not even as the least of them deserve; but I pray that His infinite mercy may wish to hear this my confession of them.[101]

She directed that her body be buried in the sepulcher of the Franciscan monastery in the Alhambra at Granada, clothed in the Franciscan habit, but with the proviso that if Fernando should choose to be buried elsewhere, that

---

[100]Santa Cruz, *Crónica*, p. 303 (ch. LXXII).
[101]Isabel the Catholic, *Testamento y codicilo* (Madrid, 1956), pp. 13-16.

her body be brought to lie beside him. If for any reason her body could not be buried in Granada, she directed that it be buried in the Church of San Juan de los Reyes which she had built in Toledo; and if that were impossible, in the monastery of St. Anthony in Segovia—the city where she had lived in her youth, and been crowned. She made special provision for the permanence of her grants to her childhood friend Beatriz de Bobadilla and her husband, and a number of other property dispositions of particular importance. Once again she formally designated Juana her heir; but that section of her Testament was followed immediately by a long prohibition against her successors granting governmental and ecclesiastical offices in Spain to foreigners (which clearly she felt might be done in Juana's name). Isabel went on to say that if Juana were not in Spain when she died (as evidently she was most unlikely to be), or if "she does not wish to, or is unable to exercise authority in the governance of these kingdoms," that Fernando should govern and maintain the realm until her grandson Prince Charles reached the age of majority, which she specified as twenty. She further charged her daughter and son-in-law to be obedient and respectful to Fernando and to work closely with him for the peace and good order of Spain, and above all to live in harmony with each other.[102]

She must have known how remote were the prospects that these charges of hers regarding Juana and Philip would be, or even could be heeded. But she had to try; she had to say it; duty required it. Now she had done her duty, and she was ready to die, whenever God called her. But Isabel the Catholic was a strong woman, strong in heart and body as well as in mind and soul; nothing in her would yield or weaken before impending death until her time had come. She lived a full six weeks after signing her will October 12. No one had expected her to live that much longer. During that time she reviewed her will in her mind, and the history of her reign—what she had done, and what she should have done that she might have failed to do. There was even a faint possibility that she might, after all, have recovered. The will to live of an exceptionally strong man or woman has often confounded the best predictions of doctors.

But by November 19 Peter Martyr wrote that all possible hope had gone.[103] It may not be only coincidental that it was probably on that day that Isabel and Fernando received another shattering letter from Brussels, written there by Ambassador Fuensalida on November 1.

During the months since she assaulted Philip's mistress, was confined by him, and descended temporarily into total madness, Juana had recovered the appearance of sanity. Despite his vow at the time of this outbreak to stay away from her, Philip apparently had begun to see her again at least occasionally. But she spent much of her time with Moorish slaves from Spain, who were

---

[102]*Ibid.*, pp. 17-18, 22-41.
[103]Peter Martyr de Anglería to the Archbishop of Granada and the Count of Tendilla, Nov. 19, 1504 (Medina del Campo), DIHE X, 88-89.

constantly giving her baths and washing her hair. Both Philip and her doctors objected to this, and eventually he ordered the slaves out, declaring that they would be replaced by Flemish ladies. But Juana would not let the slaves go. When Philip returned from Holland she tried to confront him, but he evaded her and went to his room; she followed him there, a furious argument ensued, and he dismissed her and stayed away from her for almost a week. Then they met again and had several more arguments, until Philip finally locked her in her room, located directly above his. All through the night Juana hammered on the floor, first with a board, then with a rock, and finally with a knife, shouting wildly: "Lord, speak to me, I want to know if you are there!" The next day she threatened a hunger strike and demanded to be let out, saying she would die before she ever again did anything he wanted. He released her, but went away with the renewed intention of never seeing her again.[104]

It was Fernando alone who answered Fuensalida, on November 20. Isabel was now beyond writing letters, though Fernando's letter indicates that he told her the contents of Fuensalida's letter of November 1, and the tone of parts of the reply has in it much of Isabel. The reply speaks of Isabel's and Fernando's deep grief for the condition of their daughter. It condemns Philip in the harshest terms of any letter written during Isabel's life-time (this part sounds more like Fernando on his own), excoriating him for dealing behind their back with France and for joining the Treaty of Blois. It calls on him to treat Juana kindly and gently and not to beat her, even if she "knows not what she does," because treating her harshly will only make her sickness worse. Philip should let her have Spanish servants instead of Flemish, even if not the objectionable Moorish slaves. Recognizing that especially under these circumstances Philip would be tempted to come to Spain without his wife to take the crown following Isabel's death, Fernando instructs Fuensalida to "say plainly" to Philip that if Isabel dies, Juana must come with him to be crowned, for without her no one in Spain would accept him.[105]

Meanwhile Isabel's meditations on her reign and her responsibilities were about to bear one last fruit in a long codicil which she added to her will November 23. In addition to further provisions for particular people and places, the codicil called for a thorough review of the manner in which funds assigned by the Church for the conduct of war against the Moors in Spain and in North Africa were being spent, to make sure that none were being diverted to other purposes; for an examination into the legality of a widely used tax called the *alcabala* to see if in fact it had been intended to be perpetual when imposed by the kings who preceded her; for a much more thorough codification of

---

[104]Gómez de Fuensalida to Isabel and Fernando, Nov. 1, 1504 (Brussels), *Correspondencia de Fuensalida*, pp. 297-301.

[105]Fernando to Gómez de Fuensalida, Nov. 20, 1504 (Medina del Campo), *ibid.*, pp. 309-310.

Spanish law than had ever been accomplished before; and—most significantly—charging Fernando, Juana, and Philip to make a special effort to protect the natives of the newly discovered lands across the Atlantic from injury and harm inflicted by their Spanish subjects, and to bring the Indians to the Faith by actively supporting missionary work among them.[106]

When the codicil was drafted and ready, Isabel was just able to scratch the famous, oft-made signature, *Yo la Reina* ("I the Queen") at the end of it. The tremulous, spidery, barely legible letters reveal the extremity of her physical weakness.[107] But her mind and spirit were still strong, steady and luminous as they moved through her last few days and nights upon earth toward the golden door at the end of the trail for one who knew and had served her Lord and Savior so well, and loved Him with all her heart.

Isabel the Catholic died in a simple building overlooking the main plaza of Medina del Campo, a little after the noon Angelus hour, November 26, 1504, with her beloved husband Fernando and her lifelong friend Beatriz de Bobadilla at her bedside.[108] She died at peace with God and man, aware that there were great stresses and dangers ahead, but knowing she had done her duty as best she could. She had done it far better than her humility would ever permit her to know on this earth.

The tributes that followed rained down glory upon her earthly remnant and her triumphant soul. We shall look at four of them. First, her husband's, on the day she died:

> Today, upon this date, it has pleased Our Lord to bring to Himself the most serene Queen Lady Isabel, my most dear and most beloved wife. Although her death is for me a greater hardship than any that could have come to me in my life—part of this grief which pierces my heart is for what I have lost in losing her, and part for what all these kingdoms have lost—yet since she died as holy and as Catholic as she lived, we may hope that Our Lord took her into glory, to a better and more lasting kingdom than what she had here.[109]

Then from Peter Martyr, her devoted and profoundly admiring counsellor, ambassador, and advocate, writing to her former confessor the Archbishop of Granada, and to his good friend the Count of Tendilla:

> My right hand droops for sorrow. . . . The Queen has breathed out her great and illustrious soul, excelling in brilliant achievements. Earth has

---

[106]Isabel the Catholic, *Testamento y codicilo*, pp. 64-68.

[107]William H. Prescott, *History of the Reign of Ferdinand and Isabella the Catholic*, ed. John F. Kirk (Philadelphia, 1872), III, 182.

[108]Chronicle of Valladolid, CODOIN XIII, 219; Galíndez de Carvajal, "Anales Breves," CODOIN XVIII, 309; Miller, *Castles and the Crown*, p. 233.

[109]Fernando to the Constable of Castile, Nov. 26, 1504 (Medina del Campo), in Rodríguez Valencia, *Isabel en la Opinion*, I, 7.

lost its most precious adornment. Never was it known before now, never was it read and recorded, that God and nature formed a person worthy to be compared with her in the feminine sex or in the ability to lead. . . . None could fail to know, during the life of this Queen, her courage in her undertakings, her constancy in struggle. . . . Her tenacity in rooting out vice, in promoting virtue, is better known to you, who participated in her work, than to me or to others. With but one exception, among the women whom by decree of the Supreme Pontiff our religion venerates in the catalogue of the saints, which one showed a more fervent veneration of piety, purity, and honesty? Not only was she an example to all women of chastity during her life, she could rightly and reasonably be called Chastity herself. After the Immaculate Virgin Mother of God—for whom it appears this prophecy was made—it could be applied to her as well: "For the Lord has created a new thing on the earth: a woman protects a man." [Jeremiah 31:22] Under feminine cover, that is, under the body of a woman, dwelt a strong and bold spirit. Meditating upon all this, we cannot fail to mourn, beginning with ourselves, continuing with all the inhabitants of these kingdoms, and ending with all Christendom, the loss of this mirror of virtue, refuge of the good, scourge of the evils that through so many years assaulted Spain. Those, like us, who knew her spirit, her words, and her actions, must rejoice. We may be sure that her soul, called to the highest heaven, transformed to the new order of celestial spirits, sits in close proximity to the Most High.[110]

Third, the near-contemporary historian Alonso de Santa Cruz, who was too young at the time of her death to have known her personally, but knew many who had known her:

She was most chaste and filled with a complete honesty, well collected in her words and never showing immodesty. Never was she seen discomposed in person, never were her works badly done, never were her words ill said. From this we must believe that her thoughts were holy and just.

She was a faithful friend, subject and very loving to her husband, favoring women well married and the enemy of those who were not. [She was] Catholic and most Christian, most faithful to God, a most merciful mother to her subjects and a most just queen to her vassals. She was given to contemplation, occupying herself continually with the Divine Office. She was very devout, and had great charity for all religious.[111]

While Isabel was enduring the four months of her mortal illness, the greatest of all her subjects, the discoverer of half the world, the man who had given her country the material key to predominant national power for the next 150 years, was wending his weary way back home from his anticlimactic fourth voyage. On August 13, 1504 he had finally reached Santo Domingo after losing

---

[110]Peter Martyr de Anglería to the Archbishop of Granada and the Count of Tendilla (dated Nov. 22, 1504 from Medina del Campo, but the date must be in error by at least four days, since we know that Isabel died on November 26), DIHE X, 90-91.

[111]Santa Cruz, *Crónica*, I, 304-305 (ch. LXXIII).

his ships and being abandoned on Jamaica for nearly an entire year. On September 4 a journeyman publicist, sometime seaman, and very amateurish Italian navigator named Amerigo Vespucci wrote a mendacious letter, later published, in which he claimed to have sailed on the first voyage to discover a continental mainland in the Indies. What Vespucci had actually done was to sail with a murderous pirate named Alonso de Ojeda who followed Columbus' track to the Venezuelan coast in 1499, the year after Columbus discovered that coast, looking for pearls; and to sail again two years later with the Portuguese captain Gonçalo Coelho to collect logwood on the coast of Brazil. But by predating his first voyage to 1497, writing a vivid though largely imaginary account of it, and making himself its hero, Vespucci convinced enough European scholars and writers of the truth of his claims to have the new continent named for him.[112]

On September 12 Columbus sailed for Spain from Santo Domingo. The voyage was troubled and slow; in October the ship in which he was travelling (he was now merely a passenger, not the captain) lost its mainmast. On November 7, nearly two months after his departure from Hispaniola, he arrived at Sanlúcar at the mouth of the Guadalquivir River, and made his way upriver to Sevilla. His letters to the dying queen went unanswered. Crippled by arthritis and gout, he was unable to set out on the long overland journey to Medina del Campo far to the north. The news of Isabel's death, when it came to him, meant the death of all his remaining hopes, the end of his career; for he had no other real friend at court.[113]

But he thought first, not of himself, but of her. On December 3 he wrote his son Diego about her. If Isabel knew what was being said of her in these first days after she left Earth, of all the tributes after her husband's it might have been these words from Christopher Columbus that would have pleased her most:

> The most important thing is to commend lovingly and with much devotion the soul of the Queen our lady, to God. Her life was always Catholic and holy, and prompt in all things in His holy service. Because of this we should believe that she is in holy glory, and beyond the cares of this harsh and weary world.[114]

---

[112]Morison, *Admiral of the Ocean Sea*, p. 658; Samuel Eliot Morison, *The European Discovery of America: the Southern Voyages* (New York, 1974), pp. 276-297.

[113]Morison, *Admiral of the Ocean Sea*, pp. 658-660.

[114]Columbus to his son Diego, Dec. 3, 1504 (Sevilla), in Rodríguez Valencia, *Isabel en la Opinion*, I, 254.

12
Achievement and Sanctity

Fernando reigned a little more than eleven years after the death of his glorious queen. They were strange years, for him and for Spain—shifting, troubled, confused, during which no man, including the King, could be quite sure where his true loyalty lay, nor who his rightful Queen might be and what he owed her.[1] Through the ebb and flow, the storm and the darkness, one figure stood like a rock: Francisco Ximénes de Cisneros, Archbishop of Toledo, primate of Spain, regent of Castile in Fernando's absence. More even than Fernando, who had lost so much when he lost Isabel, the hawk-faced ascetic whom Isabel had chosen for the highest office in the Church in Spain brought all of them through to the beginning of a new era, when Isabel's grandson Charles ruled Spain and became the Holy Roman Emperor. Isabel might well have been disappointed in Fernando; she would have felt vindicated in, and humbly grateful to Cisneros. In the end, what she had built survived every peril, to become the supreme bulwark of the Catholic Church and of Christendom in the sixteenth century.

Upon Isabel's death, Fernando at once proclaimed Juana Queen of Castile, with himself as governor of that realm in her absence, as Isabel's testament had provided. (He, of course, remained as lawful King of Aragon.) Many advised him not to proclaim Juana Queen, in view of all that was known or suspected about her condition; but he did it anyway. No plausible explanation for this action in terms of Machiavellian politics is possible; he can

---

[1]The ensuing summary of events during the remaining years of Fernando's reign after Isabel's death (November 1504 to January 1516) is based primarily upon the excellent and well documented account of Manuel Fernández Alvarez in Ramon Menéndez Pidal, director, *Historia de España*, Volume XVII: "España de los Reyes Catolicos" (Madrid, 1969), Part 2, pp. 645-729. No adequate coverage of this period has appeared in English since William H. Prescott's 150-year old *History of the Reign of Ferdinand and Isabella the Catholic* (Philadelphia, 1872; originally published in 1837), III, 210-423. Roger B. Merriman's *The Rise of the Spanish Empire in the Old World and in the New* (New York, 1918), II, 318-350 is very brief and sketchy, and Townsend Miller, *The Castles and the Crown; Spain 1451-1555* (New York, 1963), pp. 235-302, for all the extraordinary brilliance and beauty of its prose, is increasingly affected by a highly unrealistic view of Juana's psychological condition. Despite Miller's protests, the evidence is overwhelming that she was in a psychotic condition for much, though not all of the time after her mother's death.

only have done it out of respect for Isabel's memory and the explicit language of her testament, and for the love that he had borne her.

But politics, driven by so many human needs and aspirations and demands, changes so rapidly that even the most brilliant mind can never forecast it in detail nor take account of all eventualities, even of the near future, in a testamentary document. That is especially true where the mind of one of the persons most centrally involved is losing or has lost its sanity. Isabel's testament had appointed her husband administrator and, in effect, regent in the absence of her disturbed daughter, or in case of her daughter's incapacity. Absence was clear enough. But Isabel could not specify, and was wise enough not to try to specify, just how incapacity would be determined.

Fernando's rule was quickly challenged by those Castilian noblemen who wanted most to rid themselves of the strong hand of royal authority and return to the unrestricted self-aggrandizement of their kind during the reign of another mentally disturbed monarch, Isabel's predecessor Henry IV. The leader of these predatory aristocrats was the Duke of Nájera; a prominent ally of his was, as we might have expected, the Marqués of Villena, son of Isabel's ancient enemy. It is sadder and more surprising to find the Count of Benavente, son of Isabel's doughty champion, and the Duke of Medina Sidonia among their ranks. These nobles and others objected to Fernando's calling the *cortes* of Castile to meet at Toro within a few weeks of Isabel's death, and still more to his presenting reports to it of Juana's mental condition as a basis for a formal declaration on her capacity to rule, which the *cortes* agreed to make. They began writing to Brussels, urging Philip to come at once to Spain with Juana to override Fernando's authority.

Fernando sent an agent named Conchillos to obtain a letter from Juana designating him governor and administrator of Castile. She signed it, but it was intercepted, and Conchillos was thrown into prison in the Netherlands. Then someone (presumably Philip) had her sign a letter to her father saying that she was much improved in health and was resolved to remain with her husband.[2] In April 1505 a treaty between Philip and Louis XII of France provided that Philip would support Louis' claims to both Milan and Naples in return for French support in securing his control of Castile. Striking back immediately, Fernando opened negotiations with the French court in May for his marriage to the French princess Germaine de Foix, with their children to inherit Naples. By the

---

[2]This letter contained an ugly reference to her mother, implying that Juana's fits of jealousy of Philip and his mistresses echoed similar fits of jealousy by Isabel about Fernando and his extramarital affairs, which differed from her daughter's only in having been kept from the public. Though Fernando undoubtedly had some extramarital liaisons after his marriage to Isabel, there is no evidence other than this self-serving letter (which was probably not actually written by Juana) to show that Isabel ever had a violent reaction to them, or that these brief escapades had any significant effect on their relationship with each other.

terms of the reservation in the oath sworn by the *cortes* of Aragon to Juana and Philip in October 1502, a son born to Fernando by a second marriage would displace Juana as heir to Aragon and its Italian dominions. Castile, however, would remain in the hands of Juana and Philip, or their son Charles, after Fernando's death. The unification of Spain which Isabel and Fernando had brought about would be destroyed.

Fernando married Germaine in October 1505. No act in all his life has been more sharply condemned—and with reason. There was an element of spite in it, of desperation. Galling though the prospect of Philip, as consort of his mad daughter, taking over his own Aragon must have been to him, Isabel had built for the ages, not for a single generation; to cast away the unification of Castile and Aragon that he and she had achieved together was folly and betrayal. It broke faith with Isabel before she was a year in the grave. Fernando was a highly skilled negotiator and intriguer; but without Isabel, he lacked the long view and the moral sheet-anchor that she had always given him.

But now, at long last, when Isabel was beyond suffering and tragedy, the Grim Reaper appeared in her service. Probably because of Fernando's advancing age, he and Germaine conceived only once. The baby was born May 3, 1509. He was a son, and was named Juan. But he died before midnight on the same day that he was born. So Fernando's maneuver failed for lack of an heir, and Castile and Aragon remained united.

The affront to Isabel's memory which most Castilians saw in Fernando's remarriage deprived him of most of his remaining support in that realm, forcing him to make an agreement with Philip's ambassadors at Salamanca in November 1505 that he and Philip and Juana would rule jointly. Because of the treaty sealed by Fernando's marriage to Germaine, Louis XII would not this time let Philip and Juana cross French territory. So they sailed from the Netherlands in the dead of winter, almost died in a savage winter storm in the Bay of Biscay which drove them into English ports, and finally arrived at La Coruña in Galicia in April 1506. In Spain Philip avoided Fernando as long as he could. When at last he had to meet him, he came protected by thousands of armed men. Fernando shrewdly came to the parley unarmed (in a famous exchange with the Count of Benavente, who appeared with a cuirass under his clothes, he felt the Count's bulging chest and said: "Why, how fat you have grown!"). He yielded rule of Castile to Philip in return for recognition of his oft-disputed title to Naples, the continued control of the three great Castilian military orders, and the revenue of the Indies. Philip accepted these terms. A secret clause declared that Juana was incapable of ruling and should have no part in government. Scarcely were these negotiations completed when Fernando swore before three of his counsellors that the agreement had been made under duress and was therefore null and void, that he had wished to liberate Juana and regain the government of Castile. Nevertheless the agreement was confirmed publicly (except for the secret clause) at a little village called Villafáfila.

Soon afterward the *cortes* of Castile conducted a debate on whether Juana should be publicly adjudged incapable of ruling on account of mental illness. Admiral Fadrique, after a long interview with her, refused to support such a judgment; Archbishop Cisneros, on the basis of much more experience with her dark history, favored it. In the end the *cortes* took no action. But a vicious circle had now been established. Though Juana probably did not know of the secret clauses of the Agreement of Villafáfila, the debate in the *cortes* had alarmed her. She was still rational most of the time—certainly rational enough to fear for her liberty and safety. She knew that insane people were usually locked up, and began to have an obsessive fear of castles in which she might be imprisoned, refusing to stay in them even for a night. This unbalanced her still more, while reports of it further damaged her reputation.

During the summer of 1506 Philip gave lucrative gifts of land and castles and official appointments to his close associates, both Flemish and Spanish, and Castile spiralled back down toward the anarchy from which Isabel had rescued it as dispossessed nobles fought with the newcomers over these awards. In the midst of it all, in September, Philip was suddenly taken ill. Though he was only 28 years old and had been remarkably healthy, within a week he was dead.

Fernando had gone to Italy two weeks before to secure his hold on Naples. That is probably a sufficient alibi to save him from the charge of poisoning, since he would have been unlikely to leave the country if he knew that Philip was about to die. But Philip's death was so sudden, so improbable, so completely unexpected, and so opportune for so many aggrieved people, that suspicion of its natural character has lingered ever since.[3] Whatever the explanation of his demise, its effect on Juana was catastrophic. She went immediately from a condition of occasional insanity to being out of touch with reality most of the time. Her psychosis was not yet total; she had remissions, and periods of partial rationality. But they were now exceptional. She refused to sign any document, vehemently rejected the company of all women, and would move about only at night. On All Saints day, November 1, 1506, she insisted on opening Philip's coffin, and the next month she took it from its tomb and carried it about the countryside with her. She kept her husband's mouldering corpse with her for more than two years—one of the most macabre stories in the world's history—until at last, in February 1509, Fernando took it away from her and locked her up for the rest of her life in the frowning old

---

[3]Analysis of the question is not helped by mindless repetition by many fine historians, even in the medically sophisticated twentieth century, of the old wives' tale that the cause of Philip's fatal illness was drinking too much cold water after vigorous exercise. If that were a cause of death, half the population of the United States would be dead because of it.

castle at Tordesillas.

Fernando did not return immediately from Italy on the news of Philip's death, but wisely entrusted Archbishop Cisneros with the desperately difficult task of restoring order in this disintegrating situation. All men trusted the Archbishop (while all definitely did not trust Fernando). Despite widespread hunger, economic depression, and pestilence during 1507, Cisneros was successful; when Fernando finally came back to Spain in August of that year, almost all opposition to him had evaporated. Juana, who seems to have still had some feeling for her father, agreed immediately on his return to sign a surrender of all governmental authority in Castile to him, despite her refusal to sign almost any other document after Philip's death. The rebellious nobles made their peace with Fernando, and on Fernando's request Pope Julius II made Cisneros a Cardinal.

In 1509 and 1510 the magnificent Spanish soldiers undertook an extraordinary career of conquest along the coast of Muslim North Africa, regaining it for Christendom from Melilla to the border of Tunisia, and Tripoli in Libya as well. However, Fernando then became deeply involved in Italy again, when Pope Julius II formally invested him with the crown and scepter of Naples and he joined a league with Venice and the Papacy to keep the French from challenging his rule there. During the ensuing war with France the North African Muslims regained all the Spanish had taken from them, but Fernando retained Naples after a bloody battle between the Spanish and Swiss on one side and the French on the other, fought near Ravenna in 1512. An outgrowth of this new war with France was Fernando's conquest of Navarra, permanently joining the greater part of that small country which lay south of the Pyrenees, to the main body of Spain. Thus the Pyrenees became the Spanish frontier (except for Roussillon, which lay north of it) as it has remained ever since (with the French eventually regaining Roussillon).

By the time of the Battle of Ravenna it was clear that Fernando, who turned sixty that year, would in all probability never have a child by Germaine, that all of Spain would pass to the heir of Philip and Juana. All their children were in the Netherlands except the King's boy namesake, now nine years old, who had been born in Spain when Juana was forced to remain there in 1503, and had never left. Fernando tried to gain the succession for him, but his advisors and the various *cortes* and above all Cardinal Cisneros would not hear of it; there had been far too many succession controversies already. As Fernando lay on his deathbed in January 1516, Prince Charles was just a month short of his sixteenth birthday. He was heir by clear right to all his father would have inherited if he had lived, and his mother if she had been sane—all Spain, all the Netherlands, and as soon as his grandfather Maximilian died, in all

ISABEL OF SPAIN

probability the Holy Roman Empire.[4]

He was an awkward, unprepossessing boy, with a small thin body, a narrow face, an ugly underslung jaw, and hesitant speech. Few saw great potential in him; many thought to take advantage of him. The worldly-minded paid no heed to the impact upon him of the characters of the two adults closest to him, who became almost his foster father and mother: Adrian of Utrecht, later the holy Pope Adrian VI, the last non-Italian Pope before John Paul II; and his Aunt Margaret, so briefly the wife of Isabel's only son. Born and baptized at Ghent, Charles had spent all his life in the Netherlands. There was no enthusiasm for him in any part of Spain—at best, a reluctant acceptance of his legal claims, at worst a firm determination to oppose him and the foreign parasites he was expected to bring with him when he came. Without the unwavering support of 80-year-old Cardinal Cisneros, he would have had little chance to prevail in Spain despite his unquestionable legal title to the throne. But the iron-souled primate Isabel had chosen, drawing on his last wells of strength, gave all he had left in him to the young prince, holding Spain together for the full year that intervened between Fernando's death and Charles' arrival, and during the first tumultuous weeks after his arrival. It was the last contribution, and one of the greatest, of Francisco Cardinal Ximénes de Cisneros to the Church as to the country he had loved and served so well.

For Charles—though often traduced in his time and since, as by modern historians who tend to be hypercritical of him whatever their orientation—saved Christendom. In constant journeys, on endless roads, upon the seaways of the Atlantic and the Mediterranean, in Spain, in Portugal, in Italy, in Germany, in the Netherlands, in North Africa, through forty demanding, punishing years, from 1516 to 1556, he fought infidel Turks, heretic Protestants, and perfidious French to maintain the house of faith into which he and his glorious grandmother Isabel the Catholic had been born. For thirty-seven of those years he was Holy Roman Emperor Charles V; in that position, in that era, his defection to the Protestants would have instantly destroyed the Catholic Church and the society and government and world-view it had formed, in all but a few isolated corners of Europe. He knew how widely the Church had been corrupted; but, living in Spain and seeing what his grandmother and Cardinal Cisneros had done for the Church there, he knew that it could be rescued and cleansed. Through most of his long reign Charles called again and again for the great reforming council that he knew must be held; it began at Trent under his patronage, though its work was not completed until after his death. Somehow he also found time and energy to concern himself with the sufferings of the Indians in the New World, to order comprehensive legal protection for their

---

[4]Choice of the Holy Roman Emperor was still theoretically elective, but the Holy Roman Emperor had been the Habsburg heir since 1438 and was generally expected to remain so.

liberty and prohibition on their enslavement, and to demand (though not always with success) that his governors in the New World enforce these "new laws." He stood behind his Aunt Catherine through all her splendid fight against the efforts of King Henry VIII of England and his advisors to destroy her marriage.

When Charles had expended almost the last of his energies in the discharge of these overwhelming duties, exhausted and helplessly crippled by gout at 56, he abdicated from all his thrones and crowns and retired to the monastery of Yuste in the heart of Spain, to spend his last two years in prayer and penance, in a room hung with black in mourning for his mother who had plumbed the utmost depths of human suffering. Charles I of Spain, Charles V of the Holy Roman Empire, grandson of Isabel the Catholic, did everything she could ever have prayed and dreamed and hoped that a son and heir of hers might do. Confronting Martin Luther face to face at the Diet of Worms in 1521, he fully matched any of her greatest moments, while calling upon her spirit and her heritage, when he told the man whose mission was to cleave Christendom asunder:

> Ye know that I am born of the most Christian Emperors of the noble German nation, of the Catholic kings of Spain, the Archdukes of Austria, the Dukes of Burgundy, who were all to the death true sons of the Roman Church, defenders of the Catholic Faith, of the sacred customs, decrees and uses of its worship, who have bequeathed all this to me as my heritage, and according to whose example I have hitherto lived. Thus I am determined to hold fast by all which has happened since the Council of Constance. For it is certain that a single monk must err if he stands against the opinion of all Christendom. Otherwise Christendom itself would have erred for more than a thousand years. Therefore I am determined to set my kingdoms and dominions, my friends, my body, my blood, my life, my soul upon it.[5]

In Charles V and what he did lies a very significant and substantial part of the achievement of Isabel the Catholic. Charles was conscious of it, not only in what he said to Luther and in other tributes to his forebears, but especially in the Spain he found when he arrived there in 1517, and came to understand better and better and to love more and more during all the rest of his life—the one country he ruled that he could always count on, the only people that never let him down. This was the Spain his grandmother, above all, had created. Charles took the Spanish into his heart and they took him into their hearts. Though born in a foreign land, arriving without a word of their language, he has

---

[5]Karl Brandi, *The Emperor Charles V* (Atlantic Highlands NJ, 1965), p. 131. This is, in the writer's opinion, much the best of the many biographies of Charles V available in English, though there is need for an even more comprehensive one in several volumes. In Spanish, we have the monumental 999-page Volume 20 in *Historia de España* directed by Ramón Menéndez Pidal, "La España del Emperador Carlos V" by Manuel Fernández Alvarez, 4th ed. (Madrid, 1986).

become one of their supreme national heroes, his name still on their lips four hundred years later, *Carlos Quinto*. When he chose to leave the world, seeking a place to rest and pray and contemplate and die, there was never any doubt that the place he would choose would be in Spain. Of Yuste where he went, he said simply: "Here it is forever spring."

Such was Isabel's legacy. In conclusion, we should review and behold the tangible achievements of her life and reign, and the signs of sanctity in her soul that emerge into history.

She took a country that under her pathetic half-brother had become the laughingstock, the whipped dog of Europe, and made it the greatest power in the world; and she did this by no harsh and domineering rule, but by bringing justice and peace, integrity and incorruptibility, care and honor with her wherever she went. Above all, she brought love—the love she bore her people and the love they bore her. Europe had capable kings in her time, but none who would have been able to face down a rioting mob of hundreds with only three companions as she did at Segovia when her daughter was shut up in the castle there in 1476. She could do that only because of the love she gave to her people and received from them.

By her marriage to Fernando, and the love that sealed it and the unity and harmony of both of them in action that she crafted, she not only unified Spain, but performed superlatively the combined duties of queen, wife, and mother that so often seem incompatible. Through thirty-six years of the most intimate public and private union, it was always *tanto monta, monta tanto, Isabel como Fernando*—Isabel amounts to Fernando, Fernando amounts to Isabel.

Though Fernando as a great warrior and general played an indispensable part in the tremendous victory over Muslim Granada that crowned and completed the longest crusade, the evidence is overwhelming that it would not have been achieved without Isabel. More than once during the ten years required to attain that total victory, Fernando wavered and was distracted; Isabel was ever constant. Whenever she was needed, she answered the call. She marshalled the troops, sent the food, and brought up the guns. When morale faltered, she came in person to the battlefront, to the camps outside the besieged cities, to inspire her soldiers; and she inspired them as no woman but St. Joan of Arc has ever done.

When a lone and penniless sea rover from Genoa came to her with a plan and a dream so unique, so otherworldly that few others—and none in positions of authority—had been able to follow it even in imagination, Isabel brought it to reality. Her patronage of Columbus was directly and essentially responsible for the greatest geographic discovery in history, for the opening of a new world and eventually for the baptism and conversion of hundreds of millions of souls who had never heard of Jesus Christ before the admiral she sent across the unknown sea reached them. That the beginning of their conversion was unnecessarily delayed was not her fault; she made every possible effort to launch and facilitate it, and to protect the native Americans to whom she always felt a responsibility equal to the responsibility she felt for her own people of Castile. Three days before she died, her last public act featured a charge for their protection; some of her last thoughts on earth surely were for them.

The year that Columbus returned triumphantly from the voyage in which he discovered America, Isabel began the great reform of the Church in Spain. She was the first to launch it, two years before she found and elevated its clerical leader, Archbishop Cisneros, to the primacy of the Spanish Church, using all her personal and political influence on the Borgia Pope to induce him to install in this office a man so very different from him. Cisneros deserves great credit for the thoroughness and lasting effects of the reform, which required a priest and a bishop to fulfill it; but that reform was Isabel's in conception, formulated and first put into practice while Cisneros was still living in a hermit's hut. It is no exaggeration to say that this reform, which Isabel began and Cisneros completed, saved the Catholic Church not only in Spain, but in Europe; for without the Catholic strength and unity of Spain, Charles would have found it almost impossible to preserve the Church elsewhere. Protestantism would have triumphed, then divided and subdivided as its nature dictates; all unity in Christendom would have been lost. Well-instructed Catholics know that the Church cannot be destroyed; but it has no guarantee of survival in any particular part of the world. Isabel's reform, running straight against the tide of Renaissance manners and morals, changed history fundamentally. She might well have called it her supreme achievement, if her humility would have permitted her to recognize it as such.

During the last seven years of the three decades of her reign Isabel bore crosses and endured sufferings that most men and women have hardly imagined, let alone endured; she saw ahead the shadow of destruction by death and madness of all that she and Fernando had built. But she never lost her confidence in God, and died at peace with Him. In His good time her work was confirmed, and her grandson did what her children had been unable to do.

As part of her essential task of unifying Spain and bringing it justice and peace and good order, she founded the Spanish Inquisition. The black legend that later grew up about it has brought much unjustified reproach upon her for that action. In fact the Inquisition, as she established it, was very much needed in Spain. Despite occasional abuses—some severe—it remained for centuries the most popular and most trusted tribunal in the country, sparing it the horrors of civil war and revolution, and much private revenge and calumny based on ethnic prejudice. Some of the methods it used and the punishments it inflicted are rightly criticized, but none were unique to the Spanish Inquisition; they were common to judicial proceedings in all countries during that age, as much in those which later became Protestant as in those which remained Catholic.

Her expulsion of all the Jews from Spain in 1492 was an unjust act, though not without provocation. But in a fallen world no one, not even a saint, who rules for thirty years is just in every official action, no more than any man or woman, however holy, who lives nearly that long fails to commit some sin. There was so much justice associated with every aspect of Isabel's life and rule that the balance tips overwhelmingly in her favor.

Isabel's achievements as a queen make her not only the greatest woman ruler in history, but at least arguably the morally best and the most just woman ruler in history. But sanctity demands more even than that. Great as her grandson Charles was, extraordinary and indispensable as were his accomplishments for the Church, for Christendom, and for his country, one could not seriously make a case for his canonization. With Isabel, one can.

There can be no possible doubt or question that from the very earliest notices we have of her, in her girlhood, until her last hour in the house overlooking the main square of Medina del Campo, Isabel the Catholic lived a life of prayer. Again and again, especially at critical moments in her life, though never failing even in the rare times of tranquillity, we hear of her devotion to prayer, her assiduity in prayer, the length of time she spent in converse with God.[6] That her prayer had power, that God did respond to it, was amply proved very early in her life by the fate of Pedro Girón; but there were many other examples of His response to her prayers, as she surmounted immense and apparently insuperable obstacles during the war of the succession with Portugal, and during the war against Granada. In her last years, when she bore her cross with Christ, most of her prayers were not answered from the world's viewpoint; but then she was with her Lord in Gethsemane, when His prayers were not answered either—from the world's viewpoint.

She lived the Commandments. She loved God with all her heart, with all her soul, and with all her mind. She forgave those who had wronged her—again and again we see her doing so, especially in the early years of her reign when dealing with the fractious nobility; when she let justice take its course without the alleviation of public mercy, it was only because she was convinced her primary duty to secure the realm required her then to wield the sword God gives to every legitimate government. She loved her people, the poor, the suffering captives of the Canary Islands and of the Indies. She did not envy nor covet; one may search all her writings and actions in vain for examples of petty jealousy or spite toward anyone with whom she ever had to deal. She honored her father and her mother, though they had left her a princess alone among designing, predatory men. She loved her husband and her children with a profound, almost consuming love. In the family circle she was a dutiful wife,

---

[6]See the many examples cited by Vicente Rodríguez Valencia in *Articulos del Postulador sobre la fama de santidad, vida y virtudes de la Sierva de Dios Isabel I, Reina de Castilla* (Valladolid, 1972), *passim.*

submissive to her husband, seeing no contradiction in that with her public place as his full equal, Queen of Castile beside King of Aragon. No more chaste ruler ever graced a throne; no more chaste woman ever sat by a fireside with her husband and children. No breath of scandal ever touched her personal life—though she lived at court in Renaissance Europe, where scandal was rampant, expected, assumed, when even the Pope had illegitimate children.

She crowned her goodness with humility. No one who reads Isabel's letters and reviews her actions with any serious reflection can doubt the profundity and sincerity of her humility, revealed with special clarity by all that we know of her relationship to her first confessor, Bishop Hernando de Talavera. It was before him that she gladly knelt upon making her first confession to him; it was to him that she wrote, when Fernando lay in the shadow of death following the assassination attempt of December 1492, blaming herself and her sins for what had happened to her husband. We may well imagine that her humility caused her to ask herself many times in her last years how much personal responsibility she bore for what had happened to Juana; but her resolute realism and common sense, even in those dark and foreboding years, rescued her from the perversion of humility which is self-contempt and despair. One of Satan's favorite weapons against the holy, temptation to excess in seeking virtue—"spiritual gluttony," as St. John of the Cross calls it—never touched her. She knew and practiced all the cardinal virtues—prudence, justice, temperance, and fortitude—in an exalted, indeed heroic manner. She maintained them in the face of an avalanche of personal grief in her last seven years that would have destroyed a weaker soul, and used that grief to bring her closer to God.

Her contemporaries uniformly and repeatedly testified to her extraordinary virtues, as have most historians since. Even those who vehemently disagree with some of her policies as Queen (such as her establishment of the Inquisition in Spain), cannot deny her spotless moral integrity, her total commitment to the Catholic Faith and its moral teachings, the harmony of her life with her belief, and the justice and benevolence of her rule in general. Some have argued that more of the credit for the achievements of her reign belongs to Fernando than is customarily accorded him. That would have pleased Isabel, who was always more than willing to give her beloved husband credit for anything they did together. But in evaluating such claims, the historian need look no farther than a comparison of the record of Fernando without Isabel to their record together, to see where the greatest credit is due.

Isabel's life and virtues have particular relevance to an age more and more characterized by flight from faith, morality, chastity, and responsibility, where prayer is neglected, humility is doubted, and many people become very uneasy when contemplating real and uncompromising justice. Every age needs to be reminded especially of the virtues it characteristically lacks, but wherever possible through a personality not only holy but at least in some significant ways congenial to the time. Many aspects of Isabel's personality are of timeless appeal: her sincerity, her forthright honesty, her clear and direct mind and speech, her warmth and deep feelings, her love for her husband and her children. Her achievements as a woman will inevitably appeal to an age which is giving special emphasis to the scope of women's potential to contribute to society and to do well most if not all of the things that men have customarily done in the past. Her care and concern for foreign peoples of a different race than hers will strike a chord in a century which has lavished care and concern upon such people. Yet the memory of Isabel must be as incompatible with compromise on any fundamental tenet of faith or morals as Isabel herself would have been.

She deserves the honors of the altar, on or soon after the five hundredth anniversary of the discovery of her Admiral Christopher Columbus that changed history forever by opening a new world to bring new hope and opportunity to the old.

Bibliography

This is by no means an exhaustive bibliography of the literature available on Queen Isabel. It is limited to sources actually consulted in the preparation of this biography (not necessarily always used in the final form of the text, nor cited in the notes). For the convenience of the reader without a good command of Spanish, English sources (relatively few) are listed separately. French sources are listed with the Spanish.

A. MANUSCRIPT SOURCES

Most of the important source material about Queen Isabel is now in print (though for many centuries much of it was not). However, there remain numerous letters from her and Fernando pertaining to political, military, and religious affairs that have not been printed. These are mostly found in the early national archives kept at the castle of Simancas near Valladolid, under the headings Diversos de Castilla; Estado, Castilla; Patronato Real (relating primarily to religious affairs); and Registro General de Sello.

B. PRIMARY SOURCES
(historical narratives and documents contemporary with,
or written within living memory of Isabel)

In English:

Ayala, Juan de. *A Letter to Ferdinand and Isabella, 1503*, tr. & ed. Charles E. Nowell (Minneapolis, 1965).

Bergenroth, G. A., ed. *Calendar of Letters, Dispatches, and State Papers relating to the Negotiations between England and Spain, preserved in the Archives of Simancas and Elsewhere*, Volume I: Henry VII, 1485-1509 (London, 1862).

Columbus, Christopher. *The Log of Christopher Columbus*, ed. Robert H. Fuson (Camden ME, 1987).

Columbus, Ferdinand. *The Life of the Admiral Christopher Columbus*, tr. & ed. Benjamin Keen (New Brunswick NJ, 1959).

Jane, Cecil, ed. *Select Documents Illustrating the Four Voyages of Columbus* (London, 1930), 2 vols.

Morison, Samuel Eliot, tr. & ed. *Journals and Other Documents on the Life and Voyages of Christopher Columbus* (New York, 1963).

In Spanish or French:

Baeza, Hernando de. *Las cosas que pasaron entre los reyes de Granada desde el tiempo de el rey don Juan de Castilla. Relaciones de algunos sucesos de los últimos tiempos del reino de Granada*, ed. E. Lafuente Alcántara (Madrid, 1868).

———. "Una continuación inédita de la Relación de Hernando de Baeza," ed. Juan de Mata Carriazo, *Al-Andalus* XIII (1948), 431-442.

Bernáldez, Andrés. *Memorias del reinado de los Reyes Católicos*, ed. Manuel Gomez-Moreno and Juan de Mata Carriazo (Madrid, 1962).

Carriazo, Juan de Mata, and R. Carande, eds. *El Tumbo de los Reyes Católicos del concejo de Sevilla* (Sevilla, 1969-1971), 5 vols.

Crónica incompleta de los Reyes Católicos, 1469-1476 (anonymous), ed. J. Puyol (Madrid, 1934).

Crónicon de Valladolid, *Colección de documentos inéditos para la historia de España*, Volume XIII (Madrid, 1848).

Enríquez del Castillo, Diego. "Crónica del Rey Enrique el Cuarto," in Cayetano Rosell y López, ed., *Crónicas de los reyes de Castilla*, Volume 3 (Volume 70 in Biblioteca de Autores Españoles, reprinted Madrid, 1953).

Fernández de Madrid, Alonso. *Vida de Fray Hernando de Talavera, primer Arzobispo de Granada*, ed. P. Felix G. Olmedo (Madrid, 1931).

Galíndez de Carvajal, Lorenzo. "Anales breves del reynado de los Reyes Catolicos," *Colección de documentos inéditos para la historia de España*, Volume XVIII (Madrid, 1851).

———. "Crónica de Enrique IV," text in Juan Torres Fontes, *Estudio sobre la "Crónica de Enrique IV" del Dr. Galíndez de Carvajal* (Murcia, 1946).

García Oro, José, ed. *La reforma de los religiosos españoles en tiempo de los reyes católicos* (Valladolid, 1969) [documents].

Garrido Atienza, Miguel. *Las capitulaciones para la entrega de Granada* (Granada, 1910) [documents].

Gaspar y Remiro, M., ed. "Documentos sobre Granada," in *Colección de documentos inéditos para la historia de España*, Volume VIII (Madrid, 1842).

———. *Ultimos pactos y correspondencia intima entre los Reyes Católicos y Boabdil* (Granada, 1910).

Gómez de Fuensalida, Gutierre. *Correspondencia* (Madrid, 1907).

Historia de los hechos de don Rodrigo Ponce de León, marqués de Cádiz (anonymous), *Colección de documentos inéditos para la historia de España*, Volume CVI (Madrid, 1893).

Isabel la Católica. *Testamento y codicilo* (Madrid, 1956).

Ladero Quesada, Miguel Angel. *Los Mudejares de Castilla en tiempo de Isabel I* (Valladolid, 1969) [study and documents].

Lalaing, Antoine de. "Voyage de Philippe le beau en Espagne en 1501," in

Collection des Voyages des Souverains des Pays-Bas, ed. L. P. Gachard, Volume I (Brussels, 1876).

Marineo Sículo, Lucio. *Sumario de la clarissima vida y heroycos hechos de los catolicos reyes don Fernando y doña Ysabel de immortal memoria* (Madrid, 1587).

Memorias de Don Enrique IV de Castilla, Volume II: "La Colección Diplomática del mismo Rey" (Madrid, 1913).

Münzer, Jerónimo. *Viaje por España y Portugal en los años 1494 y 1495*, tr. & ed. Julio Puyol (Madrid, 1951).

Oviedo y Valdés, Gonzalo Fernández de. *Memorias (Quinquagenas de la nobleza de España)*, ed. Juan Bautista Avable-Arce (Chapel Hill NC, 1974), 2 vols.

Palencia, Alonso Fernandez de. *Crónica de Enrique IV* (translated from the Latin original), ed. Antonio Paz y Melia (Madrid, 1904-09), 3 vols. (Volumes 257, 258, and 267 in Biblioteca de Autores Españoles).

Paz y Meliá, Antonio. *El cronista Alfonso de Palencia* (Madrid, 1914) [documents].

Peter Martyr de Anglería. "Epistolario" (translated from the Latin original), in *Documentos inéditos para la Historia de España*, published by Duque de Alba et al, Volumes IX (Madrid, 1953) and X (Madrid, 1955).

Pulgar, Hernando del. *Crónica de los reyes católicos*, ed. Juan de Mata Carriazo (Madrid, 1943), 2 vols.

Rodríguez Valencia, Vicente. *Isabel la Católica en la opinión de españoles y extranjeros, siglos XV al XX* (Valladolid, 1970), 3 vols.

Rumeu de Armas, Antonio, ed. *La política indigenista de Isabel la Católica*, Volume II [documents] (Valladolid, 1969).

Santa Cruz, Alonso de. *Crónica de los reyes católicos*, ed. Juan de Mata Carriazo, Volume I (Sevilla, 1951).

Sanz Arizmendi, C., ed. "Documentos relativos a los reyes Católicos sobre sucesos y negocios de Andalucia después de la conquista de Granada," *Colección de documentos inéditos para la historia de España*, XI (Madrid, 1846) and XIV (Madrid, 1849).

Serrano, Luciano, ed. "Documentos referentes a la prisión de Boadil en 1483," *Boletín de la Real Academia de la Historia* LXXXIV (1924).

Suarez Fernandez, Luis, ed. *Política internacional de Isabel la Católica; estudios y documentos* (Valladolid, 1965), 5 vols.

Torre y del Cerro, Antonio de la, and Luis Suarez Fernandez, eds. *Documentos sobre las relaciones internacionales de los Reyes Católicos* (Barcelona, 1949-66), 6 vols.

—————, eds. *Documentos referentes a las relaciones con Portugal durante el reinado de los reyes católicos* (Valladolid, 1958-63), 3 vols.

Valera, Mosén Diego de. *Crónica de los reyes católicos*, ed. Juan de Mata

Carriazo (Madrid, 1927, 1941).

————. *Epistolas* (Madrid, 1878).

————. *Memorial de diversas hazañas*, ed. Juan de Mata Carriazo (Madrid, 1941).

Vallejo, Juan de. *Memorial de la vida de fray Francisco Jiménez de Cisneros*, ed. Antonio de la Torre (Madrid, 1913).

C. SECONDARY SOURCES
(historical narratives written after living memory of Isabel)

In English:

Blake, J. W. *European Beginnings in West Africa, 1454-1478* (London, 1937).

Bradford, Ernle. *A Wind from the North; the Life of Henry the Navigator* (New York, 1960).

Cameron, Ian. *Lodestone and Evening Star* (New York, 1966).

Collis, John S. *Christopher Columbus* (London, 1976).

Diffie, Bailey W. and George D. Winius. *Foundations of the Portuguese Empire, 1415-1580* (Minneapolis MN, 1977).

Hibbert, Christopher. *The House of Medici: its Rise and Fall* (New York, 1974, 1980).

Kamen, Henry. *Inquisition and Society in Spain* (Bloomington IN, 1985).

Kendall, Paul M. *Louis XI, the Universal Spider* (New York, 1971).

Lea, H. C. *History of the Inquisition of Spain* (New York, 1906), 4 vols.

Lunenfeld, Marvin. *The Council of the Santa Hermandad; a Study of the Pacification Forces of Ferdinand and Isabella* (Coral Gables FL, 1971).

Mattingly, Garrett. *Catherine of Aragon* (New York, 1941).

Merriman, Roger B. *The Rise of the Spanish Empire in the Old World and the New*, Volume II: "The Catholic Kings" (New York, 1918).

Merton, Reginald. *Cardinal Ximenes and the Making of Spain* (London, 1934).

Miller, Townsend. *The Castles and the Crown; Spain 1451-1555* (New York, 1963).

————. *Henry IV of Castile* (Philadelphia, 1972).

Morison, Samuel Eliot. *Admiral of the Ocean Sea; a Life of Christopher Columbus* (Boston, 1942).

————. *The European Discovery of America; the Southern Voyages* (New York, 1974).

Pastor, Ludwig von. *History of the Popes from the Close of the Middle Ages*, Volumes IV-VI (St. Louis, 1914).

Peters, Edward. *Inquisition* (New York, 1988).

Prescott, William H. *History of the Reign of Ferdinand and Isabella the Catholic* (Philadelphia, 1872), 3 vols.

Prestage, Edgar. *The Portuguese Pioneers* (London, 1933).

Purcell, Mary. *The Great Captain; Gonzalo Fernández de Córdoba* (London, 1962).

Robertson, Ian. *Blue Guide to Spain: the Mainland*, 3rd ed. (London, 1975).

Sanceau, Elaine. *The Perfect Prince* [King John II of Portugal] (Barcelos, Portugal, 1959).

————. *Reign of the Fortunate King* [King Manuel I of Portugal] (Hamden CT, 1969).

Taviani, Paolo. *Christopher Columbus; the Grand Design* (London, 1985).

Walsh, William T. *Characters of the Inquisition* (London, 1940).

————. *Isabella of Spain; the Last Crusader* (New York, 1930).

In Spanish or French:

Alonso de Ojeda, José. *Palencia por la reina Isabel!* (Palencia, 1953).

Amezúa y Mayo, A. de. *La batalla de Lucena y el verdadero retrato de Boabdil* (Madrid, 1915).

Ballesteros Gaibrois, Manuel. *La obra de Isabel la Católica* (Segovia, 1953).

————. *Valencia y los Reyes Católicos* (Valencia, 1943).

Benito Ruano, Eloy. *Toledo en el siglo XV; vida política* (Madrid, 1961).

Bosque Carceller, Rodolfo. *Murcia y los Reyes Católicos* (Murcia, 1953).

Cereceda, Feliciano. *Semblanza espiritual de Isabel* (Madrid, 1946).

Chacón Jimenez, Francisco. *Murcia en la centuria del quinientos* (Murcia, 1979).

Clemencín, Diego. *Elogio de Isabel la Católica* (Memorias de la Academia de la Historia, Volume VI) (Madrid, 1821).

Cuartero y Huerta, Baltasar. *El Pacto de los Toros de Guisando* (Madrid, 1952).

Durán y Lerchundi, Joaquín. *La toma de Granada y caballeros que concurrieron a ella* (Madrid, 1893), 2 vols.

Encinas, Alonso de. *Madrigal de las Altas Torres, cuna de Isabel* (Madrid, n.d.).

Esteve Barba, Francisco. *Alfonso Carrillo de Acuña* (Barcelona, 1943).

Fernández, Fidel. *Fray Hernando de Talavera* (Madrid, 1942).

Fernández de Retana, Luis. *Cisneros y su siglo* (Madrid, 1929), 2 vols.

————. *Isabel la Católica, fundidora de la unidad nacional española* (Madrid, 1947), 2 vols.

Fernández Dominguez, José. *La guerra civil a la muerte de Enrique IV* (Zamora, 1928).

Ferrara, Orestes. *Un pleito sucesorio; Enrique IV, Isabel de Castilla y la Beltraneja* (Madrid, 1945).

Fuertes Arias, Rafael. *Alfonso de Quintanilla, contador mayor de los Reyes Católico* (Oviedo, 1909).

Garcia Oro, José. *Cisneros y la reforma del clero español* (Madrid, 1971).

Garcia-Villoslada, Ricardo. *Historia de la iglesia en España . . . de los siglos XV y*

XVI (Madrid, 1979), 2 vols.

Ladero Quesada, Miguel Angel. *Castilla y la conquista del reino de Granada* (Valladolid, 1967).

Llanos y Torriglia, Felix de. *Asi llegó a reinar Isabel* (Madrid, 1927).

Llorca, Bernardino. *La Inquisición en España* (Barcelona, 1936).

Manzano Manzano, Juan. *Cristóbal Colón; siete años decisivos de su vida, 1485-1492* (Madrid, 1964).

Menéndez Pidal, Ramon, ed. *Historia de España*, Volume XVII: "España de los Reyes Católicos, 1474-1516," by Luis Suárez Fernández, Juan de Mata Carriazo and Manuel Fernández Alvarez (Madrid, 1969), 2 vols.

Modesto Sarasola, Francisco. *Vizcaya y los Reyes Católicos* (Madrid, 1950).

Ponce de Leon y Freyre, Eduardo. *El Marqués de Cádiz, 1443-1492* (Madrid, 1949).

Rodríguez Valencia, Vicente. *Artículos del postulador sobre la fama de santidad, vida y virtudes de la Sierva de Dios Isabel I, Reina de Castilla* (Valladolid, 1972).

————— and Luis Suarez Fernandez. *Matrimonio y derecho sucesorio de Isabel la Católica* (Valladolid, 1960).

Rodríguez Villa, Antonio. *Bosquejo biográfico de Don Beltran de la Cueva* (Madrid, 1881).

—————. *La Reina Juana la loca* (Madrid, 1892).

Rumeu de Armas, Antonio. *Itinerario de los Reyes Católicos, 1474-1516* (Madrid, 1974).

Serrano, Luciano. *Los Reyes Católicos y la ciudad de Burgos (1451-1492)* (Madrid, 1943).

Silio y Cortés, César. *Isabel la Católica, fundadora de España* (Valladolid, 1938).

Silva, Alberto. *Doña Juana la loca (1479-1555)* (Madrid, 1957).

Sitges, J. B. *Enrique IV y la excelente Señora* (Madrid, 1912).

Suárez Fernández, Luis. "En Torno al Pacto de los Toros de Guisando," *Hispania* 23 (1963), 345-365.

Suberbiola Martínez, Jesús. *Real Patronato de Granada; El arzobispo Talavera, la Iglesia y el Estado Moderno (1486-1516)* (Granada, 1982).

Tarsicio de Azcona, P. *La elección y reforma del episcopado español en tiempo de los reyes Católicos* (Madrid, 1960).

—————. *Isabel la Católica; estado crítico de su vida y su reinado* (Madrid, 1964).

Torres Fontes, Juan. *Itinerario de Enrique IV* (Murcia, 1953).

—————. *Don Pedro Fajardo, adelantado mayor del reino de Murcia* (Madrid, 1953).

—————. *El príncipe don Alfonso, 1465-1468* (Madrid, 1973).

Val, Isabel del. *Isabel la católica, princesa* (Valladolid, 1974).

Vicens Vives, Jaime. *Historia crítica de la vida y reinado de Fernando el Católico* (Zaragoza, 1952).

————. *Juan II de Aragon 1398-1479; Monarquía y Revolución en la España del Siglo XV* (Barcelona, 1953).

Index

Alphabetization of Spanish names presents particular difficulties because of the frequent use of compound last names in which the principal name used and the break between first and last names are often unclear (especially to the reader unfamiliar with Spanish) and because in the fifteenth and sixteenth centuries many "last names" were patronymics (used by the Spanish more as we would use a "middle name") or simply a designation of the town from which the named person came. Another problem is whether and when to use a personal name or a noble title.

This index alphabetizes by the last name of a compound or cross-references from it, and by titles of nobility with cross-reference when a personal name is also used for the same individual. Only reigning kings and Popes are alphabetized by first names. English rather than Spanish alphabetical order is used. All place names are entered by their Spanish spelling rather than their anglicized form, if any.

Abdallah "El Zagal" 152-155, 163, 165-167, 172, 173, 178-179, 186, 189-190, 192-194
Abdurrahman III, Emir of Córdoba 5-6
Aben Comixa, Yusuf 200
Abruzzi e Molise 313
Abul-Hassan, Muley, King of Granada 158, 51, 152, 156, 160-161, 168, 172
Acklins Island (Bahamas) 222
Acuña, Fernando de 133
Adrian VI, Pope 354
Aegean Sea 118
Afonso V, King of Portugal 14, 24, 25, 30, 41, 44, 48, 49, 123-125, 127-128, 134
    fights War of the Succession with Castile 77-79, 82-84, 86-97, 103
    orders exploration of the African coast 118
    death 143
Afonso, Prince of Portugal (son of King John II) 236
    negotiations for marriage to Princess Isabel 128-129, 142-143, 155-156, 187, 195
    marriage to Princess Isabel 197-198, 274
    death 198, 200-201, 206, 283, 320
Africa 7, 8, 9, 12, 116-119, 149, 165, 170, 184, 188, 194, 196, 230, 238, 282, 294
Africa, North 3, 117, 145, 179, 267, 300, 345, 353, 354
Africa, West 298, 304
Aguado, Juan 2674-265
Aguilar, Alfonso de, lord of Montilla 124, 154
Aguilar, Alonso de 312

Ajarquia, Battle of (1483) 152-155, 157, 160
Alaejos 36
Alagon River 19, 83
Alarcos, Battle of (1195) 9
Alaska 230
Alba, Duke of 85
Albaicín 297-302
Albelda "the white" 5
Alberche River 38, 83
Albi, Cardinal of 50, 60
Albornoz, Iñigo López de 96
Albret, Charlotte d' 291, 294
Albret, Jean d' 305
Albuera, Battle of (1479) 127
alcabala (tax) 345-346
Alcáçoba, Treaty of (1479) 128-129, 236
Alcalá de Guadaira 49
Alcalá de Henares 62, 64, 80, 104, 124, 168-171, 280, 324, 326, 327, 330, 331
Alcántara (town) 79, 127
Alcántara, Order of 126
Alexander VI, Pope (SEE ALSO Borgia, Cardinal Rodrigo) 64, 225, 239, 274, 289-291
    election as Pope 217-218, 225
    character 217, 218, 242
    Isabel's attitude toward 217-218, 225, 238
    divides non-Christian world between Spain and Portugal 238-239, 250-251
    and Church reform in Spain 243, 257-260, 287-288, 291, 357
    death 331
Alfonso I, King of Aragon 8, 44

Alfonso V, King of Aragon 13, 245
Alfonso I, King of Asturias 15
Alfonso II, King of Asturias 4, 6, 8, 15
Alfonso III, King of Asturias 5, 15
Alfonso IV, King of Asturias, 6
Alfonso V, King of León 7
Alfonso VI, King of Castile and León 7, 15
Alfonso VII, King of Castile and León 8, 15
Alfonso VIII, King of Castile 9-10, 15, 159
Alfonso IX, King of León 9-10
Alfonso X, King of Castile 11, 15
Alfonso XI, King of Castile 11-13, 15, 23, 180, 192
Alfonso II, King of Naples 246, 254
Alfonso, Prince of Castile (brother of Isabel) 18, 21, 23-29, 32-35, 39, 71, 81, 130
Algeciras 11-13, 180
Algerbi, Abraham 181-182
Algeria 145
Alhama 146-151, 156, 157, 161-163, 166, 167
Alhambra 201-202, 310, 314, 343
Alhendín 196
Aljubarrota, Battle of (1386) 13-15, 45
Almansur 6, 10
Almazán 265, 271
Almería 137, 145, 163, 178, 186, 193-194, 311
Almodóvar 163
al-Muleh, Bulcacin 200
Alora 160, 164, 165
Aloyn, Madame de 337
Alpujarras 302-303, 305, 311
Alvaro of Portugal 182
Amazon River 19, 83
Andalusia 8-10, 15, 23, 24, 29, 48, 49, 83, 99, 110-112, 114, 121, 124, 129, 152-154, 158, 159, 161, 167, 168, 176, 178, 189, 192, 199, 207, 219, 302
Andarax 303
Anglería, Peter Martyr de SEE Peter Martyr de Anglería
Anne of Brittany, Duchess and Queen of France 289, 332
Antequera 13, 15, 49, 153
Antwerp 253
Apulia 137, 313, 323, 329
Arabian Sea 294
Arabic 2, 296
Arabs 244
Aragon 8, 11, 13, 14, 21, 23, 39, 41, 44-46, 48, 50, 52-54, 58, 60, 63-65, 69, 71, 73, 75, 98, 107, 109, 128, 129, 132, 159, 185, 186,

225, 243, 245, 266, 286, 307, 312, 313, 327, 330, 351
   cortes of 143, 158-159, 162, 259, 282-283, 286, 321, 323-325, 351
   Inquisition in 161-162, 168
   royal succession in 281-284, 321, 323-325
Arana, Diego de 232
Aranda de Duero 68-69
Aranjuez 324
Arbues, St. Peter 168
Archidona 148, 173
Arcos de la Frontera 166
Arévalo 18-22, 25, 27, 28, 33, 49, 52, 77, 84, 88-90, 106, 182, 272
Arian heresy 3
Arias, Juan, Bishop of Segovia 47, 58, 59
arquebus 330
Arronches 79
Arthur, Prince of England 188, 247, 261, 269, 273, 291, 295, 306, 316
   death 319-320

Baena 167
Baeza 48
Bahama Islands 220-222, 229
Baltanás, Battle of (1475) 88-91, 101
Barcelona 24, 64, 65, 126, 143-144, 225, 236-239, 243, 244, 329, 331
Barcelona, Treaty of (1493) 228, 239, 245, 252, 254
Bariay Bay 212
Barletta 323-324
Barrientos, Bishop Lope 27
Barrionuevo 297, 298, 300, 301
Bartolomé the shepherd 105
Basilicata 313, 329
Basques and Basque provinces 6, 62, 68, 87, 98, 100, 157
Bayona 236
Bayonne 317
Baza 186, 189-193, 195, 197
Beatriz, Princess of Portugal 45, 126, 142-143, 155, 195
Beatriz de Bobadilla, Marquesa de Moya 20, 25, 33, 50-51, 66, 68-69, 73, 79, 100-103, 133, 163, 175, 181-182, 192, 204, 209, 319, 344, 346
Belalcázar, Fray Juan de 182, 184
Beltrán de la Cueva 21, 26, 27, 37, 131
Benamaquis 164-165
Benavente, Count of (Rodrigo Pimentel) 26, 68, 74, 88-91, 101-102, 121, 123, 171,

175, 295
Benavente, Count of (son of Rodrigo
    Pimentel) 350-351
Benedictines 185, 243
Benevento 291
Berbers 2
Berdejo 54, 55
Berenguela, Queen of León 10
Bermeja Mountains 311
Bernáldez, Andrés (historian) 81, 160, 169,
    198, 209, 278
Bernáldez, Juan 177
Besançon, Archbishop of 307-309, 324, 326
Bidasoa River 24, 41, 97
Bigornia, Pass of 54
Bilbao 98
Biscay, Bay of 24, 73, 272, 351
Black Death 12, 15, 23
Blanca, Queen of Castile 18, 37
Blois 317
Blois, Treaty of (1504) 341
Boabdil (Abu Abdallah), King of Granada
    151, 152, 163-164, 172-173, 178, 181, 190,
    192-196
    Spanish capture of 155-156
    surrenders Granada 200-201
Bobadilla, Beatriz de SEE Beatriz de
    Bobadilla
Bobadilla, Francisco de 293, 305, 309-311
    death 322
Bobadilla, Pedro de 100
Boccaccio, Giovanni 245
Bohemia 255, 317
Bojador, Cape 117-118
Boleyn, Anne 316
Borgia, Caesar 218, 253-254, 289, 291, 294,
    314, 323, 331-332
Borgia, Cardinal Juan 246, 253
Borgia, Cardinal Rodrigo (SEE ALSO
    Alexander VI, Pope) 63, 64, 66, 67, 109,
    136, 162, 217
Boulier, Marcial 338
Brazil 214, 251, 304, 348
Brett, Stephen 316
Bristol 276
Brittany 341
Brotherhood, Holy SEE Holy Brotherhood
Brussels 260, 286, 287, 290, 308, 309, 316,
    325, 336, 344, 350
Bryce, James (historian) 268
Buil, Fray 239, 248, 250, 263-265
Buitrago 37

Burgo de Osma 52, 53, 55, 57, 69, 93
Burgos 17, 84, 88, 90-92, 97, 98, 100, 129,
    156, 272, 275, 338
Burgos, Alonso de, Bishop of Cuenca (later
    Palencia) 136, 139, 150, 209, 295
Burgundy 60, 103, 119, 308, 313, 355

Cabeza de Vaca, Pedro Núñez 54
Cabezas del Pozo 51
Cabot, John 276
Cabra, Count of 124, 155, 157, 164, 167-168,
    173, 289, 315
Cabral, Pedro Alvarez 304
Cabrera, Andrés de 51, 66-70, 73-, 77, 79,
    97, 100-103, 123, 139, 163, 175, 209
Cabrero, Juan 204-205
Cáceres 112, 127
Cádiz 115, 225, 238, 240, 247, 263, 265, 310,
    318
Cádiz, Marqués (later Duke) de (Rodrigo
    Ponce de León) 23, 24, 49, 120-122, 124,
    131, 143-144, 155, 163, 238, 252
    meets Queen Isabel for the first time
        114-115
    leader in the war for reconquest of
        Granada 146-154, 156-157, 160, 164-
        167, 172-174, 176-179, 181-183, 185-
        186, 191, 193, 199
    death 215
Caesar, Julius 38
Calabria 261, 313, 329
Calatayud 54, 57, 266
Calatrava 9
Calatrava, Order of 9, 26, 82, 151
Calicut 282, 284, 293
Calixtus III, Pope 52, 117
Cambil 168
Cameroon 18
Campania 313, 314
Canary Islands 9, 116-120, 128, 171, 176,
    177, 212, 214-215, 236, 284, 292, 358
    evangelization of the natives 63-64, 120
    attempted enslavement of the natives
        196-197, 216
    Columbus in 216
Cangas de Oñis 3
Cantabrian Mountains 3
Cantalapiedra 90, 111, 112, 132-133
Cao, Diogo 184
Caonabo 248
Cap Haitien 231
Cape Verde Islands 284

Capua 314

Caraffa, Cardinal 217

caravel, design of 170, 214

Cárdenas, Alonso de (Master of Santiago) 107, 121, 127, 132, 149, 152-153, 164

Cárdenas, Alonso de (grandson of the above, son of Gutierre) 276

Cárdenas, Gutierre de 52-56, 66, 73-74, 76-77, 91, 106, 112, 121, 122, 149, 173, 178, 181, 191-193, 201-, 210, 238, 258-259, 315, 317, 327-328

Cardeñosa 34

Carib Indians 248, 263

Caribbean Sea and region 220, 230, 277, 322

Carmona 163

Carrillo, Alonso, Archbishop of Toledo 22, 26-28, 31-33, 35-38, 41, 43, 47, 52, 53, 60, 62, 64-66, 68-71, 73-78, 135, 210, 218, 242, 256, 257

    rescues Princess Isabel 51

    marries Princess Isabel and Fernando 57-58

    rebels against Queen Isabel 80-82, 88-89, 91-92, 94-95, 104

    final degradation and death 123-124, 151

Cartagena 252

Cartagena, Bishop of 47

Cártama 165

Cartello (courier) 272

Carthusians 59

Carvajal, Alonso Sánchez de 310

Casas, Bartolomé de Las SEE Las Casas, Bartolomé de

Cascais 236

Castañar 211

Castañeda, Count of 76

Castile 1, 6-10, 12, 13, 18, 21, 23, 25, 27-31, 38, 39, 41, 44-47, 49-53, 57, 59-64, 66-68, 70, 73-79, 83-85, 88-90, 92, 97-100, 104, 106, 107, 109-111, 113, 116, 119, 120, 122, 123, 125, 128-133, 135, 137, 141, 147, 149, 158, 159, 168, 174, 185, 192, 197, 203, 207, 216, 229, 244, 256, 260, 275, 281, 286, 289, 291, 307, 311, 313, 325, 333, 334, 337, 350-353

    cortes of 13, 47, 62, 68, 98, 129-133, 135, 154, 281-282, 287, 289, 321, 324-326, 350, 352

Castro, Count of 56

Castronuño 36, 37, 86, 95-96, 106, 111, 112, 116, 132-133

Catalonia 23, 24, 45, 50, 64, 128, 129, 143, 158, 181, 228, 243, 271, 330

Cavarrubios 111

CATHERINE, PRINCESS (daughter of Isabel and Fernando) 200, 280, 295, 306, 321, 341, 355

    birth and baptism 168-169

    appearance and character 270-271, 315

    negotiations for marriage to Prince Arthur of England 188, 247, 261, 269, 273, 294, 295, 341

    marriage to Prince Arthur of England 309, 314-316, 320

    negotiations for marriage to Prince Henry of England 320-321, 328-329, 332

Cayo Moa, Port 224

Cazorla 259

Cebreros 83-84

Celestine III, Pope 9

Cephalonia 314

Cerignola, Battle of (1503) 329-330

Chacón, Gonzalo 19, 33, 35, 52, 66, 76-77, 103, 131, 173, 327

Chanca, Dr. Diego Alvarez 248

Charles V, Emperor (Charles I, King of Spain) 230, 293

    birth 304

    as a child, during Queen Isabel's lifetime 308, 314, 327, 336-339, 341, 344

    as King and Emperor 349, 351, 353-356, 358

Charles VIII, King of France 15, 188, 225, 228, 240, 273, 275, 313

    appearance and character 245

    invasion of Italy 245-247, 251, 257, 260-261, 273, 294, 295

    death 289

Charles of Anjou 245

Chigales 98

China 3, 205, 219, 223, 229

China Sea 118

Chios 118

Christendom 268-269, 304, 347, 354-355, 358

Cid, El (Rodrigo Diaz de Vivar) 7, 15

Cidi Ceibona 298

Cieza 110

Cifuentes, Count of 83, 153-154, 311-312

Cisneros, Cardinal Francisco Ximénes de, Archbishop of Toledo 210-211, 242, 275, 283, 285, 290, 334, 349, 352-354

    as confessor of Queen Isabel 211, 180

appointed Archbishop of Toledo 256-260
as reformer of the Church 243-244, 266-267, 287-288, 291, 302, 334, 354, 357
and the conversion of Granada 295-302, 311-312
Cistercians 136, 185
Claudia, Princess 314, 317, 327, 329, 336, 338, 341
Climent, Felip 53
Coca 50, 51
Coelho, Gonzalo 348
Coelho, Nicolau 294, 304
Cogullado 237
Coimbra 7
Coín 165
Colmeñares, Juan de 227-228
Coloma, Juan de 205
Colonna, Cardinal Giovanni 253
Columbus, Bartholomew 185, 249-250, 276, 292
COLUMBUS, CHRISTOPHER 33, 192, 275, 277, 304, 311, 315, 325, 360
Genoese origin 119
appearance and character 119, 169
alleged Jewish ancestry 169
arrives in Portugal 118-119
first meeting with Queen Isabel 169-170
project of reaching the Indies 170-171, 176, 184, 188-190, 201, 203-207
first voyage (1492-93) 211-216, 219-225, 228-236
between first and second voyages 236-239
second voyage (1493-96) 238, 244, 262-265
third voyage (1498-1500) 276, 282, 284, 292-293
arrested and chained 309-310
fourth voyage (1502-04) 318, 321-323, 347, 348
treatment of the Indians 197, 229-230, 262-265, 292-293
last tribute to Isabel 348
Columbus, Fernando 204
Columbus, Diego (brother of Christopher) 249-250
Columbus, Diego (son of Christopher) 215, 348
Concepción, Port 228-229
Concepción de la Vega 292
Conchillos 350

Congo River 184
Constance, Council of 134, 355
Constantinople 3, 136, 143, 159
conversos 67, 138-139, 162, 207-209, 288
Córdoba 3, 6, 7, 10, 11, 49, 67, 124, 125, 129, 149-151, 156, 159, 161, 163, 164, 166, 167, 172-174, 176-179, 185, 188, 229
Córdoba, Emirs of 5, 15
Córdoba, Gonzalo de (the "great captain") 164, 199, 200, 238, 247, 303, 314, 340
military commander for Spain in Italy 252-253, 255, 261, 275, 295, 305, 313-314, 323, 324, 329-330, 332, 336, 341-342
Córdoba, Iñigo de 289
Coronil, El 157
cortes, political character of 129
Cortés, Hernán 89, 239
Coruña SEE La Coruña
Cosa, Juan de la 215, 231
Costa, Cardinal 217
Costa del Sol 166
Costa Rica 323
Council, Royal 132, 277
and Columbus' first voyage 203-205, 212
Covadonga 3, 15, 180, 202
Coyanza 7
Crooked Island (Bahamas) 222
Crusades 136
Cuba 229, 263
exploration by Columbus 222-224, 249, 262
Cubillas 111, 112
Cuéllar 37
Cuenca 129, 135

Damascus 2
Dávila, Pedrarias 32
Daza, Juan 243
Delfino, Gil 291-292, 337
Despeñaperros Pass 8-10, 15, 31, 43, 148, 159
Devon 316
Deza, Diego de 188, 240-205, 288
Dias, Bartholomew 184-185, 188, 206, 282
Dominica Island (West Indies) 248
Dominican Republic SEE Hispaniola
Dominicans 59, 267
Dordux, Ali 183-184
Drake, Francis 316
Dueñas 56, 60, 61, 91, 100
Duero River 6, 55, 68, 69, 79, 84, 86, 90, 93,

94, 105, 106, 265, 271
Duvaliers of Haiti 230

Eanes, Gil 118
Easter 1, 16, 17, 149, 152, 159, 177, 195, 198,
    237, 288, 318, 323
Ebro River 6, 8, 126
Écija 161, 167
Edward I, King of England 316
Edward the Black Prince 12
Egypt 3, 190
Eleanor, Princess 287, 308
elephants 118, 129
Elna 71
encomienda SEE repartimiento
England 141, 169, 188, 199, 228, 246, 271,
    274-275, 277, 279, 315-316, 328-329
Enríquez, Enrique 258, 300
Enríquez, Admiral Fadrique SEE Fadrique
    Enríquez, Admiral
Eresma River 101
Ermesinda, Queen of Asturias 3, 75
Espés, Ramón and Gaspar 54, 57
Espina, Fray Alonso de 139
Estrada, Duke Fernando de 328-329
Ethiopia 205
Eugenius IV, Pope 215
Évora 198
Évora, Bishop of 127
Extremadura 71, 79, 109-112, 125-128

Fadrique, King of Naples 289, 312-314, 338,
    341
Fadrique Enríquez, Admiral 26, 27, 51, 60,
    65, 203, 334, 352
Fáfila, King of Asturias 3
Fajardo, Pedro (Adelantado of Murcia) 82,
    303
Fáñez, Alvar 8
Farnese, Giulia 217
FERNANDO, KING OF ARAGON
    (husband of Queen Isabel) 39, 60, 100,
    109, 115, 116, 119-121, 129, 135-136, 143-
    144, 171, 197, 221, 223, 234, 240-242, 261,
    263, 271, 290, 291, 293, 331, 336, 359
    appearance and character 44
    negotiations for marriage to Princess
        Isabel 46-48, 50-51
    journey to marry Princess Isabel 52-58
    marriage to Princess Isabel 58-59, 63
    personal letters to Isabel 71-72, 81-82,
        84-85, 177, 180-181, 321

as Prince of Castile 61-62, 64-66, 68-72
joint rule of Castile with Isabel 74-77
in the war of the succession with
    Portugal 78-88, 90-97, 104-107, 111-
    112, 123-128
and the establishment of the Holy
    Brotherhood 97-98
administration of justice in Castile 110,
    122-124, 132-133, 175-176
and Roussillon 125-126, 158-159, 228,
    239-240, 262, 271, 323, 330-332
becomes King of Aragon 128
and the reconquest of Granada 158-152,
    154-168, 172-174, 176-187, 189-196,
    198-202
and Church reform 135-136
supports Inquisition in Aragon 162
attempted assassinations of 181-182,
    224-228, 359
and Columbus 204-206, 237-239, 310,
    317-318
and the Treaty of Barcelona 228, 239
and the Italian wars 245, 247, 252, 255-
    256, 294-295, 329-331, 341-342
named, with Isabel, "the Catholic kings"
    274
and the death of Prince Juan 278-279
and the succession to the thrones of
    Aragon and Castile 280-283, 285-286,
    307-308, 318-319, 321, 323-327
and the conversion of Granada 298-303,
    311-313
and his grandson Charles 336, 338-339
and Queen Isabel's last illness and death
    340, 342-343, 346
and Queen Isabel's last testament 344-
    346
final tribute to Queen Isabel 346
and the succession fo Queen Isabel in
    Castile 349-352
death 353-354
Fernando I, King of Castile 7, 159
Fernando II, King of León 9
St. Fernando III, King of Castile and León
    10, 11, 15, 145, 259
Fernando IV, King of Castile 11
Fernando of Antequera, King of Aragon 13,
    15, 44-45
Fernando, Prince (son of Philip and Juana)
    327, 337, 339, 353
Fernando de la Cerda, Prince 11
Ferrante (Fernando) I, King of Naples 143,

245, 246, 252
Ferrante (Fernando) II, King of Naples 254, 255
Ferrante, Prince of Naples 314
Ferrer, Juan 47
Ferriz, Pedro, Bishop of Tarazona 134-135
Fez 109
Flanders 260, 268, 271, 273-274, 286, 304, 307, 309, 316, 324, 325, 331, 333, 334, 337
Florence 134, 237, 251, 341
Florida 220
Fonseca, Bishop of Córdoba 317, 334
Fonseca, Archbishop of Sevilla 31, 36, 37, 41, 50-51, 62, 65
Fonseca, Alonso de 283
Fonseca, Antonio de 166, 252, 254
Fonseca, Juan de, Archbishop of Sevilla 238
Forli 294
Fornovo, Battle of (1495) 255
Fortune Island (Bahamas) 222
France 57, 63, 65, 75, 96, 97, 103, 119, 188, 204-205, 225, 228, 240, 261, 273, 281, 289, 313, 316, 324, 326, 327, 333, 337, 341, 342, 354
    invasions of Italy by 244-247, 251-256, 294, 313-314, 323, 329-331, 336
Franciscans 59, 104, 107, 190, 211, 243-244, 257, 260, 267, 287-288, 291-292, 337, 343
Franco, Nicolás 109, 120, 136, 139
French Revolution 242
Fruela I, King of Asturias 4
Fuensalida, Gómez de 287, 307-309, 316, 317, 325, 336, 338, 340, 342, 344-345
Fuenterrabía 97, 317
Fuentesauco 93
fueros 68, 98

St. Gabriel the Archangel 343
Gaeta 330, 336
Galicia 88, 109, 133, 154, 163, 171, 175-176, 185, 215, 236, 351
Galíndez de Carvajal (historian) 300
Galíndo, Juan Fernández 18
Gama, Paul da 294
Gama, Vasco da 207, 277, 282, 284, 293-294, 304
García, King of Asturias 5
García Fernández, Count of Castile 6
Garigliano River 333
Garigliano River, Battle of (1503) 336
St. Gennadius 5
Genil River 147, 163, 173, 174

Genoa 118-119, 251
Gerald the Fearless 9
Germaine de Foix, Queen 350-351, 353
Germany 268, 331, 338, 354
Gerona 50
Ghent 304, 354
Gherardo, Cardinal 217
Gibralfaro 179
Gibraltar, Rock of 2, 7, 11, 12, 15, 23, 24, 73, 115, 202, 311
Gibraltar, Straits of 116, 145, 149, 196
Gijón 4
Girón, Pedro (Master of Calatrava) 26, 29-31, 43, 272, 358
Godfrey of Bouillon 290
gold 118, 161, 224, 231, 232, 237-238, 247, 248, 262, 264
Gómara 53
Gomera Island SEE Canary Islands
Gomes, Fernando 118
González, Count Fernán 157
Gonzalo de Córdoba SEE Córdoba, Gonzalo de
Good Hope, Cape of 185, 206, 277, 282, 294
Gozco 199
Gracián de Sesé 49, 71, 93
Granada 8, 11, 13, 14, 23, 110, 114, 137, 138, 142, 203, 207, 225, 240, 243, 244, 261, 293, 305-306, 310, 314-316
    kingdom of: population, size, resources 145, 147
    division of the kingdom 151
    final war for its reconquest 143, 144, 146-152, 155-161, 171, 176-178, 180-181, 184-187, 189-190, 192-196, 198-202, 241, 252, 320, 358
    surrender of 200-203, 207
    Inquisition extended to 288
    conversion of 296-303, 311
    burial of Isabel and Fernando in 343-344
Granada, Treaty of (1500) 313-314, 329
Great Inagua Island (West Indies) 223-224
Gredos Mountains 38, 83
Guacanagiri 231, 248
Guadalajara 67, 129
Guadalete River 145, 146, 180
Guadalhorce River 160, 164-166
Guadalquivir River 10, 113, 116, 133, 348
Guadalupe, shrine of the Blessed Virgin Mary at 111-112, 125, 172, 234, 239, 248, 265, 281, 315, 318
Guadalupe, Our Lady of 230

Guadalupe Island (West Indies) 248
Guadarrama Mountains 22, 37, 38, 64, 80,
    83, 101, 106, 111, 115, 129, 148
Guadiana River 79
Guadix 181, 189, 193, 194
Guanahani Island SEE San Salvador
Guanches 119, 196 (SEE also Canary
    Islands)
Guernica, tree of 68, 98
Guesclin, Bertrand du 12-13
Guinea coast of Africa 64, 114, 118-120, 128
gum mastic 118
Guyenne, Duke Charles of 44, 50, 60, 62
Guzmán, Alonso Pérez de, "the Good" 11
Guzmán, Fernán Pérez de (historian) 14
Guzmán, Leonor de 12

Habsburgs 247, 253, 260, 268, 269, 286, 308,
    317, 354
Haiti SEE Hispaniola
Haro, Count of SEE Velasco, Pedro
Hassan "the Old" 189, 193
Henry I, King of Castile 10
Henry II of Trastámara, King of Castile 12-
    13, 15
Henry III, King of Castile 13, 15
Henry IV, King of Castile 2, 14, 18, 20-27,
    34-38, 41-43, 38-51, 57-58, 64, 66-68, 97,
    104, 109, 121, 124, 130-131, 164, 182, 187,
    210, 218
    rebellion against (1465-68) 27-29, 32-34,
        81, 85
    Princess Isabel declared his heir SEE
        Toros de Guisando, Pact of
    denounces Isabel's marriage to
        Fernando 59-63
    reconciliation with Princess Isabel 69-70
    death 71-74
    burial at the shrine of Guadalupe 112
Henry, Prince of Aragon 13-14
Henry "the Navigator," Prince of Portugal
    14, 64, 114, 116-118, 170, 184, 188, 214,
    277, 282
Henry VII, King of England 187, 269, 271,
    273, 276, 291, 295, 309, 316, 320, 328-329
Henry VIII, King of England 169, 261-262,
    280, 320, 328-329, 332, 341, 355
heresy 141
Hermandad, Santa SEE Holy Brotherhood
Herrera, Diego de 120
Hieronymites 59
Hippo 3

Hispaniola 223, 230-232, 237, 238, 240, 247,
    263, 265, 305, 318, 323, 348
    discovery 224
    exploration by Columbus 225, 228-229
    first colonization 248
    Columbus' governorship of 250, 262-
        265, 292-293, 304, 325
    Bobadilla's governorship of 309-311
    Ovando's governorship of 322
Hitler, Adolf 141, 209, 230
Hojeda, Alonso de SEE Ojeda, Alonso de
Holy Brotherhood 97-100, 109, 123, 132,
    164, 185
Holy League 255, 260-262
Holy Roman Empire 181, 262, 268-269, 341,
    354
Holy Sepulcher 190
Honduras 323
Horn, Cape 230
hospitals, field 160, 161
Huéjar 303
Huelva 212, 215, 237
Huete 104
Hungary 317
Hurtado, Martin 155
Hurtado de Mendoza, Diego, Archbishop of
    Sevilla 173, 257, 328
Hurtado de Mendoza, Pedro 259
Hus, John 134

St. Ignatius of Loyola 140
Illora 173
Imola 294
India 3, 170, 188, 206-207, 294, 304
Indian Ocean 277, 292, 294
Indians (of the Americas) 197, 222-223, 229-
    230, 238, 248, 262, 264, 276, 310, 354-355
Innocent III, Pope 9
Innocent VIII, Pope 161-162, 167, 174, 184,
    185, 217
Inquisition, Spanish 161, 168, 288
    establishment in Castile 139-142, 242
    procedures of 140-141
    use of torture 142
    establishment in Aragon and Catalonia
        161-162, 185
    establishment in Valencia 162
    and the Jews 207-208
    establishment in Granada 288, 296
Inter caetera (bull of Pope Alexander VI)
    238-239, 250
Iran 205

Ireland 169
ISABEL, QUEEN OF CASTILE
  birth 1-2, 15-16
  infancy 17
  childhood at Arévalo 18-20
  at the court of Henry IV 21-32
  establishes her claim as heir to the
    throne of Castile 32-39
  personal appearance 35, 241
  personal religious life 124-125, 211, 234,
    347
  marriage 41-52, 56-59, 124, 350, 356
  personal letters to Fernando 172
  from marriage to coronation 59-72
  coronation 72-74
  joint rule of Castile with Fernando 74-77
  war of the succession with Portugal 78-
    92, 96-97, 103-108
  makes peace with Portugal 126-128, 142-
    143
  miscarriage, loss of son 83-84
  establishes Holy Brotherhood 97-100
  rescue of her daughter Isabel in Segovia
    100-103
  administration of justice in Castile 109-
    116, 120-127, 133, 175-176
  at the *cortes* of Castile (1480) 129-133
  and the reform of the Church 133-136,
    210-211, 241-244, 256-260, 266-267,
    287-288, 292-292, 302, 337-338, 354,
    357
  on the election of Pope Alexander VI
    217-218, 225, 238
  and the Inquisition 139-142, 161-162,
    357, 359
  and the reconquest of Granada 143-144,
    146, 149-152, 154-161, 163-168, 172-
    174, 176-187, 189-196, 198-202, 356
  attempted assassination of 181-182
  and the attempted assassination of
    Fernando 224-228
  and Christopher Columbus 169-171,
    188-190, 201, 203-206, 211, 221-223,
    237-239, 247-250, 262-266, 276-277,
    284, 292-293, 310, 317-318, 347-348,
    356-357
  protector of native populations of
    Spanish colonies 197, 230, 263-265,
    304-305, 310, 346, 357-358
  expulsion of the Jews from Spain 207-
    210, 358
  and the Treaty of Barcelona 228, 239

  and the Italian wars 247, 252-253, 261-
    262, 294-295, 332
  and the marriages of her children 288-
    277, 295, 314-315, 319-320, 328-329,
    341
  and the death of Prince Juan 277-279
  named, with Fernando, "the Catholic
    kings" 274
  and the succession to the thrones of
    Castile and Aragon 280-287, 289-290,
    305-309, 317-321, 324-325
  and the conversion of Granada 298-303,
    311-312
  and the insanity of her daughter Juana
    325-331, 333-337, 339-340, 344-345
  and her grandson Charles 327, 336-339
  last illness, last testament, and death
    342-347, 349-350
  achievements (summary) 356-358
  holiness 358-360
Isabel of Portugal, Queen of Castile
  (mother of Queen Isabel) 1-2, 14, 17-19,
  22, 25, 27, 33, 272
ISABEL, PRINCESS (daughter of Isabel
  and Fernando) 60, 75, 79, 98, 105-106,
  163, 166, 168, 169, 174, 179, 181, 185, 186,
  192, 194, 196, 201, 236, 248, 270, 295, 314,
  321
    rescued by her mother in Segovia 100-
    102
    negotiations for marriage to Prince
      Afonso of Portugal 128-129, 142-143,
      155-156, 187, 195
    marriage to Prince Afonso of Portugal
      197-198
    widowhood 198, 200, 320
    marriage to King Manuel of Portugal
      269-270, 274, 277, 280
    as heir to Castile 281-285
    death 285, 293, 299, 306
Isabel, Princess, daughter of Philip and
  Juana 316
Isabela (Hispaniola) 248, 264
Islam 156
Italy 13, 44, 45, 63, 118, 127, 186, 237, 238,
  245, 273, 312, 324, 331, 337, 341, 353, 354
  French invasions 228, 240, 244-247, 251-
    256, 294, 313-314, 329-330, 336
ivory 118

Jaén 24, 25, 31, 67, 129, 148, 168, 175, 189,
  191, 192, 259

Jamaica 249, 323, 348
St. James (Santiago) 5, 9, 15, 113, 122, 202
James I, King of Aragon 10, 145
Japan 170, 219, 223
St. Jeanne de Valois 289
Jem, Prince 247, 254-254
Jeremiah, Prophet 260
Jérez de la Frontera 115, 120, 121, 146
Jerusalem 103, 137, 190
Jews 67, 138-140, 145, 207-210, 274, 311-312
Jiménez, Sancho 9
St. Joan of Arc 356
Joanna II, Queen of Naples 245, 256, 313
St. John the Baptist 343
St. John the Evangelist 122, 129, 166, 343
St. John of the Cross 359
John I, King of Portugal 13, 14
John II, King of Portugal 41, 43, 92-95, 109,
    118, 127, 143, 155-156, 170, 176, 188, 195,
    198, 206-207, 209, 236
John, Crown Prince of Portugal, grandson
    of Queen Isabel 309
Juan II, King of Aragon (father of
    Fernando) 21, 23, 24, 64-65, 68, 71, 72, 97,
    106, 125-126, 158, 228, 245
    blindness cured by operation 39-40
    seeks marriage of his son Fernando to
        Isabel 43-47, 49-50, 52-54, 56
    death 126
Juan I, King of Castile 13, 14, 15, 45
Juan II, King of Castile 1, 13-15, 17-18, 102
JUAN, PRINCE (son of Isabel and
    Fernando) 128, 143, 144, 159, 163, 168,
    169, 185, 186, 188, 192, 197-199, 201, 226,
    238, 314
    birth and baptism 122-123
    appearance and character 270-271
    negotiations for marriage to Princess
        Margaret of Austria 247, 253, 260, 268
    marriage to Princess Margaret of
        Austria 268, 274-276
    death 277-279, 286, 299, 306, 320-321,
        328
Juan, Prince, son of Fernando and
    Germaine de Foix 351
Juan "the Pacer" 54-55
Juana, Queen of Castile (wife of Henry IV)
    20-22, 25, 36-38, 41, 43, 77
Juana Enríquez, Queen of Aragon (mother
    of Fernando) 39, 44
Juana "la Beltraneja" (daughter of Queen
    Juana of Castile, wife of Henry IV) 22, 27,

34, 41, 59-62, 72, 73, 86, 124, 129, 142
    claims throne of Castile 77-78, 80, 83, 88,
        103, 134
    abandons claim to throne of Castile 128
JUANA, PRINCESS (daughter of Isabel
    and Fernando) 42, 132, 144, 156, 159, 163,
    169, 199, 201, 269, 304, 314, 316, 338, 341
    birth and baptism 129
    appearance and character 270-271
    negotiations for marriage to Archduke
        Philip of Austria and Burgundy 187,
        247, 253, 260
    marriage to Archduke Philip of Austria
        and Burgundy 268, 271-274, 316, 330,
        332, 337, 339-340, 344-345
    insanity of 272, 281-287, 290, 305, 325-
        328, 330-331, 333-337, 339-340, 344-
        345, 349-353
    succession to the thrones of Castile and
        Aragon 286, 305-309, 313, 316-319,
        321, 323-324, 342, 344, 349-351
Judge, Joseph 222
Julius II, Pope 332, 341, 353

Kenya 282
Knights of Rhodes 137

La Coruña 176, 315, 351
La Guardia, "Holy Child" of 207-208
La Higuerela, Battle of (1431) 14-15
La Mancha 8, 31, 148
La Mota 33-337, 340
La Mejorada 339
La Navidad SEE Navidad
La Rábida monastery 169, 188, 201, 203,
    211-212, 215, 237
La Serna, Miguel López de, Bishop of the
    Canary Islands 197
Lagos 119
Laino 261
Lalaing, Antoine de (historian) 317, 318,
    326
Lanjarón 303
Laredo 271-272, 316, 337
Las Casas, Bartolomé de 216, 229-230, 237,
    265, 293
Las Navas (near Avila) 99
Las Navas de Tolosa, Battle of (1212) 9, 10,
    12, 15, 159
Las Zubias 199
Ledesma 93
Lemos, Count of 164, 171, 175

León (country) 5-10, 15, 176
León (city) 5, 7, 129
León, Rodrigo Ponce de SEE Cádiz, Marqués de
Leonor, Queen of Castile 13
Lérin, Count of 303
Leyte Gulf, Battle of (1944) 90
Libya 353
Liguria 63
Lille 273
Lisbon 185, 236, 237, 277, 294, 304
Logroño 5
logwood 348
Loja 147, 149-152, 155, 162-163, 172-175, 177, 180
lombards (cannon) 159-161, 164, 165, 168, 173, 183, 189
Long Island (Bahamas) 222
longbow 172
López, Rodrigo (Treasurer) 182-183
Lorca 186
Louis XI, King of France 24, 41, 44, 60-61, 65, 66, 96, 97, 103, 125, 158, 245
Louis XII, King of France 289, 291, 294, 295, 305, 313, 316, 317, 324, 332, 341-342, 350-351
Low Countries SEE Netherlands
Lubia 55
Lucas, Miguel 21, 24, 67
Lucena, Battle of (1483) 155, 157
Ludlow 316, 320
Luna, Alvaro de 14, 17-19, 30, 48
Luna, Count of 70
Luna, Juana de 48
Luna, Pedro de (Antipope) 14
Luther, Martin 355
Lyons, Treaty of 329-330, 336

Machiavelli, Niccolò 134, 245, 251
Madeira 118, 119, 171, 212
Madrid 6, 26, 36, 38, 62, 64, 66, 79, 80, 95, 96, 104, 109-111, 121, 122, 129, 148, 151, 152, 168, 171, 237, 241, 244, 289, 291, 318, 324, 326, 327
Madrigal de las Altas Torres 1, 4, 16-18, 23, 36, 50, 51, 65, 69, 90, 93, 98, 124, 172, 277
Madroño, Battle of (1462) 23
Mafia 244
Málaga 137, 145, 150-152, 160, 165, 166, 174, 178, 303, 311
    siege and capture of by Isabel and Fernando 177, 179-184, 189, 191-193

malaria 331
Maldonado, Alfonso 100-103
Maldonado, Rodrigo 176
Malines 260
Mamelukes of Egypt 190
Mancha, La SEE La Mancha
Manrique, Archbishop of Sevilla 161
Manrique, Gómez 123
Mantua, Marquis of 331
Manuel I, King of Portugal 289, 294, 321
    marriage to Princess Isabel 269, 274, 277
    expulsion of the Jews from Portugal 274
    in Castile after the death of Prince Juan 281-285
    marriage to Princess Maria 304, 306, 309
maravedi, value of 132
Marchena, Fray Antonio 169, 171, 188, 201, 212-213
Marden, Luis and Ethel 222
Margaret, Archduchess of Austria 247, 257, 260, 267, 268, 273-274, 320, 329, 332-333
    marriage to Prince Juan 274-276
    appearance and character 275
    miscarriage after Prince Juan's death 280-281
    in the Netherlands 308, 354
Margarit, Pedro 249-250, 265
Maria of Portugal, Queen of Castile 12
Maria of Aragon, Queen of Castile 14
MARIA, PRINCESS (daughter of Isabel and Fernando) 159, 163, 169, 200, 274, 280, 341
    birth and baptism 150
    appearance 270
    marriage to King Manuel I of Portugal 304, 306, 309
Marimón, Chief Inquisitor for Catalonia 162
marriage, Catholic 34-36
Martin "the Humane," King of Aragon 13
Martinique 322
Mary the Blessed Virgin 5, 10, 123, 169, 202, 226, 234, 343, 347
Matienzo, Sub-prior Tomás de 286-287, 290, 305, 307
Mattingly, Garrett (historian) 305
Maximilian, Emperor 246, 247, 252-255, 260, 268, 294, 295, 317, 329, 341, 353
Mazariegos, Pedro de 90
Medellín 127-128, 239
Medellín, Countess of 126-127
Medici family of Florence 251

Medici, Giuliano de 134
Medici, Lorenzo de 134, 251
Medici, Piero de 251
Medina del Campo 27, 33, 85, 93, 98, 106, 143, 146, 148, 171, 172, 277, 333, 338, 339, 342, 346, 348, 358
Medina del Campo, Sentence of (1465) 27
Medina del Campo, Treaty of (1489) 187-188
Medina del Rioseco 60-62
Medina Sidonia, Duke of (Enrique de Guzmán) 23, 24, 49, 83, 99-100, 114-116, 121, 123, 124, 148, 163, 164, 188, 350
Medinaceli, Count of 53, 54
Medinaceli, Duke of 188, 203, 237
Mediterranean Sea 74, 82, 136, 137, 354
Melilla 353
Melindi 282
Melun, Monsieur de 337
Membrilla 121
Mencia de la Torre 50-51
Méndez, Diego 323
Mendoza family 37, 41, 43, 46, 64
Mendoza, Cardinal Pedro González de 66, 68, 70, 73-77, 80, 88, 94, 101-102, 122, 130, 135, 139, 167-168, 171, 178, 181, 186, 188, 192, 194, 201, 203, 211, 237, 242, 257
    appointed Cardinal 64
    appointed Archbishop of Toledo 151-152
    death 244, 256
Mendoza, Hurtado de SEE Hurtado de Mendoza
Mercado, Gumiel de 56
Mérida 10, 126-128
Mesopotamia 3
Messina, Straits of 253, 255
Mexico 89, 230, 239
St. Michael the Archangel 343
Miguel, Prince (son of Princess Isabel and King Manuel of Portugal) 285-287, 289-292, 305-306
    death 306-308, 312, 321
Milan 255, 261, 291, 294, 305, 312-314, 317, 341, 350
Miller, Townsend (historian) 72, 278, 318, 349
Moclín 167, 173-175, 180, 196
Moguer 212, 214-215, 237
Mohammed II the Conqueror, Sultan of the Turks 136-137, 143
Monroy, Alonso de 126-127

Monserrat, Nicholas 233
Monteagudo 54
Montefrío 174
Montiel, Battle of (1369) 12-13
Montoya, Pedro de, Bishop of Burgo de Osma 52, 53, 56
Montserrat, shrine of the Blessed Virgin Mary at 226
Moors 2-3, 5-14, 23, 24, 100, 114, 117, 144-160, 163, 165-166, 173-174, 177-187, 189, 191-194, 259, 261, 286, 296-303, 311-312, 317, 320, 345
Morena Mountains 31
Morillo, Miguel de 139
Moriscos 312
Morison, Samuel Eliot (historian) 214, 220-222, 236
Morocco 9, 116, 145, 196, 209
Moura 142-143, 155-156
Moya, Marqués de SEE Cabrera, Andrés de
Moya, Marquesa de SEE Beatriz de Bobadilla
Mozambique 282
Munguía, Battle of (1471) 62
Münzer, Dr. Hieronymus 241, 244, 270-271
Murcia 10, 11, 74, 82, 110, 129, 186-187, 302
Muslims 2-4, 7-11, 14, 67, 136, 138-140, 145, 160, 161, 165, 179, 182, 190, 194, 200, 207, 223, 257, 284, 296-298, 300-301, 353

Nájera, Battle of (1367) 12
Nájera, Duke of 350
Namibia 184
Nanni, Fray Francisco 287
Naples, Kingdom of 13, 228, 239-240, 245-247, 251-257, 261, 294-295, 305, 312-314, 323, 329-330, 333, 336, 338-341, 350-353
Natal 185
Navarra 6, 12, 24, 128, 262, 353
Navarrete (historian) 222
Navidad, La (fort in Hispaniola) 232, 248, 250
Nebuchadnezzar, King of Babylon 209
Nemours, Duke of 329-330
Netherlands 103, 187, 268, 281, 286, 287, 308, 313, 326, 327, 333, 337, 350, 353, 354
Newfoundland 251, 276
Nicaragua 323
Nicholas V, Pope 37
Niña (Columbus' ship) 214-216, 221, 224, 231-237, 264-265, 304
Niño, Juan 214

Normans 244

Ocaña 43, 48-50, 52, 71, 90, 107, 258, 287-289, 299, 324
Ocoa Bay 322
Odiel River 212
Ojeda, Alonso de 348
Olias 318
Olmedo 98, 101
Olmedo, First Battle of (1445) 14
Olmedo, Second Battle of (1467) 32
Orbigo River 5
Ordoño I, King of Asturias 5
Ordoño II, King of Asturias 5-6
Ordoño III, King of Asturias 6
Orinoco River 284
Ortega, Juan de 97
Ortego de Prado 147, 162
Orsini, Orsino 217
Ostia 246, 252, 253, 275
Osuna, Bernaldino de 152
Otranto 137-139, 143
Ottoman Empire SEE Turkish Empire
Ovando, Nicolás de 310, 318, 322-323

Pacheco, Juan (for a time Marqués of Villena) 20-33, 35-36, 38-39, 41, 43, 46, 48-52, 57, 59-71, 73, 77, 93, 106, 109, 112, 121, 126, 277
Pacheco Pereira, Duarte SEE Pereira, Duarte Pacheco
Pacific Ocean 89
Padilla, Maria de 12
Palencia, Alonso de (historian) 42, 50, 52-54, 56, 57, 96, 101, 113, 153
Palermo 244-245
Palestine 190, 252
Palos 169, 188, 201, 203-205, 211-215, 236, 237
Pamplona 6
Panama 323
Papal state SEE Rome and the Papal state
Paredes, Count of (Rodrigo Manrique) 106, 121
Parma 255
Pascual, Juan, Bishop of Burgos 267
St. Paul 3, 343
Paul II, Pope 30, 37, 46, 47, 58, 59, 63
Pavia 246
Pazzi conspiracy 134-135
pearls 348
Pedro III, King of Aragon 245

Pedro, King of Castile 12-13, 15
Pelayo, King of Asturias 3, 8, 15, 75, 180
Peleagonzalo, Battle of SEE Toro, Battle of
Peñafiel 69, 70, 88
Peralta, Pierres de, Constable of Navarra 43, 46, 47
Peraza, Beatriz de 196-197, 216
Peraza, Fernán 196-197
Pereira, Duarte Pacheco 117
Pereira, Nun'Alvares 13
Pérez, Fray Juan 201, 212
Perpignan 65, 240
Persia 3
Peru 230, 239
St. Peter 343
Peter Martyr de Anglería 186-187, 199, 211, 218, 225, 240, 259, 270, 276, 278, 279, 284-285, 306, 325-328, 330, 340, 344, 346-347
Philip, Archduke of Austria, Prince of Burgundy and the Netherlands 268, 269, 286, 295, 304-306, 316, 329, 335-336, 338-339, 341
    negotiations for marriage to Princess Juana 187, 253-254, 260
    marriage to Princess Juana 273-274, 316, 330, 332-333, 337, 339-340, 344-345
    as heir apparent, with Juana, to Castile 306-309, 313, 316-319, 321, 323-327
    royal succession in Castile 342, 350-352
    death 352
Philip II, King of Spain 269, 316
Philip III, King of Spain 312
Philippa, Queen of Portugal 14
Phoenicians 117
Piacenza 246
Piccolomini, Cardinal Francisco (Pope Pius III) 331
Pilate, Pontius 209-210
Pina, Ruy de (historian) 236
Pineda, Juan and Pedro de 154
Pinta (Columbus' ship) 214-216, 221, 224, 232-233, 236
Pinzón, Martín Alonso 213-214, 216, 219-221, 224, 232-234, 236-237
Pinzón, Vicente Yáñez 213-214, 224, 231, 235, 236, 304
Pisa 251, 341
Pius II, Pope 47, 58
Pius III, Pope SEE Piccolomini, Cardinal Francesco
Pizarro, Francisco 239
Plantagenets 14

Plasencia 84
Plasencia, Count of 26, 27, 41, 49, 77, 78, 83
Plymouth 316
Poggibonzi 255
Polaris 219, 233
Polo, Marco 117, 118
Polvoraría, Battle of (878) 5, 15
Ponce, Dr. Felipe 289
Ponce de León, Manuel 252
Ponferrada 164, 175
Porres, Juan de 86
Portland 273
Porto Santo Island 171
Portocarrero, Luís Fernández 149, 151, 157, 160
Portugal 11, 24, 28, 41, 45, 48, 57, 64, 77, 79, 83, 95, 97, 103, 114, 119, 126-129, 143, 193, 198, 209, 234, 236, 238-239, 244, 250-251, 277, 281-283, 289, 304, 305, 320, 354, 358
   exploration along the western coast of Africa 116-118, 170, 184-185, 206-207, 236, 282
Prado, Ortega de SEE Ortega de Prado
Prats, Francisco des 242
"Prester John," legend of 117, 205, 238
Protestants 242, 260, 269, 280, 302, 338, 354, 357
Ptolemy, Cladius 284
Puebla, Dr. Rodrigo Gonsalvi de (Spanish ambassador to England) 261, 320, 329, 341
Puerto Rico 233, 248
Pulgar, Fernando de (historian) 103, 113, 130, 140, 167
Pyrenees Mountains 24, 65, 125, 202, 225, 240, 317, 330, 333, 353

Qa'it Bay al-Ashraf Saif ud-Din, Sultan of Egypt 190
quadrant 233
Quevedo, Juan de 338
Quintanilla, Alonso de 97, 99, 100, 171, 188, 190

Rábida, La, monastery of SEE La Rábida monastery
Rada, Rodrigo de, Archbishop of Toledo 10, 12
Ramires, Francisco 312
Ramiro I, King of Asturias 4
Ramiro II, King of Asturias 6, 15
Ramiro III, King of Asturias 6
Ravenna, Battle of (1512) 353

Raymond of Burgundy 8
Raymond of Toulouse (the crusader) 290
Reconquest of Spain from the Moors 2-16, 75, 99, 110, 114, 117, 132, 144, 158-159, 164, 174, 190, 199, 202, 207, 223, 263, 296, 302, 304
Reggio di Calabria 255
repartimiento system 293
Rhodes, siege of (1480) 137
Riario, Cardinal Raffaelo 134-136
Ribera, Diego de 92
Ribera, Juan de 83
Richard the Lion-Hearted, King of England 290
Richmond 329
Rieux, Marshal de 337
Roderick, King of Spain 3, 145, 180
Rojas, Francisco de 247
Roldán, Francisco 292-293
Romagna 294
Rome and the Papal state 253, 268, 275, 331
Romero, Juan 97
Ronda 144, 165-167, 303, 311
Roussillon (Rosellón) 24, 65, 71, 125, 158-159, 225, 228, 239-240, 262, 271, 313, 323, 330-332, 353
Rovere, Cardinal Giuliano della (later Pope Julius II) 162, 246, 252, 253
Ruiforco, monastery of 6
Ruíz, Francisco 299

Saavedra, Fernán Arias de 121
Sagrajas, Battle of (1086) 7
Sahara Desert 116-117
Saint Jean de Luz, Treaty of (1478) 125
Salado River, Battle of (1340) 12, 15
Salamanca 51, 79, 98, 129, 176, 277-278, 351
Salamanca, University of 176, 188, 210
Salcedo 297, 300
"Salic law" of France 75
Salobreña 196
Salses 332
Salzela 211
Samaná Bay 232
Samaná Cay (Bahamas) 222
San Martín de Valdeiglesias 83
San Martín, Juan de 139
San Nicolás, Puerto (Hispaniola) 225
San Salvador Island (Bahamas) 221-222
Sánchez, Bishop of Ciudad Rodrigo 37
Sánchez, Guillén 54
Sancho I, King of Castile 6

Sancho II, King of Castile and León 7
Sancho III, King of Castile 9
Sancho IV, King of Castile 11
Sancho el Mayor, King of Navarra 7
Sande, Ruy de 195
Sanlucár de Barrameda 116, 458
Santa Cruz, Alonso de (historian) 218, 272, 273, 285, 291, 318, 326, 332, 340, 347
Santa Cruz of Córdoba, Abbess of 338
Santa Fe 199, 201, 203, 204
Santa Fe, Capitulations of (1492) 205
Santa Hermandad SEE Holy Brotherhood
Santa Inés of Córdoba, Abbess of 338
Santa María (Columbus' ship) 214-215, 220-221, 224
    shipwreck of 231-232
Santa Maria de Nieva 68
Santa Maria Island SEE Azores Islands
Santander 271, 275
Santángel, Luis de 204-206
Santarem 198
Santiago, Order of 9, 26, 27, 48, 77, 106-107, 109, 121, 126, 132
Santiago de Compostela 7, 8, 10, 15, 122, 175-176, 244
Santiago de Compostela, Archbishop of 315
Santillana, Marqués of 41, 46
Santo Domingo 264, 292, 309, 310, 322, 347, 348
Santo Dolmingo de la Calzada 156
Scales, Lord (Anthony Woodville) 172-173
Sardinia 228, 313
"Sargasso Sea" 219
Savelli, Cardinal Giovanni Battista 253
Savonarola, Girolamo 251, 255
Savoy 246, 332
Segovia 1, 22, 23, 26, 27, 32, 36, 64, 66, 70, 72, 73-75, 78, 79, 85, 97, 98, 100-105, 109, 129, 148, 171, 182, 210, 283, 286, 295, 331-334, 344, 356
Seminara, First Battle of (1496) 261
Seminara, Second Battle of (1503) 329
Seneca 170
Senior, Abraham 209
Sepúlveda 64
Sesé, Gracián de SEE Gracián de Sesé
Setenil 161
Sevilla 10, 11, 15, 49, 74, 83, 100, 113-116, 118, 121-124, 129, 133, 139-140, 142, 146, 148, 154, 157, 161-163, 167, 190, 192, 195, 198, 219, 237, 239, 244, 264, 282, 296, 298, 302, 305, 317-318, 348

Sforza, Cardinal Ascanio 217-219, 225, 246, 253
Sforza, Catarina 294
Sforza, Duke Lodovico 294, 304
Shah Rukh 205
Shropshire 316
Sicily 13, 44-46, 244-245, 247, 252-255
Siena 255
Sierra Leone 118
Sierra Nevada 200, 201
Siete Iglesias 111, 112
Sigüenza 210
Sigüenza, Bishop of 46
Silos, Chronicler of 5
Simancas 6, 28, 64
Simancas, Battle of (939) 6, 15
Sintra 236
Sistine Chapel 217
Sixtus IV, Pope 59, 62, 63, 103, 104, 107, 109, 123, 124, 134-137, 161
slavery
    of blacks in Portugal 118, 119
    of blacks in Castile 119-120, 298
    of Canary Islanders 120, 196-197
    of Indians 230, 262-263, 292
Solís, Alonso de, Bishop of Cádiz 113
Sona, Bishop Luís de 166
Soria 129
South America 284, 292
Spain 2, 3, 6-9, 11, 44, 45, 52, 63, 120, 134, 137-139, 161, 170, 180, 187, 192, 194, 195, 197, 203, 206, 208, 209, 221, 225, 228, 232, 234, 238-239, 241, 242, 247, 250-251, 253-257, 261-262, 268, 269, 271, 274, 275, 277, 280-282, 284, 288, 291, 295, 305, 308-311, 316, 317, 322-324, 326, 327-333, 336-339, 341-343, 348, 349, 351, 353, 358
Stalin, Joseph 141, 230
Stúñiga family 84, 88, 92, 119, 126
Suárez Fernández, Luís (historian) 136
Swiss infantry 329-330, 353
Syria 3, 190

Tagus River 25, 41, 43, 79, 198, 236, 277
Taino Indians 263
Talavera 127
Talavera, Hernando de 139, 181, 185, 209, 346
    as Isabel's confessor 124-125, 359
    at the *cortes* of Toledo in 1480 130-131
    headed commission to investigate
        Columbus' project 171, 176, 184, 188,

204-205
  as Bishop of Granada 200-201, 211, 296-
    298, 300-301, 303
  Isabel's letter to, on the attempted
    assassination of Fernando 226-227
Talavera, Synod of 288
Tamerlane 205
Tapía, Diego de 68
Taranto 314
Tarazona 158-159, 259
Tarifa 11
Tariq 161
Tendilla, Count of 201, 218, 297-300, 303,
  346
St. Teresa of Avila 140
Thule, Ultima 170
Tinto River 212, 214, 236
Toledo 5-8, 34, 64, 79, 80-84, 107, 109, 111,
  122-124, 127, 129, 130, 132, 149, 159, 244,
  267, 281, 283, 285, 289, 318-319, 321, 324
  Church of San Juan de los Reyes in 107-
    108, 122, 166, 211, 320, 344
  cortes of (1480) see Castile, cortes of
Toledo, Pedro de, Bishop of Málaga 184
Tordesillas 81, 85, 87, 89, 93, 96, 100, 101,
  106, 353
Tordesillas, Treaty of (1494) 250-251
Tormes River 79, 93
Toro 84-89, 91-94, 96, 100, 104-106, 129,
  277, 350
Toro, Battle of (1476) 94-98, 109, 142, 166
Toros de Guisando, Pact of (1468) 38-43,
  46, 48, 49, 56, 57, 60, 61, 76, 83-84
Torquemada, Tomás de, Inquisitor-General
  of Castile 140-142, 161-162, 288, 295
Torre, Mencia de la SEE Mencia de la
  Torre
Torrelaguna 210
Torremolinos 166
Torres, Captain Antonio de 247-248, 250,
  262-263
Torres, Diego de 196
Torres, Juana de 310
Tortosa 66
Toscanelli, Paolo 171
trade winds 171, 219-220, 223-224, 231, 233,
  249
Trent, Council of 134, 288, 354
Treviño, Count of (Pedro Manrique) 56, 93,
  133
Trinitarians 338
Tripoli 353

Trujillo 49, 52, 71, 93, 100, 112, 126, 127,
  239
Trujillo, Treaty of SEE Alcáçoba, Treaty of
Tudela, League of 21, 24, 26, 32, 38, 41
Tunisia 181, 353
Turin 246
Turkish Empire 136-138, 143, 159, 190, 246-
  247, 252, 304, 314, 354
Turks Island SEE Bahama Islands
Turones River 93
Tyrol 294

Ubeda 10, 192
Uceda 210
Uclés 104, 106-107, 109, 121
Ulloa, Juan de 91, 105
Ulloa, Rodrigo de 91
United States of America 230
Ureña, Count of 82, 312
Urraca, Queen of Castile 8, 44, 73
Ushant 316
Utrera 121-122, 126, 157
Utrera, Battle of (1483) 157

Vaca, Pedro 53
Vaca, Pedro Núñez Cabeza de SEE Cabeza
  de Vaca, Pedro Núñez de
Vaeza, Antón Rodríguez de 70
Valdejunquera, Battle of (920) 6
Valdelozoya 60-61
Valdés, Francisco de 86, 90-91
Valencia 8, 50, 64, 66, 128-129, 162, 196,
  218, 244
  cortes of 144
Valencia de Alcántara 277-278, 280
Valera, Diego de (historian) 56, 57, 72, 146
Valladolid 18, 52, 54, 56, 57-60, 64, 78-79,
  81, 84, 85, 88, 91-93, 98, 129, 243
Vatican Library 213-214
Vega Real (Hispaniola) 264
Velasco family 41
Velasco, Iñigo, Constable of Spain 275
Velasco, Pedro de (Count of Haro) 42, 45,
  46, 48, 62, 70, 76, 80, 92, 105
Vélez Málaga 177-180
Velletri 254
Veneriis, Antonio de, Bishop of León (later
  Cuenca) 38, 58-59, 63, 135
Venezuela 282, 348
Venice 255, 331, 341, 353
Vera 186
Vera, Pedro de 196, 197

Vergara, Pedro de, Bishop of León 135
Vermudo II, King of León 6, 7
Vermudo III, King of León 7
Vespucci, Amerigo 348
Vignaud, Henri 171
Vigo 236
Vikings 4, 116
Villacastín 26
Villafáfila, Agreement of (1506) 351-352
Villalón, Dr. Andrés de 78, 120, 176
Villarrubia de las Ojos 31
Villena, first Marqués of SEE Pacheco,
  Juan
Villena, second Marqués of (Diego
  Pacheco) 48, 73, 77, 78, 80, 82, 86, 88, 89,
  92, 93, 104, 110, 112, 350
Virgin Islands 248
Virgin Mountains 31
Visconti, Cardinal Ascanio 187
Vitoria 100, 157, 158
Vivero, Juan de 52, 57-59
Vizcaya SEE Basque provinces

Wales 316
Walvis Bay 184
Warbeck, Perkin 295
Watling's Island (Bahamas) 222
westerlies, prevailing (winds) 171, 223-224,
  232-233
Worcester 320
Worms, Diet of (1521) 355
Wyclif, John 134

Xaragua 292
Ximénes de Cisneros, Cardinal Francisco
  SEE Cisneros, Cardinal Francisco
  Ximénes de

Yahia el-Nayer 193
Yeguas River 172
Yepes 43-44
yoke and arrows 76, 108
Yuste 355-356

Zafra, Fernando de 200, 302
"Zagal, El" SEE Abdallah "El Zagal"
Zahara 144-146, 157, 161-163
Zalamea de la Serena 318
Zamora 5, 6, 74, 83, 86, 88, 90-96, 98, 129
Zamora, Dr. Nuño Ramires 120
Zaragoza 45, 53, 54, 56, 185, 186, 218, 225,
  266-267, 282, 283, 285, 287, 288, 289, 321,
  324, 326
Zaragoza, Archbishop of 54, 135-136, 242,
  256
Zeli, Hamet 179, 181, 183, 189
Zoraya, Queen of Granada 151, 156